BUSINESS MARKETING

HOUGHTON MIFFLIN COMPANY   Boston   Toronto

Dallas   Geneva, Illinois   Palo Alto   Princeton, New Jersey

BUSINESS MARKETING

Andrew C. Gross
Cleveland State University

Peter M. Banting
McMaster University

Lindsay N. Meredith
Simon Fraser University

I. David Ford
University of Bath

Sponsoring Editor: *Diane McOscar*
Managing Development Editor: *Patricia L. Ménard*
Senior Project Editor: *Margaret M. Kearney*
Senior Production/Design Coordinator: *Karen Rappaport*
Senior Manufacturing Coordinator: *Marie Barnes*
Marketing Manager: *Robert Wolcott*

We would like to dedicate this book to

Our students, colleagues, teachers, and mentors who taught us

Our families—parents, spouses, children—who encouraged us, especially MSP, Wendy, Susie, and Jenny

Our practitioner friends and acquaintances who inspired us

Cover design by Ellen Conant.

Cover illustration by Richard Newton, courtesy of Renard Represents, New York.

Exhibit 14-3: Adapted table from *Advertising: A Decision Making Approach* by Charles H. Patti and Charles F. Frazer. Copyright © 1988 by the Dryden Press, reprinted by permission of the publisher.

Printed in the U.S.A.

Library of Congress Catalog Number: 91-72686

ISBN: 0-395-56083-7

23456789-DH-96 95 94

CONTENTS

CHAPTER 5   **MARKETING RESEARCH AND MARKET INFORMATION SYSTEMS**   **136**

CHAPTER 8   TECHNOLOGY AND THE INDUSTRIAL MARKETPLACE   275

CHAPTER 17   BUSINESS MARKETING STRATEGY, PLANNING, AND IMPLEMENTATION   630

CASES IN BUSINESS MARKETING   657

PREFACE

Business marketing is a relatively new term. It replaces two other terms, *industrial marketing* and *organizational marketing.* Yet another term is *business-to-business marketing.* In fact, all these terms are equivalent and can be used interchangeably. They signify situations in which individuals or groups purchase products or services for resale, for use in producing other goods, and for daily operations of an enterprise. The range of such offerings is indeed vast. Business marketing encompasses large aircraft, raw materials, truck fleet maintenance, business advisory services, institutional feeding, tiny electronic circuits, and telecommunications. Companies, partnerships, institutions, and governments are the customers.

Our goal in this text is to convey the growing importance of a major field of business activity that has suffered some neglect over the years. Throughout the book, we attempt to

- Show the dynamic and complex nature of the business marketplace in a global, comparative framework;

- Analyze the action, the actors, and the audience by exploring what business marketers do, both those who buy and those who sell;

- Explore both the broad policies and the specific practices in the field of business marketing—not just what is done, but how it is done;

- Reveal which competitive strategies and tactics work well, with special reference to selected industries, organizations, and situations.

The authors come from different countries and with diverse experience in academia, industry, and government; thus, we can bring a richer, broader perspective to the discussion at hand. Because our background includes many areas, it is natural for us to adopt a combined outlook, encompassing both managerial and social perspectives. We think that users of the book benefit when the text brings such diverse perspectives into play.

While we stress the importance of companies, partnerships, and individual entrepreneurs, we recognize that business marketing is carried out by a host of government agencies, not-for-profit institutions, and groups such as trade, industry, and technical associations. We note, too, that although business marketing is carried out in and among highly industrialized nations, such activity is also an integral part of the economies of developing and industrializing nations. Finally, we recognize that no concrete wall exists between business marketing and consumer marketing. Indeed, we applaud creative marketers who cross the border in either or both directions. Flowers are now being delivered to offices and industrial-grade cleaning compounds find loyal users in households.

ORGANIZATION

Business Marketing is organized into 17 chapters. Chapters 1 and 2 focus on the environment of business marketing and show the links between industrial and consumer goods. Chapters 3 and 4 explain organizational buying and selling behavior. Interaction of buyers and sellers is probed and purchasing as a major activity is discussed at this point. Chapters 5 through 8 look at the driving forces and elements in business marketing, including the roles played by marketing research, segmentation, and technology. Competitive and cooperative behavior of industrial enterprises is discussed at some length. Chapters 9 through 15 focus on the marketing mix, emphasizing the nature and characteristics of goods and services, distribution channels and logistics, pricing policies, and promotion practices in the business marketplace. The text comes to a close by looking at evaluation and control systems in Chapter 16 and at strategy and planning in Chapter 17. Following the chapters are twenty-two cases that provide in-depth examples of a variety of business marketing activities.

UNIQUE FEATURES

Though our book is in the mainstream of business marketing, observing many traditions, it also offers some special features:

- Instead of an individual chapter on global marketing, the book offers global examples in each chapter.

- While thinking globally, business marketers must act locally; adaptation to special conditions is stressed where and when appropriate.

- Illustrations, cases, mini-cases, and videos show actual, lively examples of what is happening in the field.

- The discussion emphasizes not only what, who, where, and when, but also the how and why of business marketing.

- The multi-faceted and complex nature of the industrial marketplace is described, analyzed, and evaluated, to show both the macro and micro aspects of the issues.

LEARNING AND TEACHING AIDS

Each chapter opens with an outline and the major objectives, and closes with a list of the key terms and concepts and a set of challenging discussion questions. Business Marketing in Practice boxes in each chapter offer short but relevant stories of business marketing in action. The cases at the end of the book provide in-depth examples of a business marketing event, problem, or issue. For adopters of the book, we offer a set of videotapes consisting of two hours of stories highlighting individual companies and their experiences.

The Instructor's Resource Manual provides detailed answers to the discussion questions at the end of each chapter and a brief analysis of how to handle each of the cases at the end of the text. Our answers are just one possibility; creative students and instructors may wish to consider other acceptable responses. The manual also includes a guide to the videos, with suggestions for integrating the videos into the class. The Test Bank portion of the manual offers a complete set of multiple-choice questions and answers for each chapter, along with several essay questions and suggested answers. Finally, the manual includes a set of 100 transparency masters that do not duplicate the exhibits in the book, but rather complement and supplement them.

ACKNOWLEDGMENTS

Many people have assisted us in the writing of *Business Marketing*. We appreciate their contributions to the book, and we are grateful for their helpful comments and suggestions. We acknowledge the following Cleveland State University students for their assistance during manuscript preparation: Noah Iafigliola, Stephane Liozu, Mary Kay McManamon, Steven White, Jackie Woldering, Theresa Eady, and Ramesh Sharma. We extend special thanks to the following reviewers:

Joseph A. Bellizzi
Arizona State University

James R. Brown
Virginia Polytechnic and State University

E. Raymond Corey
Harvard University

Tamer Cavusgil
Michigan State University

C. Anthony di Benedetto
Temple University

Nermin Eyuboglu
Baruch College

Abbie Griffin
The University of Chicago

Robert R. Harmon
Portland State University

Jon Hawes
University of Akron

Robert D. Hisrich
University of Tulsa

Lloyd C. Hodges
University of Illinois-Urbana/Champaign

Shreekant G. Joag
St. John's University

Alvin Kelly
South Carolina State College

Sylvia Keyes
Bridgewater State College

Ron LeBlanc
Idaho State University

Donald K. Macintyre
Bentley College

Frank S. McCabe
Northern Illinois University

Jim Narus
Wake Forest University

William Rodgers
St. Cloud State University

David Savino
Ohio Northern University

James A. Stephens
Arizona State University

Fred Trawick
University of Alabama-Birmingham

D. Charles White
California State Polytechnic
University-Pomona

Jerome Williams
Pennsylvania State University

ABOUT THE AUTHORS

Peter M. Banting is Professor of Marketing and International Business at McMaster University in Hamilton, Ontario. He received his doctorate from Michigan State University and is a Senior Fellow of the Academy of Marketing Science. He has been a Visiting Professor at the University of Science and Technology in Beijing and at Nankai University in Tianjin, both in the People's Republic of China, as well as at universities in Japan, England, and Canada. Professor Banting has done extensive consulting for both government and industry, and his articles and contributions have appeared in several journals, including *Industrial Marketing Management, The Business Quarterly,* the *Journal of Business and Industrial Marketing,* and *European Research.*

I. David Ford is Professor of Marketing in the School of Management at the University of Bath in Bath, England. He received his doctorate from the University of Manchester in England. Professor Ford is a founding member of IMP, an international group of researchers who have carried out a number of large-scale, multi-country studies in industrial marketing and purchasing. This work can be found in *International Marketing & Purchasing of Industrial Goods: An Interaction Approach* (John Wiley) ed. H. Hakansson, and he recently edited *Understanding Business Markets* (Academic Press). He has served as Visiting Professor at the University of Texas at Austin and regularly gives management seminars in many countries.

Andrew C. Gross is Professor of Marketing and International Business at Cleveland State University, in Cleveland, Ohio. He received his doctorate from Ohio State University. He has been honored as a distinguished teacher and has received two Fulbright awards for lecturing and research in his native Hungary. He has been a

Visiting Professor at McGill University and McMaster University, the University of New South Wales in Sydney, and the University of Economics in Budapest. He has worked in several industries and assisted in founding Predicasts, Inc., a market research and publishing firm, and has acted as a consultant to various U.S. and overseas companies. His articles have appeared in the *Columbia Journal of World Business*, the *European Journal of Marketing, Industrial Marketing Management*, and many others.

Lindsay N. Meredith is Professor of Marketing at Simon Fraser University in Burnaby, British Columbia, where he also received his doctorate. He has done considerable consulting in the private sector as well as for crown corporations and government agencies, specializing in market demand estimation for new and existing products and services, market segmentation studies, marketing decision support systems, and the development of customer profiles. Professor Meredith's many articles have been published in *Industrial Marketing Management*, the *International Journal of Advertising* and Harvard's *Review of Economics and Statistics*.

Where to Reach Us

We are available to you and are genuinely interested in your comments, corrections, and criticism. We welcome contributions from you for future editions, be they mini-stories, examples, cases, or statistics. You can reach us by mail, phone, or fax, and are welcome to drop in on our classes for a face-to-face talk. Let us hear from you!

Peter M. Banting
Michael G. DeGroote
  School of Business
McMaster University
Hamilton, Ontario
CANADA L8S 4M4
Tel: (416) 529-7070 × 3969
Fax: (416) 527-0100

Andrew C. Gross
College of Business Administration
Cleveland State University
Cleveland, Ohio 44115
USA
Tel: (216) 687-4744
Fax: (216) 687-9354

I. David Ford
School of Management
University of Bath
Bath, England BA2 7AY
UNITED KINGDOM
Tel: 022 582-6726
Fax: 022-582-6473

Lindsay N. Meredith
Faculty of Business
Simon Fraser University
Burnaby, British Columbia
CANADA V5A 1S6
Tel: (604) 291-3653
Fax: (604) 291-3404

Learning and teaching are not spectator sports. We hope that by using this book, whether as a student who purchased it or as an instructor who adopted it, you will benefit. In turn, we would like to learn from you! Please, do give us your comments and criticisms by mail, phone, or fax.

BUSINESS MARKETING

1

INTRODUCTION TO BUSINESS MARKETING

For whom will you work in your first full-time job? Most marketing students picture themselves as product managers in charge of Crest toothpaste at Procter & Gamble, or handling the Nescafé coffee account for Nestlé. They have studied introductory marketing with professors and texts that describe consumer products and services, and probably have gone on to take other courses, such as consumer behavior or advertising. But they have not been exposed to the world of business marketing. Although more than 60 percent will be employed by companies that market to businesses, less than 2 percent will have studied business marketing in college.[1]

AN OVERVIEW OF BUSINESS MARKETING

Marketing delivers a standard of living. In the case of business marketing, this standard is delivered to business organizations, public agencies, and not-for-profit institutions of all kinds, large and small. What is this standard and how is it delivered? The standard is what clients or customers expect: information and quality products and services, priced right, and distributed at appropriate locations. Delivery may be around the corner or across the ocean. A small service station repairs and maintains the truck fleet of another enterprise just down the street. A crucial aerospace component is sent via air express, on short notice, from North to South America. Financial or health care advice is flashed instantly by telephone, fax, or satellite from England to Hungary or from Australia to Indonesia.

Exhibit 1–1 is a simplified view of the buying and selling activities of the three major participants in business markets: private, profit-making organizations of all kinds and sizes; public institutions (government agencies) at all levels from local to international; and not-for-profit institutions, ranging from clinics to churches and trade associations to science museums. Although the chart shows the arrows going one way, any enterprise can be both a seller and a buyer. Thus, a computer service organization purchases parts and other items from its suppliers and sells

EXHIBIT 1–1   A Simplified View of Buyers and Sellers in Business Marketing

THREE MAJOR CATEGORIES

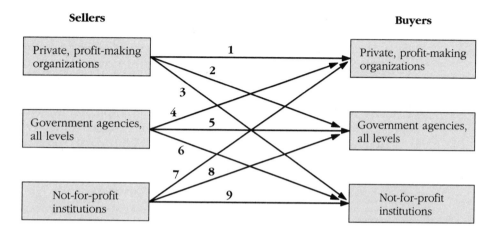

Line 1: A foundry or plastic moulder sells parts to a truck manufacturer.
Line 2: A computer service company bids on a federal government contract.
Line 3: A furniture manufacturer ships beds to hospitals and pews to churches.
Line 4: A federal government agency offers geological maps to explorers.
Line 5: A state sewage authority connects a local public agency to its line.
Line 6: A space agency supplies satellite photographs to high schools.
Line 7: A health care firm bids for the contract of a large chemical firm.
Line 8: An orchestra performs for a major government conference.
Line 9: A chamber of commerce gives export advice to a trade association.

sophisticated custom software packages to clients in both the public and private sectors.

Do business marketing organizations cater to household consumers (families and individuals)? Yes, indeed. For example, an office equipment firm might expand its markets by selling modular furniture and small computers to families with teenagers who will use these items for homework. A company that makes industrial adhesives and cleaning compounds may offer its products to household users. Or, an industrial security firm may decide to begin protecting luxury homes.

What about the reverse? Do companies that offer consumer goods and services attempt to penetrate industrial markets? Yes, indeed. A producer of soaps and detergents for the home may decide to bid on a contract to supply a hospital or museum. A florist delivering to homes may want to broaden its client base by trying to place green plants in both downtown and suburban office buildings.

Consumer and business markets can overlap. In this text, however, we will focus on businesses that sell to or buy from other businesses. We will study organizational buying behavior and the methods of measuring the size and characteristics of a potential business market.

The term *business marketing* suggests that organizations deal with other organizations in a sort of faceless fashion. But keep in mind, each and every organization is made up of many individuals with diverse backgrounds and characteristics. Business-to-business transactions involve people-to-people relations. Yes, there are teams of sellers; yes, there are many groups in the buying firm who influence the purchase. Ultimately, however, it is individuals who deal with other individuals. It is essential to consider the perceptions, expectations, and motivations of these individuals if we are to achieve an understanding of business marketing.

Here is an interesting dialogue that illustrates this point, and reveals a major gap between buyers and sellers:

PURCHASING AGENT: We require just-in-time delivery.

SALESPERSON: My company will do better than that. We'll deliver your parts before you need them.

About 90 percent of purchasing professionals understand immediately the humor in that dialogue, but only 50 percent of sales professionals recognize that it is a joke.[2] Although humorous, the anecdote indicates that there is a serious problem. In the 1990s, sales managers must address this problem if they hope to achieve rapport with individual purchasing agents.

As we enter the field of business marketing, we should note two phenomena. First, there is an incredible richness and variety to the field. Products and services can be simple or complex. Goods can range from small items such as pencils or nails to assembly lines, printing presses, and aerospace missiles. Services can be as elementary as tightening a screw to refurbishing a nuclear reactor. They can range from filling out forms to complex medical, financial, or technical consultancy. Prices can range from a fraction of a cent for processing a payroll check to millions of dollars for building a jumbo jet aircraft. Distribution can be near or distant, and invariably involves numerous decisions about dealers, agents, warehouses, trucks, and trains. Promotion decisions can range from placing a simple advertisement in the yellow pages to participating in a large trade show. Planning marketing strategy and coordinating the marketing mix are truly challenging tasks that are performed in a continuously changing environment.

Second, there is a jargon or special vocabulary in business marketing, just as there is in any other functional area of business, sports, medicine, or any discipline. To communicate with other business marketers it is necessary to speak their language. We will highlight key words and concepts throughout this book to help you become familiar with the business marketer's vocabulary. You are now set to explore the exciting world of business marketing—a field that is four times larger than consumer marketing.

BUSINESS MARKETING TERMINOLOGY

As the first step in your study of business marketing you will need to become familiar with some marketing terminology as it is used in this text.

Marketing is the creation and adaptation of products and services to provide greater utility or value to customers than do competing products and services. Marketing involves selection of potential customers (target markets) and management of the marketing mix (product, price, place, and promotion).

The **marketing concept** includes three key ideas: (1) the principal focus of the marketing manager is to provide customer satisfaction; (2) the entire

BUSINESS MARKETING IN PRACTICE

Hitting the Nail, But Not on the Head

For decades, the Steel Company of Canada shipped trainfuls of Stelco common nails from its plant to all parts of the nation. Year after year, boxcar after boxcar of nails went to the market. Stelco did not know who was using those mountains of nails or for what purposes they were being used, nor was it of any real concern to Stelco management. Nails were being bought. That was all that mattered—until Stelco developed a brand-new kind of nail with a spiral thread.

The new nail was a revolutionary fundamental innovation after sixty years of absolutely no significant changes in the common nail. Stelco executives couldn't have been more delighted. They were certain that their new Ardox nail would almost completely replace the common nail.

And why not? It was stronger. It could be driven straight and true, guided smoothly into the wood by those spiral grooves. It provided less chance of splitting the wood while being driven. It held wood more tightly. Carpenters could use fewer Ardox nails to obtain the holding power of more common nails. And the Ardox nail was inexpensive.

Yet after two decades on the market, Ardox nails still had not reached their expected sales volume. Why? How could one of North America's largest steel mills have missed their sales target by so much? Although a number of reasons could be given, the main one is that Stelco didn't know who was buying and using their nails.

Of course, the company knew the immediate customers to whom they were selling nails. Stelco was selling to hardware and industrial distributors. They were selling nails by the boxcar. But what happened to those boxcars of nails after distributors in every part of the country had unloaded them? Who actually bought and used nails? Who were Stelco's real customers? How many were builders, contractors, carpenters, repair people, and handymen? How did they decide what kind of nail to buy? Would they welcome a technically better nail? To whom should Ardox nails be advertised?

Although many contributing factors prevented the Ardox nail from fulfilling management's expectations, the main problem was inadequate knowledge of end users' behavior, perceptions, and purchase motivations.

Source: C. S. Kidd, Sales Manager, Merchant Products, Steel Company of Canada, Ltd., as related to Peter Banting, Ph.D., Professor of Marketing, McMaster University, Hamilton, Ontario.

organization must be coordinated as an integrated system in which all employees and departments are aware of their roles in the organization/customer relationship and work together to maintain that relationship; and (3) the long-range goals of the organization (profit, stability of employment, service to society, a favorable public image, and so forth) must be fulfilled.

A **consumer** is an individual who purchases goods and services for self-gratification. Self-gratification may result from using the purchase (such as the enjoyment obtained from eating a chocolate candy bar or watching a rented videotape) or from giving the purchase to another person (such as the pleasure the buyer experiences in anticipating the appreciation that will be exhibited by the recipient of the gift).

A **business marketer** is an individual or an organization that sells goods and services to other businesspeople, businesses, institutions, or organizations. The business marketer may also be called a *business-to-business marketer* or *seller.*

A **business buyer** is an industrial or business purchaser who buys for reasons other than self-gratification. Typically, the purchase or rental is made for one of three reasons: (1) to incorporate the product or service into the products or services that the organization produces (for example, General Motors purchases laminated safety glass for auto windshields); (2) to facilitate the operation of the organization (for example, IBM purchases automobiles for its salespeople); or (3) to resell the product or service (for example, a retail store purchases packaged food products to resell immediately, without any modifications, to consumers). The terms *business buyer, buyer, industrial buyer, organizational buyer, buying organization, client, purchasing agent, purchaser, buying center, acquisitions officer,* and *customer* are all roughly equivalent.

Business marketing is the marketing of products and services to organizations rather than to households or ultimate consumers. The purchase is made, not for self-gratification, but rather to achieve organizational objectives. Business marketing is also called *business-to-business marketing, industrial marketing, commercial marketing, institutional marketing, government marketing,* or *organizational marketing.*

BUSINESS MARKETING DEFINED

In past years, texts dealing with business marketing were titled "Industrial Marketing," and many courses in business schools today are still called "industrial marketing." However, the term *business marketing* offers a more realistic and comprehensive image of the nonconsumer marketing world. It avoids the confusion that may arise when, for example, a firm manufactures hair shampoo and then sells it to distributors and retailers. Although the product in such a case clearly is a consumer product, the decision-making and purchasing behavior of the distributor or retailer is very different from that of a consumer. Thus we find that business marketing is employed throughout the distribution channel up to the time of sale of the product to the retailer.[3]

In business marketing, the purchasing decisions throughout the distribution channel are based on very rational economic considerations involving such issues as potential demand, inventory levels, shelf-space availability, promotional support offered by the manufacturer, and profitability of the product—considerations that normally do not play a role in a consumer's buying decision process.

Business customers usually are organizations rather than individuals (although there are many single-proprietor businesses in operation). Business customers' requirements typically are thoroughly specified and more technically complex. Furthermore, the success, the economics of operation, and the profitability of the organization are strongly dependent on what items are purchased, how they are purchased, when they are purchased, and the reliability and consistency of supply of those goods.

Business marketing also encompasses a range of organizations that do not have profit as a primary goal. Government agencies—federal, state, municipal, and local—are considered business markets. So too are such institutions as hospitals, churches, prisons, schools, colleges, and universities. Even the YMCA and the Red Cross can be classified as part of the business market. Again, the justification is that their evaluation of competing suppliers and their products tends to be more formalized and professional, and more carefully evaluated against the institution's objectives. Thus, the buying decision processes of nonprofit organizations are more similar to decisions made by profit-making businesses than to the self-gratifying purchase decisions arrived at by consumers.

BUSINESS PRODUCTS DEFINED

Some products can be identified clearly as industrial products: forklift trucks, bulldozers, pallets, injection molding machines, cream separators, and jet engines are a few. Others, which appear to be industrial or business products, may find customers among groups of consumers. Vans, originally intended for commercial deliveries, have become popular family vehicles. Cellular telephones are finding their way into private vehicles for personal use.[4] When consumers become attracted to business products, responsive marketers may adapt those products to suit the newfound market's needs more closely. A good example of this is the huge consumer market that now exists for video cameras, which in past years were the domain of commercial television broadcasters.

Still other products with little or no adaptation may be considered either business or consumer products, depending on the circumstances in which they are purchased and used. For example, identical computers may be found in word processing applications in the office and in the home. And what about flowers and plants? In the home we know they are consumer goods. But in the office, they play the role of business goods.

BUSINESS MARKETING IN PRACTICE ■■■■■■■■

Business Pager Marketers Watch Consumers

Businesses buy pocket pagers to communicate urgent messages to their executives. Individuals who operate their own businesses buy pocket pagers to ensure that they quickly receive messages from a secretary or answering service. These pocket pagers are bought for business purposes and form part of the huge business market. Indeed, more than 15 million businesspeople around the world carry an electronic pager—a small box, about the size of a cigarette pack, that beeps to announce the arrival of a message.

But hundreds of millions of consumers wear wrist watches. With advances in miniaturization, it is now possible to build a pager into a wrist watch. Such a wrist watch pager costs about the same as a good watch and keeps absolutely perfect time. Major pager marketers want to develop this market to make the pager a consumer item with appeal beyond its current business niche. They can imagine Mom and Dad wearing a pager so the kids or the babysitter can reach them. Marketers also hope that businesspeople who feel uncomfortable wearing a pager on their belt or searching around for one in a purse will like the watch pager.

"It's taking the technology and making it smaller, putting it into a form that is very user friendly," states Motorola's Robert Walz. Motorola, based in Schaumburg, Illinois, is one of the fifty largest industrial companies in the United States, with annual revenues approaching $10 billion. Motorola already has a large pager business that complements its cellular communications products. In fact, cellular telephones may be driving some of the growth in paging, according to Walz. Rather than publish a cellular telephone number and pay for all the incoming calls, some people are using pagers to screen their cellular messages, returning only the ones that they want to pay for.

Motorola has joined with Timex Corporation of Middlebury, Connecticut, to sell the Motorola Wrist Watch Pager for about $300. There's also a monthly fee of between $10 to $25, depending on location. AT&E Corporation of San Francisco and Hattori Seiko Co. Ltd. of Japan (the maker of Seiko watches) are launching a similar product called Receptor, which is based on a different paging technology and which will be able to provide global paging. Receptor lists for $225, and the monthly fee ranges from $12.50 to about $35.00, depending on whether it is used for local, national, or international paging.

AT&E president Charles Skibo says the company's market research indicates that one of every two Americans would like a wrist watch pager, that 53 percent of the existing pager market would switch to a wrist watch pager, and that 33 percent of all U.S. businesses would like to have wrist watch pagers.

Source: Adapted with permission from Geoffrey Rowan, "Timing the Pager Market," (Toronto) *Globe and Mail*, August, 27, 1990, pp. B1, B2.

More prosaically, consider toilet paper. A consumer product? Definitely. Or is it? Not so when purchased by a university or an industrial plant. In those settings it is facilitating the operation of the organization. And as a business product, it must be marketed in a different manner than it is to consumers. Business buyers are concerned less with its squeezable softness, pastel colors, or fresh forest scent and more with its timely delivery, quantity discounts, and dollars and cents.

BUSINESS PRODUCT CLASSIFICATION

Consumer goods are classified as convenience goods, shopping goods, specialty goods, and unsought goods.[5] The basis for this classification system is the variability in the buying behavior of consumers. Thus consumer goods are classified according to *how people buy.*

With business goods, there is a remarkably low degree of variability in buying behavior (see Exhibit 1–2). Consequently, the consumer goods classification system does not help business marketers classify business goods. Since most businesses follow the same pattern of search, evaluation, approval, and purchase for goods and services, we must find a classification scheme that points out other types of differences in product groupings. The traditional method of classifying business products is based on *how the goods are used.* This system consists of the seven categories listed in Exhibit 1–3 and described in the following sections.

Capital Equipment and Investments

Capital equipment and **investments** require significant financial expenditure. Thus, marketers may have to extend credit to the buyer, assist the buyer in securing funds or loans, or offer the buyer leasing agreements. The high cost of capital expenditures also means that the buying organization's top executives will be involved in the purchase decision. Capital equipment and investments can be subcategorized into land, buildings, and other companies; single-purpose equipment; and multipurpose equipment. Capital equipment items are always installed in a fixed location.

Land, Buildings, and Other Companies.   Land, buildings, and other companies (takeovers) typically involve lengthy negotiations and are the largest investments a firm will make. Associated professional business services—such as environmental

---

EXHIBIT 1–2   The Business Buying Decision Process

1. Recognition of needs
2. Definition of characteristics and quantity of item needed
3. Development of specifications to guide procurement
4. Search for and qualification of potential sources
5. Acquisition and analysis of proposals
6. Evaluation of proposals and selection of suppliers
7. Selection of order routine
8. Performance feedback and evaluation

Source: Patrick J. Robinson, C. W. Faris, and Y. Wind, *Industrial Buying and Creative Marketing* (Boston: Allyn & Bacon and the Marketing Science Institute, 1967), pp. 13–18.

EXHIBIT 1–3 Business Goods Classification

	Standardization or Grading	Used Across Various Industries	Risk of Obsolescence	Requires High-Level Approval	Credit Necessary	Emphasis on OEM Specifications	Delivery is Important
Capital equipment and investments							
Land, buildings, other companies		M	M	P	M		
Single-purpose equipment			P	P	P	P	
Multipurpose equipment	P	P		P	P		
Accessory equipment	P	P					
Component parts							
Standardized	P	P				P	P
Custom			P			P	P
Process materials	P	P				P	P
Maintenance, repair, and operating (MRO) supplies	P	P				M	M
Raw materials	P	P				P	P
Services							
Technical					P		
Nontechnical		P					P

P=present   **M**=may be present

impact studies, architectural design, and financial intermediation—may be purchased prior to and during the capital project acquisition decision.

Single-Purpose Equipment.   Typically, **single-purpose equipment** is custom-made for only one company or industry. For example, a conveyor system is custom-designed to traverse a certain factory configuration at a specific speed and carrying a stated maximum load. Alternatively, a certain leather-stitching machine might only be useful to plants in the shoe manufacturing industry. Customized equipment requires much interaction and negotiation between the technical sales and service people of the seller and the engineering staff of the client.

Older custom-made equipment can pose problems. Because of its specialized nature, it is extremely difficult to find buyers for used single-purpose equipment. Thus, if the buyer's products change rapidly (requiring different production equipment) or if the single-purpose machine is easily made obsolete by technological innovation in the machine-producing industry, the buyer faces high risk levels. Consequently, buyers of single-purpose equipment plan for shorter replacement periods and have to put more money aside annually for equipment replacement. All of these factors suggest that the astute business marketer may have to extend credit terms or help the client secure a loan if a sale of new equipment is to be consummated. Mainframe computer manufacturers have addressed this problem by providing trade-in schemes and offering leasing terms to their customers.

Multipurpose Equipment.   **Multipurpose equipment**, such as boilers, compressors and hoists, is used by most manufacturing industries. Such equipment has a **horizontal market**—that is, a market extending across many industries. The product life cycle tends to be quite long, resulting in lower risk of obsolescence and longer replacement periods. The broad market for these products guarantees relatively easy sale of used equipment, and indeed, used equipment brokers play a role in bringing together buyers and sellers of older machines. The standardization of multipurpose equipment means that business marketers do not have to be involved in as much detailed selling, service, or negotiation with customers as in the case of single-purpose equipment.

Accessory Equipment

Accessory equipment includes such readily movable items as spot-welders, hand-held drills, and forklift trucks in industrial settings, and personal computers and furniture in office settings.

Accessory equipment and machines are standardized, and their marketing involves routine selling and negotiation. Their relatively lower cost permits most to be considered current-expense items—that is, their cost can be charged as an expense in the purchase period rather than having to be deducted in portions over several years of operation, as is the case for capital equipment purchases. Thus accessory equipment does not require high-level executive approval prior to purchase. High demand and extensive horizontal markets for accessory equipment permit the use of distributors.

Component Parts

Component parts are manufactured items, subassemblies, or completely assembled units that are incorporated into the buyer's final product. There are two types of components: standardized and custom. **Standardized components** conform to industry-accepted dimensions and performance specifications. Batteries, tires, and headlights are examples of standardized components in the vehicle market. In other industries, items such as fractional horsepower motors, integrated circuits, ball bearings, and LED (light-emitting diode) displays exhibit the standardization inherent in this class of component parts. Such products can be held in inventory by distributors and sold "off-the-shelf." **Custom components**, on the other hand, can involve elaborate specifications. Forgings, castings, automotive windshields, and timing motors are examples of custom components designed to the exact specifications of the buyer.

Because many components wear out with use and need replacement, they have the potential for significant replacement sales. Also, the manufacturer using the components to build a product may buy substantial volumes of components and be a very important customer for the component supplier.

Original Equipment Manufacturer (OEM).   The purchaser that uses component parts in some larger, final product is called an **original equipment manufacturer (OEM)**. Thus, in the automotive business, Chrysler is an OEM, and the component parts purchased by Chrysler (windshields, tires, door handles, and so forth) are referred to as OEM parts. The manufacturers that sell components to Chrysler are called OEM parts suppliers. Component parts suppliers must not only rigorously meet OEM specifications, but also ensure that the quality of the components is consistent and that their delivery is reliable so that the OEM can hold inventories at a low level. Japanese OEMs, such as Toyota, have achieved extremely low inventory costs by demanding that their suppliers provide **just-in-time (JIT)** deliveries.[6] (JIT is discussed in greater detail in Chapter 4.) This indicates that business marketers must use short, direct channels of distribution to capture OEM business.

After-Market.   Some components—such as treads in crawler tractors, vehicle batteries, tires, headlights, fan belts, and air and oil filters—are subject to degradation or wear and present a sizable market, called the **after-market** or **replacement market.** Where such components do not lose their identity in the final product, it is possible to establish brands, such as Fram filters, Firestone tires, and GE headlights. Many component manufacturers vie for a share of the after-market. For any component—say, auto tires—one of these competitors is the OEM parts supplier. The rest are called **will-fit component suppliers** (see Exhibit 1–4).

EXHIBIT 1–4   The Component Business for Automobile Tires

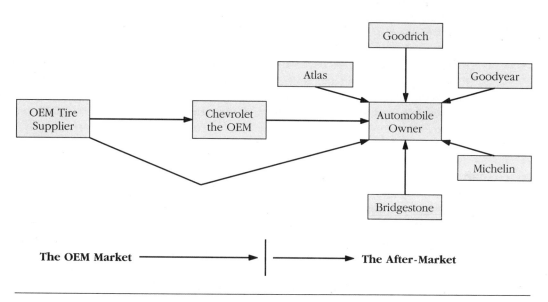

The OEM Market ⟶ | ⟶ The After-Market

The implications of the after-market can be important to the business marketer. First, the user of a $20,000 product that requires a replacement component will be relatively insensitive to price. The after-market, therefore, can be quite lucrative. Second, when it comes time to replace a degraded component, a significant proportion of OEM product owners feel more confident when they purchase the OEM part rather than a will-fit part. Third, the existence of several competitors hotly contesting after-market business suggests that the part manufacturing firm that is the designated OEM supplier will have a distinctive competitive advantage over all of the will-fit part suppliers. Fourth, potential component suppliers will be willing to yield price concessions to the OEM, not only to obtain the substantial production-run order of the OEM, but also to win the **follow-on business** of the more profitable (per unit) after-market. Fifth, business marketers in the after-market all use a **pull strategy** in advertising their components—that is, they promote their products to final OEM product owners, who in turn place a demand for these products on the suppliers, thus "pulling" the product down through the marketing channel. For example, the tire manufacturers in Exhibit 1–4 all advertise directly to consumers. Finally, such advertising also may help influence the OEM in the choice of which component manufacturer to select as the OEM parts supplier.

Process Materials

Process materials are manufacturing materials that tend to lose their identity and may even be indistinguishable in the final product. Examples of process materials are sheet metals, textiles, cement, chemicals, and electrical and electronic circuit wiring. Process materials that are indistinguishable in the final product include the additives used in lubricants, fuels, and antifreezes; the filler and other ingredients in pharmaceutical pills; and the ingredients in cake mixes. Process materials usually are standardized or graded and are sold by specification. The replacement market for process materials is not substantial. The business marketer may have to provide some technical assistance to customers, finds price competition keen because competing suppliers are readily available, and must provide reliable delivery because the customer's production is dependent on availability of materials.

Maintenance, Repair, and Operating (MRO) Supplies

Maintenance, repair, and operating (MRO) supplies are used to facilitate operation of the organization but do not become part of the final product in the way that component parts and process materials do. Maintenance and repair items include cleaning agents and tools, paints, and light bulbs. Operating supplies include such items as lubricants and coolants for factory machinery, heating fuels, gasoline for company vehicles, and office supplies, such as envelopes and printer, fax, and reproduction papers.

These items are characterized as having extensive horizontal markets and are relatively low cost, current-expense items. They are usually purchased routinely, in small quantities, and do not require high-executive approval. The MRO supplier's marketing efforts are similar to those associated with consumer products, and typically the channel of distribution for MRO goods is relatively long and indirect. The exception is when long-term **systems contracts** are negotiated, for perhaps a year's anticipated needs.

Raw Materials

Raw materials are the products of the fishing, lumber, hunting, aquacultural, agricultural (farming, livestock), and extractive (petroleum, gas, and mining) industries. Sources of raw materials tend to be geographically concentrated—for example, industrial diamonds are found chiefly in South Africa; oil in Texas, Alberta, and the Arab states; bauxite in Guiana; nickel in northern Ontario; and cotton in the southern United States. Sixty percent of the world's rhodium comes from South Africa, 20 percent from the former Soviet Union (now the Commonwealth of Independent States), and 10 percent from Canada.

In contrast, less geographic concentration is exhibited by meat rendering. This industry recycles a wide variety of livestock, poultry, and fish by-products into commercial products, such as tallow and meal. Tallow is used in the production of soaps, cosmetics, and paints. Meal is used primarily in animal feed, pet foods, and fertilizer.

Swings in raw materials supplies can have a severe influence on their prices. For example, rhodium is used extensively in automotive catalytic converters to reduce the nitrous oxide in exhaust fumes, and to a lesser extent in chemicals, electronics, and glass. In a period of six months, the price of rhodium climbed from $1,746 an ounce in December 1989 to $3,425 an ounce on June 27, 1990. One week later, it had skyrocketed to $7,000 an ounce.[7] Industrial users scrambled to seek substitutes for rhodium, ran their inventories down to critical low levels, and announced increases in the prices of products using rhodium.

Because of volatility of supply and sometimes extreme price fluctuations, raw materials markets may exhibit **vertical integration**. That is, companies buy the firms that supply raw materials, thus providing an assured source of supply and a more predictable acquisition price. The large Canadian steel manufacturer Stelco owns iron ore mines, operates pelleting plants at the mine sites, and ships the concentrated iron pellets to its Hamilton, Ontario, steel-making furnaces in unit trains. This vertical integration not only assures stability in raw materials supplies and prices, but also provides economies in transportation.

In nonintegrated industries (industries with little vertical integration, such as beef production and apple growing), raw materials are graded or otherwise specified by government or the supplying industry. Many raw materials can then be marketed through brokers.

Business Services

Business services are the fastest-growing segment in industrialized nations. In 1985 the share of services in the gross domestic product (GDP) of developed market economies averaged 61 percent, compared with 55 percent in 1965.[8] Business services may be *technical,* such as computer repair contracts, or *nontechnical,* such as janitorial service. Nontechnical services usually can be sold across horizontal markets. Typically, the reliability of delivery of the service is important.

Business services are often purchased from sources outside of the organization because they can be performed more quickly, more reliably, or more inexpensively by specialists who make the service their full-time activity. The buying organization also may avoid investment in equipment and supplies that are necessary to perform the service. For example, nondestructive testing of metal parts can be accomplished with nuclear bombardment from the port of a nuclear reactor, but no industrial manufacturer would acquire a nuclear reactor to test a few hundred (or even a few thousand) pieces a year.

If the service rendered is highly technical in nature, the buying organization can "rent" expertise, rather than hiring and underutilizing its own full-time expert. Thus an organization may purchase the services of a patent attorney, a marketing research consultant, or an advertising agency from time to time, or even a litigation lawyer when circumstances so warrant.

Even a nontechnical service, such as janitorial work, can involve higher levels of technology than one would expect. Fifteen thousand employees of

ServiceMaster Co. of Downers Grove, Illinois, provide contract housekeeping and plant maintenance to industrial plants, health care facilities, and educational institutions. The firm achieves high efficiency through extensive employee training and research and development on cleaning chemicals and equipment. For example, ServiceMaster devised a battery-operated, cordless vacuum cleaner that permits the company's housekeepers to vacuum twice as fast as they could with conventional equipment.[9]

As a business "product," services are treated as a current-expense item. Nevertheless, their purchase may be negotiated at fairly high executive levels in the buying organization, particularly if union jobs may be replaced by the externally purchased service.

Because services are intangible, it is important to focus the marketing effort on managing the personal relationships between service personnel and contact people within customer organizations. Research indicates that although business customers have few problems conceptualizing the benefits of a new service, they do have difficulty in evaluating the quality of service.[10] Providing the customer with evidence relating to the intangible (and often invisible) services can be helpful in this regard. Thus, whenever possible, the business marketer should create tangible reminders that the service has been performed. For example, after applying fertilizer or insecticide, a landscaping service might stick a small notice in the lawn indicating the type of treatment and the date before leaving the work site. The key point is that business marketers should strive to communicate to customers the quality of the service they provide.

Other Business Product Classifications

It is obvious that the traditional business product classification system was developed mainly to categorize products, materials, and services being purchased by manufacturing companies. In that context it is a very useful system because the operational implications for business marketers can be derived from it. However, this traditional system may be less adequate in nonmanufacturing circumstances. Chapter 3 introduces the Robinson, Faris, and Wind Buygrid model, which groups products according to the novelty of the purchasing situation in the buying organization. Chapter 9 presents yet a third classification approach, based on the degree of customization or adaptation of the product.

DIFFERENCES BETWEEN BUSINESS MARKETING AND CONSUMER MARKETING

Some marketers contend that "marketing is marketing" no matter where or by whom products and services are bought and sold.[11] To the extent that the marketing concept is incorporated into the strategy and tactics of the organization, this is true. However, many others, including the authors of this text, contend that business marketing differs so substantively that it deserves special attention. In some cases the differences are a matter of degree or emphasis. Yet other aspects of business marketing are unique.

This section examines differences between business marketing and consumer marketing with respect to market structure, marketing philosophy, buyer behavior, purchasing decisions, marketing research, product/service mix, promotion, distribution mix, and price (see Exhibit 1–5). Each of these topics will be discussed in more detail in the chapters that follow. After examining the points developed in this section, you can decide for yourself whether business marketing is different from consumer marketing.

Market Structure

Market structure refers to the characteristics used to describe the group of organizations that buy the products and services of a business marketer. These factors include competition, demand, price elasticity of demand, market and buyer size, and location of the market.

Competition.   Business markets have fewer sellers and decidedly fewer buyers in any market segment than do consumer markets. Competition in business markets tends to be more oligopolistic (fewer sellers and many buyers), whereas consumer markets are more monopolistic (many buyers and sellers, and differentiation among competing products).

Demand.   Whereas consumers initiate a **direct demand** with their purchases, the demand for business products or services depends on the level of activity that the buying organization (the business marketer's customer) can generate in its own markets. Thus business demand is *derived* (second- or thirdhand, or more). This **derived demand** would not exist if the customer organization, in turn, could not find customers or clients for its own products or services.

Demand Levels.   The organizational buyer may use a piece of production equipment to produce 10,000 units per year. Thus, a second machine is required only if sales are expected to exceed 10,000 units. As a result, there is no direct one-to-one relationship between the customer's (for example, a retailer's) sales fluctuations and the business marketer's sales. This accentuates the swings in derived demand, making sales to business buyers far more volatile than changes of demand experienced in consumer markets by a retailer.

Reverse Elasticity.   When organizational buyers see prices start to decline, they may postpone buying in the expectation of obtaining an even lower price later. The opposite holds if the organizational buyer anticipates continuing price increases. In this case, when prices begin to rise, more volume than is immediately

EXHIBIT 1–5   Differences Between Business Marketing and Consumer Marketing

	Characteristic	*Business Marketing*	*Consumer Marketing*
Market Structure	Competition	Oligopolistic	Monopolistic
	Demand	Derived	Direct
	Demand levels	More volatile	Less volatile
	Reverse elasticity	Frequent	Infrequent
	Total market size	Larger	Smaller
	Size of buying unit	Group	Individual
	Market geography	Concentrated	Diffuse
Marketing Philosophy	Market segmentation	Emporographics	Demographics
	Investment requirements	Strategic	Tactical
	Market perspective	Global	Regional/national
	Tactical marketing emphasis	Profit performance	Market share
	Innovation	Technology-push	Demand-pull
	Buyer/seller interaction	Relationship	Transactional
	Reciprocity	Frequent	Rare
	Key accounts	Important	Nonexistent
	Customer education	Strong	Weak
Buyer Behavior	Customer/prospect mix	Small	Large
	Order size and frequency	Large, infrequent	Small, frequent
	Purchasing motives and skills	Rational, professional	Emotional, self-gratifying
	Contractual penalties	Common	Never
	Buying power	Strong	Weak
	Vendor loyalty	Strong	Weak
	Purchase involvement	Greater	Smaller
Purchasing Decisions	Decision-making process	Complex, lengthy	Simple, short
	Accounting/tax considerations	Important	Unimportant
	Purchase risk	Very high	Low
Marketing Research	Orientation	Strategic	Tactical
	Research approach	Empirical	Inferential
	Questionnaire terminology	Technical	Nontechnical
	Precision of data	Rough estimates	Statistical precision
	Costs of projects	Low	High
Product/ Service Mix	Product life cycle	Shorter	Longer
	Product specification	Customized	Standardized
	Branding	Corporate family	Individual product
	Purchase timing	Requirement planning	Immediate use
	Degree of fabrication	Value-adding stages required	Mostly finished goods
	Type of packaging	Protective	Promotional
	Services	Much more, pre- and post-transactional	Less, point-of-purchase
	Equipment compatibility	Good	Poor
	Consistency of quality	Critical	Not vital
	Industrial design	Less frequent	More frequent
	Systems selling	More frequent	Less frequent

EXHIBIT 1–5   Differences Between Business Marketing and Consumer Marketing (*cont.*)

	Characteristic	*Business Marketing*	*Consumer Marketing*
Promotion	Promotional emphasis	Personal selling	Mass advertising
	Promotional objectives	Preparing for sales call	Positioning product and firm
	Promotional themes	Rational, factual	Fanciful, imaginative
	Role of salesperson	Problem solving	Persuasion
	Sales promotion tools	Specification sheets, catalogs, direct mail, trade shows	Coupons, samples, point-of-purchase displays
Distribution Mix	Channel length	Short, direct	Long, indirect
	Channel complexity	Complex	Simple
	Product knowledge	Strong	Weak
	Channel coverage	Direct, exclusive	Intensive, selective
	Delivery reliability	Crucial	Not critical
Price	Competitive bidding	Common	Rare
	Price negotiation	Common	Rare
	Leasing	Common	Rare
	Product life cycle costs and benefits	Important	Usually ignored
	Discount structures	Complex	Straightforward
	Promotional pricing	Seldom used	Frequently used

needed is purchased to avoid paying even higher prices later. Such **reverse price elasticity of demand** is infrequent in consumer markets.

Total Market Size.   Business markets include not only the various early, value-adding stages of manufacturing and distributing consumer goods, but also the sales of business goods and services to manufacturing, processing, commercial, institutional, and government organizations. As a result, the business market is significantly larger—indeed, four times larger—than the consumer market.[12]

Size of Buying Unit.   The organizational buying unit—often called **central buying unit (CBU)**, **decision-making unit (DMU)**, **multiple buying influence (MBI)**, or **buying center**—usually involves several individuals. One reason is that various departments of an organization are affected by the purchase. For example, in the factory, the purchase of certain machinery may affect output quality (quality control department), the plant manager's budget, machinist productivity (the union), the acquisition of funds (finance department), the engineering department, and a purchasing agent. Another reason is that many minds often can make a better decision. A third point of view is that group membership removes the decision-making responsibility from any single individual. This can be quite useful if the decision turns out to be a poor one. For the business marketer, the group of people involved in the purchasing decision represent a veritable "who's who" in the buying organization. Each individual imposes different perspectives, expectations, and requirements on the purchase. In contrast, the consumer purchase usually involves an individual or, at most, one or two family members.

Market Geography.   Think of oil, and Texas, Alberta, and Iran come to mind. Similarly, cutlery manufacturing suggests Sheffield, England, and Toledo, Spain. Pittsburgh, Pennsylvania, and Hamilton, Ontario, are associated with steel production. The Detroit/Windsor and Oakville, Ontario, areas are North American automobile manufacturing centers. Birmingham and Coventry are centers of British motor vehicle production. Semiconductors and integrated circuit manufacturers have congregated in "Silicon Valley" near San Francisco, around Route 128 near Boston, and in "Silicon Valley North," near Ottawa. In industry after industry, business marketers tend to concentrate geographically because of the availability of natural resources or of a skilled work force, the distribution advantages, or the desire to be close to customers. Thus, business markets tend to be geographically concentrated, and business marketers travel significant distances from one cluster of customers to another. Consumer markets are more diffuse, generally spread out according to population location.

Marketing Philosophy

The concepts or philosophies of business marketing differ substantially from those of consumer marketing. One basic difference we have already mentioned is that consumer goods are usually classified according to how they are purchased (convenience, shopping, specialty, unsought), and industrial goods are categorized according to their use or buying situation (task) or degree of customization. Other significant differences occur in the areas of market segmentation, investment requirements, market perspective, tactical marketing emphasis, innovation, buyer/seller interaction, reciprocity, key accounts, and customer education.

Market Segmentation.   Consumer marketers use demographics (age, income, location) and sociopsychological dimensions (attitudes, preferences, personality, lifestyle) to segment their markets. Business marketers, on the other hand, use **emporographics** (industry, end market served, level of technology, ownership), SIC (Standard Industrial Classification) codes, and characteristics of the buying units (number of influences, ad hoc versus standing committees, centralized versus decentralized, annual volume of purchase) to segment their markets. (Market segmentation is discussed in detail in Chapter 6.)

Investment Requirements.   Business marketers tend to have higher strategic investments—that is, investments in capital equipment and research and development (R&D). For example, it takes $100 million to build a silicon fabrication line, and a computer chip manufacturer must have several of them to be competitive.[13] Consumer marketers' investments are more tactical—that is, directed more toward marketing activities (researching their huge customer base and promoting to mass markets).

Market Perspective.   Consumer marketers typically seek regional or national markets because their products are created to appeal to local tastes and they can find sufficient sales volumes at home. Business goods and services are less dependent on regional tastes and preferences. Furthermore, their specialized technologies and limited applications often require that customers be sought abroad to achieve economic production volumes and to justify high R&D costs and capital investments. Even a country with a large production in, for example, electronic equipment, may import as much as it exports. Business marketing must, therefore, have a more global perspective of markets, in terms of both customers and competitors.

Tactical Marketing Emphasis.   Most consumer marketers are concerned with seeking market share and sales volumes (frequently hoping for future profit as a result). Business marketers are more likely to have a sizable share of highly segmented, smaller, specialized markets, resulting in more restricted sales volumes. Thus, business marketers tend to focus on profit performance and profit improvement in the short run.

Innovation.   In consumer markets, innovation involves greater emphasis on style and incremental changes to products that can justify model changes. Innovation tends to be more of a **demand-pull** type (new products are developed as a result of assessment of consumer needs and wants). In contrast, innovation in business markets is characterized by R&D **technological-push** and radical-breakthrough developments that may revolutionize entire industries. An example is the creation of the transistor, which came from Bell Labs' research efforts and quickly replaced vacuum tubes in the electronics industry. No amount of identifying unsatisfied consumer needs could have led to the development of the transistor.

Buyer/Seller Interaction.   Because business marketers deal with a smaller number of customers, frequently on a face-to-face basis, they are more sensitive and responsive to their customers' requirements. In that sense, business marketers are far more customer oriented than are consumer marketers. Consumer marketers' relations with customers usually are distanced by long, indirect channels of distribution and are reduced to a mass of transactions made at "arm's length." Organizational buyers and sellers usually enter stable, long-term relationships in which each depends on the other for continuing business success. Thus, strong loyalty is developed between buyer and seller in organizational markets.

Reciprocity.   Frequently in business markets, two organizations could be buyers of each other's products or services. For example, an automobile manufacturer requires computer word processors, and a computer manufacturer requires automobiles for its sales force. In such a situation, **reciprocity** may be practiced: "I'll buy from you if you buy from me." Business marketers frequently use reciprocity as a tactic to win sales in the business market. This situation rarely is possible in the consumer market.

Key Accounts.   Within the customer base of a business marketer there usually are from a dozen to as many as a hundred customer firms that the marketer designates as **key accounts**. These are firms whose business is so important that its loss could significantly impair the marketer's sales volume, profitability, or corporate image. Clearly, the marketer must maintain close contact with these important customers to maintain its supplier status. No similar situation exists in consumer markets.

Customer Education.   For many business marketers, customer education is an important part of the marketing strategy. IBM gained a successful **niche** in the mainframe computer market by sending its representatives to spend periods of months, even years, in the customer's company, working side by side with the customer's staff to write and run programs and help them learn how to use IBM equipment. Typically, business and industrial equipment has more complete instruction manuals, specification sheets, and repair and maintenance books than does consumer equipment.

Buyer Behavior

Business buyer behavior depends on a number of factors. Business buyers have more personal contact with suppliers, buy infrequently but in large quantities, and tend to be very objective and professional in buying. Because their dollar purchases are large, they can penalize nonperforming suppliers, but are very loyal and work closely with reliable suppliers.

Customer/Prospect Mix.   Markets are composed of customers and those who may in the future become customers (prospects). Whereas consumer marketers' customer bases range from the thousands to the hundreds of thousands and, for some, the millions, business marketers' customers range from as few as one major buyer to a few thousand. For this reason, business marketers tend to be closer to their customers and more in tune with customers' buying behavior.

Order Size and Frequency.   Although the number of customers in organizational markets may be small, their orders tend to be quite large in number of units, dollar value, or both. For example, a university with 10,000 students typically orders 6,500 F40CW fluorescent light tubes; 7,400 F40CW/RS/EW Econowatt fluorescent light tubes; and 6,000 60-2watt incandescent light bulbs per year. Organizational buyers purchase for inventory and sometimes calculate **economic order quantities (EOQ)** when buying supplies, components, and materials. EOQ is the number of units calculated to minimize the sum of ordering costs and inventory costs. Purchasing departments may purchase supplies using systems contracts with the vendor, under which they contract to purchase an entire year's supply of an item from a single vendor. The university in the previous example, for instance, buys lighting supplies under such a systems contract, with orders delivered only once a month. In contrast, consumer buyers purchase in small quantities and frequently.

Purchasing Motives and Skills.   The purchasing motives of organizational buyers relate to maintaining and furthering the organization's goals. These motives are rational, economic, objective, and profit or efficiency oriented compared with the more emotionally based, self-gratifying motives underlying consumer purchases.[14] Business buyers are technically qualified purchasing specialists. Their career experiences in purchasing are augmented by attending continuing training courses and seminars in buying. In large companies they may specialize in the purchase of certain commodities and products. For example, farm equipment manufacturers, such as J I Case or John Deere, typically employ an individual who specializes in purchasing paints and other coatings. The central buying unit of a retail chain such as Sears employs different purchasing people who are specialists in buying home entertainment products, housewares, clothing, home furnishings, and so on.

Contractual Penalties.   Organizational buyers may build substantial penalties for shoddy work or nonperformance into contracts with their suppliers. For example, a contract may specify that the business marketer must pay $1,000 for every day's delay in delivery of an order, or even higher penalties for delay in the construction of a building or in the completion of machinery installation in a plant. Such penalties are never part of consumer markets.

Buying Power.   If an industrial manufacturer's plant is running under capacity, or a customer's order today has the potential of significant follow-on business in the future, or if the order represents a sizable portion of the marketer's business, the customer can exert a strong influence on the business marketer's price, product design, delivery, and other dimensions of the business. Such buying power never exists in consumer markets. The aggressive use of buying power by a purchasing officer to encourage or persuade a supplier to sell a product or service that more closely meets the buyer's particular requirements is called "reverse marketing."[15]

Vendor Loyalty.   Organizational buyers often exhibit strong loyalty to their current or in-supplier. In general, **vendor loyalty** is a characteristic of the strong interdependence between organizational buyers and their suppliers. The industrial buyer who changes vendors faces high **switching costs**, such as the effort of training a new supplier in the intricacies of the buyer's particular business, the possible loss of confidential trade secrets if the supplier is abandoned, and the high cost of identifying and qualifying an alternative supplier. In contrast, consumer loyalty to specific retailers or product brands is weak, and the consequences of brand or supplier switching are not serious to the consumer.

Purchase Involvement. The organizational buyer's involvement in a purchase is much greater than that of a consumer. The business buyer must plan the firm's requirements and specify technical and delivery details of the purchase, frequently with the assistance of the supplier. The business buyer may help the supplier develop the capability to supply what is needed,[16] may negotiate for many months with the supplier, and must monitor supplier performance over the life of the contract.

Purchasing Decisions

Purchasing decisions can be complex and lengthy and usually involve several people in the buying organization. They also have tax and accounting implications for the firm. Furthermore, the business buyer must evaluate the risks inherent in the purchase.

Decision-making Process. The organizational purchasing decision process typically is complex, involving several functional areas of the buying organization, each with different points of view.[17] Committees discuss the pros and cons of a purchase using documented data, proposals, purchase specifications, competitive bids, vendor analyses, and reports. Business buyers also often have the option of making a product or providing the service themselves rather than simply buying it. The organizational decision-making process is observable and progresses through distinctive stages (see Exhibit 1–2). It can also be quite lengthy. For example, the purchase of two executive jets for several million dollars by a U.S. manufacturer involved thirty-seven participants, took a year and a half for the decision to be reached after the need had been identified, and received final approval from an eighteen-member top-corporate-officer committee.

In contrast, the consumer purchasing decision process is relatively simple and short. It takes place in the buyer's mind and cannot be observed. Although consumers may be able to make a product or provide a service themselves, this option is generally not as available to the consumer as it is to the business buyer.

Accounting/Tax Considerations. In business markets, the way purchases are accounted for—for example, current or capital expense, depreciation method, distribution of cost—and the tax implications of the purchases will affect what is purchased, the timing of the purchases, and how the goods and services are bought. Product life cycle costs (operating and disposal costs) may be more important than acquisition costs. In consumer purchases, accounting or tax considerations are rare.

Purchase Risk. The business buyer's risk can be very high. It is greatest in the new-task situation, in which the buying situation has not been encountered before. Risk is least in the straight-rebuy situation, in which purchasing involves simply reordering. But even in a straight rebuy there are risks, such as the delivery risk (late or incomplete shipment or damaged goods). Performance risk is reduced by

Babcock & Wilcox Gains a Foothold in China

Babcock & Wilcox, a wholly owned subsidiary of McDermott International Inc., has been in the business of making steam boilers since 1867. Looking for a high-growth area to exploit in the twenty-first century, the company approached the People's Republic of China, whose per capita consumption of electric power is only one-thirtieth of that of the United States, but whose population exceeds 1 billion (four times the U.S. population). As China becomes more industrialized, this largest market in the world will require more industrial steam to produce electricity, and more steam boilers. In August 1986 a joint venture between Babcock & Wilcox and the Beijing Boiler Works began operation under the name of Babcock & Wilcox Beijing Company Ltd. Despite a shortage of skilled workers, a material procurement system in which state-supplied material can be obtained only twice a year (resulting in costly inventories), extra packing costs to protect products from rougher railway handling, higher finished-goods inventories due to railcar shortages, and the high cost of maintaining expatriate employees in Beijing (more than $150,000 per year per family), the company is operating profitably.

"The huge potential of the Chinese business market makes marketers' eyes light up as they project what will happen when China is using as much electricity per capita as the United States," states Paul P. Koenderman, vice president and general manager of Babcock & Wilcox, International Division. "Because we believed that we could not expect to export manufactured goods to China on an ongoing basis when the country becomes capable of being self-sufficient, we concluded that a joint venture was the only way we could participate in the Chinese market in a meaningful and long-term way. Also, we expect that our Chinese venture will help us compete elsewhere in the future."

The formation of the alliance illustrates the problems, perseverance, patience, and long periods of time that business marketers often must sustain in their efforts to do business in international markets. It took Babcock & Wilcox three years to gain a foothold in China, as is shown in the chronology of events that followed its decision to seek a Chinese market:

1983	October	First meeting in Beijing
1984	February	Technical meetings in Beijing
	September	Chinese officials visit Babcock & Wilcox
	November	B&W evaluates manufacturing facilities in Beijing
1985	March	Feasibility study negotiations in Beijing
	April	Visit to Beijing by B&W vice president
	May	President of Beijing Machine Building Corp. visits B&W
	June	B&W president visits Beijing
	August	Negotiations in Beijing
	October	State Economic Commission vice minister visits B&W
	October	Joint venture contract signed in Beijing
	November	Contract and feasibility study submitted to Chinese government
1986	January	First group of B&W people moves to China
	February	Joint venture contract approved by Chinese government
	June	Chinese government issues business license
	August	Babcock & Wilcox Beijing Company Ltd. begins operation

Source: Paul P. Koenderman, Vice President and General Manager, Babcock & Wilcox, International Division, as related to Terry Seawright, business marketing lecturer and consultant, Toronto, Ontario.

purchasing from large, well-known, and reputable companies and by continuing to buy from the same supplier (vendor loyalty). In the U.K. machine tool industry, for example, 60 percent of machine purchases are from suppliers from which the buyer has previously purchased.[18] Consumers' purchases also involve risk, usually proportional to the dollar value of the purchase. But in most cases the risk is relatively minor, and the consumer simply switches to a competing product (e.g., a different brand of candy bar) or doesn't buy the item again if dissatisfied.

Marketing Research

Marketing research studies in business markets usually are conducted by the marketer's own staff among key accounts because the jargon or vocabulary of the particular industry must be understood by the researchers. Studies are broad and strategic in scope, seek general information rather than precise data, and are low in cost.

Orientation.   Business marketing research is more strategically focused than is consumer marketing research. Each project tends to be unique with a specific goal in mind. Examples of business marketing research include economic forecasting, new-product potential and acceptance, and value analysis. Consumer marketing studies are more concerned with tactical issues, such as product tests, measurement of advertising effectiveness, package design, and data collection for establishing sales quotas and evaluating sales territories. Consumer studies typically involve repeated and continuous surveys to determine trends.

Research Approach.   Business marketing involves empirical studies and personal contact with customers. Usually business marketing research surveys the entire group of key customer accounts and samples the remainder of the customer base. In contrast, consumer marketing research depends heavily on inferential, statistical techniques. Organizational researchers are typically the business marketer's in-house personnel. Consumer marketers more frequently use external research specialists.

Questionnaire Terminology.   Business marketing researchers must be conversant with the specialized terminology of the business and knowledgeable about relevant industry technologies and products. Consumer researchers require little, if any, product or industry knowledge and may communicate on any language level that provides mutual understanding with the people being interviewed.

Precision of Data.   Business research projects tend to seek rough (order-of-magnitude) estimates through unstructured interviews, whereas consumer research studies use highly structured questionnaires yielding precise measurements bracketed by statistical confidence limits.

Cost of Projects.   Generally, business research entails relatively low cost compared with the very high-cost studies conducted for consumer marketers. Lower costs come from doing more secondary and less primary research and from using smaller samples.

Product/Service Mix

The product/service mix is an area of marketing with the greatest number of differences between consumer and business markets. Business products have shorter product life cycles, are less likely to be branded, and are precisely specified by buyers for a future use. Packaging is mainly for protection, and services associated with the product are extensive. Business products usually are manufactured to specific industry technical and quality standards, but functionality overrides their aesthetics. Often total systems are offered to provide comprehensive solutions to the business customer's needs.

Product Life Cycle.   The business **product life cycle (PLC)** is shorter than that of consumer products because of the rapidity of technological change and innovation in business markets.

Product Specification.   Organization products involve far more customization to the customer's technical requirements and specifications than do consumer products, which for the most part have been prespecified by the supplier, are standardized, and cannot be adjusted or modified. The consumer usually can only select from a smorgasbord offering.

Branding.   Business products generally are identified by a corporate family brand, such as Caterpillar tractors, whereas consumer products are more frequently identified by individual product brands, such as Tide laundry detergent.

Purchase Timing.   Consumers usually buy products for immediate use, whereas organizations buy products to fit a requirement planning sequence. Consequently, businesses typically purchase products to be stored in inventory before they are needed for actual use.

Degree of Fabrication.   Most consumer goods are purchased as finished end products. A large portion of business purchases are materials and components that must undergo further value-adding stages.

Type of Packaging.   Packaging performs two major functions: protection of contents and promotion. The protection aspect is more important in business product packaging, whereas promotion plays the more significant role in consumer product packaging.

Services.   Organizational customers demand and receive more services in association with products than do customers in the consumer market, and **pre- and posttransaction service** is proportionately greater in the business market. Business market services range from delivery services to technical services. In contrast, consumers expect and find more **point-of-purchase services**, such as credit and display services, and receive fewer pre- and posttransaction service.

Equipment Compatibility.   Business buyers expect various pieces of equipment they purchase to match and work well together. For example, electronic broadcasting, time-coding, and editing equipment must conform to industry technical standards and mounting panel dimensions. In contrast, consumer equipment, such as household appliances, exhibits a wide variety of technical specifications and dimensions and is unlikely to match well, even when offered by the same manufacturer.

Consistency of Quality.   The smooth and uninterrupted operation of a business organization depends on the uniform and predictable quality of its inputs. These characteristics are not critical to consumers and are less prevalent in consumer products.

Industrial Design.   **Industrial design** creates products that are not only functional, but also aesthetically pleasing and ergonomically sound—that is, they compensate for the limitations of the human body. Good industrial design is more often encountered in consumer products than in business products.

Systems Selling.   **Systems selling** involves offering a complete package of products and services, including design, installation, and service, thereby providing a comprehensive solution to a customer's requirements and problems. IBM's offering of hardware, software, maintenance, and in-company customer training is an example of systems selling. Far more systems selling is available to organizational buyers than to consumers.

Promotion

Business promotion focuses on rational, economic themes. Personal selling dominates the business marketer's promotion mix. The salesperson primarily seeks to solve business customers' problems, and often is supported by a group of inside (telephone) salespeople. Business advertising is used to prepare the customer for the sales call and is augmented by a range of sales promotion tools, including trade shows.

Promotional Emphasis.   Because the organizational buyer requires the help of the supplier in solving technical problems and because the buyer negotiates with the supplier, the business marketer's promotion mix emphasizes personal selling.

Consumer marketers must reach multitudes of customers and therefore use mass promotion techniques, with the heaviest emphasis on advertising.

Promotional Objectives.   The cost of personal selling is extremely high, averaging $259 per sales call in 1989 business markets.[19] Hence, the objective of organizational promotion is to prepare the customer for the sales call by presenting information about the selling organization, its product lines, its customer mix, and its areas of specialization. Then, during the sales call, the salesperson will be able to devote valuable time to the more difficult and productive activities of problem solving and negotiation, rather than answering a lot of questions for which the customer should already have answers. Consumer advertising concentrates more on positioning products relative to competing products.

Promotional Themes.   Messages directed to organizational buyers emphasize factual, rational, and economic issues, such as technical specifications, performance characteristics, and enhancement of the customer's efficiency and profits. In contrast, consumer appeals are more emotional and stress feelings and self-image. Consumer promotional claims are more imaginative and less factual.

Role of the Salesperson.   The business salesperson is primarily a technical problem solver, providing information and solutions. Product training is extensive, and the salesperson usually has a thorough background and experience in the industry. In contrast, the consumer salesperson recognizes that there are many similar competing solutions for the consumer's needs and therefore relies less on information and more on persuasion. Consumer salesperson training focuses less on product knowledge and more on developing selling techniques. **Inside salespeople—** salespeople who contact customers solely by telephone—are widely used in the business market. They inform customers of inventory levels and product availability, solve customer problems over the telephone, and solicit new prospects for outside salespeople to visit. Inside salespeople are not used extensively by consumer marketers.

Sales Promotion Tools.   Organizational sales promotion makes more use of specification sheets, catalogs, direct mail, trade shows, and exhibits. Consumer marketers, on the other hand, rely more on couponing, sampling, and point-of-purchase displays.

Distribution Mix

The distribution mix differs between consumer and business marketing. Business channels are shorter but more complex, and channel members have greater product knowledge. More direct, selective, or exclusive channels are used, and delivery reliability is crucial.

Channel Length.   Business distribution channels tend to be short and direct because of the customer's needs for technical assistance and assured delivery. The geographic concentration of business customers facilitates shorter channels and provides sufficient sales volume to support dealerships, branches, and direct calls by salespeople. Channels for consumer products usually are much longer and more indirect.

Channel Complexity.   Although business channels generally are shorter, they tend to be more complex than channels for consumer products because of the many different types of businesses and classes of customers that make up organizational markets. A manufacturer of an industrial product such as refrigeration equipment may sell to the federal government, to OEMs in several different industries, to contractors, to repair and maintenance companies, and through various types of distributors and manufacturer's agents in different territories. In contrast, a manufacturer of a consumer product such as corn flakes would sell to supermarkets, hotels, restaurants, and convenience stores through a food broker.

Product Knowledge.   Business channel members must be thoroughly familiar with the technical aspects of the products they handle and the industries and commercial organizations to which they sell. In contrast, retailers' product knowledge is weak. Retailers concentrate on maintaining inventories, providing product display, and offering credit and delivery service.

Channel Coverage.   Because of the mass of buyers and the diffuse nature of consumer markets, consumer marketers most frequently use intensive and selective channels of distribution. Smaller numbers and greater concentrations of customers in organizational markets provide more opportunities for business marketers to use direct or exclusive distribution approaches.

Delivery Reliability.   Late delivery, misdirected shipments, and damaged goods, although annoying, nevertheless usually are not disastrous for consumers. On the other hand, in business markets reliability is crucial and has a direct impact on profitability. Shipment expediting and vendor performance analysis are therefore important functions in business markets. Organizational customers may also negotiate JIT arrangements, impose nonperformance penalties on their suppliers, and periodically evaluate various logistical alternatives.

Price

Because acquisition costs represent a large proportion of a business's total costs and have a direct impact on profit, organizational buyers use every means to achieve better supply prices. Consumers do not engage in such meticulous analysis and generally tend to be less price sensitive than business buyers. Organizational buyers frequently use competitive bidding and negotiation to arrive at a purchase agreement. Leasing is another means of avoiding large capital outlays. Business marketers must pay particular attention to the customer's evaluation of the cost and benefits of the purchase throughout the product's life cycle. Business marketers usually offer customers a complex of discount opportunities but rarely trade off lower price as an alternative to promotion.

Competitive Bidding.   Organizational buyers make extensive use of **competitive bidding**, ranging from the less formal solicitation of quotations to the very formal sealed-bid tender requests that are used by government agencies to avoid any appearance of underhandedness. Some companies have policies requiring a minimum number of price quotations for every acquisition. Price comparisons in consumer markets are usually informal, are often based on impressions rather than facts, and are usually limited to homogeneous shopping goods.

Price Negotiation.   **Price negotiation** is a common practice in business markets, with various tradeoffs in specifications and product/service requirements changing throughout the negotiation process. In the high-level economies of North America, Europe, and Japan, consumers generally accept or reject the prices offered to them, and little if any negotiation is involved in the transaction.

Leasing.   Organizational customers often use **leasing** as an alternative to financing a large purchase because of the current-expense balance sheet implications of leasing versus ownership. Consumers seldom use leasing arrangements.

Product Life Cycle Costs and Benefits.   The price of a purchased business product is only one of the various cost considerations evaluated by organizational buyers. A manufacturing customer when buying a production machine must consider the lifetime costs and benefits of the purchase. These might include such factors as faster machining speeds, higher output, lower energy consumption, lower maintenance costs, lower repair costs, lower downtime for setup, greater functional flexibility, higher resale price as used equipment, or lower disposal costs. A manufacturer, considering several alternative components to purchase, might also evaluate their prices, benefits, and costs in terms of value added from the end customer's perspective. This is part of a manufacturer's value analysis of the product's manufacturer.

An intermediary in the distribution channel must consider how long a particular purchase will incur inventory costs. A business organization must also consider the effect of a purchase on its employees and the union. All business buyers must weigh the effects of technological (and style) obsolescence on purchases and their potential for adaptation, modification, or upgrading as technology changes. These considerations may make the acquisition price considerably less important than the lifetime costs and benefits for the organizational purchaser. Such careful evaluations are not as common in consumer markets.

This product is being advertised to consumers. What kind of appeal is used?

Courtesy of 3M Corporation.

Discount Structures.   Many business products are marketed under published **list** or **book prices**. A complicated set of discounts is subsequently applied to the list price. These discounts depend on such factors as

- The class of customer (government, distributor, dealer, and user)
- The volume of purchase (single-purchase quantity, annual requirement)
- The services performed by the customer on behalf of the seller (discounts for advertising, delivery)
- The seller's need for business (to provide work for an underutilized manufacturing plant)
- Industry and competitive conditions

Notice how the appeal for the product changes when it is advertised to business markets.

THERE'S NO SUCH THING AS A LITTLE STAIN.

A little ketchup on the upholstery is enough to kill the joy of a new car. That's why Chevrolet selected interior fabrics with Scotchgard™ Protector for their 1990 cars.

Mill-applied, locked-on Scotchgard™ Fabric Protector adds value to cars because most spills wipe right up before they become stains.

It also adds saleability. Because Scotchgard™ brand is the best known name in protectors and again this year it is being backed by a multi-million dollar, global advertising campaign.

Add saleability and value to your cars with Scotchgard™ Protector. Contact 3M Protective Chemical Products Division, Automotive Industry Center, 2100 Telegraph Road, Southfield, MI 48034-4269, 313-827-6919. Because even a little stain is too much.

© 3M 1990

98-0211-5077-0

Scotchgard Protector

Innovation working for you™ **3M**

Courtesy of 3M Corporation.

- The probability of follow-on business
- The perceived relative buying/negotiation power of the buyer

Unlike the discount structures for business products, consumer discounts are more straightforward.

Conclusion

Now that we have examined some of the differences between marketing to consumers and marketing to business customers, you can see that the unique characteristics of business markets require awareness, understanding, and special attention by the business marketer. One qualification should be mentioned: as with any contrast, the situation is never entirely black or white. Indeed, it is often the exception that proves the rule. Nevertheless, the distinctions between markets that we have identified generally hold true.

BUSINESS MARKETING: AN INTERNATIONAL PERSPECTIVE

Are business marketers internationally minded? Some are and some are not. Should they be? Yes, most or almost all of them should be. Why? Because their customers may be abroad as well as at home. Business marketers' suppliers may come from across the street, but they are just as likely to be from across the continent, or across the ocean in a different hemisphere. Today we speak of the global village, where everyone is interconnected. The U.S.–Canada Free Trade Agreement is one example of just how close such connections can become. Interdependency is very much the case for businesses, large or small, that cater to other businesses. Exporting and importing are not just the domain of the largest firms. Whether large or small, whether in traditional or high-tech sectors, the astute marketer should look widely for both clients and suppliers.

Examples of International Business Marketing

Let us consider four specific sectors, two of them making goods (forging plants and water treatment chemical firms), and two of them offering services (geographic information services and small package delivery). What stands out in each of these examples is that selling and purchasing are important and complex processes. There is much competition, but it is also possible to have cooperative or joint ventures. Technology plays a role in many of these fields. The four P's of marketing (product, price, promotion, and place) are important, but so are conducting market research, formulating a strategic plan, establishing controls, and motivating fellow workers. In short, many operational steps are involved; a vision of the future is also a necessity. We will not cover all these aspects in the following examples, but we shall unfold them in the chapters to come.

The Field of Forging.   Like old-time blacksmiths, modern forging plants heat and treat various metals, then hammer and press them into various shapes. Forging improves the durability and strength of metals, so products—such as axles, crankshafts, and hand tools—can withstand stress. The modern forging firm uses sophisticated furnaces, computers, and instruments because clients demand blemish-free output. Viking Forge of Streetsboro, Ohio, and Impact Forge of Columbus, Indiana, both located in the heart of the U.S. Midwest, offer precision forgings with strict tolerances to customers at home and abroad. They can compete successfully against European and Asian forging shops because they have modernized their plants and equipment.[20]

Water Treatment Chemicals.   These compounds are used to cleanse both incoming water and outgoing wastewater. For many years, business firms thought that such spending was wasteful, but under government and public pressure they have realized that pollution control is a must. Water treatment chemicals firms made their big breakthrough when they demonstrated two things to their clients. First, they emphasized that it may be cheaper to buy chemicals rather than water treatment equipment. Second, they showed that by keeping water pipes clean, energy savings can be effected. Among the leading firms are Betz Laboratories and Nalco Chemical of the United States, Degremont of France, and Portals of England. They vie for domestic and foreign markets, often using technological advances as a competitive edge. Many of these firms publish handbooks and encourage their staff to offer technical advice; these steps are seen as a goodwill gesture as well as a "soft-touch" selling technique.[21]

Geographic Information Systems.   Computerized mapping is a promising technology that is poised to become one of the fastest-growing industries in the United States and worldwide. Who are and who will be the customers for such "spatial databases"? Large banks, insurance companies, retailers, and transportation firms are the most likely to buy. They want to know where their customers are, where potential clients reside, and even where competitors' branches are located. But so far mostly utilities and government agencies have signed up to obtain these digital maps. In the United States alone, there are over 70,000 government agencies. So, the future is rosy for such firms as Geovision, Intergraph, and ESRI, three of the leading U.S. firms. They are now looking at foreign markets, especially at metropolitan areas in Europe, Asia, and Latin America. A detailed geographical information system can show all land records and infrastructure, thereby assisting municipal governments to become more effective in delivering local services.[22]

Small Package Delivery.   Small package delivery has been a booming business ever since Fred Smith thought of the idea as an undergraduate student at Yale University. He established Federal Express, with a hub in Memphis, Tennessee. All packages are flown to Memphis, sorted by destination, and then re-shipped by overnight air cargo. Meanwhile, TNT in Australia and DHL in Europe have established their own routes and delivery system. UPS, an American firm, also has expanded overseas. The size of the market differs sharply from one region to another. FedEx was hoping to duplicate its success in the United States into rival turf in Europe. The company found, however, that whereas the U.S. market has 3 million express packages going from one state to another each day, the intra-European traffic amounts to only 130,000 packages (in 1992). In short, there are too many

BUSINESS MARKETING IN PRACTICE ████████████████

The U.S.–Canada Free Trade Agreement

The Free Trade Agreement (FTA) between the United States and Canada, which took effect on January 1, 1989, is another milestone in the realignment of world markets. Canada and Japan were the only members of the Organization for Economic Cooperation and Development (OECD) that did not belong to a significant trade area prior to 1989. We will likely see three major trading blocs emerge in the near future: the European Community (EC), Canada/United States/Mexico, and Japan/Pacific Rim. The realignment of world markets has been one of the catalysts to corporate restructuring, and the trend to globalization undoubtedly will continue unabated. The next catalyst is the initiation of the EC in 1992.

Business marketing will not see immediate major changes because of the FTA. Duty came off several products on January 1, 1989, but no revolution took place. Duties are scheduled to be removed over a ten-year period, but both nations are working on shortening this time span. Eighty percent of goods currently traded between the United States and Canada are tariff free. In the longer run, certain sectors of the Canadian business market will see change:

Industry	Impact of the FTA on Canadian Business
Energy	Increase in revenue and profits
Fisheries	More investment in Canadian Maritime Provinces
High technology	Restructuring of North American facilities
Financial industry	Canadian company investment in the United States Heavier U.S. competition in Canada
Garment industry	Slowdown (country-of-origin limitations)
Wine industry	Decline in Canada
Publishing	Restructuring, expansion in the United States
Utilities	Growth in exports to the United States
Leather industry	Decline in Canada
Services	Easier access to both countries, growth
Food industry	Little change (nontariff barriers remain)
Automobiles and parts	Little change
Resources	Little change (relative values of Canadian and U.S. dollar are very important here)
Steel	Restructuring, increased competition

In addition to the changes already mentioned, the FTA is likely to result in the following three opportunities and/or problems for the Canadian business marketer:

Cost/Service. Cost to Canadian buyers of goods from U.S. suppliers could be reduced by the amount of the duty. The reduced cost may or may not be passed on, depending on market conditions, and could change competitiveness. For example, Bull Worldwide Information Systems buys printers from France, whereas many Canadian competitors source from their U.S. parent companies. In a price-sensitive market, a 5 to 10 percent reduction in cost enjoyed by competitors may spell disaster for the Canadian manufacturer. Service by U.S. companies in the Canadian market may improve now that barriers are being dismantled.

Likewise, Canadian businessmen will now be able to visit U.S. clients without having to undergo detailed interrogation by U.S. customs and immigration officials at the border. The alternative for these businessmen was to travel constantly with a set of golf clubs and lie about the trip being for pleasure, just to avoid the time-consuming red tape.

Government Procurement. The FTA eliminated national preference on all (U.S. and Canadian) government procurement valued at more than U.S. $25,000. On the surface and according to government releases, this should open up an increased U.S. market of U.S. $3 billion; however, 80 percent of this market was already covered by the Canada–U.S. Defense Production Sharing Agreement. Thus the potential market expansion for Canadians selling to U.S. governments is closer to $600 million. From this must be subtracted the various set-asides not covered by the FTA. Two large barriers still must be overcome by a Canadian company seeking U.S. government contracts: the lack of awareness of the new rules by many procurement officers and the extremely complicated and difficult process involved in selling to the U.S. federal government. The sheer size and bureaucracy, not to speak of the complex federal, state, and local regulations, are enough to discourage even the most aggressive and optimistic Canadian company. U.S. access to Canadian procurement seems easier, and competition here should increase.

Market Information. The demand for U.S. market information (government and nongovernment) should increase as more and more Canadian firms start to view their market as North America.

The FTA offers advantages to business marketers in the United States and to their Canadian counterparts. Awareness of the effects of the FTA on Canadian businesses will help United States businesspeople compete with Canadian companies and will suggest areas in which opportunities exist for cooperation and joint ventures with Canadian firms.

Source: Contributed by Knud B. Jensen, Professor, School of Business Management, Ryerson Polytechnical Institute, Toronto, Ontario.

couriers and too much overcapacity; so for now, FedEx has stopped delivering between cities in Europe. The desire to capture markets continues, however, and rivals will square off again and again.[23]

Entering Foreign Markets

Why should business marketers enter the international arena? The reasons are many and usually can be attributed to a combination of forces. Domestic markets may be saturated, mature, or highly competitive. As a result, growth in sales, profits, and market share may be hard to achieve. In contrast, foreign markets may appear attractive—less competition, less saturation. It is also possible to line up partners abroad who can assist in the tasks of local distribution and promotion. Lower costs in foreign settings are often a great attraction. Possibly, the business marketer may wish to gain access to information—knowledge about local conditions, local technology, and local labor skills. Of course, the size and characteristics of foreign markets must be considered and weighed judiciously. For example, in the mid-1980s, Sherwin Williams, a major U.S. paint manufacturer, thought that its line of automotive and architectural paints would find a ready market in prosperous West Germany. Instead, the company found that particular market to be mature and very

EXHIBIT 1–6   The Spectrum of International Business Involvement

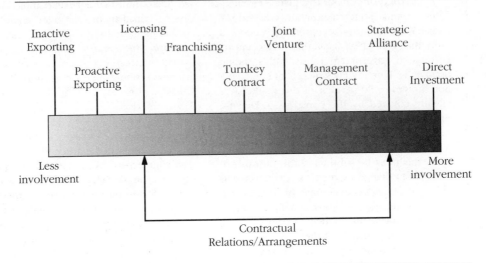

competitive. On further investigation, it entered the Caribbean market, specifically Jamaica. Although the size of this market was not nearly as large as West Germany's, it was viable because the people in Jamaica kept their cars and houses for a long time. So, Sherwin Williams was able to sell paints to dealers in large quantities.

How should business marketers enter foreign markets? The easiest way is to fill orders, called inactive exporting. Many business marketers, however, now solicit export orders in a proactive mode. After "learning the ropes," they may enter into contractual arrangements of various kinds, including licensing, franchising, joint ventures, strategic alliances, turnkey contracts, and management contracts. Finally, they may make direct investments in factories, offices, and laboratories abroad and commence operations on foreign soil. Direct investment is the most risky, but it can also be the most rewarding. Exhibit 1–6 illustrates all of these possibilities and the degree of involvement.

A LOOK AHEAD

In this chapter you have learned some of the concepts and language of business marketing. Both will be explored in greater depth as you progress through this book. Chapter 2 presents the concept of derived demand and its implications. The use of telescopic marketing is advocated, the "boom-bust" volatility of derived demand is explained, and a demand evaluation model is developed. The key message of Chapter 2 is to know your customers' customers.

Chapter 3 develops the factors affecting business buying decisions, introduces the concept of the buying center, and presents the Robinson, Faris, and Wind Buygrid. This chapter stresses the importance of the business marketer assuming responsibility for appropriate management of the buyer-seller relationship.

The marketer's need to understand the customer leads us to Chapter 4 and an examination of how purchasing is effected. Companies may have the choices of making or buying products, passively responding to marketers' offerings or actively developing their suppliers, using value or vendor analysis, and implementing just-in-time purchasing. That buyers use such approaches emphasizes the importance of developing good buyer-supplier relationships.

Information about customers and markets is essential to support effective business marketing decisions. Chapter 5 discusses how marketing research is used to uncover such information. Business marketers make extensive use of secondary sources, or desk research. Primary research, although it is more expensive to obtain, is also used to create new intelligence.

To match the organization's offering of goods and services to the needs and expectations of chosen groups of customers, the business marketer must be able to create macro- and microsegments. Chapter 6 explains the techniques of segmentation to choose targets, win clients, and retain customers.

No matter how carefully the business marketer segments markets, competitive forces play a significant role in determining a firm's success. Chapter 7 examines different facets of rivalry, concluding with eight minicases that describe rivalry in mature and emerging industries. The chapter also looks at alternatives to competition.

Intense competition from developing countries with lower labor costs has forced North Americans and Europeans to reexamine their sources of competitive advantage. One of the most important of these is technological strength. Chapter 8 discusses innovation, technology transfer, and technological forecasting. Minicases of technology-marketplace linkages in five industries illustrate the dynamics of technological innovation in business markets.

All business products, whether high-tech or low-tech, experience a life cycle. The fact that sooner or later they will die implies that a business must develop a stream of new products to assure continuity and growth of profits. Chapter 9 examines domestic and international new product development processes, together with product deletion decisions, niche marketing, industrial design, and strategic product approaches.

Business services have become the fastest-growing part of the product/service mix. Chapter 10 explores the unique characteristics of business services that make their creation, positioning, branding, promotion, and pricing so different from product marketing, both domestically and internationally.

Business pricing focuses attention on the costs of the business product or service to the buying organization, and the extent to which the marketer's offering yields added value to the operation of the customer's business. Chapter 11 discusses negotiation, competitive bidding, and pricing for export.

Marketing intermediaries, including industrial distributors and manufacturers' agents, are an alternative to the business marketer's dealing directly with the client organization. The use of intermediaries, the focus of Chapter 12, involves an understanding of the behavioral aspects of channel management and motivation.

Physical distribution decisions require the marketer to analyze the cost/benefit tradeoffs of different alternative methods of handling plant and warehouse location, order management, transportation, inventory management, packaging, and materials handling. Chapter 13 discusses the total cost approach to logistics.

A third of all business promotion costs are devoted to informing, convincing, and preselling current and potential customers through advertising, sales promotion, and publicity. Chapter 14 guides us through campaign development to achieve a balanced and consistent promotional effort.

The other two-thirds of business promotion costs are devoted to personal selling. The first part of Chapter 15 examines recruitment, selection, training, motivation, supervision, and compensation of the industrial sales force. The second part deals with sales force planning, organization, and control.

Chapter 16 considers two approaches to help the business marketer identify problems and opportunities: the internal system, which produces information from the company's invoice system, and the external system, which generates intelligence from a customer profile databank.

The final chapter of this text provides a framework for developing the firm's strategy and marketing plan. Chapter 17 cautions that all strategy/planning components must function in harmony with one another to produce a successful business marketing outcome.

Now that you have an overview, let us proceed to examine the distinctive features of business marketing in greater depth. Examples of how companies respond to the challenges of business marketing will demonstrate the exciting possibilities for innovative approaches used by business marketers.

SUMMARY

Marketing delivers a standard of living by creating products and services that provide utility to customers. Marketers are guided by the marketing concept of the total enterprise operating as an integrated system to provide customer satisfaction and to achieve its organizational goals. Business marketers choose to provide satisfaction to other businesspeople and businesses, government institutions, and nonprofit organizations. These customers purchase goods and services to incorporate in the goods and services that their firm produces, to further the operation of their organization, or to resell the goods (as an intermediary).

Consumers are individuals who buy for self-gratification and whose purchase motives are in large measure emotionally based. In contrast, business markets are composed of organizations whose purchases are mainly rationally and economically motivated.

Consumer goods are classified as convenience goods, shopping goods, specialty goods, and unsought goods. Business products may be classified according to *use* into seven main categories: capital equipment and investments; accessory equipment; component parts; process materials; maintenance, repair and operating (MRO) supplies; raw materials; and business services. Two other classifications systems may also be used. The Buygrid Model groups products according to the newness of the purchasing situation in the buying organization. The third approach is based on the degree of customization.

Although business markets are four times larger than consumer markets, and more than 60 percent of marketing students will be employed as business marketers, less than 2 percent have studied business marketing in college. One contention is that "marketing is marketing," so business marketing training is redundant. But the differences between business marketing and consumer marketing are both substantial and significant. These differences exist in the areas of market structure, marketing philosophy, buyer behavior, purchasing decisions, marketing research, product/service mix, promotion, distribution mix, and price.

Astute business marketers recognize that to compete effectively they must source their inputs from the best suppliers throughout the world. They also recognize the importance of seeking customers globally. A range of market entry methods is available for business marketing in foreign markets.

This chapter has defined the scope of business marketing and has introduced some of the concepts and vocabulary used by business marketers. It concludes with an overview of the main issues to be explored in successive chapters.

Key Terms and Concepts

marketing
marketing concept
consumer
business marketer
business buyer
business marketing
capital equipment
investments
single-purpose equipment
multipurpose equipment
horizontal market
accessory equipment
component parts
standardized components
custom components
original equipment manufacturer (OEM)
just-in-time (JIT)
after-market
replacement market
will-fit component suppliers
follow-on business
pull strategy
process materials

maintenance, repair, and operating (MRO) supplies
systems contracts
raw materials
vertical integration
business services
market structure
direct demand
derived demand
reverse price elasticity of demand
central buying unit (CBU)
decision-making unit (DMU)
multiple buying influence (MBI)
buying center
emporographics
demand-pull
technological-push
reciprocity
key accounts
niche
economic order quantities (EOQ)
vendor loyalty
switching costs

product life cycle (PLC)
pre- and posttransaction service
point-of-purchase services
industrial design
systems selling

inside salespeople
competitive bidding
price negotiation
leasing
list (book) prices

Discussion Questions

1. Why is it important to avoid the term *consumer* when referring to organizational buyers?

2. Can a product be both a consumer and a business product simultaneously? If it is physically the identical product, why would it be important to classify it as either a "business" or a "consumer" product?

3. Why is the consumer goods classification system of little use to business marketers?

4. Why are products such as ice cream, nylon stockings, and fishing rods considered "business" products when they are marketed to retail stores? What are the implications of classifying them in this manner?

5. Name three examples of systems contracts in the consumer market. How do they differ from systems contracts in business markets?

6. Organizational buyers are typified as being more rational than consumers. Describe three situations in which business buyers may appear to be behaving in a more emotional way.

7. Why is the term *industrial marketing* falling from favor and being replaced by the term *business marketing*?

8. Why do you think only 2 percent of college marketing students have studied business marketing?

9. Trace the impact of the greater geographical concentration of business customers on the marketing strategy (target market and marketing mix) decisions of business marketers.

10. A manufacturer of portable electronic pagers for business use anticipates that the product is likely to become popular among consumers and is planning to enter and develop the consumer market. What problems relating to marketing will the firm probably encounter?

Endnotes and References

1. James D. Hlavacek, "Business Schools Need More Industrial Marketing," *Marketing News* 13 (April 4, 1980): 1; Peter LaPlaca, *Journal of Business and Industrial Marketing* 3 (Winter 1988): 3.

2. "Selling in the New Environment," *Sales Manager's Bulletin,* Special Report #1217, September 30, 1989, Section 11, pp. 1–2.

3. An alternative way of differentiating between consumer and business markets is to define consumer purchases as final transactions, whereas business purchases are intermediate transactions that are always followed by subsequent transactions in which the buyers now play the role of sellers. See C. M. Sashi, "Structural Differences Between Business and Consumer Markets," *Quarterly Review of Economics and Business* 30 (Summer 1990): 69–83.

4. Mary Gooderham, "Private Calls, Public Airwaves," (Toronto) *Globe and Mail,* July 17, 1990, p. A4.

5. Gordon McDougall, Philip Kotler, and Gary Armstrong, *Marketing* (Scarborough, Ontario: Prentice-Hall Canada, 1992), pp. 223–225.

6. P. A. Dion, Peter M. Banting, and Loretta M. Hasey, "The Impact of JIT on Industrial Marketers," *Industrial Marketing Management* 19 (February 1990): 41–46.

7. Carolyn Leitch, "Rhodium Hits $7,000 an Ounce," (Toronto) *Globe and Mail,* July 5, 1990, p. B9.

8. John H. Dunning, "Multinational Enterprises and the Growth of Services: Some Conceptual and Theoretical Issues," *Service Industries Journal* 19 (January 1989): 7.

9. Kate Bertrand, "Servicemaster: Focus on Employees Boosts Quality," *Business Marketing* (April 1988): 58.

10. Ulrike de Brentani, "Success and Failure in New Industrial Services," *Journal of Product Innovation Management* 6 (December 1989): 239–258.

11. For arguments against distinctions being made, see Edward F. Fern and James R. Brown, "The Industrial/Consumer Dichotomy: A Case of Insufficient Justification," *Journal of Marketing* 48 (Spring 1984): 68–77; Diane L. Kastiel, "Why Johnny Can't Market," *Business Marketing* (November 1986): 100–105.

12. According to the *Survey of Current Business* (Washington, D.C.: U.S. Department of Commerce, August 1988), 1987 manufacturers' sales were $2,408 billion, wholesalers' sales were $3,928 billion, and retail sales were $1,510 billion.

13. Mark Potts and Peter Behr, *The Leading Edge* (New York: McGraw-Hill, 1987), p. 83.

14. This statement may be tempered by the idea that individuals within organizations "choose" behaviors in purchasing situations. See John F. Tanner, Jr., "Predicting Organizational Buyer Behavior," *Journal of Business and Industrial Marketing* 5 (Summer/Fall, 1990): 57–64. A contrary view is presented in Paul Sherlock, "Business Buying Decisions Are Rational Nonsense," *Business Marketing* (June 1991): 57.

15. David L. Blenkhorn and Peter M. Banting, "How Reverse Marketing Changes Buyer-Seller Roles," *Industrial Marketing Management* 20 (August 1991): 185–191.

16. David L. Blenkhorn and Peter M. Banting, "Should North American Parts Suppliers Learn Japanese?" *The Journal of Business and Industrial Marketing* 7 (Winter 1992): 37.

17. Peter M. Banting, David Ford, Andrew C. Gross, and George Holmes, "Generalizations from a Cross-National Study of the Industrial Buying Process," *International Marketing Review* 2 (Winter 1985).

18. Malcolm T. Cunningham and J. G. White, "The Behavior of Industrial Buyers in the Search for Suppliers of Machine Tools," *Journal of Management Studies* (May 1974).

19. Cahners Advertising Research Report No. 542.1G (April 1991) (based on a random mail survey of 4,000 business respondents).

20. T. W. Gerdel, "As Technology Changes Forging, U.S. Shops Get More Competitive," *The Cleveland Plain Dealer,* March 31, 1992, pp. 1F–5F.

21. Andrew C. Gross, *Water Treatment Chemicals, 5th ed.* (Cleveland, Ohio: Predicasts, 1984), updated with news items from chemical journals.

22. "The Delight of Digital Maps," *The Economist,* March 21, 1992, pp. 69–70.

23. "Pass the Parcel," *The Economist,* March 21, 1992, pp. 73–74.

2

THE NATURE OF DEMAND IN BUSINESS MARKETS

CHAPTER OUTLINE

- To understand the importance of the business marketer's customer's customer
- To learn how a firm can stimulate derived demand
- To learn how to develop a step-by-step demand evaluation model

One of the keys to effective marketing of business goods and services is an understanding of the buying behavior of the individuals and institutions that comprise industrial and organizational markets. Buying behavior results in demand—registration of business and institutional needs in real terms. Demand is the expression of the business's requirements in terms of the quantities and the qualities (specific attributes) of goods and services to be purchased.

The level of demand in business marketing is frequently expressed in terms of the dollar amounts that buyers have spent or that potential buyers are willing to spend. Other broad indicators of demand include estimates of industrial activity expressed in such terms as manufacturers' new net orders, new plant and equipment expenditures, book value of manufacturing inventories, average monthly manufacturing payrolls, and value of manufacturers' shipments.[1]

These broad measures of demand represent the collective needs or requirements that are expressed in the buying behavior and purchasing patterns of many institutions, organizations, commercial enterprises, and individual businesspeople. Although these measures are useful in economic forecasting, business marketers eventually seek to understand the behavior of customers and potential markets at a more immediate or micro-level—that is, the demand for their particular company's products and services. Thus we find that demand can be viewed in many different ways. In this chapter we will examine demand, paying particular attention to the business marketing implications of derived demand. Then we will explain a systematic method for analyzing and evaluating demand for a product or service in a defined geographic region.

DEMAND DEFINED

Demand can be defined as the volume of a specific product a defined customer or customer group in a particular geographic area buys during a specified period of time. Thus demand is a single number. For example, U.S. demand for cold-rolled automotive steel sheet in 1992 was the total dollar volume shipped to U.S. automobile manufacturers from January 1, 1992 to December 31, 1992.

Such a number could have taken other values, higher or lower, depending on the marketing programs undertaken by the sellers in the market, and on the relative buoyant or depressed state of the economic environment. In 1982–1983, and again in 1990–1992, it was easy to recognize that the strongest influence on

BUSINESS MARKETING IN PRACTICE ■■■■■■■■■■

The "Good Book" Is Good Business for Paper Producers

The Bible is the answer to paper marketers' prayers. Sales are enormous and virtually recession-proof. In fact, demand for Bibles often picks up when the economy turns down. Nonprofit distribution of Bibles (such as by Gideons International) steams ahead regardless of economic conditions. Even commercial sales of Bibles are generally believed to be countercyclical, rising during recessions.

"When the economy is rolling along, people don't need religion," explains Tom Freking, vice president of R.R. Donnelley & Sons Co. of Chicago, a leading U.S. printer, whose revenues from printing Bibles totaled $30 million in 1988.

Linda Peterson, director of advertising and communications for Zondervan Corp., a major Bible publisher based in Grand Rapids, Michigan, estimates the annual U.S. wholesale market at $100 million. Zondervan claims a 31 percent market share for its New International Version.

Only a handful of North American paper-makers vie for Bible printers' orders. The production challenges in making very thin, strong, and opaque paper are daunting. But the reward is a premium price. Ross Morrison, president of RBW Graphics, a leading Canadian Bible printer, says a typical grade of lightweight Bible paper sells for 89 to 95 cents Canadian per pound, compared with about 57 cents for magazine-quality paper and only 35 cents for newsprint.

Two Canadian paper manufacturers, E.B. Eddy Forest Products Ltd. of Ottawa, Ontario, and Fraser Inc. of Edmunston, New Brunswick, have zeroed in on this specialty paper niche market, in which the highest-quality paper still is provided by such European firms as Cervakoski Oy of Finland. Premium price and countercyclical derived demand make this niche market particularly attractive.

Source: Adapted with permission from (Toronto) *The Financial Post,* January 14–16, 1989, p. 19.

---

demand was the depressed state of the economy. As steel mills, auto manufacturers, and other major machinery and equipment companies cut production and closed down entire plants, their suppliers felt the pangs of deep recession even more severely. Of course, the environment affecting demand includes a number of forces, including political, legal, and societal in addition to the major one, the state of the economy. But it is important not to overlook the effect of marketing programs on demand. Despite severe recession in 1982, the markets for videogames and video recorder units boomed, and therefore so did the demand for their electronic components and parts. Similarly, demand for Bibles is considered recession-proof, and the derived demand for high-quality Bible paper is regarded as countercyclical.[2]

Direct Demand

Direct demand is generated by individuals who buy goods and services to satisfy their own personal needs. The end objective of the purchase is personal gratification in one way or another. In this role, we are known as "consumers." We are not buying to further the ends of a business or to make a profit. Even in our purchases for gift giving, the end result is our personal gratification at seeing the pleasure of the gift recipient. Consumer direct demand is the origin of all other demand.

Derived Demand

On the other hand, purchases made by business buyers, institutions, and organizations are expressions of **derived demand**—that is, they are derived from the demand generated by the customers or clients of the organization.

A commercial enterprise or institution is in business to satisfy the expectations of its customers and potential clients. As we describe in Chapter 1, business goods and services are purchased for incorporation into the products the organization manufactures, to facilitate operation of the organization, or for eventual resale.[3] If the firm had no clients or customers, it would have no need to buy anything.[4]

The Chain of Derived Demand

A company manufactures ball-point pens. Its customers are consumers. Thus the demand for these pens is a direct demand. The pen company buys metal ball-tips, plastic barrels, and ink to make the pens. Each supplier to the pen manufacturer is supplying into a business market and faces a derived demand. If consumers buy more pens (direct demand), then the suppliers are called upon to deliver more plastic barrels, ink, and so on (derived demand).

Note that each of these suppliers, in turn, purchases materials and supplies from other firms. Thus a **chain of derived demand** is established, with suppliers several times removed depending on the initial consumers' direct demand for pens to generate derived demand for their products.

Exhibit 2–1 illustrates the chain of derived demand traced back through several states of business supply. In this instance, the consumer's direct demand for automobiles initiates the original equipment manufacturer (OEM) to order wet-cell batteries from a battery manufacturer. This is a derived demand. The battery manufacturer must purchase battery acid (derived demand), and the supplier of acid must order metal drums (derived demand) in which to ship the acid. But since the acid will corrode the metal drums, they must be lined with plastic. This initiates a derived demand for plastic drum liners, which in turn generates a derived demand by the liner manufacturer for plastic materials.

Exhibit 2–2 diagrams material flow in the flexible urethane foam industry as an illustration of derived demand. A variety of basic materials are assembled and transformed into intermediate goods, which in turn are molded for use in three major end-user segments: furniture/bedding; apparel/carpeting/packaging; and transportation. What happens at the level of the ultimate consumer is extremely important to these end-user segments. Thus, for example, furniture and bedding manufacturers must ask themselves if members of the baby-boom generation born in the 1950s will buy such items from them or if they will ask their parents for hand-me-downs. Carpet-makers have to determine whether there is a trend toward

The demand for BF Goodrich wheels and brakes is derived from the demand for airline travel.

Courtesy of BF Goodrich Commercial Aircraft Wheels and Brakes.

or away from carpeting relative to linoleum, parquet, and other competing materials. Finally, the transportation equipment firms must analyze patterns of car, truck, and aircraft purchases. Sales of big cars could be declining, but the decline may be compensated for by a trend toward family purchases of two small cars if both spouses work. Or, more or less foam may be called for in aircraft seats according to engineers' specifications or users' wishes.

EXHIBIT 2–1   The Chain of Derived Demand: An Example from the Automotive Market

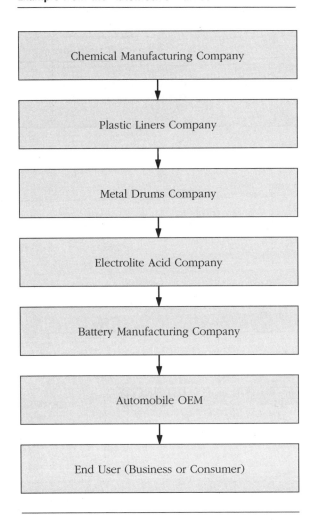

Chemical Manufacturing Company

↓

Plastic Liners Company

↓

Metal Drums Company

↓

Electrolite Acid Company

↓

Battery Manufacturing Company

↓

Automobile OEM

↓

End User (Business or Consumer)

Companies engaged in making intermediate goods take their cues from manufacturers catering to the end-use markets. Thus, Carpenter and Tenneco, makers of urethane foam, are continuously looking to see if fewer orders by one sector can be made up by sales to others. If General Motors signals that it is budgeting less for purchases of foam, then Tenneco may aggressively pursue Kroehler or Mohasco. Tenneco may also go after foreign markets or seek out new car producers in the United States, such as Honda and Hyundai. The reflection of household purchases back to the first line of manufacturers must be watched closely by the second and third line of firms farther back in the channel of derived demand.

EXHIBIT 2–2   Flexible Urethane Foam Industry Structure and Material Flow Illustrating Derived Demand in the United States (material flow in millions of pounds)

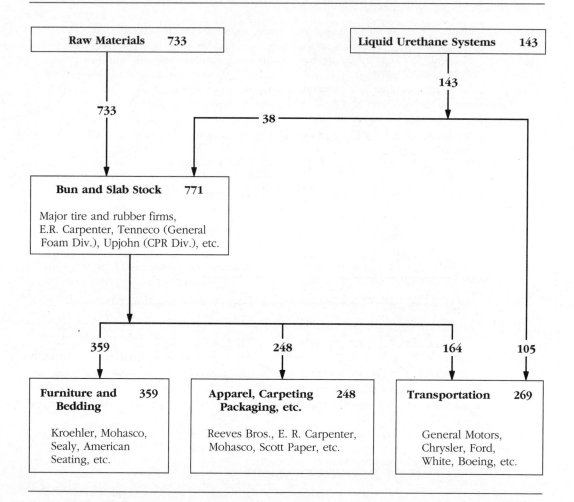

Such tracings of chains of derived demand can be helpful to business marketers in understanding some of the conditions and factors influencing their sales. All too often business marketers are so concerned with satisfying the expectations of immediate customers that they neglect to monitor conditions affecting their customers' markets. It is, however, crucial for business marketers to keep track of their customers' customers.

If, for example, a technological breakthrough made it economical for OEMs to replace acid batteries with another source of electricity, such as a fuel cell, the

BUSINESS MARKETING IN PRACTICE ▮▮▮▮▮▮▮▮▮▮▮▮▮▮▮▮▮▮▮▮▮▮▮▮▮▮

GE Analyzes Its Customers' Customers

According to Michael A. Carpenter, vice president for corporate business development and planning at General Electric, "There are two levels of understanding of customers. One being, what does my customer want from me to allow me to do business with him more effectively, the other being what are the pressures on my customer—or on my customer's customer—that are changing the way he views the world, changing his strategy, and therefore will have an impact on me. Let me give you an example: In the motor business, we sell to a compressor manufacturer, the compressor manufacturer will sell to a room air-conditioner manufacturer or to a central-air-conditioner manufacturer. It's one thing to say, 'Aha, this is an important customer, what have I got to do to serve him better?' It's another thing to

say, 'Aha, if I were his customer, the thing I really worry about is the Japanese taking over the air-conditioner business, and my problem is how do I stay competitive as a compressor manufacturer, and what are all my options in thinking that through—and therefore, what are the implications for me as his motor supplier? How can I help him achieve his objective?'"

Analyzing such information, GE hopes it can figure out both how to serve its customers better and, by implication, how to steal a march on its competition.

Source: Mark Potts and Peter Behr, *The Leading Edge,* Copyright © 1987 (New York: McGraw-Hill Book Company), p. 31. Reprinted with permission of McGraw-Hill, Inc.

---

derived demand for electrolytes, metal drums, liners, and so forth would virtually disappear in the supply lines for automotive batteries. If, on the other hand, the price of oil (hence gasoline) were to skyrocket, the direct demand for automobiles would shrink, and this shrinkage would be passed on as a reduction in derived demand for batteries.

THE IMPLICATIONS OF DERIVED DEMAND

The concept of derived demand is perhaps the most important idea in business marketing—one with many significant implications for the marketing mix. Changes in the business marketer's price may shift market shares among competitors but are not likely to affect overall industry demand. Price elasticity of demand (relative price sensitivity) depends on how crucial reliability is to the buyer and the profit impact on the buyer of the price change. The business marketer's promotional efforts may benefit from use of a telescopic marketing strategy. In distribution, changes in demand may be magnified by the acceleration effect, the whiplash effect, inventory policies, speculation, and discontinuities associated with capital goods purchases.

Price and Profit Impact

Derived demand carries three implications for the pricing of business products and services: difficulty in expanding overall demand, relative price insensitivity, and in certain situations, relative price sensitivity.

Difficulty in Expanding Overall Demand.   Generally speaking, some rule-of-thumb ratio can be established to estimate overhead, administration and sales costs, and profit as a percentage of the cost of goods. If we assume that these components amount to 50 percent of the price of any finished product, the other 50 percent would be the cost of materials. However, in most cases the cost of materials is much lower than 50 percent of the cost of the finished product. Consequently, if the business marketer is able to reduce the cost of purchased materials, the cost savings that can be passed on to the end-market consumer will be very small. Thus it is virtually impossible to expand total market demand by lowering the price of a component sold in the business market. For example, if the price of a $50 automobile battery is reduced by $5, and that reduction is reflected in a lower price of the automobile, it is highly improbable that even one more automobile will be sold as a result. At best, the only influence a lower price will have is to shift shares of the given market among competing suppliers. Shifts in market share are, however, likely to generate reactive price cuts by competitors, with the eventual lowering of profit margins for all.

Relative Price Insensitivity.   In industries in which industrial products feed production lines, the customer is likely to view price as relatively unimportant in comparison with such supplier attributes as assurance of stability in product specifications and reliability in consistently meeting delivery dates.[5] The buyer will pay more to prevent breakdown in capital equipment and to keep the assembly line moving. A slightly higher cost of supplies in such a case is a small price to guarantee against downtime (the period during which equipment cannot be used) and to avoid the cost of paying workers who cannot produce output.

Organizational buyers are also willing to pay a higher price if purchases promise to make their products more attractive to the customer. Again, business marketers must keep in mind their customer's customers.

Relative Price Sensitivity.   In comparison with the direct-demand consumer market, in which personal gratification and even whim may lead to purchases without great concern for price, derived demand tends to respond more often to pressure on price. One reason for this is the profit-generating potential of any cost reductions the business buyer can achieve. If, for example, Sony earns a return of 5 percent on sales revenue, the company must sell $100 worth of radios to earn $5 profit. On the other hand, if the company can cut its costs by $5, this represents immediate profit. Often it is much easier to find cost savings than to increase sales by twentyfold. Because of this immediate impact on profits, business buyers often place great pressure on their suppliers.[6] However, business marketers can insulate themselves from such pressure if their product or service plays a critical role (as in the case of assembly-line supplies) or if they have created a competitive advantage for their product or service.

Promotion

Because of derived demand, business marketers must direct promotional efforts to more targets than just their immediate customers. They may need to use **pull promotion** to increase derived demand by stimulating their customer's customers to specify the marketer's specific material, component, or service—thus *pulling* the product through the distribution channel from a lower level. Thus a manufacturer of fluorescent lighting fixtures, such as General Electric, might send salespeople to visit architects and might advertise in architectural journals to induce architects to specify GE fixtures rather than those of competitors, even though the actual buyer, the immediate customer, is the contractor, not the architect.

What this means is that the multiple buying influences at the customer level (production, finance, quality control, plant managers), all of whom may be recipients of promotional messages, may be joined by another layer of multiple buying influences at the customer's customer level.[7] Given a sufficient promotional budget and demonstrable results from effective pull strategies, the business marketer's task may become extremely complex.

Telescopic Marketing Strategy.   Telescopic marketing is a somewhat more sophisticated technique using promotion to increase derived demand for a business marketer's product or service.[8] In **telescopic marketing**, the marketer stimulates direct demand for an end product containing the marketer's product. This in turn increases derived demand for the business good or service. Thus telescopic marketing is something more than a simple pull promotion strategy.

In a **pull promotion strategy**, the marketer sells a product through the distribution channel, with no intervening manufacturing or processing stage. General Foods advertises Tang orange drink powder to consumers to *pull* the product through the wholesale and retail distribution channel. The product, Tang, is sold exactly in the form it left the factory. Furthermore, in such a pull strategy, the qualities promoted, and the product and qualities purchased by the consumer, are the same as those sold by General Foods.

In a **telescopic marketing strategy**, the marketer sells to an intermediate manufacturer or processor. Consequently, the product, component, or material undergoes an intervening manufacturing or processing stage before it is purchased by the end customer. Furthermore, the product or qualities promoted in telescopic marketing and bought by the end customer are products or qualities *other* than the specific item sold by the telescopic marketer.

Exhibit 2–3 illustrates these two strategies. A quarter of a century ago, soft drinks, such as Coca-Cola, were sold only in bottles. When Coca-Cola advertised "Have a Coke" to consumers, the company was using a pull promotion strategy.

EXHIBIT 2–3   Telescopic Marketing Versus Pull Promotion

```
┌─────────────────────────────────────┐
│             Steel Mill              │ ─────────────┐
└─────────────────────────────────────┘              │
              │                                       │
              ▼                                       │
┌─────────────────────────────────────┐              │
│       Metal Can Manufacturer        │              │
└─────────────────────────────────────┘        Telescopic
              │                                 Marketing
              ▼                                       │
     ┌──────────────────────────────────────┐        │
 ◀───│      Soft-Drink (Soda) Bottler      │         │
 │   └──────────────────────────────────────┘        │
 │            │                                       │
 │            ▼                                       │
 │   ┌─────────────────────────────────────┐         │
 │   │      Retailer (Supermarket)        │          │
 │   └─────────────────────────────────────┘         │
 │            │                                       │
Pull          ▼                                       ▼
Promotion ┌─────────────────────────────────────┐
 └──────▶ │      Consumer (Household)          │ ◀────
          └─────────────────────────────────────┘
```

About that time, steel mills were searching for ways to increase their tonnage of sales. One of their products, tin plate, was being used to package foods. It occurred to steel mill executives that beverages such as colas and other carbonated drinks also could be packaged in cans. The result was a highly successful telescopic marketing strategy.

Billboard, magazine, and newspaper advertisements across the country encouraged consumers to "Buy Carbonated Drinks in Cans." The advertised virtues of canned beverages included such qualities as no heavy bottles to carry home, easily disposable, no sticky insect-attractive bottles to return to the store, no deposit, chills more quickly in the refrigerator, and so forth. These advertisements were placed by the steel mills but were not promoting the steel mills' product, tin plate. Indeed, the advertisements did not even indicate who the sponsor was. They simply promoted beverages in a new form. As shown in Exhibit 2–3, promotion by the steel mill aimed at the carbonated beverage bottlers, retailers, and ultimate consumers is telescopic marketing since the benefits being communicated refer to a product (the canned drink) that has undergone further manufacturing operations and is substantially different from the tin plate sold by the mill.

Another extremely successful example of a telescopic marketing strategy is the promotional campaign launched several years ago by Du Pont to encourage consumers to buy carpets made from Du Pont's 501 nylon fiber. Du Pont stressed the advantages of such carpets. But Du Pont doesn't make carpets. Their fiber undergoes further processing. It is woven by carpet manufacturers in various parts of the country in different styles and designs. The Du Pont telescopic strategy was so successful that it virtually displaced all leading fibers used in carpeting.

Du Pont is notable as a business marketer that has used telescopic marketing extensively. Although the company does not make fry pans, waffle irons, pots, pans, or crepe makers, through telescopic marketing it has generated a significant demand for its nonstick surface material Teflon, used with all these products. More recently Du Pont has used the same strategy to generate derived demand for its SilverStone premium nonstick surface material (see Exhibit 2–4). By 1990, 90 percent of skillets and 45 percent of saucepans were nonstick.[9]

Du Pont's new product, Micromattique polyester microfiber, is also being marketed telescopically to consumers who buy wearing apparel. William J. Tuchey, marketing manager for Micromattique, states, "We have a unique marketing position. We're supporting a product that goes to the consumer yet we're three or four steps removed from the actual manufacturing process."[10]

Telescopic marketing is not just the prerogative of giant companies. A Canadian plastic-film maker, Leco Industries Ltd., whose film is bought by manufacturers of plastic sheets, bags, and rolls, traditionally advertised in trade publications and through direct sales calls on the relatively few converters of its products. But to generate derived demand for its film, Leco would have had to advertise in dozens of trade publications. Instead, the company chose to market telescopically, using television to reach supermarkets, dry cleaners, and other stores that were potential buyers of the end products.[11]

Factors Permitting Use of Telescopic Marketing.   Not every business marketer can use a telescopic marketing strategy. Since the company is promoting something other than the identifiable product it manufactures, competitors can also benefit from its efforts. Thus a company that is considering telescopic marketing should have a high market share in the product. Stelco already had 70 percent of the Canadian tin plate market when it telescopically marketed beverages in cans.

Alternatively, if a generic product has many competing suppliers, they may choose to group together as an association to promote the product telescopically. Sheep farmers have done this with their "wool mark," as have the Florida Citrus Growers with their promotion of frozen orange juice.

Telescopic marketing is a feasible strategy for products or processes that are patentable (such as Du Pont's SilverStone or Searle's NutraSweet)[12] or that have high entry barriers (as in tin plate manufacture). As already mentioned, telescopic marketing is made much easier if the business marketer's customers represent a

EXHIBIT 2–4   Du Pont's Use of Telescopic Marketing

Source: Courtesy of EI du Pont de Nemours & Company.

high market share in the industry (Leco's customers were all of the manufacturers using plastic film in their products). Lastly, the end market must be sufficiently large to generate enough derived demand for the product to warrant the investment in telescopic promotion.

Telescopic marketing is likely to bring the greatest derived-demand benefits if current penetration of end markets is small. But the shrewd marketer also must consider the availability of direct and indirect substitutes and how long they will take to eat into the new market.[13] For example, aluminum cans have now displaced most tin plate cans in the carbonated beverage business.

The state of the economy is another variable affecting the feasibility of a telescopic marketing strategy. Since in telescopic marketing the product or service is not immediately identified with the business marketer, the marketer receives no spin-off benefits, which it would in the case of institutional advertising. Since the marketer's benefits depend solely on the sale of other companies' products, telescopic marketing is more risky in a poor economy.

Finally, the marketer should weigh the advantages and disadvantages of the item to be promoted from the perspective of the manufacturers, processors, and other channel members intervening between the marketer and the end user. The new item should have obvious advantages to these channel members or, at the very least, lack negative attributes. It is extremely difficult to use telescopic marketing effectively if the transition costs to channel members are high.

Distribution

The chain of derived demand forms a channel of distribution characterized by dramatically wide swings in inventories and expectations. This **boom and bust volatility** can be caused by shifts in tastes and preferences at the consumer direct-demand level, by inventory policies, by technological developments, or by changes in economic conditions. It is exacerbated at times by the speculative purchasing of organizational buyers.

The Acceleration Effect.   A change in direct demand at the consumer level has an **acceleration effect** on the business market. For example, assume that it takes $300 worth of raw materials, which undergo processing, to make $500 worth of processed material, which in turn undergoes a fabrication stage to become $600 worth of finished product—one hundred units in all. These one hundred units sell at $10 each to yield total sales of $1,000. If demand drops 10 percent, from one hundred to ninety units, the demand for fabricated product is reduced to $540 ($600 $\times$ 0.9). Similarly, the demand for processing is reduced to $450, and the demand for raw materials to $270. Thus the ten-unit, or $100, reduction in demand at the consumer level has had the effect of reducing the demand for goods in the business market by $140.

Not only is the overall business demand decreased by a larger absolute amount than the decrease in consumer demand, it is also likely that distributors, jobbers, and retailers, which base their inventory levels on some multiple of current sales, will further reduce their inventories. This will have an accelerating or multiplying effect on inventory levels back through the channel.

The Whiplash Effect.   The small fluctuations in retail demand that are reflected in inventory patterns at each level of the channel are called the **whiplash effect**. For example, assume that the typical retailer figures an inventory requirement on the basis of sixty days' supply of goods to meet the current sales level. The retailer might check inventories every two weeks, place an order with the distributor, and

BUSINESS MARKETING IN PRACTICE ■■■■■■■■■■■■■■■■■■■■■■■■■■■

Alcoa Reintroduces Aluminum TV Dinner Trays for the Microwave

In the 1960s, the Aluminum Company of America (Alcoa) was the major U.S. supplier of aluminum foil, selling foil into a $270 million market to such firms as Alcan Package Foil Division, Federal Foil, and Ekcola division of Packaging Corporation of America. These firms manufactured the metal trays for television dinners sold in the consumer market by such TV dinner manufacturers as Swanson. But when consumers began buying microwave ovens, which carried warnings not to place metal in the oven, Alcoa's foil sales plummeted, and TV dinners on plastic trays and other composite materials displaced those with metal trays. Because Alcoa had not monitored changes in the consumer market that could influence derived demand, management had not anticipated that the advent of microwave ovens in the home would generate a decline in demand for aluminum used in making metal trays.

To recapture aluminum sales, Alcoa engineers designed a new aluminum foil-based TV dinner tray that could be heated in the microwave. Research by the aluminum companies and independent laboratories showed that the new aluminum foil-based containers were perfectly safe to use under proper guidelines in microwave ovens. However, the companies manufacturing trays for TV dinners did not believe that aluminum foil-based trays would be acceptable to consumers. Alcoa responded by conducting mall intercept interviews and focus group interviews to demonstrate consumer acceptance of the new product. The positive results of these interviews convinced tray manufacturers, and in November 1988 Alcoa obtained its first $2 million contract for foil in the new application. By conducting research at the consumer level Alcoa was able to prove that a derived demand for aluminum foil in microwave TV dinner trays could be regenerated.

Source: Thomas S. Brown, Marketing Manager, Foil Products, Alcoa, as related to Peter Banting, Ph.D., Professor of Marketing, McMaster University, Hamilton, Ontario.

---

receive delivery two weeks after the order is placed. With relatively stable demand, adequate cycle quantities are on hand, and there is sufficient safety stock to cover delivery delays. Distributor and manufacturer inventories would be managed in a similar fashion.

Exhibit 2–5 shows a retail sales increase in period 1, with a corresponding decrease in retail inventory. The retailer bases inventory restocking on the expectation that sales will remain at the new higher level and orders accordingly. The sales increase, however, is not permanent, and in period 2, sales fall back to their former level. The retail inventory remains low until the restocking cycle is complete, then rises to the new planned higher level in period 3. When the anticipated higher level of sales does not materialize, the retailer allows the inventory to fall back to its former level. At the distributor level, these effects take longer to make an appearance and are more pronounced. Similarly, at the manufacturer level, the delay in orders generated by the initial retail sales increase is even longer, and the relative magnitude of the increase is even greater. The whiplash effect can thus be characterized as exhibiting both a *phase shift* and an increase in *amplitude.*

EXHIBIT 2–5   The Whiplash Effect in the Chain of Derived Demand

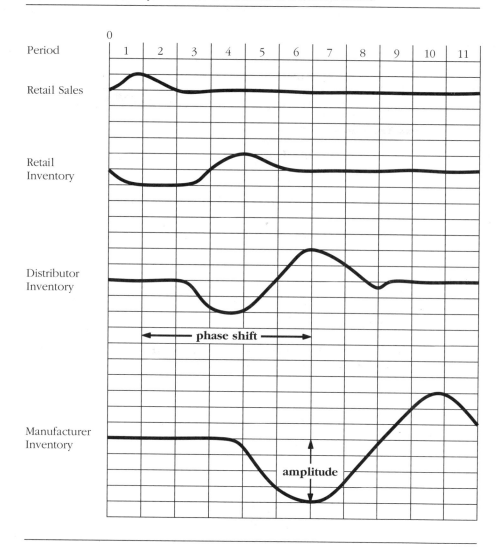

Although the whiplash effect has been illustrated using retail sales as they reflect back to the manufacturer, the concept applies equally to other channels of supply for business goods. The major implication of the whiplash effect is that the farther removed in the chain of derived demand the marketer is from the end user (whether consumer or business buyer), the more vulnerable the marketer is to large demand changes when they are least expected. They are unexpected because of the amplitude change through the channel; they are large because of the phase shift. Once again, it is critical that marketers be aware of the behavior of their customer's customers.[14]

Fortunately, marketing research at the end-user level will generally alert the business marketer to direct-demand changes in ample time for corrections to be made. Such corrections might include building for inventory, operating extra shifts in anticipation of sales swells, and allowing inventory to run down in anticipation of sales declines. Of course, in this illustration, only one anomaly in sales was carried through the chain of derived demand. In reality, the fluctuations are continuous, and more difficult to track. Thus, in addition to generating reliable sales forecasts and monitoring actual end-customer purchases, the business marketer should also be conversant with various channel members' inventory requirements, turnover rates, and order cycle times. Computerized integration of materials requirements planning (MRP) with distribution resources planning (DRP) can help the firm adjust to fluctuating demand.[15]

Volatility in Longer Channels.   When organizational buyers are trying to assure adequate supplies of components and material for production in their company, they too will establish an inventory objective for each item they buy. This is usually sufficient for a particular production run or, on long runs, for some time period, say sixty or ninety days. The inventory objective is based on forecasted sales of the particular products, perhaps for the next six or twelve months. Just as in the preceding retail example, increased demand for the consumer or business end-product and optimism about continued high demand lead the buyer to increase inventory objectives, whereas pessimism and decreased sales reduce these objectives considerably. Thus **demand volatility** for supplies and components in longer distribution channels is the result not only of shifts in demand, but also of inventory policies and expectations.

Demand for High-Technology Components.   The marketer of high-technology components is in a particularly tricky situation.[16] Demand for such products can be highly elusive. Astute buyers know that manufacturing costs and total costs of products in high-tech industries are apt to drop as production efficiency increases over time. Thus buyers may hold off offers until the last minute. For example, in the six months between the initial decision by Telcom Research (a Burlington, Ontario-based manufacturer of time-coding equipment for videotape editing) to manufacture a product using a microprocessor chip and the time when the design was finalized, the cost of the chip decreased from $8.15 to $5.00. Telcom purchased a sample shipment of chips to use in the prototype assembly but postponed the main order until the last minute, by which time the cost of the chip had dropped to $4.79. The dynamic demand conditions and the rapid innovation in the high-tech field tax the marketer's timing skills in matching market demand while avoiding competitive attacks.

Demand Volatility in Capital Goods.   Often the hardest-hit industries during economic recessions are the capital goods (production machinery manufacturing) industries. They also rebound more quickly in good times.

An example of this boom-and-bust cycle in the capital goods industries is given in Exhibit 2–6. Here a manufacturer uses ten machines, each producing ten units

EXHIBIT 2–6   The Boom and Bust Cycle in Industry

Year	Consumer Demand for Product A (units)	Percentage Change in Product Demand	Production Machines Needed (units)	Industrial Demand for New Machines (units)	Percentage Change in Machines Purchased
1	100	0	10	1	0
2	100	0	10	1	0
3	110	+ 10.0	11	2	+ 100.0
4	130	+ 18.1	13	3	+ 50.0
5	130	0	13	1	− 66.6
6	100	− 23.0	10	0	− 100.0

Source: Staudt/Taylor/Bowersox, *A Managerial Introduction to Marketing*, 3e, © 1976, p. 162. Adapted by permission of Prentice-Hall, Englewood Cliffs, New Jersey.

of product A. One machine wears out each year and must be replaced to maintain steady output. However, when a small (10 percent) increase in consumer demand occurs for product A, an additional machine must be bought (year 3). Thus, the demand for the capital good is increased by 100 percent. Conversely, between years 5 and 6, when consumer demand drops 23 percent, demand for the capital good drops by 100 percent. An example of these wide fluctuations in demand for capital goods occurred in the 1982 recession year, during which a 1.8 percent decline in the U.S. economy was accompanied by a 3.8 percent decline in capital outlays.

MARKET EVALUATION

Given all the factors that can influence demand for business products and services, the business marketer needs a systematic, structured approach to demand evaluation. An analytical framework developed by one of the authors of this text ties together a wide range of analytical tools related to both marketing and microeconomic theory (see Exhibit 2–7).[17] This demand evaluation approach

■ draws attention to a wide range of market environment factors that pose either direct or potential impacts on the company's products and

■ links together a number of individual analytical techniques to create a comprehensive evaluation process.

It differs from more commonly used methods of market analysis (such as standard forecasting or monitoring techniques), which tend to concentrate more on sales alone.

EXHIBIT 2–7   A Demand Evaluation Model

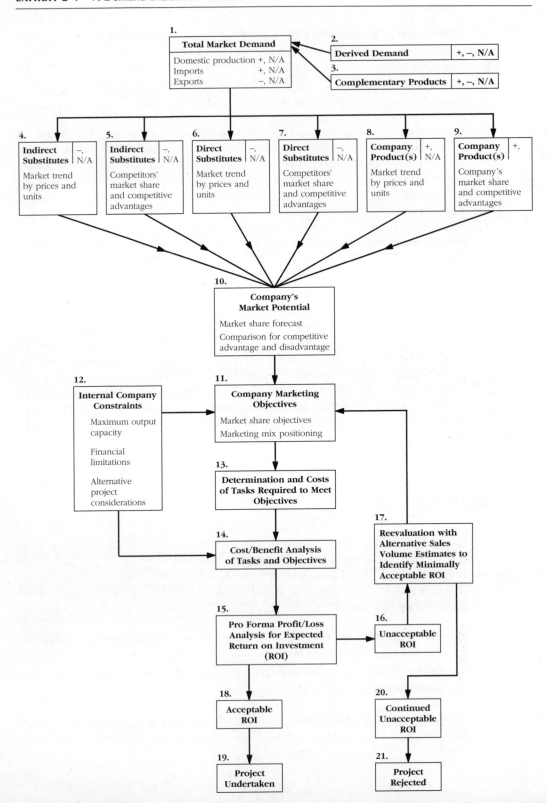

In addition to employing the traditional tools of forecasting and monitoring, business marketers need to make every attempt to assess indirect impacts on their product offering—such as derived-demand factors, complementary products, and indirect substitutes—and to assess comparative advantages and disadvantages of their total product relative to that of their actual and potential competitors.

The need for this expanded approach is becoming ever more apparent as the competitive arena continues to grow from regional, to national, to international in scope. The implications of this trend are twofold. First, competition can be brought to bear from a much greater range of competitors. A greater range of competitors brings with it increased potential for various forms of comparative advantage, be it cheap labor or technological sophistication. Second, international competition and the trend toward distant market development force the firm to consider longer forecasting or planning horizons. Trends such as these mean that the firm must assess a greater range of factors that will ultimately affect demand for its specific products.

The demand evaluation model in Exhibit 2–7 is meant to be used as a supplement to, and not a replacement for, standard forecasting and market monitoring procedures. It is entirely possible, however, that information generated by the model may cause management to reevaluate data acquired from other forecasting and monitoring procedures. It is designed to aid in evaluation of both current and new markets.

The signs $+$, $-$ and N/A are interpreted as follows:

$+$ indicates data input reflecting conditions that are expected to exert a positive effect on the firm's actual or potential available market.

$-$ indicates an expected negative impact on the firm's actual or potential market.

N/A means that the market factor in question either does not exist or is not applicable to the firm's deliberations regarding the market under consideration.

Components of the diagram are most suited to analysis of larger geographical or national markets (because data are most readily available at these levels). However, managers should at least consider the elements of the model in their deliberations regarding smaller markets. Quantification of some model components may be extremely difficult, but this is preferable to committing errors of omission, which sometimes can have disastrous consequences.

In the following discussion, the numbered headings provide easy reference to the numbered boxes in Exhibit 2–7.

The Total Market Demand (1)

The total market demand for a given product category is composed of domestic production, imports, and exports (see box 1 in Exhibit 2–7). The export component carries a negative sign in the evaluation scheme to avoid overestimation of the total market size in the trading area of interest. The *N/A* designation should be applied to innovative products since prior data regarding the product class will be nonexistent.

Derived Demand (2)

Considerations of derived-demand effects are important for both long-term planning and short-term forecasting. Long-term planning for major additions to capital plant and equipment is contingent upon determining the health of key markets over time. The condition of business markets is very often dependent on consumer markets. Thus the business product planner must be aware of market trends in the consumer sector that may exert an impact on demand for the business product. For example, a multinational minerals producer was seriously considering a large capital addition to increase plant capacity. Research of the derived demand market supplying electrical toys, flashlights, calculators, and watches indicated, however, that manufacturers were switching away from the types of battery that rely on the firm's mineral output. In this instance, the marketing vice president concluded that the shifting demand caused by the consumer sector manufacturers would adversely affect the firm's battery-manufacturing customers and ultimately the demand for the firm's own product.

Review of derived-demand factors to obtain leading indicators can aid short-term forecasting of sales volume. The advantage of this approach is that it allows the firm to fine-tune production levels and prices so that inventories remain in balance. For example, forest products producers monitor housing starts, loan applications, and interest rates in the consumer housing sector in an effort to predict short-term demand for structural wood products.

The importance of derived demand to the firm is a function of the degree of impact exerted by such demand and the number of alternative markets available. Firms that are dependent on a single end-use market should be especially concerned with derived-demand issues.

The plus, minus, and *N/A* designations for the derived-demand category indicate the range of influence this factor can exert on the business market.

Complementary Products (3)

The impact of **complementary products** (which are used together, such as shoes and shoe laces) on demand for a firm's output varies both by degree and direction of dependency. For example, demand for computer disks is a function of computer sales, but computer sales are not wholly dependent on sales of computer disks. When sales of the company's output are dependent on sales of the complementary product, the business marketer needs to carefully monitor trends in the complementary product market. This information must then be integrated with the firm's sales forecasting efforts.

As with the derived-demand category, a plus sign for the complementary products evaluation would indicate an expected positive impact on the total market size—for instance, when the complementary product market is expanding and creating a growth in demand for the firm's product. A minus sign would indicate the reverse situation. The *N/A* designation would result if there were no complementary product relationships, or if the relationship were of a very minor degree, or if the direction of dependency ran totally from the complementary product to the firm's product.

Indirect Substitutes (4 and 5)

Boxes 4 and 5 in Exhibit 2-7 are designed to make the business marketer aware of the dangers posed by **indirect substitutes** (other products that perform the same function, such as motive power provided by a gasoline engine or by an electric motor) for the firm's product.[18] The definition of what constitutes an indirect substitute when considered in too wide a context can create a complex and cumbersome evaluation problem. On the other hand, too narrow a definition may cause the marketer to exclude potential threats that may have serious consequences for company sales (especially if the indirect substitute has comparative advantages). When there is even a remote possibility of substitution, the marketer should investigate the product further.

BUSINESS MARKETING IN PRACTICE ▰▰▰▰▰▰▰▰▰▰▰

Titanium Displaces Graphite

For forty years major oil refineries, such as CONOCO, supplied sponge coke, resin, and pitch to manufacturers of graphite anodes used in electrolytic cells by chemical companies, such as Hooker Chemicals and Dow Chemical, to produce chlorine gas. Manufacturers of graphite anodes included Stackpole, supplying half of the demand, Union Carbide, Arico Speer Carbon, and Great Lakes Carbon.

In 1968 a more expensive but superior anode of coated titanium was developed. None of the anode suppliers believed that the chemical companies would buy the new dimensionally stable anode (DSA) until a precipitous decline in graphite anode demand occurred between 1975 and 1979. Indeed, it took until 1986 before the last cells using graphite anodes in the United States were shut down.

Despite its higher price, acceptance of a technologically superior DSA anode by the chemical industry totally displaced the demand for conventional graphite anodes and derived demand for coke, resin, and pitch from major oil refiners. The moral: Keep your eyes on your customer's customer.

Source: Ron Braund, Sales Manager, Graphite Materials Division, Carbone of America, as related to Peter Banting, Ph.D., Professor of Marketing, McMaster University, Hamilton, Ontario.

The indirect substitution of floppy disks for conventional film to generate magnetic images in "filmless" cameras will affect not only the manufacturers of conventional films, but also the derived demand for silver. Half the global demand for silver is from the makers of film.[19]

Observation of distant markets can be useful if indirect substitutes have been known to penetrate those trading areas. The implication is that successful substitutes will ultimately diffuse to most other markets.

Box 4 focuses on the dynamic, quantitative aspects of indirect-substitute penetration of the market. Market trend information is useful to the extent that the analyst can gain insight into how quickly the indirect substitute is capturing market share from the product class it is displacing. Data on price movements and units sold allow analysis of market volatility. Price adjustments to changing demand and supply of the indirect substitute can also be analyzed. For example, the market analyst of a large multinational company was asked to evaluate the future sales potential of a sash and door mill the corporation was considering for purchase. Although the growth trend in this product class was acceptable, the market analyst found the trend in residential housing starts was far in excess of that shown by the sash and door industry. Since the two products were complementary, their growth trends should have been similar. A check of indirect substitutes revealed that metal window frame and door producers were displacing business from wood manufacturers. Needless to say, the company did not purchase the mill.

Box 5 shifts attention to some qualitatively judged aspects of the indirect substitute: estimates of its market share and its competitive advantages. The business marketer should try to determine whether producers of the indirect substitute have increased their market share over time and if so, through what particular marketing mix and competitive advantages. For example, a U.S. firm invested approximately $3 million in a mill to produce exotic wood paneling such as Indian rosewood, teak, and mahogany. Selling prices ranged from $25 to $425 per sheet. The company, however, failed to investigate Japanese entrepreneurs who were producing imitation grained panels for the same market. Their selling prices were from $5 to $20 per sheet. The U.S. firm did not believe the products were even indirect substitutes until the mill went into bankruptcy. Only then did further market research indicate that consumers could not differentiate between the two products from a distance of eight feet! Since the Japanese producers were able to imitate the exotic wood quality at a fraction of the cost, contractors naturally chose to install the cheaper of the two alternatives.

The minus signs in boxes 4 and 5 indicate that the impact of indirect substitutes, if they exist, should be used to scale down the size of the total market available. *N/A* applies in the absence of such substitutes.

Direct Substitutes (6 and 7)

Business marketers are much more familiar with the direct-substitution problem since behavior of direct competitors has an ongoing impact on the firm. The analysis of **direct substitutes** (that is, competing brands of the same type of product) is similar to that used for indirect substitutes. Familiarity with direct competitors, however, implies that the analysis can be somewhat more detailed.

Note again that data regarding market share and competitive advantage are used to scale down expectations regarding the total market available. The rationale is that taking business from direct competition, although certainly not impossible, is more difficult than garnering sales in a market of equal size that is free of competitors. It is preferable to err on the conservative side in estimation of total market size. Given the enviable situation that no direct competition exists, the *N/A* evaluation is used.

Company Product(s) (8 and 9)

Marketers should analyze their own product package along the same lines used for analyzing direct and indirect substitutes. Evaluation of the market trend for the marketer's product gives dynamic perspective to the product's market share calculations, especially if the market structure is volatile by nature or in rapid transition (for example, commodities markets, electronics industries). Without such a perspective, market share calculations conducted at some specific point in time can be misleading. As with direct and indirect substitutes, marketers must also evaluate the competitive advantages of their firm's marketing mix here.

In evaluation of the total market size, the market trend (box 8) and market share (box 9) associated with the company's output are considered positive factors since there is some accumulation of loyalty and goodwill. Similarly, in box 9, competitive advantages of the firm's marketing mix should make a positive contribution to company sales.

If the firm is considering a new-product introduction, no market trend history will be available, hence the *N/A* option in box 8.

Company's Market Potential (10)

After taking into consideration all of the issues identified in boxes 1 through 9, the marketer is ready to undertake the more traditional calculations of the company's market potential stipulated in box 10. The actual **market potential** is a function of the factors previously discussed.

Before any sales volumes and revenues can be estimated, however, the marketer must make a final qualitative analysis of the product and the company's competitive advantages and disadvantages compared with those of all sources of competition. An objective assessment is crucial.

Since the remaining procedures in Exhibit 2–7 are quite well known to marketers, we will not analyze them in detail here.

Company Marketing Objectives (11)

The business marketer needs to determine market share objectives interactively with cost considerations in the pro forma profit/loss analysis in box 15 (hence the feedback loop). Marketers must also consider the impact on the marketing mix of new products and expansion of existing product lines. For example, when introducing new products, marketers should be wary of "**cannibalizing**" the market share of existing product lines, especially if the existing products provide larger profit margins than the new additions.

Internal Company Constraints (12)

Assuming the project survives the marketing review, other corporate constraints come into consideration, such as maximum capacity output, financial limitations, and alternative project considerations. Corporate constraints may again be considered in greater detail when the marketer undertakes a cost/benefit analysis of tasks and objectives (box 14).

Evaluation of Tasks and Objectives (13 and 14)

The marketing literature in this area is well developed. The evaluation of tasks and objectives includes setting objectives, determining the tasks required to reach the objectives, determining the costs of the tasks, and performing a cost/benefit analysis of the tasks and objectives. Tasks and objectives may include achieving such factors as minimum or target growth, profitability, market share, completeness of product line, and reinforcement of a particular corporate image.

Pro Forma Profit and Loss Analysis (15)

This field of analysis is also well developed. One cautionary note is in order, however. Return on investment (ROI) calculations focus attention on expected profits. In many instances, marketers conduct a series of tests to locate the profit-maximizing size of investment for the project. The results may not be consistent with the company's longer-run requirements in terms of sales revenue generation or market position; that is, there is a tradeoff in terms of short-run and long-run profitability.

   If the return on investment is acceptable, the project is undertaken (boxes 18 and 19). An unacceptable ROI (box 16) leads to a reevaluation feedback loop through box 17.

Reevaluation for Acceptable ROI (17)

The search for an acceptable ROI through the pro forma profit and loss analysis is an *iterative* (repeating) process. The most common problem with the procedure is ensuring that the projected sales revenue, which the company must acquire for profitability, is actually realistic. Economies of scale that reduce operating expenses often occur at larger output volumes. Consequently, marketers may tend to overestimate potential market share or volume in the search for the optimal operating range. The validity of the entire pro forma profit and loss exercise rests on producing a realistic *and achievable* sales volume objective. To the extent that this figure is biased, the remaining steps in the analysis become meaningless.

Through the reevaluation process the marketer makes another attempt, starting again with marketing objectives (box 11), to locate a viable ROI. In the event that the marketer cannot project a realistically achievable corporate market share and sales revenue, the exit procedure leads through box 20 to box 21 and the project is rejected.

The preceding flow-diagram approach provides a conceptual synthesis of factors pertinent to business demand evaluation. This model was designed with four specific goals in mind:

1. To integrate a number of economics-based concepts (boxes 1–9) into a marketing context to broaden the analytical base used for demand evaluation
2. To provide a framework designed to tie each of the numerous individual marketing concepts into a unified and cohesive plan for demand evaluation
3. To apply a sequential ordering to all elements of the model for purposes of organizing the evaluation procedure
4. To indicate the viability of selected components within the model by demonstrating their application in a number of "real world" examples

Given the trend toward international competition, it is no longer sufficient to concentrate on the company and its interaction with a few local direct competitors. Markets and entire industries are disappearing and being created with ever-increasing rapidity. Corporate survival in the future may depend on the ability of management to detect fast-changing, seemingly remote market forces—and to prepare for them.

SUMMARY

Business demand is defined as the volume of a specific product a defined customer or customer group in a particular geographic area buys during a specified time period. Direct demand is generated by consumers' purchases, which are based on personal gratification. In contrast, business buyers purchase goods and services for use in the products and services that they, in turn, produce for facilitating the operation of the enterprise or for resale. Thus business purchases are not an end in themselves but rather depend on demand generated by others. Business demand therefore is a derived demand. Indeed, business demand can be traced back through a chain of derived demand to a consumer direct demand that initiates the sequence.

Of greatest importance to the business marketer is recognition of the implications of derived demand for the business marketing mix. Price may be used to shift market share away from competitors but most likely will prove ineffective in expanding total market demand. The customer may apply pressure on the business marketer's price if dollar purchases are sufficiently large that a price reduction will add significantly to the buyer's profit. But if the customer is concerned that late delivery or inconsistent input quality may prove costly, the buyer is likely to be less price sensitive.

Although institutional promotion and pull promotion are useful, some business marketers use a telescopic marketing strategy to increase derived demand for their company's offering. Telescopic marketing is a promotional technique for increasing derived demand for a business product or service by stimulating direct demand for an end product or service containing the business marketer's good or service. The product or qualities promoted in a telescopic marketing strategy (and bought by the end customer) are products or qualities other than the specific item sold by the telescopic marketer.

A number of conditions allow the use of telescopic marketing. The telescopic marketer's product should have a high share of the market supplying the end user's product that is telescopically promoted, or competing suppliers should be willing to share the costs of the promotion. The telescopic marketer should have a patent on the item supplied, have know-how that is difficult to acquire, or enjoy some other high entry barriers that preclude competitors from benefiting from the promotion. The telescopic marketer's customers should have a high share of the market in the end-use industry. The end market should be large enough to yield a good return on the telescopic marketing investment. Direct and indirect substitutes should be unlikely to divert the newly generated derived demand from the telescopic marketer's product or service. The general economy should be healthy. Finally, the new item should have obvious advantages for channel members as well as for end users.

In distribution, the erratic "boom and bust" volatility of derived demand stems from a number of sources, including shifts in direct demand that cause an acceleration effect; management's inventory policies that lead to a whiplash effect and demand volatility for supplies and components in longer business channels of distribution; technological developments that affect prices of supplies and lead to speculative buying behavior; and economic cycles that are magnified by the purchases of capital goods.

The chapter concludes with a model for evaluating the demand for existing and new business products and services. The model begins with known values of domestic production, imports, and exports; it then examines the impacts of derived demand, complementary products, and direct and indirect substitutes. Company products are analyzed and a market potential for the company is estimated. Next the business marketer checks to see that corporate marketing objectives are being met and that other corporate constraints are not being violated. Since it costs money to achieve objectives, these costs must be estimated and weighed against the benefits they create. Calculations of returns on investment can be reevaluated using different estimates of sales volume to arrive at a realistically achievable corporate market share and sales revenue. The model provides a structured approach to the analysis of the market and its impact on the firm.

The key message of Chapter 2 is that marketers must be aware of the behavior of their customers' customers.

Key Terms and Concepts

demand
direct demand
derived demand
chain of derived demand
pull promotion
telescopic marketing
pull promotion strategy
telescopic marketing strategy
boom and bust volatility

acceleration effect
whiplash effect
demand volatility
complementary products
indirect substitutes
direct substitutes
market potential
"cannibalizing"

Discussion Questions

1. What conditions are necessary for a company to employ a telescopic marketing strategy?

2. Under what conditions could a business marketer expand the total demand for a product class using pricing strategy?

3. Why is the customer's customer so important to the business marketer?

4. Discuss relative price sensitivity and relative price insensitivity in business marketing.

5. A manufacturer of fine paper sells through distributors to various printers. The market-ing manager is considering using a pull promotion strategy. Should advertising be directed at printers? At publishing companies? Since there are multiple buying influences at each level, how would this affect the promotion strategy?

6. Identify direct and indirect substitute products for paper.

7. Discuss the possibility of the "paperless office" and its implications for business marketers.

Endnotes and References

1. Statistics on these demand indicators are published annually in such sources as *Survey of Current Business, Business Conditions Digest, Predicasts,* and *Sales and Marketing*

Management's "Survey of Industrial Purchasing Power." For countries other than the United States, see *Worldcasts,* a statistical quarterly.

2. (Toronto) *Financial Post,* January 14–16, 1989, p. 19. Demand that is countercyclical resists and can even move in a direction opposite to the growth or decline in the economic cycle.

3. Examples are found in J.A.F. Nicholls and Sidney Roslow, "Two Faces of the Industrial Marketing Transaction: A Buyer and Seller Framework for Goods and Services," *Journal of Business and Industrial Marketing* 3 (Summer 1988): 46.

4. In an examination of need recognition by organizations, this point is often overlooked. See Kjell Gronhaug and Alladi Venkatesh, "Needs and Need Recognition in Organizational Buying," *European Journal of Marketing* 25 (1991): 17–32.

5. Louis J. DeRose, "Meet Today's Buying Influences with Value Selling," *Industrial Marketing Management* 20 (1991): 87–91.

6. See, for example, Barbara C. Perdue and John O. Summers, "Purchasing Agents' Use of Negotiation Strategies," *Journal of Marketing Research* 28 (May 1991): 175–189.

7. Mark Potts and Peter Behr, *The Leading Edge* (New York: McGraw-Hill, 1987), p. 31.

8. Telescopic marketing strategy is a concept suggested by Dr. I. A. Litvak of York University, Toronto.

9. Vivian L. Gernand, "Fantasies for Sale: Marketing Products That Do Not Yet Exist," *Journal of Business and Industrial Marketing* 6 (Summer/Fall 1991): 36.

10. Kate Bertrand, "This Is Not Your Mother's Polyester," *Business Marketing* (May 1991): 12.

11. (Toronto) *Globe and Mail,* February 23, 1972, p. B4.

12. Harvey Skolnick, *Business-to-Business Marketing,* November 23, 1987, p. B15.

13. Direct and indirect substitutes are discussed later in this chapter.

14. This discussion does not consider the consequences that buyers must face when their suppliers cannot meet their order, and the subsequent implications for the supplier. See, for example, Paul A. Dion, L. M. Hasey, P. C. Dorin, and J. Lundin, "Consequences of Inventory Stockouts," *Industrial Marketing Management* 20 (1991): 23–27.

15. Joseph G. Ormsby and Dillard B. Tinsley, "The Role of Marketing in Materials Requirement Planning Systems," *Industrial Marketing Management* 20 (February 1991): 67–72.

16. For a definition of "high-technology," see Rowland T. Moriarty and Thomas J. Kosnik, "High-Tech Marketing: Concepts, Continuity, and Change," *Sloan Management Review* (Summer 1989): 7–17.

17. This demand evaluation model was developed by Lindsay Meredith of Simon Fraser University, Burnaby, British Columbia.

18. The concept of substitution in market demand evaluation is not new. E. Jerome McCarthy and Stanley Shapiro, on p. 236 of *Basic Marketing* (Homewood, Ill.: Irwin, 1975), discuss the application of G. T. Borchert's "Design of the Marketing Program for a New Product," published in *Marketing's Role in Scientific Management,* ed. Robert L. Clewett (Chicago: American Marketing Association, 1957).

19. Bud Jorgensen, "New Photography Developments Are Negative for Silver," (Toronto) *Globe and Mail,* April 12, 1989, p. B6.

3

BUSINESS BUYER BEHAVIOR

- To be able to analyze the factors that affect business buying decisions and to decide which factors are likely to be important in different situations

- To understand that each business purchase is a process over time and to be able to analyze specific purchases and plan marketing activity to relate to each stage in the buying process

- To be able to categorize different purchases according to what is being bought, the experience of the buyer, and the uncertainties that the buyer faces

- To be able to decide which marketing abilities are appropriate to the different uncertainties that buyers face

- To understand the nature of buyer/seller relationships as part of an overall portfolio and to understand the issues in building a strategy for that portfolio

All companies buy a wide range of different products and services from suppliers from many countries. They may buy highly complex technical products that are specially designed or developed to their particular requirements, as when Boeing or McDonnell Douglas buys a flight control system for one of its new airplanes. Sometimes a company may buy a single large machine tool that costs many thousands of dollars and affects the future direction and strategy of the company. In contrast, the automobile industry also buys many small, low-priced components that are delivered regularly in large quantities. But if any of these tiny components has a habit of failing in use, then the business customer runs the risk of losing its reputation for the quality of its own products. If a whole batch of components is delivered to the wrong quality standard, then the customer's production schedule will be disrupted, perhaps involving layoffs and financial losses. At the other extreme, companies also buy low-value, routine, and relatively unexciting products, such as lubricating oil or envelopes.

Companies will buy these different products in quite different ways. The way they buy will also depend on how sure they are about exactly what they want and how much they know of what is available in the market. Perhaps the product is a standardized commodity, such as sheet steel, which the company buys frequently from a number of regular suppliers. These purchases will be very different from buying a new computer software package for running the company's production, a purchase that may be fraught with risk and uncertainty. Many business purchases are made automatically by computer when the stock of a particular product reaches a certain low point. Others involve deep consideration over many months or even years. Some purchases are made entirely by a single purchasing clerk, whereas others consist of a complex process involving many people in product development, production, research, and finance, all of whom will have different ideas about what the company should buy.

Sometimes the business marketer is like a consumer marketer, who launches a marketing mix of product, price, promotion and distribution at a large part of the market, as when the business marketer is selling paper towels or lubricants. In other cases, the business marketer may have to tailor the firm's product to the particular requirements of a single customer company or even to the wishes of separate individuals within that company. In such cases a close relationship between buying and selling companies often develops—one that may last for many years, such as the relationship between Boeing and General Electric for the development of several generations of jet engines. This is quite unlike the marketing of consumer products—few of us, for instance, have ever met anyone from Kellogg or Procter & Gamble. It would be most unlikely for these companies to modify their cornflakes or toothpaste to suit our individual requirements. Good business marketers have a clear understanding of their company's relationships with all its actual or potential customers; of whether those relationships should be close or distant, complex or simple; and of what, if any, aspects of the company's offering should be modified in each case.

In this chapter we try to answer a number of questions that are important to understanding business buyer behavior and the nature of the relationships between buying and selling companies in business markets. These questions are as follows:

1. What are the factors that affect buying decisions and who is involved in buying?

2. What is the process of business buying and how does that process vary for different purchases and under different circumstances?

3. What are the motivations of the business buyer and what abilities does a marketer need to be able to respond to them?

4. What are the characteristics of buyer/seller relationships and what do these mean for the business marketer?

FACTORS AFFECTING BUYING DECISIONS

No buying decision is ever taken in isolation. Each decision is influenced by factors having to do with the buying company and the individuals who are involved. In this section we examine these factors using an analysis model developed by Webster and Wind in 1972 that has formed the basis of many later attempts to understand business buying.[1] As shown in Exhibit 3–1, this model groups the various factors into four levels of buying influences: environmental, organizational, buying center, and individual.

Environmental Factors

The Webster and Wind model divides environmental factors affecting the buying decision into six categories: physical, economic, technological, legal, political, and cultural.

EXHIBIT 3–1   Levels of Influence on Business Buying

Environmental factors	Physical, economic, technological, legal, political, cultural
Organizational factors	Technology, goals and tasks, actors, structure
Buying center factors	Roles, resources
Individual factors	Status, politics, ethics

Source: Based on Frederick E. Webster and Yoram Wind, "A General Model of Organizational Buying Behavior," *Journal of Marketing* 36 (April 1972) 12–19.

Physical Environment.   The physical environment affecting the buying firm consists of the geographical spread of the firm's suppliers and customers. This factor will affect the firm's costs and the extent of the logistical problems it may face in actually getting the products it has bought. For example, many firms that buy large quantities of components for continuous production favor suppliers that are located in close proximity to their plant. Having a close supplier helps the company keep a reduced inventory and facilitates just-in-time (JIT) delivery schedules. Some suppliers have even had to relocate their production to retain business with this kind of customer.

Economic Environment.   The economic environment consists of the general situation of economic growth or recession, interest rates, and corporate profitability, within which all firms operate. One frequently neglected aspect of the economic environment is the fact that a company's purchases are often directly related to its own sales or order situation. For example, shipments of beer in the United States rose by 2.7 percent in 1990. Part of this growth was due not to the industry's marketing efforts, but to stockpiling by distributors and retailers ahead of a federal tax increase at the beginning of 1991. This price increase and the effects of the recession on purchasing power made brewers expect shipments to be down 3 to 5 percent in 1991. Trucking companies could expect a corresponding downturn in demand for their services, and manufacturers of brewing and canning equipment could expect an even greater downturn as reequipment decisions were postponed and the industry became even more concentrated.

Technological Environment.   The technological environment refers to the current technologies in particular industries and the rate of technological change. These factors strongly affect marketing conditions. For example, in the United States, the vast majority of cars have gasoline engines. In Europe, a significant number use diesel engines, and this proportion is growing. A U.S. manufacturer of vehicle engine components trying to sell products in Europe would thus have to cope with a very different technological environment and quite different customer requirements.

The technological environment facing firms is often related to the political environment. Consider, for example, the airline industry. During the first month of

BUSINESS MARKETING IN PRACTICE ▰▰▰▰▰▰▰▰

Prestige Motivates Corporate Jet Purchases

The recession has hit the flight plans of many big companies, and the days of executives jetting around the continent in expensive aircraft may be numbered. Even top managers are under pressure to justify using executive jets, which can cost between $2,000 and $3,000 an hour to fly.

"There used to be the image for a lot of companies that these planes presented perks and prestige," says John-David Lyon, president of the Ottawa-based Canadian Business Aircraft Association.

To keep costs down through the recession, some companies are selling their corporate jets and using commercial airlines or chartering planes from specialist operators, such as Execaire Inc., of Dorval, Quebec, the largest aircraft management company in Canada. Some of the biggest names in Canadian business, including Ranger Oil Ltd. of Calgary, Petro-Canada, Algoma Steel Corp. Ltd. of Sault Ste. Marie, Ontario, and Olympia & York Developments Ltd. have sold their aircraft and switched to charters. Other companies that are keeping their corporate jets are using firms like Execaire to rent their planes out for charter flights, thereby recapturing some of their costs.

Source: "Recession Prompts Firms to Sell Corporate Jets" (Toronto) *Globe and Mail,* July 21, 1992, p. 85. Adapted with permission.

---

the Gulf War, companies tried to reduce their trans-Atlantic air travel, resulting in a 60 percent increase in videoconferencing calls between the United States and the United Kingdom. International companies, such as the California-based computer company Amdahl, are now installing videoconferencing facilities in their headquarters for European operations. Amdahl reports that to send three executives across the Atlantic costs $24,000 plus the cost of lost time. The new video facilities cost about $12,000, which is only a small fraction of the company's $2 million travel budget. These developments in the technological environment can be expected to have a detrimental effect on future growth in the airline business.

Legal and Political Environment.   The legal and political environment within which business buying takes place refers to the ways in which government legislation affects purchasing, directly or indirectly. For example, environmental protection legislation directly affects which products can be bought or sold in some countries. Also, employee protection or labor union laws in some countries will indirectly affect companies' profits and hence their ability to buy some products. This means that companies must be fully aware of the legal and political environment before they enter new international markets.

Cultural Environment.   The cultural environment of a buying company includes all those national attitudes and beliefs that affect the way business people operate. A buying company's cultural environment can strongly affect its attitude toward suppliers, as is illustrated in Exhibits 3–2 and 3–3. Exhibit 3–2 shows how

EXHIBIT 3–2   European Marketers' Assessment of Buyers from Different European Countries

	Buyers				
	French	German	Italian	Swedish	U.K.
1. We like dealing with these buyers.	116*	119	127	149	129
2. Business with them is based on mutual trust.	89	75	94	108	122
3. They are loyal to suppliers.	63	75	7	74	82
4. They are easy to cooperate with.	118	109	88	144	117
5. They understand suppliers' problems.	12	−16	−17	53	36
6. They have a favorable attitude toward foreign suppliers.	9	−30	60	58	8
7. They are easy to make friends with.	66	48	60	89	109
8. Cultural differences are not a problem.	45	25	63	80	63
9. Language differences are not a problem.	−52	−19	7	68	8

*Weighted scores based on responses to a five-point scale. The higher the score, the stronger the agreement. Negative scores indicate disagreement.

Source: Reprinted with the permission of the Macmillan Press Limited from Peter W. Turnbull and Malcolm T. Cunningham eds. *International Marketing and Purchasing*, 1981. Copyright © 1981 by The Macmillan Press Limited.

experienced European business marketers assessed the attitudes of buyers from different European countries. Each score in the exhibit measures the extent to which suppliers agreed with the statement as applied to buying companies from five important European countries. For example, statements 2 and 8 seem to show that these suppliers believed that there was less trust between them and German customers as compared with customers from the other European countries, and that cultural distance seemed to be more of a problem when dealing with German buyers. Statement 6 shows that German buyers also seemed to have less favorable attitudes to foreign firms. Also noticeable is the marked lack of loyalty that suppliers experienced with Italian customers (statement 3). These ratings have clear lessons for any U.S. supplier seeking to expand its sales into Western Europe.

Exhibit 3–3 shows the views of the same European marketers about the attitudes of buying companies from each of the countries toward new technology and joint development of new products by buyer and seller. The marketers believed that German buyers were much more interested in new technology than were U.K. buyers. But perhaps because of their attitude toward foreign firms, German buyers were much less interested in joint product development with suppliers than were Swedish buyers.

The data for this study were collected some years ago, but it is the opinion of the researchers that the results are still largely valid. Marketers must realize that any business purchase takes place within a cultural environment that affects the ways in which customers will buy and hence the way in which they must be ap-

EXHIBIT 3–3   European Buyers' Interest in New Technology and Joint Product Development with Suppliers

Buyers	Interest in New Technology	Interest in Joint Product Development
French	81*	23
German	108	26
Italian	87	15
Swedish	132	60
U.K.	66	31

*Scores are weighted averages of European marketers' agreement with each statement on a five-point scale. The higher the score, the stronger the agreement.

Source: Reprinted with the permission of The Macmillan Press Limited from Peter W. Turnbull and Malcolm T. Cunningham eds. *International Marketing and Purchasing*, 1981. Copyright © 1981 by The Macmillan Press Limited.

proached. For example, the data in Exhibit 3–2 indicate that in approaching German customers, marketers must take into account that language differences are much more of an issue than they would be in Sweden. Additionally, foreign marketers in Germany must cope with a lower appreciation of the seller's problems and may have to work harder to establish mutual trust.

Cultural knowledge gained by selling in foreign markets can also help the business marketer compete with foreign marketers at home. For example, a U.S. marketer may be faced with a Swedish competitor in the U.S. market. If the U.S. marketer also sells into the competitor's home Swedish market, the U.S. marketer will have learned something about the requirements of Swedish customers, such as the importance of joint product development. The U.S. marketer will also have seen how the Swedish competitor copes with these requirements and can then apply this knowledge against that competitor in the United States.

Organizational Factors

Organizational factors affecting business buying behavior relate to the buying organization itself: its technology, its goals and tasks, the actors involved in buying, and the organization's structure.

Technology.   The many dimensions of technology are discussed in more detail in Chapter 8. For our purposes here we will emphasize a few technological issues that particularly affect how businesses buy. First, to a large extent a customer company is not simply buying products from a supplier, but buying the technologies on which that product is based. These include the suppliers' skills and knowledge in developing, designing, and manufacturing the product. No buying company can know everything about what goes into its products, and so it relies on the technology of its suppliers. For example, an automobile manufacturer relies on the technical knowledge of tire makers to contribute to the road holding and safety of its vehicles. It also relies on the technology of fuel injection equipment manufacturers to ensure the performance and economy of its engines. In contrast, when the automobile manufacturer buys steel, it may be quite confident in knowing exactly what type of steel is right for its particular application, but it probably knows little about precisely how that steel is made. Thus the way in which a company buys a product, and indeed what it buys, are strongly affected by its level of knowledge of the technologies on which the product is based.

The way in which a company buys will also depend on whether the product has been designed by the company or by a supplier. When the buying company has developed its own design for a component, it will seek suppliers that are willing to make to its design (or blueprint) and are able to offer the best combination of quality, service, price, and delivery. We call this **"make to print."** Under these circumstances, the buying company will not need, nor will it be willing to pay for, the design skills, or **product technology**, of the seller. Instead, it will be paying for the seller's skills in manufacturing the product to the appropriate standards and consistency. We refer to this as the seller's **process technology**.[2]

Some companies decide to rely as much as possible on their own technologies. Thereby they increase their research and development costs but hope to reduce the cost of what they buy. Others rely much more on the skill and inventiveness of their suppliers and develop close and long-term relations with them. It has been suggested that a large part of the competitive advantage achieved by Japanese automobile makers over their U.S. competitors is due to their superior relations with component suppliers. Some suppliers may not be prepared for this kind of participatory relationship. For example, a Detroit firm that wanted to bid on making seat pans for Kawasaki's U.S. motorcycle plant was unable to do so because Kawasaki did not provide its bidders with detailed design specifications. Kawasaki's blueprints simply called for 12-gauge cold-rolled steel, gave key dimensions, and described the desired finish.[3] The Japanese company's strategy was built on the idea of its suppliers *adding value* to its products through their technological improvements. In other words, Kawasaki wanted to use the product technology of its suppliers. The U.S. supplier, however, was used to simply making to the stated requirements of customers and probably did not have the design capability to provide product enhancement.

Goals and Tasks.   Increasingly, U.S. business buyers are adopting an approach to their suppliers that is much closer to that of the Japanese. This approach involves making a longer-term commitment to suppliers to achieve value and quality improvement, as opposed to frequently changing suppliers to achieve a short-term price advantage. These two different approaches have many implications for the relationship between selling and buying companies and mean that the business marketer must examine in great detail the strategy and the specific purchasing goals and tasks of the particular buying company. Thus, business marketing is less about assembling a marketing mix that is then offered to a wide, undifferentiated, and relatively passive market than it is about tailoring the marketer's offering to the precise requirements of each customer company.

Actors.   Another factor affecting buying decisions at the organizational level is the philosophy and motivation of the customer company's individual personnel, or **actors.** We can expect managers to have different attitudes to buying depending on whether they consider themselves technologists or marketers. Their attitudes will also be different if they are more concerned about the long-term development of their company or its short-term profit. Thus we may expect a very particular set of requirements from a buying company in which the culture of the management is centered on product excellence, such as Mercedes-Benz. Individuals involved in making purchase decisions in such companies will tend to emphasize product reliability and performance rather than price. This approach contrasts sharply with the buying philosophy of the chief executive of another European company: "We regard our customers as the financial institutions, not the people who buy our companies' products. We are in the business of buying companies rather than running them."[4] Such a company obviously has a very short-term view of its operations and is interested in asset-stripping the companies it buys. It is very unlikely that any supplier to such a company could expect to develop a long-term relationship with its managers or that they would be interested in major new-product initiatives.

Structure.   The final organizational factor affecting buying decisions is organizational structure—that is, the way in which the buying function is related to the rest of the organization and in particular to the management of the company's operations.[5] In some companies the buying function is decentralized, with offices in each manufacturing plant that report directly to local management. Each of these local offices may have to be visited separately by the marketer's sales force. Buyers in these offices are likely to be very concerned with issues that are important to local managers, such as reliability of deliveries and ease of using products. In other companies, buying may be centralized at corporate headquarters, far away from local managers. Buyers in these companies are more likely to be concerned with what is important to the senior buyers, such as negotiating lower prices and standardizing the products that are used across the whole company so as to obtain quantity discounts.

Buying Center Factors

The third group of factors influencing business buying behavior relate to the buying center. The **buying center** consists of those people in the organization who are involved either consciously or unconsciously in the buying process. The marketer needs to know the roles performed by different members of the buying center and the resources available to them to help them make their purchase decision.

Roles.   Buying center roles are those of initiator, user, decider, influencer, buyer, and gatekeeper. The **initiator** is the person who recognizes that the company has a problem or requirement. The initiator is not always someone inside the buying company because the company may not realize that it has a problem or may be unclear as to its requirements. We have already seen that buying companies often rely on the technological knowledge of their suppliers. In this case a salesperson from a potential supplier may initiate the buying process by pointing out a current problem or possible improvement. The potential users of a product may also initiate the purchase process or may act to constrain the process by ruling out certain types of products, problem solutions, or manufacturers on the grounds of unsatisfactory previous purchases or poor reputation. For example, the large French software house GSI has been successful in selling Tolas, an order-processing, inventory, and distribution software package in the United States. The buying process for new software may be initiated by a financial manager because of poor order processing or an inventory control problem. The manager may favor purchasing Tolas. However, the purchase could be constrained by the final users of the software in the data-processing departments, who may want to continue using IBM computer equipment. They may argue that Tolas should not be considered because it is designed to run on Digital equipment.

Most often it is the users of a product who draw up the initial specification for what is to be sought from the market. They may favor a particular supplier so strongly that they act as de facto **deciders**. It is often very difficult to spot when a purchase decision is actually made, either because organizations often move toward a particular decision through a process of "creeping commitment" or because the **influencers** in the company are so skilled at lobbying that the decider's role is little more than to act as a rubber stamp.

There may be many influencers in a buying company. Exhibit 3–4 shows some of the influencers in the purchase of welding rods. Welding rods are consumable operating items costing less than a dollar each. They are used in very large quantities by a wide range of companies, ranging from the constructors of nuclear power plants to farmers who need to repair a broken plow. The actual welders who use the products have a powerful influence on what should not be bought even though their formal influence in the buying process is nonexistent. If welders decide that the product is difficult to work with, they will not work with it. Exhibit 3–4 also shows how the different influencers have different requirements of the same simple welding rod. The welders are interested in speed, elimination of cleaning time, and output per week. Obviously, ease of operation is important to them, as is the appearance of their final product. Price is less important to the welders than it is to the workshop foreman or a buyer. A company metallurgist would seek to influence the purchase decision in the direction of products having the highest technical quality, the widest applicability to poor steel, and the greatest capability of producing strong welds. Additionally, many buying companies are strongly influenced by their peers in other similar companies. Good business marketers know who the most influential companies in an industry are and cultivate them carefully.

EXHIBIT 3–4   Who Is Interested in What? Different Influencers' Requirements of a Welding Rod

| | Influencer | | | | |
Requirement	Welder	Foreman	Welding Engineer	Buyer	Metallurgist
Electrode price		X		X	
Welding speed	X	X			
Elimination of cleaning time	X	X			
Output per week	X	X	X		
Ease of operation	X				
Appearance of final product	X		X		
Strength of weld			X		X
Applicability to poor steel	X	X	X		X

These "reference sites" can then be used as a source of recommendation to other buyers.

Buyers are the people whose formal task it is to select a supplier and arrange the terms of a deal. For many repeat purchases or lower-value items, the buyer will be the sole member of the buying center. For the purchase of major capital equipment, the buyer's role may simply be to search for and evaluate suppliers and to present this data to other center members. We will look more closely at the buyer's role later in this chapter.

Companies can only make purchase decisions on the basis of the information they have available. **Gatekeepers** are the buying center members who control that flow of information. Most commonly, the buyer is the gatekeeper, or first point of contact for the salesperson. The salesperson may make a presentation and leave product information with the buyer but won't know if that information is going to be passed on to other members of the buying center. Often secretaries act as gatekeepers, and salespeople employ a host of techniques to get past the secretary and communicate directly with an important influencer or decision maker in the purchase process.

Resources.   A second aspect of the buying center influencing buying decisions is the resources that the center has available to aid in decision making. These resources include information and expertise. Some companies have a purchasing research department that is able to assist in the buying process by assessing supply markets, product trends, and the characteristics of individual suppliers and products. But in many companies, purchase research is less well developed than is market research. When purchase research is undeveloped, the business buyer is likely to be more dependent on suppliers for information and will have more difficulty in evaluating different competing offerings.[6]

Individual Factors

Business purchases are not made by companies but by individuals within those companies. This means that we need to understand the requirements and motivation of these individuals, as well as those that are stated by the company. Three factors relating to these individuals influence buying decisions: the buyer's status, organizational politics, and the ethics of buying.

Buyer's Status.   The business buyer's status in the buying organization may play a role in the buying decision. Business buyers are often paid less than marketing people of similar seniority, and some buyers occupy a relatively low-status position in the organizational hierarchy. This situation is gradually changing as companies are becoming more aware of the importance of skilled and well-trained buyers. But it is still possible that a business buyer may take pleasure in buying from a prestigious company or gain a sense of achievement and importance by buying expensively. Also, business buyers are often similar to consumers and may know only a little about the technicalities of what they are buying. Like consumers, they may reduce their risks by insisting on well-known brand products that conform strictly to existing industry standards. In this way they hope to avoid criticism by others in their company.

Organizational Politics.   Buying can often be part of organizational politics, and buyers may use a number of tactics to increase their influence in the company.[7] For example, a buyer may "bend the rules" for someone in the company either in return for a favor or to show that the buyer has the power to act independently. Buyers often value information provided by salespeople if it increases their influence over others in the company.

Organizational politics can also be used by business salespeople for their own advantage. For example, someone selling photocopying or facsimile machines may exploit the fact that some first-level managers will see this equipment as a mark of independence and status. The salesperson may also emphasize the alternative of leasing these products so that the initial cost is less than that at which senior management approval is needed.

Ethics.   The individual motivations of people in a buying company present a question of ethics for the marketer. Marketers must think carefully about whether they are manipulating the wishes or vanities of individuals in a company at the expense of the customer company's well-being and, incidentally, the marketer's own long-term best interests. Many companies prohibit even the smallest gifts from suppliers, and there is strong legislation against corrupt practices in business buying. Nevertheless, some business buyers will seek or be offered a personal inducement

BUSINESS MARKETING IN PRACTICE ▮▮▮▮▮▮▮▮▮▮▮

Overstepping Ethical Bounds

Research in the past focused on what practices are considered ethical or unethical in buyer/ seller relationships. These investigations focused on a firm's offer regarding price, delivery, and so on. But such studies covered only a limited set of possible salesperson's activities. A recent survey extended the research and focused on buyer ethical opinions. What do buyers feel is right and wrong? I. F. Trawick and J. E. Swann interviewed a total of 187 purchasing professionals in the southeast and north-central United States. The survey consisted of several statements describing particular gift-giving situations; respondents were asked to rate these situations as ethical, neutral, or unethical. The results are below:

	Percentage Believing Situation Is:		
*Situation**	Ethical	Neutral	Unethical
1. Buys lunch for purchasing agent	56	40	4
2. Provides entertainment for buyer such as sporting event tickets	17	47	37
3. Gives customer $10 Christmas present	20	50	30
4. Gives customer $25 Christmas present	11	38	50
5. Gives customer $50 Christmas present	6	23	71
6. Gives prospect $10 Christmas present	9	30	61
7. Gives prospect $25 Christmas present	5	17	78
8. Gives prospect $50 Christmas present	5	13	82

*Situations have been shortened for brevity.

Trawick and Swann list six specific recommendations for salespeople:

1. Do not offer or give a gift of even nominal value ($10) to a prospect.

2. Do not assume that low-cost gifts or entertainment beyond a business lunch will be welcomed by current customers. Know your customer before providing a nominal gift. Gifts worth $25 or more should be avoided.

3. Don't create an impression that you will give preferential treatment to purchasers that you personally like.

4. Avoid the temptation to pressure the buyer for concessions by alluding to reciprocal buying or the economic power of the supplier.

5. Don't put your interests as a salesperson ahead of those of your customer by giving incomplete or misleading information.

6. Do not bypass purchasing with "back-door" selling.

Source: I. F. Trawick Jr., and J. E. Swann, "How Sales People Err with Purchasers: Overstepping Ethical Bounds," *The Journal of Business and Industrial Marketing,* Vol. 3 (Summer 1988), pp. 5–11. Adapted with permission.

to favor one particular supplier. Giving or accepting such a bribe is not only unethical and illegal, it also weakens the position of both parties in any future transaction. In particular, it means that both buyer and seller are likely to be pressured to
give or take additional gifts in the future, or even to be blackmailed by the threat
of disclosure.

THE PROCESS OF BUSINESS BUYING

The business buying process varies widely. Exhibit 3–5 shows a simplified version
of the Robinson, Faris, and Wind **Buygrid**, which helps categorize the process in
different circumstances.[8] The Buygrid is widely used in business to make sense of
different types of purchasing and the process which these purchases go through.
We will use the Buygrid to examine the categories of purchases, known as the buy
classes. We will also look at different types of products, and the stages in the buying
process, known as the buy phases. Finally, we look at the business buying process
in practice.

Buy Classes

Purchases may be categorized into three **buy classes** according to the newness of
the buying situation: new-task, straight-rebuy, and modified-rebuy.

EXHIBIT 3–5   The Process of Business Buying by Classes

Buy Phases	*Buy Classes*		
	New-Task	Straight-Rebuy	Modified-Rebuy
Identification of need			
Establishment of specification			
Identification of alternatives			
Evaluation of alternatives			
Selection of suppliers			
Performance feedback			

Derived from P. J. Robinson, C. W. Faris, and Y. Wind, *Industrial Buying and Creative Marketing,*
1967, p. 14. Reprinted by permission of the author.

New-Task.   In **new-task purchases** the company is buying a product or service for the first time or, more properly, facing a problem for the first time. In this buy class the company will have to evaluate a wide range of possible problem solutions or suppliers. The process tends to be time consuming and involves a number of people.

Straight-Rebuy.   **Straight-rebuy purchases** are repeat purchases of products or services, many of which are triggered automatically when existing stocks reach a certain level, as in the case of office supplies, such as paper, pens, or envelopes. The buyer has little involvement in the purchase and makes no evaluation of competing brands before simply repeating the purchase of the same brand as last time. Straight-rebuys constitute the majority of business purchases. Companies simply do not have the resources to evaluate each purchase on every occasion, and often the low value of the items means that reevaluation is not worthwhile.

Organizations may also opt for a straight-rebuy because of lack of resources to evaluate alternative purchases, the possible risks in changing suppliers, or sheer inertia. There are considerable costs and risks to both buyer and seller in switching from an established relationship, as will be detailed when we examine the nature of buyer/seller relationships later in the chapter.

Modified-Rebuy.   **Modified-rebuy purchases** are purchases in which the buyer is reevaluating a product or service that has been bought before. There will be less evaluation than when the buyer has no experience or skill in the purchase, as in a new-task situation, but much more than in a straight-rebuy.

Types of Products

The buy classes are a useful shorthand for categorizing purchasing situations. However, the traditional product classifications—capital equipment/investments; accessory equipment; component parts; process materials; maintenance, repair, and operating (MRO) supplies; raw materials; business services; and so forth—also have implications affecting the buying process. Some purchases of products or services are so important that on each occasion there will be thorough evaluation. This is likely to be the case for some capital goods, whereas for MRO items there may not be any real evaluation, even when the products are purchased for the first time. In MRO purchases, convenience and availability may be more important than specification or even price. The buyer will simply order among the products available from a particular distributor, possibly under a contract that provides for a discount across a wide range of product items. Parts and materials form a middle category in which the discretion of the buying organization is at perhaps its greatest. Here the buyer has scope for cost reduction and product improvement by working effectively with a number of different suppliers.

Buy Phases

The process of business buying is not carried out in isolation by the buying company alone. Instead, it is a process of interaction between the buying company and potential suppliers, which will be seeking to influence the process to their advantage. These suppliers can be separated into the **in-supplier**, which is already supplying the company, and the **out-suppliers**, which are trying to displace it. We can describe the buying process as going through five stages, called **buy phases**: identification of need, establishment of specification, identification and evaluation of alternatives, selection of suppliers, and performance feedback. In an actual purchase, however, the buy phases are not clear-cut. The marketer who wishes to influence the buyer often faces the difficult task of finding out exactly which stage the buying company is at in the buying process.

Identification of Need.   The in-supplier is in a stronger position than other suppliers to sow the seeds of need recognition in the buyer's mind. A business can often carry on for years with an unrecognized problem or inefficiency. It is the task of the business marketer's promotional activity, either through advertising or using sales calls or telemarketing, to raise this problem in the mind of the buyer.

Establishment of Specification.   Even if it isn't the supplier that starts the buyer thinking about a problem, a salesperson can sometimes influence a buyer to specify a problem solution in a way close to the supplier's offering—for example, "Zenith Model AK49 compressor, or equivalent." A marketing company therefore needs to use its sales force to gather intelligence about when and where buying companies are thinking of making a purchase. This task is very much more difficult for out-suppliers. Trade directories and suppliers' catalogs are very important to both the buyer and the marketer during the specification phase because for many design problems, an engineer may simply refer to a general directory or to the catalog of a specific supplier's products for a problem solution.

Identification and Evaluation of Alternatives.   We have already noted that buying companies tend to buy from the same source of supply as before unless there is some positive reason to change. This may mean that there is little evaluation of alternatives. On the other hand, when the buying company is seeking a new product, it may have great difficulty in identifying a supplier that is either able or willing to produce a product to meet the buyer's particular requirements. In either case, the business buying process is not one of reaction to the sales and marketing efforts of sellers. More often it is a process of search and evaluation of a number of suppliers that may be more or less able to deal with the customer or willing to make efforts to meet its requirements. Chapter 4 discusses new-product buying in detail.

Selection of Suppliers and Performance Feedback.   The actual selection of a supplier is the direct outcome of the evaluation in the previous buy phase. The selection decision, however, may be made by a different person in the organization—by someone who was not involved in the earlier evaluation process. This situation has occurred in a wide range of companies in different international markets.[9]

Just as a purchase does not start at the point at which the order is signed, neither does it finish at the point at which the product is delivered. The buying company will seek to evaluate performance of the product in use, the cost of the product over its life, and the quality of the supplier's back-up service. This evaluation constitutes **performance feedback** and will be a major factor in determining what will be bought next time and from whom it will be bought. Chapter 4 looks at performance evaluation in greater detail.

The Business Buying Process in Practice

Exhibit 3–6 shows some of the distinctive features of fourteen different purchases in the new-task, modified-rebuy, and straight-rebuy classes.[10] In these examples, a new-task/modified-rebuy purchase took as long as five years to complete, there were as many as six people in the buying center, different people were the initiators of the buying process in the different buy classes, and different factors were critical in choosing among suppliers.

EXHIBIT 3–6   Characteristics of the Business Buying Process for Different Buy Classes

Characteristics of Buying Process	*Buy Class and Number of Purchases*	
	New-Task/Modified-Rebuy ($n = 7$)	Straight-Rebuy ($n = 7$)
Length of time	7 months–5 years	1 week–7 months
Number in buying center	3–6 members	2–3 members
Source of contact with suppliers	Buyer, plant or project manager, engineer	Buyer
Initiators of buying process	Manager, other suppliers, engineers	Buyer, user
Critical factors in purchase	Price, product, performance, delivery, guarantee	Delivery, price, terms of payment
Composition of buying center	Fluctuates	Buyer and fluctuates
Reasons for supplier contact by customers	Modifications desired, incapable suppliers, dissatisfaction	Depletion of stocks, dissatisfaction
Postpurchase evaluation	Informal	Informal

Source: Reprinted by permission of the publisher from "Organizations Buying in New Tasks and Rebuy Situations," by Peter Doyle, Arch G. Woodside, and Paul Michell, *Industrial Marketing Management,* vol. 8, 7:11. Copyright 1979 by Elsevier Science Publishing Co., Inc.

MOTIVATIONS OF THE BUSINESS BUYER

Like consumers, business buyers are subject to a wide variety and complexity of buying motives, and it is rare for either group to buy for just one reason. In this section we first list some of the criteria that business buyers may apply in making their decisions. We then look at the different uncertainties that motivate businesses in making their purchases. Finally, we look at the different abilities a marketer needs to satisfy buyers' requirements.

Buyers' Criteria

The choice of supplier for a particular product could be influenced by any combination of such factors as convenience, specification, life cycle cost, delivery, reputation of the supplier, after-sales service, technology, reciprocity, product range, and expertise.

Convenience.   The convenience offered by a product refers to the extent to which it is compatible with the customer's existing products and procedures.

Specification.   The specification for a product includes its required performance and versatility. These requirements may be expressed in clear, quantitative terms, or more loosely as the need for "high quality." However, the quality of any product cannot be defined absolutely and can only be evaluated against its fitness for a particular use. Assessments of the quality of a single product can vary between different applications and different customers.

Life Cycle Cost.   The **life cycle cost** of a product consists of the product's initial price plus the costs of using the product over its useful life. Often minimizing the life cycle costs is of greater concern to the buyer than simply buying at the cheapest price. Other buyers may choose to minimize their initial outlay and accept higher life cycle costs.

Delivery.   For some customers, speed of delivery will be important. Others will be more concerned with reliability of delivery, and some will demand both.

Reputation.   Some companies will place great emphasis on the reputation of the supplier in making their decision, rather than concentrating on assessing the quality of the product itself.

After-Sales Service.   Some customers will question very closely the ability of a supplier to ensure the continuing effectiveness of the product in use. The quality of this **after-sales service** and support by the supplier may outweigh the importance of initial price or product performance.

Technology.   Some products are based on entirely new technologies. It may be very important to a buyer to keep up with such technological changes. In this case the buyer may be prepared to trade off the new technology against a lower level of reliability from the product.

Reciprocity.   Many companies both buy from and sell to each other. This can mean that a company will agree to buy a particular product, even though the product may offer lower performance, just so that it can ensure a reciprocal sale of its own products. This reciprocity can influence the buying decision.

Product Range.   A customer may buy a particular product because it is from the same company that supplies a range of other products to the customer. Often the customer will be able to negotiate a favorable deal across the whole range.

Expertise.   When a buying company is purchasing a product for the first time, it may be unsure about which is the right product for its particular requirements. In this case it is likely to buy from a company that it believes has the expertise to advise it, even though that company may not offer the best prices.

Buyers' Uncertainties

Understanding the problems and uncertainties facing buyers is vital for marketers if they are to provide successful solutions and reduce these uncertainties. Buyer uncertainties can be grouped into three categories: need, market, and transaction uncertainties.[11]

Need Uncertainty.   The purchase of goods and services is relatively straightforward when the company is sure of precisely what it wants. However, the company's needs may be difficult to determine, such as when buying a complex machining center, and this **need uncertainty** will strongly influence the way the company buys.

When buyers have high need uncertainty, they are more likely to look toward current suppliers or well-known brands—witness the well-known adage "No one ever got fired for specifying IBM." In other words, the reputation of IBM provides comfort for the buyer with high need uncertainty. Only more experienced computer buyers would have low enough need uncertainty to feel confident about purchasing "brandless" generic computer products. Studies have also shown that those buyers with high need uncertainty are less likely to buy products from foreign suppliers.[12]

Market Uncertainty.   Sometimes a market may consist of a wide diversity of types of products, or it may be changing rapidly with a succession of new and different offerings. In these cases buyers face **market uncertainty**. They will be concerned about keeping track of the rapid technological and product changes in

the market and the different offerings of suppliers. A buyer with high market uncertainty will place great emphasis on market scanning and will be less concerned
about establishing a close relationship with a single supplier than is the buyer with
need uncertainty. A close relationship with a single supplier means that the buyer
may receive improved service or that the seller may modify a product to suit the
buyer's requirements. But a close relationship with a single supplier in a time of
high market uncertainty means that the buyer loses the advantage of access to the
technology of alternative suppliers. Under conditions of high market uncertainty
the buyer is more likely to favor two or more parallel suppliers.

A good example of high market uncertainty in both the consumer and business
markets occurred recently during the time of rapid product introductions for personal computers. Buyers were often faced with the choice of buying now or waiting for the rumored introductions of faster, more powerful, cheaper offerings in
the near future. These market conditions led to the growth of such magazines as
What Computer? This magazine includes a great deal of new-product advertising
and reviews, thus serving the buyer's need for information at a time of rapid
change.

Transaction Uncertainty.   The buyer may also face problems with suppliers—
perhaps they are located overseas, or perhaps their reliability is in doubt. In such
cases the buyer has high **transaction uncertainty**. To avoid transaction uncertainty buyers are likely to emphasize the importance of building contacts with
potential suppliers and gathering information from them. (Another well-known
business adage is "No one ever buys from a stranger.") Buyers may also try to
increase the likelihood of getting what they need by using such formal procedures
as vendor rating. Chapter 4 discusses these procedures in greater detail.

Marketers' Abilities

The various uncertainties facing buyers result in ever-changing requirements. Marketers have two abilities they can use to satisfy these requirements: problem-
solving ability and transfer ability.[13]

Problem-Solving Ability.   The seller's problem-solving ability is important when
the technology in a product is new or changing very rapidly. At this time buyers
will have great difficulty in choosing among alternatives, and the seller may be able
to capitalize on its much greater knowledge of the product to solve the buyer's
problems. This means that the customer is buying the seller's problem-solving skills
as well as the product's characteristics, and this may mean that the seller can command a higher price.

Transfer Ability.   Later, as buyers become familar with a particular product, they
will have a better understanding of the capability and imperfections of different suppliers. The buyer then will not need and will not be willing to pay for the seller's

problem-solving abilities. Instead, the buyer has transaction uncertainty, and questions of price and delivery are of major importance. The most important characteristic of the seller at this time is the ability to deliver an undifferentiated product to the buyer quickly, reliably, and cheaply. This is the seller's **transfer ability**.

To succeed in today's market, a marketing company must develop the abilities that match the buyers' uncertainties *at that particular time.* Many companies fail because they offer abilities that the current market does not require. For example, a U.K. company was a pioneer in developing special nickel alloys for use in jet engines, petrochemical plants, and so forth, where the alloys had to withstand extremes of heat, acidity, or vibration. The firm's customers often did not know what alloy specification would suit their requirements (high need uncertainty) and would seek the problem-solving ability of the alloy company. The firm would develop an alloy with a specification to suit the customer's problem at no charge to the buyer. Research and development costs were recouped through the subsequent sales of the product to the customer. Over time, these special alloys became used in a wider variety of applications from vehicle engines to domestic appliances. Customers got to know the products well, and they became standard items. The U.K. company found that its customers started to enquire what the price and delivery would be for these more common items. The company's expensive research and development, slow deliveries, and high prices meant that it faced competition from narrow-range, low-price producers and also from wholesalers that had good transfer ability, offering rapid delivery of standardized products at low prices. It was only after a painful period of adjustment that the company shifted its resources away from problem solving to transfer ability.

CHARACTERISTICS OF BUYER/SELLER RELATIONSHIPS

One way to understand business marketing is to see it as establishing and developing a portfolio of relationships with customers. This means that the business marketer has the task of managing these relationships, and each purchase and delivery of goods is just one, albeit very important, episode in such a relationship. Each episode is affected by the overall relationship with the supplier and in turn may affect the whole relationship. For example, failure to deliver on time or giving an impression of being uncaring can spoil the seller's reputation with the buyer and the likelihood of future sales. We first look at the process of relationship development in business markets and then at the implications of the **buyer/seller relationship** for the business marketer.

The Process of Relationship Development

Buyer/seller relationships evolve over time. This is particularly the case with relationships that center on important purchases, such as component parts or capital goods, rather than routine, off-the-shelf items, such as standard operating supplies. By looking at the stages in the **relationship development process** we can examine the problems of starting, developing and managing relationships. These tasks are faced by both buyer and seller companies, because both have an important stake in the success of their relationships. Sellers need to develop and retain business, and buyers need to ensure that they continue to obtain the products they want at the best value possible.[14] The process of buyer/seller relationship development is illustrated in Exhibit 3–7. Buyer/seller relationships between companies are often said to parallel the relationships between people in a marriage. You may wish to explore this analogy as we describe the stages in the relationship model.

EXHIBIT 3–7   The Development of Buyer/Seller Relationships in Business Markets

1 *The Prerelationship Stage*	*2* *The Early Stage*	*3* *The Development Stage*	*4* *The Long-Term Stage*	*5* *The Final Stage*
			After Several Major Purchases or Large-Scale Deliveries	In Long-Established Markets
Evaluation of New Potential Supplier	Negotiation or Sample Delivery	After Contract Signed or Delivery Build-Up		
Evaluation initiated by:	Experience low	Experience increased	Experience high	Business stable and based on historical ways of dealing with each other
Particular episode in existing relationship				
General evaluation of existing supplier performance	Distance high	Distance reduced	Distance minimum	
Efforts of out-supplier				Vulnerable to competitive entry
Other information sources	Commitment and adaptation low	Actual commitment increased; perceived commitment demonstrated by informal adaptations	Actual commitment maximum; perceived commitment reduced	
Overall policy decision				
Evaluation conditioned by:				
Experience with previous supplier				
Uncertainty about potential relationship	High investment of management time; few benefits	Increasing formal and informal adaptations; benefits increase	Extensive adaptations; benefits reduced by lack of attention	
"Distance" from potential supplier				

Source: From H. Hakansson, ed. *Industrial Marketing and Purchasing: An Interaction Approach.* Copyright © 1982 by John Wiley & Sons, Ltd. Reprinted by permission of John Wiley & Sons, Ltd.

The Prerelationship Stage.   We have already noted how inertia affects business buying. Buying and selling companies may continue to deal with each other over a long period with relatively little attention to the alternative suppliers or customers available to them. A buyer's decision to consider a new potential supplier can be triggered for a number of reasons, such as a particular episode in a current relationship. For example, a major bicycle manufacturer had bought all its tires for many years from a single large supplier. This supplier had become complacent and made a series of price increases. The latest increase happened to coincide with the appointment of a new purchasing manager in the bicycle company. The manager was eager to make his reputation and immediately ordered an investigation of alternative potential suppliers. He soon ruled out a switch to another large tire manufacturer and instead switched after a short time to a number of small suppliers in the Far East. The new suppliers were prepared to manufacture tires to the buyer's specification, with the buyer's own name imprinted on the tires rather than theirs. Thus a long-term relationship that was important to two very large companies collapsed following a single initiating episode.

Sometimes a company will carry out a general review of an existing supplier's performance, perhaps as part of a continuing vendor-rating procedure. This review may lead to a decision to evaluate new potential suppliers. The sales or promo-

---

Continental Bank outlines the depth of its interactions with business clients.

Produced by Fallon McElligott Advertising. Photography by Rick Dublin.

tional efforts of an out-supplier or information received from others in the industry may also trigger a buyer to evaluate new suppliers. Finally, the customer may seek to evaluate new potential suppliers as a result of an overall policy decision. For example, the British computer company ICL has been making major efforts to expand into the rest of the European Community (EC). As part of this expansion effort it has sought to increase its European orientation by switching to suppliers from within the EC unless it has no alternative. This policy has had a detrimental effect on suppliers from non-EC countries, such as the United States.

For whatever reason, the buyer's decision to evaluate new suppliers will not be casual, and its evaluation of any new supplier will be strongly influenced by its experience with its current and other suppliers. Thus the customer may choose a new supplier mainly for its supposed consistency of product quality if the existing supplier has performed badly in that area.

The "distance" between the buyer and a new supplier is likely to be considerable and affects their ability to understand and cooperate with each other. The *physical distance* between them is likely to restrict communication. The *social distance* is the extent to which people from the buying and selling companies are unfamiliar with each other's ways of working and thinking. *Cultural distance* concerns differences in norms, values, or practices between companies in different regions or countries. *Technological distance* refers to differences between the technological skills of the two companies. Obviously, contacts will be different between companies when they involve a product that both companies understand well, as opposed to a customer's first purchase of a particular piece of high technology. Technological distance is likely to be reinforced when the two companies are from different countries and hence the individuals involved are from different cultures. *Time distance* refers to the length of time between initial discussions and the likely time of product or service delivery. The longer this time is, the less the two companies are likely to feel committed to each other in the early stages of their dealings. They also tend to feel more uncertain about the potential costs and benefits of dealing with each other when the fruits of their relationship are a long way in the future. To build a successful relationship with a customer a marketer must be aware of which aspects of distance are important to the customer and take clear steps to reduce them.

The Early Stage.   Stage 2 in the development of a buyer/seller relationship is when negotiations take place about what precisely is to be supplied or when samples of product are delivered. If the relationship is successful at this stage, the distance between the firms will gradually decrease. They begin to know each other on a social as well as a professional level. The marketer also demonstrates commitment to the customer by devoting time to development of the relationship.

One way for the marketer to show commitment is by making adaptations to suit the buyer's requirements. In this way the marketer hopes to gain the benefits of increased commitment from the customer in return. It is common in some markets for a special product to be developed for a single customer. We refer to this as a **formal adaptation**. Perhaps more significant in showing commitment are the informal, noncontractual adaptations that the supplier may make, such as altering a delivery schedule or making a minor product change.

Of course, the marketer must control the adaptations it makes for a buying company because they can involve considerable costs. The buying company may also show its commitment to the seller by making adaptations to its own products, production, or payment terms to accommodate the seller. By demonstrating commitment the buyer tries to ensure that it receives the seller's attention and the seller's best efforts in tailoring products or production to the buyer's requirements. It is not unknown for buyers to talk of "competing for suppliers"—not because of any absolute shortage of product, but because there is a shortage of technically advanced and adaptable suppliers that will be committed to the buyer in the long term.

The early stages of a buyer/seller relationship involve investment of considerable management time in meetings, negotiations, and the discussion of design and delivery issues. At this early stage, both sides will see few benefits from their efforts. The buying company has not yet acquired a new, stable, quality product offering tailored more or less to its requirements, and the seller does not have the certainty of a new valuable customer.

The Development Stage.   As their relationship develops in stage 3, the buyer and seller companies grow closer to each other. This stage is reached after a contract has been signed or the delivery of continuously purchased products has built up. The two companies become more used to each other's ways of living and working, rather like individuals do after they have been married for some time. They show how important they feel the other party is by making more **informal adaptations** to meet each other's requirements. In this way both their actual commitment and their perceived commitment increase.

Sometimes a marketer can most clearly show its commitment by overcoming a particular problem for the buyer. For example, a British manufacturer of foundry equipment supplied product to a French customer. The product was installed and immediately failed in use. As always seems to happen, this failure occurred late on a Friday afternoon. However, the supplier company responded immediately to a request for help and solved the problem over the weekend. On the following Monday morning it showed the French buying company how it could avoid any repetition of the failure in the future. By demonstrating strong commitment to the customer in solving this problem, the relationship subsequently developed from strength to strength.

Informal adaptations have benefits for both companies in the relationship. The buying company has an increased likelihood of offerings tailored to its requirements. The seller company has assured sales to a buyer that may be more understanding of its problems and less likely to make unreasonable demands. The extent of these benefits to each party determines whether the buyer will choose to commit to a close relationship or choose to play the market. In some product areas buyers gain considerably by having product, production, or service tailored to their particular requirements. In other areas these benefits are not necessary, and the buyer will be inclined to play the field. Sometimes sellers gain by having a development contract with a certain customer or by having an assured outlet for a production facility. Other times a seller may choose to sacrifice the security of a stable customer for the short-term-profit advantage of selling a standardized offering to a wider range of customers.

The Long-Term Stage.   There is a danger that as individuals or companies grow close to each other, they may start to take each other for granted. This is where the buyer/seller relationship moves into stage 4. After several major purchases or large-scale deliveries, both sides will know each other very well. As with a long-married couple, the distance between buying and selling companies may be at a minimum, and both will be strongly committed to each other. However, the opportunities to demonstrate this commitment may be less. For example, product and production modifications may have occurred some years before, which may lead the buyer to form an impression that the seller is no longer trying to serve the buyer's needs. Here again the marriage analogy is appropriate. Both parties in a marriage or a buyer/seller relationship can drift into ways of working or living that can cause the other party to evaluate someone else. For example, the seller's defect rate on a product for a particular customer can gradually become out of line with the improvements of other potential suppliers, perhaps because the seller is concentrating its efforts on new products for new customers. The danger is that this lack of attention and the unwillingness to invest in the buyer/seller relationship, as in a marriage, can lead to divorce.

The Final Stage.   Stage 5 in the buyer/seller relationship is reached only in very long-established markets. Examples in the United States are those industries that for many years were relatively immune to foreign competition, such as the steel, automobile, and textile industries. The industry members became used to a relatively comfortable level of competition, or at least to a form of competition with which they were familiar. Many suppliers drifted into complacency and operated in traditional, noninnovative ways. Of course, when an industry slides into this state, it is very vulnerable to the actions of new, foreign suppliers that may have inadequate knowledge of conventional methods of doing business. These new suppliers may offer levels of innovation and adaptation beyond the experience of the domestic buyers and sellers. The result is that many relationships break up, with buyers building new relationships with foreign partners. Thus from stage 4 or stage 5 the model cycles back to stage 1 and the evaluation of a new potential supplier.

This model of the development of buyer/seller relationships does not mean that all long-established relationships must fail. Good management can ensure that the relationship carries on indefinitely, satisfying the requirements of both companies. For example, in the automobile industry, A. O. Smith has successfully supplied components to General Motors for over fifty years.[15] The firm bases this success on the quality of its product as well as its continuing commitment and planned adaptation to the customer's requirements.

Implications of Buyer/Seller Relationships for the Business Marketer

The buyer/seller relationship model presents clear implications for the business marketer.

Relationship Management.   The complexity of the buyer/seller relationship means that for a successful relationship to develop, **relationship management** is needed. The marketer must develop and manage relationships with each customer company. As the out-supplier, the marketer must determine the nature of any inadequacies that a customer sees in its current supplier. On the other hand, the marketer must carefully measure and evaluate the sales effort, product, or production resources that it devotes to each of its customers so that it can satisfy the customer's requirements while not allowing the customer to take these resources for granted. Even more important, a seller must not let its relationship with a customer become fixed and unresponsive and hence provide the buyer with an incentive to seek another supplier.

Because of the importance of buyer/seller relationships to the business marketer, we need to reassess the role of the salesperson, who is perhaps best thought of as a "relationship manager." It is the salesperson's task to coordinate the many different contacts between different people in the two companies, who are all performing different tasks. Many problems can arise if all parties are not working well together. For example, at the exact time that a salesperson from one company was visiting a customer and negotiating a new order, the seller's finance department called the customer and threatened to cut off supplies if an invoice was not paid immediately!

Relationship Audits.   As well as the operational management of a single relationship, marketers have a **strategic management** task in dealing with all the company's portfolio of relationships. A salesperson involved in detailed interaction with customers may have difficulty in seeing each relationship in a wider perspective. An overall marketing view must be taken of how the company will allocate its resources and efforts among different customers, including such decisions as for which customers it should use its limited product development facilities, for which it should change its production schedules, and on which it should concentrate it sales and service efforts. The basis of this strategy is an audit of the company's relationships. A **relationship audit** must involve answers to at least the following questions:

- What is the likely sales and profit potential of this relationship?
- What resources are required to fulfill this potential?
- Does the likely return justify this investment when compared with the potential in other relationships?
- Where do the threats to the development of this relationship come from?
- What is the contribution of this relationship to the company's overall

operations? Does it provide a strong cash flow, is it the source of joint product development that will enhance the company's general market position, and does it provide entry to other similar customers?

- Are the current efforts devoted to this relationship appropriate to the company's overall strategy?

- Are we too dependent on this customer?

- Are our ways of dealing with this customer appropriate both to its needs and our strategy, or are they dealings based on habit or history?

SUMMARY

The business marketer must be able to analyze the many different environmental factors that may affect each single buying decision: physical, economic, technological, legal and political, and cultural. The marketer must also understand that business purchases vary widely, depending on the requirements of the buying company and its skills and experience. Additionally, business buying is carried out by a number of people, and the marketer must strive to identify each of these and the roles they are performing at different stages in the process of buying. Business buyers have a variety of motivations, and the marketing company must tailor its abilities to meet the real requirements of buyers at any one point in time.

As well as examining individual buying decisions, the marketer must be aware that these form part of an overall relationship between buying and selling companies. The marketer's task is to determine whether the buyer needs a close, complex relationship or a more distant one, and which is in the marketer's best interests. The marketing company must manage each relationship over the different stages of its life. It must also develop a strategy for all current and potential relationships as part of a portfolio, so as to maximize the contribution of each to the company's profitability.

Key Terms and Concepts

"make to print"	buy classes
product technology	new-task purchases
process technology	straight-rebuy purchases
actors	modified-rebuy purchases
buying center	in-supplier
initiator	out-suppliers
deciders	buy phases
influencers	performance feedback
buyers	life cycle cost
gatekeepers	after-sales service
Buygrid	need uncertainty

market uncertainty
transaction uncertainty
transfer ability
buyer/seller relationship
relationship development process

formal adaptation
informal adaptation
relationship management
strategic management
relationship audit

Discussion Questions

1. This chapter made reference to the large number of people from a marketing company who might be in contact with those in a buying organization. How should the marketing company decide who should be involved in contacts with customers? How should it manage these contacts for maximum marketing effectiveness?

2. A manufacturer of computer equipment is seeking to enter a new market overseas. Advise the manufacturer on the sort of questions it should ask and the sort of information it will need about the buying process for its equipment in order to develop a sound marketing strategy.

3. Describe the type of sales activities that would be appropriate at different buy phases in the purchase process for (a) a new-task purchase, (b) a modified-rebuy purchase, and (c) a straight-rebuy. To what extent is the salesperson able to influence the purchase process after the initial sales presentation?

4. Assume that you are a salesperson with the task of developing sales to two groups of business customers. One group has long-established relationships with single suppliers, and the other changes frequently among different suppliers. Explain how you would assess the requirement of companies from the two groups. What would you expect these differences to be and how would your sales approach cope with them?

5. This chapter has separated the members of the buying center into a number of categories: users, deciders, buyers, and gatekeepers. Discuss the ways in which a marketing company can reach and influence these different groups and whether personal or impersonal media are likely to be more or less successful.

6. Assume that you have been appointed to a position of marketing manager in a small manufacturer of either (a) industrial production machinery or (b) specialized industrial components used in the aerospace industry. Explain how you would develop a strategy for building relationships with important potential customers. How would your strategy be different from one that could be developed by a large company in the same industry and what would be the advantages and disadvantages you would have as a small competitor?

7. This chapter has suggested that companies can compete on the bases of their problem-solving ability and their transfer ability. How would the way in which marketing was organized be different between companies whose orientation was toward problem solving and those that concentrated on transfer ability?

Endnotes and References

1. Frederick E. Webster and Yoram Wind, "A General Model of Organizational Buying Behavior," *Journal of Marketing* 36 (April 1972): 12–19.

2. David Ford, "Develop Your Technology Strategy," *Long Range Planning* 21 (1988): 85–95.

3. Roy D. Shapiro, *Toward Effective Supplier Management: International Comparisons,* Harvard University, Division of Research, Working Paper 9-785-062, 1985.

4. Peter Doyle, "Marketing and the British Chief Executive," *Journal of Marketing Management* 1 (1987): 121–132.

5. Frederick Webster, *Industrial Marketing Strategy,* 3rd ed. (New York: Wiley, 1991), p. 37.

6. Bob Hardwick and David Ford, "Industrial Buyer Resources and Responsibilities and the Buyer-Seller Relationship," *Industrial Marketing Management* 1 (1988): 3–26.

7. George Strauss, "Tactics of Lateral Relationship," *Administrative Science Quarterly* 7 (September 1962): 161–86.

8. P. J. Robinson, C. W. Faris, and Y. Wind, *Industrial Buying and Creative Marketing* (Boston: Allyn and Bacon, 1967).

9. Peter Banting, David Ford, Andrew Gross, and George Holmes, "Similarities in Industrial Procurement Across Four Countries," *Industrial Marketing Management* 4 (1985): 133–144.

10. Peter Doyle, Arch Woodside, and Paul Michell, "Organizations Buying in New Tasks and Modified Rebuy Situations," *Industrial Marketing Management* 8 (1979): 7–11.

11. Hakan Hakansson, Jan Johansson, and Bjorn Wootz, "Influence Tactics in Buyer-Seller Processes," *Industrial Marketing Management* 5 (1977): 319–332.

12. Hakan Hakansson and Bjorn Wootz, "Supplier Selection in an International Environment: An Experimental Study," *Journal of Marketing Research* 12 (1975): 46–51.

13. Hakansson, Johansson, and Wootz, "Influence Tactics in Buyer-Seller Processes," pp. 319–332.

14. David Ford, "The Development of Buyer-Seller Relationships in Industrial Markets," *European Journal of Marketing* 14 (1980): 339–353; see also Barbara Bund Jackson, "Build Customer Relationships That Last," *Harvard Business Review* 63 (November–December 1985): 120–128.

15. John McMillan, "Managing Suppliers: Incentive Systems in Japanese and U.S. Industry," *California Management Review* (Summer 1990): 38–55.

4

BUSINESS PURCHASING

CHAPTER OUTLINE

- To understand the nature and scale of the purchasing task facing companies and its implications for business marketing
- To understand the contribution of purchasing toward using fewer suppliers
- To understand the longer-term strategies and approaches to corporate buying that purchasing companies may adopt
- To be able to assess the trends in relationship management as carried out by buying companies
- To know how purchasing companies assess suppliers and how they seek to manage products and prices

It may seem strange for a textbook on business marketing to include a chapter on business purchasing, particularly when that chapter immediately follows one on business buyer behavior. The reason is simple. The business marketer must understand the tasks of a purchasing function and the problems that individual buyers face. It is not enough simply to be able to analyze the purchasing process. The marketer must understand how the purchasing task fits into the customer's overall organization and the contribution it makes to corporate profitability. Only then can the marketer work toward solving the customer's problems, thereby achieving profit for both buyer and seller.

Business purchasing is sometimes referred to as *procurement,* and individual buyers who work in a purchasing department are sometimes called *procurement agents. Sourcing* usually has a wider meaning than simply buying a product. It includes the location and evaluation of suppliers as well as the negotiation and buying task. Through this chapter we will refer to purchasing, the purchasing department, and individual buyers.

Purchasing is changing. Traditionally it simply reacted to those in the company who asked for something to be bought. It also reacted to the sales efforts of potential suppliers when they came to call. In recent years purchasing has become more proactive. Buyers carry out vendor approval checks before they will consider buying from a supplier, and they negotiate long-term agreements with suppliers so that all the divisions of their company can obtain price discounts.

Purchasing is also becoming more strategic. Companies are more aware that their competitive success depends on the quality of their suppliers and the products they deliver. Buying companies increasingly see their suppliers as a vital technological resource that can complement and reinforce their own technological assets and product development. This strategic orientation means that the purchasing function is more closely involved with other functions in the organization and with supplier companies in developing new products, processes, and quality improvements.

Despite the obvious contribution that an effective purchasing department can make to an organization's competitive success, the importance of purchasing is still often underrated by companies themselves. Also, textbooks on purchasing often concentrate on the routine, "mechanical" aspects of the task, such as the forms and procedures for placing, monitoring, and controlling delivery. These aspects are important, but they are the equivalent of order processing for the sales function. Just as marketing is more than running a sales office, so is buying much more than order processing. In this chapter we will concentrate on the major strategic aspects of purchasing and on how purchasing affects the development of strategy for the business marketer.

Business purchasing has many similarities to business marketing. Both require an understanding of markets and competitive activities. Both involve skill in negotiation, and buyers have a purchasing mix that corresponds to the marketing mix. For the buyer, it is important to buy the right product at the right price. Buyers are also concerned about distribution and the logistics of getting the product at the right time and at the lowest cost. Finally, buyers have an equivalent task to sellers' promotion; they have to locate suitable suppliers and often convince them to supply their requirements.

Chapter 4 looks first in more detail at the contribution purchasing makes to business success and in particular at the growing scale of bought-in products and services in many companies. It also highlights the effects of improvements in purchasing performance on company profitability and product quality and suggests some of the reasons why this contribution is not more fully appreciated by managers. The chapter then concentrates on some aspects of strategic purchasing, including the growing trend by companies to use fewer suppliers, how strategic purchasing relates to technology strategy in companies, the question of centralization of decision making in purchasing, and long-term strategy in purchasing.

Also covered in Chapter 4 is how purchasing companies manage and develop their relationships with suppliers; many companies, for example, are moving toward more cooperative and less adversarial relationships with their suppliers. The chapter explains how business buyers assess the suitability and performance of suppliers, and then it concentrates on two critical areas in the purchasing task: product management and purchase price management. Finally, the chapter looks at the impact of the just-in-time (JIT) approach on purchasing.

THE CONTRIBUTION OF PURCHASING

Purchasing's importance to corporate success can be illustrated in three ways: first, by the scale of purchased items as a proportion of a company's total expenditures; second, by the profit impact of an improvement in purchasing performance; and third, by the effect of good purchasing on product quality and performance.

The Scale of Buying

A typical manufacturing company nowadays spends at least half of its sales revenue on purchased parts, materials, and services—often twice as much as it spends on payroll. The proportion of total costs spent in purchasing goods and services is known as the **scale of buying** and varies between industries. For example, few companies in the drug industry spend more than 25 percent of the total cost of goods sold on outside purchases.[1] In contrast, because of the increasing use of electronic components and bought-in subassemblies, purchased items can account for more than 70 percent of the cost of goods sold in other industries, such as the computer industry.

The Effects of Purchasing on Profits

Suppose a company spends $5 million per annum on purchases and has sales of $10 million, with a profit margin on sales of 10 percent, or $1 million. If the company were able to reduce materials costs by 5 percent, it would save $250,000, thus increasing its profits by 25 percent. To achieve the same increase in profits by sales revenue, the company would have to increase sales by $2.5 million, or 25 percent. Thus a 5 percent reduction in the cost of purchased items has the same profit contribution as a 25 percent increase in sales.

The Effects of Purchasing on Product Quality

The buying company seeks to manage its supplier relationships to achieve quality in the broadest sense over the long term. **Product quality** means both consistency of performance across all purchases and up-to-date product technology. Many companies have a long way to go to reach the levels of quality necessary to compete in today's markets. The vast majority of American manufacturers still tolerates a 1 to 3 percent defect rate in purchased products.[2] This level of quality translates to 10 thousand to 30 thousand defects per million incoming parts.

Many companies are now taking a **just-in-time (JIT)** approach to production management. JIT seeks to reduce the capital tied up in inventory by taking deliveries from suppliers in frequent small quantities and only as required. Under JIT there is virtually no inventory of purchased goods awaiting inspection in the customer's factory, and therefore any quality defect can disrupt the company's entire production flow. JIT systems can only tolerate incoming defect levels of less than 100 parts per million. Under these circumstances the quality and consistency of purchased items are absolutely vital to a company's production and profitability. (The impact of JIT on purchasing is discussed later in the chapter.)

Appreciation of Purchasing's Contribution

Purchasing departments have traditionally been relatively low-status or low-reward areas when compared with marketing and sales, despite purchasing's potential contribution to profits and product quality. There are a number of reasons. First, much of purchasing consists of the routine and clerical tasks of order processing, which tends to reinforce the erroneous view that purchasing is a mechanical activity with little scope for strategic thinking. Second, many companies see the main contribution of purchasing as cost reduction, which means that the competitive advantage of excellence in purchased goods and services is largely underestimated or ignored. Finally, the contribution of purchasing is often misunderstood because it is actually very difficult to judge the performance of either an individual buyer or a purchasing department as a whole.

For example, when a salesperson brings in an order worth $1 million, the achievement is obvious. On the other hand, if the items that a buyer purchases increase in cost by 2 percent over a year, is this success or failure? If the inflation rate on those items is 6 percent per annum, a 2 percent increase might be regarded as success. Similarly, it may be even more difficult for a company to compare the "quality" of products or services it receives with what its competitors are obtaining or what it could expect with "better" buyers. Later, this chapter describes some of the ways in which purchasing can be assessed. For the moment we should note that the "simple" task of buying the right product at the right time and at the right price, as well as all the other buying tasks, is becoming much more complicated.

STRATEGIC PURCHASING

Strategic purchasing is the buyer's equivalent of strategic marketing. It consists of major decisions about the future aims and direction of the purchasing function, how it will contribute to corporate objectives, how it will be organized, and how it will deal with other functions in the company. One aspect of the future direction of buying is the trend toward using fewer suppliers, and this has clear implications for marketers. Another issue is how purchasing strategy relates to the overall technology strategy of the company and the related question of when a company should choose to make a product for itself and when it should choose to buy from another company. Two more issues of strategic purchasing concern the centralization or decentralization of purchase decision making and the long-term aspects of purchasing strategy.

Using Fewer Suppliers

Recently, many companies have made the strategic decision to move toward fewer or even a single supplier for many of their purchased products. Fewer suppliers means closer relationships between buyer and seller and greater commitment on the part of both. When suppliers believe that customers are committed to them, they in turn are more likely to commit themselves to greater product quality and customer service. This type of relationship may involve rigorous inspection and

BUSINESS MARKETING IN PRACTICE ■■■■■■■■

Comparisons of Purchasing Patterns in Different Nations (Equipment, Materials, Components)

Can we generalize the industrial buying process across time and across countries? Are there major similarities or differences in procurement—that is, purchasing patterns—in different nations? Do the similarities apply equally to equipment, materials and components?

These are just some of the key questions that three of the four authors of this text (P. Banting, D. Ford, and A. Gross) tackled, with the cooperation of other colleagues in Australia, France, and Hungary (G. Holmes, R. de Maricourt, and J. Beracs). The basis for the research came from two studies in the United States sponsored by *Scientific American* in 1950 and 1970, and a study by Buckner in the United Kingdom in 1967. Our follow-up studies were carried out in the 1980s and early 1990s in Australia, Canada, France, Hungary, the United Kingdom, and the United States.

Our studies focused on two key process industries: (1) paper and pulp and (2) chemical and allied products. We interviewed purchasing directors using the same four-page mail questionnaire utilized in the earlier surveys. We looked at the different stages of the buying process: (1) Who is most likely to initiate a purchasing project? (2) Who surveys alternatives? (3) Who determines specifications to be met? (4) Who surveys available makes and chooses suppliers from whom to invite bids? (5) Who evaluates submitted materials for accord with specifications? and (6) Who decides which supplier gets the order?

Basically, we found that many different departments (or functional areas) are involved, not just the purchasing people. However, the nature of the departmental or group involvement will vary, depending on what items are involved. There are strong similarities between acquisition of material and of components, but not with equipment. Different functional areas are involved at different stages. As a general rule, purchasing plays a major role at the initial and final stages—who initiates a purchasing project and who decides which supplier gets the order. Research is involved at the early and intermediate phases, whereas operations, design, and production engineering play a strong role—active or supportive—through much of the purchasing process. Top management is involved in buying high-priced equipment. Finance and sales departments have little involvement.

Similarities among the four English-speaking nations are striking, and the differences are very few. There are also more similarities than differences between this group of nations and Hungary and France. In a nutshell, differences in the industrial purchasing process have more to do with what is being purchased than with the country of the buyer. These findings should give confidence to business marketers that at least there are similarities in the process of buying, even though the attitudes of buyers may differ.

Source: P. Banting, D. Ford, A. Gross, and G. Holmes, "Similarities in Industrial Procurement Across Four Countries," *Industrial Marketing Management* 14 (May 1985): 133–144, and "Generalisations from a Cross-National Study of the Industrial Buying Process," *International Marketing Review* 2 (Winter 1985): 64–74; P. Banting, J. Beracs, and A. Gross, "The Industrial Buying Process in Capitalist and Socialist Countries," *Industrial Marketing Management* 20 (1991): 105–113; R. Maricourt, F. Malige, A. Gross, and P. Banting, "Comparison of Industrial Purchasing: France and English-speaking Nations," forthcoming.

certification by the customer as well as a program of education of the supplier by the customer.[3]

This approach to purchasing suits the current need for rapid changes in product range and hence the need for close liaison with the suppliers of components for new products. The fewer suppliers a company has, the simpler its administrative procedures and the more it can know of and be able to use the capabilities of its suppliers. Fewer suppliers also means that the buyer is more important to each and can use this factor in price negotiations. On the other hand, fewer suppliers means that the customer is dependent on those suppliers to a much greater extent than if it were "playing the market."

Buying from one supplier, or **single sourcing**, is a way of linking the skills and technologies of suppliers with the purchasing firm more efficiently and effectively. This is so that the buyer's products incorporate the best of the skills and capabilities of both the purchasing company and its suppliers. Of course, not all purchases should or even can be single-sourced. The use of a number of different suppliers is vital when the supply market for a product is unstable because of product shortages or because suppliers are unreliable in deliveries or product quality. Also, when technology is changing rapidly or producing a wide variety of different offerings, the buyer is more likely to require more than one source. **Multiple sourcing** keeps buyers in touch with developments and prices in different companies rather than being overly dependent on the skills of a single supplier.

Supplier Reduction Programs.   Companies often find that the number of suppliers they have for any one product tends to increase over time. This is due to the efforts of different marketers, the decentralization of buying decisions, and poor sharing of information between different people involved in buying. Having too many suppliers often means that the company cannot use its purchasing strength to achieve low prices and good attention from any one of them. In recent years, some companies have undertaken major reductions in the number of suppliers for each product area. Such a company can negotiate group discounts that apply throughout the organization for purchases from suppliers on an "approved list" or "short list."

Japanese Practice.   It is often thought that single sourcing is used frequently in Japanese industry and is a major factor in Japanese success. Many Japanese companies are acutely aware of the advantages of close relationships with suppliers, especially when development work is involved. Nevertheless, these companies single source only when appropriate and not automatically. For example, in a sample of eighty parts purchased by Toyota, 28 percent were single-sourced, 39 percent had two suppliers, 19 percent had three suppliers, and 15 percent had between four and seven suppliers. Similar figures were also found for Honda.[4]

Analysis for Single Sourcing.   Decisions on single sourcing are neither simple nor taken once and for all time. These decisions form a major part of purchasing strategy and involve the purchasing function in both long-term and detailed short-term analysis of suppliers. The original equipment manufacturer needs to know a lot about a supplier before risking its product line on a single source.

Purchasing Strategy and Technology Strategy

Purchasing strategy is not just about single-sourcing decisions. It also builds on analysis of the purchasing company's technologies and on its overall technology strategy. Technology issues in business marketing are fully considered in Chapter 8. Here we are concerned with technology as it affects purchasing strategy.

Technology Strategy.   A company's **technology strategy** includes decisions on what new technologies it needs and how it should acquire them. For example, the company can rely on its own R&D or form a joint venture with another company to develop a technology, or it can license the technology from a company which has already done the development. Technology strategy also includes decisions on how best to exploit the organization's technological strengths. The company can use technologies in its own products and processes or form joint ventures with partners to exploit particular applications, or license a technology with other companies for them to use in their products.[5]

Purchasing Strategy.   **Purchasing strategy** is closely related to technology strategy. All companies have limited R&D resources. They must decide which parts of their products they will design and develop for themselves and for which parts they will rely on the designs of their component suppliers. A second decision they face is whether to make the part themselves or to buy it from a supplier. We will deal with this "make-or-buy" decision shortly. If the company does decide to buy the part it has designed, it will seek suppliers to manufacture that design. This is known as **"make to print."** For other parts of its products the buying company will rely on the design and development skills of its suppliers. Turning design and development over to a supplier is often a very long-term and strategic decision because once the company withdraws from development in a particular area, it will be very difficult for it to return and catch up. Thus purchasing decisions are closely related to the company's R&D decisions and to its basic strategy concerning which skills and technologies it wishes to develop. Clearly, these decisions will be influenced by the purchasing department's assessment of the skills of suppliers and the quality of the company's relationship with them.

External Resources.   The buyer's task with suppliers can be described as managing the company's external resources. External resources become more important and increasingly technological as the proportion of bought-in items grows and the rate of technological change accelerates. The buyer must develop and control the relationship with suppliers if the company is to gain maximum competitive advantage from the skills of its suppliers. Japanese companies have been very successful in managing these relationships to achieve innovative new-product development (see the Business Marketing in Practice box on pages 112–113). Their approach involves a team of people from different functions, including buying, and close cooperation with suppliers. A Japanese manager's description of new product development at Fuji-Xerox nicely illustrates this approach:

> We ask our suppliers to come to our factory and start working together with us as early in the development process as possible. The suppliers also don't mind our visiting their plants. This kind of mutual exchange and openness about information works to enhance flexibility. Early participation on the part of the supplier enables them to understand where they are positioned within the entire process. Furthermore, by working with us on a regular basis, they learn how to bring in precisely what we are looking for, even if we only show them a rough sketch.[6]

A Longer-Term Approach.   Paradoxically, the more rapid the rate of technological change, the more the buyer must take a long-term focus in evaluating suppliers. Considerations of price, quality, and reliability are still of great importance to the buyer. However, they are often qualifying factors—standards that a supplier must reach to be considered. Increasingly buyers are looking to match their technology strategy with the skills of the supplier and its commitment to further development on the buyer's behalf.

The development of long-term technology strategy within buying companies changes and enhances the buyer's role. Buyers need to know much more about each supplier's product and production technologies, potential, and investments. Information exchange between buying and selling companies becomes even greater, and the marketing task facing the selling company becomes even more complex.

Make or Buy

Make or buy is a common expression in purchasing, referring to whether a company should make a particular item itself or buy it in from a supplier. Obviously, these decisions are vital to the business marketer seeking to sell to a customer. We may think that a buying company could make such decisions by simply comparing the cost of making a product with the price of buying it from a supplier. But many buying companies now realize that the situation is more complex and relate make-or-buy decisions to their long-term strategy. Despite this, a survey of make-or-buy decisions in the United States, Canada, and the United Kingdom found that there were wide variations in the way make-or-buy decisions are made in different companies.[7] Three different approaches to make or buy are outlined in Exhibit 4–1: the operational/cost-based approach, the business approach, and the policy approach.

The Operational/Cost-Based Approach.   The **operational**, or **cost-based, approach** is the most common approach to make-or-buy decisions. In this approach, decisions are made individually according to the immediate cost savings or

BUSINESS MARKETING IN PRACTICE ■■■■■■■■

Buyer/Seller Relations in Japan

We tend to imagine that Japanese industrial success has been built just on the exploits of major well-known companies, such as Honda, NEC, Canon, and so forth. In fact, these companies in turn build their success on their relationships with a network of often very small suppliers. The Japanese system of buyer/seller relations can be illustrated by the interorganizational network between Fuji-Xerox and Toritsu-Kogyo, one of its primary subcontractors.

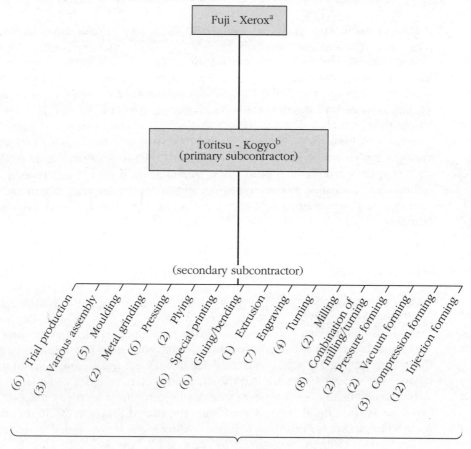

[a]Has other primary subcontractors.
[b]Serves as subcontractor for other manufacturers.

Toritsu-Kogyo is a fairly large subcontractor by Japanese standards, with sales of about $7 million and fifty employees. Most of the secondary subcontractors have fewer than ten employees. The division of labor in this system means that each of the secondary subcontractors acquires a high level of skill in one specialized area as well as a high level of competence in problem solving. This means that they can respond very effectively to special requests from their customers and to changes in the environment. Perhaps most important, these secondary subcontractors are tied closely to Fuji-Xerox via the primary subcontractor.

Source: Kim B. Clark, Robert H. Hayes, and Christopher Lorenz, ed., *The Uneasy Alliance: Managing the Productivity-Technology Dilemma.* Boston: Havard Business School Press, 1985, p. 364. Reprinted by permission.

operational advantage. There are a number of reasons for companies to take an operational approach to make-or-buy decisions. First, a company may buy products or services to avoid paying unionized labor within the company. Second, the type of approach is related to who initiates the make-or-buy decision. Only 3 percent of North American companies report that senior management—which could be expected to take a long-term view—is involved in initiating make-or-buy decisions.[8] Instead, in the United States the finance function—which would tend to focus on immediate costs savings—is most likely to take the initiative. A third rea-

EXHIBIT 4–1   Different Approaches to Make or Buy

	Basis of Approach	*Examples*	*Problems or Drawbacks*
Operational/ cost-based approach	Decisions taken individually to achieve cost savings or operational advantages	Subcontracting transport, printing, or peak load manufacturing	Failure to achieve all possible savings; no relationship to any overall company strategy
Business approach	Proactive approach to make or buy based either on a system of continuing evaluation or broader cost/operational criteria	Use of multifunctional team (materials, finance, legal) that assesses any departmental activity for cost savings by buying-in	Decisions may be based on short/medium-term cost savings, which are cyclical. Buying-in decisions may lead to strategic shortcomings
Policy approach	Based on an overview of the strategic direction of the company and its technological strengths and weaknesses	Activities based on single-minded concentration on core/essential technologies	Difficulty in integrating business policy/ technology strategy/ purchasing organization

Source: B. Cotton, D. Ford, D. Farmer, and A. Gross, "Make or Buy and Technology Strategy" (Paper presented at the 6th IMP International Conference on Industrial Marketing and Purchasing, Milan, Italy, 1990).

son for the operational approach is the general short-term orientation of many managers. As many as 92 percent of executives in U.S. manufacturing industries receive annual bonuses under bonus schemes that tend to reward short-term, visible, measurable performance. Short-term performance improvements can often be achieved by buying things rather than making them in-house.

The final reason for a cost-based approach centers on the opportunity to achieve cost advantages by subcontracting manufacture to a foreign supplier, which may have lower labor and materials costs. For example, one U.S. manufacturer moved the production of its pumps to an offshore supplier and achieved lower costs and increased competitiveness. It should also be noted that such a move may not incur a quality penalty. A components manufacturer claimed not only lower costs by buying from overseas but also achieved quality improvements. It has also been suggested that some companies move manufacturing from their own U.S. plants to overseas companies to avoid tough environmental legislation in the United States. This form of cost reduction raises strong ethical issues for management.

Business Approach. In the **business approach** to make-or-buy decisions, a company carries out a thorough review of each department's activities to see whether cost savings can be achieved by buying the products or services the department is responsible for. Commonly this review is done by a multidisciplinary team, but decisions may still be made on the basis of short- or medium-term cost advantage. The problem with a short- or medium-term approach is that it may be cheaper and more advantageous to buy a component for a period of perhaps three years, but then the cost advantages may swing back toward own-manufacture. Unless costs are monitored constantly, a firm can suffer serious disadvantages in the longer term. For example, a company can shut itself out of a major technological area vital to its future by abandoning its own development and manufacture in that area. Such a consequence could make any short-term cost savings seem very bad value for money indeed.

Policy Approach.   The **policy approach** is quite rare among companies today. It is built on a clear view of the strategic direction of the company and its technological strengths and weaknesses. Black and Decker provides an interesting example of this approach. The company has a single-minded dedication to excellence in the production of fractional horsepower electric motors and their automated assembly into powered appliances. These activities are Black and Decker's distinctive technologies. The company takes the view that it should not fill its plant with anything that it does not have to do, particularly if this limits its capacity to produce its final product. In other words, it should concentrate on making what is essential and what it is excellent at. Other things should be bought. Black and Decker believes that companies face pressure to "fill the plant" and increase contribution toward fixed overheads, especially under adverse market conditions. It sees this as a short-term view based on an inadequate analysis of true costs. Black and Decker takes a very careful long-term view of which activities it should keep in-house and which should be carried out by suppliers and devotes great efforts to managing these external resources.

Finally, it should be emphasized that a policy approach to make or buy does not necessarily mean a vast increase in buying. A company may decide that it must retain its operations in certain key areas. These areas are the activities that add the most value to the company's products and hence are the prime source of its profits. Also, some activities are so critical to the company's future that it could not risk letting its knowledge of them decline or become dependent on others for them.

Implications for the Business Marketer.   There appear to be good opportunities for business marketers because more companies are seeking cost and performance advantage by buying products rather than making them. However, few business marketers have developed the skill of explaining the advantages of buying rather than making to take advantage of these opportunities. In the aforementioned survey of make-or-buy decisions in the United States, Canada, and the United Kingdom, 52 percent of U.S. buying companies reported that no supplier had been responsible for them starting to consider buying something rather than making it, and the figures for Canada and the United Kingdom were even higher—63 and 80 percent, respectively.[9] It is clear that few marketing companies are analyzing the problems of their potential customers so that they can increase mutual profitability by helping to solve them.

Corporate Purchasing

Corporate purchasing refers to those purchase decisions that are made at the corporate level rather than by local buyers. The amount of corporate purchasing depends on the extent to which the company has centralized its purchasing. In **decentralized purchasing** buyers are located in individual operating units and report directly to local management. Decentralized purchasing allows a buyer to give rapid service to the local unit. However, the local buyer may only buy a small amount of any one item and also may not be aware of everything that is happening in the supply market for a particular product. In **centralized purchasing** a single buyer at corporate headquarters specializes in each product area and buys all of the company's needs at one time and therefore may be able to negotiate a lower price.

Many companies try to achieve the benefits of both centralized and decentralized purchasing by negotiating companywide contracts or group purchase agreements for what are often called **strategic purchased items**. These are items that represent major costs for the company or that are vital to its competitive advantage. By buying these items centrally, the company hopes to take advantage of its buying power to achieve the best possible prices or to bring to bear specialized knowledge on strategic items. Local buyers receive information on these corporate deals and place orders to take advantage of them. An example of a major cost item for a manufacturer of consumer durables would be electric motors. For a hamburger chain, beef would be an item affecting competitive advantage and would require great expertise in buying.

Long-Term Strategy

Buying companies face a hierarchy of problems. At the short-term, detail level are the issues of order processing, quality checking, and delivery reliability. At the more strategic level is the question of managing and developing the company's relationships with its suppliers. Even more strategic is the issue of long-term security of supplies. For example, in a highly automated industry such as electronics or automobile manufacturing, the savings from even a large price reduction on a single component are much less than the costs associated with stopping the production line for one day because of a shortage of that component. A longer-term stoppage could bring the whole future of such a company into doubt.

Security Precautions.   Buyers' concerns over supply security have traditionally led them to a number of precautions: they use dual sourcing in the case of vital components; they keep inventory in a neutral warehouse away from labor union control, and they monitor closely the labor relations records and labor contract timing of suppliers. More recently the advantages of single sourcing and the pressure to reduce inventory have meant that companies have had to balance security of supply against the advantages of a close relationship with a single supplier. This situation emphasizes the importance of supplier selection and relationship management, subjects we address later on in the chapter.

Supply Market Changes.   Companies also have to cope with the potential long-term changes that can occur in supply markets. The past twenty years have seen violent changes in technology, inflation rates, raw material costs and usage, and product availability. More of these changes will occur in the future, and a strategic approach to predicting and planning for them is a necessity.

Development Suppliers.   One aspect of this strategic approach is for a buying company to designate its best suppliers as **development suppliers** with which it will jointly develop major technological changes. The policy of a major U.S. automobile manufacturer operating overseas illustrates this approach and can be outlined as follows:

■   To obtain a considerable proportion of components from foreign sources to counteract supply difficulties in one of the countries in which it manufactures.

■   To reduce the number of suppliers in each product group, while at the same time retaining dual sourcing wherever possible.

■   To impose conditions on suppliers to establish "security stocks" that will counteract supply difficulties.

- To make individual buying groups responsible for long-term future planning of supplies in particular products.

- To explicitly designate some suppliers as development suppliers. The company plans to buy increasing volumes from these suppliers of both the current generation and the next generation of products. The company places considerable emphasis on these development suppliers and stresses the importance of close relationships with them.

This corporation summarized its attitudes toward long-term suppliers as follows:

> We can tolerate mistakes by suppliers. We can't tolerate them stopping the line. If they have a problem we would expect them to talk to us, explain the problem and we would be prepared to help. One supplier didn't tell us of a developing problem until it was too late. There was no trust and so we dropped that supplier.

There is a high level of contact between this company and its development suppliers. The company provides information on its plans and where the supplier fits in, and it is willing to help these suppliers develop their technology to better serve the company.

Another engineering company split the orders for an important component between two suppliers. This was not just to ensure competition between them, but also so that the buying company was involved long-term in both of the competing technological solutions to its problems. One of these suppliers was from overseas because the buying company was also concerned about a possible future supply shortage in a new type of component. It wanted to build a relationship with several possible suppliers to ensure its own supplies in the future.

RELATIONSHIP MANAGEMENT AND SUPPLIER DEVELOPMENT

Relationship management and **supplier development** follow from the development of a coherent purchasing strategy and a sound purchasing organization. The goal is to achieve a reliable and prosperous supplier base so that the company can look forward to continuing high-quality and technologically advancing products. The prosperity of suppliers is of course crucial to the customer's own success. A supplier in financial difficulties will not be able to afford to develop new products, and a supplier that feels aggrieved at its treatment by a customer is unlikely to be committed to that customer in the future.

The first issue in relationship management is to understand the impact on a customer's profitability of poor supplier relationships. Second, there is a distinction to be made between an adversarial approach to suppliers and one that is nonadversarial. It is often difficult to achieve a nonadversarial approach, but there are some clear advantages. Finally, it is important to examine the true costs of changing a supplier. These costs may often outweigh any short-term price advantage.

Supplier Relationships and Profit

Exhibit 4–2 shows graphically how poor supplier relationships can reduce profits. We will use the example of a manufacturer of consumer durables (e.g., refrigerators or home laundry equipment) that is buying components (e.g., motors and switches) for use in its production process.

The diagram starts at the left-hand side with "Buying for Price" (box 1). **Buying for price** refers to a situation in which the buyer's main or even sole concern is to achieve the lowest possible price for the products being purchased. There is nothing wrong with trying to buy at a low price. The danger comes when this approach means that the buyer is blind to the real costs of buying a particular product, which are much more than the original price paid. We will see that these

EXHIBIT 4–2   Supplier Relationships and Profit

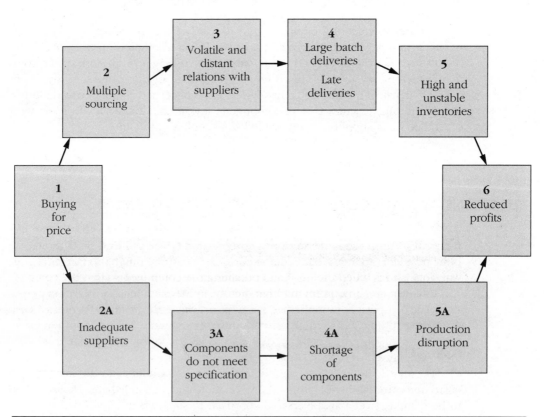

Source: Based on J. Bache, R. Carr, J. Parnaby, and A. M. Tobias, "Supplier Development Systems," *International Journal of Technology Management* 2 (1987): 219–228.

can include the costs of a product's poor performance when compared to an alternative as well as the costs of late deliveries or even of product failure in use.

The company that buys for price will probably use multiple sourcing (box 2). For example, the company may be concerned to ensure continuous supply of important components, such as motors or compressors, in the event of problems with one supplier. If the buyer does use multiple sourcing, it may find that it has a volatile and distant relationship (box 3) with each of its suppliers. These relationships are likely to be based more on formal contracts because of the lack of trust between companies that do not know each other well. These contracts are often short-term with frequent, typically annual rebidding and with suppliers chosen largely on the basis of price. One effect of this approach is that product deliveries do not match the customer's requirements, but only the vendor's existing production schedule. This can mean that the buyer receives large-batch or late deliveries (box 4) of components, which can lead to high or unstable levels of inventory (box 5). The carrying costs of these inventories will reduce profitability (box 6) in the mature and price competitive market for consumer durables. In contrast, a buyer that has a close relationship with suppliers, possibly with a single source for each component, will not be able to transfer orders between suppliers in this way. But the buyer will be able to avoid the problem of volatile relationships with distant suppliers (box 3).

A policy of buying for price and maintaining a distant relationship with suppliers may also lead to inadequate suppliers (box 2A). These suppliers will naturally pay great attention to their prices and hence to reducing their costs. They will have less incentive or resources to invest in longer-term projects, such as good production and quality control systems. These suppliers are also less likely to concentrate on developing improved components to meet the particular requirements of a customer, which may switch to another supplier tomorrow to save 50 cents on the price of a motor.

These inadequacies in the suppliers can mean that vital components don't meet specification (box 3A). The customer may have to invest in extra inspection for these components and may face a shortage of components (box 4A), which will lead to production disruptions (box 5A) and hence reduced profits (box 6). If the problems are not identified, the customer's customer may also face excessive warranty claims when the product containing the components fails in use.

This example may seem extreme, but the problems it highlights are very common. The ideas we have described were in part developed by the director of manufacturing strategy for a major automobile manufacturer.

Adversarial Purchasing

The success of Japanese companies has led some American companies to move away from what has been described as the traditional adversarial model of

BUSINESS MARKETING IN PRACTICE ▬▬▬▬▬▬▬▬

An Example of Adversarial Purchasing

A large multiproduct group in the paint industry uses foreign suppliers extensively, its main aim being to achieve lower purchasing costs than other firms in the industry. It is very concerned with buying achievements obtained against suppliers. The company's buyers emphasize the following tactics in their relations with suppliers:

- Buying at prices below those quoted on suppliers' list prices.

- Paying accounts later than specified by suppliers.

- Treating suppliers' intended price increases as a buying challenge and adopting one of several bargaining ploys: (1) threatening to change suppliers as a bluff; (2) changing suppliers, but only temporarily; (3) delaying the timing of price increases and insisting on buying inventory before the price rises become effective.

Buying at below price is, of course, a common and legitimate aim of a buyer, but late payment may be regarded as unfair tactic that would be frowned on in many companies and would certainly not build up trust between buyer and seller. The company also tries to make its suppliers dependent on it by drawing them into a progressively dependent relationship. It then uses this dependency to force through lower prices. Suppliers are initially chosen for their capacity and delivery capability, provided that they are technically adequate. The company then insists on being treated as a "favored customer" in any subsequent supply shortage. The firm appears to have a low regard for suppliers and considers many to be "almost as big crooks as we are."

You may wish to consider the effects of this approach on the long-term dealings between this buying company and its suppliers and whether this approach is in the best long-term interests of the company.

Source: M. T. Cunningham, *International Marketing and Purchasing of Industrial Goods,* 1982, p. 269. Copyright © 1982 by John Wiley & Sons, Ltd. Reprinted by permission of John Wiley & Sons, Ltd.

purchasing relationships. In **adversarial purchasing** the buyer sees the supplier as an enemy and sees the purchasing process as a contest between buyer and seller, with a clear winner and loser. This approach is still very common and is illustrated in the Business Marketing in Practice box above.

The move away from traditional adversarial purchasing often means simply replacing low price as the criterion for vendor performance with a set of additional criteria, such as quality and delivery reliability. The purchasing organization and its approach do not change. This has been labeled the **new adversarial approach**.[10] An example of this approach is the American car maker that sought to improve supplier quality a few years ago with the following memo to many of its suppliers: "Effective immediately, it is the policy of all divisions of the corporation to reject in its entirety any shipment received that contains even one item with any error."

Nonadversarial Purchasing

Terms such as *partnership purchasing, vendor as co-maker,* and *preferred supplier systems* all refer to attempts to break down the antagonism between buyers and supplying companies and to maximize the benefits of cooperation in **nonadversarial purchasing**. Such cooperation has specific benefits for new-product development, which we shall look at shortly. More generally, a good indication of the aims of buyer/seller cooperation can be seen in Xerox's approach.

Xerox reduced its suppliers from three thousand to three hundred and increased its investment in the remaining relationships. Limiting the number of suppliers concentrates Xerox's buying resources. The company also benefits from the economies of scale in buying and the lower costs that come as suppliers move through their learning curve. Closer contact between suppliers and a designated relationship manager reduces the uncertainty in dealing with suppliers. Not only does better information mean that the supplier is more dependent on Xerox, but also that Xerox is better able to understand the supplier's problems. The preferred supplier system also emphasizes investment in training of suppliers in quality and production and inventory techniques. Xerox aims to more than recover the costs of this investment by improved quality and reduced testing. More generally, the company seeks to increase its suppliers' commitment to their relationship with Xerox. This commitment shows in continuous improvement in products and production processes.

Switching Costs

Before developing a relationship with a supplier, a buying company must ensure that it has selected the right supplier. Exhibit 4–3 shows some of the difficulties that both sides face if they choose to sever their relationship at any time—the **switching costs**. A supplier will have to introduce its product to a new customer, perhaps in prototype form. The customer will have to test the product, and if the test is successful, both sides will have the costs and task of training the customer's personnel. Both sides may face production changes. The seller may have to cope with the buyer's requirements for a change in materials or design, or perhaps with enhanced quality control. The buying company may also have to modify its own products or production processes to accommodate the new product, and both sides may have to adjust their logistical systems. But perhaps the most important switching costs are the last two in Exhibit 4–3. They both concern time and can be summarized as the time necessary to get to know each others' abilities, requirements, culture, and ways of doing business. Both sides have to build a relationship that can cope with the inevitable problems that emerge between buyer and seller. The value of an existing relationship, the costs of switching, and the inertia that tends to develop in all organizations help to explain why buyer/seller relationships tend to be long lasting.

EXHIBIT 4–3   Source of Switching Costs in Buyer/Seller Relationships

Activity	Source of Switching Costs	
	Supplier	Customer
New product introduction	Supplying prototype and test data; training customer's staff	Testing a new product; training own staff
Production	Changing materials, design, equipment to meet customer's needs; special quality control; especially rapid production	Changing product, design, or production methods to accommodate the supplier; special quality control
Logistics	Special stockholding and delivery requirements	Special warehousing and handling
Product development and technical service	Time needed to get to know customer's problems and technical staff	Time needed to understand supplier's technical resources and staff
Buying, selling, and administration	Time required to get to know the customer, his or her staff, and ways of doing business; special documentation and procedures	Time required to get to know supplier, his or her staff, and ways of doing business; special documentation and procedures

Source: Reprinted by permission of the publisher from "An Interactional Approach to Organizational Behavior" by N.C.G. Campbell, *Journal of Business Research,* vol. 13, pp. 35–48. Copyright 1985 by Elsevier Science Publishing Co., Inc.

ASSESSING SUPPLIERS

The business buyer must assess a supplier's product performance, quality, production capability, financial soundness, and overall trustworthiness before any relationship is established and must continue **supplier assessment** at intervals throughout the relationship. The initial assessment of a supplier is particularly important because the buyer will not have the resources to carry out such a thorough analysis for each subsequent purchase. Many continuous, low-value purchases are only assessed infrequently—a fact that can be understood by analogy with consumer purchases. Imagine how long a grocery shopping trip would take if we reassessed every purchase we made—for example, comparing every detail of the nutritional value and cost per ounce of each brand of breakfast cereal.

The basic ideas on the assessment of suppliers were developed many years ago.[11] Initial supplier assessment needs to cover several areas, which extend beyond narrow concerns with product specification. Exhibit 4–4 lists some of the areas that need to be questioned. Very often companies rate suppliers on a numerical scale, as shown in Exhibit 4–5. This method provides a way of comparing suppliers against target scores. The specificity of such rating devices enables the buyer to separate out different requirements and avoid the "halo effect," in which

EXHIBIT 4–4   Initial Assessment of a Potential Vendor

1. Who are the key people (functions, experience, education)?
2. What are vendor's design/development procedures?
3. What are its inspection procedures?
4. Does it have a good quality control department?
5. What are its planning, scheduling, and inventory control systems?
6. What is its stock and material control system?
7. What is its current financial position?
8. What is its current and projected volume of business?
9. What is its cash flow situation?
10. What accounting systems does it use?
11. How does it calculate its production and labor costs?
12. What is the company's personnel and union situation?
13. Will designated individuals be assigned to our account?

Source: Developed from L. J. DeRose, *Negotiated Purchasing* (Boston: Materials Management Institute, 1962), pp. 2–6 to 2–9.

EXHIBIT 4–5   Vendor Rating of an Existing Supplier

	Below Average	Average	Above Average
	2 Points	4 Points	5 Points
Personnel Capabilities			
Caliber/availability of sales/technical personnel			
Management progressiveness			
Technical knowledge of supervision			
Competence of technical staff and management			
Technical field service availability			
Cooperativeness on design problems and engineering changes			
Labor relations			
Facilities Capabilities			
Capable of producing anticipated volume			
Reserve production capacity			
Commitment to other customers			
Up-to-date methods and equipment			
Geographical location			
Financial ability to stand behind failure of product			
Profit-making enterprise			
Investing capital in organization			

Source: L. J. DeRose, *Negotiated Purchasing* (Boston: Materials Management Institute, 1962), pp. 2–16, 2–17.

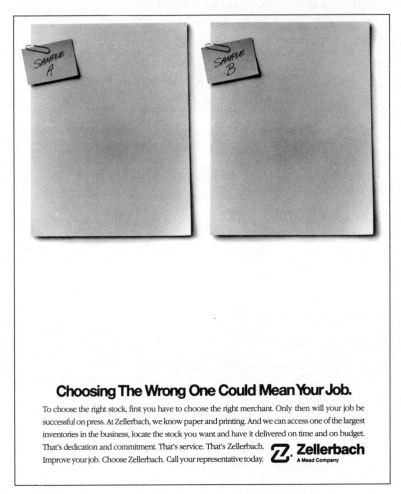

suppliers that perform well on one noticeable dimension are considered to be "excellent," even though they may lapse on other dimensions that are less easy to assess. Rating scales also help avoid a supplier's being condemned for a single instance of low quality due to a machine breakdown in an otherwise impeccable record of service.

More recently, suppliers have gone beyond basic rating and developed such devices as a "supplier award of excellence." The Ford Motor Company has even published in the national press a list of suppliers that have achieved high standards, with Ford's thanks for their work. This form of advertising is an excellent way to remind consumers of Ford's commitment to quality.

PRODUCT MANAGEMENT

Supplier evaluation is about deciding from whom a company should buy. **Product management** for the buyer concerns the quality and specification of what should be bought. Product management is a broad issue, but three aspects have particular relevance to the buyer: value analysis, the costs of a supplier's failure to meet the buyer's quality requirements, and the buyer's role in product development.

Value Analysis

The business buyer is often unable to take a unilateral decision on what the company should buy. Instead, buyers work with other departments to ensure that the "right" product is bought. Generally, the development of a specification involves both technical and commercial considerations. Although technical issues may lead in determining requirements, the buyer will try to ensure that an engineering department does not specify a specially made component when a standard, lower-priced item is readily available. Similarly, the buyer wants to make sure that raw materials are not bought to a higher specification of purity than is required for the purpose intended.

This is not simply an ad hoc activity that takes place when an opportunity to buy a cheaper product presents itself. Buyers are involved in a **value analysis** program that seeks to reduce costs on all items made by the company as well as those purchased from suppliers by seeking answers to the following questions:

Can a cheaper material be used?

Can an alternative tooling arrangement be used at current production volumes?

Are the limits and tolerances too tight?

Costs of Quality

It is obvious that the concept of quality to the professional buyer is not the same as the concept of quality used in consumer advertising. Instead of a "quality" car, or shoes "made to the highest quality standards," the buyer will be concerned with quality as fitness for a specific purpose. The buyer needs to assess the costs of a product's failure to meet the specific quality standards. Again, the buyer will quantify these issues and may use a **quality cost analysis** like that shown in Exhibit 4–6. This scheme lists the costs incurred in buying from three suppliers under the headings of defect prevention, defect detection, and defect correction. Finally, it records the costs to the buying company of complaints and lost sales. These costs may far outweigh the initial purchase price of any product. Supplier A has caused the customer to incur high costs in defect correction and in complaints and lost sales. These costs amount to nearly 30 percent of the value of the purchases from

EXHIBIT 4–6   Quality Cost Analysis

	Supplier		
	A	B	C
Cost of defect prevention			
Qualifying visits	250	250	250
Laboratory tests	200	200	200
Specification revision	300	—	—
Cost of defect detection			
Incoming inspection	600	600	600
Processing inspection reports	1,200	1,200	1,200
Cost of defect correction			
Manufacturing losses	1,590	150	200
Handling and packing rejects	1,500	280	600
Cost of complaints and lost sales	13,200	—	2,043
Total	18,840	2,680	5,093
Total value of purchases	63,820	67,947	84,896
Quality cost ratio (%)	29.5	3.9	5.9

Source: D. Ford, "Purchasing Price Management," in *Purchasing Management Handbook,* ed. D. Farmer (London: Gower, 1985), p. 138.

that supplier and contrast strikingly with the quality costs of supplier B, which were only 3.9 percent. Thus the costs of buying from supplier A were much greater in total than the costs of buying from supplier B, even though the value of the purchases was less. Supplier C sold products worth $85,000 but achieved a quality cost ratio of only 5.9 percent. It too could be judged a much better supplier than A.

Purchasing and Product Development

Marketing textbooks almost always include a chapter on product development and how the marketing manager carries out the task of researching customer requirements, developing the product, and bringing it successfully to the market. This is a very one-sided view of product development and does not describe accurately what often happens in business markets.

Alternative Forms of Product Development.   New products are developed in three ways, as illustrated in Exhibit 4–7. In the traditional, manufacturer-initiated approach, new products are developed by the technical skill of a company on the

EXHIBIT 4–7   The Initiator of Product Development

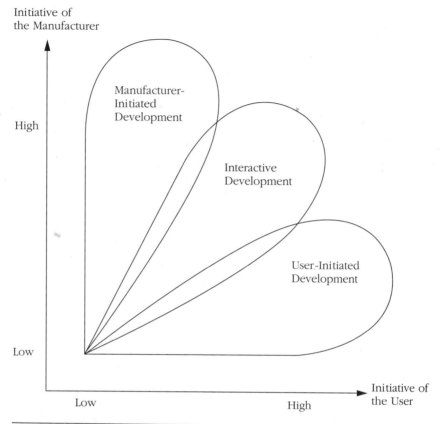

Source: H. Hakansson, "Product Development in Networks," in *Industrial Technological Development: A Network Approach,* ed. by H. Hakansson (London: Croom Helm, 1987), p. 86. Reprinted by permission.

basis of its market research and are then sold to as wide a market as possible. At the opposite extreme is the user-initiated approach, in which product development is initiated by the buying company, which then seeks potential suppliers willing to manufacture to its design. A very large proportion of product innovations in business markets are in neither of these categories, however, but are developed through collaboration between the buying and selling companies. This is known as **interactive product development.**[12]

Managing Interactive Product Development.   We have already emphasized the importance for a buying company of using the skills and technology of its suppliers in developing new products, and we have noted the success of Fuji-Xerox in this respect. Exhibit 4–8 contrasts the Japanese approach to product develop-

EXHIBIT 4–8   Parts Manufacturing in Japan and the United States

OEN / Supplier	Market Needs Assessment	R & D	Design	Test	Specs	In-House Production	Contract Out	Assembly	Shipping
Market Needs Assessment									
R & D									
Design									
Test									
Specs									
In-House Production									
Contract Out									
Assembly							○ United States		
Shipping							● Japan		

Source: Reprinted by permission of the publisher from "What It Takes to Supply Japanese OEM's," by D. C. Blenkhorn and A. H. Noori, *Industrial Marketing Management,* vol. 19, p. 28. Copyright 1990 by Elsevier Science Publishing Co., Inc.

ment with the methods still common in much of North American industry.[13] In the Japanese approach the customer company (the original equipment manufacturer, or OEM) goes through a sequence of activities from market and needs assessment through R&D, design, and testing to the final development of the specification. The supplier of components goes through a similar series of steps, commencing with recognition of a functional need at the same time or even in advance of the OEM. Japanese OEMs want their suppliers to provide leading-edge technology, not just to respond to the OEM's formulated requirements.

In U.S. companies the OEM assembler carries out the product marketing research and the R&D work to develop a specification more in isolation from its supplier, which tends to become involved only after the specification has been finalized. The stages are similar after specification, but there is a critical difference between the two approaches. In the Japanese approach the OEM is working together with the supplier to pool views of future requirements and product and production technologies.

The interactive approach to product development has been followed increasingly by Western companies in recent years. Consider this example of a small paint manufacturer. Unlike the larger antagonistic buyer described in the Business Marketing in Practice box on page 120, this small company, which manufactures medium-quality paints, bases its buying strategy on the recognition that it has very limited purchasing power over suppliers because of its own small size. The company uses the minimum number of suppliers possible in each product category and tries to build up long-term relationships and cultivate customer and supplier loyalty to one another. As the business grows, it retains its original suppliers rather than seeking multiple sources, so as to consolidate the close relationships established. A main element of the company's buying strategy is to choose large suppliers because it believes that large suppliers are more reliable. More important, the company can draw on the technical and product development skills of the large suppliers and so reduce its own product development.

PURCHASE PRICE MANAGEMENT

Despite the growing emphasis placed on product quality and technical advancement, the price paid for products is still of major importance to the buyer. It is now common for companies to require their buyers to negotiate with suppliers to reduce price on an annual basis. According to one business marketing manager with Borg Warner, Inc.:

> Now we're going to a five-year rolling contract where productivity increases are built in, and where we reduce the price × percent each year for five years. In fact, two Borg Warner executives met with a [buyer in an OEM firm] recently, and agreed to sell their transmission for less than they sold it four years earlier.... They're talking about a lower price next year.[14]

There are two main activities in purchase price management. The first is **pricing analysis,** the process by which buyers analyze the costs of potential suppliers as a basis for price negotiation. The second activity is the development of formulas to adjust a contract price for movements in supplier costs over time. Purchase price also has an important function in the way in which individual buyers are rewarded.

Pricing Analysis

Some buying companies do not rely solely on the negotiating skills of their buyers to control prices. Instead, these companies may establish an analytical basis for assessing the initial and subsequent prices for particular products. This procedure is most applicable for continuously or regularly purchased items. It involves the buyer in seeking a cost breakdown from the supplier before the purchase takes place. For example, such a cost breakdown may indicate the following:

	% of Total Price
Raw materials	35
Labor	25
Overhead	25
Profit and administration	15

Suppose that after this initial breakdown has been supplied, the supplier seeks a 10 percent price increase. The justification given by the supplier is that its labor costs have increased by 15 percent. However, the buyer can say that labor costs only represent 25 percent of the product's price. This will mean that only a 3.75 percent price increase can be justified.

Contract Price Adjustments

Some price adjustments are formalized into a contract price agreement. Such agreements are not only for continuously purchased products, but also for products that may be delivered a long time after the initial order is placed. For example, a large piece of production machinery can be specified and ordered for delivery in two years' time. Both parties may agree to an adjustment in price to cope with any cost increases in the intervening period. An example of a contract price formula is given in Exhibit 4–9. Here, the final invoiced price (P_1) will vary from the initial price agreed to in negotiation (P_0). This variation will be due to increases in materials costs (M) and wage rates (S) over the last three-fifths of the period of the contract. The formula for variation is built up using a breakdown of fixed costs, materials, and wages agreed in the initial negotiation.[15] Of course, the use of any such formula-based pricing arrangement is based on a willingness of the supplier to share its cost information with the buyer. This openness indicates a similar level of trust in capital purchases to that which we have described as emerging in many of the relationships between companies for the purchase of components.

Price as a Measure of Purchasing Performance

Because price is expressed in quantitative terms it is a convenient measurement of a buyer's performance. There have been a number of attempts to evaluate the performance of buyers using a formula based on the price achieved as well as a series of other factors. Exhibit 4–10 illustrates a purchasing rating formula developed for the U.S. Air Force. This formula measures the performance of buyers by the volume of work they do, expressed as the number of different products (lines) bought and the proportion of high-value items. Also included is the number of

EXHIBIT 4–9   Contract Price Adjustment for a Capital Purchase

$$P_1 = \frac{P_0}{100}\left(a + \frac{bM_1}{M_0} + \frac{cS_1}{S_0}\right)$$

P_1 is the final invoiced price for the item which will vary from the original price at the date of quotation due to movement in the cost of the relevant materials and wages.

P_0 is the initial price at the date of quotation.

M_1 is the mean of the price for the materials concerned over the last 3/5ths of the period of the contract.

M_0 is the initial price for the same materials at the date of quotation.

S_1 is the mean of the wages of shopfloor personnel over the last 3/5ths of the period of the contract.

S_0 is the initial wages for the same staff at the start of the contract.

abc are the contractually agreed proportions of the initial price at the following percentages:

    a—fixed proportions at 15 percent
    b—materials at 44 percent
    c—wages and social charges at 41 percent

Source: B. Farrington, *Industrial Purchase Price Management* (London: Gower, 1980), pp. 144–145. Reprinted by permission.

EXHIBIT 4–10   U.S. Air Force Purchasing Rating Formula

The buying rating formula is based on seven variable factors:

$$\text{Standard output} = \left[\frac{x_1 + 2(x_2 + 10x_3)}{x_4}\right] \times \left[1 - \left(\frac{x_5}{2} + \frac{x_6}{x_2 + x_3} - \frac{x_7}{x_1}\right)\right]$$

where:

x_1 = line items (number of items purchased per month, regardless of quantity per item)

x_2 = actions under \$2,500 (this includes the vast majority)

x_3 = actions over \$2,500 (these estimated to take 10 times longer to handle)

x_4 = number of manhours worked in a month

x_5 = delinquency rate (percent of orders shipped late)

x_6 = major and minor errors (one point for major errors, 0.25 for minor errors)

x_7 = cost savings (one point for saving under \$100, two points for over \$100).

A *minor error* is defined as the failure to act on requisitions within 30 days or the failure to mention a delivery date on the order.

A *major error* would include the failure to include required legal clauses and the failure to obtain competitive bids.

Source: O. Davies, "Measuring Purchasing Performance," in *Purchasing Management Handbook*, ed. by D. Farmer (London: Gower, 1985), p. 321. Reprinted by permission.

major and minor errors that are made. The rating scale attempts to include the cost savings that the buyers have achieved. We have already noted that the factor of cost savings is difficult to estimate in measuring any buyer's performance. The price achieved by the buyer and the cost savings that this represents have little value in assessing the buyer's performance unless we compare that price with some internally generated standard, industry norm, or performance target. Many companies seek to compare the prices achieved by their buyers over a year against a preset forecast of cost movements. Alternatively, they may try to assess achievement against a cost minimization program.

It is important for business marketers to understand not only the motivations of the companies they deal with, but also those of the individual buyers. Marketers must assess the rewards given to those buyers and the emphasis placed on cost reduction, supply security, or attempts at technological and quality advancement.

JUST-IN-TIME (JIT)

Many of the developments we have outlined in this chapter have blurred the lines that separate buying and selling companies. Companies are enmeshed in a series of supply and product development relationships with many other companies around them. This means that the boundaries of each company are increasingly open. For example, product development often takes place through a supplier and buyer working together. Just-in-time (JIT) is one of the developments that have encouraged close buyer/seller relationships. JIT has blurred the boundaries between buyer and seller and strengthened the importance of the buying department.

The fundamental aim of JIT is to remove inventory from the manufacturing chain of successive buyer/seller relationships. A buying company may wish to eliminate its inventory to avoid carrying costs. If the company achieves this simply by requiring suppliers to carry its inventory, the supplier's costs increase, and it will seek to pass these back to the customer through increased prices. JIT involves inventory reduction or elimination through delivery of the necessary items at each stage in a manufacturing chain exactly when they are required. For this to be achieved, very precise systems of production control are required in all the companies involved. Often this takes the form of the Japanese *kanban* method of parts supply, perfected at Toyota's production facilities in Japan. The *kanban* system helps eliminate wasted production time and costly inventory build-up by ensuring that only the required number of parts are built and then delivered just in time to the line for assembly. JIT is not a quick technological fix for a company. It involves a major philosophical change, not only within the separate buying and supplying companies, but also in the relationship between them. When successful, its effects can be dramatic. For example, when Burlington Industries ships denim to one of the nation's leading sportswear makers, the truck is not loaded with a random sequence of rolls as for most denim customers. Instead, the cloth arrives in a particular sequence so that the customer can immediately unload it, spread it, and cut it.[16] JIT has frequently been referred to as a philosophy and is a good example of the philosophical changes occurring in business buying that affect the business marketer.

SUMMARY

This chapter has examined some of the problems, activities, and plans of buying organizations. The whole basis of marketing thought is that the marketing-oriented company places itself in the position of its customers and tries to understand their requirements. It then looks back at itself and sees how it can tailor itself to match these requirements. It is necessary for business marketers to devote great attention to understanding the emporographics and expectations of their customer base. Business marketers must also be aware of the intricate details of customers' internal operations, the tensions and conflicts that exist in the company, its purchasing strategy and motivation, and the problems and procedures of the individual buyers and the purchasing function as a whole.

Business purchasing can be seen as an activity with much in common with business marketing. Both are market based, and both operate on the periphery of their organizations. They not only carry out their more obvious functions but also serve as a window onto the world for their companies. The main difference between the two is that marketing is a high-status and highly paid activity, whereas buying is still often low status, low paid, and restricted to the mundane operational aspects of its work. As a result, many companies lose the major profit opportunities that improved purchasing can achieve. Perhaps more important they miss the great contribution toward the development of their overall strategy that can be provided by the only department that has close links with the organizations providing the main external inputs to the company's products.

Chapters 3 and 4 emphasize the importance of the relationship between buying and selling companies. These relationships are at their closest in Japanese business, and European companies have realized for years the value of close relationships as an alternative to "playing the market" for short-term gain. However it is only recently that American buying organizations have moved toward a strategy that seeks to take advantage of closer relationships.

It is vital for business marketers to see themselves as problem-solvers for their business clients and as part of their production process. The marketer is someone who carries out the task of establishing, developing, and managing buyer/seller relationships for mutual profitability. The ability to carry out these tasks depends very heavily on analysis and understanding of business buying.

Key Terms and Concepts

scale of buying
product quality
just-in-time (JIT)
strategic purchasing
single sourcing
multiple sourcing
technology strategy
purchasing strategy
"make to print"
make or buy
operational (cost-based) approach
business approach
policy approach
corporate purchasing
decentralized purchasing
centralized purchasing

strategic purchased items
development suppliers
relationship management
supplier development
buying for price
adversarial purchasing
new adversarial approach
nonadversarial purchasing
switching costs
supplier assessment
product management
value analysis
quality cost analysis
interactive product development
pricing analysis

Discussion Questions

1. You have been employed as a buyer within a large industrial company. Your manager asks if you would be interested in taking a job in marketing. Produce a short report for the manager detailing the advantages that your buying experience would bring to a marketing job and the kind of problems you think a buyer would face in making this change.

2. Explain the steps you would go through in seeking new suppliers for a particular industrial product from an overseas country, in line with your organization's strategy of diversifying supply sources.

3. Produce a report that defines and describes the following terms: *supplier evaluation, supplier development, relationship management,* and *supplier selection.* Explain the value of each concept to the practicing business buyer.

4. Explain the advantages and disadvantages of single-source and dual-source suppliers for an industrial product.

5. Many of the techniques of supplier relationships we have examined in this chapter seem to have their origin in Japan. Are they equally applicable to the United States? What problems might U.S. companies have in adopting them?

6. Produce a report for a purchasing manager listing the reasons why it may not be a good idea to always buy from the cheapest supplier.

7. Examine the alternative strategies available to a buying company to improve the quality of the products it purchases.

8. Produce a report for the chief executive officer of a company explaining why the CEO's purchasing staff should be paid the same salary as the marketing staff.

9. Produce a report for a business marketing manager outlining the implications for the company's operations of the adoption of JIT by a number of its customers.

Endnotes and References

1. Dean Ammer, *Materials Management and Purchasing,* 4th ed. (Homewood, Ill.: Richard D. Irwin, 1980).

2. D. W. Dobler, D. N. Burt, and L. Lee, *Purchasing and Materials Management,* 5th ed. (New York: McGraw-Hill, 1990).

3. D. N. Burt, "Managing Suppliers Up to Speed," *Harvard Business Review* (July-August 1989): 127–135.

4. John McMillan, "Managing Suppliers: Incentive Systems in Japanese and U.S. Industry," *California Management Review* (Summer 1990): 38–55.

5. David Ford, "Develop Your Technology Strategy," *Long-Range Planning* 21 (1988): 85–95.

6. Ken-ichi Imai, Ikujiro Nonaka, and Hirotaka Takeuchi, "Managing New Product Development: How Japanese Companies Learn and Unlearn," in *The Uneasy Alliance,* ed. K. B. Clark, R. H. Hayes, and C. Lorenz (Boston: Harvard Business School Press, 1985), pp. 337–375.

7. Barry Cotton, David Ford, David Farmer, and Andrew Gross, "Make or Buy and Technology Strategy" (Paper presented at the Sixth IMP International Conference on Industrial Marketing and Purchasing, Milan, Italy, September 1990).

8. Ibid.

9. Ibid.

10. Roy D. Shapiro, *Toward Effective Supplier Management: International Comparisons,* Harvard Business School, Division of Research, Working Paper 9-785-062 (1985).

11. Lee J. DeRose, *Negotiated Purchasing* (Boston: Materials Management Institute, 1962).

12. Hakan Hakansson, "Product Development in Networks," in *Industrial Technological Development: A Network Approach,* ed. H. Hakansson (London: Croom Helm, 1987), pp. 84–128.

13. D. L. Blenkhorn and A. H. Noori, "What It Takes to Supply Japanese OEM's," *Industrial Marketing Management* 19 (1990): 21–30.

14. Douglas Williams, "Suppliers' Viewpoint: Learning New Contract Rules," *Automotive Industries* (December 1986): 61.

15. Brian Farrington, *Industrial Purchase Price Management* (London: Gower, 1980).

16. Malcolm T. Cunningham, "Britapaints and Colorex: The Purchasing Strategies of Two Paint Manufacturers," in *International Marketing and Purchasing of Industrial Goods,* ed. H. Hakansson (New York: Wiley, 1982), pp. 267–270.

5

MARKETING RESEARCH AND MARKET INFORMATION SYSTEMS

CHAPTER OUTLINE

- To realize that managers and analyists must cooperate in the task of executing action-oriented marketing research in a creative fashion

- To demonstrate that marketing research must be a process of continuous feedback and that progressive organizations must operate information centers

- To become familiar with the wide variety of available information sources in both printed and electronic formats

- To show the dominant role of surveys in business marketing research and the ways in which higher response rates can be ensured at reasonable cost

- To learn the techniques of estimating market potential and the methods of forecasting market demand

- To identify and describe various topics that market researchers investigate, such as market size, buying influences, and competitors' characteristics

Business marketing decisions can range from the apparently trivial to the truly significant. Consider the following three examples: When is it better to call on Ken Jones, the purchasing director of Widgetmasters—on a Monday or a Tuesday? Evidence from practitioners indicates that midweek is slightly preferable to Mondays or Fridays. Should we establish a new distribution channel for truck parts in Western Europe? An existing network is likely to be less costly, but the products may not get the full attention of distributors; a cost/benefit study may be conducted for a clear-cut answer. How big is the global market for computer software and what are competitors doing to increase their market share? The answers can come from a commercial study already published, from collecting recent articles, or from doing a major new survey.

Marketing research is aimed at learning about markets and about marketing activities. Such research is not done for its own sake, but to help managers make better decisions. Clearly, findings lead or should lead to analysis, advice, and then action. Such action then serves as input to information repositories, as illustrated in the upper part of Exhibit 5–1. Decision makers want evaluation and recommendations, not just computer printouts containing pages of text and columns of numbers. Managers seek information that is actionable; it can then be termed *intelligence,* or *refined information.* But how can such information be generated? How can the quantity of information be reduced and its quality upgraded? What sources should be consulted to achieve this distillation and what methods should be employed to gather needed items?[1]

Business marketers have come to rely on diverse sources of information: their own ideas and experiences; internal operating reports; contacts with customers, suppliers, and outside experts; a random sample of published items; and surveys by their own research staff. In the past, the last category offered static reports and presented only single scenarios. There is a gap, however, between research analysts

EXHIBIT 5–1   Conceptual Framework for Information Flow and Market Research in an Organization

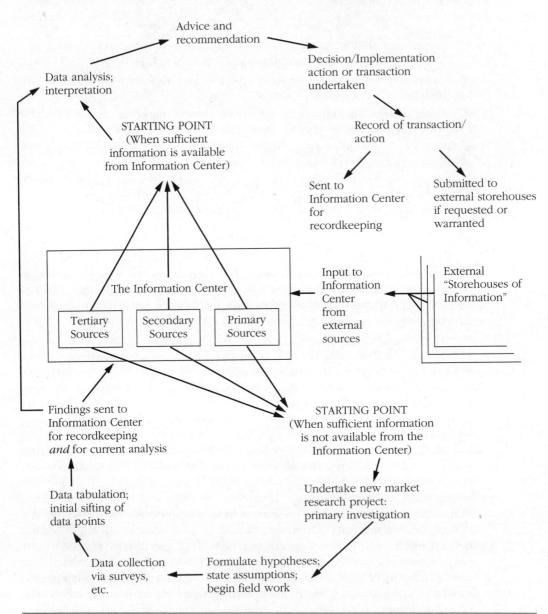

Source: Based on information from Samuel A. Wolpert of Predicasts, Inc. and William M. Weiss of The Freedonia Group, both of Cleveland, Ohio.

and managers. Analysts like to emphasize elegant methods, powerful techniques, and complexity; managers want brief statements, speedy solutions, and flexibility. But the two groups are talking to each other, and giant strides have been made on both the information-gathering and analysis fronts in the past decade.[2]

Market researchers and managers have discovered that they can now tap into vast databanks, internal and external. They can go "on-line" electronically and query giant databases, such as BRS and Dialog, many miles away. Shelves of books, journals, and indexes are now condensed into compact disks, such as Wilsondisc and Silver Platter, which can be spun and tapped for short abstracts or full text. "What if?" questions can be answered, and multiple scenarios can be developed. On the primary research front, findings from surveys can be readily tabulated and analyzed, thanks to software packages such as SAS and SPSS. Making sense of all that information and gaining access to it still require human ingenuity, however.[3]

In this chapter we will take you on a guided tour of how the intelligence-gathering function is carried out in marketing. First, we tackle the information center as the hub of such activities. Next, we look at the richness, diverse types, and different levels of published information. Then we focus on how original, primary surveys can be executed and high rates of response achieved. Next, we investigate the manner in which market size can be estimated and forecast. Finally, we look at the growing field of competitive intelligence and some other special topics in business research.

MARKETING RESEARCH AND INFORMATION SYSTEMS

Enterprises, large and small, need road maps to know where they are and where they are going. Boeing, Airbus, and McDonnell Douglas must study the current inventory and the future needs of airline companies before they manufacture new aircraft. Pansophic Systems, specializing in software for banks, should probe whether bank mergers will shrink its markets. Machine tool makers, such as Giddings and Lewis and Cincinnati Milacron, must find out what benefits users are looking for. To provide better service, the Jack & Jill Copier Repair Center needs to learn where new and used machines are installed. Government bureaus must decide whom or what to enumerate and whether to take a complete count (census) or just a sample. A trade association needs to cater to its membership and thus may decide to use a survey to profile its members. In sum, all companies, government agencies, and nonprofit organizations engage in marketing research.

The investigation in each of these cases should lead to action. Marketing research is done not for its own sake, but as an aid to decision-makers. In this section we focus on the information center, which is not a physical place but the working hub of data gathering. We look at the nature and diversity of information and the manner in which it can be delivered efficiently to managers.

The Information Center

Traditionally, marketing research has been carried out on a project-by-project basis, with emphasis on original surveys. Whenever a major problem arose, the solution would be to initiate a new survey; the marching orders would go out to collect data, analyze findings, file the report, and make recommendations. This kind of market research, illustrated in the lower part of Exhibit 5–1, is still widely practiced. The work can be carried out by a competent staff in-house, or it can be assigned to outside specialists, such as independent market research agencies, university research bureaus, or individual experts. Either way, such studies are indeed original and offer financial rewards as well as prestige to those associated with executing such assignments. However, they are also costly undertakings in terms of time and funds.

Many enterprises today have therefore established a marketing **information system** or a corporate **information center**. In addition, they have extended their contacts with outside centers—often known as databanks, databases, specialized libraries, or information clearinghouses (see the center of Exhibit 5–1). A company may both buy from and sell information to such depositories. What organizations have learned is that it pays to gather information on a *continuous* basis from both inside and outside sources. One key to the success of any corporate information center is classifying, storing, indexing, and then retrieving millions of information bits. Organizations have also learned that access to the vast storehouses of information, both internal and external, for those who need information has to be easy.

Information centers are a combination of a traditional corporate library and equipment ranging from computers to fax machines. A skillful staff uses the resources of the center to gain access to information from near and far. We can compare the information center to a war room maintained by military authorities. It is a nerve center where incoming news is collated with existing knowledge and where new information requests are processed quickly, based on need. The heart of the information center consists of primary, secondary, and tertiary levels of information, which may originate from both external and internal sources. Primary sources include such documents as corporate files and government reports; secondary sources consist of items such as journals and news releases; tertiary sources include indexes, abstracts, and digests. These items may come in print or electronic format and are discussed in detail later in the chapter.[4]

Progressive organizations *combine* the idea of original market research and the concept of the information center. In effect, the central and lower parts of Exhibit 5–1 reinforce each other. The ongoing information process may suggest problem areas requiring specific projects to be carried out. Conversely, field research can indicate that certain data should be collected on a regular basis. As a general rule, however, the starting point for an investigation has shifted; now most studies begin by tapping the holdings of the information center in-house and by searching external sources *before* embarking on a new survey (see the old and new starting points in Exhibit 5–1). For example, when Betz Laboratories, Nalco Chemical, and other water treatment chemical companies want to expand their marketing activities, they look first to their information centers for insights; then they tap outside storehouses for additional input; only as a last resort do they commission a new survey.[5]

The Nature of Information

Information is a most unusual resource, whether it comes as text or numbers, from internal or external sources, or as a result of an ongoing or a one-time search. Information is reusable, portable, expandable, and compressible. Using information still leaves it available to others. The real value of information derives from organization; when properly arranged, information becomes **intelligence** or knowledge; it moves from commodity to a more valuable, specialty status. Indeed, a vast information industry exists, catering to millions of users. Information takes on value when properly managed, not because there is so little of it, as in years past, but because there is so much of it! Compressed, precise, relevant "data bits" are preferred over computer printouts and reports gathering dust on shelves.

The complex flow of information shown in Exhibit 5–1 indicates that the process is a dynamic one of renewal, feedback, and interaction at all times. New inputs must be absorbed and related to data gathered in the past. The challenge is to tackle the flood of information from both special projects and ongoing retrieval in a way that will make the information attractive to decision makers. Then, when a course of action is decided upon or a transaction is made, new bits of information have to be absorbed and entered into the system, as in the following example.

Foxboro, a U.S. company, receives an order for a large cluster of instruments to be used in the plant of a specialty chemical manufacturer in Germany. Foxboro records the sale on corporate ledgers and eventually in its annual report. Because the order represents a significant export shipment, Foxboro also reports the transaction to government inspectors for public documentation. All these records are considered **primary sources** of information because the information is recorded for the first time by those involved in the transaction. Instrument and chemical journals then report the sale; these are the **secondary sources** of information. Condensed articles will find their way as short sentences into printed or electronic abstracts, digests, and indexes; these are considered **tertiary sources**. Assume now that a competitor searching a database finds news of the transaction and, as a result, increases its marketing efforts. Conversely, the competitor can leave the battlefield. Either way, published sources (the competitor's annual report, newspaper articles, abstracts, and so forth) record the action, and the underlying information base is further enhanced for all participants.

The Delivery and Diversity of Information

Of course, it is not sufficient to create vast databanks, whether internal or external. Both analysts and managers need access to information so they can transform it into useful knowledge—that is, marketing intelligence. Two key considerations are,

How easily can users gain *access* to the needed data? and How *quickly* can the databank *deliver* the data? If the need is immediate, the delivery must be instantaneous. This is happening today in military, medical, and credit-check activities. But in today's fast-paced world, marketing managers too wish to learn quickly about such topics as a shift in sales, a change in competitors' prices, or new promotional techniques. Telecommunication, well-designed databases, and skilled staff enable marketing managers to monitor the marketplace, to take action, or to react to moves initiated by others. As in other aspects of business life, speed is important. Market researchers can no longer afford to tell managers that the report will be ready in six months; decisions may have to be made in a few hours or days.[6]

The amount and type of marketing information desired will vary with the information seeker's position in the organization. This is partly a matter of rank or job title, partly a matter of assignment or function. A senior marketing vice president prefers an executive summary and concise advice in a few paragraphs and may ask for supporting documents if and when needed. A sales manager in the field would like detailed statistics on the performance of key products, the significance of national accounts, and the role of the sales force. The manager may need and indeed receive some of this information immediately, but other items will take time to gather. The challenging task for the research analyst is to deliver the right quantity and quality of information in the right form—and on time. Such work depends on the holdings in internal or external databanks or a combination of the two. Only if such sources fail will an original survey be undertaken. Consider the following examples.

Inquiry.   A marketing manager wants to gain insights on the activities of domestic competitors, especially their pricing practices. The analyst goes on-line and extracts data from internal and external databases. This retrieval should yield sufficient knowledge, probably in the form of price quotations. Note that while carrying out this task, the analyst gains an understanding of both the manager's needs and the capabilities of the databank; the search process thereby becomes more efficient on the next round.

Orientation.   The manager wants to understand the replacement tire market in France and the demand for truck components in Central America. Here too it makes sense to tap the internal as well as external databanks. Brief abstracts may serve at the start, but full-text retrieval is possible too. If these fail to yield sufficient information, published multiclient or off-the-shelf studies may be bought from outside vendors. If none of the above yields sufficient knowledge, a primary survey may be carried out by in-house or outside experts.

Retrospective Search.   The director of purchasing at a large hospital in Canada wishes to find out what software applications exist in the field and which ones are most popular in the United States and the United Kingdom. This information is likely to require a thorough, sophisticated electronic search of various databases, plus a possible review of business, health care, and software journals. Still, it is unlikely that a new survey has to be commissioned.

"What If?" Scenarios.   Various spreadsheet and related software programs now permit experimenting with diverse scenarios, such as different pricing, promotional, or distribution schemes. Total marketing simulation games with sophisticated features are available. A machine tool maker can utilize these programs, making assumptions about competitors' moves based on an analysis of their activities as gleaned from published abstracts. Graphs can be displayed and altered at will; telephone or video teleconferences can be convened. When new information arises, it can be built into the data files, the spreadsheets, and the simulation exercises. Expert systems are becoming popular; these are artificial or machine intelligence programs for computers that emulate human decision makers concerning the best course of action under given conditions.

Selective Dissemination.   Managers can now tell the research staff in the information center that they wish to receive specific updates on areas of their interest. They will receive abstracts and digests; if details are needed, the full text can be printed out. Major gaps in the information center may require acquisition of new data files or gaining access to giant databases in an ongoing fashion. Again, depending on the topic and the time frame, a primary survey may or may not be undertaken by the in-house staff or an outside agency.

EXISTING SOURCES OF INFORMATION: INTERNAL AND EXTERNAL

Research can be primary or secondary. For many years, the former has been praised, no doubt promoted by market research organizations seeking business and by academic writers fond of "breaking new ground." There is nothing wrong with this quest except, as just documented, it is often not cost effective. Furthermore, one-time or one-sector studies often provide only temporary insights. We are starting to see primary longitudinal and cross-sectional studies, which are more valuable. The former offer analysis over long periods of time; the latter permit industrial and international comparisons. Typical of these categories are surveys of buying practices in several nations between 1950 and 1990 and polls of U.S. purchasing managers in regard to both current and expected orders in various industries.[7] **Primary research**—by companies, government bureaus, and academics—will continue to play a major role, but its undertaking will have to be strongly justified in terms of cost/benefit calculations. This applies especially for single projects but is valid even for ongoing, comparative surveys.

Secondary research is the term given to those tasks that involve tapping existing sources. This path looks less glamorous than primary investigation, but as discussed, it is frequently more effective. There is a tendency to view this veritable gold mine of sources in dichotomous schemes: internal versus external, printed or electronic, domestic versus foreign, published versus unpublished, abstract versus full text. In fact, such categories tend to overlap. The important point is to appreciate the vast variety of sources and the mode of access to them. Public libraries, information firms, and computer database specialists now offer training for both managers and analysts in formulating search strategies—that is, identifying the appropriate sources and the ways of tapping them quickly. Such training can make managers become skilled analysts and thereby dispense with the hiring of a large research staff, whether in-house or outside. Who is better equipped to know what information is needed than the manager who will act upon it? We are witnessing this combination of operating and research duties in many firms.[8]

Our primary task in this section is to show efficient ways of tapping into existing sources of information. Generally, this implies using information already at hand within the organization and then choosing a specific path among external sources. Accessing information from printed and electronic media is both an art and a science. Care must be exercised in the gathering and in the interpretation phases. It is possible to encounter "information overload" and to lose sight of the investigation. Accuracy is an especially important issue that must be addressed.

Internal/Unpublished Sources

The starting point in any secondary research should be the set of internal files that already exists in organizations. Evidence is strong that small and large companies, government bureaus, and institutions have a wealth of information at their fingertips, yet fail to make full use of the underlying data. There are internal statistics on characteristics of customers, seasonal sales patterns, frequency of purchases, export shipments, and other relevant business activities, but they may be hidden in folders or file drawers. To serve as valuable marketing information the files must be located, organized, and shared with all colleagues who can make use of them.

Well-run organizations are creating in-house information centers that keep track of their own marketing transactions as well as the activities of others, such as competitors, suppliers, and regulators. Establishing an information center is important, but it is equally crucial to make the contents easily available to all those who can benefit from them. Providing access must be viewed as important as accumulation. Access can be offered via user-friendly machinery, software, instructions, newsletters, and other ways of dissemination. As new information comes into the organization, it should be cross-referenced to existing tabulations and text. In most cases, the contents of the corporate information center are not available to outsiders. However, government and university research bureaus often maintain unpublished files that outsiders can obtain upon request, either free or for a fee.

The Three Levels of Published Sources

Three major levels of public information are identified in the flow diagram of Exhibit 5–1 as primary, secondary, and tertiary; they are listed again in Exhibit 5–2 with several key examples cited. But what are the characteristics, the advantages, and the disadvantages of these three levels? In what sequence should they be used?

EXHIBIT 5–2   Guide to Selected Published Sources of Information

Primary Sources

International	*UN Demographic Yearbook* (United Nations)
	UN Statistical Yearbook (United Nations)
	World Development Report (World Bank)
	IMF Statistics (International Monetary Fund)
	OECD Countries—National Accounts (Organization for Economic Development, Paris)
	EC Statistics (European Community)
	IDB Annual Report (Inter-American Development Bank)
National	*Statistical Abstract of the United States* (U.S. Department of Commerce)
	USDC Census Reports (U.S. Department of Commerce)
	Census of Manufactures
	Census of Service Industries
	Survey of Current Business (U.S. Department of Commerce)
	U.S. Industrial Outlook—Annual (U.S. Department of Commerce)
	U.S. Tariff Commission Reports
	Canada Yearbook (Statistics Canada)
	Korea Yearbook
	Statistical Yearbook of Hungary
Company and Institutional	Annual and "10K" reports (especially in the United States)
	Bank newsletters and reports
	Filings with government agencies (export/import data, etc.)
	Trade association surveys
	Annual reports of nonprofit institutions
	Research reports from universities
	Foundation grant reports
	Scientific and technical societies

Secondary Sources

General Business Publications	*Business Week*
	Fortune
	The Economist
	Forbes
	L'Expansion
Specific Trade/ Industry Publications	*Aviation Week*
	Computerworld
	Coal Age
	Datamation
	Electronics
Newspapers	*Wall Street Journal*
	Wall Street Transcript
	The Times (United Kingdom)
	Financial Post (Canada)
	Australian Financial Review
	Figyelo (Hungary)

(continues)

EXHIBIT 5–2   Guide to Selected Published Sources of Information (*cont.*)

Tertiary Sources and Special Publications

Indexes
Business Periodicals Index
Canadian Business Periodical Index
Public Affairs Information Index
Predicasts F & S Indexes (United States; Europe; rest of world)
Public Affairs Information Index

Abstracts
Dissertation Abstracts
Chemical Abstracts
Employment Abstracts

Databases
On-line Databases (see Exhibits 5–3, 5–4, and 5–5)

Directories
Consumer Yellow Pages; Business to Business Yellow Pages
Dun & Bradstreet Million Dollar Directory
Standard & Poor List of Companies
Thomas Register of American Manufacturers
Encyclopedia of Associations
Books in Print (United States)
British Books in Print (United Kingdom)
Ulrich's List of Periodicals
Business International
SRI International (Stanford Research Institute)
Disclosure
Value Line
Standard Rate and Data Service
Commerce Clearing House
Euromonitor

Primary information sources consist of text, statistics, and other data that originate from those individuals and organizations that are responsible for the actual transactions or for recording them for the first time. Examples in the private sector include corporate annual reports, customer surveys, credit rating bulletins, and trade association news releases. Examples in the public sector include the census of manufacturers and census of services, export shipments, and state government expenditures. Advantages of primary information are originality, completeness, few errors, and fast transmittal of the data within the organization. Disadvantages are bulkiness, delays in the release of the data, possible—indeed, likely—revisions, and the fact that the compilation has not been subjected to any form of evaluation.

Secondary information sources condense and rearrange primary information for periodic transfer to users. This category includes journals and newspapers of all kinds (general, industry, trade, technical, professional, and so forth), government bulletins, bank and brokerage house reports, and consultants' newsletters.

BUSINESS MARKETING IN PRACTICE ▰▰▰▰▰▰▰

The *Yellow Pages* as a Market Research Tool

According to many market researchers, the *Yellow Pages* telephone directory is an effective and inexpensive tool for market research. There are now competing *Yellow Pages,* including those available in on-line format. As a general rule, there are two volumes, *Consumer Yellow Pages* and *Business to Business Yellow Pages.* The latter is, of course, of primary importance to business marketers, but even the former can be useful since some business marketers cater to professionals working in home offices. The *Yellow Pages* can be and is used to identify competitors, to locate suppliers, to pinpoint distributors, and to define a trading area. By turning to the index and specific advertisements in the *Yellow Pages,* one can retrieve product information and understand industry terminology.

In a study of the U.S. computer service industry, the authors of this text found the *Yellow Pages* to be an excellent supplement to the *Census of Manufactures,* published by the U.S. Department of Commerce, and to various volumes published by trade associations. By checking the *Yellow Pages* we could identify whether certain firms operated in certain areas. The top fifty computer service organizations did operate in almost all of the top twenty-five cities, but there were variations in terms of the services they offered in different cities. Data processing and facility management were more prevalent in New York, Detroit, Dallas, and San Francisco. Software and related programming assistance proved to be more popular in Boston, Philadelphia, Houston, and Los Angeles. The explanation of these differences lies in the nature of the businesses in those cities—for example, high tech in Boston, automotive in Detroit. Such findings alert entrepreneurs to business opportunities and also signal the extent to which some markets may be saturated.

The advantages at this level include compression of the data along with the reduction in irrelevant content; in other words, we get highlights. The disadvantages consist of less complete information on a less timely basis, with possible errors in processing and in transmittal.

Tertiary information sources systematically condense, arrange, and classify material from primary and secondary sources. Included here are the various abstracts, digests, and indexes that sort the vast world of primary corporate and government reports and the secondary world of journals and news releases. Many of these sources are now available in both hard copy (print) and electronic format (on-line, compact disks). The key advantages here are compactness, the tapping of many sources, classification, and even evaluation. Disadvantages include the time lag in availability (often weeks or months after the primary and secondary sources appear), the loss of details because of compression, and possible transcription errors.

The generation of information at the three levels naturally follows the sequence just outlined. But the utilization of information should follow just the opposite route, as noted above and shown in Exhibit 5–1. Why? Because the tertiary sources offer the richest variety but most compressed form of information. This level affords the luxury of browsing, yet conserves time. Indexes and abstracts refer back to journals and newspapers; we may choose to look up some of these secondary sources, while ignoring others. Finally, from the tertiary and secondary levels, we can go to primary corporate reports and government documents, but again only if warranted. This sequence applies whether we seek data on products or markets, prices or promotion, domestic or foreign settings, industry or firm statistics. Admittedly, many nations do not have as vast a tertiary or secondary source information base as the United States, the United Kingdom, or Canada.[9]

Accessing Information

How do we gain access to the wealth of published information? While we could go directly to the creators of information (companies, government bureaus, and so forth) or ask journal publishers to send out copies, we just argued that this would be ineffective. In short, we should start our search by going to indexes, abstracts, and digests—those listed at the tertiary level of Exhibit 5–2. The printed versions are in fact reference volumes on the shelves of most public and college libraries; some corporations also selectively subscribe. Certain indexes appeared in the past on microfilm or microfiche, but the modern way to search is electronically. Electronic or computerized access to the tertiary level is easy and cost effective. In many cases we can even tap secondary sources since index publishers now have permission to offer the full text of articles.[10]

There are several ways to gain electronic access to published information, but two popular routes, for both libraries and companies, are CD-ROMs (compact disk/ read only memory) and on-line. In either case, users sit at computer terminals, call up abstracts or indexes, and then conduct a search by subject, industry, company, name, and so forth. Databases once available only on-line can now be stored on disks. Such disks are sold outright for thousands of dollars, yet growth has been rapid. In 1988 there were fewer than 200 public databases using the CD-ROM format, but by mid-1991 the figure grew to 1,500.

Although the CD-ROM format is gaining in popularity (under such names as Wilsondisc, Silver Platter, and so forth), on-line remains popular because it allows access to giant databases stored in vast information warehouses. Here too the growth has been phenomenal, attesting to the increasing popularity of the electronic medium among companies, institutions, and even individuals. The rapid rise in on-line databases, on-line services, and subscribers is shown in Exhibit 5–3. Subscribing to an on-line service is relatively simple; all the user needs is a personal computer, a modem (a computer/phone link), a telephone line, and a contract. What is more difficult is to choose among the many offerings and to devise an effective search strategy.

Thousands of databases are available from hundreds of on-line service firms, but not all databases are available from all on-line suppliers; users must shop around. Some key business databases are ABI/Inform, Business Periodicals Index, and PTS Prompt. The producers of databases (e.g., UMI/Data Courier for ABI/In-

EXHIBIT 5–3   The Growth of Databases, On-Line Services, and Subscribers in the United States, 1980–1990

	1980	*1982*	*1984*	*1986*	*1988*	*1990*
Number of Databases[a]	400	965	1,878	2,901	3,699	4,465
Number of Database Producers[b]	221	512	927	1,379	1,685	1,950
Number of On-Line Services[c]	59	170	272	454	555	645
Number of Gateways[d]				35	59	88
Number of Subscribers (thousands)						
General Interest			326.1	677.0	1,018.6	
Business/Financial			377.1	558.6	726.6	
Scientific/Technical			229.2	345.8	404.5	

[a]Databases: Computer-readable collections of data available for interactive access by users from remote terminals or microcomputers. Databases can be "reference" (bibliographic or referral) or "source" (numeric, textual, numeric-textual, full-text, etc.).
[b]Database producers: Suppliers of databases, primarily publishers of print indexes and abstracts journals, but also publishers of other reports who transform and submit the data on magnetic tape to on-line vendors.
[c]On-line services or vendors: Time-sharing firms, network information services, remote computing services, etc., who provide access to databases.
[d]Gateways: Any computer service that acts as an intermediary between users and databases; several categories exist.
For further details, see *Directory of On-Line Databases,* p. viii.

Sources: Lines 1–4: *Directory of On-Line Databases, 1991* (New York: Cuadra/Elsevier, 1991), p. v.
Lines 5–7: *Information Industry Factbook 89/90* (Stamford, Conn.: Digital Information Group, 1989), p. 229.

form, H. W. Wilson Company for Business Periodicals Index, and Predicasts for PTS PROMT) sell their output to on-line services such as BRS, Dialog, Nexis, and Reuters. Some popular databases and their characteristics are listed in Exhibit 5–4, but there are many more. Comprehensive listings can be found in the *Directory of On-Line Databases* and *Computer Readable Databases,* both of which offer assistance in choosing the right database.

How much do the electronic services cost? The use of CD-ROMs in public and college libraries is free so far, but they have become so popular that usage is often restricted to a half hour per person. Companies buying computer indexes in CD-ROM format can expect to pay about $2,500 per compact disk per year if they already subscribe to the index in the printed format. Some vendors give discounts to college libraries. On-line services are priced differently; the charge to users depends on the vendor, volume, mode, and time of usage. Information wholesalers charge an hourly rate plus a small fee for each abstract printed; information retailers ask for an up-front fee plus various charges according to what is being processed. A typical daytime charge for database access is about $100 per hour, but less in off-peak hours (as of 1992). If items are downloaded to a personal computer or if they are sent by mail from the vendor, the per item fee is less than if the abstracts or text are printed right on-line.

EXHIBIT 5–4   Features of Five Key Business Databases in On-Line and CD-ROM Format

•21• ABI/INFORM

Former Name: Abstracted Business Information

Type: Bibliographic

Subject: Administration & Management; Business & Industry—International

Producer: UMI/Data Courier

On-line Service: BRS Information Technologies; BRS Information Technologies, BRS/After Dark; Thomson Financial Networks Inc., CORIS; Data-Star; OCLC On-line Computer Library Center, Inc., OCLC EPIC; DIALOG Information Services, Inc.; DIALOG Information Services, Inc., Knowledge Index; Executive Telecom System International (ETSI), Human Resource Information Network (HRIN); ORBIT Search Service; Mead Data Central, Inc. (MDC), NEXIS; European Space Agency (ESA), Information Retrieval Service (IRS)

Conditions: Subscription to OCLC EPIC Service required, with differential charges for OCLC member Institute and library schools; annual subscription to ETSI/HRIN required; subscription to Mead Data Central required

Content: Contains more than 550,000 citations, with abstracts, to the periodical literature in the areas of business and management. Covers more than 800 international periodicals in these subject areas: accounting and auditing; economics; electronic data processing (EDP) systems and information science; engineering management; finance and financial management; health care; law and taxation; management science; marketing, advertising and sales management; personnel, employee benefits, and labor relations; banking; insurance; public administration and government; real estate; and telecommunications. A hierarchical classification system allows users to create broad topical subsets before applying specific search terms. Five areas are covered by the classification codes: business environment (e.g., economic conditions, social policy), management function (e.g., public relations, planning, information management), industries and markets, article treatment (e.g., company specific, product specific), and organization codes (e.g., small business, non-profit institution).

NOTE: Also contains the complete text of selected articles from 100 major publications since 1991.

Language: English.

Coverage: International

Time Span: BRS, BRS/After Dark, Mead Data Central, and OCLC Online Computer Library Center, 1971 to date; ETSI/HRIN, 1980 to date; all other services, August 1971 to date.

Updating: Monthly

Alternate Formats: CD-ROM; magnetic tape

•3382• PTS PROMT

Alternate Name: Predicasts Overview of Markets and Technology

Type: Bibliographic; full-text

Subject: Business & Industry News—International; Corporate Finances—United States; Economics—United States Regional; Investing & Investments; Labor & Employment; Products & Vendors

Producer: Predicasts

On-line Service: BRS Information Technologies; BRS Information Technologies, BRS/COLLEAGUE; Thomson Financial Networks Inc., CORIS; Data-Star; VU/TEXT Information Services; NIFTY Corporation, NIFTY-Serve

Content: Contains more than 1.5 million citations, with abstracts and selected full texts, to the worldwide business literature on companies, markets, products, and technologies for major international, national, and regional manufacturing and service industries. Covers new products and technologies, mergers and acquisitions, capital expenditures, market data, product sales, marketing strategies, foreign trade, and regulations. Sources include more than 1200 business, financial, and trade magazines, newspapers, newsletters, reports, and COMLINE News Service, providing abstracts of articles and news originally published in Japanese. Corresponds to *PROMT* (Predicasts Overview of Markets and Technology) and includes information from the following Predicasts databases: PTS Aerospace/Defense Markets & Technology, PTS Annual Reports Abstracts, PTS Marketing and Advertising Reference Service, and PTS New Product Announcements/Plus (described in separate entries).

Language: English

Coverage: International

Time Span: 1972 to date (varies by service)

Updating: Daily or weekly

Alternate Formats: CD-ROM

•3383• PTS U.S. Forecasts and PTS International Forecasts™

Type: Full-text; numeric

Subject: Economics—International; Economics—United States

Producer: Predicasts

On-line Service: Data-Star; DIALOG Information Services, Inc.

Content: Contains citations and data from published forecasts in trade journals, business and financial publications, key newspapers, government reports, and special studies. Coverage ranges from thousands of detailed products to entire economies, including

EXHIBIT 5–4   Features of Five Key Business Databases in On-Line and CD-ROM Format (*cont.*)

forecasts, products, industries, demographics, and national income. Records generally contain historical base period data for one year, a short-term forecast, and a long-term forecast. There are currently more than 1 million records on-line. The files correspond to *Predicasts Forecasts* and *Worldcasts*.

Language: English

Coverage: U.S. and International

Time Span: DIALOG, July 1971 to date; Data-Star, 1978 to date.

Updating: Monthly

•601• Business Periodicals Index (BPI)

Type: Bibliographic

Subject: Business & Industry—International

Producer: H.W. Wilson Company

On-line Service: BRS Information Technologies; BRS Information Technologies, BRS/After Dark; BRS Information Technologies, BRS/COLLEAGUE; H.W. Wilson Company, WILSONLINE; OCLC On-line Computer Library Center, Inc., OCLC EPIC; OCLC On-line Computer Library Center, Inc., OCLC FirstSearch Catalog

Content: Contains about 515,000 citations to articles and book reviews in more than 340 business periodicals. Includes feature articles, interviews, biographical sketches of business leaders, book reviews, research developments, new product reviews, and reports of associations, societies, and conferences. Covers such general topics as accounting, advertising, economics, finance, management, marketing, and occupational health and safety, as well as such specific industries as banking,

the chemical industry, and real estate. Corresponds to *Business Periodicals Index*.

Language: English.

Coverage: Canada, France, Germany, The Netherlands, Switzerland, U.K., and U.S.

Time Span: July 1982 to date

Updating: Twice a week; about 5500 articles a month.

Alternate Formats: CD-ROM; magnetic tape

•2438• KOMPASS EUROPE (EKOD)

Former Name: European Kompass On-line (EKOL)

Type: Directory

Subject: Business & Industry Directories—Europe; Mailing Lists & Labels—Europe

Producer: Reed Information Services Ltd.

On-line Service: Thomson Financial Networks Inc., CORIS; Reed Information Services Ltd., KOMPASS Online

Content: Contains references to about 300,000 companies in 12 western European countries. Includes company name, address, contact numbers, languages used, number of employees, names of company officers, and codes for products manufactured, distributed, imported or exported. Corresponds to information published in the *Kompass* directories.

Language: English; French; German; Italian; Spanish

Coverage: Western Europe

Time Span: Current information

Updating: Quarterly

Alternate Formats: CD-ROM

Source: Reprinted by permission of the publisher from *Directory of On-line Databases*, pp. 4, 84, 344, and 480. Copyright 1992 by Elsevier Science Publishing Co., Inc.

How can a business market researcher make effective use of these electronic media? The search strategy can be learned through trial and error, but a better way is to attend a half- or full-day seminar offered by database producers or on-line service vendors. At such sessions, often free, the potential user receives a manual, a fee schedule, instructions, and a chance to perform sample searches. A search can be performed by industry code, product name, country, company name, and so forth. Key words or codes can be combined, making the search cost effective. (Such combinations are known as Boolean algebra or Venn diagrams.) If there are too many items, the search is truncated (cut back); if too few, the search is expanded or a new database may be chosen. A skilled researcher can perform the task in a few minutes, so the $100 per hour fee is not an obstacle.

Accuracy and Errors

How accurate is the information found in the printed and electronic media? Specifically, can one have confidence in the statistics? (We are concerned here with the actual data, not the possibility of transcription errors.) The topic of **accuracy** received little attention in the past, and even now only a few business economists and government statisticians are at work dealing with the subject. According to one pioneer in the 1960s, "economics is a one-digit science," and the range of error is about 10 percent for industrialized nations and 20 percent for developing countries that do not have a tradition of good data collection. Our own estimate, based on global and country research on various industrial products, indicates that statistics should be regarded with at least a 5 percent range of error for developed nations in the Western Hemisphere and a 15 percent range for other regions.[11]

What accounts for this state of affairs? The causes include poorly trained poll takers, ambiguous survey forms, misguided classification schemes, deliberate misinformation, or evasion from tax collectors. According to a recent article, even the most widely used indicators do not reveal much and can be misleading.[12] What can be done about this situation? Common sense, experience, and digging further are the first line of defense. A major U.S. Department of Commerce survey of pollution control equipment in industrialized nations reported the size of the Belgian market to be five times as high as that of the Netherlands.[13] Any analyst familiar with these two small nations (roughly equal in size, population, and level of development) would recognize that one of the statistics must be in error. The dilemma was resolved by analyzing the detailed statistics and by taking ratios such as pollution spending as a percentage of gross national product. It was found that the Belgian data mistakenly included labor and construction, not just equipment. A second line of defense is to collect information from as many divergent sources as possible and to conduct cross-checking. Composite or consensus figures prove superior to any single source.

BREAKING NEW GROUND: CONDUCTING PRIMARY RESEARCH

No matter how vast the storehouse of published market information is nor how easy access becomes to all the items therein, many business marketing problems require primary research. As argued above, it is best to search published sources first and then follow up by primary investigation if needed. Sometimes the review of published data and the task of gathering fresh information are taken in parallel. A complex scheme ensues, and activities need to be dovetailed. In a follow-up on the global pollution control market study cited above, newer national government yearbooks and international agency reports had to be analyzed. At the same time, the investigator contacted foreign consulates in the United States and statistics bureaus in foreign capital cities by mail and phone and even in person.

SRDS (Standard Rate and Data Service) provides companies with abundant information about local and national media.

ASAP. SRDS.

Accessibility.
  It's what makes SRDS so essential to the media professional. It's having the important facts you need to know about more than 58,000 media options right at your fingertips, wherever you go.
  When you need information, you need it now. SRDS gives you the tools. So that you can find the solutions.

The media's medium.
Call 1-800-323-4588.
In Illinois, 708-256-8333.

Reprinted with permission from Standard Rate and Data Service, 1992.

Primary market research starts usually with problem recognition or issue-specific questions. Topics, as we shall see, can be very wide-ranging indeed. Information needs, potential sources to contact, and corporate resources to carry out the project are determined. A decision is likely at this stage on make or buy—that is, whether to do the work in-house or to give it to an outside agency. The next step involves choosing the proper techniques and developing "dummy" or pro forma tables in which findings will be entered. Data collection and data tabulation follow, including the creation of graphs and charts. The information gathered is analyzed and interpreted; it is then usually presented in a report. Analysts must draw out the highlights and make policy recommendations. Findings are not only reported, but are also recorded in the organization's information center. When primary research is done on an ongoing basis—for example, tracking client satisfaction on a monthly basis—the format remains the same; the key advantage of such studies is that the results permit comparisons over time.

Research Topics

Business marketing research deals with a wide variety of topics. Surveys in the 1970s and 1980s indicate that the following subjects were the most frequently pursued: market potential, market share and sales analysis, and short- and long-range forecasting. Other popular topics investigated included pricing patterns, competitive products, and distribution channels. In contrast, consumer panels, corporate responsibility, and most aspects of advertising received much less attention.[14] The explanation for this discrepancy lies in the characteristics of industrial goods and services. There is obviously more concern with big-ticket items, multiple buying influences, and technology than is the case for consumer goods companies. Business marketing also involves more personal selling and less mass communication than does the marketing of consumer goods.

Some business marketing researchers, however, now contend that industrial goods companies would be wise to engage in such activities as motivation research, focus group interviews, and test marketing. Tracking studies that show client satisfaction, month in and month out, are becoming popular. National Market Measures, a small firm in the Midwest, carries out such studies for manufacturing, transport, and health care organizations. Another trend is for business marketers to confer one on one with customers to ascertain what benefits they seek in products and services delivered. Finally, more emphasis is being given to analyzing the effectiveness of promotional campaigns as the costs of sales force, advertising, and trade show exhibitions keep rising sharply.

Types of Business Marketing Research

The three major categories of business marketing research are exploratory, descriptive, and causal. **Exploratory research** is the simplest and cheapest. As its name implies, it looks only at identifying problems and alternative courses of action. Such investigation points out opportunities for further work and is useful in exploring vulnerable product features or promotion schemes. **Descriptive research** is concerned with events, transactions, and trends. Topics can range from sales territory assessment to market share analysis and from product line deletion to pricing decisions. This type of work, which assists greatly in the understanding of market phenomena, usually necessitates field research, as opposed to less costly desk research. **Causal research** seeks to identify cause-and-effect relations. Hypotheses are formulated, tested, and then accepted or rejected. Such work requires precision, much time, and many dollars; yet we are beginning to see some applications in the areas of product evaluation and buyer behavior.

Research Techniques

The three major techniques for executing primary research are observation, experimentation, and surveys. **Observation** is useful for noting activity or behavior, but it will not reveal the motivation behind the action. One popular application of the observation technique is at trade shows, where trained observers or television cameras record how long visitors linger at each exhibit booth. Observation should be as unobtrusive as possible. **Experimentation** involves adjusting variables in a real or artificial setting, in the field or in the laboratory. Either way, experimentation is limited to collection of data on current behavior, and it finds few applications. Two exceptions are field experiments with the test marketing of new products and laboratory experiments with buyer behavior. **Surveys** are by far the most popular primary research technique in business marketing and involve questioning individuals or groups about current and past activities.[15]

ORGANIZING AND EXECUTING BUSINESS SURVEYS

Questioning individuals and groups in large and small organizations is no small task—incisive probing is both an art and a science. But survey forms can be tested and refined, and interviewing skills can be taught and learned. There are a host of powerful statistical techniques that can extract meaningful information from the underlying data. At the same time, there is no doubt that intangible elements enter into the process. Creativity can and does have an impact on the design, execution, and interpretation of surveys.

Business market surveys extend to a wide variety of topics, ranging from acceptance of new products to price sensitivity and from buying intentions to customer satisfaction. Reaching respondents and gaining their cooperation is essential, especially since both the population and the sample tend to be small. As a general rule, qualified respondents are not easy to identify. Response rates will vary depending on whether the survey reached the "right party." Skilled interviewers are hard to find or costly to train; ideally they must have interpersonal, business, and technical skills. As a result, even small surveys may carry a high price. In some cases, the sales force can collect data, but marketing researchers must use this alternative with care. The three major survey techniques—in person, mail, and phone—and their key features are shown in Exhibit 5–5. In discussing each technique, we shall refer to practices pursued at Parker Hannifin, a major fluid power

EXHIBIT 5–5   Features of the Three Survey Methods Used in Industrial Marketing Research

Consideration	Personal Interviews	Telephone Interviews	Mail Interviews
Cost	Highest cost per respondent; depends on length, fee for interviewer, travel	Lowest cost per respondent, but costs can rise as qualified respondents are sought	Moderate cost, but expenses rise with higher postage cost plus second- and third-wave mailings
Time	Most time consuming; can be very long with open-ended questions and/or call-back features	Least time consuming, especially if qualified respondent is located quickly	Moderate, but can take time if the nonrespondents are sent second- and third-wave mailings
Information quality	Can elicit complex, in-depth information	Can elicit in-depth information if prior contact is made and/or if shared vocabulary exists	Can handle only moderately complex information
Information quantity	Can obtain much; superior to other modes, especially in regard to open-ended questions	Limited, but a conversational tone helps rapport	Much depends on the interest and effort that the respondent must give
Nonresponse	Relatively low as a result of face-to-face contact	Can be difficult to ensure correct respondent	Hard to control who responds and number responding
Interviewer error and bias	Hard to detect and control; try for rapport (but interviewer may bias respondent)	Hard to control; some anonymity; hard to develop trust	Can be done with good pretest; survey form can be returned anonymously
Flexibility	Most flexible; interviewer can elaborate, use visual aids, etc.	Flexible if the probing is creative; still limited (e.g., cannot observe)	Rather inflexible; little probing possible; takes time to implement in full

Source: Based in part on W. E. Cox, Jr., *Industrial Marketing Research* (New York; Wiley/Ronald Press, 1979), pp. 246–251 and other marketing research and marketing principles books.

company headquartered in Cleveland, Ohio, with operations and markets around the world. Parker Hannifin is useful as an example because its procedures are typical for many business marketing firms.[16]

Personal Interviewing

Although the personal interview technique requires significant time and budget commitment, it is used widely because it produces high response rates and achieves close cooperation. Personal interviewing is truly superb when it comes to capturing expert opinions, new ideas, and in-depth information, including motives and attitudes. Many large organizations, including Parker Hannifin (PH), like to combine personal interviews with a tour of their facilities, followed by a social affair. PH may seek permission to record respondents' answers for subsequent analysis. When outsiders conduct personal interviews, videotaping can be useful but should be done with permission. Interviewer bias is one limitation of face-to-face surveys, but it can be overcome by two-person teams, auditing, and monitoring the quality of the exchange throughout the session.

Interviews may be conducted with all potential respondents or on the basis of sizable probability samples; in either case, results are amenable to statistical analysis. Personal interviewing of a few experts (judgment sampling) or of interested parties (convenience sampling) is also popular. Skilled interviewers can elicit useful data in both cases, at a relatively low cost. Experts can identify key technological trends. Focus groups are useful for getting reactions to new product ideas, old advertisements, pricing changes, or competitors' programs. One survey found that minor annoyances affect major purchases. For example, charging extra for a training manual was considered so petty as to lose the business. Though focus groups are often considered too soft or qualitative by some academic writers, they are becoming popular among practitioners. Such group interviews are especially useful as an exploratory step to further research.[17]

Mail Surveys

When the target audience for a survey is large and widely scattered, survey forms sent in the mail prove to be ideal. Mailing lists can be developed in-house or bought from agencies that specialize in compiling qualified prospects—for example, 4,500 specialty chemical plant engineers or 5,800 maintenance technicians. Commercial lists sell for about $75 per 1,000 names. But even the best lists become dated as people move, transfer, get promoted, or retire. PH notes a significant increase in undeliverable envelopes in recent years, in some cases reaching 5 to 8 percent of the total sent out.

Mail surveys cost much less than personal interviews, but they are not inexpensive. PH estimates its current expenses for mail questionnaires at about $3 per piece. This sum includes typing, printing, envelopes, postage, and even a $1 incentive included with each survey. The $3 cost does not include pretesting, processing, and analysis, which precede or follow the survey. As postage and printing costs rise, telephone surveys start to look more attractive. Another good possibility is facsimile transmission; this procedure uses the telephone but also provides a document or paper trail.

Achieving high response rates is not easy in mail surveys. There is some disagreement about what constitutes an acceptable response rate. Historically ARF, the Advertising Research Foundation, advocated 80 percent, but others argue that 50 percent is sufficient. Achieving even the latter figure is difficult as surveys proliferate. Various ways of increasing response rates are shown in Exhibit 5–6. PH found that enclosing a $1 bill helps significantly, but even with this incentive, PH's

BUSINESS MARKETING IN PRACTICE

Mailing Lists: How to Get them, What They Offer

Although a business marketer should always accumulate lists of current customers, prospects, competitors, suppliers, expediters, and so forth, it is not always possible to compile a full directory. This is especially true when it comes to pinpointing potential clients. Magazines and journals in a particular industry offer a list of subscribers, but such lists may be incomplete. Several large and small organizations specialize in lists that they offer for sale. The lists can offer the following:

- National, state, and local coverage

- Large versus small business listings, by name and address

- Specific telemarketing prospects

- Companies listed by size (shipments, employees) and by industry code

- Specific names from various directories

- Computer elimination of duplicates

- Customized listing, at extra charge

- Complete direct mail services, at extra charge

But beware: some lists may be dated; others may contain duplicates despite assurances to the contrary. People move, get transferred, or promoted. Companies merge, product lines are phased out, business functions may be eliminated. Attempt to obtain information on how the list was compiled, by whom, and when.

There are many vendors of mailing lists. The following are some of the major vendors:

- American Business List

- Dun & Bradstreet

- Dunhill

- Donnelly

- Market Data Retrieval

- National Business List

- R. L. Polk

- A. Zeller

The vendors themselves are subject to change because of new entrepreneurs, mergers, and failures. Some vendors specialize in certain industries or occupations. Outside the United States and Canada, it is more difficult to obtain up-to-date mailing lists, but mailing lists are readily available in Europe and Australia. In certain European countries the trade directories are very good and can be used to act as a substitute for the purchase of mailing lists.

best response rates are in the 40 to 50 percent range. Researchers' experience in various Western nations indicates that altruistic appeals with some incentive (money or a small gift) work well, especially with professional, technical, and managerial groups.[18]

Questions in mail surveys should be thoroughly pretested. The questions should be brief, clear, and specific. Sensitive ones should be omitted or put at the end. Although short survey forms are preferable, complex topics can be handled if the audience is receptive. One mail survey by PH was designed to elicit detailed answers on the characteristics of metering pumps. A total of 7,700 forms sent to specialists in oil refining, chemical, and other process industries yielded a 45 percent response rate. PH gained useful insights on respondents' preferences, and the survey allowed the company to cut back the variety offered in its product line.

EXHIBIT 5–6   Methods for Improving Response Rates in Industrial Market Surveys

Activity (Steps Taken)	Effect on Response Rate
Preliminary notification	No increase in response rates
Monetary incentives	Increased response rate, with the rate increasing as value of incentive rises
Nonmonetary incentives	Increased response rate, but not as significantly as with monetary incentives
Type of postage	Higher response rates on stamped return envelopes than business reply envelopes; no significant difference between stamp and no stamp
Personalization	No significant difference in response between personally addressed and "Dear Sir" letters
Anonymity	Positive effect on response rate as sensitivity of issue increases
Colored survey form	No significant impact
Type of appeal	
Altruistic	Improves response rate
Typed/handwritten	No effect
Deadlines	No significant effect
Types of questions	Closed-ended questions get much better response than open-ended
Follow-up mailings	Second- and third-wave mailing have positive effect

Source: Based on and adapted from D. Jobber, "Improving Response Rates in Industrial Mail Surveys," *Industrial Marketing Management,* 15 (1986): 183–195.

Telephone Surveys

For many decades now, the telephone has been a quick and inexpensive way to reach busy people. Even while potential respondents in organizations are busy in the shop, office, or meeting room, they have a compulsion to answer a ringing telephone. Long-distance calls are more impressive, and some interviewers deliberately choose this route. While there is a sense of immediacy to cooperate, there is also a tendency to terminate a telephone interview. Some respondents may refuse to talk either because the caller's credentials cannot be verified or because they cannot remain anonymous. But once engaged, they tend to cooperate and complete the interview. The interviewer's opening phrases and quick establishment of rapport with the potential respondent are crucial in all phone surveys.[19]

The telephone is a powerful instrument in reaching the right party, but the process is not simple. Consider an assignment that calls for reaching individuals ordering aluminum foil for packaging and other applications. The surveyor may have to go through the following sequence: phone operator or receptionist, buying clerk, assistant purchasing director, engineering supervisor, and project engineer.

This is an exhausting exercise, but a phone call is more likely to reach the right person than would ordinary mail or even special delivery.

Phone surveys also tend to yield more timely results, higher completion rates, and lower costs than do mail questionnaires. PH reports completing phone polls in a matter of days and with response rates as high as 80 to 90 percent. Direct costs of such phone surveys are estimated by PH at about 50 cents per minute plus overhead. Another company, AGA Gas, had to act quickly to find out if it could pass on to customers a sudden increase in its insurance rates; a phone survey showed that it could do so. In yet another phone survey of trade show attendees, AGA Gas contacted 400 persons in a few days to seek their reaction to its exhibits and achieved an 83 percent response rate. PH, AGA Gas, and many other medium- and large-size firms tend to utilize leased long-distance lines when conducting their phone surveys, a step that keeps costs down.

Telephone surveys are simpler in North America than in many other countries for several reasons: common language, available directories and lists, respondents who are conditioned to being approached this way, and more openness on the part of individuals and companies. As surveys proliferate, however, the potential respondents may be more reluctant to collaborate. Even now, experience indicates that certain regions of the United States, particularly the Midwest and South, yield better cooperation than that obtained from the East and West Coasts. Evidence from Europe shows an increase in the use of telephone surveys, but in other regions of the world this method is not yet widely embraced.

Telemarketing, EDI, E-Mail, and Fax

Telemarketing is commonly perceived as selling over the phone: finding and qualifying sales prospects, reaching marginal accounts, or introducing a new service. Electronic data interchange (EDI) uses dedicated telecommunication lines to expedite purchase orders, shipments, and inventory adjustments between vendors and clients. Electronic mail, or e-mail, is popular among professional groups for exchange of messages over public networks. Facsimile, or fax, machines can send and receive printed documents over the phone. Faxing has become so popular that some recipients object to junk fax and may be reluctant to reveal their numbers.

Although these techniques assist in carrying out portions of the marketing program, especially transactions or transfers, they are also used for marketing research purposes. Telemarketing can register inquiries or complaints from clients over toll-free phone lines. The results can be tabulated to find out where improvement in service is warranted. Similarly, EDI, e-mail, or fax can be used not just to solicit or expedite orders, but to notify suppliers and customers about new standards, distribution policies, and discounts. Market research can be carried out on the basis of tallying the results. For example, tabulations are kept on how the number and size of orders increase in relation to price cuts. Companies should be always ethically correct, however, and avoid misleading respondents. For example, a tie-line dedicated to registering complaints or to expediting shipping should not be used to conduct a direct sales pitch.[20]

Qualifying Interviewers, Interviewees, and Survey Forms

In both personal and telephone surveys, skilled interviewers are essential, yet many companies think that anyone can ask questions, especially on the phone. The evidence indicates otherwise: training, supervision, and motivation are essential. Monitoring the process is also highly recommended to avoid interviewer burnout. Using the sales force for marketing research may seem like a sensible solution at times, but extensive training is warranted, since the two activities require different skills and behavior. Manville, the insulation company, found this out quickly when the members of its sales force received only a half-day training session on the topic of a complex product. Thus, the sales force could neither sell effectively nor properly collect the reaction from potential clients.

Although respondents cannot be trained, they can be qualified. Thus, the administrators of surveys need to develop proper lists of prospects. Potential lists, user lists, and qualified lists are just some of the terms to distinguish well-prepared rosters from those that are labeled "unqualified lists." The more specific the list is—complete with names, titles, addresses, and telephone (or fax or e-mail) numbers—the better the job can be executed. Response rates of 70 to 80 percent can be achieved for highly qualified lists, compared with 20 percent for unqualified ones.

The link between interviewers and interviewees is the survey form. Constructing the questionnaire remains an art as much as a science. Questions should come in proper sequence, and the phrasing should be free of ambiguity. The key is to have a streamlined interview in which the discussion flows in a smooth and friendly fashion. The opening is especially crucial in personal and telephone interviews. The first minute can and should establish credibility, competence, and rapport. Identification should be followed by stating the purpose of the study and the benefits to the party being interviewed. Some advocate stating the time it will take to complete the interview, but others prefer not to do so. However, interviewers should never mislead and never try to sell under the guise of a survey. Questions may be structured or open ended, but they should be pretested in a pilot study. The overall survey form can be linear or in a grid format. Generally, interviewing is best done during the middle of the week and during working hours. Some top managers can be reached at 7 A.M., but the survey had better be one in which they are keenly interested.

From the authors' experiences in various industries in three nations (as full-time workers and part-time consultants), the best approach is to act modestly, yet appear to be knowledgeable. This means acquiring the jargon or technical terms of the industry from journals or from early conversations with experts. Another rule of thumb is to give information before asking for it; this comes across as a friendly, less threatening approach. A typical productive statement followed by a question would be, "You know, Mr./Ms. Jones (in some cases, Joe or Jane), my estimate of the industry leader's market share is in the 25 to 30 percent range. Others say it can be as high as 35 percent. What do your estimates show?" This approach is called horsetrading, or bouncing-and-bracketing the data, and results in a cordial and mutually advantageous exchange rather than in a one-sided, unproductive conversation.[21]

Data Analysis

Upon completing any survey, it is a good idea for the interviewer to go through a debriefing process, listing the sources contacted, techniques utilized, and any follow-up steps promised to respondents. Otherwise, valuable information will be lost. Then comes the task of tabulation, processing, and analysis of the statistics. Even if the survey results are entered on a computer, data may have to be transposed, rearranged, and sifted. Data analysis must be coupled with the original problem definition, the issues to be addressed, interpretation of statistics, and sound judgment regarding the policy implications of the findings.

The appropriate techniques for processing the data can be found in dozens of statistical, market research, business, or social science research textbooks. Descriptive statistics, in the form of frequency charts and cross-tabulations, can reveal much about the underlying data. Researchers increasingly use inferential statistics and multivariate methods to extract further meaning from the data collected. These techniques, which include regression, cluster, factor, and conjoint analysis, show the relationships between variables and pinpoint meaningful differences between groups. Powerful, yet relatively easy-to-use software packages now exist (from SAS, SPSS, and many others) that handle the task of tabulating, computing, and even interpreting the quantitative data. Presentation graphics are available, making the data come alive in the report.[22]

One popular advanced statistical technique is conjoint analysis. This technique provides for modeling tradeoffs among product attributes that buyers will accept. The procedure allows quantifying the relative impact that each attribute has on product preferences. The results are then used as input for the next step, perceptual mapping. This graphic display shows how the respondents perceive competing sets of products relative to each other or to an ideal product. The pictorial representation shows an organization's strength vis-à-vis its competitors. The process can also reveal gaps in the marketplace that a company can fill with an appropriate offering, such as lighter weight or faster delivery. An office furniture company used conjoint analysis to study the attributes of its product line among three segments: purchasing agents, office workers, and outside consultants. It was then able to position its offerings and also its advertising campaign accordingly.[23]

Cost Considerations

Many organizations, especially small companies, avoid primary research because of five myths. They view the undertaking of surveys as (1) relevant only for major decisions, (2) too costly, (3) too sophisticated, (4) too aggressively promoted by poll takers, and (5) yielding findings that may never be put into action. A key task for the in-house or the outside market research staff is to dispel such myths. Analysts can do so by explaining the costs and benefits of their work. They should keep the goals simple, the procedures practical, and the reports understandable. Managers who commission a survey or other primary research should ask for cost estimates and should not be afraid to negotiate a realistic fee. But what is realistic or reasonable? Shopping around helps in determining that.

A prominent Midwest market research agency submitted a proposal to a diversified, Ohio-based manufacturer calling for an extensive telephone survey of both users and those who influence purchasing decisions. A quick calculation revealed that the fee amounted to about $40 per contact when all costs were included. The company then turned to its own small group of analysts and found the equivalent in-house figure to be $15 per contact, so the outside firm did not have a chance. In another survey, an instrument maker wished to ascertain the type of control panels used by electric utilities in four states. Short calls to purchasing departments and power plant operators brought results, with a total survey cost of under $5,000. In contrast, a three-year study of advertising effectiveness in various industries ran over $100,000 because precisely controlled market tests were conducted, tracking the frequency and impact of the advertisements. Yet this costly research proved to be controversial later on, just the same. Critics were not fully convinced that it always pays to advertise in a recession.

Surveys conducted during the 1980s found that business marketing organizations spent less than 0.5 percent of sales on market research, a far lower percentage than consumer goods firms. Although four out of five industrial enterprises had an in-house marketing research department, most of them had only one full-time person working in that section. About 75 percent of the responding firms undertook primary surveys, but only about 25 percent used outside research agencies. It is possible to argue that business marketers should spend more, but it is also possible to contend that consumer goods companies overspend and overstaff.[24]

MEASURING AND FORECASTING MARKETS

As noted earlier in the chapter, the most frequent assignment for business researchers is to analyze markets, specifically market size and market characteristics. First of all, decision makers must know whether markets are large or small and whether they are growing, declining, or stable. Are the markets fragmented or concentrated, stable or volatile, high tech or low tech, regulated or unregulated? Where are the actual *and* potential customers at home and abroad? What are their present budgets and plans for buying? How can customers be grouped or segmented? Understanding an organization's current market is a key step for many reasons. It helps in serving old clients and in locating new customers; it reveals purchase patterns and exposes opportunities. An incisive market assessment frequently suggests the need to alter existing products and services or aids in creating new ones. It can assist with distribution strategy, helping to locate new warehouses. Knowing the size and key features of the market can also aid in establishing sales territories, sales force compensation schemes, and advertising budgets.

At first sight, it seems easy to ascertain market size and market characteristics. But, in fact, it is a complex estimating process, even when good published statistics, access to databases, and budget for conducting surveys are assured. The explanation lies in attempting to define a market, in the wide variety of actual and potential customers, and in fast-changing conditions. Consider the example of a software package aimed at budget officers in the financial sector. What is the total number of such professionals? Are savings and loan institutions to be targeted or just banks? Could the market potentially encompass budget officers in nonfinancial organizations? Should the company count related financial or multipurpose software programs? Does it make a difference if users have an IBM or an Apple Macintosh computer? Analysts must continuously wrestle with definitions.

Consider other areas. What about the market potential for fertilizers: Should it include farms or industrial park lawns too? Should the demand analysis for office cleaning include only office buildings, or offices within factories and stores as well? Ideally, a company would like to know the absolute market potential, the relative market potential, and its own sales potential. **Absolute market potential** is the upper limit on demand for the entire market. It is the size of the market if all prospective buyers make a purchase during the year under current conditions. **Relative market potential** is the upper limit on demand within a given sector of the market, such as a geographic region or an industry. In the financial software example above, for example, the market analyst would ascertain the purchases of all banks in selected Midwest states. **Sales potential** refers to the maximum amount of sales a given firm can expect while competing for market potential against other firms. After the fact, sales potential converts to that company's market share.[25]

In this section, we look at various ways of estimating market potential, specifically the build-up and breakdown techniques. We also investigate a wide variety of qualitative and quantitative forecasting methods, citing where each one seems appropriate. Finally, we look at some specific examples that illustrate applications of ascertaining both current and projected market size.

Estimating Techniques for Market Potential

Absolute market potential is an elusive concept, but it indicates a goal to aim for in the long run. Sales potential is relatively easy to estimate, because a company knows its own sales patterns and can estimate additional efforts that may be needed to increase sales. Of greatest interest is relative market potential, because it is a realistic, specific objective for an industry vis-à-vis its client base. Relative market potential can be estimated in one of two ways. A complete count (census) or a sampling process can be used; primary survey or published sources can both be utilized.

Breakdown or Top-Down Method.   The **breakdown approach**, also called the **top-down method**, is based on having available aggregate statistics in the form of a time series—for example, 1970–1990 data. In some cases, marketing researchers may be able to obtain the set of numbers desired directly from a source, such as a government bureau or a trade association. A new census may be taken if there are only a few producers and users. More likely, however, researchers must derive the statistics from broader data by computing ratios in which one set of time series is a subset of another. (We shall see an example of this applied to forecasting in the next section and in Exhibit 5–11). Another solution is to relate one set of data to another set of variables. For example, employment and output per hour worked in an industry can be used to estimate shipments; those in turn act as a proxy for consumption data. Assumptions may be needed in this case about inventory, carry-over, and so forth.

Build-up or Bottom-up Method.   With the **build-up approach**, or **bottom-up method**, research begins with statistics from current customers and potential clients; however, some may refuse to reveal the information, forcing researchers to "guesstimate." Data from each establishment are added up to obtain the total for all end users and/or for the whole geographic region. The inquiry can be a public or private undertaking. A census or full enumeration is appropriate for concentrated markets and where orders are high in value, but units are few. Examples are civilian aircraft, medical imaging equipment, or insurance for supertankers. Sampling is used for markets that are not highly concentrated and in which many low-value, high-volume items are involved, such as truck parts, software programs, and office cleaning services. An example of the build-up method is shown in Exhibit 5–7.

In practice, neither method is used in isolation; rather the methods tend to be *combined* in a creative fashion. The process can then be compared to tunneling from two ends, with two teams boring from opposite directions until they meet in the middle. In the case of the market for software, the top-down method consisted of relating the software to computer equipment and computer services. The bottom-up method consisted of adding up vendors' shipments of specific software.[26]

Forecasting Techniques

Forecasting is an irresistible endeavor: who would not like to know the future? All private sector companies, government agencies, and nonprofit institutes like to predict the demand or market size for their products or services. The very notion of planning calls for constructing a picture of things to come. Many market researchers are eager to try their hands at this task. Yet the road is full of peril, pitfalls, and setbacks. Improved models are constantly touted, but the accuracy of past projections are ignored. Some humility, however, is in order. Even global market modelers now speak of "offering insights," as opposed to exact predictions.

There are two major classes of forecasting techniques, qualitative and quantitative; each has a number of subcategories, as shown in Exhibit 5–8. There are distinct advantages and disadvantages to the two major categories and to each specific technique. Applications vary for different time horizons, industry or product categories, and external conditions.

EXHIBIT 5–7   Estimating Market Potential Using the Build-up Method

Problem:	Estimate the market for plastics in new trucks and buses for California in 1991 (hypothetical situation)
Product:	Molded plastics
Application:	New trucks and buses
Geographical area:	State of California
Time series:	Value of shipments
Latest data:	1988
Estimate:	1991
Sources:	*U.S. Census of Manufacturers* and *U.S. Industrial Outlook* (U.S. Department of Commerce); State of California vehicle data; "Survey of Industrial and Commercial Purchasing Power," *Sales and Marketing Management*; Trinet, Inc., etc.

Step 1   Production of vehicles

	Units (thousands)		Average price	Value of shipment (mil $)	
	USA	*Calif.*	*(thousand $/unit)*	*USA*	*California*
Trucks	520	42	45	23,400	1,890
Buses	65	7	32	2,080	224

Step 2   Plastics use

	Value (mil $)	Vehicle value from above (mil $)	Usage or ratio	Apply ratio to California	Value (mil $)
Trucks	2,050	23,400	0.0876	$0.0876 \times 1890 =$	166
Buses	175	2,080	0.0841	$0.0841 \times 224 =$	19

Step 3   Growth in Production

	1988–1991	Apply to California data	
		1988 (mil $)	*1991 (mil $)*
Trucks	3.5%/year	$(1.035)^3 \times 1890 =$	2095
Buses	1.5%/year	$(1.015)^3 \times 224 =$	234

Step 4   Usage rate of plastics in vehicles to increase 10% over 3 years, 1988–1991: (based on input from plastics and vehicle manufacturers)

Trucks	0.0876 + 10% over a 3-year span = 0.0964
Buses	0.0841 + 10% over a 3-year period = 0.0925

Step 5   Apply new usage rate to California data to obtain revised 1991 estimate:

	1988 (mil $) × usage	1991 (mil $)	as compared to 1988 (mil $)
Trucks	$2095 \times 0.0964 =$	202	vs. 166
Buses	$234 \times 0.0925 =$	22	vs. 19

EXHIBIT 5–8   Forecasting Methods

Part A: Qualitative Techniques

Name of Technique	Description of Approach	Application and Time Horizon
Sales force estimates	Combining and averaging estimates by sales force	For forecasts by territory, client; SR and IR
Users' expectations	Asking clients about their views of demand in general and planned requirements	Capital goods, special orders; SR and IR
Executive jury or panel	Combining views of top executives or managers with special expertise	Existing or new product scenarios; IR and LR
Delphi panel	Group of experts making successive rounds of forecasts with feedback until consensus is reached	New products and technology; LR

Part B: Quantitative Techniques

Name of Technique	Description of Approach	Application and Time Horizon
Naive forecast/ trend fitting	Simple extrapolation extending historical data	For mature products; SR and IR
Simple moving average	Using historical pattern, keep adding latest data	Standard goods and inventory; SR and IR
Exponential smoothing	Weighted moving average (recent data given more weight)	Standard goods and inventory; SR and IR
Data decomposition	Consider secular, cyclical, seasonal, irregular variation	For products with such variability; SR, IR, LR
Chain ratio analysis	Series of key ratios related sequentially	Linked products and usage patterns; LR
Autoregressive moving average	Math model, computer selection, combination technique	Various goods and services; SR
Simple or multiple regression	Relates company data to external factors	Good for broad indicators, variable goods; IR
Econometric models	Series of related equations describing economy and industry	Generic products, can tie sales and promotion; SR, IR
Leading indicators	Tie corporate data to other leading series	General business conditions and sales; IR and LR
Diffusion index	Percent of economic indicators going up and down	Tying company data to changes in economy; SR
Input-output coefficients	Interindustry flow of goods; constant technology	Usage of various materials; SR
Product life cycle	Analysis of introductory, growth, maturity, decline stages	For new or growing products; SR and IR

Notes: SR = short run; IR = intermediate run; LR = long run.

Qualitative forecasting techniques involve interviewing knowledgeable people within the organization, such as members of the sales force or key managers; outside experts; and users, influencers, and buying agents (both current and potential). Advantages of such methods include the wide variety of sources, consideration of "quantum" changes in the environment, and the relatively low cost of gathering the data. The disadvantages are that the information so gathered is subjective, rests on unstated assumptions, and hence is not usable for simulation. Contradictions and inconsistencies cannot be fully resolved in a positive vein, but the wide range of views may yet reveal insights.

Quantitative forecasting techniques include two subsets—namely, time series analysis and causal methods including complex models. The "quant" procedures have become popular in the past twenty-five years, but they have been roundly criticized as well. Advantages include stated assumptions, simulation possibilities using computers, and low costs once the model is built. Disadvantages include problems with inconsistencies and data gaps; ignoring effects of technological, social and other changes; and ignoring expert or public opinion. Quantitative techniques are far better for the short run (under one year) than the intermediate or long run (one to four years and five years plus, respectively). Forecasting software, such as Autobox, Forecast Master, 4cast/2, and Statgraphics, is available for personal computers. But beware: the output is only as good as the input.

As was the case for the top-down and bottom-up methods for estimating market potential, the two major forecasting techniques are used in conjunction with each other. **Combination** (also called **composite** or **consensus**) **forecasting** attempts to incorporate the best features of the qualitative and quantitative methods. Combination forecasting emulates the real world wherein the diverse plans of many individuals and organizations are converted into mutually consistent happenings. At its simplest, the technique involves averaging everyone's forecast. Often it turns out that such averages work better than any individual forecaster, short or long run. At its most complex, the method involves a conceptual framework or analytical model relying on diverse inputs and numerous equations, coupled with intuition and judgment. This method is also used to build different alternative futures, called *plausible scenarios.*

Combination forecasting means looking beyond a single time series; it calls for relating a given product line both to its components and to broader aggregates, in a historical and projected time frame. For example, in the case of computer workstations, combination forecasting would look at memory units, disk drives, and so forth (the components) and at the total data processing in the office or the plant (the overall electronic network). Most important, it would consider applications, past and future. Exhibit 5–9 shows combination forecasting applied to tires. Advantages of this method are the inclusion of diverse views, the ability to handle data gaps, consideration of new developments, and better accuracy for the long run. The disadvantages include difficulty of simulation, problems in judging ratios or relationships, the need for a vast quantity of input, and high costs.[27]

Why do forecasts go wrong? What can be done to correct this situation? Several signs suggest that there is a strong bias toward optimism; managers cherish

EXHIBIT 5–9   Elements in Combination Forecasting for Rubber Consumption

Published forecasts on rubber consumption

Published forecasts of synthetic rubber production and exports as well as rubber imports

Published forecasts of automobile tire requirements per car

Published forecasts of automobile registrations and replacement tire demand

Published forecasts of total tire production

Historical trend in rubber consumption per tire

Mathematical verification (e.g., number of tires per car, which has been declining from 5 to 4; no "real" spare tire)

For foreign countries: possible interpolation and extrapolation for missing data, based on level of economic development (e.g., Italy is between France and Spain in per capita income)

Source: Based on information from Samuel A. Wolpert of Predicasts, Inc., and William M. Weiss of The Freedonia Group, both of Cleveland, Ohio.

market researchers more when their projections show fast growth rates. Other factors accounting for erroneous forecasting include the researcher's inability to step outside narrow boundaries; price-performance failures—that is, over- or underestimating; and misjudging acceptance of new technology. So what is the solution? Here are a few guidelines: Ask fundamental questions about markets, focus on cost/benefit analysis, and emphasize alternative technologies. Always challenge assumptions, downplay precedents, and look outside your own industry. Building scenarios is also highly recommended; Royal Dutch Shell reputedly had much success with this technique. Scenarios or plausible futures are structured analytical narratives, not just pure numerical estimates. They indicate possible paths toward goals, not just the point of arrival—that is, the exact number. Scenarios work well under different sets of assumptions and conditions; but they must be described in great detail.[28]

Specific Applications

In this section we take a look at three distinct markets; a low-tech, a medium-tech, and a high-tech sector. We show both the historical situation and the forecasts made; some narrative analysis is also provided; an exhibit supplements the story in each case.

Copy and Computer Paper.   A manager with a major U.S. consulting firm claims that analysts need take only four steps to forecast total market demand for any good or service: (1) define the market, (2) divide the total industry demand into its main components, (3) forecast the "drivers" of demand in each segment and project those that are likely to change, and (4) conduct sensitivity analyses to understand the most critical assumptions and to gauge the risks to the baseline forecast. The key task is to identify the underlying forces that drive demand. The key mistake is to assume that relationships now will continue unaltered in the future.

These tenets are then applied to the paper industry, which is segmented into twelve end-use categories, and the four largest categories are investigated in detail. The drivers of demand for reprographic paper—that is, paper used in copiers and computer printers—are shown in Exhibit 5–10. The demand for such paper has

EXHIBIT 5–10   Short-Term Forecasting of Total Market Demand for Reprographic Paper, 1978–1986, Using Graphic Method ("Drivers of Demand")

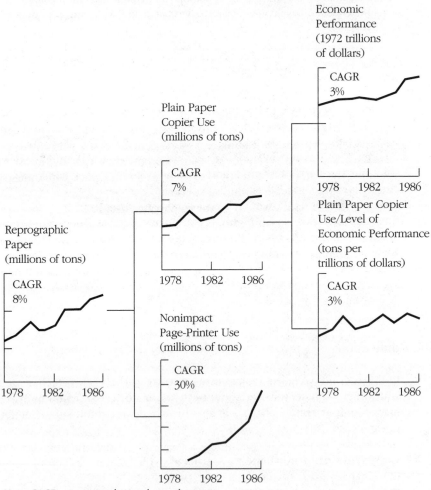

Note: CAGR = compound annual growth rate.

shown fast growth due to a sharp decline in copying costs, increases in the volume of computer printing, reduced costs for the toner in the copying equipment, and savings in clerical time and equipment depreciation. To judge future demand both qualitative and quantitative techniques are used, including regression analysis.[29]

The Global Market for Water Pollution Control Equipment.   Several surveys looked at the demand for water pollution control equipment at the end of the 1970s, with findings reported in various reports and journal articles.[30] To update such work, a new literature search was carried out and one of the authors conducted personal interviews with private and public sector officials in industrialized nations during the early 1980s.[31] Published sources that ranged from field reports to statistical yearbooks proved to be of use, but the most recent data emerged from the interviewing process.

Forecasts of market size were then undertaken for a total of fifty nations, with the horizon extending to 1990. Both breakdown and build-up methods were used to estimate market demand, and both qualitative and quantitative techniques were used. The use of the breakdown approach is illustrated for one nation in Exhibit 5–11. The essence of the breakdown approach in this case is chain ratio analysis. This means moving from broad to specific indicators in a logical fashion. Each successive time series is estimated as a percentage of the previous one. Such percentages, like absolute numbers, may rise, but they can also decline. Absolute spending for water pollution tends to increase to keep pace with industrial activity. However, relative water pollution spending decreases, since a higher share of the cleanup budget now tends to go for solid waste disposal.

The build-up approach was more difficult and could be achieved only in part. However, it proved to be a good check on the breakdown technique. Specific product shipment data came from companies and trade associations. A typical question was, "How many filtering devices did you ship during each of the last five years to municipalities and to industrial end users?" Refusal of some firms to cooperate proved to be one obstacle. Other problems were differences in terminology, classification, and accounting practices.

Applying "combination forecasting" meant using qualitative and quantitative techniques. It also meant investigating both specific components of water pollution control equipment (screens, filters, pumps, and so forth) and the broader aggregates (all pollution control equipment, including those for air and solid waste). The major drivers of demand in each nation proved to be the ability and willingness of key sectors—usually government agencies and manufacturing and utilities—to spend money on the cleanup task. Other forces ranged from changes in industry operations (eliminating a particularly dirty process, for example) to regulations and degree of enforcement.[32]

Telecommunication Equipment.   The story of electronics is the success story of the past forty years. There is an oft-quoted tale comparing the world of electronics with the world of cars: If the same progress had been made in both areas, we would all be driving Rolls-Royce luxury cars, getting one hundred miles to the gallon. But although accomplishments in electronics and specifically in computers

EXHIBIT 5–11   Forecasting the Water Pollution Control Equipment Market in the United Kingdom, 1979–1990, Using the Breakdown Method and Chain Ratio Analysis

Item	Market Estimate 1979	Forecast for 1985	Forecast for 1990	Annual Growth Rate (%) 1990/1979
Population (million persons)	55.9	56.3	56.7	0.1
GDP/capita (75 $)	4,510.0	4,760.0	5,380.0	1.6
Gross Domestic Product (GDP) (bil 75 $)	252.4	268.0	305.0	1.8
% for GFCF	17.2	18.7	19.4	
Gross Fixed Capital Formation (GFCF) (bil 75 $)	43.4	50.1	59.2	2.9
% for NFI	45.5	46.7	48.0	
Nonresidential Fixed Investment (NFI) (bil 75 $)	19.8	23.4	28.4	3.4
% for PC spending	8.7	8.2	7.7	
Pollution Control (PC) expenditure (mil 75 $)	1,715.0	1,920.0	2,190.0	2.2
% for WPC spending	75.0	72.0	69.0	
Water Pollution Control (WPC) expenditure (mil 75 $)	1,285.0	1,380.0	1,510.0	1.5
% for WPCE	8.9	9.0	9.0	
Water Pollution Control Equipment (WPCE) (mil 75 $)	115.0	123.0	136.0	1.5
Industrial Production Index for UK (1975 = 100)	110.0	112.0	130.0	1.5

Note: All dollar figures are in constant 1975 U.S. dollars.

Source: MCB University Press Limited. A. C. Gross, "Global Competition for Environmental Markets: The Case of the Water Pollution Control Equipment Industry," *European Journal of Marketing* (Spring 1986), p. 24. Used by permission.

and communication are amazing, a slowdown can be expected even in this field as offices, plants, and homes become saturated with hardware.

In examining the market for such equipment, four key drivers loom important: research and development, aggressive entrants, creative financing, and government intervention. However, these driving forces play different roles in different nations. For example, although relative research spending is similar in Japan and the United States, Japan spends much of its funds on civilian research and development and emphasizes the development side. In contrast, through the 1980s, the United States stressed military-related research. Japan also has tighter restraints on foreign competitors than does the United States, and this has an impact on market size and activities.

Forecasts in this case were developed on the basis of total market measures, relying on industry shipment statistics and end-use patterns. Sources included international agencies, governments, trade associations, and a host of private sector

EXHIBIT 5–12   Market Estimates and Forecasts for Telecommunication in Japan, 1980–1990

Item	Market Estimate, 1980 (mil $)	Forecast for 1985 (mil $)	Forecast for 1990 (mil $)	Annual Average Growth Rate 1980–1985 (%)	1985–1990 (%)
Telephone	3,976	4,829	5,302	4.0	2.0
Telegraph, telex, data transmission	183	232	267	4.9	3.0
Satellite communications	7	12	19	10.9	9.0
Mobile radio and radio telephone	45	62	69	6.8	7.0
Paging systems	13	16	18	4.9	2.0
Cable television	66	120	128	16.2	6.0
Total	4,289	5,277	5,833	4.1	2.0

Source: G. Ara et al., *World Telecommunications Market* (Ottawa, Canada: University of Ottawa, Faculty of Business and Federal Department of Communications, 1983), pp. 72 and 105; relying on A. D. Little, Inc., *World Telecommunications Survey I*: (Boston: ADL, 1981); and *Electronics,* January 13, 1982.

publications. Estimates of market size and growth rates to 1990 were based on various trends already visible in the late 1970s.[33] The first set of figures were then revised in the mid-1980s because of changes in the field; these revised figures are shown in Exhibit 5–12. In a fast-moving field such as telecommunications, constant revision of forecasts is a must. If an update were made in the 1990s, several changes would have to be taken into account. For example, telex communication is fading fast, whereas fax transmission is booming. Japan is also opening its markets more to foreign entrants.

OTHER TOPICS IN BUSINESS MARKETING RESEARCH

Although business marketing research focuses mainly on market size, present and future, and the role of the marketing mix, other topics are also the subjects of investigation. Assessing the nature of buying influences, evaluating vendors, and gathering competitive intelligence are three significant areas: knowing to whom a firm sells, from whom a firm buys, and who a firm's competitors are is just as important as knowing market size and market characteristics.

Buying Influences

A key finding reported in Chapter 3 on buying behavior is that knowing the purchasing director is not enough. Many studies show that especially in medium and large organizations, sellers must consider all members of the buying center who have an influence on the purchase. These influences range from top management to design engineers and from the research staff to production personnel. The authors of this book have investigated buying patterns in the chemical and paper industries of four nations—Australia, Canada, the United States, and the United Kingdom—building on earlier surveys. This comparative project continues in the 1990s, with extensions to France and Hungary. The payoff comes in gaining knowledge about the impact of different departments on purchasing decisions.[34]

What are the practical implications of such investigation? It can show members of the sales force how to direct their efforts, in a specific way, when calling on companies. For example, when equipment and process lines are being altered, operation engineers have a major impact at the early stages of the procurement process. Research and development managers have a voice in the purchase of natural and manufactured materials. Accordingly, the approval of such parties must be sought; they do not write the purchase contract, but they have a major influence on it. So calling on the purchasing department is only the initial step in the sales process.

Vendor Selection

Vendor evaluation at first glance has little to do with marketing research. But the way in which a company buys and from whom it buys are just as significant as how it sells and to whom. Indeed, it is possible to argue that $1 saved on purchasing is far more significant than the 5 cents earned from selling $1 worth of goods. Thus it is not surprising that members of the market research department, familiar with evaluating buyer characteristics, are also called on to judge the sources from which the organization gets its goods and services.

Ongoing reviews of current suppliers and one-time evaluation of the qualifications of bidders on a given contract need to be carried out. In a typical vendor-rating process, each criterion is given a weight, and subjective judgments are expressed in numerical terms on a scale of 1 to 5 or 1 to 10. Dimensions evaluated include reliability, product quality, price, delivery, and technical competence. Ratings assist in managing vendor relations, including feedback to vendors showing them how they can improve. Market researchers can assist in constructing evaluation forms and in the subsequent analysis of the vendor ratings. Such work can be as much a contribution to corporate strategy and profits as sizing up markets.[35]

Competitive Intelligence: How It Is Gathered

Gathering information on competitors is similar in sequence to marketing research in general. But the focus is different, and the assembly of data points is more complex. Trials and errors abound; frequent setbacks occur; blind alleys are not unusual; false witnesses may emerge; competitors may make countermoves. But persistence and skillful investigation pay off. **Competitive intelligence** is an ethical and legal alternative to industrial espionage. Careful reading of available data and

BUSINESS MARKETING IN PRACTICE ▰▰▰▰▰▰▰▰▰▰▰▰▰▰▰

The Inquiring Mind, the Persistent Attitude

What makes a good market researcher? A curious mind! An in-depth investigation can be compared to starting a new business or to solving a detective story. There will be ups and downs, small successes and failures, false leads and contradictory results. There may be no clear-cut road map, just some hints and clues. Each piece of the jigsaw puzzle must be patiently fitted in.

Getting to know the market usually means getting to know actual and potential customers. Some of these may be privately held small companies. The same may be true for competitors. Where can you go to find out about such organizations? Industry and product directories are obvious starting places. *Ward's Directory* has a thorough listing of privately held firms. The *Wall Street Transcript* has "Roundtable" discussions on specific industries, with many small participants mentioned. You should browse through journals and look at news items, especially on corporate changes, new products, and processes. Using surveys to elicit names of competitors is a good idea. But be sure you list a few names and then leave open spaces on the form for listing others.

Some unusual places to gather information on market size, products, competitors, and so forth, include credit reports, property transactions, patent filings, stock brokerage and bank reports, trade shows, technical seminars, and the numerous databases (not just business-oriented ones). One useful database to search is *Dissertation Abstracts*. Many times doctoral theses reveal much about an industry and key players in it. Distributors and other intermediaries are excellent sources of information since they deal with a wide variety of corporate contacts and product lines. But always start with your internal sources; the missing piece of the puzzle may already be in your own corporate files, but in another department.

Sources: L. M. Fuld, *Competitive Intelligence* (New York: Wiley, 1985); A. Krigman, *Researching Industrial Markets* (Research Triangle Park, N.C.: Instrument Society of America, 1983); and P. Sherlock, *Rethinking Business to Business Marketing* (New York: Free Press, 1991).

talking openly to good personal sources can provide more insights than hidden microphones, trespassing, and bribery.

The commitment of senior executives to a competitive intelligence system is crucial. The next step is one of problem definition: Who are the company's competitors, actual and potential? What are their plans? Organizations, of course, must be concerned not just with their current rivals, but as much or more with new entrants, substitute goods, and the threat of vertical integration by suppliers and customers. For example, metal can manufacturers must consider glass and plastic bottle companies as much as they consider other can makers. Giant AT&T is competing against MCI and US Sprint in telecommunication. AT&T also confronts computer makers, having bought NCR, and is battling Visa and MasterCard, having issued its own credit card. In pollution control, the battle is between equipment or chemical firms, which stand ready to clean up, and consulting engineers, who can redesign process lines and stop the waste at the source.

Market researchers should gather data on all facets of the marketing program, not just focus on goods and services. Distribution, pricing policies, and promotion schemes must be studied. Sources to be tapped include in-house information, publications of competitors, and third-party reports. Data on hand can include engineers' impressions of rivals' products at trade shows and their judgments about the competitors' levels of technical expertise. Similarly, members of the sales force need to be debriefed after visiting clients. Publications of competitors, including annual reports, direct-mail fliers, press releases, trade publications, and speeches of executives before financial analysts, should be carefully studied. Third-party sources are suppliers, customers, utilities, government bureaus, watchdog groups, and consultants. Generally, it is advisable to proceed simultaneously on many fronts. Do not wait with field operations until all published information is gathered. Do not set up elaborate files too early; remain flexible.

Creative competitive intelligence operations include scanning unusual published sources and talking to people who really know what is going on. Case studies gathered by professors, reports issued by university research bureaus, and abstracts of dissertations provide useful insights. For example, the authors of this book and other consultants believe sales can be estimated by knowing the number of employees. A rule of thumb is that many manufacturing firms average $120,000 per employee, whereas service companies average revenues of $250,000 per employee. Other sources for gathering information on competitors range from regional magazines and small-town journals to credit reports and city directories. The U.S. Department of Commerce computes various ratios, such as land per building and employees per square foot, that provide clues to shipment data. Environmental impact statements can reveal much about the operations of chemical companies. Data available from public utilities can offer clues to the economic activity of firms in a region. The best personal sources of information are people who deal with day-to-day operations: shippers, packagers, salespersons, product managers, tellers, brokers, and agents.[36]

Observations or visual sightings can also be useful, but beware of false leads. Counting one kind of corrugated boxes shipped may not be a true measure of that firm's shipments because of multiple sources and use of other packaging material. Counting boxcars on a railroad siding without noting their serial numbers is likely to result in an over- or undercount. Aerial photography is a possible intelligence tool, but Du Pont successfully sued a flying service company for taking photos of a facility under construction. Whether one can rummage through, much less remove, the garbage of another organization is another gray area.

Wherever there is intelligence there will be counterintelligence. Companies used to offer plant tours; now practically no one does. Organizations used to encourage their top executives to make detailed statements before security analysts; now legal experts and public relations specialists scrutinize speeches and handouts. Universities and research institutes had open-door policies; now there are restrictions, and even insiders must demonstrate a need to know. Meeting rooms are electronically swept for listening devices; computer passwords are changed quite frequently; scrambler phones are popular. Still, people do listen in on cellular phones (legal in many cases), and computer hackers have not been punished as much as security staff would like. The fact remains that competitive intelligence and counterintelligence are being practiced actively by reputable companies.

Competitive Intelligence: Legal and Ethical Limits

Knowledge is power; information can be valuable. In highly competitive situations, companies and organizations attempt to obtain an edge. Many consider obtaining such an edge a gray area in which boundaries are blurred between what is right and what is wrong. Yet it is possible to establish both legal and ethical guidelines. Thus, in the United States, the hundred-year-old Sherman Act expressly prohibits fixing prices or carving up markets. The "great electrical conspiracy" of 1959 showed that even high-level executives are not immune to prosecution and prison terms. More recently, however, high-tech firms have been granted permission to join research consortia and exchange technical ideas. In each nation it pays to understand the judicial system as it applies to business rivalry. Some countries allow or even encourage cartels, price stability, and insider trading, whereas others prohibit advertisements that disparage competitive products.

In regard to ethical considerations, cultural and corporate business practices also vary from country to country. A useful list suggested by Wade in 1965 still seems applicable: Acceptable sources are public documents, market surveys, financial reports, journals, trade show exhibits, released corporate brochures, analysis of competitors' products, and disclosures made by rival firms' employees obtained without subterfuge. Unethical are camouflaged questioning, observation under secret conditions, false job interviews, hiring an employee away to get specific information, and hiring private investigators. Illegal are trespassing on rivals' property, bribing employees or suppliers, planting an agent, wiretapping or eavesdropping, theft, blackmail, and extortion.[37]

How do companies and corporate executives act and react in light of these guidelines? Some are not concerned about espionage; some brag about counterespionage. Still others dismiss the topic: "How can it be classified or secret when I read it in . . . heard it in. . . ." But the most revealing evidence comes from repeated polls of attendees at seminars on competitive intelligence conducted during 1974–1984. Findings are shown in Exhibit 5–13. The bar graphs show that each company and each manager view themselves as almost clean, whereas competitors are strongly suspected of shady practices. This is compelling evidence that much hypocrisy exists on the ethical front. About 80 percent of the attendees at competitive intelligence seminars claimed that there is much pressure to get a competitive edge and to do "twilight work" (meaning: unethical, but not illegal)—not an encouraging picture![38]

Yet there are strong signs that ethical considerations will play a far greater role in the decade of the 1990s than they did in the 1980s. The frantic acquisition binge and the floating of junk bonds have abated; several prominent financial figures were found guilty of unethical and illegal conduct. Manufacturers are now aggressively

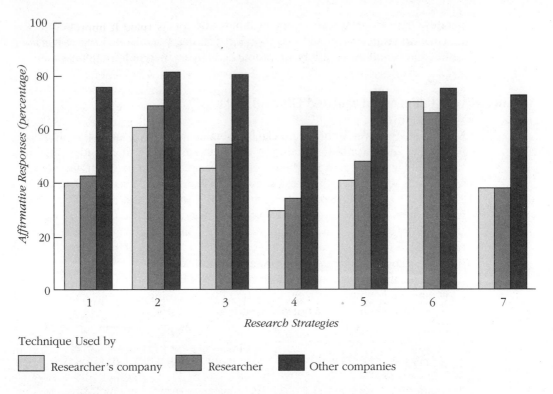

Technique Used by

☐ Researcher's company   ☐ Researcher   ■ Other companies

Research Strategies

1. Researcher poses as a graduate student working on a thesis. Researcher tells source that dorm phones are busy, so researcher will call back rather than have phone calls returned. This way, researcher's real identity is protected.
2. Researcher calls a company vice president while he or she is at lunch, hoping to find the secretary, who may have some information but is less likely to be suspicious about researcher's motives.
3. Researcher calls competitor's suppliers and distributors, pretending to do a study of the entire industry. Researcher poses as a representative of a private research firm and works at home during the project so that the company's identity is protected.
4. The competitor's representative is coming to a local college to recruit employees. Researcher poses as a student job seeker to learn practices and some other general information about the competitor.
5. The researcher is asked to verify rumors that the competitor is planning to open a new plant in a small southern town. The researcher poses as an agent from a manufacturer looking for a site similar to the one that the competitor supposedly would need. Researcher uses this cover to become friendly with local representatives of the Chamber of Commerce, newspaper, realtors, etc.
6. Researcher corners a competitor's employee at a national conference, such as an American Marketing Association meeting, and offers to buy drinks at the hotel bar. Several drinks later the researcher asks the hard questions.
7. Researcher finds an individual who works for the competitor to serve as an informant to researcher's company.

Source: P. Maher, "Corporate Espionage: When Market Research Goes Too Far," *Business Marketing,* October 1984, p. 60, quoting J. Endean of Washington Researchers. Reprinted with permission of *Business Marketing.*

pursuing piracy of their products. In the 1980s courts ruled it improper to use information competitively if it was obtained during negotiations that were later terminated. Similarly, courts now enforce agreements that require that knowledge given in confidence cannot be disclosed later on. Thus Data General successfully sued a competitor copying the design of one of its minicomputers even though circuit drawings were given earlier to thousands of users. More and more companies establish and enforce codes of conduct, and more college courses stress ethical considerations in business transactions. Some firms are generously supporting ethics seminars and institutes.[39]

SUMMARY

The task of business marketing research is to support decision making. This means transforming information into intelligence. It is simply not sufficient to gather thousands of data points, write long reports, and offer diverse views. The task often involves a thorough yet quick search of published information, then coupling it with primary investigations. It also means subjecting the data to appropriate analysis and presenting the findings in meaningful charts and tables. It means making recommendations and offering policy guidelines for implementation.

Compared with previous decades, researchers and managers will be facing an information overload in the 1990s, not a shortage. Making sense of the vast data files available both in-house and from outside sources is a challenging task. However, the job is made easier by user-friendly devices and instructions. Searches of databases can take place using compact disks and on-line facilities. Either way one gains access to a wealth of statistics and descriptions in either abbreviated or full-text form. But the task involves good literature search strategies.

Primary market research can involve some experimentation and observation, but surveys remain the most popular tool for gathering new input. Personal, mail, and telephone surveys are utilized widely; each one offers distinct advantages and disadvantages. Due to cost and speed considerations, however, phone surveys are becoming more and more popular. In reaching busy people in the workplace, it is best to work with qualified lists. Building rapport with respondents should result in relatively high response rates.

The most frequently assigned research task is to assess present markets and to project the size of future markets. This work also involves an assessment of the characteristics of the marketplace; conditions, both in and especially outside the organization, may change rapidly. The current size of existing markets can be estimated using either the breakdown or the build-up method; the combination of the two is preferable. In a similar fashion, although there is a wide variety of qualitative and quantitative forecasting techniques for estimating the size of future markets, the preferred solution is to utilize a combination of techniques.

Other topics included in marketing research are as varied as marketing itself. They can range from buying behavior to vendor analysis, from the role of promotional tools to the impact of pricing changes, and from product attributes to evaluating delivery performance. Currently, one major topic gaining importance is competitive analysis, which is concerned with analyzing rivals. This task is as important as analyzing customers and must be carried out in an ethical fashion. There are now guidelines to judge the appropriateness of various methods of competitive analysis.

Key Terms and Concepts

information system
information center
intelligence
primary sources
secondary sources
tertiary sources
primary research
secondary research
accuracy
exploratory research
descriptive research
causal research
observation

experimentation
surveys
absolute market potential
relative market potential
sales potential
breakdown approach (top-down method)
build-up approach (bottom-up method)
qualitative forecasting techniques
quantitative forecasting techniques
combination (composite or consensus)
    forecasting
competitive intelligence

Discussion Questions

1. Business organizations like to go beyond selling existing goods to their present markets. They seek to sell existing products to new markets, new products to current markets, and new goods to new markets. Does the market research task differ in each of these cases?

2. Assume the same setting as in question 1. Discuss how the techniques or methods of collecting information may differ in each of those situations, with reference to both level of sources and level of investigation (primary versus secondary).

3. An upcoming chapter (Chapter 8) focuses on technology and especially on high-tech industries, such as electronics, aerospace, and biotechnology. Do you think market researchers face a disadvantage since the field in each case is changing rapidly?

4. Chapters 1 and 2 refer to original equipment

and to the replacement market. If your assignment calls for investigating the tire market for new trucks and the tire market for existing trucks, will your sources and methods differ between the two cases?

5. In another chapter of the book, we note that business marketers go after consumer goods markets (e.g., Loctite is now selling adhesives for households), and that consumer goods firms are shipping to business markets (florists delivering to offices). Do the market research assignments differ in these two situations?

6. This chapter cites three levels of sources—tertiary, secondary, and primary levels of information—and suggests that you start at the tertiary level. Do you see any valid exceptions to this rule?

7. In business market research we tend to work with smaller samples than is the case for con-

sumer goods. Should we, as a result, have less confidence in the findings?

8. Although the chapter emphasizes the prevalence of surveys in business marketing research, experimentation and observation are mentioned as two other ways of conducting a primary investigation. Cite examples in which these two means of gathering new data can be useful.

9. Often the single best source of marketing information is "the expert." Where can you find these experts? Who are they? How would you go about locating them? Suggest as many creative ways as you possibly can, in diverse industries.

10. Should there be a nationwide or industrywide standard for interviewers? Financial planners can now attend courses and become "certified." Should similar procedures be instituted for market research interviewers?

11. It is far easier to work with a list of specific names and phone numbers than with just corporate names. Who publishes lists of executives, managers, and so forth, and how quickly do such lists become obsolete in your view? Take a look at three directories at least.

12. What advantages and disadvantages do you see in using the same survey form that others have used already? (*Note:* Start collecting survey forms if possible.)

Endnotes and References

1. A. C. Gross and S. A. Wolpert, "Marketing Information: New Directions, Vital Issues," *Australian Marketing Research* (June 1980): 253–266; A. C. Gross and S. A. Wolpert, "New Information Technology Impacts Business Hierarchy," *Infosystems* (October 1979): 128–132. See also M. A. Dressler, R. Beall, and J. I. Brant, "Decision Support Systems," *Industrial Marketing Management* (March 1983): 50–60.

2. For the academic contribution, see W. E. Cox, Jr., *Industrial Marketing Research* (New York: Ronald/Wiley, 1979). For a blend of academic and practitioner contribution, see N. A. Stacey and A. Wilson, *Industrial Marketing Research* (London: Hutchinson, 1963); A. Rawnsley, ed., *Manual of Industrial Marketing Research* (Chichester, U.K.: Wiley, 1978); I. Maclean, ed., *Handbook of Industrial Marketing Research* (London: Kluwer-Harrap, 1975). For the practitioner viewpoint, see C. H. Kline & Staff, *Industrial Marketing Research* (Fairfield, N.J.: Kline, 1979); A. Krigman, *Researching Industrial Markets* (Research Triangle Park, N.C.: Instrument Society of America, 1983); D. D. Lee, *Industrial Marketing Research* (Westport, Conn.: Technomic Publishing, 1978).

3. A. C. Gross, "The Information Vending Machine," *Business Horizons* (January–February 1988): 24–33; A. C. Gross, "Analyzing and Forecasting World Markets," in M. Simai and K. Garam, eds., *Economic Integration* (Budapest: The Press of the Hungarian Academy of Sciences, 1977), pp. 113–129; condensed in A. C. Gross, "Accurate Forecasting of World Industrial Markets," *Marketing News*, September 18, 1981, p. 18.

4. See S. A. Wolpert and J. Wolpert, *The Economics of Information* (New York: Van Nostrand, 1987), for a good overview, and see Exhibits 5–3 and 5–4 in this chapter for further details.

5. See P. M. Chisnall, *Strategic Industrial Marketing* (London: Prentice-Hall International, 1985), especially Chapter 4 on marketing research. See also D. Sommers, "Industrial Marketing Research Helps Develop Product/Market Strategies," *Industrial Marketing Management* 12 (March 1983): 1–6.

6. Gross, "Accurate Forecasting of World Industrial Markets," p. 18; Gross, "The Information Vending Machine," p. 24; A. C. Gross, "World Computer Markets," *Columbia Journal of World Business* (Spring 1974): 13–23.

7. P. M. Banting, D. Ford, A. C. Gross, and G. Holmes, "Similarities in Industrial Procurement Across Four Countries," *Industrial Marketing Management* 14 (May 1985): 133–144.

8. Based on conversation with industrial managers at various conferences as well as at corporate locations. See also such new works as P. Sherlock, *Rethinking Business to Business Marketing* (New York: Free Press/Macmillan, 1991), especially pp. 33–58. See also Wolpert and Wolpert, *The Economics of Information*; S. A. Wolpert and W. M. Weiss, *Business Information Research Seminar* (Cleveland: Predicasts, 1980); and various marketing research books cited in endnote 2.

9. S. Douglas and S. Craig, *International Marketing Research* (Englewood Cliffs, N.J.: Prentice-Hall, 1983) and selected articles in *European Journal of Marketing, International Marketing Review, Journal of Global Marketing,* and *Journal of International Business Studies* during the 1980s.

10. See the following books: K. Y. Marcaccio, ed., *Directory of On-Line Databases* (New York: Cuadra/Gale, 1992); *Information Industry Factbook* (Stamford, Conn.: Digital Information Group, 1989); K. Y. Marcaccio, ed., *Computer Readable Databases,* 6th ed. (Detroit: Gale Research, 1989); and L. C. Smith, ed., *Questions and Answers: Strategies for Using the Electronic Reference Collection* (Champaign-Urbana: University of Illinois Graduate School of Library Science, 1989). For articles on the topic, see such journals as *On-Line, On-Line Review,* and *CD-ROM Professional.*

11. The classic book on this topic is still O. Morgenstern, *On the Accuracy of Economic Observations,* 2nd ed. (Princeton, N.J.: Princeton University Press, 1963). See also Gross, "Accurate Forecasting of World Industrial Markets," p. 18.

12. O. M. Mervosh, "The Indicators Don't Indicate Very Much," *Business Month* (December 1987): 55–57.

13. The USDC study is *Global Market Survey: Air and Water Purification and Pollution Control Equipment* (Washington, D.C.: U.S. Department of Commerce, 1976). For an update of this study, see A. C. Gross, "Global Competition for Environmental Markets," *European Journal of Marketing* 20 (1986): 22–34.

14. Based on D. W. Twedt, ed., *Survey of Marketing Research* (Chicago: American Marketing Association, 1983 and prior years). This is a survey of topics and techniques used by industrial and consumer goods firms. See also B. A. Greenberg et al., "What Research Techniques Are Used by Market Researchers in Business," *Journal of Marketing* 41 (April 1977): 62–68.

15. For recent practitioner-oriented articles on research techniques, see T. Eisenhart, "Closing the Research Gap," *Business Marketing* (April 1991): 22–23, and his earlier articles in the same journal. See also M. Katz, "Use Same Theory, Skills for Consumer, Industrial Marketing Research," *Marketing News,* January 12, 1979, p. 16; W. E. Cox, Jr. and L. V. Dominguez, "The Key Issues and Procedures of Industrial Marketing Research," *Industrial Marketing Management* 8 (March 1979): 81–93. On surveys, see a practical, well-written volume, A. Payne, *The Art of Asking Questions* (Princeton, N.J.: Princeton University Press, 1965).

16. This section is based partly on an unpublished study by Edith Phillips, "Applications of Various Market Research Methods in the Industrial Sector," M.B.A. research paper, Cleveland State University, 1988. Ms. Phillips worked for Parker Hannifin and is now with AGA Gas, Inc.

17. B. G. Yovovich, "Focusing on Customers' Needs and Motivations," *Business Marketing* (March 1991): 41–43. For earlier contributions, see J. L. Welch, "Researching Marketing Problems and Opportunities with Focus Groups," *Industrial Marketing Management* 14 (November 1985): 245–253; and R. C. Inglis, "In-Depth Data: Using Focus Groups to Study Industrial Markets," *Business Marketing* (November 1987): 78–82.

18. Phillips, "Applications of Various Market Research Methods in the Industrial Sector"; D. Jobber, "Improving Response Rates in Industrial Mail Surveys," *Industrial Marketing Management* 15 (August 1986): 183–196; S. J. London and C. J. Dommayer, "Increasing Response to Industrial Mail Surveys," *Industrial Marketing Management* 19 (August 1990): 235–242.

19. Phillips, "Applications of Various Market Research Methods in the Industrial Sector," and communication with Michael Marvin, Market Research Manager, Parker Hannifin, Cleveland, Ohio, May 1991. See also Jobber, "Improving Response Rates in Industrial Mail Surveys," pp. 183–196; and A. B. Blankenship, *Professional Telephone Surveys* (New York: McGraw-Hill, 1977). Based also on experience with phone surveys at National Market Measures of Cleveland, Ohio, 1989–1991.

20. Yovovich, "Focusing on Customers' Needs and Motivations," and others say quite clearly: Never mix market research with selling activities.

21. A. R. Andreason, "Cost-Conscious Marketing Research," *Harvard Business Review* (July–August 1983): 74–79.

22. There are now many good volumes on presentations and computer graphics, e.g., C. Wildner, *Presentations Kits: Ten Steps for Selling Your Ideas* (New York: Wiley, 1990); M. W. Holcombe, *Presentations for Decision Makers* (New York: Van Nostrand Reinhold, 1990); and E. R. Tufte, *Envisioning Information* (Cheshire, Conn.: Graphics Press, 1990). Numerous journals, e.g., *Desktop Publishing,* also deal with this topic.

23. P. Green and V. Srinivasan, "Conjoint Analysis in Marketing Research," *Journal of Marketing* 54 (October 1990): 3–19. See also R. van den Heuvel, "The Measurement of Attribute Importance for Industrial Products," *Proceedings of the Budapest Seminar on Industrial Market Research* (Amsterdam: ESOMAR, 1982): 185–194.

24. Andreason, "Cost-Conscious Marketing Research," and Twedt, *Survey of Marketing Research.*

25. Cox, *Industrial Marketing Research,* especially Chapter 7, Market and Sales Potential, pp. 144–176; see also Sherlock, *Rethinking Business to Business Marketing,* especially pp. 49–51.

26. A. C. Gross, *Computer Services* (Cleveland: Predicasts, 1983).

27. Combination forecasting has been practiced since 1960 at Predicasts, Inc.; see their three key publications, *Predicasts, Worldcasts,* and *Basebook.* It is now embraced by many academics and practitioners, including R. Eggert, publisher of *Blue Chip Indicators,* which shows general economic forecasts of the top fifty U.S. economists. See also such volumes as S. Wheelwright and T. Makridakis, *Forecasting* (New York: Wiley, 1987); S. Armstrong, *Long-Range Forecasting* (New York: Ronald, 1985). See also D. M. Georgoff and R. G. Murdick, "Manager's Guide to Forecasting," *Harvard Business Review* (January–February 1986): 110–120, and various articles in the *Journal of Forecasting.* For computer-based forecasting, see Dick Berry, *Forecasting Sales with the PC* (New York: Quorum Books, 1988).

28. P. R. Stokke et al., "Scenario Planning," *Long Range Planning* (April 1990): 17–26; M. Werner, "Planning for Uncertain Futures," *Business Horizons* (May–June 1990): 55–58; W. Whipple, "Evaluating Alternative Strategies Using Scenarios," *Long Range Planning* (June 1989): 82–86; and "Making the Most of Both Worlds—Scenario Building at Royal Dutch Shell," *Management Review* (September 1990): 59–61.

29. F. W. Barnett, "Four Steps to Forecast Total Market Demand," *Harvard Business Review* (July–August 1988): 28–38, especially p. 34.

30. USDC, *Global Market Survey.*

31. Gross, "Global Competition for Environmental Markets."

32. Ibid.

33. G. Ara et al., *The World Telecommunications*

Market (Ottawa, Canada: Faculty of Business, University of Ottawa, 1983), relying on A. D. Little & Staff, *World Telecommunications Survey* (Cambridge, Mass.: A. D. Little, Inc., 1980).

34. Banting et al., "Similarities in Industrial Procurement Across Four Countries."

35. See F. E. Webster, Jr., *Industrial Marketing Strategy,* 2nd ed. (New York: Wiley, 1984), pp. 45–47, and journals such as *Purchasing* and *Purchasing World.*

36. See L. M. Fuld, *Competitor Intelligence* (New York: Wiley, 1985); L. M. Fuld, *Monitoring the Competition* (New York: Wiley, 1987); John Endean, *Finding Company Intelligence* (Washington, D.C.: Washington Researchers, 1985); M. M. Kaiser et al., *Understanding the Competition: A Practical Guide to Competitive Analysis* (Washington: Kaiser & Associates, 1983); C. M. Vella and J. J. McGonagle, Jr., *Competitive Intelligence in the Computer Age* (Westport, Conn.: Greenwood Press, 1987); J. Kovach, "Competitive Intelligence," *Industry Week,* November 12, 1984, pp. 50–53; and D. M. Lambert et al., "Industrial Salespeople as a Source of Market Information," *Industrial Marketing Management* 19 (May 1990): 141–148. *Note:* the term *competitive intelligence* appears to have been used as early as 1959 in a Harvard Business School monograph which received very little publicity at the time.

37. R. W. Stewart and M. A. Hiltzik, "Industrial Espionage Is Big Business," *Best of Business* 4 (Fall 1982): 96–101; P. Maher, "Corporate Espionage: When Market Research Goes Too Far," *Business Marketing* (October 1984): 51–66, and P. Maher, "Getting the Information You Need, Whatever It Takes," *Business Marketing* (October 1984): 64–65, both relying on research done by John Endean of Washington Researchers. This group has subsequently published a book: *Finding Company Intelligence* (Washington, D.C.: Washington Researchers, 1985). For viewpoints from a U.K. perspective, see R. Bottom, Jr. and R. J. Gallati, *Industrial Espionage: Intelligence Techniques and Countermeasures* (Stoneham, Mass.: Butterworth, 1984) and P. A. Heins, *Countering Industrial Espionage* (Leatherheads, U.K.: 20th Century Security Education, 1982).

38. Endean, *Finding Company Intelligence.* See also Exhibit 5–13.

39. See such recent volumes as Jack Behrman, *Essays on Ethics in Business* (Englewood Cliffs, N.J.: Prentice-Hall, 1988); N. E. Bowie and R. Duska, *Business Ethics,* 2nd ed. (Englewood Cliffs, N.J.: Prentice-Hall, 1989); R. E. Freeman, ed., *Business Ethics* (New York: Oxford University Press, 1991); G. Laczniak and P. Murphy, *Marketing Ethics* (New York: Free Press, 1985), and T. Donaldson, *The Ethics of International Business* (New York: Oxford University Press, 1990). Several corporations (such as Andersen Consulting) and colleges (such as Bentley College) now sponsor summer seminars and even year-round centers on business ethics. For a recent commentary, see B. J. Feder, "Helping Corporate America Hew to the Straight and Narrow," *New York Times,* November 3, 1991, p. F5. Companies cited as having ethics sections are Dow Corning, General Dynamics, Nynex, Pacific Bell, and Texas Instruments.

6

SEGMENTATION OF BUSINESS MARKETS

CHAPTER OUTLINE

- To understand how business customers can and should be classified into different groups called segments and why such segmentation is important to business marketers

- To be able to identify the three major bases for segmentation and analysis: macro—general or objective; intermediate; and micro—specific or subjective

- To recognize different bases of segmentation and then combine them in various business markets

- To understand how the "nested approach" can encompass the major bases of segmentation and to learn how this procedure works in a cost/benefit framework

- To study applications and specific examples of segmenting in various industries and in both local and global markets

- To understand why segmentation must occur prior to target marketing, product positioning, and strategy formulation

Just as individuals match their skills to the demands of the labor market, so suppliers offer their goods and services in line with what organizations want and seek. What offerings should be made to commercial and industrial companies, to government and nonprofit agencies? Knowing "what the market wants" means knowing the buying patterns of current clients and their reasons for purchasing. Similarly, potential customers and their characteristics must be studied. A successful business must do more than study the "market out there"; it must anticipate needs and offer innovative ideas, products, and related services. Those marketers succeed best who cultivate existing customers *and* who create new clients.

Organizational customers may be actual or potential, large or small, concentrated or scattered, in the private or public sector, and in domestic or foreign markets. They may belong to one or several industrial categories; their purchasing can be frequent or occasional, of an emergency or routine nature. The groups or individuals in the buying organizations may be risk takers or risk avoiders; they may be sophisticated or naive. Lumping all clients together makes little sense in view of such diversity, and studying each individual customer is too cumbersome. Elementary schools differ in characteristics from colleges, and they both differ from the business world as Apple, Compaq, IBM, Next, and other computer makers found out early on.

The task of **market segmentation** is, therefore, to divide the market into meaningful categories and then approach them with appropriate offerings. The division is meaningful when customers in each category are similar to each other but distinct from members of other categories. Thus elementary schools resemble each other, although their purchase policies can be different from state to state. In that case, geographic location may be a crucial variable. Small firms have less formal but possibly more innovative buying patterns than large companies. Food service organizations, such as ARA and Sysco, know that their offerings should be different to college cafeterias than to senior citizen residences.

Segmentation, like other marketing activities, is a dynamic process. Once a supplier makes a decision about serving certain segments and specific clients, it has to keep on refining its skills and offerings. The relationship between supplier and buyer will continue to evolve; commitment or loyalty bonds may develop. Finding new customers is important; retaining old ones is crucial. Knowing the practices of both can assist greatly in the marketing task.

A large supplier of forest products knows that lumber has many applications: log cabins in national parks, benches in schoolyards, wooden pallets in warehouses, housing components, and parquet flooring for corporate boardrooms. How should segmentation take place? Which segments should be targeted? Where do new opportunities lie? A manufacturer of truck parts faces a similar decision process. Should it cater to original equipment makers or the replacement market? Where is faster growth, in domestic or foreign models? Do fleet buyers differ from those who buy only a few trucks at a time?

Service organizations face much the same task. Consider a company whose strength is maintaining and repairing rugged laundry equipment used by hospitals, motels, the military, and various cleaning establishments. Should it cater to all of them or just to a few segments? Should it go after new markets? A business information firm, such as Reuters, disseminates news to stockbrokers, mutual fund managers, investor groups, and the media. Ideally, it must identify, segment, and evaluate each distinct client base. It must "make sense from diversity" and then position its offerings accordingly. Organizations must decide whether to cater to many segments, a few selected segments, or a single segment. In sum, the key task is to pinpoint market opportunities.

THE NATURE OF MARKET SEGMENTATION

Markets consist of many actual and potential clients. The essence of market segmentation involves categorizing customers according to certain conditions or criteria. Such classification is not a meaningless exercise but a crucial step before any further action is taken. After segmentation, the desirable categories will be targeted and approached with the right marketing mix. Knowing the clientele as much as possible and then matching them with appropriate product and service offerings form the essence of positioning and marketing strategy.

The Basic Criteria

What are the ways for identifying users and distinguishing them from each other? Five criteria must be met for pinpointing a market and its subcategories. The market and its specific segments should be measurable, substantial, accessible, stable, and compatible.[1] *Measurability* means that information on location and other characteristics of buyers is available. A given market or segment is *substantial* when it is sufficiently large in size and/or is likely to have future potential. Having *access* means that a supplier can retain old customers and pinpoint new ones. *Stability* implies that customers have staying power and that a relationship can be established between supplier and clients. *Compatibility* is the degree of similarity between sellers and buyers in regard to risk taking, service standards, and corporate style. Let's apply these criteria to a fictitious company headquartered in the city of Toronto.

Northern Flight manufactures and markets helicopters across Canada. Current buyers include companies, government agencies, and large hospitals from the province of Quebec to the Yukon. These markets are measurable, significant, and stable. Compatibility with purchasers exists by understanding the purpose for which clients utilize the helicopters. They are used for flying into remote areas (by mining firms), inspecting forest or crop growth (by a government agency), and for making emergency runs (by clinics). The company refines its segmentation further and draws up a chart such as Exhibit 6–1.

Northern Flight is eager to enter foreign markets but will cater only to civilian users as it makes neither attack nor defensive military units. Its analysis indicates that purchase patterns by industries and government units will be similar in other countries, though some applications may differ. First, the company looks at the United States, then to Central and South America. How big are these regional markets? Then it considers the size of the global market.

Northern Flight's inquiry leads to a geographic distribution pie-chart such as Exhibit 6–2, Part A. Clearly, the North American market is dominant when it comes to the existing fleet. There will be new purchases in this region, but many units will be sold for replacement. The market is already sizable, but it is more saturated than others. Future growth will be faster in other regions. This is evident by the demand pattern for new units seen in Exhibit 6–2, Part B. The geographical distribution of shipments clearly will differ from that which now prevails for the existing fleet.[2]

Within each major region of the world, Northern Flight gathers data on segments by type of ownership and by application. Knowing its present capabilities and future plans, the company elects to pass up the emergency medical markets. Instead, it chooses to direct its marketing activities toward forestry, oil exploration, and mining companies as well as those government agencies that carry out aerial inspections. Northern Flight thinks that such clients can be easily identified in developing nations eager to market their natural resources, at the same time protecting their environment. Given its multilingual staff and its understanding of large organizations, Northern Flight thinks that a sound relationship can be achieved between itself and buyers.

Now let us consider Heli Supply House, a small fictitious British firm, which makes components for helicopters and offers maintenance and repair services. This company has limited staff and lacks funds to go worldwide, so it emphasizes only

EXHIBIT 6–1   Market Segmentation for a Helicopter Company by Three Possible Variables

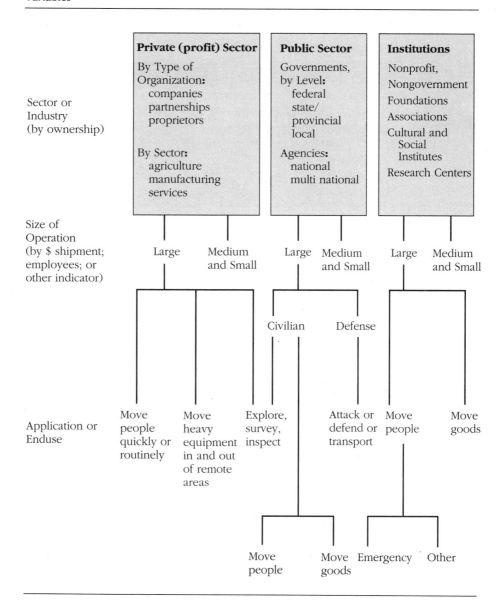

EXHIBIT 6–2   The World Market for Civilian Helicopters, 1990

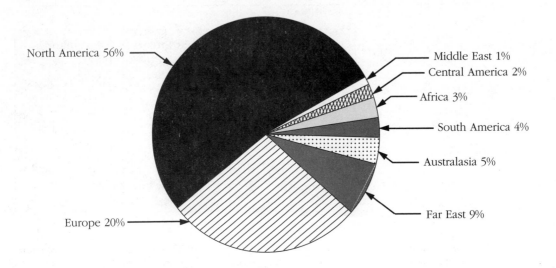

A. Worldwide Distribution of Existing Helicopter Fleets (a total of 18,656 helicopters)

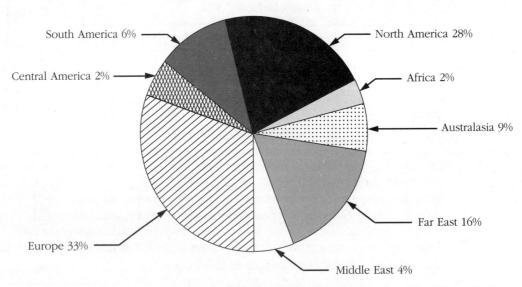

B. World Market Share of New Helicopters

Note: Central America includes the Caribbean.

Source: G. Endres, "The World Civilian Helicopter Market," *Interavia Aerospace Review,* January 1991, pp. 70–71. Reprinted by permission of *Interavia Aerospace Review.*

its home market, Western Europe, and North America. These are substantial and stable markets. In these regions Heli Supply House must identify the makers of helicopters. It should have no problem in gaining access to them and establishing compatibility. The next step is to identify those that carry out the maintenance of helicopters. This is more difficult. Is such activity carried out at manufacturing sites, at the heliports of the owners, at neutral sites, or at a combination of such places? The company must find the answers and explore the implications of its findings for a successful marketing strategy.

The Bases for Segmentation

Assuming the five conditions cited above are satisfied, we are ready to proceed with the idea of segmentation. The concept is not a new one. As early as 1934, one author stated, "The first step in analyzing an industrial market is to divide it . . . into particular groups of prospective and present users to whom to appeal."[3] But what the bases for such action would be was not made clear. Should it be location, type of industry, size of firms, or some other objective bases? Over successive decades, academics and practitioners suggested additional bases for segmentation, including subjective measures, such as urgency of application or buyers' personal characteristics. In addition, a debate ensued over whether segmentation should be on a single basis (say, location), dual bases (say, industry and size of order), or multiple bases (three or more factors).

A comprehensive, multistep approach to segmentation is shown in detail in Exhibit 6–3. The merit of this nested scheme lies in having a continuum from objective to subjective bases for segmenting. Another way of describing this situation, in terms of the diagram, is that we should move from general (or macro) to intermediate to specific (or micro) bases for segmenting. In total, five distinct bases are identified: organizational demographics (emporographics), operating variables, purchasing approaches, situational factors, and personal characteristics. As we move gradually inward, the task of obtaining the needed information becomes more difficult, but also more rewarding. Too often we speak of markets only in terms of industry and location, when in fact it is desirable to identify the personal characteristics of individuals or teams.[4]

Which single basis do companies use most frequently for segmenting? What dual or multiple bases enjoy popularity? Is there one recommended route? The answers to such questions are not simple. Indeed, we devote the rest of the chapter to exploring such topics. But one truth emerges already at this point: there is no ideal or single solution applicable to all situations.

A study of the literature reveals that companies use the easily observable or objective factors, such as industry or location, most frequently. Many practitioners favor this route for its simplicity and ease of application. Published information is also geared toward such factors. Just think of the reference volumes cited in the previous chapter that identify industry, location, and company size. But to learn more details about various industrial sectors and firms, analysts use subjective bases. Recent studies show that purchasing policies, applications, and risk percep-

EXHIBIT 6–3   The Nested Approach to Segmentation: Macro, Intermediate, and Micro Bases

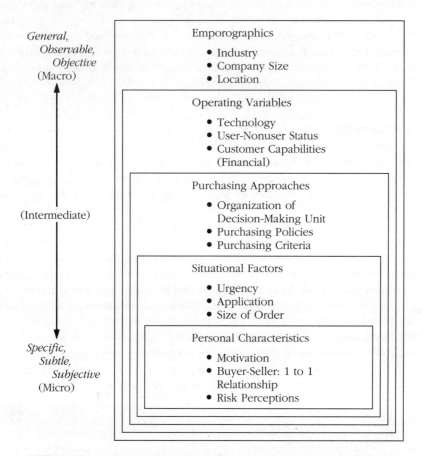

General,
Observable,
Objective
(Macro)

Emporographics

- Industry
- Company Size
- Location

Operating Variables

- Technology
- User-Nonuser Status
- Customer Capabilities (Financial)

(Intermediate)

Purchasing Approaches

- Organization of Decision-Making Unit
- Purchasing Policies
- Purchasing Criteria

Situational Factors

- Urgency
- Application
- Size of Order

Specific,
Subtle,
Subjective
(Micro)

Personal Characteristics

- Motivation
- Buyer-Seller: 1 to 1 Relationship
- Risk Perceptions

Source: Thomas V. Bonoma and Benson P. Shapiro, *Segmenting the Industrial Market* (Lexington, Mass.: Lexington Books, D. C. Heath and Company, 1983), p. 10. Reprinted with permission.

tions are possible ways of segmenting large groups of engineers and plant managers. In other cases, the combination of industry, location, user status, and team behavior proved useful for both segmenting purposes *and* subsequent activities such as product positioning, pricing, and promotion.[5]

Misapplications of Segmentation

In this chapter we shall look at several applications of segmentation. Before doing so, let us examine three common misapplications of market segmentation: over-concern with demand level, needless searching for identification, and myopic views of product forms.[6] The reason for this: we can often learn more from mistakes than from success stories.

Typically, marketers pay more attention to current users than to potential ones, claiming that it is always easier to keep a client than to find one. Similarly, they like to focus on heavy as opposed to light users because 80 percent of sales come from 20 percent of users. These two views are correct, but in mature markets (for example, the United States, Canada, and Europe), it is also smart to look at nonusers and light users. A good example of how this works is the case of water treatment chemicals. For many years, such compounds were used almost exclusively by utilities and manufacturers. However, office buildings and shopping malls now also need such chemicals for both pollution control and energy savings. Stressing this powerful combination has generated a fast-growing market for progressive firms.

A second possible misapplication of segmentation is the needless search for identification, often based on key objective factors, such as location, industry, or size of organization. Having the facts on hand makes little difference if one cannot act on them. For example, we know that the major steel mills are clustered between Pittsburgh and Chicago in the United States and in the Ruhr Valley of Germany, and we know their exact location and size. But this knowledge is of limited use to the makers of measuring instruments because most mills are not being modernized and some have shut down. It is, therefore, far better to focus on the modern, though smaller, minimills that are able to use such controls and meters. These mills can be found in rural locations, away from industrial valleys.

The third misuse occurs when business marketers are concerned with the broad form of the product or service instead of the specific needs of users. This results in a myopic view of both segmentation and marketing action. For example, to satisfy certain clients, makers of blowers and fans had to move well beyond the generic problem of circulating air to consider the specific problem of removing noxious fumes. Another example is that of regional trade show organizers, who found that they could successfully appeal to high-tech exhibitors who had become disenchanted with the cost and anonymity of participating in vast national trade shows. Narrowly focused, smaller shows met with approval from both exhibitors and attendees in New England and southwestern states.[7]

Beyond Segmentation

The comprehensive nesting diagram of Exhibit 6–3 provides an overview of the various bases of segmentation and serves as a guide for the remainder of the chapter. But it says nothing about the relationship between segmentation and marketing activities. How do these two facets relate to each other? Clearly, companies do not undertake segmentation for its own sake, but because it can serve as a platform for action. Segmentation can effectively link an organization to the external environment. It influences product positioning and other elements of the marketing mix.

Any organization, large or small, should have a vision. What is our mission? What is the fundamental rationale for having this business? At one level, the answer is to create customers, but at another level it is also about technical leadership, growth, profits, quality, and stakeholder satisfaction. (Stakeholders are shareholders, employees, customers, suppliers, and even the general public.) These objectives can best be achieved by planning and by formulating strategy. At the operating level, organizations must translate these objectives into tactical decisions. This means matching the relevant segments to be served with appropriate products and services.[8]

At the end of the chapter we relate segmentation to marketing strategy in detail, but here is a brief, specific example. The jet engine makers General Electric, Pratt & Whitney, and Rolls-Royce serve Airbus, Boeing, and McDonnell Douglas, the large jet aircraft firms. The plane makers sell their output to large commercial airlines, such as Air France, Lufthansa, United, and many others. There is pressure on *all* parties to provide less noisy *and* more fuel-efficient planes. On short hops over cities, the first factor is crucial; on long journeys, the second factor is more important. There are other factors that add up to varied requirements for the airlines and provide a rationale for segmentation by the aircraft and engine manufacturers. The task of segmenting, then, directly influences product design and positioning.

THE MACRO BASES FOR SEGMENTATION

The broad objective or **macro bases of segmentation** shown at the top of Exhibit 6–3, are the size of buying units, the type of industry, and location.

A Note on Terminology

Demographics is the term used when segmenting consumer markets according to such variables as the size of population, location of residence, age, occupation, or level of education. (The term comes from *demos,* a Greek word meaning "people.") These demographic variables serve as the macro or objective bases for segmenting the market for consumer goods and services. We shall use the word **emporographics** as the industrial equivalent of demographics.[9] (The term comes from *emporium,* also a Greek word, meaning "a place of commerce" or "trading area.") Emporographics encompasses the macro or objective bases for segmenting business markets—that is, the size of buying unit, type of industry, and location.

Size of Buying Unit

Who gets the most publicity in the pages of the business press as a general rule? The big organizations, of course, such as those on the *Fortune* 500 and *Forbes*

1000 lists in the United States and the *Financial Post* 500 and *Globe & Mail* 1000 lists in Canada. In Europe and Japan, we continuously find references to the top ten, twenty, or fifty leading firms in journals such as the *Financial Times, Les Echos,* and *Business Tokyo.* Similarly, in the developing nations, the largest private and public enterprises can be readily identified.

The giant companies are given much publicity because they command the resources, in terms of employees, physical assets, and sales. In most nations they dominate the mining, manufacturing, transportation, communication, and utility sectors. For example, the top 100 manufacturing firms in the United States account for one-third of all corporate assets and sales; in Canada the dominance is even more pronounced. Globally, as cited above, three companies account for all large civilian aircraft, and another three make all the jet engines. A total of nine telecommunication companies capture 90 percent of the world market. Single, giant PTTs (post, telephone, and telegraph) firms dominate in many nations in Europe and elsewhere, although some are being broken up, as was AT&T in the United States.

Medium-size firms, members of the middle market, are those in the $50 million to $500 million range in terms of annual sales, although these are arbitrary figures. According to several observers, this is a substantial, yet growing marketplace.[10] Medium-size companies usually have a balanced product line and purchase a wide variety of goods and services. However, some do divest subsidiaries or spin-off divisions. Conversely, successful medium-size firms are often absorbed by larger ones. (For example, in water treatment chemicals, Mogul, DuBois, and Calgon, all medium size, were bought by Dexter, Chemed, and Merck.) In such cases, the process of segmentation must be performed again and again.

Up-to-date lists of medium-size firms, like those of large ones, are available in numerous directories. Size, address, plant location, industry code, names of key executives, and so forth, are shown in detail in such directories as *Dun & Bradstreet, Moody's, Standard & Poor,* and *Ward's* in the United States, *Canadian Trade Index* in Canada, and the *Kompass* volumes for Europe.

Many small vendors operate as suppliers to large and medium-size firms, because the bigger firms are sizable, accessible, and (until recently) stable. This is often a sensible solution, although the purchasing policies and styles of larger organizations may prove to be incompatible with some small suppliers. In the midwestern states, many small foundries, metal fabricators, and plastic molders have ceased serving GM, Ford, and Chrysler since the Big Three now prefer to deal with fewer and larger suppliers. Other small firms, hoping to be vendors to the U.S. plants of Honda, Toyota, and Nissan, found that the Japanese brought their own suppliers. As some large firms close, downsize, or decentralize, the task of reaching their buying centers becomes more challenging. Small firms know that relying on a few key accounts is a risky policy and have diversified their clientele.

Small companies often look to other small firms as their most likely customers. They understand well each other's practices and constraints. Small firms are often trendsetters in their activities, and they can thus serve as proving grounds without undue risk taking. For example, small high-technology firms offer electronic products with new features. At the same time, they buy trendy furniture, fitness equipment, and flowering plants for their offices. (Of course, small firms sell and buy many everyday goods and services, ranging from word processors to freight expediting.)

Many small firms are privately or family owned and may be difficult to locate. Still, there are numerous volumes listing them, including those already cited, state or major city directories published by Harris and chambers of commerce, and membership rosters of industry or trade associations. Specialized mailing lists can be purchased from commercial sources. Successful enterprises, including the 50 or 100 showing the fastest growth rates over five years, are listed in *INC., Business Week,* and the *Wall Street Journal.* These and other journals give details on specific U.S. firms as "small companies worth watching." The situation is similar in other countries as entrepreneurs start up new ventures. There are many "roundtables," or informal groups of small businesses whose activities are publicized. In short, information is readily available on small firms, too.

Type of Industry

A classification scheme for industrial establishments and their shipments has been pioneered by the U.S. government. This categorization, called the **SIC (Standard Industrial Classification) code**, has received wide acceptance by both the public and private sectors. Its equivalent at the international level is the **ISIC (International Standard Industrial Classification) code**, which is also enjoying popularity. A company classifying its client base according to the SIC code can compare its sales data with existing statistics. This is a major advantage and reinforces the popularity of the SIC code. Data on the divisions, plants, and shipments of other firms are also available on the basis of the SIC code, usually in private sector publications (for example, *Dun & Bradstreet Market Identifiers*).

Exhibit 6–4 shows examples of the SIC categorizing procedure. Major divisions of the economy are given one-digit codes, key industries within those divisions get two digits, and subsectors of the industries get additional digits. Each category is relatively homogeneous, especially at the four-digit level. Some publications, such as *Predicasts,* will carry statistics on a seven-digit basis, so further details become evident. The SIC code has been used to construct input-output tables showing interindustry transactions. The SIC code allows market analysts to browse for comparative data. When information gaps occur, it is possible to extrapolate or interpolate to levels at which data are more plentiful.

The SIC system has definite problems, however. The classification procedure can get out of date as technical and structural changes occur in the economy. Long after computers, biotech compounds, and robotics came into existence, they still had no proper SIC codes. Some SIC codes, even at the four-digit level, contain dozens of products, causing a clutter problem (see Part C of Exhibit 6–4). Related items are not always assigned in proximity to each other. Fully harmonizing the SIC code with the classification schemes of other nations is an ongoing task. Market analysts are constantly at work reconciling export and import statistics between two or more nations.[11]

EXHIBIT 6–4   The Standard Industrial Classification (SIC) System

Part A: Major Divisions

Division	Description of Major Industry	2-digits
A	Agriculture, Forestry, Fishing	01 to 09
B	Mining	10 to 14
C	Construction	15 to 17
D	Manufacturing	20 to 39
E	Transport., Communic., Utilities	40 to 49
F & G	Wholesale & Retail Trade	50 to 59
H	Finance, Insurance, Real Estate	60 to 69
I	Services excl. whse & ret. trd.	70 to 89
J	Public Administration	91 to 97
K	Nonclassifiable	99

Part B: Subcategories of a Major Division

35	Industrial & Commercial Machinery; Electronic Computers
357	Computer & Office Equipment
3571	Electronic Computers
3577	Computer Peripheral Equipment

Part C: Detailed Description of One 4-Digit Category

3577 Computer Peripheral Equipment, Not Elsewhere Classified

Establishments primarily engaged in manufacturing computer peripheral equipment, not elsewhere classified, including printers, plotters, and graphic displays. Establishments primarily engaged in manufacturing modems and other communications interface equipment are classified in Industry 3661.

Card-punching and sorting machines
Card-type conversion equipment, computer peripheral equipment
Computer output to microfilm units, computer peripheral equipment
Computer paper tape punchers and devices, computer peripheral equipment
Decoders, computer peripheral equipment
Disk pack inspectors, computer peripheral equipment
Document entry conversion devices, computer peripheral equipment
Graphic displays, except graphic terminals: computer peripheral equipment
Input/output equipment, computer: except terminals
Key-disk or diskette equipment, computer peripheral equipment
Key-tape equipment: reel, cassette, or cartridge

Keying equipment, computer peripheral equipment
Keypunch/verify cards, computer peripheral equipment
Magnetic ink recognition devices, computer peripheral equipment
Media-to-media data conversion equipment, computer peripheral equipment
Optical scanning devices, computer peripheral equipment
Plotter controllers, computer peripheral equipment
Plotters, computer
Printers, computer
Punch card equipment: card readers, tabulators, collators, sorters, and interpreters
Tape cleaners, magnetic: computer peripheral equipment
Tape print units, computer peripheral equipment

Source: *SIC Manual 1987* (Washington, D.C.: USGPO, 1987).

The most vexing problem is to pinpoint exactly what each industry, establishment, or plant makes and therefore what each is likely to purchase. The reason for this problem is that the data for a given facility reflect primary and secondary activities at the four-digit level. Consider Mid-Ohio Machinery, which ships $85 million worth of engines and turbines (SIC 3510) and $75 million worth of construction machinery (SIC 3530). All the data relating to Mid-Ohio's business activities would be under the category that shows the highest number. This can occur even though the company is very active in other lines of business. To overcome this problem, the U.S. Department of Commerce provides two corrective measures, called *specialization ratio* and *coverage ratio*.[12] Major improvements in the SIC code are to be found in the latest (1987) edition of the *SIC Manual*, a standard reference text.

In the final analysis, the SIC remains a good tool for segmenting markets, planning sales territories, estimating market and sales potential, and doing market research in general. This is especially true for categories that show high specialization and little diversity in their shipments and whose purchases therefore are likely to be quite narrow and well defined. Annual surveys by various government and private agencies show the importance of four-digit categories at state, county, and metropolitan area level. As one expert put it, "Half the marketing managers in the USA can improve their performance by utilizing the SIC system to a greater extent."[13]

Geographic Location

Knowing the location of actual and potential customers assists greatly in sizing up and segmenting markets. Good decisions in this area have a major impact on planning distribution centers and promotional campaigns. The first step is to pinpoint the resources or facilities of a given industry. Where are the mines, mills, or offices? Exhibit 6–5 shows that proven oil reserves are clustered in different regions of the world; they are highly concentrated in the OPEC (Organization of Petroleum Exporting Countries) nations of the Middle East.

The segmenting of markets by location has different implications in different industries. A resource-based industry such as lumber and a manufacturing industry such as food processing have to consider the distances that their output must be shipped to reach buyers. This consideration must then be balanced against the desire to be close to their raw input and suppliers. Light manufacturers such as electronic component makers and service industry companies such as leasing offices have fewer problems in regard to being distant from their customers and suppliers. It is true, however, that being geographically close is reassuring to users. This applies especially for maintenance and repair firms.

Market segmentation by location goes beyond locating specific clients in given cities, states, or countries. Marketers need to know other economic and business statistics on a geographic basis to do their planning. Exhibit 6–6 shows differences in cement supply and demand on a regional basis in the United States and the

EXHIBIT 6–5   Proven Reserves of Crude Oil Worldwide

In thousand million barrels

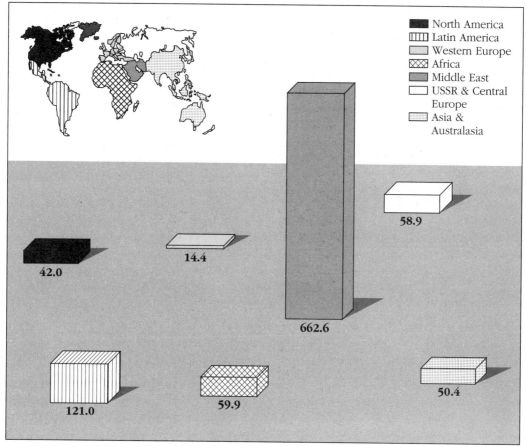

The height of each region is proportional to its reserves. This highlights the dominant position that the Middle East holds in terms of the world's total proved reserves of oil.

Source: *British Petroleum Review of World Energy* 1990. Reprinted with permission.

extent to which the needs of cement purchasers can be fulfilled from production facilities in that region. The figures also reveal that in certain regions, notably the Northern Mountain region, there is not sufficient capacity for doing so. In this case, shipments from other geographic regions play a major role in meeting the shortfall. Such geographic statistics can be used to identify opportunities for locating new cement plants and for catering to clients in those regions.

Over the years several volumes that assist the marketer in carrying out economic geographical analysis have been published. These include many volumes

EXHIBIT 6–6   Supply and Demand Relationship for Cement in the United States by Geographic Regions, 1989–1990 (ratio of consumption to domestic clinker capacity, expressed in percentages)

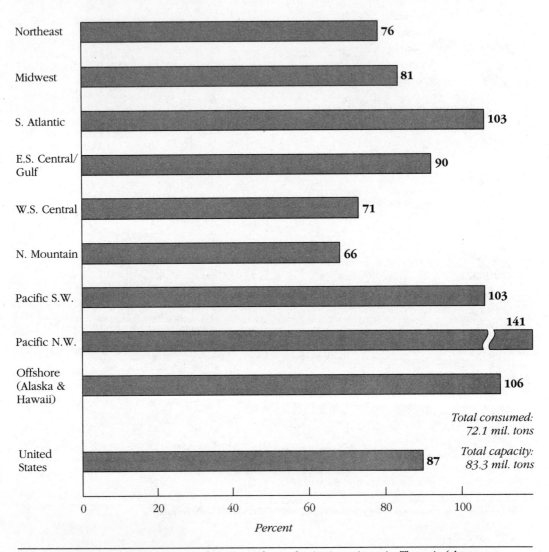

Note: Consumption/capacity ratio is not the same as the production/capacity ratio. The ratio (shown as a percentage) reflects a utilization situation. The table can be used to judge regional balance or imbalance.

Source: J. Breckling, *The U.S. Market for Cement and Related Materials* (Cleveland: Leading Edge Reports, 1989), 185–187.

from the U.S. Census Bureau (censuses of manufacturing, services, agriculture), state publications, the *Rand McNally Commercial Atlas,* special issues of *Sales & Marketing Management* on industrial and commercial purchasing power, and a host of directories. Equivalent public and private sector publications can be found in Australia, Canada, Japan, and Europe, and even for some developing nations. Many of the volumes are becoming available in electronic format.[14]

At the global level, volumes being published currently include *The World Development Report, World Resources,* and the statistical yearbooks and surveys by the United Nations, the Organization for Economic Cooperation and Development (OECD), and many other multinational bodies. Publications from such bodies as the Asian Development Bank give clues to regional data. The books provide both location and industry data, though frequently with a lag of two to three years. Knowing which minerals are mined at what locations across the globe serves as a key input to a maker of mining equipment. Similar reasoning applies to manufacturing and service industries.

Combining Size, Industry, and Location

Macro bases such as those just discussed can be used singly, but such emporographics prove to be more meaningful in combination. Knowing where clients are located, to which industries they belong, and how big they are can assist the marketing manager in the segmentation process. Few companies can serve all possible markets. Focusing on a limited set of actual and potential customers while knowing much about their characteristics and then adjusting the product or service line makes sense, whether we consider old-line or new industries.

Segmentation is coming to the marketing of small computers. IBM believes that "a world of niche computer outlets, paralleling the rise of specialty stores in other fields, will promote increased use of computers in specific businesses."[15] This giant company, known as Big Blue, identified more than forty growing market segments, such as accounting, auto repair shops, and beauty salons. In similar fashion, a Sears Business Center in Chicago is focusing on attorneys, while a Computerland franchisee in Indianapolis is targeting small newspapers. To be successful, each of these vendors will have to study the characteristics of these customers.

The computer services industry is different from the computer equipment industry, but segmentation is appropriate here too. Computer services fall into four categories: data processing, software, consulting, and turnkey systems. Although all four can be found in all regions of the United States, there are distinct differences reflecting the underlying demand and usage patterns by clients. Knowing this and knowing who is moving in and out of a given state or city gives an edge to the astute marketer. For example, software development is proportionally higher in Boston, Los Angeles, and Houston. Data processing is relatively more intense in New York, Detroit, and San Francisco. Such patterns reflect the clustering of distinct industries, nonprofit institutes, and government agencies in these urban locations.[16]

Where should a young entrepreneurial computer service firm locate and what sectors should it cater to? This depends in part on the expertise of its managerial and technical labor force. But another input is identification of the potential client base in terms of emporographics or macro bases. Published data, ranging from government statistics to phone directory listings, indicate that routine data processing is still in demand in New York, Washington, and Los Angeles. In contrast, the market for such services is saturated in Denver, Miami, and Seattle. Computer consultancy services sprang up around Boston, and in urban areas in neighboring states.

BUSINESS MARKETING IN PRACTICE

Segmenting the Markets of Eastern Europe for Telecommunication and Computer Equipment

The year 1989 will be famous forever as the year of drastic changes in the small nations of Eastern Europe. The Iron Curtain and the Berlin Wall came tumbling down as East Germany, Poland, Hungary, Czechoslovakia, Bulgaria, and Romania began a concerted move toward political freedom and a market economy. All of these nations are eager in the 1990s for an infusion of Western capital, technology, specific equipment, and services.

The countries of the region differ sharply in their inventory of existing equipment and in their ability to absorb new technology. This is especially true in the field of telecommunication. Probably each nation constitutes a distinct segment. Telephones per one hundred people show sharp differences: the number stood at about fourteen for Czechoslovakia and about eight for Hungary toward the end of the 1980s. However, the growth rate is higher for Hungary, at about 5 percent per year, versus about 3 percent for the nation of Czechs and Slovaks.

The telecommunication solutions for many of these nations are different from those of Western European countries where reliable fixed-link networks exist. It is conceivable that for some Eastern European nations the best solution will be to leap-frog using a mobile telecommunication network. In such cases, mobile telephones may be used to expand quickly and to avoid the traditional five-year waits for telephone service to organizations and households. In one success story, the Hungary Post Office and U.S. West are joining forces (Westel) to provide cellular telephone service, starting in Budapest, the capital city.

In the case of computer hardware and software, skilled Eastern European technicians imitated the features of Western goods and services, such as those of IBM, Digital Equipment, Apple, and Microsoft. In some cases, there were many patent, trademark, or copyright violations or some pilfered goods obtained on black markets. As a result, however, many people have training and insights in working with such equipment and software, which is one reason why Western firms see a lucrative base from which to expand. Again, as with the field of telecommunications, the situation differs from nation to nation, and even within industries in a given country. Thus each Eastern European country and its key industries will constitute a distinct segment for Western firms.

Source: Based on selected news items in *Marketing News* and *Electronic News* during 1991, and T. Kelly, "Telecommunications in the Rebirth of Eastern Europe," *OECD Observer* (December 1990–January 1991): 19–22.

Segmentation according to macro bases plays a major role in foreign markets as well and indeed in the global marketplace as a whole. The helicopter market used as an example at the beginning of the chapter showed the importance of knowing which regions will be growing fastest. The paint industry in the United Kingdom provides another illustration on how industry, location, and application can be combined. End users for paint are divided into consumer and business markets, with the latter then subdivided into automotive, decorative, and all other markets. The "all other" category includes paints for aircraft, marine, factory upkeep, and other uses. Within the marine applications, further breakdown is achieved by probing which end users need weatherproof quality paint. The marine market is also broken down by location—for example, seaside cities with large shipyards versus small harbors with pleasure yachts or small boats.[17]

Another example from the paint industry involves the U.S. giant firm of Sherwin Williams taking a look at the automotive and architectural paint markets on a global basis. Sherwin Williams, like many other firms, judged that lucrative markets for its paints would be in developed nations because of high per capita income and the large stock of existing cars, trucks, and buildings of all kinds. However, the competition in Europe proved to be intense, and entry into Japan was difficult. The company found its markets in Central America, especially Jamaica, where many old cars and old structures needed a fresh coat of paint. Competition was also less keen.[18]

Although segmentation along emporographic dimensions in existing markets is a good practice, care should be taken not to exclude potentially lucrative new markets. This is especially true for new materials and equipment. Consider the initial use of nylon—in an area of textiles known as warp knits. Subsequently, nylon found major uses in tire cords, garments, and carpets. Similarly, reinforced plastics first found applications in the defense sector, where material strength was a key requirement. Now such plastics are used extensively in recreational vehicles, such as kayaks, canoes, and sailplanes; reinforced plastics may yet be used widely in commercial vehicles.

THE INTERMEDIATE BASES FOR SEGMENTATION

Where do the macro bases for segmentation end and where do the intermediate bases start? As the nesting diagram in Exhibit 6–3 illustrates, there are no hard lines of demarcation, but rather a continuum. Overlap is a common occurrence among the macro, intermediate, and micro bases of segmentation. The **intermediate bases of segmentation** are, roughly, the middle three nests: operating variables, purchasing approaches, and situational factors. The overlap between macro and intermediate bases can be seen easily in the case of technology. It is part of the intermediate group in Exhibit 6–3, yet it was also cited in the macro section because technology is tied to the notion of industry (some industries are high-tech, some are old-line sectors). Similarly, location has a relation to usage; just think of de-icing chemicals.

Operating Variables

Operating variables include some important distinguishing characteristics: user status, technical features, and customer capabilities. All of these descriptors may serve as ways of segmenting the existing and potential client base. As before, they may be used singly or in combination.

Usage Rate.   Segmentation of clients on the basis of usage occurs usually along the following lines: heavy, moderate, and light users. The challenge is to retain heavy users, at the same time remembering that light users can develop into significant clients. It is important to recognize also that related goods and follow-up services can be useful for approaching clients for further sales. For example, progressive chemical firms not only offer compounds in bulk or in small quantities, but carry out testing and monitoring to see if the chemicals perform as promised and to show that pollution does not occur.

An important division for business marketers is the one between original equipment makers (OEMs) and the replacement market. Quite frequently, the OEM field is dominated by large vendors and is difficult to penetrate. In such cases, the replacement market or after-market may look attractive. Examples include the sale of tires, batteries, and servicing for truck and car fleets; instruments for chemical, paper, and other process companies; computer peripheral equipment and consultancy for large and small offices; and architectural services for building renovation.

High usage rates may imply frequent repeat orders for small quantities *or* occasional sizable orders. The vendor is well advised to know what role its products and services play in the buyer's activities. In the 1970s, hardware played a major role in the data processing field. By the 1980s, software became more important. Companies that correctly perceived this shift in each client's activities did far better than those that chose to specialize in hardware or software exclusively.

Customer Capability.   By understanding the nature of the customer's business (including knowing the client's clients), the relationship becomes one of trust, and the account may enjoy a steady increase. Loyalty bonds refer to both trust and longevity. Such bonds are based on the parties knowing and assisting each other.

Strong ties are often prevalent in the case of basic commodities, factory parts, and office supplies. The result is the *straight-rebuy* situation, described in Chapter 3. Even in such situations, it pays to know the manner in which the client operates. The *modified-rebuy* and *new-task* situations represent opportunities for vendors to become first-time suppliers and thereby make the "short list." Such lists, often disavowed or secret, are made up of preferred vendors that are solicited to bid or

BUSINESS MARKETING IN PRACTICE ▪▪▪▪▪▪▪▪▪▪

Marvin: Real-World Window Sales

Marvin Windows is an eighty-year-old company, still small, but growing rapidly in recent years, with sales rising from $44 million in 1981 to $230 million in 1988. The firm has gained a competitive edge through segmentation. It caters to influential segments with highly specific advertising campaigns, sales tactics, and product literature.

In the early 1980s, Marvin identified the following three distinct groups: *remodelers; building supply dealers;* and *builders and architects.* It then developed messages for the various segments—after studying their interests, awareness levels, and behavior. Marvin looked at trade publishers' research and also conducted surveys. Then it formulated messages for each customer group based on the findings.

Remodelers want windows that fit existing spaces and minimize installation labor charges, thus making their prices more competitive. Marvin positions itself as the made-to-order window manufacturer with advertisements for remodelers that highlight its ability to provide replacement windows identical in size to the originals.

In addressing *building supply dealers,* the company focuses on how its windows enhance their profitability. The dealer advertisements explain that Marvin's products require no reseller inventory because they are made to order and shipped as needed, thereby lowering dealers' inventory costs and making their prices more competitive. The advertisements also stress how the products' unique appeal to the end user can mean profit to the dealer.

Builders and architects have similar needs for windows that range from elaborate and decorative to merely functional. Marvin's advertising campaigns to those two segments stress design flexibility that will meet both aesthetic and budgetary constraints.

Customers and others say that Marvin's segmented advertising has strengthened its competitive position vis-à-vis adversaries such as market leader Andersen Corporation.

Source: Kate Bertrand, "Divide and Conquer—Market Segmentation," *Business Marketing,* October 1989, p. 50. Reprinted with permission of *Business Marketing,* October 1989.

to approach with a proposal for a transaction that, of course, may then turn into a long-term commitment or relationship.[19]

Technology.   The ties that bind the global village together are the various forms of telecommunication. Several choices exist for transmittal of voice, data, and picture, but telephone lines are still the most vital. The extent to which nations and organizations expect the latest in equipment and services governs the way in which telephone companies respond to their needs. Exhibit 6–7 shows the kind of information that is vital to providing state-of-the-art facilities. This chart reveals not only the size of each national market in terms of subscriber lines, but also the extent to which transmission and switching networks are digitized. Lower figures indicate bigger market opportunities for vendors of telephone equipment.

EXHIBIT 6–7   Segmenting the West European Telephone Network Market by Degree of Digitalization, 1990

Country in Europe	Subscribers (main lines) millions	Degree of Digitalization %		
			Switching	
		Transmission	Local	Long-distance
Belgium	4.0	50	29	75
Denmark	3.0	85	23	40
France	27.0	70	70	75
Germany	28.6	50	3	22
Greece	4.5	15	15	25
Ireland	1.2	70	65	85
Italy	21.7	45	25	36
Luxembourg	0.2	35	8	10
Netherlands	6.3	95	35	15
Portugal	19.5	70	20	30
Spain	12.2	47	5	45
United Kingdom	20.0	100	42	90

Source: European Conference of Postal and Telecommunications Administrations (CEPT) and Commission of the European Community, quoted in D. Ypsilanti and R. Mansell, "Reforming Telecommunications Policy in OECD Countries." *OECD Observer,* October–November, 1987, p. 20, based on plans by network operators as of that date (1987). Reprinted by permission.

Another example comes from a related high-tech field, namely computers. One of the key building blocks of personal computers is the chip or microprocessor. Two large U.S. firms, Intel and Motorola, are battling it out, with Intel holding a commanding 66 percent of the global market in 1991. Motorola's obsession with technological excellence delayed new products at a critical time. The corporate infighting between the champions of a new technology and defenders of a successful older one made things worse. Meanwhile, Intel knew what specific features its customers, the large computer firms, wanted, and it aggressively promoted its line of chips to IBM, Apple, Compaq, and others. Soon, Intel's chips became the standard. The moral of the story, often repeated in other high-tech fields, is to match technology to customer requirements.[20]

A particularly powerful segmentation technique is to consider multiple product applications in relation to alternative functions. A case in point occurred in Japan, where technical innovation is characterized by steady improvements. This is in contrast to the United States, where many companies seek breakthrough technologies. Currently, Japanese researchers are working hard to combine three basic fields: electronics, mechanics, and optics. Areas of applications range from printing machinery to medical equipment, from machine tools to aerospace. The firms involved must probe various applications and ask what problems they can solve for their clientele.[21]

Purchasing Approaches

Why do some buyers place orders much in advance, whereas others wait until the last minute? Which departments get involved (and in what sequence) in surveying alternative makes, determining specifications, bid invitations, and supplier selection? Answers to these and similar questions are important to vendors for purposes of segmenting, for dealing with both policies and people, and for positioning the product or service offered to the target markets.

Purchasing Policies and Practices.   Fortunately, as discussed in Chapters 3, 4, and 5, we know much more now about industrial procurement in industrialized nations than before. Major similarities exist in the purchasing patterns of companies in the United States, the United Kingdom, Australia, and Canada. Comparisons will be soon available on whether the findings apply to firms in France, Hungary, and other nations. The authors of this book found that the way in which materials, equipment, and components are bought in English-speaking nations is highly similar. Other, earlier studies in the United States also showed consistency over time.[22]

As a result of such research, we can be confident about the way in which the different functional departments in a company become involved in the purchasing process—both across national borders and over time. These results are applicable to manufacturing sectors, especially the paper and chemical industries. However, the procurement process may be different in primary sector (agriculture, forestry, and mining) industries and in the various service industries (utilities, trade, and transport).

Whenever feasible, vendors should obtain written documentation, beyond oral understanding, about the purchasing practices of their clients. Topics covered may include policies on reciprocity, gift giving, the way in which bids are sought, and special arrangements for minority contractors. Two key areas are worth investigating: (1) Is purchasing centralized, decentralized, or a combination of the two (for example, capital goods bought at headquarters, routine orders at branches)? (2) Does the client prefer a system solution or does it wish to buy separate components for assembly?

Purchasing Criteria.   Traditional business buying occurs along the familiar lines of seeking quality products, prompt delivery, a fair price, and follow-up service. These terms are explained or elaborated on in several chapters of the book. Here we are concerned with their implications for the actual purchase. What is prompt delivery? Can clients be classified according to how fast they wish goods to be delivered? Certainly, United Parcel Service, Federal Express, DHL, TNT, and others are testing the boundaries of small package delivery in this respect. Overnight delivery over vast distances, even at a high price, is important to some clients.

Several studies highlight the tradeoffs that clients are willing to make. For example, in a comparative survey of identical laboratory instruments bought by companies and hospitals, technical support proved to be more important to the industrial segment, whereas service loomed more significant to the clinics. Comparing the purchase of valves and pumps in the United Kingdom and Canada, delivery reliability ranked first in both nations. However, having test facilities ranked near the top in the United Kingdom, but quite low in Canada. In contrast, prompt quotation was perceived as a key aspect in Canada, but not in the United Kingdom.[23]

Service Level.   Although price is often cited as a key consideration (most often by large users), many clients focus on such service issues as reliability, ability to obtain emergency deliveries, and the quality of technical assistance. It may be useful, therefore, to segment customers according to common service requirements. As a general rule, the more service is required, the more localized must be the offerings by the vendor. There is no substitute for being near and readily available to clients.

Consider the different kinds of distributors shown in Exhibit 6–8. Clearly, what is significant in such cases—in regard to "relevant" market size and hence segmen-

EXHIBIT 6–8   Looking at Distributors' Business by Selected Segmentation Bases

Type of Distribution Business	*Determinants of Relevant Market Size*		*Scope of Market*
	Value-to-Bulk*	Service Level	
Electronic components (fill a bill of materials)	Very high	Low (reasonable order cycle time)	National
Food wholesaling (to grocers)	Moderate	Moderate (weekly deliveries)	Regional
Metal service centers	High	Moderate (custom processing, minimum order cycle time)	Regional
Food service (to hotels/ restaurants)	Moderate	High (daily deliveries)	SMSA†
Convenience stores	Moderate	High ("fill in" food purchases on ad hoc basis)	SMSA†
Newspaper delivery	Low	Very high (daily deliveries)	Local

*Value-to-bulk = dollar value to physical volume.
†SMSA = standard metropolitan statistical area (urban area).

Source: N. Novich, "Distribution Strategy," *Sloan Management Review,* 12/e (Fall 1990): 75. Reprinted by permission of *Sloan Management Review.*

tation—are the value-to-bulk ratios and the service levels to be provided for different industries or operations. When service levels demand daily contact or deliveries, as in the case of food service to hotels, the scope of operation will be local in character. Conversely, when service level can be low in terms of order cycle time, as in the case of electronic components, the market can be national in character. Of course, accurate and prompt delivery is still needed in all cases.

Situational Variables

Situational variables are the last of the intermediate bases of segmentation. Situational variables are closely related to operating and purchasing variables on the one hand and to the micro bases of team and individual buyer characteristics on the other. Situational considerations are such aspects as *urgency* and *application* and the nature and *size of the order* placed by a client. Another factor that can be equally important here is whether clients are seeking standardized or customized solutions. Service level expectations, referred to above, can also come into play.

An example for segmenting by situational variables comes from the field of information retrieval. This is a highly complex industry in which users differ sharply in regard to the kind of information need and in regard to the speed with which they need it delivered. These two aspects are explored in Exhibit 6–9. Military and medical specialists are two groups that seek instant information. When lives are at stake, every second is crucial. In contrast, archivists are content with information delivered a few days late. Workers seeking skill improvement are also not in a big hurry. Note that segmenting is not by industries in the chart, but rather by function or occupation. Suppliers of information must find out which groups need data quickly and are willing to pay for fast service compared with those who can tolerate a waiting period. Vendors can thus target selected user groups and position their services.[24]

THE MICRO BASES FOR SEGMENTATION

Beyond macro and intermediate segments lies the realm of **micro bases of segmentation**. At this juncture, we are looking at the groups and individuals in the buying center, their decision-making style, their technical sophistication, and their attitude toward risk taking. Such considerations are similar to topics we touched on in Chapters 3 and 4 when we looked at organizational buying behavior and purchasing practices. We concluded that looking at the purchasing agent is hardly enough; we must study the individuals and groups who are influential or who have veto power over the procurement.

EXHIBIT 6–9   A Perceptual Map of the Information Industry Segmented by Speed of Delivery and Urgency of Need

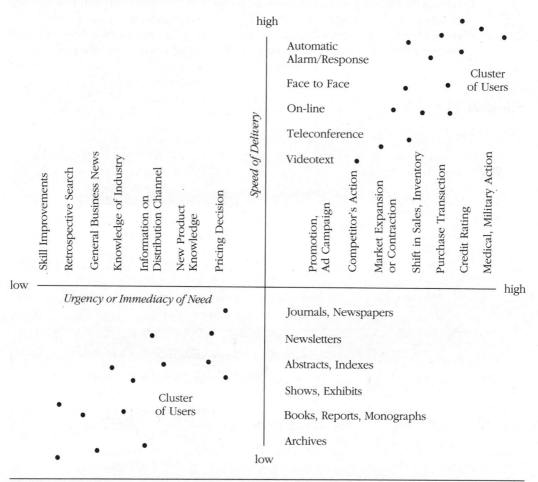

Note: Each dot represents a possible position occupied by an information company.

Source: A. C. Gross, "The Information Vending Machine." Reprinted from *Business Horizons*, January–February 1988, p. 29. Copyright © 1988 by the Foundation for the School of Business at Indiana University. Used with permission.

Buyer-Seller: One on One

It is clearly at the micro level that we can speak of strong ties or loyalty bonds between seller and buyer. There are cross-currents in all industrial sectors and in local or national economies. Some observers say that long-term commitments are on the rise because of a desire for stability, the complexity of transactions, and clients' preference for dealing with fewer vendors. Others contend that under the pressures of cost cutting, corporate downsizing, and outsourcing, loyalty bonds are bound to erode. In industries characterized by rapid change and keen competition, suppliers are often played off against each other.[25] The ties between seller and buyer usually take years to build but can erode rather quickly.

Business customers as a rule are ready to switch vendors under the following circumstances: dissatisfaction with an existing vendor's price, quality, or service; the retirement, transfer, or death of a key contact, such as a sales force member who had called on the client for decades; and changes in requirements—for example when a factory switches to a new material. In times of turbulence—such as inflation, shortages, or reorganization—loyalty bonds become frayed. Such situations represent threats to present vendors and opportunities for would-be suppliers that are on the outside looking in.

Once loyalty bonds are established, relationship selling should still be cultivated. No individual or company is sold forever even on the best product. Thus, once the relationship has evolved from a transaction to a relationship or commitment style of operation, a continuing dialog is still required. Such discussion can take a number of different formats, especially when it comes to selling add-ons, peripherals, or follow-up items.

Individual Characteristics

In this section we descend to the most specific level of segmentation: the demographic and psychographic characteristics of individuals. The more we know about them, the better we can execute the task of segmentation and the subsequent task of delivering value.

Background, Function, and Responsibility Level.   Research has shown that the greater the similarity between the salesperson and the prospective client, the higher the probability of the sale. When the background, education, and corporate rank of individuals match each other, there is a sense of camaraderie, even a notion of a partnership. This is enhanced when the selling organization designates an individual to be resident troubleshooter at the site of the customer. Common sense and protocol dictate that young salespersons should not call on upper-level managers with years of experience and expertise.

Members of the buying center, those who influence purchase decisions, look at complex products and services in terms of the primary and secondary benefits they offer. Such benefits can range from financial returns to product features, from ease of operation to ease of replacement. The salesperson should note these and point out benefits not considered. Trying to change preferences or benefit rankings, however, is not advisable. It is wise to stress different aspects of the offering to the members of the buying center who come with differing wish lists. Thus, a computer network can be described as productivity enhancing to top managers, as cost-effective to purchasing agents, and as user friendly to those who work with it on a daily basis.[26]

Preferences, Motivation, Sophistication.   Whereas the background, title, and function of individuals can be ascertained with relative ease, it is much harder to learn about their attitudes, especially in regard to risk taking. Although findings in this regard are not plentiful, several insights are beginning to emerge. A few firms even commissioned research focusing on industrial psychographics—that is, the study of personality traits and behavior of individuals in organizations.

These studies investigated at length the characteristics of engineers, managers, and other functional groups influencing the purchase of industrial air-conditioning equipment. Questionnaires measured product awareness, perception, and preferences at the individual level, as well as satisfaction with existing products and levels of service and attitudes toward risk taking. In the end, the studies identified several microsegments, as shown in Exhibit 6–10. Clearly, there is homogeneity within groups, and there are salient differences between any two groups. Such findings suggest which product features, promotional schemes, and cost emphasis would work best.[27]

In another study, the authors argue that the three layers of managers in any organization—that is top, middle, and lower—can be described as having high, moderate, and low levels of sophistication.[28] The characteristics of the three

EXHIBIT 6–10   Issues of Importance to Selected Groups in the Purchase of Industrial Cooling Systems

Group or Microsegment	Key Importance	Less Importance
Production Engineers	Operating cost Energy savings Reliability Complexity	Initial cost Field proven
Corporate Engineers	Initial cost Field proven Reliability Complexity	Energy savings Up-to-date
Plant Managers	Operating cost Use of unproductive areas Up-to-date Power failure protection	Initial cost Complexity
Top Managers	Up-to-date Energy savings Operating cost	Noise level in plant Reliability
Heating, Ventilating, and Air Conditioning Consultants	Noise level in plant Initial cost Reliability	Up-to-date Energy savings Operating cost

Source: Reprinted by permission from J. M. Choffray and G. Lillien, "Assessing Response to Industrial Marketing Strategy," *Journal of Marketing,* April 1978, p. 30.

EXHIBIT 6–11   Segmenting Industrial Buyers by Extent of Sophistication

Sophisticated	*Moderately Sophisticated*	*Unsophisticated*
Top management	Middle management	Lower management
Heavy exposure to trade/professional magazines	Some exposure to travel, professional magazines	No exposure to trade/professional magazines
Next heaviest readers of consumer magazines	Heaviest readers of consumer magazines	Infrequent readers of consumer magazines
Large majority are members of professional association	Half are members of professional association	Few are members of professional association
Large majority go to trade shows	Half go to trade shows	Few go to trade shows
Middle level of education	Highest level of education	Lowest level of education
Oldest and most experienced	Middle in age and experience	Youngest and least experienced
Slightly less confident than moderately sophisticated about buying decisions	Most confident about buying decisions	Least confident about buying decisions

Source: Reprinted by permission from N. J. Church and R. McTavish, "Segment Buyers 'Sophistication' to Reach Industrial Markets Efficiently," *Marketing News,* September 16, 1983, p. 8.

groups are described in Exhibit 6–11. This three-way, simple breakdown needs further study and validation by type of industry, size of organization, and other variables. The descriptors, if valid, do suggest the marketing efforts that could be undertaken. For example, marketers can approach top managers via advertisements in professional journals and at trade shows; middle managers, through consumer journals; and lower-level, less sophisticated managers, via the telephone or in person at the office.

COMBINING DIFFERENT BASES

There are several ways of combining the different bases of segmentation. Marketing managers do this regularly on a formal or intuitive mode. Combinations are generally useful, but constant tinkering or expansion may not be worthwhile. Each refinement must be weighed in terms of its potential costs and benefits.

Industry, Application, and Benefits

Computer terminals are as familiar today as typewriters were a decade ago. But they are put to far more different uses than typewriters ever were. Retailers use them for customer service: checking credit, sales records, follow-up. Manufacturers use them for order entry and for inventory control as well as in dedicated networks and factory operations. A survey found that despite different uses, the desired benefits are the same across applications and participants. Service ranked first, followed by reliability, vendor reputation, software, compatibility, and delivery.[29]

Still, it was possible to distinguish two distinct groupings by clustering industrial sectors and benefits. Manufacturers, wholesalers, and retailers insist on low price and ease of operation. They also want highly competent salespeople calling on them. In contrast, business service firms, such as consultants and financial institutions, desire a broad offering of hardware and software—that is, variable configuration. They insist on the supplier having a solid reputation, a spotless image. In sum, one cluster is price conscious; the other is quality conscious.

What are the implications of the above findings for marketers of these computer terminals? A major market leader with a solid reputation should cater to risk-averse, safety-minded clientele. It should stress premium quality, and it can demand a premium price. In contrast, a small vendor with less visibility can emphasize low prices and lack of frills. But it should still field a highly competent, knowledgeable sales force calling on the manufacturing, the wholesale, and the retail trade sectors.

Users and Psychographics

In the consumer goods area it is not unusual for organizations to look into the personality traits and behavior of their customers (usually in a nonintrusive fashion). But it is still a rarity for industrial firms to do this. A major producer of adhesives and sealants, however, decided that it wanted to learn more details about its client base of engineers. Loctite was convinced that this broad community of technical experts had significant subcategories whose behavior was worth exploring.[30]

Loctite hired its advertising agency, Mintz & Hoke, to look at users versus nonusers first. The agency identified three types of engineers by behavioral dimensions such as dependency, risk avoidance, competence, and competitive spirit. Users matched the characteristics of early adopters, whereas nonusers matched the profile of followers. Users proved to be risk avoiders, but they would take on responsibilities and assist others. Nonusers were even more intense risk avoiders; they also reacted to stress by worrying and looked skeptically on new ideas.

The report submitted by Mintz & Hoke to Loctite also identified three types of engineers with distinct characteristics. Design engineers view themselves as innovators and as problem solvers, but they do not respond to appeals that call for them to operate in such a mode. They like to use charts that prove that using certain technology results in a specific level of performance. Production engineers are concerned about making errors and are risk avoiders. Plant maintenance engineers see themselves as creative problem solvers and as unsung heroes. They are visually literate, like live demonstrations, and prefer photos over charts for proof.

On the basis of these results, Loctite concluded that promoting new applications to current users and stepping up promotional efforts to potential users would be far better than reformulating its products. Loctite also chose plant engineers as the primary audience to whom it would appeal. Such appeal would use photos of products rather than charts. The design and production engineers, however, would continue to get charts that give details about products in a more formal fashion.

Technology and Buying Factors

The requirements of any industrial organization, according to one group of researchers, consist of two broad facets: technical parameters and buying factors. The first category includes all the technical specifications demanded that are "the irreducible capabilities that will be accepted." They are the initial criteria, whether speaking of standard or customized products. The second category includes all other factors, such as quality, price, delivery, vendor reputation, and even personal benefits supplied.[31]

This scheme is applied to a maker of fans and blowers. Starting with the generic notion of moving air, this company has to match up its product line with the technical needs and nontechnical requirements of users. Technical aspects relate to the volume of air and the pressure under which it must be moved. Another consideration is air quality, such as whether fresh air is to be circulated or noxious fumes are to be removed. The buying factors of prime importance in this example are service, reputation, and reliability. This scheme, the authors claim, ensures that the seller focuses on those aspects that buyers will value the most.

Emporographics and Product Application

Some academics and practitioners advocate that segmentation can best be accomplished when macro bases are considered simultaneously with the application or use of the product line. An example of this approach can be seen in the case of Works, a new software program developed by Microsoft for IBM and IBM-compatible personal computers. Microsoft deliberately chose this application as it developed other programs for Apple Macintosh computers. Microsoft then looked at specific industries, occupations, and functions. Users were classified along two dimensions: first-time versus experienced and single versus multifunction. Finally, Microsoft developed certain features for different national and local markets.[32]

In essence, Microsoft utilized sequential segmentation for its software program. First, it chose the hardware environment. Next it specified the type of use by function, occupation, and then by customer attributes. Finally, it identified foreign markets where Works could be adapted to the native language. This procedure can pinpoint the existence or lack of large market segments for certain product applications (types of use) and whether buyer behavior would vary a lot or little in the segments. Microsoft learned that markets in some countries are sufficiently large to support segment-oriented strategies for several applications. In these nations, it is also cost effective to develop tailor-made promotion and distribution. For smaller markets, such an approach would not be proper.

SEGMENTATION AND MARKETING STRATEGY

Segmentation is a conscious decision to identify clusters of potential clients who are similar in their buying, usage, and evaluation patterns. The procedure is a means of getting to the goal of serving "the right clients." However, although many segments may be attractive, the vendor may not have the capabilities to serve all attractive clusters. A choice must be made: some segments will be served, others will not. The chosen ones are called *targets* or *niches,* and the strategy aimed at them is **targeting** or **niche marketing** (see Chapter 9). After segmentation and targeting, the vendor can develop the appropriate marketing mix and the relevant marketing strategy for all of the chosen clusters.

Because targeted segments value the products or services offered, they should consist of eager and willing buyers. Many analysts now advocate thinking narrowly and use such terms as *supersegmentation, micromarketing,* and *mininiches.* "It has been said that in an age of global markets and mammoth competitors, the most successful marketers will be those that fight . . . neighborhood by neighborhood . . ."[33] For business marketers, the notion of neighborhood means moving from office park to office park, from industrial district to industrial district, and from one government agency to another. Put briefly: Think globally, but act locally!

After segmentation, targeting, and niche marketing comes **product positioning**. This term is close to the notion of both product image and corporate image, which are always linked together. The key objective is to position the vendor in the client's mind as the first choice for the product or service in question. Currently, for computer mainframes, IBM is number one, but for personal computers, Apple and Compaq come to mind most readily, and Sun Microsystems is the current leader in workstations.

Segmentation, Strategy, and Positioning: An In-Depth Example

To understand the most comprehensive approach to segmentation, look again at Exhibit 6–3. Now let's apply this five-step, nested procedure to a specific company, utilizing a cost/benefit framework. This example should illustrate how segmentation can serve the cause of product positioning and marketing strategy.

Consider a major security equipment company, Sensortag, which is marketing a product line of electronic security tags. These tags can be attached to a wide

Lockheed's small but powerful target audience learns about defense.

Innovation

THE ROMAN EMPIRE AND MILITARY AIRLIFT Perhaps the most remarkable thing about the Roman Empire was that, at its greatest geographic extension, its security was assured by a mere thirty legions. From Scotland to Egypt no more than 180,000 regular troops kept the Empire in tranquility.

The key to this manpower-efficient defense was the metalled road.

Metalled roads provided a great logistic advantage over ordinary dirt highways, which could not support the traffic of a marching legion (around 6,000 troops and a like number of animals). Even in dry weather, movement was restricted to about twelve miles per day. In rain and snow, dirt roads were churned into quagmires, and movement stopped altogether.

But on their extensive network of paved, engineered roads, the Roman troops could march thirty miles a day—in all weather. Legions could be quickly shuttled around the empire to respond to unrest in one province, or the invasion of another. In this way, Rome could afford a much smaller defense establishment than the geographic size of her empire would suggest.

In the late 20th century this lesson of strategic and tactical mobility is still apt. For the United States, with our global commitments, our Roman roads are our airlift fleet.

Presently that logistic potential is adequate to respond to small scale crises around the world. But in the event of a major outbreak overseas, and given the strength of our current airlift fleet, there has been some debate as to our ability to protect our worldwide interests.

Flexibility is critical to an efficient defense. Julius Caesar understood it. All Romans understood it. It was the primary reason for their paved roads. Without them, the Roman Empire would not have lasted as long as it did, for the mere knowledge that legions could be on the scene within weeks was usually sufficient to keep the peace.

In the near future, the knowledge that overwhelming American force might be on the scene within hours would give pause to potential enemies. And that, in the final analysis, would be the most efficient defense of all.

Lockheed
Giving shape to imagination

Roman road at Timgad, Algeria

Courtesy of Lockheed Corporation.

variety of goods, such as garments, housewares, and other items, to prevent pilferage by both customers and employees. Such tags can be attached in retail stores, but they can also be installed by manufacturers or wholesalers. The tags differ in size and shape, depending on the type of store and the items to which they are attached. Tags are to be removed when a sale is made.

Sensortag thinks that approaching manufacturers and wholesalers would be a time-consuming, expensive process. Large retail establishments appear to be the best choice in the United States as well as in Western Europe and Japan. The tags are costly, but large stores receive volume discounts. Segmentation beyond location and type of store is implemented along additional macro, intermediate, and micro bases. At each level, the organization takes a close look at costs and benefits. The anticipated costs are those of research, design, production, transport, and overhead. The expected benefits are revenues, profit, image, market share, competitive

BUSINESS MARKETING IN PRACTICE ■■■■■■■■■■■

Lucrative Segments in Continuing Education

As full-time undergraduate enrollments stabilize or decline, the field of continuing education provides a lucrative alternative market for colleges and universities. But to cater to people and organizations, institutes of higher education must be able to compete against many other institutions, ranging from profit-making firms to chambers of commerce and from individual lecturers to major conference organizers.

How should the market be segmented in this case? Many advocate that occupations, functions, or job titles be used rather than industries. This means offering short and long courses to architects, bankers, engineers, and nurses. Some suggest that continuing education be offered on the basis of high-interest topics to groups of individuals. There is also debate concerning whether to offer skill upgrade courses on a general basis to all comers or to go in-house and offer such courses to employees of one company. A few universities now award master degrees without residency requirements; courses are given on cable television.

Another issue is whether to give degrees, certificates, or other tangible proof of completing courses and seminars. The American Management Association (AMA) is offering "ceu's" or continuing education units; it is one of the more formidable competitors. Some colleges now cooperate with the AMA. A few organizations award degrees, even though they are not universities. General Electric has a fine reputation for its own in-house programs.

Dangers exist in this field. Some universities have segmented the market well and then targeted groups that appeared able and willing to take continuing education courses. For example, several institutes of higher education focused on engineers and scientists in the high-tech sectors. But when the market declined for some high-tech goods and services and when large electronic firms cut back on employment, enrollment declined sharply, and the universities also had to cut back.

edge, and control. It is imperative to relate the costs to benefits at each successive segmentation step. This is done in a straightforward way in Exhibit 6–12.

At the macro level, Sensortag chose highly industrialized countries where mass merchandising is the rule. Large department stores, major discount chains, and selected clothing stores are good candidates. Catalog stores and independent firms are ruled out. At the intermediate level, the firm is looking at technology, purchasing criteria, and application. For example, it has to learn how easily the tags can be attached and removed in the store by the store personnel. If the size of the order is sufficiently large, can long-term, favorable credit terms be extended to the store? Finally, at the micro level, Sensortag has to understand the risk-taking philosophy of store managers, their perception, and their motivation.

While Sensortag originally thought that its product line would be of interest to a wide variety of retail merchants, it had to make choices on stores it would or could serve. Segmentation proved to be valuable in this regard. But the decision to serve some stores and not others also included an assessment of its own re-

EXHIBIT 6–12   Coupling the Nested Approach to Segmentation with Cost/Benefit Analysis for a Maker of Electronic Security Tags (used to prevent shoplifting in stores)

Segmentation Basis and Subcategories	Implications for Cost/Benefit Analysis
Macro Bases	
Type of retailer	
Department store chains	Most likely possibility; contact now
Variety store chains	Too dispersed and items are low priced
Specialty (boutique) shops	Enough salespeople in store; no need for tags
Size of client	
Large accounts	Competitive situation, but worth tackling
Medium to small accounts	Definite possibility but only later on
Intermediate Bases	
Operating variable	
Well-financed customers	Can pay us on time (30 days net)
Medium financial capability	Likely to delay payment; may default
Purchasing approach	
Centralized purchasing	Easy to deal with headquarters
Decentralized purchasing	Possible, if individual store is large
Mixed purchasing	Presents complex bureaucracy
Situational factor	
Very urgent need (now)	Hot prospect; contact immediately
Less urgency, still wanted	Soft-sell approach now; more aggressive later
Can wait approach by client	Defer for several years; build data base
Micro Bases	
Motivational factor	
High concern with security	Signifies likely buyer; will be responsive
Medium to low concern	Keep in reserve; approach later on
Risk-taking consideration	
Willing to try new product	Will be highly receptive; will buy or influence
Limited risk taking	Future possibility

sources, the action of competitors, and the likely demand patterns from the various segments. All of the above then had to be put into a cost/benefit framework.

Having decided to serve certain target markets at a given point in time, Sensortag may continue to pursue additional niche marketing. This means finding specific, possibly narrow segments. One such niche may be high-fashion boutiques as opposed to ready-to-wear merchants. The boutique managers may insist that the tags be very small and unobtrusive. These stores do not wish to give their customers any idea that they would suspect them of shoplifting. Some boutiques may not even purchase tags, because they have enough salespeople. Thus, Sensor-tag may have to consider whether to cater to boutiques. If it chooses to go ahead, it will have to devise an appropriate marketing strategy and a proper marketing mix program to cater to this narrow segment.

Examples from the Service Sector

Market segments in the service sector often have to be rethought as specific customer segments. The key here is the expectation of different clients. Other considerations refer to the nature of services, especially the fact that services cannot be stored. Consider a hotel catering to both business people and family travelers. It is now contemplating a cost-cutting measure, such as automatic check-out upon departure. Although business travelers will see this service as time saving and courteous, families may view it as jarring and impersonal. Clearly, a hotel wanting to cater to both sides has to make proper provisions for each. The automatic checkout would be played up in the business press, whereas advertising in consumer magazines would assure tourists of personalized service.[34]

Now consider the segmentation, niche marketing, and positioning strategy of a small expediter of urgent letters and small packages. Eastern Connection is truly minuscule in comparison with Federal Express and United Parcel Service. The company owns two hundred trucks, but no planes for direct air service. Sales are currently only $20 million per year, a very small slice of the $8 billion regional market, the Eastern Seaboard. The company operates only in large cities, such as Boston, New York, and Washington. The majority of its customers have more than half their mailings in the Northeast.[35]

So how can Eastern Connection go up against big rivals and still charge less? It has cleverly segmented the market and then targeted only heavy users in the large cities of the region. The next step was to offer highly competitive rates and better service to these clusters. For packages of 3 to 5 pounds it charges $11 to $18, compared with FedEx's $27 to $33. Delivery is door to door by 9:00 A.M. rather than by 10:30 A.M., and Eastern will pick up packages as late as 11:30 P.M. It also coordinates its trucks with available air service by others as requested, on a twenty-four-hour-per-day basis. The company expects to emulate the giant firms by developing computer tracking of packages, and it is even thinking about servicing the West Coast.

Eastern Connection does not have the promotional budget of a UPS or Federal Express. What can it do to establish itself as a viable, cost-effective alternative? Its messages should show that the company is already going that extra mile for its client base by offering earlier delivery and later pickup. Eastern emphasizes this message in direct-mail brochures, in selective business journals, and over the telephone, but the company will not purchase costly commercials on television networks or even local stations.

For our final example, we go back to the information industry featured in Exhibit 6–9. As we noted earlier, this is a complex field because just about every business has a need for data processing, software, and professional advice. But computational and other tasks differ greatly in size and characteristics from industry to industry, from occupation to occupation, and from function to function.

Information industry participants have carved out many specific niches—for example: (1) large private, intensive-care clinics and hospitals; (2) engineering and architectural firms with fewer than fifty employees; (3) small and medium-size insurance companies with strict record-keeping needs in highly regulated states; (4) makers of pesticides subject to environmental reviews; and (5) trucking firms whose drivers need quick credit approval or cash on a twenty-four-hour basis at any one of 4,500 locations across the United States.[36]

Users differ in regard to the urgency of their needs and to the extent that unique software is desired. Fast service and customizing come at a higher price. Vendors in such cases stress the values provided, such as on-time performance and follow-up service. In the opposite situation, reliability and raw computing power would be emphasized. Pricing would be related to volume in this case, and promotion would reinforce this stance. One of the great fears of information providers is that the buyer will decide to take the operation "in-house." So vendors attempt to demonstrate at each turn how effective they are. But what constitutes effectiveness (i.e., value given vs. cost savings) tends to differ from one situation to the next.[37]

SUMMARY

Market segmentation is really about making choices. It is about knowing one's own strength, studying the competitive environment and other external factors, and then identifying market opportunities. To pinpoint the possibilities, most companies must make choices. The world is a complex and unforgiving marketplace. Few companies can serve as the single source to a wide variety of clients. There are few universal industrial products and business services (the exceptions may be paperclips, pens, telephones, and terminals). In short, the vast majority of offerings need to be tailored to markets. Indeed, the analysis of actual and potential clients should come even before a product is created, much less offered.

Thus, segmentation is the marketer's way of looking at a multihued, complex, and dynamic world of business customers with varying needs, wants, and expectations. They differ in how they perceive, use, and evaluate products and services offered by competing vendors. Segmentation is a way of clustering, classifying, and analyzing actual and potential clients. By going through this process, one gains a better understanding of buyers. An appropriate marketing program is then prepared, which will vary according to the characteristics of the groups and subcategories identified.

Segmentation can occur along various dimensions, but the framework of the nested approach assists in proceeding in a logical fashion. First and foremost, we need to learn about the observable or macro bases, the organizational demographics, which we have labeled emporographics. These are geographic location, industry, and size of the buying unit. Next, we have the three intermediate bases: operating variables (technology, user status), purchasing approaches (policies, criteria), and situational factors (urgency of need, application, order size). Finally, there are the micro or subjective bases: group and individual characteristics, such as motivation, perceptions, and attitudes, especially in regard to risk-taking.

Although it is possible to cover all bases, to move across all five nests, the practice of segmentation often dictates shortcuts and the use of just a few bases. We have given examples of single-basis and multivariate segmentation, as well as using the total, five-nest approach. No matter what bases are used, marketers are advised to consider the action of segmenting in terms of costs and benefits and to treat it as a dynamic process. Each additional step of refinement is likely to involve both expenditures and returns. The process must be continuous as the underlying clientele is not static, but shifting all the time.

After segmenting has taken place, the marketer faces the task of selecting among several clusters and catering to those chosen. This is a challenge. It calls for a good match between the characteristics of the market(s) and those of the product(s). The markets selected are labeled target markets. Catering to them has been called niche marketing, because each niche has to be approached with a rather unique combination of the marketing mix. When this is done right, the niches become what has been termed "pockets of profitability." To do the job right, continuous monitoring and feedback from members of each niche are strongly recommended.

Blending the correct product, price, promotion, and distribution into a meaningful, complete offering can be thought of as product positioning. The idea behind this notion is to give customer requirements a central place and to think of oneself as a client would. We must decide on the position we wish to occupy in the client's mind. Are we to be low-cost providers or known as the most reliable in the business? Are we stressing defect-free goods above all or offering service twenty-four hours per day, seven days per week? Creating images about one's product and one's total business in the minds of others is no small task. Indeed, it is a special blend of art and science.

Before we can execute a grand marketing strategy, we must establish a good marketing program, ranging from correct product positioning to the appropriate promotion. Before we can do that, we must choose the right target markets and potentially lucrative niches. And before that, we must have an understanding of the total market and its major divisions. In short, we must embark on an incisive segmentation procedure. This chapter should assist you in this all-important task. As the various sections demonstrate, there is seldom a quick, simple, or single approach. The alternatives and illustrations provided, however, should light the way toward sensible solutions.

Key Terms and Concepts

market segmentation
macro bases of segmentation
demographics
emporographics
SIC (Standard Industrial Classification) code
ISIC (International Standard Industrial
   Classification) code

intermediate bases of segmentation
micro bases of segmentation
targeting
niche marketing
product positioning

Discussion Questions

1. Should a manufacturer of "everyday industrial products," such as nails, screws, bolts, and nuts, forget about segmentation since its product line is likely to have broad appeal? Why or why not?

2. Some writers claim that entry into a particular market by an industrial company means a greater commitment than a comparable decision by a consumer goods firm. Offer reasons why this is likely to be so.

3. Exhibit 6–1 classifies users into three major categories: the private, for-profit sector; governments at all levels; and nonprofit, nongovernment institutions. Now assume that your organization is in the business of food vending to various users. Does it make any difference where you classify a state university or a veterans' hospital? Explain.

4. Some years ago, Union Carbide marketed a water-cleansing system, known as Unox, that removed contaminants from wastewater. The company classified users into three groups: urban industrial, urban municipal, and rural light industrial users. Does this threefold breakdown make sense? What might have been the basis or bases for segmenting the end users?

5. Assume you are a sales representative for an instrument company calling on technicians and scientists in industrial and government laboratories. Should you make a distinction between private and public labs? Should you study the characteristics of the people in the lab, including their attitude toward risk taking?

6. Two widely used bases for segmentation (macro level) are industry and location. Cite several examples of your own in which a combination of these two macro bases would prove to be highly useful.

7. In a book entitled *Winning and Keeping Industrial Customers,* Barbara Jackson writes about two kinds of marketing—relationship and transactional. In discussing relationship marketing, she refers to strong loyalty bonds and committed clients. In describing transactional marketing, she writes about multisourcing, switching suppliers, and choosy clientele. Does this two-way breakdown make sense to you in light of the chapter material? Explain.

8. In the book cited in the previous question, Barbara Jackson also speaks about high switching costs and high perceived exposure in the case of relationship marketing in contrast to much lower costs of switching and lower perceived exposure in the case of transactional marketing. How can a company find out if indeed clients face high or low switching costs (to another product, service, technology, vendor, and so forth)?

9. The buying center in any organization is not a physical place as much as it is a grouping of people with influence and/or decision-making power about purchases. Does it make sense to segment the managers and others belonging to such a center? Explain.

10. Two distinct markets that manufacturers have considered for a long time are the "new" or "original equipment" market versus the "existing" or "replacement" market (see, for example, Exhibit 6–2). Do you think this two-way division is applicable in any way to companies that offer services, such as repair, maintenance, and so forth?

11. The publishers of *SMM, Sales & Marketing Management* magazine, have published a *Survey of Industrial & Commercial Buying Power* based on the SIC code and geographic location (see Chapter 5). However, this survey is being discontinued, or rather being made available for a substantial fee. Would you advocate that a small company buy into this survey? Why or why not?

12. Gather articles on segmentation from two key journals: *Business Marketing* and *Industrial Marketing Management.* Look over the past three years. Do you find that the articles use single or multiple bases? Macro, intermediate, or micro bases?

Endnotes and References

1. There are several lists that suggest "validation criteria" for segmenting, some of them showing six, seven, or more criteria. These criteria are not the same as the bases used for segmenting. The criteria have to do with the more basic question: Is segmentation worthwhile, can it be done, should it be done? The bases have to do with a subsequent question: Now that we have decided to do segmentation, along what basis, dimensions, or variables should we do it?

2. The simplest way of segmenting is usually along two dimensions—for example, original equipment versus replacement (or follow-on) market, domestic versus foreign market, less developed versus industrialized nations, commodity versus specialty-oriented clientele, and so forth. But one must go deeper.

3. This quote is from J. Frederick, *Industrial Marketing* (New York: Prentice-Hall, 1934), one of the earliest books on the topic. According to F. W. Winter, "Market Segmentation: A Tactical Approach," *Business Horizons* (January–February 1984): 57–63, the acknowledged father of segmentation is Wendell Smith, who discussed the concept at length in his pioneering "Product Differentiation and Market Segmentation," *Journal of Marketing* 20 (July 1956): 3–8.

4. The two studies referred to in this paragraph are J. M. Choffray and G. L. Lillien, "Industrial Marketing Segmentation by the Structure of the Purchasing Process," *Industrial Marketing Management* 9 (1980): 331–342; and B. Donath, "What Loctite Learned from Psychographic Insights," *Business Marketing* (July 1984): 100–102.

5. Y. Wind et al., "Market-Based Guidelines for Design of Industrial Products," *Journal of Marketing* 42 (July 1978): 27–37.

6. The quote on misapplications of segmentation is from Winter, "Market Segmentation," pp. 58–59. See also the discussion on "too few versus too many segments" in B. C. Ames and J. D. Hlavacek, *Managerial Marketing for Industrial Firms* (New York: Random House, 1984), pp. 104–105, and their subsequent article, "Segmenting Industrial and High-Tech Markets," *Journal of Business Strategy* 7 (Fall 1986): 39–50. For an early review of the topic, see Y. Wind and R. Cardozo, "Industrial Market Segmentation," *Industrial Marketing Management* 3 (April 1974): 153–166. For more recent, thorough treatment, see R. E. Plank, "A Critical Review of Industrial Market Segmentation," *Industrial Marketing Management* 14 (May 1985): 79–91, and E. J. Cheron and E. J. Kleinschmidt, "A Review of Industrial Market Segmentation Research," *International Journal of Research in Marketing* 2 (1985): 101–115.

7. On this point, see K. Bertrand, "High Tech

Competition Breeds Exhibit Options," *Business Marketing* (May 1989): 70–74. Other contributions by K. Bertrand on the topic of segmentation include "Peddling the Bright Idea," *Business Marketing* (May 1989): 70–74; "Divide and Conquer," *Business Marketing* (October 1989): 49–54; and "Harvesting the Best," *Business Marketing* (October 1988): 41–50.

8. Y. Wind, "Positioning Analysis and Strategy," in G. Day et al., eds., *The Interface of Marketing and Strategy* (Greenwich, Conn.: JAI Press, 1991), pp. 387–412. For another view, see C. A. de Kluyver and D. B. Whitlark, "Benefit Segmentation for Industrial Products," *Industrial Marketing Management* 15 (1986): 273–296.

9. The term "emporographics" was created in the early 1970s by Peter M. Banting, Ph.D., Professor of Marketing, McMaster University, Hamilton, Ontario, Canada.

10. See R. Kuhn, *To Flourish Among Giants* (New York: Wiley, 1985), pp. 71–72, 87–97.

11. The latest edition is *The SIC Manual* (Washington, D.C.: USSPO for USDC, 1987). The U.S. Department of Commerce is harmonizing the SIC with its international counterpart, the ISIC. For a critical view of the SIC, see J. Couretas, "What Is Wrong with the SIC Code and Why," *Business Marketing* (December 1984): 108–115, and I. Belth, "The SIC Needs Therapy," *Business Marketing* (August 1984): 50–52. But it is "still the only game in town"—see endnote 13.

12. The U.S. Department of Commerce publishes two corrective ratios for manufacturing. See the *Census of Manufactures* (Washington, D.C.: USDC), published annually. The "specialization ratio" is the share of the primary product in the four-digit category. The "coverage ratio" compares the shipments of a four-digit industry with the total shipments of that product by all other industries. As a rule of thumb, when these ratios exceed 90 percent, the data can be considered reliable. That is because the higher the ratio, the more homogeneous the industry.

13. Gary Frazier argues in Couretas, "What Is Wrong with the SIC Code and Why," that despite shortcomings, the SIC coding system is highly useful for preliminary market research and that the federal government does a good job in this field with very limited funds.

14. The Economist Intelligence Unit publishes numerous country and product reports on a global basis from its London headquarters. For a list of all multiclient studies see *Findex* (New York: Find/SVP), published annually, which lists hundreds of titles by various market research and publishing organizations. The annual statistical yearbooks of various countries constitute a good start on such research because they often refer to public and private sources—for example, *Canada Yearbook* (Ottawa: Statistics Canada), published annually.

15. L. Hooper, "Segment Is the New Buzzword for PC Sellers," *Wall Street Journal,* June 21, 1990, pp. B-1, B-5. Similar articles can be found in *Business Week, The Economist, Fortune,* and *INC.*

16. A. C. Gross, *Computer Services* (Cleveland: Predicasts, 1983). This was a multiclient study; excerpts from it appeared in A. C. Gross, "The Information Vending Machine," *Business Horizons* (January–February 1988): 24–33.

17. P. Doyle and J. Saunders, "Market Segmentation and Positioning in Specialized Markets," *Journal of Marketing* 49 (Spring 1985): 24–32.

18. J. Breen, "The World Market for Automotive Architectural, and Industrial Paint," unpublished master's thesis, Cleveland State University, 1990, pp. 24–25.

19. The idea of a "short list" or "preferred list" has been around for many years but has been hidden or not talked about. Now that major firms such as Ford Motor and others have cut back drastically on their suppliers, but publish a list of their top performing ones, this notion is receiving more publicity and is more openly talked about. Still, some companies will not admit to it. Other firms write

"technical specs" so only a few vendors can qualify.

20. See the various endnotes in Chapter 8. See also W. Davidow, *Marketing High Technology* (New York: Free Press, 1986); F. A. Johne, "Segmenting High Technology Adopters," *Industrial Marketing Management* 13 (1984): 59–63; and R. D. Hof, "Inside Intel," *Business Week,* June 1, 1992, pp. 86–94.

21. "Some Points Concerning Optomechanics," *The Quarterly Survey of Japanese Finance and Industry* (published by the Industrial Bank of Japan, Tokyo and New York), 4th quarter, 1985, p. 10.

22. R. Erickson and A. Gross, "Generalizing Industrial Buying: A Longitudinal Study," *Industrial Marketing Management* 9 (July 1980): 253–265. This study has been duplicated for three other English-speaking nations; see P. Banting et al., "Similarities in Industrial Procurement Across Four Countries," *Industrial Marketing Management* 14 (May 1985): 133–144.

23. P. M. Banting, "Customer Service in Industrial Marketing: A Comparative Study," *European Journal of Marketing* 3 (1976): 136–145. See also G. E. Kiser and C. P. Rao, "Important Vendor Factors in Industrial and Hospital Organizations," *Industrial Marketing Management* 6 (August 1977): 289–296, and G. R. Banville and R. J. Dornoff, "Industrial Source Selection Behavior," *Industrial Marketing Management* 3 (August 1973): 251–260.

24. A. C. Gross, "The Information Vending Machine."

25. The erosion of loyalty bonds has been observed in various industries, but especially in those that are experiencing mature products—for example, in the case of chemical commodities. This portion is based in part on extended discussions with W. T. Sullivan, President Emeritus, Mogul Corporation, Chagrin Falls, Ohio, 1987–1988. On the matter of high-tech firms and suppliers, the evidence is based in part on literature cited in Chapter 8 and extended discussions with L. G. Polgar, Vice President, Marketing, Bertram Laboratories, North Plainfield, New Jersey, 1990–1991.

26. Granted that the various members of the buying center will talk to each other, this still does not negate the principle of stressing the "right" benefit to the "right" parties. This is not unethical; indeed, it is considered proper. What would be unethical is to make claims for benefits that do not exist or to make promises for service aspects that cannot be delivered.

27. See T. Bonoma and B. Shapiro, *Segmenting the Industrial Market* (Lexington, Mass.: Lexington Books, 1983) and their article, "How to Segment Industrial Markets," *Harvard Business Review* (May–June 1984): 104–110; Y. Wind et al., "Industrial Product Diffusion by Market Segment," *Industrial Marketing Management* 11 (1982): 1–8; S. Lynn, "Segmenting a Business Market for a Professional Service," *Industrial Marketing Management* 15 (1986): 13–21; and N. C. Campbell and M. T. Cunningham, "Customer Analysis for Strategic Development in Industrial Markets," *Strategic Management Journal* 4 (October 1983): 369–380.

28. N. J. Church and R. McTavish, "Segment Buyer Sophistication to Reach Industrial Markets Efficiently," *Marketing News,* September 16, 1983, p. 8. See also S. A. Sinclair and E. C. Stalling, "How to Identify Differences Between Market Segments with Attribute Analysis," *Industrial Marketing Management* 19 (May 1990): 141–148.

29. See R. T. Moriarty and D. J. Reibstein, *Benefit Segmentation: An Industrial Application, Report #82-1109* (Boston: Marketing Science Institute, 1982) and R. T. Moriarty, *Industrial Buying Behavior* (Lexington, Mass.: Lexington Books, 1983).

30. Donath, "What Loctite Learned from Psychographic Insights," and N. H. Giragosian, "A Case of Commercial Development: Loctite," *Chemtech* (October 1980): 604–609.

31. H. Brown et al., "Requirements Driven Market Segmentation," *Industrial Marketing Management* 18 (May 1989): 105–117.

32. E. Raymond Corey, *Industrial Marketing,* 4th ed. (Englewood Cliffs, N.J.: Prentice-Hall, 1991), pp. 119–120, 158–163. See also his earlier article, "Key Options in Market Selection and Product Planning," *Harvard Business Review* (September–October 1975): 119–128.

33. A. L. Stern, "In Search of Micro Niches," *Business Month* (July 1989): 60–63. See also J. F. Barone, "Niche Marketing," *Business Marketing* (November 1984): 56–62.

34. W. Davidow and B. Uttal, "Service Companies: Focus or Falter," *Harvard Business Review* (July–August 1989): 77–85; and W. Davidow, "The Ultimate Marketing Weapon," *Business Marketing* (October 1989): 56–64.

35. S. Alexander, "Small Firm's Single-Coast Strategy Delivers the Goods," *Wall Street Journal,* March 6, 1991, p. B2. The *Wall Street Journal* carries many such stories, usually on pages B1 and B2. For other stories, see *INC.* and *Venture* magazine issues (the latter journal has ceased publication recently).

36. Gross, *Computer Services.*

37. Gross, "The Information Vending Machine."

7

COMPETITION AND COOPERATION IN BUSINESS MARKETS

CHAPTER OUTLINE

- To analyze the nature of competition in a historical-economic setting and from a modern business-marketing viewpoint

- To examine the alternatives to competition, especially voluntary cooperation, such as alliances, partnerships, and consortia

- To study the basic forces driving competition in an industry: existing and new rivals, threat of substitutes, and threat of integration

- To analyze competitive behavior in action and to understand the major categories of competitive strategies and tactics

- To show how performance is measured in the marketplace and to highlight the importance of market share

- To illustrate the nature of competition in domestic and international markets and to discuss competition in specific mature and emerging U.S. industries

To compete is to strive, to contend, to vie. As individuals, we compete in sports, in social activities, and in politics, with the prize being a trophy, acceptance by peers, and being elected to an office. Motives here range from self-esteem to challenges issued by others. In the modern industrial world, we witness competition among individuals as well as companies, industries, regions, and nations. Individual, corporate, or public awards are handed out. These range from "executive of the year" to "best exhibit at the trade show" and from "top-ranked firm by return on sales" to "most friendly (translation: low tax) state government." Motives here are diverse, too. Generally, the rewards are net income, market share, growth in sales, and enhanced status.[1]

Although competition is the dominant mode among enterprises, the idea of cooperation is taking hold in such forms as joint ventures, strategic alliances, franchising, consortia, and coalitions. These cooperative arrangements can vary in duration and substance. Some are for a short-term, single venture; others require multi-year contracts and details on who will do what. Cooperation may work for those on the inside, but rivalry becomes keen against outsiders. In some instances, however, all participants may join in—for example, in a research consortium. Internationally, we hear of reciprocity, "managed trade," and "orderly marketing arrangements," which come close to the idea of cartelization, price fixing, or monopoly. Some businesses truly prefer no competitors at all, but such fortresses cannot be sustained for any length of time.[2]

THE ARENA OF COMPETITION AND COOPERATION

Where does competition really take place? It can be near and far, but in today's world, businesses must watch for rivals across the street *and* across the ocean. For

BUSINESS MARKETING IN PRACTICE

The Parable of the Playground by the Seashore

Surely you have noticed the ebb and flow of the tide at the seashore. Forever changing, the waves form new sand dunes, destroy old ones. Life at the edge of the ocean is never dull. The same is true for the way the children play. Some go off by themselves; others form groups and build a sandcastle. Then two individuals or two teams take on each other: Who can build the biggest and best-looking sand sculpture? When the creativity is exhausted, they may demolish the sandcastle and start throwing the sand at each other.

Meanwhile the older children are playing beach volleyball. They form teams and compete against each other. A bunch of new children may show up and challenge those playing. A bully or a gang may come along and issue commands to those already on the beach. A fight may ensue, or one side may yield and a compromise is worked out. The seashore has a life of its own; and so does the play or sports activity by the shoreline. Is there a pattern?

What we observe about all the activities is that change occurs all the time. We also note that both collaboration and competition exist. When games are played, we really need to know only three things:

First, what game are we playing? Is it an activity for individuals or for teams? Is it a friendly game, or have we been challenged by outsiders? Will playing this game have any consequence later on for friendship?

Second, what rules are we playing by? For example, in a pickup game with ball and bat, are we going to play baseball, softball, or cricket? In a pickup game with a football, will it be U.S. rules, Australian rules, or perhaps rugby? Is it just "kid stuff" (touch football), or is the tackling for real?

Third, who is keeping score and how seriously? Is it just the participants, or is there an impartial referee or umpire? If there is an independent rulekeeper, can that person mete out a penalty, and if so, will it be observed?

When we know these three conditions (often we know them even without discussing them), the game takes place. Tomorrow, however, there may be new games, new rules, and new rulekeepers. The fun goes on, but in a different direction.

Source: Based on conversations with the late Samuel Wolpert of Cleveland, Ohio.

two truck repair stops across from each other on a highway, the competition appears to be local. Medium-sized chemical firms seek customers in the same region, while large machine tool makers wage rivalry across the Pacific and the Atlantic oceans. However, the situation in each case can change quickly. The truck repair firms may go to national operations or even enter foreign markets. At the same time, the machine tool firms may withdraw from certain countries if rivalry gets too intense and if sales show a sharp decline. Every day in every field is a new day of reassessment.

A few giant firms enter a market only if they can be dominant. Reportedly, General Electric wishes to be a market leader or hold the number two or number three position in market share. If it cannot do so, it will withdraw from that field. But many firms are content with being number five or even number ten; even a

15 percent market share may be desirable and rewarding. Other alternatives include finding small pockets of profitability. This means carving out niches, going after narrow segments. Companies can enter related fields where rivalry is less intense, such as maintenance and repair as opposed to manufacturing. A highly creative solution is to "invent" a new industry.[3]

Just how is it possible to succeed? This, of course, depends on the definition of success and on circumstances. But progressive firms grab the initiative. They change the game or the rules of the game; they reclassify themselves or other companies. Consider the computer hardware industry over the past twenty years. The technology changed rapidly, with vast computing power becoming available in small, desktop units. At the same time, it also became desirable for small units to communicate with each other in a network. The overall result was the realignment of a major industry in terms of key product lines. The four waves of growth in computer hardware are illustrated in Exhibit 7–1. What can companies do in such a situation?

For an innovative, medium-sized electronics firm such as Sun Microsystems it would have been foolish to chase rainbows. It could not and should not compete directly with IBM, Cray, and Fujitsu in large computer mainframes or with Apple, Compaq, and Dell in small computers, which have almost become a commodity. Instead, Sun Microsystems chose to emphasize the latest technology and the corresponding product line. Sun Microsystems is now heavily committed to

EXHIBIT 7–1 Four Waves of Growth in Computers

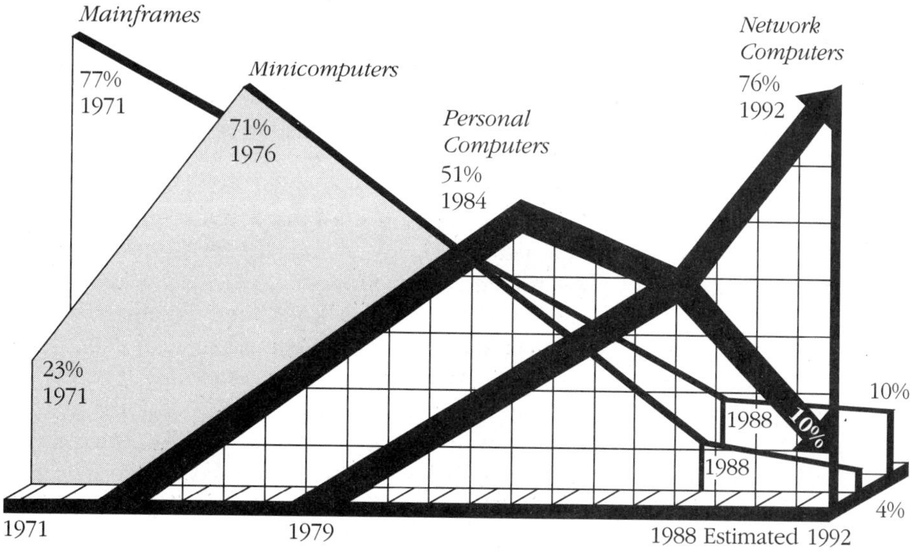

Source: S. Gannes, "IBM and DEC Take on the Little Guys," *Fortune,* October 10, 1988, p. 108.

workstations—that is, network computers. In effect, it redefined the industry and how computers are used. It is saying, let's connect the small computers; its slogan is, "the network is the system." As shown in Exhibit 7–2, Sun Microsystems has done very well. While it is not number one overall in total computer hardware, it is currently number one in its chosen line, namely workstation installations.

Meanwhile, some big computer makers entered into collaborative agreements, known as strategic alliances. A good example is IBM, which for many years chose to conduct its business in a centralized fashion and to go it alone. Now it is transforming itself by giving more autonomy to its divisions. But even more important, it has formed alliances with many small firms along technical, marketing, and financial lines. In another case, Digital Equipment Company (DEC) forged a cross-licensing exchange with Cray Research at the "high end of computing." DEC also signed cooperative agreements with Apple, Compaq, Olivetti, and Tandy to facilitate networking and to avoid bruising duplicate efforts in small computers. But it also acquired a product line from Philips to round out its offerings and to enhance its European market position.

Consider now an entirely different industry, that of making and marketing aircraft. Here we can identify four product families: (1) military planes, made by Northrop, Lockheed, and a few non–U.S. firms; (2) large civilian aircraft, made by Boeing and McDonnell Douglas of the United States and Airbus, a European consortium; (3) executive and commuter aircraft, made by Canadair, Embraer of Brazil, Gulfstream, and so forth; and (4) small units, such as those made by Cessna and Piper. Boeing and Cessna are in the same industry, but they are not direct rivals, having chosen different lines of business. It would make no sense for either to invade the other's turf. However, Cessna appears to be moving upstream, into executive aircraft.[4]

There is more to this industry than segmentation by purpose (civilian versus military) and the configuration of aircraft (by number of seats, engines, or flying range). The making of large civilian aircraft has become so costly and so complex that Boeing is finding Japanese partners, a step unimaginable just a few years ago. In a similar fashion, McDonnell Douglas is proposing to link up with Taiwanese companies. Indeed, many large firms are embarked on several joint ventures, as shown in Exhibit 7–3. Note the collaboration across different continents. There are alliances in components too; jet engine makers General Electric (U.S.) and Snecma (France) collaborated for about twenty years. Thus cooperation flourishes side by side with competition, especially when the strengths of the partners complement each other. Participants must decide in what segments they should compete, collaborate, or possibly do both.

Competitive and cooperative forces operate not just in the marketing of high-ticket items, such as aircraft or computers, but also in the case of low-cost goods and services. Distributors of small replacement parts compete aggressively in seeking the business from truck repair shops across vast distances. Copy centers go after corporate and institutional accounts, usually in a metropolitan area. Architectural and engineering design firms often submit competitive bids, but they may also combine with others. For example, the Austin Company (U.S.) found it wise to line up Japanese partners in bidding on a new airport near Tokyo.

EXHIBIT 7–2   Ranking of Major Computer Companies by Market Share in Selected Categories of Computer Hardware, at the Start of the 1990s

Part A: The Top 10 in Mainframes (large-scale systems)

Company	Nationality	Market Share
IBM	United States	44.4%
Fujitsu	Japan	11.6
Hitachi	Japan	11.1
NEC	Japan	8.5
Amdahl	United States	5.2
Unisys	United States	4.3
Groupe Bull	France	3.0
Cray	United States	2.2
Siemens	Germany	2.2
STC	United Kingdom	1.7

Part B: The Top 10 in Personal Computers (PCs)

Company	Nationality	Market Share
IBM	United States	22.3%
Apple	United States	9.6
NEC	Japan	8.3
Compaq	United States	7.7
Groupe Bull	France	4.5
Olivetti	Italy	4.1
Toshiba	Japan	3.6
Tandy	United States	3.6
Unisys	United States	3.5
Fujitsu	Japan	2.3

Part C: The Top 10 in Workstations

Company	Nationality	Market Share
Sun Microsystems	United States	21.3%
Digital Equipment	United States	17.6
Hewlett Packard	United States	12.2
Matsushita	Japan	12.2
IBM	United States	8.7
C. Itoh	Japan	6.9
Xerox	United States	4.8
Intergraph	United States	3.8
Hitachi	Japan	2.7
STC	United Kingdom	1.7

Source: Reprinted with permission of *Datamation* Magazine, June 15, 1990 © by Cahners Publishing Company.

EXHIBIT 7–3   Major International Cooperative Ventures in the Aircraft Industry

Venture	Partners	Countries	Share	Products
Airbus Industrie	Aerospatiale	France	38%	Wide-body, medium-haul,
	Deutsche Airbus	Germany	38	twin-engine aircraft (A300,
	British Aerospace	United Kingdom	20	A310, A320, etc.)
	CASA	Spain	4	
Boeing-Japan	Boeing	United States	75	Airframe, fuselage panels,
	JADC	Japan	25	wings, etc., on 7J7 program
CFM International	General Electric	United States	50	High-bypass, turbo-fan engines
	Snecma	France	50	in low-thrust market segment
International Aero	Pratt & Whitney	United States	30	High-bypass, turbo-fan engines
Engines	Rolls-Royce	United Kingdom	30	in the 25,000-lb. thrust (high-
	Japan Aero Engines	Japan	20	thrust) market segment
	MTU	Germany	12	
	Fiat	Italy	8	

Source: Reprinted with permission of Lexington Books, an imprint of Macmillan, Inc., from *Cooperative Strategies in International Business* by Farok J. Contractor and Peter Lorange, editors. Copyright © 1988 by Lexington Books.

A Historical-Economic View of Competition

The economic ideas of the eighteenth and nineteenth centuries (such as Adam Smith's "invisible hand" and Alfred Marshall's "relevant market") still have an impact on both corporate decisions and public policy measures. The economists thought that competition was highly desirable because it resulted in the lowest possible costs to customers. Governments, they said, should only prevent collusion and enforce regulations. Others argued later, however, that competition encouraged poor product quality, lower service levels, business failures, unsafe working conditions, and pollution. They noted too that intense rivalry meant that a few powerful firms could eliminate smaller ones, then raise prices or divide market shares.

Traditionally, economic analysis always focused on three distinct aspects of competition in an industry, with emphasis on how rivals related to each other and their customers.

- *Structure:* What is the market share of competitors? How high are entry barriers?

- *Conduct:* Is there any evidence of coercive pricing, misleading promotion, and so forth?

- *Performance:* Are operations efficient? How high are profit levels?

This view of competition can be dynamic, but in practice the analysis often took place at a given point of time. As a result, it yielded an imperfect view of the real world wherein new rivals, substitute goods, the bargaining power of suppliers and customers, and active government policy were not accounted for. Yet these factors continuously alter the competitive and cooperative landscape.[5]

The Modern Business View of Competition

Many business executives subscribe to the economists' view that looking at structure, conduct, and performance in a given industry is important, but they consider it only a first step. Managers do not wish to debate endlessly whether barriers to entry are too high, too low, or just right. What they wish to focus on is the dynamic nature of the marketplace: Who is entering, who is leaving? What peripheral segments can we move into or out of quickly? What about potential rivals from other industries? What about the bargaining power of suppliers and customers who can also drive us out of business? What substitute goods and services can drastically change the industry? These aspects, applicable to any industry, are displayed in graphic form in Exhibit 7–4; they form the basis for looking at competition in today's world.[6]

The schematic shown in the exhibit assumes that entry barriers in industries are not insurmountable and that technology offers substitutes. Another assumption is that restrictive regulations would be more harmful than beneficial, although some government regulation (against collusion, fraud, and selling below cost to drive out rivals) is acceptable. In this scenario, customer choice still reigns supreme, driving out inefficient or predatory producers. Shoddy products, pollution, and worker exploitation are still possible in this model. But a validation of this view of competition can be seen in the recent privatization of many state enterprises in Europe, Asia, and Latin America. Although some of the excesses of capitalism are bound to occur, they are less repulsive than the stifling nature of state bureaucracies.[7]

COMPETITIVE FORCES AND THEIR DETERMINANTS

As shown in Exhibit 7–4, five major forces drive competition: rivalry between existing competitors, the threat of new entrants to a market, the bargaining power of suppliers, the bargaining power of buyers, and the threat of substitute products or services. Each of these forces has specific applications cited for industries that market goods and services to businesses and institutions. The exhibit shows that competition is much more than rivalry among existing firms in an industry. It is that, but it is much more. Four other major forces also come into play, and they can move in both directions. The diagram, however, does not show that these forces can interact. For example, suppliers may enter an industry with technical substitutes. Finally, the exhibit says nothing about the positive or negative role that governments and other institutions can and do play.[8]

EXHIBIT 7–4   Key Forces Driving Industry Competition

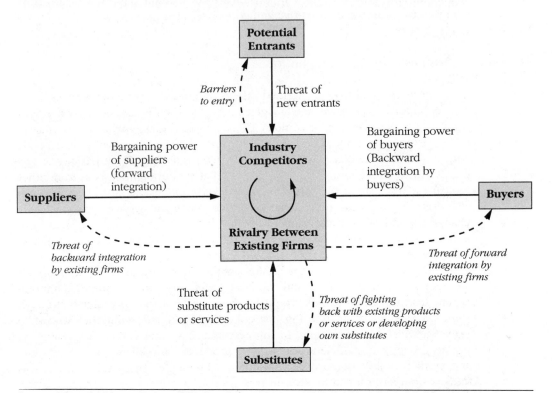

Source: Adapted with permission of The Free Press, a Division of Macmillan, Inc., from *Competitive Advantage: Creating and Sustaining Superior Performance* by Michael E. Porter. Copyright © 1989 by The Free Press. (Dotted lines and terms have been added to indicate how existing rivals in center can fight back.)

Existing Rivalry

Many factors influence how intense rivalry is among existing competitors, but the key determinant is the growth of the industry. During a fast-growth era, even weak rivals are accommodated; during years of little growth or decline, there is bound to be intense battle for market share. Other factors influencing existing rivalry are production capacity, diversity of competitors, variety of product line, switching costs of clients, and corporate commitments.

Consider the key factor first, that of growth, in the context of two different industries: steel and electronics. We can certainly characterize the former as a slow- or no-growth sector and the latter as a near-boom situation. Steelmaking is not in as good a shape as electronics, judging by various global or national market and economic indicators. Further analysis, however, reveals silver linings for steelmakers and some clouds for electronics firms. For example, some minimills are expanding, having found buyers for their narrower product lines, whereas sales of semiconductors and computers have slowed down. So although the growth issue is important, companies can prosper even in mature sectors by defining or redefining the industry they are in. They can also choose customer segments they wish to serve with specialized offerings.[9]

Let's continue the contrast between the steel companies and the electronics firms. Steel is bulky and costly to store, and it is regarded as a commodity. Although there is value added, it is not very high, except for specialty steel. There is much overcapacity, despite the fact that major producers have closed several large steel mills. In contrast, semiconductors represent much value added; storage costs are not a major burden; and capacity can be readily adjusted. Distinct designs are possible as in the case of standard versus application-specific chips. There are even brand wars between Intel and Motorola, with numbers taking the place of brand names. Companies have become more aggressive as well as more flexible.[10]

The remaining determinants reflect a variety of corporate factors in the industry. These range from corporate identity to so-called exit barriers. In the steel industry, companies that retained their original names, such as Armco, Bethlehem Steel, and Inland Steel have an advantage over those that switched to conglomerate status, such as USX (formerly U.S. Steel) and LTV (which absorbed Republic Steel and Jones & Laughlin). Ryerson Steel, a steel distributor, and Nucor, an aggressive minimill, emphasize their dedication to customizing and service rather than just offering slabs of steel. Exit barriers are quite real, ranging from having specialized assets to labor contracts and other obligations that must be honored. These come into play before a plant can be shut down. But the hope that business will improve governs many participants in steel and even electronics. For example, Steve Jobs, who now heads up Next Computer, is struggling to emulate his original success at Apple. Many software firms are hanging on despite losses; they may not be the next Microsoft or Lotus, but they hope to be another Borland or Novell.[11]

New Entrants

The most direct threat to existing rivals comes from business units that wish to participate in sales and profits in an industry. New rivals may come from the domestic or the foreign front and from adjacent or unrelated industries. Such newcomers are seldom welcome, yet they often have a beneficial impact. They stir up the existing body of competitors, spur innovation, bring lower prices, and offer better service to customers. Emerging industries are more likely to be invaded, because of the potential for sales and profits. Mature industries are more likely to have entrenched firms with significant market shares and loyalty from their customers. Although the ties that bind vendor and client can be strong, commitments come under strain when new entrants offer price advantages or when long-trusted sales representatives quit or retire.

The major barriers to new entrants are cost differentials, product differentiation, government policy, and possible retaliation by those already in the industry.

Studies conducted during 1950–1990 in industrialized Western nations show that industries have widely divergent barriers to entry; some are high and some are low. As a result, some industries are still highly concentrated with established players; others have fragmented greatly. Much investment is required to enter capital-intensive industries, such as machinery, utilities, and transportation, compared with business services and wholesale trade. As a general rule, product or service differentiation poses a greater barrier to new entrants than do cost disadvantages. Government policy can also assist or hinder the entry of new firms through contract awards, antitrust policy, enforcement measures, and subsidies. New entrants should expect retaliation; for example, large steel mills are now fighting back against the upstart minimills.[12]

Consider now the global electronics market, in which U.S., Japanese, and European companies participate. Subsectors of this industry range from the small chips to the equipment used to make these semiconductors, from personal computers to telecommunication software. Aggressive entry by Japanese firms has crowded out both U.S. and European companies in many sectors, as can be seen in Exhibit 7–5.[13] There is some resurgence now in both the United States and Europe in semiconductors and in other electronics goods, including computers. This is not because the firms in the electronics industry of Japan became less aggressive. Rather, other factors came into play, ranging from innovation to encouragement of partnerships. Outside political pressure put on the Japanese government-industry alliance also had an impact. Finally, imaginative firms can redefine an industry and resegment markets. We noted this in the case of Sun Microsystems earlier. It is also true for progressive software firms, such as Novell and Banyan, that seek to interconnect small and large networks.[14]

Power of Suppliers and Buyers: The Threat of Integration

In transforming products and services from a lower to higher value stage, the two important contacts for any firm are its suppliers and its clients. Under ordinary circumstances, both are looked upon as valuable partners. But what happens when organizations are threatened by their customers or by their suppliers? This is not unusual. Customers may decide to perform an operation or produce a good themselves; we then speak of clients doing **backward integration**. In a similar way, suppliers can exercise their economic clout and carry out the job; in this case suppliers do **forward integration**. Conversely, existing firms can and do contemplate invading the realm of their suppliers and customers by integrating backward or forward. Integration, in short, is always a double-edged sword. Factors that influence integration in either direction include cost and profit considerations, bargaining power, price sensitivity, corporate resources, and the nature and volume of business with suppliers and clients. Integration does not always have to take place; threat of action (i.e., bargaining power) may be enough to achieve a desired goal.

A well-known example of customer power is the attempt of General Motors to replace the robots used in its car assembly. In truck and car manufacturing,

EXHIBIT 7-5   Rankings in the Semiconductor Industry, Worldwide, 1980s.

Part A: Top Worldwide Semiconductor Manufacturers

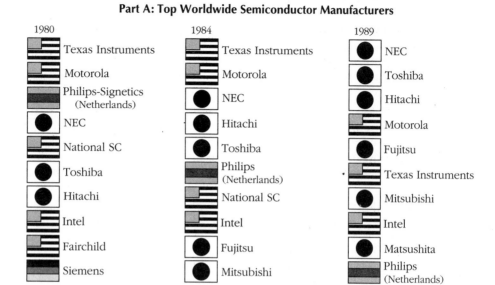

Source: Dataquest, Inc.

Part B: Top Worldwide Semiconductor Equipment Manufacturers

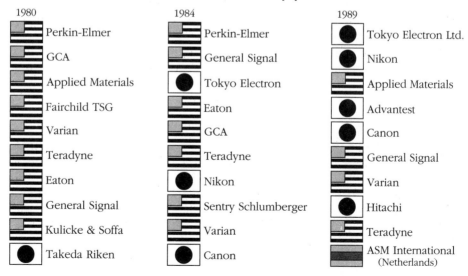

Source: VLSI Research Inc.

Source: Adapted with permission of The Free Press, a Division of Macmillan, Inc., from *Cracking the Japanese Market: Strategies for Success in the New Global Economy* by James C. Morgan and J. Jeffrey Morgan. Copyright © 1991 by The Free Press.

robots function in a "dedicated" or "specific application" mode. Who knows this mode better than the assembler? So GM decided to stop buying robotic equipment from vendors and contemplated making its own. However, GM knew that its expertise was not in robotics, so it formed a joint venture with Fujitsu. The new firm, called GMF, supplied both parent companies with robots and eventually other corporations as well. This way, GMF had both a captive, in-house market and an outside market.[15]

Other examples of customer power range from oilfield operations to metal fabrication. In such cases, manufacturers acquire raw material vendors to assure themselves of steady sources of crude oil, coal, iron ore, or minerals. However, the expertise to run such operations may be lacking. BHP, a very large Australian resource firm, has done a good job of finding supplies and acquiring suppliers. But some U.S. firms became disillusioned and divested themselves of raw material suppliers because they lacked the core competency in mining. With emphasis on recycling in the 1990s, many manufacturers see recycled materials as an attractive possibility and as a viable substitute for investing in raw material supplies.

Supplier power can and does occur in many industries. The chemical industries of North America, Western Europe, and Japan provide a major illustration of such action. In the past, the large producers supplied the basic chemicals to the so-called formulators. Then they realized that lucrative opportunities exist in compounding chemical specialties. Therefore, such U.S. giants as Du Pont, Dow, and Monsanto started to make and market their own industrial specialty chemicals. They even expanded their operations into chemicals intended for household use, such as antifreeze and plastic wrap. In the United Kingdom, a British maker of pine gum resins became a formulator of paper and chemical specialties. Its forward integration paid off because it correctly identified the need for new specialty chemicals in growing markets.[16]

The key reason for suppliers exerting their power and doing some forward integration is potential sales and profit growth. Another consideration is to depend less on a few large clients. Yet another factor is the need for more market information. Companies wish to learn more quickly and more directly about the preferences of the ultimate users of their product. That way they can do a better job of providing the optimal product mix and services. In the case of two large Canadian firms, Genstar integrated forward from building materials into construction of industrial buildings and even residential housing, whereas Indal moved from metal rolling into fabrication. Both firms placed emphasis on gaining early market information.[17] Much danger exists, however, in entering fields in which a firm has no expertise and no established reputation.

Substitutes: New Products and Processes

Technology offers the most interesting rivalry possibilities in the form of **substitutes**: new goods, alternate processes, and improved services. Although new technology can be absorbed by existing firms, more frequently it is the outsiders who adopt it and use it as a wedge for entering a field of industrial activity. As a general rule, the substitute material or operation is subjected to intense scrutiny in terms of cost/benefit analysis, usually along physical, chemical, or engineering dimensions and along bureaucratic requirements. For example, in the case of a new material: Will its strength and performance characteristics be sufficient? Can it meet existing government regulations or industry association standards? How will buyers react to switching costs? There is bound to be resistance if the new items cannot meet such objections. Purchase price, operating costs, and the cost of switchover must all be considered.

The substitution battle is waged in many industries, but it is especially intense in the case of packaging materials. Environmental factors play a major role, as do transportation and storage requirements. Consider, for example, beverage containers. What is the best way to bring beer, wine, soft drinks, juice, and milk to households? What do supermarkets and other outlets demand? What stacking requirements do warehouse and transport firms insist on? Makers of glass, metal, plastic, and paper containers must appeal to the beverage makers, while keeping in mind distributors and households. The battle of beverage containers during the 1980s is documented in Exhibit 7–6. Metal can makers stress advantages such as reduced weight of lighter cans, savings in storage, and ease of stacking. Glass manufacturers point to reusable or returnable bottles and stress the visibility factor. Plastic bottle makers stress the shatterproof features, whereas aseptic packagers emphasize portability and environmental considerations.[18]

Other industries offer equally interesting examples of substitution. In tire manufacturing, nylon replaced rayon. Now polyester, glass, and steel are used to reinforce tires. In the case of textile materials, synthetics made clear inroads at the expense of natural fibers, though the latter are fighting back. The cotton and wool industry groups are not standing idly by as the polyester and cellulosic fibers invade. The historical evidence is illustrated in Exhibit 7–7. In another field, the family of reinforced plastics (also known as composites) is making major gains at

EXHIBIT 7–6   Use of Different Materials for Beverage Containers

Material	1982	1988	1993*	2000*
Metal (aluminum, steel)	49.7%	52.2%	50.0%	47.7%
Glass	25.5	21.5	19.8	17.7
Paper	17.8	14.2	13.7	13.0
Plastic	7.0	10.0	12.9	16.9
Aseptic	negligible	2.1	3.6	4.7
Total: %	100.	100.	100.	100.
billion units	129.3	165.2	177.3	196.1

*estimate

Source: L. A. Weisenbach, *Beverage Containers, Industry Study #272* (Cleveland: The Freedonia Group, 1989), p. 64. Used with permission.

EXHIBIT 7–7   Consumption of Natural and Synthetic Fibers, United States, 1955–1990 (mill consumption)

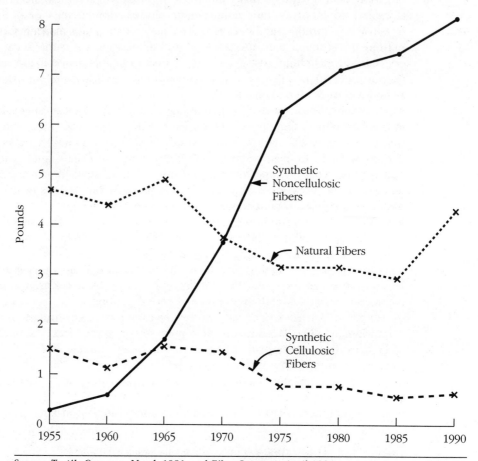

Source: *Textile Organon,* March 1981, and *Fiber Organon,* April 1991.

the expense of metals. The composites provide incredible strength and durability and are especially valued in such demanding applications as high-speed aircraft, helicopters, and space vehicles. Composites now enjoy many other applications, beyond aircraft and aerospace; they are utilized increasingly in gears, pistons, boats, and racing cars.[19]

COOPERATION: AN ALTERNATIVE TO COMPETITION

Competitive activities are truly ingrained in modern life, ranging from sports to education, from the entertainment world to religious organizations. But it is in the economic sphere that the competitive forces are most visible. Yet viable alternatives to rivalry do exist in all areas, including the industrial world. Cooperative and collaborative linkages are becoming more popular among businesses in the 1990s. Cooperation is a formal or informal partnership between two or more enterprises to work together, usually on a specified project for a specified period. Various voluntary forms and mandated forms of collaboration are feasible. Cooperation occurs most frequently when two firms have complementary strengths to offer each other. Collaboration among many firms happens usually when resources are to be preserved.

Cooperating or partnering between two firms can create several economic benefits: access to new markets or different channels; process innovations; shorter lead times for product development; cost savings; and improved market feedback. We already cited examples of such benefits resulting from partnerships in the aircraft and computer industries. Natural resources are often finite, so an orderly agreement on dealing with scarce supplies may prove acceptable to all. This can apply to rare minerals, air traffic space, or radio frequencies. Allocation may be made by the parties involved, or government may play a role. Other resources, such as skilled labor, technical know-how, and capital requirements may also be lacking in some enterprises. Rather than make major expenditures to acquire these or to have a supplier furnish them, firms may enter into a temporary collaborative arrangement.[20]

Voluntary Cooperation

There are two different styles of **voluntary cooperation** among business firms. **Formal cooperation** can take several forms; most popular are licensing, franchising, and joint ventures. These forms have a tradition of many decades, especially in international business. They are used when the parties wish to demonstrate to outsiders, including clients and competitors, that they joined forces. There are announcements and specific contractual arrangements. **Informal cooperation** takes the form of alliances, partnerships, coalitions, and consortia. Such arrangements are relatively new but are growing rather rapidly, especially in international settings. They are used when the partners want little visibility or publicity. There may not even be a written agreement, especially if a trial period is contemplated. Common to both types is the expectation that the mutual assistance pact will be of benefit to both (or all) parties involved.[21]

Licensing calls for the transfer of technical ideas from one business entity to another. A license is a permit to use a patent or nonpatentable ideas in exchange for specific lump sum payments called fees or royalties. For example, some years ago, Eaton (U.S.) gave a license to a maker of material handling equipment in Scotland (U.K.) to use its forklift patents. Eaton realized that it could be putting the other firm into competition with itself, but the fees constituted steady income over several years. To protect itself, Eaton may not have offered its latest technology, or it could have included a noncompetition clause. Finally, Eaton may have had an

BUSINESS MARKETING IN PRACTICE ▬▬▬▬▬▬▬▬▬▬▬

When Competitors Agree to Cooperate

Cooperative arrangements exist among competitors in business markets. There is a rough analogy with consumer goods markets in which a major tire maker, such as Goodyear, sells tires under its own brand name but also manufactures tires for sale by independent merchants that are then sold using a private or dealer brand. Another rough analogy is when Perrier uses Pepsi's distribution network in the United States to market mineral water, and Pepsi utilizes the Perrier distribution network in France to sell its soft drinks.

A good example of collaboration of this sort in industrial markets occurs in semiconductors. There is a long manufacturing chain in this instance, starting with crystal ingots that are processed into polished wafers. The wafers are then used by chip makers to fabricate integrated circuits and transistors. The overall process is highly complex and technical.

Wacker is a German manufacturer of both semiconductor crystal ingots and polished wafers. In addition to selling its final-stage product, it also sells ingots to a competitor, Bertram Laboratories of the United States. Bertram processes the ingots into wafers that it sells in competition with Wacker's finished products. This is done with the full knowledge and the assent of both parties.

Despite the fact that Wacker and Bertram compete in the wafer segment, each party benefits from the cooperation. This is so because the two firms have different research and manufacturing capabilities, which are especially evident in the final-stage processing. The other factor that permits the existence of the arrangement is that the two companies have access to distinct client bases as a result of established customer relationships (known also as loyalty bonds). In effect, the two have carried out a segmentation process and reached different target markets. The end result is that both Wacker and Bertram obtain greater market share than would be feasible in the absence of cooperation.

Source: Interview in January 1992 with Dr. Leslie G. Polgar, Vice President Marketing, Bertram Laboratories USA, Somerville, New Jersey.

---

option with the Scottish firm for a more full-fledged partnering later on, such as a joint venture.[22]

Franchising has been popular for many years among companies marketing consumer goods and services, but it is now used increasingly in selected industrial sectors. The key is to share the corporate name and the financial power of a well-established organization with small entrepreneurs who bring their knowledge of local conditions to the undertaking. Opportunities range from office services to pollution control equipment. Examples of franchisers are AlphaGraphics and Kinko in copying and printing, Businessland and Computerland in distribution of small computers, and Hotsy in pressure washer and heater installations.

The traditional **joint venture** represents a formal agreement to cooperate. Usually two partners join forces, creating a third company in which they hold shares on a fifty-fifty, seventy-thirty, or some other basis. Joint ventures are like human marriages; some endure, some end quickly. Average duration is only about three to five years. Surveys report failure rates from 30 to 70 percent of joint ventures studied; put differently, about half of them succeed. Joint ventures are more successful when partners are from similar corporate cultures and have related markets, products, and technologies. Greatest relative successes are reported in petrochemicals, pharmaceuticals, and metals fabrication. When a joint venture is disbanded, it should not be considered a failure; it may have been the right choice at the start and for the duration as well.

Partners in joint ventures have high hopes of achieving both cost and risk reduction, blocking competition, complementing each other's technology, overcoming trade barriers, or achieving some form of integration. With such high hopes and with thorough preparation, why should joint ventures last only for a few years? Exhibit 7–8 lists some common mistakes in joint ventures, including the causes and symptoms of their demise. Clearly, many factors are at work. What happens to the joint ventures when they are terminated? Most frequently, one partner assumes full ownership, and the other bows out. New joint ventures arise regularly, both in domestic and foreign markets in many industries. Giant AT&T tried hooking up with the Dutch giant Philips and with Olivetti of Italy. Japanese, European, and U.S. firms are now pursuing Russian partners.[23]

EXHIBIT 7–8 Common Mistakes in Joint Ventures

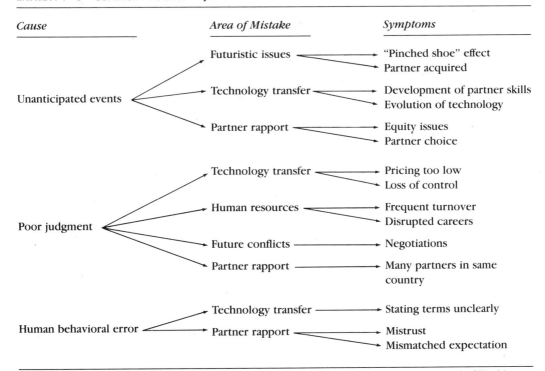

Cause	Area of Mistake	Symptoms
Unanticipated events	Futuristic issues	"Pinched shoe" effect / Partner acquired
	Technology transfer	Development of partner skills / Evolution of technology
	Partner rapport	Equity issues / Partner choice
Poor judgment	Technology transfer	Pricing too low / Loss of control
	Human resources	Frequent turnover / Disrupted careers
	Future conflicts	Negotiations
	Partner rapport	Many partners in same country
Human behavioral error	Technology transfer	Stating terms unclearly
	Partner rapport	Mistrust / Mismatched expectation

Source: M. A. Lyles, "Common Mistakes of Joint Venture Experienced Firms," *Columbia Journal of World Business* (Summer 1987): 75—77. Copyright © 1987. *Columbia Journal of World Business*. Reprinted with permission.

An **alliance**, **partnership**, or **coalition** is an informal agreement to cooper-ate, but no new firm is created and there is usually no purchase of equity (stock or shareholding) in each other. There are many working examples of such alliances in both domestic and international markets. They represent an alternative to the more traditional routes of joint venture, outright acquisition, or partial ownership purchase. Many alliances are looked on as experimental, but they are growing in importance as participants seek a pooling of resources in manufacturing, market-ing, research, or possibly all three. Cooperation in marketing is aimed at reaching markets in which the partner has more knowledge about channels; smart distri-bution is often the key to finding more customers. This applies domestically as well as in foreign marketplaces.

Examples of partnerships include Acme-Cleveland, an old-line machine tool company, hooking up with Digital Signal, a high-tech firm, in the field of laser sensors, which are used now widely for noncontact inspection. The partnership blends the high-tech expertise of Digital Signal with the market reach of Acme-Cleveland. In a similar fashion, Fuji assisted Xerox in entering the Japanese market by introducing Xerox to its key contacts, whereas Xerox can provide Fuji with copying technology and access to U.S. clients. Giant IBM has formed technical and marketing alliances with such large firms as Baxter Healthcare, First Boston, and Texas Instruments. IBM has even given up its "not invented here" syndrome and has formed alliances with small computer companies as well as taking an eq-uity position in some of them. Alliances exist not just in high-tech areas, but in other fields as well, such as metals and plastics.[24]

A **consortium** is a voluntary collaborative venture of several large and small firms, usually encouraged by government or an industry association. This hap-pened in the case of Sematech and U.S. Memories in the United States, both in the semiconductor field. The consortium came about because of concern with the loss of production and markets to Japanese competitors. But there has been squabbling among participants; some members are not eager to share their technology. Sematech still exists, but U.S. Memories is being disbanded. In a similar fashion, the high hopes for Esprit, the European telecommunication consortium, have not been realized.

Mandated Collaboration

A major alternative to competition and voluntary cooperation is **required** or **man-dated collaboration**. Such mandates go beyond the idea of a consortium, though here too the drive for joining forces can come from a government agency or an industry association. The most extreme form of mandated collaboration, carteli-zation, occurs when key companies in an industry come to the conclusion that competition is too intense and "is hurting everyone." Accordingly, they think that market shares can be allocated or that prices can be fixed. The result is a **cartel**. Cartels are not legal in the United States and many other nations, but they are tacitly or expressly allowed in some countries. Another term for those cartels that attempt to fix prices rather than allocate production quotas or market shares is **orderly marketing arrangements (OMAs)**. The use of OMAs is popular for agricultural commodities, minerals, and other natural resources. **Collusion** is less formal than either a cartel or an OMA; it is designed to sustain price levels or to allocate market shares for a certain period of time, "until conditions improve."

The best known cartel is OPEC (Organization of Petroleum Exporting Countries), to which Middle East nations, Venezuela, and Indonesia belong. This cartel first made its appearance in 1973 and caused the price of oil to quadruple and to rise again and again. Although OPEC has achieved some success, its members started violating their production quotas and thereby undermined the arrangement. The price also eroded as producers had overcapacity while users applied conservation measures. The price of a barrel of oil zoomed from $2 to $16 and then close to $40, only to fall back into the $15 to $25 category. The lesson is that even the most crucial natural resource in the industrialized world is subject to the laws of supply and demand.[25]

An example of an OMA can be seen in the action of the International Tin Council, which tried to prop up prices for four years while supplies of tin proved to be plentiful. This action was one of the few effective international commodity price supports. But the arrangement has come under attack and seems to be unraveling as the price of tin is falling. The producing and consuming nations have to honor a $400 million debt to metal dealers and commercial banks; many tin mines are now viewed as unprofitable; growing markets are hard to find. Thus ultimately, an OMA, like a cartel, is bound to fall apart.[26]

One of the most famous cases of collusion occurred in the United States in 1959. This was the great electrical switchgear conspiracy. In this case, reputable firms, despite written codes of conduct and full awareness of antitrust regulations, tried to find ways of avoiding price wars. They also wanted to maintain their customary market shares. Allis Chalmers, General Electric, Westinghouse, and others used a formula to decide when and how to bid to supply equipment to electric utilities. When the conspiracy unraveled, the companies paid fines, and for the first time, some executives served jail sentences.[27] A more recent example of collusion was the widespread bid rigging on U.S. road construction projects in the 1980s. In this case, many small contractors joined forces in over twenty states. Contractors would divide a region and agree not to compete. If an outsider dared to make a bid and disrupt the process, threats were made. In this case, too, companies were fined and jail terms were handed out to individuals. As a result of such prosecution, the number of bidders on contracts rose within a few years.[28]

Two Special Situations

It is possible to have a form of loose collaboration through an industry, trade, or professional association. This form is perfectly legal; it is neither cartelization nor collusion. Membership is voluntary, but once a company is a member, it is expected to conform to certain rules. For example, companies can be asked to adhere to certain technical or administrative standards. In turn, the association acts as an agency for its members. To the outside world, the association acts with a unified voice when lobbying, publicizing, or publishing. Several large associations often speak for a whole industry, as is the case for the American Petroleum Institute and the Pulp and Paper Institute of Canada. In setting and enforcing standards, associations portray themselves as the protectors of the public. However, in assuming that role, they may also stifle innovation—for example, when a metal group objects to installations of plastic piping.[29]

A second special situation is flying solo or acting alone. In effect, we are speaking here about unique entrepreneurs. In certain industrial sectors it is possible for a crackerjack individual or team to become so skillful that few or no direct rivals appear. Here is a short list of such special individuals (some active, others retired; some working alone, others with teams):

- Red Adair—global firefighter of major fires at oil rigs, wells, and refineries
- Ferdinando Borghetti—the master of marble quarries in both Italy and the United States
- Bill Lear—designer and builder of sleek corporate and commuter jet aircraft
- Thomas Moser—designer and builder of custom furniture for corporate offices
- Benjamin Rosen—financial angel for Ansa, Compaq, and Lotus computer companies
- Chuck Yeager—test pilot for both military and civilian high-speed aircraft

Yes, there are other fighters of oil fires, other aircraft designers, other financial angels. But the above individuals have carved out a special niche by being true pioneers, by being dedicated craftsmen, and by staying with their calling for a long, long time. Sustained creativity, constant dedication, and longevity characterize all such entrepreneurs.

A few companies can also succeed, albeit temporarily, in being pioneers. For example, Hales Testing Lab examines buildings for earthquake resistance by taking its unique ultrasonic equipment to the site. Construction Research Lab uses high-speed jetstreams in wind tunnels to check for leaks in equipment. Thinking Machines is the clear leader in parallel computing and neural networks. Firms like these are bound to have imitators over time. But by then the pioneers have carved out an image and a level of performance that may be hard to duplicate.[30]

COMPETITIVE STRATEGIES AND TACTICS: CONCEPTS AND IMPLEMENTATION

In this section, we focus on five related topics. First, we examine what paths enterprises must follow to prepare for future growth. Second, three generic competitive strategies are examined: cost leadership, differentiation, and focus. Next, marketing "battle" strategies and tactics are highlighted, in both offensive and defensive categories. Fourth, we briefly examine the marketing mix as a competitive tool. Finally, we look at selected performance measures by which competitors and competitive battles are judged. Strategy in this section refers to broad plans and large-scale operations, whereas tactics are specific, short-term arrangements designed for implementing strategy. (For further details, see Chapter 17.)

Corporate Growth Strategies and Tactics

In all situations, firms must look beyond their present circumstances and assess the direction they wish to go in the future. That is, they must plan for growth. There are three major corporate growth strategies, each with three tactics:[31]

- *Intense growth:* market penetration, market development, product development
- *Diversified growth:* concentric, horizontal, conglomerate
- *Integrated growth:* forward, backward, horizontal

Intense Growth.   In the **intense growth strategy**, an enterprise can practice market penetration—that is, selling more of its existing products to its present buyers. A second possibility is market development—offering old products to new markets. The third choice is product development—that is, selling new products to current buyers. As an illustration of all three choices for a single company, a vendor of pasta and other dry goods catering to university cafeterias can sell more food if enrollments are up. It can also then expand its services to other institutions, such as nursing homes. Finally, it can consider selling fresh vegetables and fruits to the colleges and universities.

Diversified Growth.   The **diversified growth strategy** means bringing new goods or services to new markets, either by internal development or via acquisition. In concentric diversification, the firm develops new products that are still related to its old product line. In horizontal diversification, the move is into new but related markets. Finally, the conglomerate route means new products and new markets that are not related to their existing counterparts. As a threefold illustration of diversified growth, an office furniture delivery firm in the suburbs may hire bicycle messengers for downtown delivery of small packages. It can then expand service to other cities it did not serve before. Finally, it may enter into the cellular phone business or other areas.

Integrated Growth.   In an **integrated growth strategy**, growth takes place within the firm's own industry; the three directions are forward, backward, and horizontal. In forward integration a company most frequently takes control of its distributors or customers. In backward integration, the company assumes control of its suppliers. Horizontal integration is simply the acquisition of rivals in the same industry. A fiber glass manufacturer that decides to go into boat making, acquires mining/quarrying facilities, and buys out two small rivals is engaged in all three forms of integration.

Generic Competitive Strategies

Any industrial enterprise must establish its competitive strategy by examining two distinct environments: its own and that of the external world. Such analysis is often referred to by the acronym **SWOT**. The first two letters refer to the strengths and weaknesses of the organization. What are the core competencies and the short-comings of the firm in terms of managerial talent, resources, market knowledge, and other skills? The last two letters of the acronym refer to opportunities and threats in the external environment. Which marketing channels, government policies, and promotional media are available or favorable and which appear as blockages?

Whereas an organization may have many strengths and weaknesses, there are only two basic types of competitive advantage: low cost or differentiation. There is an extreme form of differentiation that we label focus or concentration. The three generic competitive strategies of cost leadership, differentiation, and focus correspond roughly to three possible segment categories identified in Chapter 6: mass market or many segments, selected segments, and single segment.

Cost Leadership. In the **cost leadership strategy**, the organization seeks to achieve and sustain an overall cost advantage over its rivals. If it can command prices at about the industry average, it will then achieve above average profit performance because of its low-cost position. The sources of cost advantage can be varied, ranging from preferential access to raw materials to proprietary technology. But a low-cost leader must exploit all sources of cost advantage. Low-cost producers sell a standardized, no-frills product to mass markets—to many, many users. Cost leaders cited for many years were Lincoln Electric in welding equipment, Emerson Electric in motors, and Black and Decker in hand tools. As of 1990, Cargill in agricultural commodities, Alcoa in aluminum, and Wackenhut in security guard services seem to qualify. They all boast access to low-cost material, low-cost labor, and low overhead and can maintain their leadership role.

Differentiation. In the **differentiation strategy**, the firm seeks to differentiate itself in its industry by offering distinct goods and services that are highly valued by select buyer segments. It may cater to distinct groups with variations on a basic appeal, such as the latest technology (Hyster in lift trucks), speedy delivery (Federal Express in small packages), and wide reach (United Parcel Service, also in small packages). Cummins makes diesel engines for highway, marine, and agricultural applications. In each case it stresses reliability and compatibility. Caterpillar Tractor emphasizes durability of equipment, but spare parts availability and a superb dealer network even more so. In computers, IBM practiced this strategy for many years.

Focus. In the **focus strategy**, the firm will concentrate on a single segment or a narrow band of users. Competitive advantage can be achieved when its offerings match the specialized needs of this narrow segment. This focus strategy rests on the differences between a focuser's target segments and other segments to whom the industry caters. Dedication to the narrowly defined segment is a must. Two paper companies, Fort Howard and Hammermill, have both been cited as focusers. Fort Howard makes a very narrow range of industrial-grade papers, whereas Hammermill offers high-quality specialty paper for selected white-collar workers in large offices. In the high-tech area, both Amdahl and Cray deliver supercomputers to government agencies and research institutes whose demand for high-speed numerical analysis differs from that of most industrial enterprises.

Marketing "Battle" Strategies and Tactics

The idea of competition as civilized warfare experienced a resurgence in the past decade as judged by both academic and popular writings. Marketing is warfare, say these authors, with divisions employed, the sales force sent out to do battle, and the struggle being waged for market share. One can hear phrases such as "beating the other sales rep" or "vanquishing the enemy."[32] Although the ideas of military strategists may have civilian applications, it is advisable to recognize two key points. First, while there are several similarities, military engagements and marketing action have many differences. Attempting to eliminate opponents in business can bring not only retaliation, but also lawsuits and ethical objections. Second, companies often want to see their rivals stay in business and to provide stability to an industry.

Offensive strategy calls for attacking one's opponents. Specific substrategies (in a sense, tactics) are labeled frontal, flanking, encirclement, bypass, and guerrilla attacks. Offensive strategy is waged most frequently by small companies, medium-sized firms, and business divisions of larger firms. The opponents are likely to be large firms, often the market leaders. **Frontal attack** works best when there is underlying strength, such as a major cost advantage; Harnischfeger did this in large cranes. **Flanking** means finding a weak point in the opponent, such as a geographically neglected or unserved market. For a while, IBM neglected small business clients, and its rivals were able to exploit this opening. **Encirclement** is an extension of flanking; it is engaging the enemy at several locations. Businessland's taking on Computerland in distribution is an illustration. **Bypass** is a gentle maneuver entailing diversification into submarkets—for example, small robotics firms going after specialized applications rather than the larger, but more competitive automotive market. **Guerrilla attacks** are "sorties in the night" in search of niche markets. Small software firms use this strategy versus industry leaders Microsoft, Lotus, and Novell.

Defensive strategy means guarding against offensive attacks, protecting one's turf. Defensive strategies and tactics are practiced by large firms to keep out smaller ones or to signal other competitors. They need not be just reactive moves;

Caterpillar goes head-to-head with its competition—an example of comparative advertising.

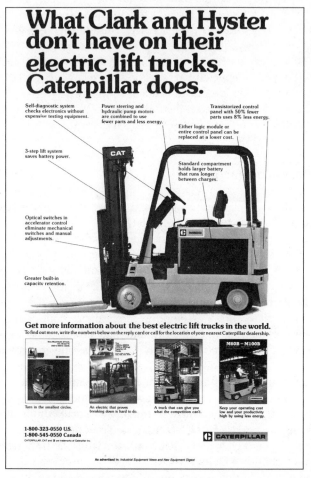

Courtesy of Caterpillar Industrial Inc.

they can be creative and proactive. Substrategies or tactics are fortification, mobility, preempting, flanking, and regrouping. **Fortification** seems like a good idea, but it works only against present rivals, not against new ones or technical substitutes. An example is the U.S. steel industry, in which the giant firms tried to fight imports and minimills. **Mobility** is just diversification under another name; U.S. Steel used this strategy in buying Marathon Oil and becoming USX. **Preemptive and flanking defense** means waging counteroffensives to protect vulnerable positions. Large chemical companies retaliated against small ones by moving from commodities into specialties. Finally, **regrouping** occurs when a position can no longer be defended, but an adjacent hill is available. General Electric regrouped when it moved from computer hardware into information services.

A company may use more than one of these moves; indeed, it can use a vast combination of strategies and tactics for different divisions, product lines, and markets. As in the military, the moves may often be announced, yet not executed. The idea is to signal opponents not to carry out their threats. The best combatants know how to choose rivals, how to keep them informed, when to engage in battle, and when not to. Good rivals understand the rules of the game, make realistic assumptions about business conditions, read signals well in regard to promotion and prices (no price wars!), and reinforce desirable features, such as product differentiation.

Possibly the most important decision that an organization makes in carrying out its marketing battles is where it wishes to confront its rivals. In other words, what location should be the battlefront? In military terms, this would call for deploying guerrillas in the mountains, not on the plain, or fighting swiftly under the sea with attack submarines rather than on the surface with slower battleships. There is no single answer here, but a good idea is to create a map of the industry and to find uncrowded locations, as is illustrated for the computer services industry (including software) in Exhibit 7–9. Note the two key dimensions in this field: extent of customizing and extent of interacting with clients. Clearly, firms have positioned themselves in all four quadrants. When they expand, it is usually in the same quadrant. Moving into another quadrant is less frequent, partly because such a move requires different expertise and partly because other companies have already entrenched themselves in other quadrants.

Utilizing the Marketing Mix

Although the marketing mix is a set of "offerings" a company makes to its customers, it can be viewed also as a set of activities distinct from that of other firms and hence a set of **competitive tactics**. Every enterprise must think of its product, price, promotion, and place (distribution) policies as vehicles to carry out its mission. How each one of the "4 Ps" is used this way will be shown in subsequent chapters; here we offer only a short glimpse.

Product.   Products or services in business markets can compete on the basis of features, but a far better approach is to emphasize benefits. Differentiation makes the good stand out; but customers want performance and satisfaction, not "bells and whistles" for their own sake. Too many business marketers still try to compete on the basis of "specs" rather than trying to find out what clients prefer. For proof of this, take a look at advertisements in trade journals, booth displays at exhibits, and catalog items and see what is being emphasized.

Price.   Price policies, when judiciously used, relay much information. The two sides of the coin, namely cost and demand, must both be analyzed. Cost leadership was noted already as a powerful tool; dominant firms with a low-cost structure can keep rivals at bay. Demand orientation is more likely to be practiced by medium and small firms. One of the most common mistakes is to price too aggressively low;

EXHIBIT 7–9   Spatial Map of the U.S. Information Industry, 1992

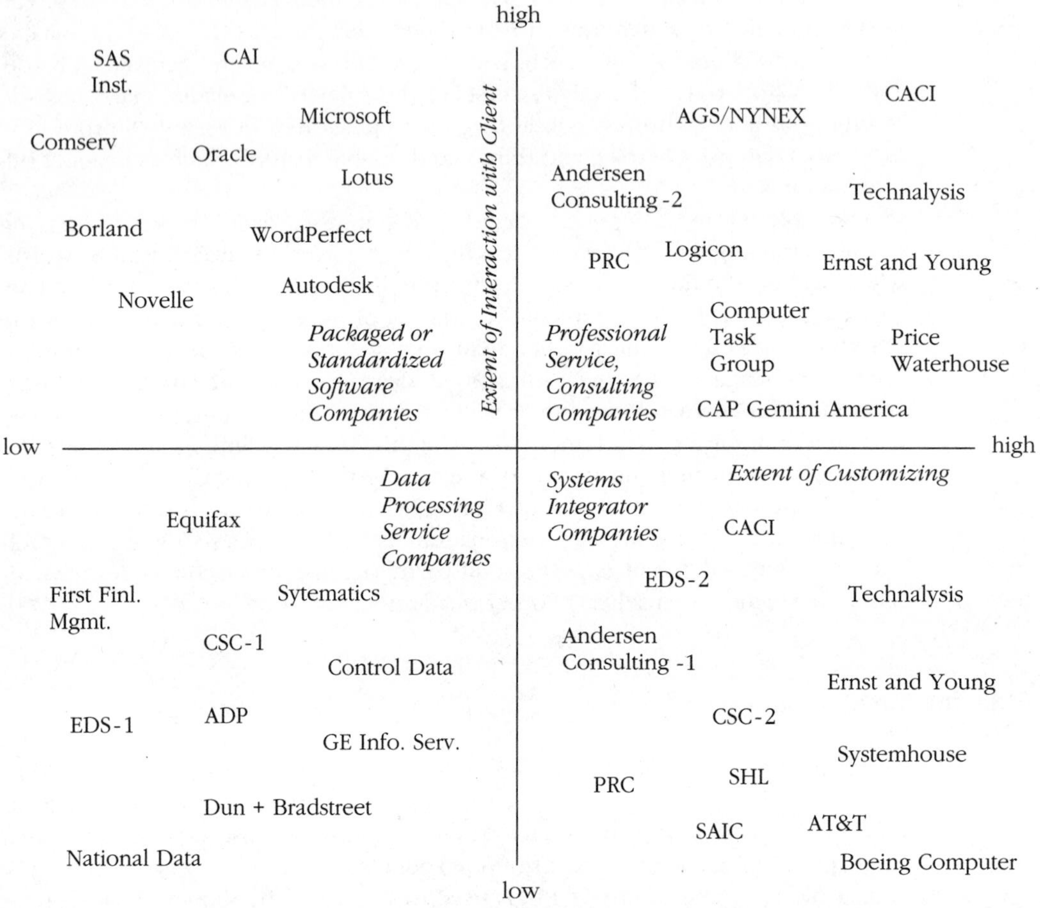

high

SAS Inst.	CAI	CACI
	Microsoft	AGS/NYNEX
Comserv	Oracle	
	Lotus	Andersen Consulting-2 Technalysis
Borland	WordPerfect	PRC Logicon Ernst and Young
Novelle	Autodesk	

Extent of Interaction with Client

Packaged or Standardized Software Companies

Professional Service, Consulting Companies

Computer Task Group

Price Waterhouse

CAP Gemini America

low ——————————————————————————————————— high

Extent of Customizing

	Data Processing Service Companies	*Systems Integrator Companies* CACI
Equifax		EDS-2 Technalysis
First Finl. Mgmt.	Sytematics	Andersen Consulting-1
	CSC-1	Ernst and Young
	Control Data	CSC-2
EDS-1 ADP	GE Info. Serv.	Systemhouse
	Dun + Bradstreet	PRC SHL
National Data		SAIC AT&T Boeing Computer

low

Source: Reprinted from *Business Horizons,* "The Information Vending Machine," January–February 1988, Figure 4, p. 29 and Figure 6, p. 33. Copyright © 1988 by the Foundation for the School of Business at Indiana University. Used with permission.

such eagerness results in rising sales and lower profits. Smart marketers tend to combine their product and pricing policies by moving their low-priced commodities into higher margin specialties. Open bids, used in public and other contract work, can reveal much about pricing behavior.[33]

Promotion.   Promotion is the front line of any marketing mix. How smoothly messages reach an audience, how good the exhibit is, and how convincingly sales-force members present themselves will determine who gets the order. Competitive comparisons are on the rise in all fields, ranging from aircraft to financial services and from paper makers to truck maintenance. Some advertising copy from Compaq, comparing its computer features to those of direct competitors, can be seen in Exhibit 7–10. Such advertisements carry even more weight when citing independent ratings.

Place.   Place or distribution channels are key contacts with clients and thus serve as focal points in talking with actual and would-be customers. An effective distribution scheme becomes a partnership that is then characterized by loyalty bonds. This means it is unwise for the client to seek out a new supplier; the cost of switching acts as a barrier. Electronic information exchanges or networks between providers of goods and the distributors further enhance the partnership arrangement.

Measuring Performance

Competition and cooperation are two major forms of business activity, both of which are culturally determined. Accordingly, what constitutes success in one

EXHIBIT 7–10   Use of Print Advertisement as a Competitive Tool: Feature by Feature Comparisons of Compaq Personal Computer with Rivals

Nobody else gives you all the advantages you get with the COMPAQ DESKPRO/M PCs	*COMPAQ DESKPRO/M FAMILY*	*ALR BUSINESS VEISA*	*AST PREMIUM II*	*DELL POWERLINE DE*	*IBM PS/2 MODEL 90*
1. Five-board modular design	Yes	No	No	No	No
2. Upgradable video without using an expansion slot	Yes	Yes	No	No	No
3. Separate I/O board for potential enhancements and ease of service	Yes	No	No	No	No
4. 14 levels of security including cable-lock provision	Yes	No	No	No	No
5. System configuration and ID number available in memory and accessible remotely	Yes	No	No	No	Yes
6. Power supply adequate for all expansion needs	240w	150w	145w	220w	194w

Note: This comparison is only a small portion of a larger two-page advertisement.

Source: Compaq Computer Corporation ad in *Computerworld*, Dec. 23, 1991/Jan 2, 1992, p. 30. Reprinted by permission.

setting can be regarded as relatively unimportant in another. For example, in the United States, most companies still emphasize short-term profits for many reasons, but mostly because financial analysts on Wall Street and top managers in large firms insist on quarterly results as true indicators (and their own pay may be tied to such measures). In contrast, for Japanese firms, growth in sales and market share is of primary interest, followed by exploitation of their competitive advantage. In developing nations, where agricultural commodities play a key role, organizations that can maintain price stability and employ many workers will be accorded much praise and given state subsidies.

We can distinguish three distinct sets of **performance measures**: (1) financial numbers and ratios, such as absolute profits or net income as a percentage of sales; (2) market indicators, such as growth in sales, market share, and market stability; and (3) marketing measures, ranging from product quality to customer service and from export orientation to corporate image rankings. Various publications have collected data on such indicators, including comparative measures, so our comments will focus on the range of measures and on their applications.[34]

Financial statistics, including absolute numbers and ratios, are frequently used to judge the status of both an industry and competitors therein. Examples can be seen in the daily newspapers and weekly journals of industrialized nations. On a quarterly or annual basis, these sources also provide "scoreboard" issues showing return on sales, return on investment, research and development spending as a percentage of sales, and many other ratios. As a rough rule, fast-growing, research-intensive, and high-technology industries exhibit higher ratios than mature industrial sectors. For example, drug companies, although competing intensely, manage to achieve very high returns. This may be due to their having carved out a lucrative niche, possessing an iron-clad patent, or "playing hardball" with generic competitors. One of the best ways to study an industry and the rivals is to classify them by size and characteristics. In short, compare and contrast same-size competitors that have roughly similar physical facilities and work force and near-identical research and promotion budgets.

Market indicators are those that focus on the growth of sales and market share. For many years, the former was emphasized; now it is the latter. Five- or ten-year growth rates in sales are still good indicators of stability for both an industry and the individual competitors. But the oil crisis of the 1970s, coupled with saturated markets, made many firms realize that the era of growth is ending in developed economies and that market share, accompanied by proper product positioning, is important. Many companies prefer to be dominant in market share, sensing that profits will then accrue. However, some managers dissent. For example, Charles Ames, formerly of Reliance Electric and Acme-Cleveland, contends that there are many strong companies that are not market leaders. Still, he admits that if a business unit has less than a 10 percent market share of a well-defined market, there is cause for alarm.

Examination of the available evidence from a variety of sources, but especially a major database called PIMS, reveals that market share is indeed a major influence on profitability as measured by return on investment. (PIMS stands for "profit impact of market strategies" and includes over 200 companies and over 2,000 lines of business.) Further analysis reveals that market share matters a lot, but it is more important in high-tech and marketing-intensive businesses than in old-line manufacturing. In the former, number one ranking can earn 35 percent return on investment as against 10 percent for rank number five, whereas in the latter the difference is about 25 versus 12 percent. Market share is also positively correlated to relative quality as perceived by customers and to industry concentration, as shown in Exhibit 7–11. When all three are high, the returns on investment are high; when the three are low, the firm is stuck in the "bottom corner." In sum, market share is shorthand for a set of underlying profit influences.[35]

Recently, indicators other than financial ratios and market share have been used to describe and analyze an industry and the participants therein. These can be specific or broad measures. They may focus on product quality, such as performance data versus specifications, percentage of product returns, and number of customer complaints. Winning the prestigious Deming Award in Japan or the Baldrige Award in the United States would be an indicator of product quality (and could then be publicized).[36] Customer service measures can range from lack of delays in delivery to percentage of orders shipped complete. Such measures can be tracked and used as input for salary schemes. Employee morale can be judged by turnover and absenteeism trends. Innovative firms can look at the number of new products introduced versus the number introduced by competitors. In a cooperative scheme, one team of bidders can judge how well it did against other bidding teams.

In the final analysis, there is no contradiction between financial health and market viability on the one hand and indicators focusing on other aspects. The first duty of a profit-making, competitive organization is to achieve good returns, especially over a period of several years. Many companies have good financial ratios, solid market share, and do well on other measures. There are exceptions; some companies earn much, but get little recognition, whereas others are admired, but the balance sheet is in trouble. Astute managers know that a company must also be responsive to its various stakeholders, such as clients, employees, and suppliers, and must earn their confidence. By doing so, it is likely to enhance both its bottom line and its image. For the industry as a whole, observers like to see stability coupled with infusion of new ideas and new products. In the case of cooperation, the duration as well as the accomplishments of an alliance or joint venture can serve as measuring rods.

RIVALRY IN STABLE AND MATURE INDUSTRIES

Mature industries are characterized by uncertainties about the rate and pattern of demand. Decline sets in as products move to commodity status. Fixed costs may be high, and many firms may be locked in by exit barriers. The struggle to hold on to market share can be bitter. The strategic options noted earlier do apply, but some firms will choose to make a definite exit by disinvestment or liquidation. In other words, they may quickly or slowly close plants and branch offices, eliminate product lines or services offered, and shift to another industry.

EXHIBIT 7–11 Market Share and Other Correlates of Profitability

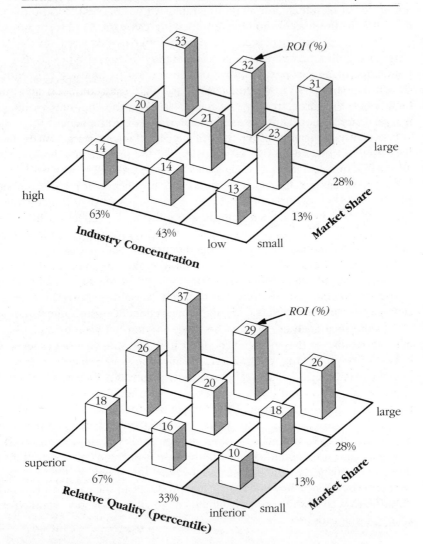

Note: Profitability is measured by return on investment.

Source: Adapted with permission of The Free Press, a Division of Macmillan, Inc., from *The PIMS Principles: Linking Strategy to Performance* by Robert D. Buzzell and Bradley T. Gale. Copyright © 1987 by The Free Press.

BUSINESS MARKETING IN PRACTICE ▐████████████████

Why Can't Outstanding Companies Remain Outstanding?

In Search of Excellence by T. Peters and R. Waterman was a popular book in the early 1980s that focused on "excellent companies." Why were these firms rated excellent? It seemed that they showed flexibility, "stuck to their knitting" (did what they do best), and got close to their customers. But just a few years later, some of these fine companies fell on hard times and could no longer be rated excellent. What happened?

Several analysts in both the popular business and the academic press soon offered some explanations, ranging from internal dissension to external pressures. Two other books, published at the end of the 1980s, offered more in-depth analysis on why the outstanding companies were no longer outstanding. A. Ghosh's *Redefining Excellence* examines the downturn in financial figures or ratios, ranging from growth in earnings and assets to returns on equity and sales. Ghosh says that the excellent firms were simply unable to sustain their lofty positions for any length of time. Why? Because these firms are also subject to the same pressures and cycles as are other firms. But this still does not fully explain the situation. Probing further for underlying causes, Ghosh cites a wide range of factors, among them domestic and foreign competitive pressures, changes in consumer preferences, overly ambitious mergers and leveraged buyouts, and restructuring that did not work out.

The other book, *The Icarus Paradox* by D. Miller, focuses on organizational behavior rather than on financial aspects. Miller thinks that the very causes of success are bound to lead to failure. Companies begin to repeat what worked in the past, and this becomes "too much of a good thing." Miller identifies four paths to failure. First, we have companies moving from craftsman to tinkerer status. Leadership in quality and low cost is replaced by too much insistence on savings, stale products, and paperwork. Second, companies move from being builders to being imperialists. Successful diversification leads to overexpansion at some point. Third, pioneer firms become escapists. Innovation is supplanted by technical overkill, extravagance, and marketing myopia. Fourth is the case of sales-minded companies becoming drifters. Good corporate image and a sufficient product line give way to infighting among business units and proliferation of products. Miller thinks, however, that rejuvenation is a possibility in each case.

Source: T. Peters and R. Waterman, *In Search of Excellence* (New York: Harper & Row, 1982); A. Ghosh, *Redefining Excellence* (New York: Praeger, 1989); D. Miller, *The Icarus Paradox* (New York: Harper Business, 1990). See also selected articles on the topic in *Business Week, The Economist,* and *Harvard Business Review* from 1982 to 1990.

Abrasive Materials

Any product that requires surface grinding or finishing makes use of a natural or synthetic abrasive material. Abrasives are used in other manufacturing operations as well, such as cleaning and cutting. Natural abrasives are diamond, pumice, and garnet; synthetic abrasives are silicon carbide and aluminum oxide. The demand for abrasives in the United States is stabilizing and may decline for the following reasons: (1) plastics, which are becoming more widely used, need less grinding and finishing; (2) heavy abrasive users, such as the steel, auto, and machinery industries, prefer worldwide sourcing; and (3) the demand for final products, such as cars and appliances, is slowing down.[37]

Given a highly mature market, we would expect producers to compete intensely for market share. Indeed, this is the situation; the top four firms control about 50 percent of the market. A major battle took place in the 1970s, and the reverberations are still being felt. Kennecott acquired Carborundum and in turn was acquired by Standard Oil of Ohio, now known as BP America. As a result of these mergers, many talented executives left the industry. Managerial decisions came slowly; quality and on-time delivery slipped. Although BP America tried to reverse the trend, it did not succeed; unable to find a buyer or a partner for the whole operation, it divested the unit piece by piece.

The result of the Kennecott-Carborundum fiasco did bring benefits to and increased market share for other producers. Norton is the largest firm in the industry and the cost leader; it is bound to engage in defensive maneuvers. Exolon-ESK and Washington Mills, which bought a division from BP America, are surviving. The full-line abrasive manufacturers have a definite advantage as they offer one-stop shopping convenience and lower prices. Small firms are stressing high quality, custom design, technical sophistication, and quick delivery. In short, we witness in this industry a good example of cost leadership by the largest firm versus differentiation and focus by small companies.

Cement

The U.S. cement industry consists of fewer than fifty producers and about fifteen importers affiliated with cement-producing firms in Canada, Mexico, and elsewhere. Entry barriers are high in terms of capital requirements for both building and running a plant; the cost of constructing a new plant runs about $200 per ton of capacity. But the potential for solid earnings is high. This makes the field attractive to newcomers, especially to foreign producers, who like the size of the U.S. market. The industry did well until 1991, when the situation for real estate deteriorated sharply. When housing starts are down and office building vacancies are up, construction slows sharply, and there is an immediate impact on cement demand.[38]

Ownership changes occur frequently as companies jockey for market share, which varies region by region. Foreign firms now own more than 55 percent of total U.S. capacity. The three largest firms are Holnam, Lafarge Coppee, and Southdown, each with about 9 percent of the market. Lafarge of France, whose profits shriveled to 3 percent of sales in 1990, still decided to spend $140 million in 1991 to purchase three competing U.S. plants in order to have a presence from coast to coast. In terms of growth strategy, the option chosen is integrated growth, with forward integration as a favored tactic—that is, buying distributors. Of the generic competitive strategies, the top three firms strive for cost leadership, but not always successfully. Others choose the focus route. Since cement is basically a commodity, product differentiation is minimal and price variations tend to be minor. Most firms meet the lowest price posted in a given region.

Along with forward integration noted above, joint ventures or alliances with construction firms are ways of bypassing intense price competition. But there is danger in moving from being just a cement maker into specific concrete products and construction. This action may merely transfer price competition down the line. Another disadvantage is that an integrated producer will encounter resistance by buyers with whom its subsidiary or partner is now competing. Finally, until recently, expansion by cement makers into construction was regarded as an unfair trade practice in the United States. But portions of the regional Midwest and Southwest markets are now vertically integrated.

Internal Combustion Engines

Internal combustion engines are normally thought of as being used for transport vehicles: autos, boats, and aircraft. But such engines find many other applications in farm machinery, construction, materials handling, power generation, oilfield pumping, and such outdoor equipment as chain saws and lawn mowers. Demand in these markets is highly cyclical; changes in annual shipments can range from 10 to 30 percent. The technology is mature, and no radical changes are on the horizon. One recent improvement is the use of microprocessors for better fuel economy. There may be increased regulation of engines for air pollution control.[39]

Many producers make more than a single type of engine and sell to a variety of customers. Different markets demand distinct features, so product differentiation is practiced. Gasoline engines offer cost, size, and weight advantages, but maintenance costs run higher and life spans are shorter than for diesels. Diesel engines are preferred in medium- to high-horsepower applications. They have a good repair record, but they cost more initially than gasoline engines. Natural gas engines are used in remote locations and may find other applications.

The industry is made up of both integrated and independent companies; they produce engines for their own use and for sale to original equipment manufacturers. Concentration is pronounced, with fewer than twenty firms dominating. Caterpillar, General Motors, and Cummins together account for 60 percent of all diesel and gas engine shipments. Briggs and Stratton has 40 percent of the gasoline engine market. These four firms take slightly more than half of the total internal combustion engine market in the United States and set the tone on marketing practices.

Price competition is keen, with Briggs and Stratton taking the cost leadership role in the gasoline engine market. This firm has been able to keep price increases relatively modest while increasing horsepower. Its advertising stresses low prices and the "made in USA" label; its major clients are Toro and Jacobson, makers of lawn mowers and other outdoor equipment. In contrast, Cummins emphasizes product differentiation in transportation, machinery, and construction. Caterpillar is also a differentiator, using its dealer network and product reliability to keep customers. Small producers wage offensive strategies against the top firms, carving out special niches. Cooperative ventures have not been popular, but there may be more of them as European and Japanese firms penetrate the U.S. market in engines as well.

Welding Equipment

Although welding is a mature process, it is in transition and is becoming known as "materials joining technology." Welding is the leading process for joining metals, but many nonmetals must also be joined. Some of these materials, such as thermoplastics, are also welded. Other processes, such as brazing and soldering, also fall into the welding category. Brazing is used for joining ceramics to metals, and soldering is used in joining electronic components.[40]

Welding is influenced by general economic trends and especially by conditions in manufacturing. Shipments of welding equipment reflect the cyclical nature of the metal products and automotive industries. Welding equipment is used in construction and in the defense sector, two bright spots until 1991, when the recession and the end of the cold war took their toll.

There are two types of companies in this industry. The first group consists of large companies; for these, welding equipment is a small portion of their total revenues. Participants are Air Products & Chemicals, BOC-Airco, Union Carbide, and Allegheny International. Some of these firms may leave the field on short notice if they find that making welding equipment does not fit their corporate mission. The second group is made up of medium-sized and small firms whose commitment to the field is strong. For Lincoln Electric, Hobart, Miller Electric, and Newcor the sale of welding equipment represents the bulk of their business.

The second group of firms shows a better financial record than the large companies on most indicators: higher profit margins, lower debt, and higher sales per employee. Industry observers attribute this record to these companies' knowledge of technology and specialization. This seems strange in light of their lower research to sales ratio. The explanation lies in several factors. Some of the smaller firms are privately held and do not reveal their research spending. The research and development function may also be integrated with production so intimately that it is hard to separate. Finally, these firms have forged stronger loyalty ties with their clients than the large firms.

Lincoln Electric of Cleveland is well known worldwide as one of the true pioneers in the field. This firm, privately held, emphasizes employee participation, productivity, and low costs. Both individual and team accomplishments are stressed, with reward in the form of large year-end bonuses. The company maintains close rapport with clients. Newcor of Detroit cultivates its relationships with Ford and General Motors, two clients accounting for half its sales. Newcor pleased these firms through differentiation, by innovating its friction and resistance welding equipment line, and by offering automated systems. Smaller firms have a focus orientation and practice offensive moves to capture niche markets. The larger firms are becoming active in the area of welding robotics and practice defensive strategy and tactics.

RIVALRY IN EMERGING AND GROWING INDUSTRIES

Youthful industries are characterized by both technological and strategic uncertainty. Rules of the game are few or nonexistent; the structure, conduct, and performance of an emerging industry unfold as the field becomes more mature. When an industry is new, there are bound to be high initial costs, especially in high-technology and capital-intensive sectors, but they are less steep in services. Access to raw materials, skilled labor, and distribution channels is likely to be difficult. Existing industries often fight back, perceiving newcomers as a threat. If demand for the output of a new industry is high at the start, there will be less infighting among competitors. Partnerships of all kinds arise when a new technology or industrial activity emerges. This is because large firms like to form alliances or joint ventures with small ones in order to gain a foothold in the new field.

Biotechnology

In just two decades, biotechnology has grown from a pure science to a broad field with many promising commercial applications. Two key factors shape the industry: scientific expertise and capital investment. Both represent significant commitment, and though early payoffs were modest, sales and profits are now on the rise. Estimates on the number of participating companies range from 600 to over 800; many firms, large and small, are staking out specific subfields. Biotechnology in the 1990s will make a major impact in agriculture, food processing, chemical manufacturing, health care, and waste degradation. Western firms are linking up with enterprises in Africa, Asia, and Latin America. This field, more than any other, is likely to have a global impact during the 1990s. Although government regulators and consumer activists are scrutinizing and criticizing biotechnology procedures, such challenges are not expected to act as a hindrance to the industry's future.[41]

As in any "hot" area, many small companies have sprung up, attracting both scientific talent and venture capital. When payoffs did not materialize quickly, the flow of funds slowed and some firms went out of business. But the promise for developing significant new products was high, so that many small firms decided to "stick it out" and others forged licensing, joint venture, or partnership deals with large firms. Today every major chemical and pharmaceutical company in the United States has a biotechnology operation in-house. There are no clear cost leaders in the field; the emphasis is on product and process differentiation. Newer and older methods compete on the basis of cost/benefit analysis. Of course, this means that clients must consider not only initial expenditures, but also the cost of switching and the cost of operating new processes—for example, fermentation.

CAD/CAM/CAE Systems

CAD/CAM/CAE is the acronym for computer-aided design, manufacturing, and engineering. Like biotechnology, it is a coordinated effort to apply new techniques to old problems, mostly in engineering. The key driving force for innovators in this field is to enhance the productivity of blue- and white-collar workers. Since the work is so varied, the basis for growth is product development and differentiation. Half a million CAD/CAM/CAE systems are used globally in such applications as engineering layout, mapping, textile pattern, and other designs. There are over a hundred vendors in the field in the United States alone, but the top five vendors dominate, each averaging about 20,000 active users. Depending on the features desired, a typical system could be purchased for between $10,000 and $50,000 as of early 1992.[42]

The industry traces its roots back to the 1950s, but the major thrust came in the 1980s, starting with units that combined hardware and software. Newer units involve software that fits into a number of standard computer platforms. This is known as "the unbundling of software." Earlier, there were problems overcoming start-up anxiety by clients, so companies spent 20 percent of their revenues on marketing and third-party consultants thrived by advising. As in biotechnology, firms became more user-friendly over time, and users are becoming more sophisticated. Small vendors use focus strategy to carve out specific niches.

The CAD/CAM/CAE sector is still high tech, still growing. But it is quickly passing from emergence into the growth phase. Price leaders are beginning to emerge, and some vendors are starting to dominate. A leading system, known as Autocad and designed to work on personal computers, has over 300,000 systems licensees. Product variety is still huge, but there are signs of standardization. There are many competitors, but a shakeout will be occurring during the 1990s, with alliances and mergers on the rise—for example, Computervision and Prime Computer.

Capital Equipment Leasing

Leasing, which is simply long-term rental for a year or more, is an alternative to purchase. Over one-fifth of industrial equipment is leased in the United States. Items leased range from computers to aircraft and from oilfield to restaurant equipment. There are two kinds of leases, operating and capital. An **operating lease** is a true lease; a **capital lease** is a conditional sales contract, providing for ownership at the end. Equipment leasing is still in its growth phase, with value of leases rising at 10 percent per year in the 1980s. Leasing is done by two major groups: manufacturers and third-party leasing firms, including banks and other financial institutions.[43]

Competition between those who wish to sell and those who wish to lease is keen, but several large firms clearly attempt to be on both sides. Manufacturers lease for various reasons. Deere and Tenneco see leasing as a way to boost sales by financing and leasing to clients who cannot afford to buy. The office and factory equipment makers do leasing primarily to gain market share and to boost earnings. Banks and other financial institutions, such as GE Credit, Commercial Credit, and Leaseway, see leasing as earning fees from credit extension.

The competition in this industry takes its characteristics from both finance and marketing. The financial arrangement must be attractive to all parties, while conforming to existing tax laws and accounting practices. Making money available at low rates is not enough; tailor-made arrangements are the rule. A broad approach and differentiation are needed for such widespread markets as office equipment. A more focused approach works for a narrower market, such as aircraft. Guinness Peat Aviation and International Lease Finance have contracted to lease one-third of Boeing's backlog of aircraft. They fulfill a key role since few airlines can afford the purchase of new jets and Boeing needs the cash to operate. But when the airline industry is in the doldrums as in early 1992, lessors are stuck with a new fleet on their hands that stands idle.

Industrial Security

This industry is a growth field because crimes against property and businesses are on the rise. Both the number of crimes committed and the apparent vulnerability of users come into consideration. In the United States during the 1980s, property crimes grew at about 5 percent per year, but stolen property crimes rose at the rate of 20 percent per year. Businesses that were hit and those that were not seem equally concerned. There is a wide variety of crimes, making the task more complex. Access to factories and laboratories must be stricter than access to offices and wholesale and retail trade facilities, where sales representatives and visitors are more frequent. Retailers want protection against both employee and customer pilferage, but they want both jobs done unobtrusively so as not to be accused of any harassment by either group.[44]

Offerings in this industry range from old-fashioned safes and locks to highly sophisticated electronic surveillance devices and from guards with or without dogs to intrusion detection units. The basic devices tend to be highly price competitive, with reliability assumed. For advanced-technology devices, quality and follow-up service are important. Vendors generally stress either their established reputation or their new technology, but usually not both. As a general rule, differentiation and focus are practiced; there is no clear-cut cost leader.

Two major groups of companies make security equipment: the large, diversified firms and the smaller specialty firms with narrower product lines. A

EXHIBIT 7–12   Composite Financial Ratios: Selected Security Equipment Manufacturers, 1987–1989

Item	Diversified/ Conglomerate Manufacturers[a]			Specialty or "Pure Play" Manufacturers[b]		
	1987	1988	1989	1987	1988	1989
Return on sales (%)	4.0	3.5	5.0	7.9	8.3	6.6
Return on assets (%)	4.8	4.3	6.3	6.7	7.7	7.0
Return on equity (%)	11.7	11.9	16.5	10.4	10.2	9.0
Current ratio	2.1	2.0	1.9	3.1	3.3	3.8
Quick ratio	1.2	1.2	1.1	2.0	2.3	2.6
Inventory turnover (times/yr)	5.6	5.8	6.2	5.6	7.3	5.9
Total debt/total assets (%)[c]	48.1	53.1	51.2	33.8	33.5	31.7
Long-term debt/equity (%)	68.6	81.4	67.4	29.1	29.3	18.0
Price/earnings ratio	13.5	11.3	10.6	8.5	13.8	11.7
Research and development spending/sales (%)	2.4	2.4	2.3	4.7	4.9	5.1
Sales per employee (000$)	83.9	87.4	98.2	79.6	92.3	87.1

Note: fiscal years vary.

[a]Diversified/Conglomerate Manufacturers' sample consists of American Brands, Figgie International, General Signal, Honeywell, Ingersoll-Rand, Nortek, Pittway, and Tyco Laboratories.
[b]Speciality or "Pure Play" sample consists of ADT, American Locker Group, Checkpoint Systems, Cohu, Detection Systems, Knogo, Napco Security Systems, and Sensormatic Electronics.
[c]Total debt defined as long-term debt plus current liabilities.

Source: Adapted with permission from E. Hester, *Security Surveillance and Monitoring Equipment* (Cleveland: Freedonia Group, 1991), p. 89.

comparison of these two groups, shown in Exhibit 7–12, reveals that the narrow-focus firms have achieved better performance, as measured by financial indicators. Investors regard them as doing a more aggressive job of marketing their wares. Conglomerates are absorbed by their quest to acquire other firms and also spend far less on research and development.

The industry has undergone restructuring during the 1980s, with some of the major firms being merged into others, including such well-known names as ADT, Emhart, Kidde, Masco, Scovill, and Yale Security. Both Western European and Japanese firms entered the U.S. market, the former via acquisitions, the latter by using their knowledge of high technology—for example, closed-circuit television monitoring. The competition is now more intense, and profit margins have eroded. Some U.S. firms have sought relief by going after global markets.

Two medium-sized firms illustrate competitive behavior in action in this field during the 1980s. Crime Controls makes heat, motion, and sound-sensing devices that are connected to a central control panel. The company emphasizes strong local presence; it acquired small firms in fast-growing population centers that have relatively high crime rates. Sensormatic Electronics makes devices to deter shoplifting. It captured a high market by catering to the needs of different retailers—for example selling heavy tags to department stores and lighter ones to drugstores. The heavy tags are also sold to some manufacturers to be put on garments at factories. Both companies stress intense growth, but Sensormatic is emphasizing diversification as well.

SUMMARY

Competition in the organizational marketplace is generally keen, whether the rivalry is across the street or across the ocean. Judging the nature of competition by looking at structure, conduct, and performance is a useful initial step. However, marketing managers need to go further and consider the intensity of rivalry among existing firms, possible entry into the market by new firms, substitutes, and forward or backward integration. New products, better processes, and improved services—often pioneered by outsiders—keep competitors on their toes.

Although competition is the way of life in many business markets, there are many alternatives, including voluntary cooperation, mandated collaboration, and some special situations. Licensing, joint ventures, and franchising are traditional ways of partnering, especially in international business. As of late, various kinds of alliances and research consortia have become popular, in both high-tech and mature industries. Other possibilities range from cartels to orderly marketing arrangements. Highly talented individuals or small teams can carve out an entrenched position. Associations can play an active role in the competitive atmosphere of any industry, especially in a domestic setting.

Corporate growth strategies include intense, diversified, and integrated growth, each of which includes a number of specific tactical steps ranging from further penetration of existing markets with existing products to entering new markets with new products. There are three generic competitive strategies: cost leadership, differentiation, and focus. Cost leaders tend to exist in more mature fields. As a general rule, most companies practice differentiation and focusing. Marketing "battle" strategies can be either offensive or defensive. Although the military analogy is not fully applicable to the industrial marketplace, the elements of the marketing mix—product, price, promotion, and distribution—act as competitive tactics. The results of competition can be judged in terms of financial indicators, growth in market share and sales, and many other measures ranging from customer service satisfaction to corporate image rankings. No single measure will suffice. It is best to compare an enterprise against its peer group.

In today's complex marketplace, it is crucial to watch one's current rivals, but it is equally important to emphasize potential competitors, often from the outside and from abroad. This is true for both mature and emerging industries. There is much action and intense jostling among participants. In mature sectors, there are uncertainties about the rate and pattern of demand. In emerging and growing sectors there is much uncertainty in regard to technology and the correct strategic path. New industries tend to attract many entrants, but a shake-out takes place as the field becomes more mature. Small firms worried about start-up costs and older firms concerned with missing an opportunity will often form alliances and partnerships.

Both competition and cooperation are accentuated today by the rapid spread of information, which, in turn, encourages taking action. Research findings, competitive challenges, cooperative arrangements, and government rulings become known quickly and are flashed around the world. Other enterprises may take immediate action in response or undertake a long-range strategic move. As some industries mature, new ones arise. Enterprises enter, leave, or alter their course of action. Change is the only constant in the arena of business interaction, whether it is along competitive or cooperative lines.

Key Terms and Concepts

backward integration
forward integration
substitutes
voluntary cooperation
formal cooperation
informal cooperation
licensing
franchising
joint venture
alliance (partnership, coalition)
consortium
required (mandated) collaboration
cartel
orderly marketing arrangements (OMAs)
collusion
intense growth strategy
diversified growth strategy
integrated growth strategy

SWOT
cost leadership strategy
differentiation strategy
focus strategy
offensive strategy
frontal attack
flanking
encirclement
bypass
guerrilla attacks
defensive strategy
fortification
mobility
preemptive and flanking defense
regrouping
competitive tactics
performance measures

Discussion Questions

1. Many business strategists and marketing managers contend that services are not as exposed to international competitive pressures as are tangible (manufactured) goods. Discuss both sides of the argument and take a stance. Cite specific examples.

2. "Steelmaking is becoming a service business. When alloys are molded to a specific weight and tolerance, services account for a significant part of the resulting product. Steel service centers help customers choose the steels and alloys they need and then inspect,

slit, coat, store, and deliver the materials" (R. Reich in *Atlantic Monthly*, February 1991, p. 40). Discuss how this trend is affecting competition.

3. The disk drive is the most labor-intensive part of a computer. So the disk drive would seem ideal for manufacturing in the People's Republic of China, which is eager to nurture technology-based industries and is overflowing with cheap labor. Do you think China can compete in this field? (Hint: Take a look at D. J. Yang, "China's Disk-Drive Industry: Ready and Willing—but Able?" *Business Week*, Oct. 17, 1988, p. 110.)

4. At the start of this chapter, the authors claim that although Boeing and Cessna are in the same industry (civilian aircraft), they are not in the same line of business. (What is this chapter's definition of *industry, business,* and *line of business*?) Can you cite parallel examples from other fields?

5. Economic textbooks contend that under so-called perfect competition the price will be given and that no one producer can alter it; the marketplace dictates it. In view of this claim, do you think that identical bids on a construction contract are a sign of pure competition or a sign of possible collusion? (Hint: take a look at R. Smith, "Incredible Electric Conspiracy," *Fortune* [April 1961]: 132–137 and [May 1961]: 161–164).

6. Select an industry association from the *Encyclopedia of Associations* (or, if you wish, the international version of this volume). Contact the association by mail, phone, or fax and ask for the following information: (1) a sample newsletter to members; (2) a list of their publications; (3) a list of research activities. In your inquiry, politely probe whether members have access to prices and pricing practices in the particular field.

7. Al Ries and Jack Trout, whom we quoted in the text, suggest that in an industry of one hundred firms, as a general rule, the leader should practice defensive warfare; next two in size should wage offensive warfare; the next three should engage in flanking; and the other ninety-four should use guerrilla tactics. Select an industry of your choice and see if this rule applies. (Note: These two authors have traditionally looked only at consumer goods firms so you will not find illustrations in their *Marketing Warfare* volume for business-to-business markets.)

8. General Motors (GM) acquired both Electronic Data Systems and Hughes Aircraft in order to diversify away from the auto and truck business. Find the companies against which these two subsidiaries of GM are now competing and see how successful they are in their quest. (Hint: look at GM's and the competitors' annual and "10K" reports.)

9. One of the most ordinary yet widely used industrial goods is the pallet. Pallets are used in every conceivable storage and warehousing activity to keep items off the floor. The pallets are traditionally made of wood, but plastics and other materials are now invading. Investigate this situation and determine the extent of substitution for wood.

10. Although companies often choose to compete on basis of product differentiation and price, they also do so via distribution. Investigate the extent to which computer firms are using such independent distributors as Businessland, Computerland, and so forth. Also take a look at whether company outlet stores, such as Digital Equipment, have or have not succeeded.

11. In the chemical industry, large firms are moving from commodities into specialty chemicals and thereby invading the turf of small- and medium-sized companies that have traditionally carved out niches. Investigate this situation for a given chemical product line—for example, automotive chemicals, water treatment chemicals, maintenance chemicals, and so forth. Do you think it is possible to emphasize brands in these areas?

12. Some managers contend that organizational design makes a difference as to how well a company can compete. One author, Robert Keidel, uses sports as an analogy in his book *Game Plans* (New York: Dutton, 1985) and

asks: "What game is your company playing?" Baseball is applicable for a team of individual stars—for example, a research lab; football for where the coach calls the plays—for example, assembly operations; and basketball where flexible coordination is the key, such as at computer or shipping firms. Do you agree with this perspective? Does this book have application to this chapter?

Endnotes and References

1. For the basis of competition in a capitalistic system see three classics: J. Schumpeter, *Capitalism, Socialism, and Democracy* (New York: Harper, 1942); J. Chamberlain, *The Roots of Capitalism* (Indianapolis: Liberty Press, 1976); and I. Kirzner, *Competition and Entrepreneurship* (Chicago: University of Chicago Press, 1973). For more recent works, see *Competition Policy in OECD Countries* (Paris: OECD, 1988); R. Brenner, *Rivalry in Business, Science Among Nations* (Chicago: University of Chicago Press, 1987); numerous government, international agency, "think tank" (institute) publications and journal articles.

2. For the cooperation side, see A. Kohn, *No Contest: The Case Against Competition* (Boston: Houghton Mifflin, 1986); J. Culbertson, *Competition: Constructive and Destructive* (Madison, Wis.: 21st Century Press, 1985); F. Contractor and P. Lorange, eds., *Cooperative Strategies in International Business* (Lexington, Mass.: Lexington Books, 1988); and journal articles.

3. For an assessment of competitiveness and entrepreneurship, mostly from a U.S. viewpoint, see *Frontiers of Entrepreneurial Research* (Wellesley, Mass.: Babson College, published every other year); R. Hisrich and M. Peters, *Entrepreneurship* (Homewood, Ill.: Dow Jones Irwin, 1991); M. Spence and H. Hazard, eds., *International Competitiveness* (New York: Harper Business, 1988); J. A. Young, ed., *The New Reality: Global Competition,* 2 vols. (Washington: U.S. Government Printing Office, 1985); J. Zysman and L. Tyson, eds., *American Industry in International Competition* (Ithaca, N.Y.: Cornell University Press, 1983).

4. This industry, like many others, has been studied at length. See A. Philips, *Technology and Market Structure: A Study of the Aircraft Industry* (Lexington, Mass.: Lexington/Heath, 1971); *A Competitive Assessment of the U.S. Civilian Aircraft Industry* (Boulder, Colo.: Westview, 1986); and *The Competitive Status of the U.S. Civilian Aviation Manufacturing Industry* (Washington, D.C.: National Academy Press for NRC, 1985). See also numerous articles in *Aviation Week and Space Technology, Air Transport World,* and *Interavia.* Two videotapes are also available: *Boeing vs. the World: The Jet Set,* and *Takeoff: Gates vs. Learjet* in the *Enterprise* series (produced by WGBH-Boston in conjunction with Harvard Business School in the early 1980s).

5. The classic economic view is summarized well in F. M. Scherer and D. Ross, *Industrial Market Structure and Economic Reform,* 3rd ed. (Boston: Houghton Mifflin, 1990); A. D. Chandler, *Scale and Scope: The Dynamics of Industrial Capitalism* (Cambridge, Mass.: Harvard University Press, 1990); and B. Carlsson, *Industrial Dynamics* (Boston: Kluwer Academic, 1989).

6. The discussion on the determinants of competitive forces in an industry is based largely on M. Porter, *Competitive Strategy* (New York: Free Press, 1980) and his *Competitive Advantage* (New York: Free Press, 1985). For related titles, also used here, see his *Competition in Global Industries* (Boston: Harvard Business School Press, 1986), and *Competitive Advantage of Nations* (New York: Free Press, 1990).

7. The best source on privatization is *The Economist,* followed by articles in *Business Week, Forbes, Fortune, The Financial Post* (Can-

ada), *The Financial Times* (U.K.), and other general business journals. Books are just starting to appear; the situation on privatization in Eastern Europe, Africa, Asia, and Latin America is still very fluid.

8. See the 1986 and 1990 volumes by Porter, *Competitive Strategy* and *Competitive Advantage,* as well as journal articles and publications on global competitiveness from the U.S. Department of Commerce (USDC) and the Organization for Economic Cooperation and Development (OECD). These and other agencies issue reports on global competition and specific industries, including the role of governments.

9. As stated already, many general business journals report regularly on major industries, as does *Industry Week* and the *Wall Street Journal* on weekdays, in some cases even carrying cover stories. Associations also issue reports—for example, in the steel industry, see the reports issued by the American Iron & Steel Institute (AISI), and for electronics, see those by the Electronics Industries Association (EIA). This is typical; your first stop for references on any industry should be the publications of the relevant industry association, followed by institute and government reports.

10. The following books focus on high-tech industries, especially electronics: W. H. Davidow, *High Technology Marketing* (New York: Free Press, 1986); W. Shanklin and J. Ryans, Jr., *Essentials of Marketing High Technology* (Lexington, Mass.: Lexington Books, 1986); and H. Riggs, *Managing High Technology Companies* (New York: Van Nostrand Reinhard, 1984). See articles in such journals as *Computerworld, Datamation, Electronics News, High Technology Business, Research & Technology Management,* and *Technology Review.* We are also grateful to J. Porter, President, Disk/Trend of Mountain View, California, for sharing his insights with us.

11. On exit and entry barriers in various industries, see journals such as the *American Economic Review, California Management Review, Journal of Business, Journal of Business Strategy, Sloan Management Review,* and *Strategic Management Journal.* See also the classic in this field: J. Bain, *Industrial Organization* (New York: Wiley, 1968). See specifically, J. Haverty and M. Kyj, "What Happens When New Competitors Enter an Industry," *Industrial Marketing Management* 20 (February 1991): 73–80. See also Scherer and Ross, *Industrial Market Structure and Economic Reform*; W. Sheperd, *Economics of Industrial Organizations,* 3rd ed. (Englewood Cliffs, N.J.: Prentice-Hall, 1990); D. Hay and D. Morris, *Industrial Organization Economics* (New York: Oxford University Press, 1990); D. Teece, *Competitive Challenge* (New York: Harper Business, 1990).

12. See the sources cited in endnote 10, journals cited in endnote 11, and articles in entrepreneurship-oriented journals, such as *INC., Journal of Small Business Management,* and *Journal of Small Business* (Canada). See also an excellent compilation in W. Adams, ed., *The Structure of American Industry,* 8th ed. (New York: Macmillan, 1989).

13. See J. Dreyfuss, "Getting High Tech Back on Track," *Fortune,* January 1, 1990, pp. 74–77; the books of D. Okimoto—for example, *The Competitive Edge* (Stanford: Stanford University Press, 1989); and J. C. Morgan and J. J. Morgan, *Cracking the Japanese Market* (New York: Macmillan/Free Press, 1991).

14. The software industry is part of the computer services industry, which in turn is part of the information industry. For three key references on the information industry, see A. C. Gross, "The Information Vending Machine," *Business Horizons* 31 (January–February 1988): 24–33; D. Raphael, "The Information Industry," *Business Economics* (July 1989): 28–34; and P. Zurkowski, "The Business of Information," in G. Roukis et al., *Global Corporate Intelligence* (New York: Quorum Books, 1990), pp. 77–90. Several reports appeared in this field during the 1980s—for example, J. McLaughlin and A. Antonoff, *Mapping the Information Business* (Cambridge, Mass.: Program on Information Resources Policy, Harvard University, 1986).

15. Cited in many business and robotics journals. See also the annual reports of General Motors and Fujitsu for an inside but not necessarily objective viewpoint. GM also made a major acquisition in the information field by purchasing Electronics Data Systems (EDS) from Ross Perot.

16. P. Doyle and J. Saunders, "Market Segmentation and Positioning in Specialized Industrial Markets," *Journal of Marketing* 49 (Spring 1985): 24–32. See also, A. C. Gross, "Global Competition for Environmental Markets: The Case of the Water Pollution Control Industry," *European Journal of Marketing* (Spring 1986): 22–34.

17. Cited in Porter, *Competitive Strategy,* p. 316.

18. We are grateful to the editorial staff of *Beverage World* magazine and the research staff of three Cleveland-based consulting firms (The Freedonia Group, Leading Edge, and Predicasts) for commentary. For further information, consult the journal *Packaging.*

19. See D. H. Middleton, ed., *Composite Materials in Aircraft Structures* (Harlow, U.K.: Longman, 1990) and G. Lubin, *Handbook of Composites* (New York: McGraw-Hill, 1982).

20. See Contractor and Lorange, *Cooperative Strategies in International Business,* and T. Collins and T. Doorley, III, *Teaming Up for the 90s: Benefits of Joint Ventures and Strategic Alliances* (Homewood, Ill.: Business One Irwin 1991). On the technology front, see J. L. Badaracco, Jr., *The Knowledge Link: Competing Through Strategic Alliances* (Boston: Harvard Business School Press, 1990), and D. Ford and C. Ryan, "Taking Technology to Market," *Harvard Business Review* 59 (March–April 1981): 117–126.

21. The general business and academic journals are now focusing on the topic. See J. Main, "Making Global Alliances Work," *Fortune,* December 17, 1990, pp. 121–126; D. Bowersox, "The Strategic Benefits of Logistics Alliances," *Harvard Business Review* 68 (July–August 1990): 36–38; R. Lynch, "Building Alliances to Penetrate European Markets," *Journal of Business Strategy* 11 (March–April 1990): 4–8; H. Crouse, "The Power of Partnership," *Journal of Business Strategy* (November–December 1991): 4–8; A. Larson, "Partner Networks," *Journal of Business Venturing* (May 1991): 173–188. Recently, *Business Periodicals Index* gave the term *strategic alliances* its own subject heading (in addition to *joint ventures* as a heading).

22. Based on documents from Eaton Corporation of Cleveland, Ohio. For a full discussion of licensing, see F. Contractor, *Licensing in International Strategy* (Westport, Conn.: Quorum Books, 1985).

23. This section relies on several articles in the Summer 1987 issue of the *Columbia Journal of World Business*; the chapters in Contractor & Lorange, *Cooperative Strategies*; and selected books of K. Harrington published in the 1980s. Historical statistics on international joint ventures have been collected by the Harvard Multinational Enterprise Project and Columbia University.

24. Based primarily on articles listed in endnote 21 as well as news briefs from *Business Week, Fortune,* and *Forbes,* summarized in *Predicasts F & S Index of Corporations and Industries.*

25. *Comprehensive Dissertation Index,* 1861–1972, vol. 26, under the subject heading, "Oil," lists over thirty doctoral theses that deal with OPEC. Some of these have projected the situation in the 1970s—for example, H. Abdel-Barr, "The Market Structure of International Oil with Special Reference to OPEC," unpublished doctoral dissertation at the University of Wisconsin, 1966. For an abstract of this thesis, see *Dissertation Abstracts,* vol. 28/03-A, p. 838; the full thesis can be ordered in print format or on microfilm. For the most comprehensive treatment of the history of crude oil and the attempts to cartelize, see D. Yergin, *The Prize* (New York: Simon & Schuster, 1991).

26. The general business press and various industry journals report on price movements as well as on attempts to cartelize. For example, precise price changes are reported for the chemical industry in *Chemical Market Re-*

porter. The annual volume *Minerals Year-book* (Washington: U.S. Bureau of Mines) gives detailed data on prices for many minerals and some other natural resources. There are also regular reports on the action of various metal councils—for example, copper, tin, etc.—and of agricultural councils that attempt to fashion "orderly markets."

27. This great collusion did not receive much publicity at the time; but see F. Cleveland, Jr., *Corporations on Trial* (Belmont, Calif.: Wadsworth, 1964), and R. Smith, "Incredible Electric Conspiracy," *Fortune,* April 1961, pp. 132–137, and May 1961, pp. 161–164.

28. S. Flex, "The Crackdown on Colluding Road Builders," *Fortune,* October 3, 1983, pp. 79–85.

29. Whether in fact trade and industry associations have been and are still acting as so-called "clearinghouses" on prices and pricing practices is a murky topic. For an overview, see C. Mack, *The Executive Handbook of Trade and Business Associations* (Westport, Conn.: Greenwood Press, 1990), and P. Millard, *Trade Associations and Professional Bodies in the UK* (London: Pergamon Press, 1988). In 1990, the U.S. airlines were accused of "signaling" each other by publishing their rates via electronic databases and reservation systems such as Apollo (United) and Sabre (American), as reported in the pages of the *Wall Street Journal.*

30. Reported in various business journals—for example, K. Steele, "Buildings Take Tests Too," *Fortune,* October 25, 1985, pp. 108–113.

31. On diversification and growth strategies, see M. Utton, *Diversification and Competition* (Cambridge: Cambridge University Press, 1979); M. Gort, *Diversification and Integration in American Industry* (Westport: Greenwood Press, 1984); G. Day, *Market Driven Strategy* (New York: Free Press, 1990); and the classic volume, H. Ansoff, *Corporate Strategy* (New York: McGraw-Hill, 1965). On the portfolio theory and practice, see any principles of marketing text. Finally,

consult R. Kuhn, *To Flourish Among Giants* (New York: Wiley, 1985), and the many outstanding volumes by Peter Drucker: *Managing in Turbulent Times* (New York: Harper & Row, 1985); *Innovation and Entrepreneurship* (New York: Harper & Row, 1985); *The New Realities* (New York: Harper & Row, 1989).

32. The three classics on military warfare are K. von Clausewitz, *On War* (New York: Pelican, 1968); B. H. Liddell Hart, *Strategy* (New York: Praeger, 1954); and Sun Tzu, *The Art of War* (New York: Dell/Bantam, 1983). Marketing as warfare is the topic in the following: A. Ries and J. Trout, *Marketing Warfare* (New York: McGraw-Hill, 1986); R. Duro and B. Sandstro, *Principles of Marketing Warfare* (New York: Wiley, 1987); and B. James, *Business Wargames* (New York: Viking Penguin, 1985). See also such journal articles as R. Calantone and C. DiBenedetto, "Defensive Industrial Marketing Strategies," *Industrial Marketing Management* 19 (August 1990): 267–278.

33. Pricing as a competitive tool has been tackled in three key volumes: K. Monroe, *Pricing* (New York: McGraw-Hill, 1989); M. Morris and G. Morris, *Market-Oriented Pricing* (Westport, Conn.: Greenwood Press); and T. Nagle, *The Strategy and Tactics of Pricing* (Englewood Cliffs, N.J.: Prentice-Hall, 1987). See also such articles as D. Shipley, "Distributor Pricing in Very Competitive Markets," *Industrial Marketing Management* 19 (August 1990): 215–224.

34. What measures to employ when judging either competitive situations or cooperative ventures has been the subject of long debate. Observers now seem to agree that you must go beyond financial indicators and even general business indicators. Still, social responsibility and other general measures of business performance have not been fully accepted as "proper indicators." It seems that a combination of the three kinds of measures is a fair way of judging what happens. The debate continues in such journals as *Business & Society Review.*

35. The relationship between market share and profitability has been probed in depth. Some say market share is key: S. Schoeffler et al., "Impact of Strategic Planning on Profit Performance," *Harvard Business Review* 52 (March–April 1979): 137–145; F. Wiersma, "Successful Share Building Strategies," *Harvard Business Review* 59 (January–February 1981): 135–144; and R. Buzzell and B. Gale, *The PIMS Principles: Linking Strategy to Performance* (New York: Free Press, 1987). For contrary views, see R. Jacobson and D. Aaker, "Is Market Share All That It's Cracked Up to Be?" *Journal of Marketing* 49 (Fall 1985): 11–22; D. McLogon, "Market Share: Key to Profitability?" *Planning Review* 9 (March 1981): 26–29; R. Alessio, "Market Share Madness," *Journal of Business Strategy* 3 (Fall 1982): 76–79; M. Lubatkin and M. Pitts, "PIMS: Fact or Folklore?" *Journal of Business Strategy* 3 (Winter 1983): 38–43. The PIMS database is produced at the Strategic Planning Institute, Boston, Mass.

36. Many articles on the importance of quality appeared during the 1980s. See, for example, L. Phillips et al., "Product Quality, Cost Position, and Business Performance," *Journal of Marketing* (Spring 1983): 26–43. The father figure in quality, specifically in quality control, is W. E. Deming, after whom Japan named its top quality award. In 1990–1991, three biographies of Deming were published simultaneously. See his book, *Out of Crisis* (Cambridge: MIT Press, 1986). In the United States, the Balrige award assumed the same prestige and status as the Deming prize; see T. Rohan, "Services Win Balrige," *Industry Week,* November 5, 1990, pp. 57–58; B. Cook, "In Search of Six Sigma (Defect Free Production)," *Industry Week,* October 1, 1990, pp. 60–65; J. Heskett et al., *Service Breakthroughs* (New York: Free Press, 1990), Chapter 7. The latest book on the topic, which also spawned a television series, is L. Dobins and C. Crawford-Mason, *Quality or Else* (Boston: Houghton Mifflin, 1992).

37. This section is based in part on D. Peters, *Abrasives and Abrasive Machinery* (Cleveland: Predicasts, 1983), updated by the *Minerals Yearbook* (Washington: U.S. Bureau of Mines, annually), with input from the Coated Abrasives Manufacturers' Institute, Abrasive Grain Association, and Grinding Wheel Institute.

38. Based in part on J. Breckling, *U.S. Markets for Cement and Ready-Mix Concrete* (Cleveland: Leading Edge, 1988), updated by the author and industry sources.

39. Based in part on J. Breckling, *Internal Combustion Engines Market* (Cleveland: Predicasts, 1983), updated by the author, industry sources, and a literature search.

40. Based in part on J. Breckling, *Welding Equipment* (Cleveland: Predicasts, 1982), updated by the author, K. Graff of Edison Welding Institute, and R. French of the American Welding Society.

41. Based in part on W. Weizer, *Biotechnological Applications* (Cleveland: Predicasts, 1983), updated by H. DeYoung, "The Greening of Biotechnology," *High Technology* (September 1984): 59–67; selected issues of *The Economist*; and personal communication with P. Bridgen of the Association of Biotechnology Companies, and R. Godown of the Industrial Biotechnology Association, both of Washington, D.C., in January 1991.

42. Based in part on N. DiGeronimo, *The Factory of the Future* (Cleveland: Predicasts, 1983), updated by a literature search and personal communication with G. Conkol of Unified Technology Center and A. Printz of Cleveland State University, both of Cleveland, Ohio, in January 1991.

43. Based in part on J. Breckling, *Capital Equipment Leasing Markets* (Cleveland: Predicasts, 1983), updated by the author in 1991.

44. Based on E. Hester, *Security Surveillance Equipment* (Cleveland: Freedonia Group, 1991), and R. McLean and E. Hester, *Electronic Security Equipment Markets* (Cleveland: Predicasts, 1984), with short comment by E. Criscuoli, Jr. of the American Society for Industrial Security of Arlington, Virginia, in January 1991.

8

TECHNOLOGY AND THE INDUSTRIAL MARKETPLACE

- To gain insights on the concept of commercialization as the complex linkage that binds science, technology, and the marketplace

- To understand how innovation (technological change) contributes to the economic growth of nations, industries, and organizations and why it can create new markets and rejuvenate old markets

- To learn the sources of funding and the performing sectors for research and development (R&D) and the indicators of R&D

- To understand the roles of inventors, innovators, imitators, users, and others involved in the invention, innovation, and diffusion of technology

- To understand the role of technology in regard to both industrialized and developing nations and both old-line and high-tech industries

- To learn about commercial payoffs, managerial implications, and the market impact of scientific and technological advances and to become aware of alternative technological and business strategies

Scientists invent it, engineers make it work. Venture capitalists back it, the sales force markets it. But what is "it," and is "it" as simple as just described? It is **commercialization** or **innovation**. It is moving from an **invention** or discovery to a trial product or pilot process, then to full-scale production, and finally to mass merchandising or niche marketing. But is it really as simple as just described? No, it is usually a far more complex process, and it often has some surprising features and outcomes.

Chapter 8 explores the relationship between science and technology on the one hand and economic growth and business marketing on the other. Although the relationship is both complex and circular, meaningful conclusions can be drawn. These can guide us to a deeper understanding of what impact **research and development (R&D)** have on both national economies and the financial well-being of enterprises. The evidence is strong that whereas any one discovery may not yield a new product or process, the totality of R&D offers the industrial marketplace many benefits. But the performers of R&D are not the only productive players. Users of the product or process contribute greatly by providing feedback; suppliers also offer good advice; and imitators often make significant improvements.

Several themes are woven in throughout the chapter. The first and most important one is that technological change is a rich tapestry, with many colors and weavers. Put differently, innovation is seldom simple, one-directional, or uniform. More often it is complex, circular, and highly diverse. A second theme is that technological advances are often disruptive to individuals, organizations, markets, or even whole economies. Yet innovation occurs, because benefits appear to outweigh the disadvantages. Progress in agriculture, advances in transportation, better health care, and faster communication all proved highly beneficial to millions

BUSINESS MARKETING IN PRACTICE ▮▮▮▮▮▮▮▮▮▮▮

Appropriate or Intermediate Technology for the Developing Nations

I say, therefore, that the dynamic approach to development, which treats the choice of appropriate, intermediate technologies as the central issue, opens up avenues of constructive action, which the static, econometric approach totally fails to recognize.

The indigenous technology of a developing country is a $1 technology, while that of the developed countries could be called a $1,000 technology (symbolically speaking). The gap is so enormous that a transition is simply impossible.... If effective help is to be brought to those who need it the most, an intermediate position is required, say a $100 technology. Put differently, choose an intermediate point between having a giant earthmover and thousands of small shovels or scoops.

Labor intensiveness and small scale lend themselves to intermediate technology, but there is more to it than that. What is crucial is to be appropriate. The idea of intermediate technology does not imply a 'going back' in history to methods now outdated ... it means a genuine forward movement into new territory, where the enormous cost and complication of production methods for the sake of labor saving and job elimination is avoided and technology is made appropriate for labor-surplus societies.

Institutional arrangements for dispensing aid are generally such that there is an unsurmountable bias in favor of large scale projects on the level of most modern technology. If we could turn official and popular interest away from the grandiose projects and to the real needs of the poor, the battle would be won. A study of intermediate technologies as they exist today already would disclose that there is enough knowledge and experience to set everybody to work, and where there are gaps, new design studies could be made very quickly. Three approaches are to transform existing techniques, adapt and reform advanced technology, or conduct field research and experiments.

Source: Excerpt from *Small Is Beautiful: Economics as if People Mattered* by E. F. Schumacher. Copyright © 1973 by E. F. Schumacher. Reprinted by permission of HarperCollins Publishers Inc.

Note: This book has had an enormous impact on thinking about the use of technology in developing nations and ultimately contributed even to major institutional changes, including the kind of projects supported by the World Bank. It is still widely quoted. The recent focus on factoring environmental damage into economic statistics also owes much to this book, which has become a classic.

---

around the globe. However—and this is our third theme—we must carefully choose the innovations we should seek out and sponsor. This is the notion of **appropriate technology** or adapting new products and processes to prevailing values, social goals, and environmental needs. Today, this may mean focusing less on giant projects and more on small-scale possibilities (for example, power plants versus solar panels). In the search for national security, a shift may occur from emphasis on nuclear weapons to productivity enhancement tools. Environmental considerations now call for considering the total life cycle of a new product, not just its initial cost and features. For example, creating less expensive, higher load-capacity or more fuel-efficient trucks is admirable, but so is finding ways for their proper disassembly or ultimate recycling.[1]

THE SOURCES OF INVENTION AND INNOVATION

Who invents and how does innovation really happen? Can it be encouraged, nurtured, and its fruits brought to market? There are two contrasting perspectives on this question: the classic view, which shows a straight line from inventing to marketing, and the more modern, complex view, which acknowledges many participants. In this second scenario, imitators and users play a significant role, and emphasis is placed on new and improved processes as much as on new products. The payoffs from innovation may not always accrue to those who make the breakthroughs or significant improvements.

The Classic View of Invention and Innovation

In our mind's eye we see the lonely inventor toiling away in the attic or basement, then suddenly crying out: "Eureka, I have found it!" The steps that follow are refining the concept, elaboration, pilot operation, production, and marketing. This classic and linear view is illustrated in Exhibit 8–1. Many observers think that this situation prevails widely even today, with research laboratories of manufacturers perceiving a need, creating a new product to fill that need, performing some product testing, and then taking the new item to market.

There is some merit and evidence for the classic view. After all, the experiments of famous European scientists, such as Faraday, Henry, Maxwell, and Kelvin, gave rise to new products and processes. Their findings laid the foundation of magnetism and electricity, which in turn resulted in the flowering of whole industries and markets. Later in the nineteenth century, Thomas Edison invented the first practical incandescent light bulb; indoor and outdoor commercial lighting installations soon followed. In the mid-1950s, the team of Bardeen, Brattain, and Shockley invented the transistor. This tiny device, which amplifies electric signals, ultimately became the basic building block in electronics, by allowing the formation of integrated circuits or "brains on chips." Semiconductors are largely responsible for the growth of the computing and communication industries. Other discoveries can be cited, ranging from atomic physics to biology, that gave rise to commercially new products and processes and then to fledgling industries and robust markets.

At this point, we should note that technological changes or innovations can occur without scientific discovery. In the eighteenth and nineteenth centuries, James Watt and others studied heat losses, designing the steam engine and other machines without being aware of the principles of kinetics and thermodynamics. In the twentieth century, progress in aviation was made by engineers, technicians, and test pilots before aerodynamic theory was fully developed. In many other fields, such as papermaking, petroleum refining, and pharmaceutical manufacturing, technological advances occurred also without scientific discoveries or fully developed theories. Thus, even in the classic view, it is possible to begin at a point

EXHIBIT 8–1   The Classic View of Innovation and Its Impact

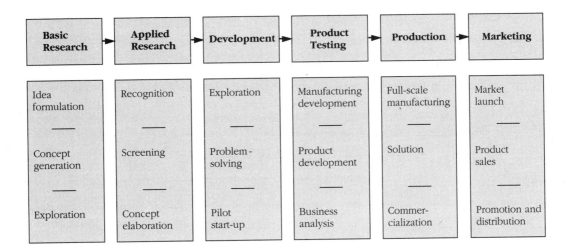

Basic Research	Applied Research	Development	Product Testing	Production	Marketing
Idea formulation	Recognition	Exploration	Manufacturing development	Full-scale manufacturing	Market launch
Concept generation	Screening	Problem-solving	Product development	Solution	Product sales
Exploration	Concept elaboration	Pilot start-up	Business analysis	Commer-cialization	Promotion and distribution

other than by basic research in laboratories. In other words, development can occur before the underlying theory is made clear. Observers note that a "nurturing, innovation-friendly" environment is more crucial in some fields than having a base of scientists and scientific knowledge.[2]

The Modern View of Invention and Innovation

Those who study inventions and innovations in the twentieth century think that a more complex, circular path of commercialization has become widely prevalent. The evidence indicates that the situation shown in Exhibit 8–2 is more frequent and more productive than the classic scenario. In this scheme, much interaction occurs between the various stages and between the many participants. Inventors, innovators, imitators, and users all make a contribution; they are all "improvers." Feedback loops, as shown in the diagram, happen often and, indeed, should be encouraged continuously. In such an atmosphere, technicians and factory workers criticize engineers, thereby improving the design and development process. Their contributions then stimulate the work of scientists in the laboratories and even suggest new theories. Those in turn can lead to discoveries or inventions, which again give rise to further innovation and improvement, and the whole roundabout sequence continues.[3]

This more complex notion of commercialization does not detract from the importance of creative ideas. Significant breakthroughs will be coming forth from individuals and from teams of researchers. What needs recognition, however, is that other aspects are equally important on the road of progress. Among these are

EXHIBIT 8–2   The Modern View of Innovation and Its Impact

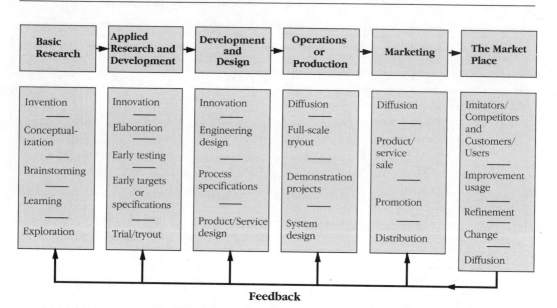

a friendly social and political environment; commitment to education of not just elite scientists, but of an overall skilled work force; easy access to a wide base of information; and feedback of all sorts from imitators, suppliers, and users. Organizing and managing the "total system" remains an elusive task that some firms and nations achieve, while others play catch-up. As shown later, a mixture of freedom and goal setting works best.

After studying a host of innovative changes in such diverse areas as material handling, engineering plastics, and scientific instruments, a team led by E. von Hippel of M.I.T. concluded that so-called **lead users** play a significant role in innovation.[4] Such early adopters tinker with solutions offered to them by the original researchers and developers. They then offer constructive criticism, make actual improvements, and may even suggest breakthrough ideas. All of these changes then form the basis for the next generation of new products and services. The suppliers of materials to manufacturers constitute yet another group that can take the lead in the innovation game. In short, outsiders, be they lead users or suppliers, become part of the creative team, often playing an equal or bigger role than the original group of innovators. Exhibit 8–3 gives a summary of the functional sources of innovation in selected fields.

While patents are awarded to new inventions, innovation seldom happens in one place, at one time, by one person. Furthermore, the individual or organization coming up with the innovation may not use it and may not be able to capture

EXHIBIT 8–3   Functional Sources of Innovation, Selected Fields

Innovation Type Sampled	Innovation Developed by					
	User	Manufacturer	Supplier	Other	NA[a] (n)	Total (n)
Scientific instruments	77%	23%	0%	0%	17	111
Semiconductor and printed circuit board process	67	21	0	12	6	49
Pultrusion process	90	10	0	0	0	10
Tractor shovel-related	6	94	0	0	0	16
Engineering plastics	10	90	0	0	0	5
Plastics additives	8	92	0	0	4	16
Industrial gas-using	42	17	33	8	0	12
Thermoplastics-using	43	14	36	7	0	14
Wire termination equipment	11	33	56	0	2	20

[a]NA = number of cases for which data item coded in this table is not available. (NA cases excluded from calculations of percentages in table.)

Source: From *The Sources of Innovation* by Eric von Hippel. Copyright © 1988 by Eric von Hippel. Reprinted by permission of Oxford University Press, Inc.

profits from it. Pharmaceutical firms are generally able to utilize the fruits of their own research. In contrast, the bar-code readers used by supermarket cashiers at check-out counters were developed by engineering companies, but with clear specification and much research help from the supermarket operators. Machinery, automotive, and other manufacturing companies in Japan, Europe, and North America that rely on and work closely with skilled suppliers often find their suppliers to be a source of useful ideas for further improvements. To repeat, much innovation consists of many small improvements, contributed by a wide variety of individuals and groups.

Another change is a shift in focus for the goals of innovation. Much emphasis has been given in the past to the creation and development of new *products*. However, many entrepreneurs and whole industries now stress that developing new or improved *processes* is equally important. Devising new ways for higher crop yields in agriculture, safer mining at the surface level or underground, and quicker means of erecting buildings and bridges can yield significant benefits for the developers and the users. Similarly, we are seeing innovative steps in factory assembly, material handling, and packaging, as well as in transportation, utilities, and communication. One example is the delivery of coal, which usually occurs by rail or trucks; now the coal is mixed with water, and the resulting slurry is sent on its way in pipelines. Another example is robotics; robots are new products, but their use in factories alters the process of assembly. In such cases, the new processes create marketing opportunities and significant new markets.[5]

THE QUEST FOR INNOVATION IN DIFFERENT NATIONS

Why is there a strong urge to innovate in many countries? Do developed nations differ from each other in the rate and direction of innovation? What are the explanations for such differences and what do they imply? Most large and small, developed and developing nations, appear committed to reaping the fruits of technological progress, but frequently they are unsure about the specific steps involved. Policies on specific goals, technology transfer, or industry subsidies are not easy to formulate.

In Search of Growth: Technology as the Catalyst

The great inventions and innovations of the eighteenth and nineteenth centuries, primarily in Europe, transformed old industries and created new ones. The Industrial Revolution brought mixed results economically and socially, but there is no doubt that it allowed faster or cheaper production of manufactured goods. Iron making, textile fabrication, machinery building, land and sea transport, and many other fields did undergo revolutionary changes. In the twentieth century, equally great advances occurred in other fields, ranging from aviation to telecommunication and from plastics making to construction. Much of this technological change has taken place in Europe, Japan, and North America, where large markets have been created with opportunities for enterprises. Thus innovation is seen as a catalyst in the economic growth of nations and in the financial well-being of industrial enterprises and individuals. As a result, a culture of innovation has been espoused, and research and development have been judged worthy of much effort and funding.[6]

At the end of the 1980s, the United States was the biggest spender for R&D in absolute terms, at about $110 billion annually, followed by Japan at about $42 billion, Germany at $21 billion, France and the United Kingdom at $14 billion each, Italy at $8 billion, and Canada at $5 billion. Smaller nations—for example, the Netherlands, Sweden, and Switzerland—registered expenditures in the $3 billion to $4 billion range. However, on a relative basis, looking at R&D spending as a share of the gross domestic product (GDP), the leader was Sweden at 3.1 percent, followed by Japan, Switzerland, and Germany at 2.9 percent each, the United States at 2.8 percent, and France and the United Kingdom at about 2.3 percent each. The most telling figures, however, are the relative levels of nondefense R&D spending; these expenditures are plotted for key nations in Exhibit 8–4. The United States has not done well in this regard as it focused heavily on weapons development.

The investments in R&D among the industrialized nations show fluctuations in both absolute and relative terms. What explains these fluctuations, and why are the paths taken regarding the type of R&D performed distinct among these nations? The different patterns in innovation among countries seem harder to explain than

EXHIBIT 8–4   Estimated Nondefense R&D Expenditures as a Percentage of Gross Domestic Product (GDP), Seven Major Western Nations, 1971–1988

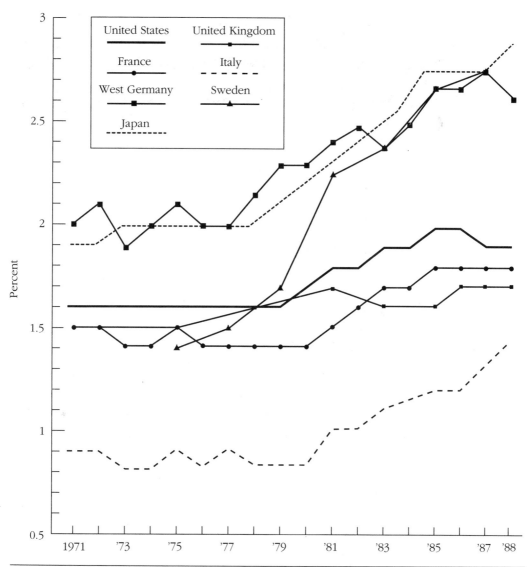

Source: *International Science and Technology Data Update,* Report #91-309 (Washington, D.C.: National Science Foundation, 1991), p. 8.

differences in R&D among industries and companies. However, conceptualization and empirical work are now beginning to pay off, yielding meaningful theories and statistics.

One of the leading theorists in this field is Henry Ergas of the OECD (Organization for Economic Cooperation and Development), a multinational statistical agency.[7] According to Ergas, three factors explain national differences: the quality of inputs (general education, scientific base, research institutions); the nature of demand (sophisticated customers calling for and aiding in constant improvements); and an effective industrial structure (allowing intense competition, yet providing ways for companies to share in the financing and diffusion of technology). As shown in Exhibit 8–5, different countries combine these factors in different ways. But governments take a lead role in shaping that combination according to the kind of activities they wish to encourage.

In the United States, the United Kingdom, and France, the national governments strongly supported research that was defense or weapons oriented, while allocating much less funding to general advancement of knowledge, health care, and agriculture. The policy was mission oriented or top down, heavily favoring large firms and major projects. In contrast, in Germany, Italy, and Sweden, the policy was bottom up or diffusion oriented, favoring state aid for education, training, and standard setting across several fields. General research, broad application of research, and industrial development were favored. In Japan, the policy was a mixture of the two approaches, with the government first encouraging a strong collaborative spirit, then taking a hands-off approach as companies caught up and even went ahead of competitors in the rest of the world.

Recent evidence indicates that the United States, the United Kingdom, and France may be moving toward the patterns shown in other developed countries. They may be changing their ways in light of political developments at home (demand for education, training, and jobs) and especially abroad. The breakup of the USSR into constituent states is forcing a move away from military-related R&D and toward more peaceful applications in Eastern Europe and in the West. Regarding the trends in the United States, an increase is likely in the share going to nondefense R&D. But the federal government is unlikely to increase its funding of R&D substantially in the coming years. It may enact more favorable federal tax laws to encourage more private sector funding. If that happens and if the short-term orientation of U.S. firms changes, we may see a sudden boost in research spending by the private sector. The key will still be bringing the new ideas to market quickly.

Industrializing and developing nations have spent modest sums on technological change until now. But the example of South Korea illustrates what can be achieved. It is spending about $2 billion annually, or 1.8 percent of its gross domestic product (GDP), on R&D and has achieved much success in world markets, competing head on against Japan, the United States, and others. Its focus is on machinery, electronics, and transport equipment. Other industrializing nations are spending less than 1 percent of their GDP on research and development. Some of them are rich in natural resources, but this is not as much benefit to them as before, since such materials can be bought on the open market and synthetics now offer alternatives. Nearness to users is not too crucial since transport costs have de-

EXHIBIT 8–5   Socioeconomic Objectives of Government R&D Expenditures, Seven Major Western Nations, 1988

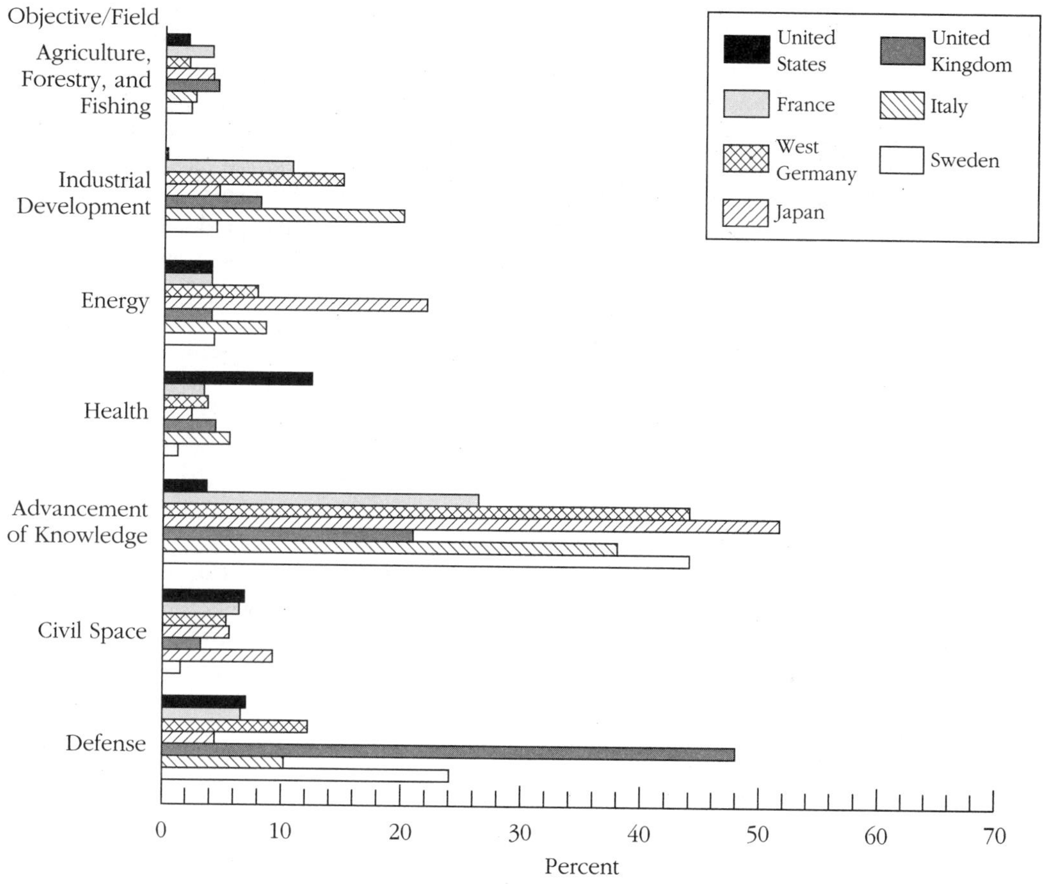

Source: *International Science and Technology Data Update,* Report #91-309 (Washington, D.C.: National Science Foundation, 1991), p. 10.

clined relative to the value of goods. The size of the domestic market is important, but often it is seldom large enough to absorb the fruits of major innovations, so foreign markets are sought. So the most promising course of action appears to be spending more money on education and technical training of the work force.[8]

Sources and Performers of Research and Development

Industrialized nations make choices about which sectors will fund and which sectors will perform research and development tasks. Traditionally, in the United

States, the federal government has played a major role in disbursement but allowed others to perform the work. At the end of the 1980s, government and industry each accounted for about one-half of the $110 billion total funding. But in perform-ance, industry set the pace at about 72 percent, followed by the government and universities at 11 percent each, with other groups accounting for the remaining 6 percent. About three-fifths of the government funds called for defense R&D, with major defense contractors doing the work. In the 1990s, patterns may change as the cold war between the United States and the former Soviet Union has ended. This development signals unique opportunities in the public and private sectors for both funding and performing R&D oriented toward agriculture, energy, health care, space exploration, and manufacturing process improvements. We may yet see a flowering of technology in these and other peaceful applications, followed by robust growth of markets. What is needed, according to many observers, is that such reorientation be followed by quicker commercialization of worthwhile ideas and concepts.

In Western Europe, the governments in the major countries (France, Germany, Italy, and the United Kingdom) provide roughly 40 percent of R&D funds, the private sector about 55 percent, and others at 5 percent. In Japan, these figures are 20, 70, and 10 percent, respectively. As noted already and as shown in a previous exhibit, the orientation in these nations, especially Germany, Italy, and Japan, has been away from the military sphere and more toward general advancement of knowledge and specific industrial development. In terms of R&D performance, governments accounted for 20 percent, universities for 15 percent, and industry for 65 percent of the total. These are rough averages for the five nations (the four European countries and Japan) at the end of the 1980s.[9]

Activity by Industries

We have noted above that R&D investment priorities differ considerably among the industrialized countries. What about the specific industrial R&D expenditures? Exhibit 8–6 shows that six fields have received the bulk of R&D funds: electrical equipment, machinery and computers, chemicals, aerospace, instrumentation, and motor vehicles. The first five fields are considered high-tech areas. The United States has chosen to emphasize aerospace, a field that is closely related to military weapons. Meanwhile, companies in other Western nations have put their funds into machinery, chemicals, and computers. It is quite true that industries that fund and perform R&D cannot always capture all the rewards from such activity, but there is evidence that many are able to do so. The R&D activities and subsequent performances of machine tool and chemical makers from Germany, electronics goods and robot manufacturers from Japan, and electrical/machinery companies from Sweden, such as Asea-Brown-Boveri, provide ample support for this view.

In the single non-high-tech area, motor vehicles, the relative R&D investment of the United States versus that of Germany and Japan is about one-half that of the other nations (see Exhibit 8–6). The automobile, truck, and bus makers of Japan

EXHIBIT 8–6   Industrial R&D Expenditures by Industry, Selected Fields, Six Major Western Nations, 1986–1987

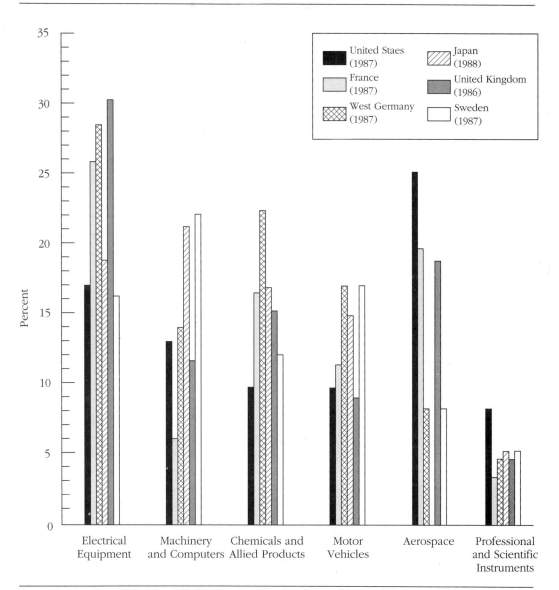

Source: *International Science and Technology Data Update,* Report #91-309 (Washington, D.C.: National Science Foundation, 1991), p. 24.

and Germany have invested in technological advances and have actually built them into vehicles in terms of better performance, smoother operating features, and "advanced gadgetry." Thus, once again, it is not surprising that the Big Three of Detroit have given up market share to Toyota, Nissan, Honda, and Mazda, as well as BMW, Mercedes-Benz, and Volkswagen-Audi. However, Chrysler, Ford, and General Motors are now emphasizing R&D again. This trend translates to smoother assembly, including more automation and better material handling.[10] Put differently, some R&D is aimed at plant productivity—that is, improving production. The other part of R&D focuses on and pays off in higher-quality vehicles, be they passenger cars, vans, trucks, or buses. In sum, the R&D investment ultimately should result in advantage in both processes and products.

MEASURING TECHNOLOGICAL CHANGE

Although many measures of technological change have been suggested, they can be classified into three categories: input, activity, and output. No single measure is really adequate, and it is not possible to understand the nature of R&D without considering all three. Even when this is done, the final results from R&D are difficult to assess because innovations are diffused widely, imitations and substitutes come into play, and users suggest improvements. However, by looking at the various indicators and their relationship and then how technological change is spreading, we can draw meaningful conclusions.

Input Indicators

The previous section emphasized the amount of absolute funds and the relative levels devoted to R&D in the major industrialized nations. We noted that the major Western nations expend about 2 to 3 percent of their gross domestic product for R&D. The allocation of funds was shown to be distinct among these countries, with the United States emphasizing defense-related research until now. As the cold war is ending and competitiveness in the marketplace is becoming an issue, U.S. patterns may begin to resemble those of other leading Western countries.

What about specific industrial sectors, not just broad categories? The pattern of R&D funding for almost twenty industries in the United States is shown in Exhibit 8–7. The big surprise in this panorama is not the relatively high rate of spending by the high-tech and other so-called glamour fields, but the fact that old-line manufacturing sectors are putting their dollars into scientific and technical knowledge. Clearly, firms in these sectors also think that there are payoffs from investing in R&D. Statistics on the R&D expenditures of major companies are also available in "scoreboard" issues of key business journals. This permits comparisons with one's competitors and with appropriate output measures. (When dealing with R&D funding figures, as with any set of statistics, one should still read the fine print. As

EXHIBIT 8–7   R&D Spending as a Percentage of Sales for Selected Major Industrial Sectors, United States, 1981–1989

Industry Sector	1981	1984	1987	1989
Semiconductors	7.5%	8.4%	9.6%	9.3%
Information processing	6.0	7.4	9.3	13.2
Computers	6.6	7.2	8.2	9.0
Drugs/pharmaceuticals	5.4	5.5	9.5	10.1
Instruments	4.5	5.5	6.0	5.8
Aerospace	4.9	4.6	4.4	4.1
Cars and trucks	3.7	3.5	3.7	3.6
Farm, construction and specialized machinery	2.7	3.4	3.0	2.6
Machine tools and mining equipment	2.3	3.0	3.7	2.0
Electrical equipment	2.6	3.0	2.4	2.3
Chemicals, excluding drugs	2.5	3.0	3.7	3.8
Telecommunications[a]	1.1	1.4	4.7	5.5
Building materials/housing	1.2	1.3	1.8	1.9
Paper and forest products	0.9	1.0	1.0	1.0
Containers	0.8	0.9	1.1	0.9
Fuel	0.5	0.6	0.7	0.8
Steel	0.6	0.6	0.7	1.0
All industry composite[b]	2.3%	2.8%	3.4%	3.4%

Notes: According to *Business Week,* surveys are of large and medium-sized firms in about thirty industrial sectors, said to represent 95 percent of all private R&D spending. Number of firms surveyed differ from year to year. Later surveys are based on Standard & Poor Compustat files. See special notes below.

[a]The jump between 1981–1984 versus 1987–1989 may not reflect reality according to some observers. Deregulation of Bell System and subsequent reclassification of the sector into operating and hardware companies may explain some or all of the discrepancy. Companies included: AT&T, ITT, GTE, Rolm, Stromberg Carlson, et al.

[b]This figure has been consistently close to the 2 percent mark (i.e., the range of 1.8 percent to 2.2 percent) for over a decade; some observers strongly doubt the jump to the 3.0 percent + range with U.S. nondefense spending on R&D showing stability.

Sources: Based on several scoreboard issues of *Business Week*: "R&D, Where Spending Is Strong," March 22, 1985, pp. 164–192; "R&D Update," July 8, 1985, pp. 86–104; "Perilous Cutback in Research Spending," June 20, 1988, pp. 139–192; and "R&D Scoreboard," June 15, 1990, pp. 197–217.

a general rule, R&D statistics do not include improvements in operations but focus on more formalized activities. At the same time, some companies now lump pollution control spending with R&D to show they care about both research and the environment. Thus, one must proceed with caution in interpreting and analyzing data.)[11]

Other input measures of R&D can be identified. One of these is capital investment in equipment and buildings devoted to the task. In other words, we can tally such things as the dollars spent on scientific instruments and research laboratory facilities. The problem is that doing so assumes full utilization of facilities in that industry, when in fact this may not be the case at all. For example, Bethlehem Steel built a magnificent research facility for steel research, only to sell it a few years later to Lehigh University, which uses it for a variety of purposes.

The number of scientists and engineers employed in the major industrialized nations can serve as an indicator of the level of effort and national priority given to science and technology. In a similar fashion, we can count degrees awarded, especially doctorates, in science and engineering. The most meaningful statistic is the ratio of scientists and engineers engaged in R&D per one thousand workers in the labor force. At the end of the 1980s, this figure stood at seven for the United States and Japan and at about five for West Germany and Sweden.[12] The average age of scientists and engineers is lowest in Japan, and some observers think this is an indicator not only of the recency of their training, but also of high future capabilities in that nation. They think so because evidence indicates that many scientific discoveries come at an early age.

Activity Indicators

Why should managers in general and marketers in particular be concerned with what scientists and engineers do in their laboratories and at their test benches? Those who analyze such activities are able to come away with insights on corporate operations. They get a glimpse of pursuits that seem promising in terms of delivering better processes and products. Whereas few organizations can claim to be excellent year after year (see the Business Marketing in Practice box on page 259 in Chapter 7), some companies are known for their innovative ways. These include 3M, Intel, and Motorola, which have mastered the art and science of running their laboratories. For example, 3M makes it a point to break up an R&D team or a laboratory when it gets too big; the company also rotates people among divisions. These firms seem more consistent than others in improving processes and bringing out new products with wide appeal to industrial clients.

A major survey of scientists in organizations conducted in the 1970s revealed some surprising results that have stood the test of time.[13] Sociologists from the University of Michigan asked scientists what would make them more productive in their laboratories. They answered almost uniformly: Let us do only professional-level work. Yet when the scientists were evaluated on various measures of professional productivity (articles published, patents obtained, peer ratings, and new prototype products), the ones who came out on top were those who had spent about 20 percent of their time on subprofessional work. Explanation: By doing some work at that level, they developed a better appreciation of the work of others, including that of technicians, marketers, and users. Then, by getting unsolicited feedback, including comments and advice on improvements, the scientists were able to sharpen their own inventive/innovative activity.

Other social scientists who studied the management of innovation uncovered more insights on what contributes to higher productivity in research laboratories.[14] An informal structure for daily work, small task forces, a set of goals, and a spirit of mission were found to enhance productivity in companies as varied as Lockheed Aircraft and Pilkington Glass. Other observers looking at electronics firms strongly endorsed the closer coupling of R&D tasks with marketing activities. This is in line with results cited earlier in regard to lead users or early adopters, who become sources of innovation. The creation of several large R&D consortia or umbrella organizations where engineers of different companies exchange "precompetitive" technical information underscores the same point. In sum, innovative enterprises will be those that encourage wide interaction between functional areas and invite feedback from outsiders, including key clients as well as researchers at other firms. These findings underline and explain the recent popularity of strategic alliances and partnerships mentioned in Chapter 7.

Output Indicators

Several measures are used to judge the output from research and development. The most obvious one would be major discoveries or inventions, but there is a lack of consensus on what is a major invention. So the following indicators are tracked on an absolute or relative basis: scientific papers published, worldwide citations or references to scientific papers, patents issued, and new products or processes. Each set has its uses, and each has some shortcomings. Social scientists pay attention to papers and citations, engineers and managers to patents, and marketers to new products and processes that can generate substantial unit sales.

Whereas the United States dominates the world scientific literature with about 36 percent of the total, other Western nations are holding on to steady shares, from a low of 2 percent for Italy to a high of 8 percent for the United Kingdom and Japan. There are variations by field of science—for example, the United States is strong in earth and space sciences, the United Kingdom in clinical medicine. The most interesting finding is the 8 percent share held by the former Soviet Union. Some astute Western businesses identified promising areas on this basis, purchased the technology, and commercialized it. Examples include the fields of physics, chemistry, metallurgy, and ceramics. Citation ratios measure the impact of scientific articles; the highest figures are held by Switzerland, Sweden, and the United States. German literature proved influential in physics and chemistry, Japanese in engineering; again, citations can yield clues to market potential.

The most traditional and a popular indicator of R&D output is patents issued. A patent is awarded in Western nations only when an invention is original, when it possesses technical feasibility, and when it has commercial applications. Current and historical statistics are available by country, technical field, national origin, and even company affiliation. Thus, patents appear to be a good measure to judge R&D output from both a technical and business viewpoint. Two factors detract from the usefulness of patent counts. First, some individuals and companies are reluctant to patent for fear of disclosing their ideas and thereby allowing others "to patent around" their inventions. Second, some discoveries are not patentable—for example, certain computer programs. On the whole, however, patents tell the story, giving insights on new ideas.[15]

Patents granted or issued have risen steadily in many countries over time. In the United States, patents issued rose from 64,000 in 1970 to 96,000 in 1989, an increase of 50 percent in less than two decades. The share going to U.S. citizens declined from three-fourths to half of the total. Meanwhile, the growth rate of U.S. patents granted to Japanese inventors nearly doubled in just five years, between 1983 and 1988. Since 1975, Japan has received more U.S. patents than any other foreign country.

There are sixteen major product fields for patents, with six areas dominant: (1) drugs and medicines, (2) office machines, (3) electrical machinery, (4) motor vehicles, (5) aircraft and parts, and (6) instruments. The distribution of patents by both major countries and major fields is shown in Exhibit 8–8. From 1978 to 1988, the U.S. patent count fell in all but one of the sixteen product fields; the Japanese share increased in all sixteen fields, with notable jumps in office and computing machines. This difference explains, at least in part, why the United States is falling behind in terms of competitiveness. Marketers and business buyers tend to espouse products that incorporate the latest technology.

New products and processes would seem to be the most popular measure for judging output from the R&D process, but there is strong disagreement on when something is new versus when it is merely an improved good or process. (As noted, many small improvements can add up to a major innovation; but these ideas may not be patentable or classified as new.) In some fields it is possible to track the number of new items. For example, in electronics and in drugs/medicines, several companies and industry associations boast that one-half of their current product line did not exist five years ago. In other areas, where the focus is on new processes, the best way to measure newness is in terms of performance. Some performance measures are speed of travel (aircraft), speed of operations (computers), tractive power (locomotives, tractors), and energy efficiency (lamps, trucks, and furnaces). Evidence is accumulating that in certain areas much progress has been made—for example, the ease and speed at which computers operate.[16] These features can then be used as a competitive tool; it is not unusual for firms to boast about newer features, faster speeds, and better performance in both print and electronic advertisements (see Chapter 7, Exhibit 7–10).

Commercial Payoffs

What business managers and marketers really wish for is to use new products and processes to increase sales, profits, and market share. To them, this is the true output or real payoff that should come from the R&D laboratories. Is it possible to draw a correlation, possibly even a causal link, among the following: R&D funding,

EXHIBIT 8–8   Patents Granted to Inventors in the United States, 1970–1989, by Year of Grant and Nationality of Inventor

Year	Patents Granted to All Countries	U.S. Origin	Foreign Origin										
			Total	Canada	France	Japan	Switzer-land	United Kingdom	Soviet Union	West Germany	Italy	Sweden	All Others
1970	64,429	47,077	17,352	1,066	1,731	2,625	1,112	2,954	218	4,435	NA	NA	3,211
1971	78,317	55,984	22,333	1,326	2,214	4,029	1,281	3,464	333	5,522	NA	NA	4,164
1972	74,810	51,524	23,286	1,241	2,229	5,151	1,305	3,167	356	5,729	NA	NA	4,108
1973	74,143	51,504	22,639	1,346	2,143	4,939	1,326	2,855	382	5,587	NA	NA	4,061
1974	76,278	50,641	25,637	1,326	2,569	5,892	1,454	3,146	496	6,153	NA	NA	4,601
1975	72,000	46,715	25,285	1,296	2,367	6,352	1,456	3,043	421	6,036	738	914	2,662
1976	70,226	44,280	25,946	1,192	2,408	6,543	1,475	2,995	426	6,180	754	1,002	2,971
1977	65,269	41,485	23,784	1,219	2,108	6,217	1,347	2,654	394	5,537	756	862	2,690
1978	66,102	41,254	24,848	1,226	2,119	6,911	1,330	2,722	412	5,850	725	826	2,727
1979	48,854	30,079	18,775	862	1,604	5,251	1,025	1,910	354	4,527	596	573	2,073
1980	61,819	37,356	24,463	1,081	2,088	7,124	1,265	2,406	460	5,747	806	822	2,664
1981	65,771	39,223	26,548	1,135	2,181	8,388	1,239	2,475	373	6,252	883	766	2,856
1982	57,888	33,896	23,992	990	1,975	8,149	1,147	2,134	209	5,408	752	685	2,543
1983	56,860	32,871	23,989	1,000	1,895	8,793	1,017	1,931	222	5,423	625	623	2,460
1984	67,200	38,365	28,835	1,206	2,162	11,110	1,174	2,271	214	6,255	794	701	2,948
1985	71,661	39,554	32,107	1,342	2,400	12,746	1,233	2,495	147	6,665	919	857	3,303
1986	70,860	38,124	32,736	1,314	2,369	13,209	1,212	2,409	116	6,803	995	883	3,426
1987	82,952	43,517	39,435	1,594	2,874	16,557	1,373	2,779	121	7,821	1,183	948	4,185
1988	77,924	40,496	37,428	1,489	2,661	16,158	1,245	2,583	96	7,307	1,076	777	4,036
1989	95,539	50,185	45,354	1,959	3,140	20,168	1,363	3,100	161	8,303	1,297	837	5,026

Note: NA = not available

Source: *International Science and Technology Data Update*, Report #91-309 (Washington, D.C.: National Science Foundation, 1991), p. 101. Based on data from U.S. Department of Commerce, Patent and Trademark Office.

new products, growth in sales or market share, and corporate profits? The answer is yes, there are certain linkages but few simple causal patterns. There is a direct relationship between R&D and sales growth as well as between R&D and productivity. However, in a major study of over 800 companies in the United States, no direct relationship was found between R&D and subsequent profit growth. Innovators carry the risk but may not fully profit from it. Imitators, users, and others may benefit more from new technologies than the pioneers.[17]

So why go on innovating? What are the complex linkages from invention to usage and business payoffs? Who really benefits and to what extent? To understand these topics and answer such questions, we turn to the topic of how technology spreads, to the diffusion or adoption of new technology.

THE SPREAD OF TECHNOLOGICAL CHANGE

Technological change may spread slowly or rapidly, depending on a number of factors. Innovators, imitators, and users all play major roles as generators and as beneficiaries of such changes. A new technology may be replaced quickly by an even newer generation, and substitution can occur quickly. Forecasting the likely paths that technological progress in different fields will take is a complex task. Still, diffusion patterns from the past and a wide variety of forecasting techniques enable us to make some intelligent estimates. The act of projecting R&D is worth pursuing, because it can improve the market planning task.

Diffusion and Substitution

Diffusion is the manner in which an innovation is communicated over time; it is the relative speed with which it is adopted. Early studies looked at the technological changes in agriculture, such as how fast hybrid corn was embraced by farmers. Later the focus turned to industrial innovations, both products and processes. Diffusion also refers to the spread of ideas among scientists, managers, companies, or the public at large. And finally, diffusion is also the story of **substitution**, as new generations of products and processes replace old ones. According to the expert who studied diffusion and substitution for decades, the following factors determine the diffusion of technology: relative advantage versus existing technology, often stated as a price/performance ratio; compatibility with existing values and habits; simplicity, or at least lack of complexity; trialability or how easily the technology can be used on a trial basis; and, observability—that is, how visible the change appears to users. Change agents, ranging from lead users (early adopters) to trade associations, from rating services to government regulators, also play a role.[18]

How fast does diffusion take place? Potential buyers seldom adopt new technologies immediately, no matter how great the advantages are. There is no universal time span as to how rapidly the diffusion occurs; just the opposite, each inno-

Early adopters such as ICI play an important role in diffusion of innovation.

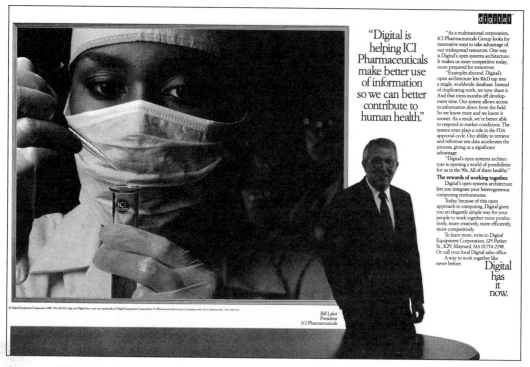

Courtesy of Digital Equipment Corporation.

vation may have its own pattern according to the impact of each factor just cited. Generally, diffusion does follow a tilted, S-shaped curve, also known as a logistics curve. What is different is the slope of each curve. The sharper the slope, the quicker the rate of diffusion. A rough average for half the major users signing on is eight to ten years and for all potential users it is usually over twenty years. Usually, there is a bandwagon effect, with the majority signing on after the pioneers have shown the way. In Exhibit 8–9, which shows diffusion of the technology for continuous casting of steel, we see that users in Japan and the European Community embraced it more quickly than did those in the United States. Note that diffusion curves are S-shaped, showing the share of all users adopting. In contrast, sales figures are bell shaped, with a downturn occurring as new generations of technologies come in to replace old ones.

Since this is a global economy, it is important to have the diffusion occur in as many countries and locations as possible, but the leading nations do not always adopt at the same rate. These points are illustrated in Exhibit 8–10. Part A shows how quickly a new process for glass making spread among countries and plants. Part B reveals differences among nations in adopting a new family of machine tools. Part C shows how the United States and Japan differed in embracing the use of

EXHIBIT 8–9   Diffusion of Steel Technology in Three Key Areas: Continuous Casting of Steel as a Percentage of Total Crude Steel Production

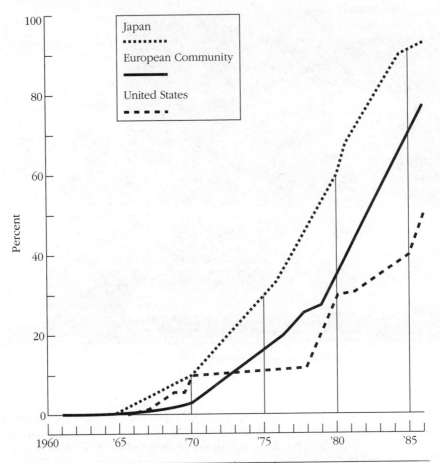

Source: Adapted with permission from G. F. Ray, "Full Circle: The Diffusion of Technology," *Research Policy* 18 (February 1989): 4; also based on author's work and U.N. statistics; partly estimated.

robots in different industries. Generally, diffusions occur quickly where and when innovations contribute significantly to productivity or profitability. However, other factors are also at work. For example, CT (computed tomography) scanners, a new set of medical imaging equipment, spread rapidly in the United States during the 1970s, in part due to the fact that the cost could be passed on to third parties. In contrast, diffusion proved slow for steel making, not just for continuous casting, but also for the byproduct coke oven and continuous annealing, which took about fourteen years to be adopted by half the major U.S. steel companies. Thinking short term, they wanted to squeeze the last dollar's worth of investment out of old equip-

EXHIBIT 8–10   Three Perspectives on Diffusion of Technology

Part A: The International Diffusion of the Float Glass-Making Process

Number of	1971	1982	1986
Manufacturers holding a license	15	30	35
Countries of the licensees	10	22	29
Float glass plants (factories)	29	88	105

Part B: The Share of Numerically Controlled Machine Tools in the Sale of All Machine Tools, by Key Countries

Country	1981	1984
Japan	13.4%	18.6%
W. Germany	1.7	7.0
France	2.7	3.7
United States	2.9	3.6

Part C: Number of Robots Per 10,000 Employees, in Selected Industries, United States and Japan, 1985

Country	Autos	Electrical Equipment	Metals	Machinery	Aerospace
Japan	245	87	16	50	—
United States	60	13	2	8	2

Source: For Parts A and B: G. F. Ray, "Full Circle: The Diffusion of Technology," *Research Policy,* 18 (February 1989), pp. 1–18. For Part C: E. Mansfield, "The Diffusion of Industrial Robots in Japan and the USA," *Research Policy,* 18 (May 1989), pp. 183–197. Reprinted by permission.

ment, unlike their European and Japanese counterparts. This eventually hindered the big steel firms and gave rise to the minimills. (Both medical imaging and steel making are discussed in more detail at the end of the chapter.)

Beneficiaries of Innovation

According to several studies, the relationship between R&D intensity and subsequent sales growth is well established, as is the link between R&D and productivity. Thus the innovating firm can capture the benefits at these levels. Furthermore, by becoming a known pioneer, an organization can develop a culture of innovation and use it to keep ahead of others. By the time imitators have caught up, the innovator has moved farther ahead. Becoming known as a pioneer, a firm can also use its specialized knowledge and experience to keep costs down. The relationship between R&D and subsequent profit growth is not significant, primarily because profitability is influenced by a host of other factors. But the studies show that a well-managed company with strong R&D and marketing functions would be profitable provided it is in a growth area. Much of the R&D spending is in "hot" or growth areas, so this should be no problem.

Can imitators capture some of the benefits of innovation? They certainly can. One scholar who followed innovations in the United States for thirty years found that imitators can make a new product for two-thirds of the cost and time that it took the innovating firm. Case studies from such diverse areas as computers, medical imaging, and video recording indicate that those who entered the field after the major breakthroughs and improved on them did very well in terms of both sales and profits.[19] Illustrations cited in the past, and even recently, told the story of the United States inventing and Japan copying and emulating. Recently, however, the Japanese have become true inventors as well as innovators (see next section for their recent achievements). Now other Asian nations, specifically Taiwan, Thailand, Indonesia, and South Korea, are the imitators. But they are also accused of not respecting intellectual property, patents, copyrights, and trademarks, especially in the field of electronics. Such piracy is hard to prosecute, but it can be pursued.

Users, of course, are often the beneficiaries of inventions and innovations, whether a process or a product is involved. Indeed, users may avoid the outlay for R&D spending altogether if another industry is able and willing to do it for them. This occurred when the telecommunication companies reaped the rewards of research performed by electronics and electrical equipment manufacturers. Generally, in the diffusion scenario, it is the large firms that become the pioneer adopters; they can afford and use the new technology. In contrast, small firms tend to wait longer as they study how to adopt the new process or product in their factories and offices. Small businesses also hope for price declines as the innovation spreads, and frequently they are not disappointed. Such declines occurred in the case of calculators, machine tools, computer hardware and software, medical equipment, and instrumentation.

Possibly the greatest beneficiaries of technological change are those organizations, be they the innovators, imitators, or users, that perceive additional applications for the new process or product in related and distant fields. This is where interaction is most noticeable, substitution is rampant, and competition becomes keen as suppliers and customers can become rivals. Large computers were first used for scientific calculations, then for data processing, record keeping, and other office operations. As memory capacity and speed of operation improved dramatically, major applications were identified by pioneering innovators, imitators, and users, ranging from agriculture to schoolwork. Gas turbines originally developed for aircraft found applications in generating electricity. When invented thirty years ago, the laser had narrow military and a few civilian applications. Now it is used in medical surgery, optical communication, spectacular laser shows, and compact disc players. The field of biotechnology is another field with extended applications, ranging from food processing to medical uses.[20]

Technological Forecasting

Studying the path and impact of past innovations requires careful analysis and is still subject to different interpretations. Predicting the future shape of products or the coming characteristics of processes is an even more difficult task. Yet **technological forecasting** is carried out; the act of doing it assists us in better managerial decisions and smoother market planning. As is the case with business and market forecasts, both qualitative and quantitative techniques may be used; a combination often works well. Many technological forecasts project higher speed, greater power, and cheaper products. But too many forecasts fail to specify the time frame or attach a degree of probability to the event. Other projections, especially in high-tech areas, are based on pure "hype and hope." Little wonder that a recent book, entitled *Megamistakes,* spoke about the errors in technological forecasting and the myth of speedy innovations.[21]

For too long we have been preoccupied with major breakthroughs, success stories, and important innovations. One of the key lessons from the past is that

BUSINESS MARKETING IN PRACTICE ▰▰▰▰▰▰

Perils and Pitfalls of Technological Forecasts—and How to Avoid Them

Technological forecasting, as the name implies, is concerned with identifying new products based on innovative technologies that will produce growth markets. It is one of the most difficult kinds of forecasts to make accurately. There are so many unknowns, and so many possible outcomes, that error appears everywhere.

It is unnecessary to exaggerate the mistakes.... Forecasters turned out to be especially poor at spotting technological trends. Most technological forecasts missed their mark not by a matter of degree, but completely, and without regard for what actually occurred years later.

Most such forecasts fail, because the forecasters fall in love with the technology they are based on and ignore the market the technology is intended to serve ... they lose perspective of common sense economic considerations. They incorrectly assume that customers will find the new technology enticing as much as they do ... those assumptions are wrong.

A close examination of the record (including the TRW Probe Project in 1966, the Kahn and Wiener Year 2000 Report, etc., etc.) indicates that only 20 to 25 percent of technological forecasts come true.

Since forecasts are highly unreliable, adopt alternative strategies. These include: scenario building, including multiple scenarios; following rather than leading; perpetually innovating; influencing the outcome (e.g., setting standards, developing the necessary infrastructure, ensuring a supply of complementary products, and lowering prices); and—the simplest of all—assuming that the future will be similar to the present.

Source: Adapted with permission of The Free Press, a Division of Macmillan, Inc. from *Megamistakes: Forecasting The Myth of Rapid Technological Change* by Stephen P. Schnaars. Copyright © 1989 by The Free Press.

innovation, more often than not, is a series of minor improvements. Second, we have seen how different groups make definite contributions. Third, we observed that innovations follow an S-shaped diffusion curve. But it is clear that new generations of technology replace old ones, well before the latter have had a chance to penetrate 60 or 80 percent of the potential client base. This is illustrated well in Exhibit 8–11, which shows what happened in electronics, pharmaceuticals, and other fields. Thus, diffusion curves must not be projected to a 100 percent saturation level. Some innovations never even take off, as shown in Exhibit 8–12. Such "flops" have many explanations, but the key point is that they simply proved not to be viable. Reasons can range from a competing process, a reluctance to switch standards, or too low a price/performance ratio.

Qualitative technological forecasts can originate from a single expert or a team of scientists, engineers, managers, users, or opinion leaders with varied backgrounds. A popular approach is the Delphi technique, which consists of successive polls. A panel of experts is asked to predict the likelihood of an event; after each round the results are fed back to the panelists to narrow the forecasts into a tighter time frame. Success has been achieved by both individuals and Delphi panels, but consistently high success scores have not been demonstrated.[22]

Quantitative methods include both simple and complex techniques, but the division into two groups is based on a different classification scheme. Growth curves, trend extrapolation, and lead-lag correlation are known as exploratory methods, because they attempt to explore the future by looking at current conditions. Using the concept of technical needs, normative methods attempt to perceive how these needs will be fulfilled by various inventions and innovations. As a rule, normative methods tend to be more complex, but their track record may not be better.

Growth curves are basically the S-shaped diffusion curves that are shown in Exhibits 8–9 and 8–11. Applications in the past included means of transportation, communication, automotive technology (from disk brakes to tires), equipment used by banks, and so forth. When an upper limit or near saturation point is reached by existing technology, the forecast will call for innovation. For example, rayon cords in tires have been followed by nylon, glass, and steel reinforcements. Fluorescent and mercury lamps came to the forefront when incandescent lighting reached its peak.

Trend extrapolation means projecting historical data in a linear, exponential, or some other fashion. This technique is often used when existing technologies have not reached a ceiling. Examples range from aircraft speed to the number of instructions that computers can process in a second. When an upper limit becomes evident, other techniques are employed.

Lead-lag correlation can be utilized for technological forecasts when two categories of goods or processes have a strong similarity or affinity to each other. Since World War I, we can observe that military aircraft have exceeded the speed of civilian aircraft by a certain margin, and we may then project this lead-lag into the future. But the story of the British-French Concorde is a warning that to fly civilians at supersonic speed is not an economic solution, but a fiasco.

Normative methods, looking at technological needs, can take different forms. It is usual to assemble both technical and business experts to study various time series in the past and to build up a holistic picture of the situation. Continuing with our transportation example, we would look at various means of moving goods and people on land, at sea, and in the air. The possibilities under land, under sea, and beyond the normal atmosphere would also be considered. Finally, alternatives to transportation would be analyzed, ranging from the phone to the fax, from dedicated tie-lines to public networks for electronic mail. When a whole set of forecasts is assembled this way, we may then construct scenarios or a series of possible outcomes. It is quite customary to construct a best, a worst, and an average scenario and to make plans accordingly.[23]

Managerial and Marketing Implications

Business marketers need to have a sound appreciation and understanding about what happens in scientific and technical pursuits. They should become familiar with the indicators of R&D, the diffusion pattern of innovation, and possible scenarios for the future in different fields. Just as financial and economic indicators and growth patterns vary from industry to industry, technological parameters will show variations. By observing the R&D scoreboards, by keeping track of new product or process announcements, and by studying related personnel and organizational changes, marketers can learn where leading edge activities take place. They can then formulate business and market scenarios and plot the outlines of likely progress.[24]

Some argue that technological changes cannot be predicted, and we have marshaled examples of failures and of pitfalls in forecasting. Additional evidence will be cited in the following sections, especially in high-tech fields that are so prone to "hype and hope." When experts have a vested interest, the marketer must be especially alert. Very few time series show growth rates of 20 percent per year over a period of a decade. Many promising technologies do not blossom because the benefits and applications are not made clear.

We can still make sensible, broad outlines and then become more specific about the shape of things to come. At this time, the innovations are likely to occur in the same areas that have been emphasized in the past ten years: resources, electronics (computers and communication), biological/medical sciences, advanced manufacturing, and transportation.

The action will be along the following lines in resources: polar and tropic exploration; deep earth, deep sea, and space mining; gasification; renewable energy sources; and recycling. In electronics, the list includes more miniaturization, personal voice/data communication, mass information systems, satellites, security/detection, and artificial intelligence. In biology and medicine, we see automated diagnostic systems, synthetic production of natural drugs, new vegetation, biomedicine, and the coupling of medical devices with software in every possible way. In manufacturing and transportation, the following are on the horizon: flexible

EXHIBIT 8–11 The Concept and the Empirical Evidence for New Generations of Technology

Part A: Typical Growth and Diffusion Patterns

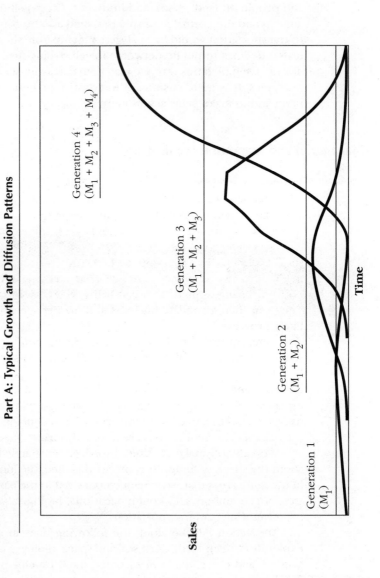

Part B: Observation and Introduction Periods

Product Class	Product	Observation Periods	Introduction Times			
			Generation 1	Generation 2	Generation 3	Generation 4
Electronics	Computer REVs	1974–1987	1970	1978	1982	1984
	Computer units	1974–1987	1970	1978	1982	1984
	Disk drives	1983–1988	1983	1986		
	Logic devices	1975–1983	1973	1975		1984
	DRAMs	1974–1984	1973	1977	1981	
	SRAMs	1975–1984	1973	1979	1982	
Pharmaceuticals	Antihypertensives	1960–1987	1954	1959		
	Blockers and inhibitors	1970–1987	1970	1983	1981*	
	Diuretics	1960–1987	1950	1963		
Consumer goods	Diapers;	1966–1987	1948	1967		
	recording media	1977–1987	1950	1975	1984	
Industrial goods	Drill bits	1971–1984	1950	1969		

*Note that calcium channel blockers (generation 2) were commercially available later than were ACE inhibitors (generation 3). There is debate within the industry about which generation is the "latest."

Source: From J. A. Norton and F. M. Bass, "Evolution of Technical Generations," *Sloan Management Review*, Winter 1992, p. 67. Reprinted with permission of *Sloan Management Review*.

EXHIBIT 8–12   Technologies That Did Not Make It Big—But (Some) May Yet Do So

Technology	Problems/Cause of Failure	Possible Comeback
Nuclear-powered airplane	Problem with transfer of nuclear-generated heat to air and with fortifying the reactor in case of crash	Comeback not likely now; but note existence of nuclear-powered submarines
Jetpack (personal jet engine)	Military lost interest in program; cannot protect flying soldier easily; tried by army, marines, etc. (but ½ hour in air at 60 mph achieved)	Engine adopted for U.S. Navy's F107 cruise missile; used at the Olympics and other spectacular events
Electromolecular propulsion	Promise to handle chemical analyses in minutes not fulfilled (e.g., blood test)	Company founder claims it will yet bring this to market
Fusion energy	Cannot solve basic problem of how to confine the fuel when it becomes superheated	Still experimenting; also, controversial cold fusion proposed
Food irradiation	Can get rid of fungi, insects, and bacteria from food, but industry sees little incentive to adopt and fears radiation label or logo	Companies focus on medical market instead, but ready to irradiate food when food companies give a signal
Rotary engine	Fewer moving parts than piston engine; runs smoothly; but some problems with seals, gas mileage, and pollution	Used successfully in Mazda RX7 and NSU Prinze Wankel and may yet become more widely used; mileage improved
Josephson junction processes	Well funded, including $300 million by IBM; promise of ultrafast, low-power device for computers, but overshadowed by improvements in silicon chip	Came to market recently in a more narrowly targeted product: super high-speed oscilloscopes
Bubble memories	Promise of data storage due to excellent feature: no moving parts and retain data after the power is off; but silicon chips and floppy disks proved to be better	Pilot production built by Texas Instruments; may yet come back
Picture phones	Much promise; very costly and not embraced by business; not full substitute for face-to-face conversation	Making a comeback in 1992 for conference calls; price is coming down sharply

Sources: H. Brody, "It Seemed Like a Good Idea at the Time," *High Technology Business,* October 1988, pp. 38–41; S. P. Schnaars, *Megamistakes* (New York: Free Press, 1989), Chapters 2, 6.

Toshiba uses technology to make information accessible and portable.

Courtesy of Toshiba America Information Systems, Inc.

and automated systems, including more robotics; more direct metal fabrication (such as the continuous casting and annealing noted earlier); chemical processes with built-in pollution controls; advanced weaving and extrusion; and streamlined traffic control.[25]

In concluding this section, an example from computer technology illustrates that what may seem spectacular to the outsider can be seen as a series of incremental improvements to the insider. Each new computer generation brought a tenfold increase in speed, a twentyfold increase in memory capacity, and a tenfold rise in reliability. At the same time, component cost was reduced tenfold, and system cost declined 2.5-fold. Such changes may not occur in other fields, but the key is to perceive what the totality of incremental changes can add up to in the long run.

TECHNOLOGY AND THE GLOBAL MARKETPLACE

We have already emphasized that technological change is most effective when it can be rolled out in an international setting. New processes and products often must find markets beyond national borders. Indeed, the real payoff comes when this occurs in ever broadening circles, as home markets may become saturated. However, this is no easy task. Science tends to be universal, with the focus on why things happen. Technology is much more local, with the concern on how things can happen. It is not the unwillingness of the rich countries or the passivity of the poor nations that prevents technological transfer. Rather it is the fact that a culture of innovation, diffusion, and substitution must be in place before the fruits of technological progress are harvested in different locations. Often, as stated, the key is the widespread education, training, and acculturation of the work force.

International Competition and Cooperation

In the industrialized nations, technology has been perceived as an excellent means of promoting economic growth, preserving jobs, and maintaining national security as well as high standards of living. Rewards have been captured by nations, industries, companies, and individuals in terms of fame and fortune. Rivalry across borders, as noted in this and the previous chapter, is alive and well across many fields. There is a race to patent, to publish papers, to test new goods and processes, and to bring them to market. In this race, Japan has been especially adept, mostly because it is quicker on many fronts. In a perceived race with the United States and to a lesser extent with Western Europe, Japan has managed to become a true inventor and innovator. Equally important, as shown in Exhibit 8–13, Japan has done its homework better than the United States in planning *and* executing its drive to bring forth new technology.

Whereas nations do compete for world markets, the actual rivalry is carried out by many organizations, institutions, and individuals. It is the linkage of government agencies, profit-making companies, scientific associations, and dozens of other groups that determines the way in which technology is disseminated and utilized. Until recently, the United States lagged behind Japan and even the European Community in encouraging dialogue and interaction between various factions. Now we are seeing the encouragement and establishment of R&D consortia with the blessing of the U.S. government. These are collaborative efforts in R&D among rival firms; they agree to cooperate in technology but not in production and marketing. Examples were cited in Chapter 7.

Cooperation in technology can take many forms, ranging from informal discussion between scientists and engineers at conferences to having cross-border

EXHIBIT 8–13   Planning and Executing Development of New Products and Processes, Japan and the U.S., 1991

Japanese companies spend more time planning . . .

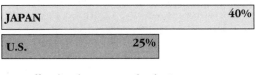

. . . suffer development setbacks in a smaller proportion of products . . .

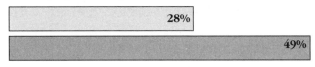

. . . and waste less of their time debugging finished products.

Japanese companies invest more of their managerial time in new products . . .

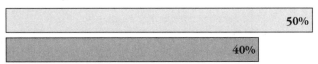

. . . and receive more revenues from them.

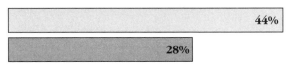

Source: Brian Dumaine, "Closing the Innovation Gap," *Fortune,* December 2, 1991, p. 59, based on work by James Swallow of A. T. Kearney Co. on fourteen top U.S. and Japanese companies. *Fortune,* © 1991 Time Inc. All rights reserved.

partnerships between two or more firms. At times international agreements may be signed, as in the case of environmental concerns—for example on river cleanup, acid rain prevention, and rain forest preservation. It also makes sense for nations and companies to cooperate in other fields. As a general rule, nations and companies develop expertise and specialize in certain areas.[26] The strengths in evolving technologies of the three key regional players—that is Europe, Japan, and the United States—are shown in the matrix of Exhibit 8–14. The expansion plans for

R&D are also illustrated. The countries and the companies may then choose to "ride the technology" in the hope of achieving a global leadership role, and they may exclude organizations and individuals outside the nation. However, we see evidence of partnership, alliances, and other forms of cooperation, even in high-technology areas. Recently, invitations have been exchanged between U.S. and Japanese consortia to join in. But competition will continue at the production and marketing stages for company-specific products and methods.

EXHIBIT 8–14   Evolving Technologies and R&D Expansion Plans in Three Key Regions

Part A: Geographic Strengths in Evolving Technologies (perception of participants)

United States	*Europe*	*Japan*
Biotechnology Aerospace composites Electronic systems Software Integrated circuits Electronic materials Artificial intelligence	Telecommunications Automotive plastics Chemicals Software	Structural/electronic ceramics Consumer electronics Automotive composites Low-cost manufacturing technologies Semiconductor equipment Electronic peripherals and components Image recognition

Part B: Primary Foreign R&D Expansion Plans

	United States	*Europe*	*Japan*
U.S. Companies		Software Telecommunications	Electronic equipment Integrated circuits Electronic systems Specialty materials Instrumentation
European Companies	Biotechnology/pharmaceuticals Electronic materials and advanced polymer composites Integrated circuits Telecommunications		Pharmaceuticals Electronic materials Semiconductors
Japanese Companies	Software Artificial intelligence Image processing	Software	

Source: Reprinted by permission from A. C. Perrino and J. W. Tipping, "Global Management of Technology," *Research Technology Management,* May–June, 1989, p. 14.

Facilitating the Transfer of Technology

Conventional wisdom holds that technology is a piece of hardware, a process for shaping a product, or a method of organization that is readily available to all. Those who have studied the topic, however, agree that technology is a set of ideas and procedures "bottled up in the system of its origin and often held in cryptic form to avoid disclosure." In short, it is not easy to transfer or transmit technical ideas from one group or place to another. Furthermore, reluctance, secrecy, security, and inertia frequently offset good will and business rationale. When attempting transfer, the technology must be appropriate to its new setting and the recipient must be flexible and ready to embrace new ideas and techniques. This process, called **technology transfer**, is usually partial and gradual; it also tends to be specific to location, timing, type of workers, and so on. Even in a highly industrialized nation and between two willing groups, technology is not easily exchanged. For example, high hopes were held out for the transfer of space technology to earth-bound problems in the United States. However, moving ideas and methods from the National Aeronautics and Space Agency to various civilian uses took much time and effort and did not always succeed.[27]

There are several ways to initiate, but not necessarily complete, the transfer of technology from one group to another. At the initial stages, scientists and engineers exchange ideas, often at conferences and then through published proceedings. Informal or formal networks are built, with information exchanged electronically or in print. At the next stage, organizations can purchase specific information and even acquire specific products and processes, but this is a more costly and complex undertaking. Nations formulate international agreements to exchange concepts and knowledge in a given field. Finally, there is indigenous technology adaptation, which is the most thorough and takes the longest, as it involves education, training, and practice. Concepts and methods from chemistry and electronics are easier to transfer than those from construction, engineering, and large-scale operations such as electric power generation and oil refining. Developing nations often need technical assistance in agriculture, building materials, and textiles, but they can easily absorb techniques for assembling advanced electronic products, as is the case in Mexico and Thailand. Organizations in Africa and Asia have been able to utilize biotechnology and computers in many areas, even forming joint ventures with Western firms.[28]

Marketing can be a way of transferring technology from one region to another, from one group to another. Creativity and managerial acumen are called for. For example, chlorine has been used as a disinfectant for cleansing water for a long time in North America. But oxygen and ozone, widely used in Europe for the same purposes, are making inroads at the expense of chlorine in both the United States and Canada. Pointing out cost savings provided one competitive advantage; another one was noting problems that occur from by-products in the chlorination process. Oxygenation and ozonation were transferred first to Canada, thereby providing trial and observation locations for potential clients in the United States. In a similar fashion, a Swedish firm, Sala Magnetics, chose to break into the U.S. market by first demonstrating its magnetic filtration process in Japan and obtaining testimonials from users in that country.[29]

Technology as a Tool in Foreign Market Entry

It may seem strange to talk about the difficulties of transferring technology and then using it as a market entry tool, but this can and does happen. Key considerations are having the appropriate technology, choosing the right mode of entry, and as always, being patient and accepting the idea that the process is often partial and gradual. The modes of entry into the arena of international business range from export, which means less risk and involvement, to investment, which means more risk and involvement, but also more control and potentially much higher rewards. In between are such possibilities as licensing the technology, forming a joint venture, franchising, and other contractual arrangements. We discussed those briefly in Chapter 7, and additional material can be found in international business and marketing textbooks. Here we look only at the way in which technology itself is involved in such situations.

Exporting technology is done usually by incorporating it in current products and even services. For example, by examining the electronic ignition and fuel injection features of German and Japanese cars, Canadian and American engineers can compare automotive technology in the three key producing areas of the world. Licensing technology means allowing others to use either patents or unpatented information in exchange for income, known as a royalty or licensing fee. There is the danger of creating a competitor, but the offset is the flow of funds and the chance of a possible joint venture with a new partner. Cross-licensing means exchanging licenses in both directions, a good idea when the parties are strong in different subfields of the same general area. When building abroad or operating a facility, the contractor brings in technology in two ways: by incorporating new products and processes into the facility and by training personnel to manage it. Companies from the United States and Canada did just this when constructing airports and operating telephone exchanges in Africa and the Middle East. Direct investment means being a corporate citizen of a foreign land, owning and running your factory, laboratory, or office on location. As a general rule, the more experience an enterprise has abroad, the more likely it is to decentralize and to share its R&D with local citizens in a beneficial, two-way exchange of information.[30]

High Technology: Is It the Cutting Edge?

Certain industries and product categories are classified as **high technology** or as **research intensive**. To qualify for this designation, the groups must show a higher ratio than the all-industry average of R&D expenditures to dollar value of shipments. The following industries are currently classified as high tech: drugs and medicines; electrical machinery; electronic components; office machinery, including computers; aerospace; and scientific instruments. Why is there special concern with high-tech fields? Because they represent cutting-edge technology, incorporating the latest or best in technical ideas. Furthermore, both high-tech products and processes show a higher sales growth rate than do non-high-tech items. This applies to domestic and especially export markets. In other words, high-tech goods and services generate healthy sales, increased profits, and a positive balance of trade for nations and firms. The world export shares of high-tech products for major nations and product fields are shown in Exhibit 8–15. Note that the United States lost and Japan gained share and that the United States dominates really in just one field, aerospace.

Policymakers in government and executives in the private sector in the United States express alarm over this loss of competitiveness, especially in global high-tech industries, but in other fields as well. Evidence that the alarm or fear is not misplaced can be found in many of the exhibits shown so far. Additional statistics can be cited—for example, the drop in the U.S. world market share in semiconductors from 50 to 37 percent between 1984 and 1988. In the 1980s the U.S. balance of trade in high-tech goods turned negative. The explanation for this state of affairs is complex, but some of the reasons have been cited before and shown in Exhibit 8–13.

To achieve technological leadership requires scanning the globe for new insights, investing in "frontier" research, integrating R&D with production and marketing more closely, establishing and promoting technical standards, and providing additional education/training to all citizens. A strong case can be made for abandoning so-called big science megaprojects and, with the end of the cold war, for phasing out costly weapon developments. By observing the above rules and by letting the United States carry the defense burden, Japan and the major Western European nations have shown a better track record in both overall productivity and in high-tech fields. But there is good reason to think the United States will rise to the challenge, as shown by proposed changes in taxation schemes related to R&D and investment, in formation of new technology-based firms, and in recent quality awards to and achievements of high-tech and other enterprises.

High-tech markets are characterized by much turbulence; insecurity; a mixture of hype, hope, and fear; government attention; and nationalistic overtones.[31] Publicity overstates the short-run market potential in almost all cases. New generations of technology can make old ones obsolete quickly, as shown in Exhibit 8–11, and as substitutes come on stream, they can create or strongly alter markets. As markets mature, R&D spending slows and an industry shakeout occurs, with large firms absorbing many small ones. This happened in certain subcategories of the drug, electronics, instrumentation, and other high-tech industries. Inventors, innovators, and entrepreneurs then move on to adjacent fields, often within the same industry. Those who stay in high tech must be prepared for a roller coaster ride.

Artificial intelligence is a high-tech area that received its impetus as an academic discipline and research field at U.S. universities in the 1950s. Growth was slow, with few practical applications. Between 1960 and 1980 came a period of

EXHIBIT 8–15   World Export Shares of Technology-Intensive Products by Country and by Product Field

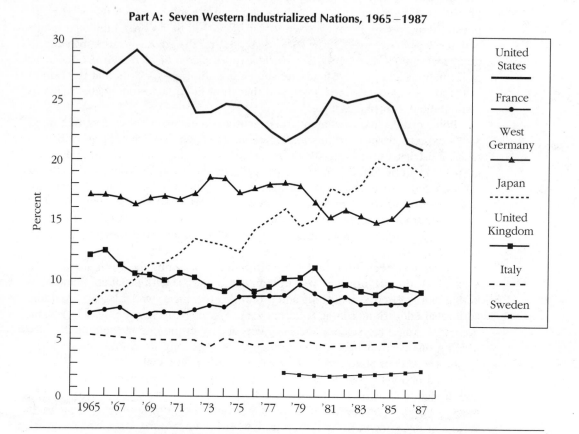

Part A: Seven Western Industrialized Nations, 1965–1987

commercialization in three subfields: natural language, robotics, and expert systems. Early applications of expert systems seemed promising. Such systems were said to be capable of emulating human experts in such diverse fields as chemistry, medicine, and finance. Then in the 1980s, years of discontent and decline set in. The key obstacles to wider use were (1) the emphasis on technical features rather than on system solutions and performance, (2) the complexity of many potential applications, and (3) the overblown promises made by technical entrepreneurs. This is very typical in high tech. Hope is raised by hype, and forecasts invariably turn out to be far too optimistic. Yet there is optimism for the 1990s. The reason is the shift to a market-driven technology, the emphasis on specific solutions rather than gadgetry, and the focus on simpler applications. The forecasts for the 1980s

EXHIBIT 8–15   World Export Shares of Technology-Intensive Products by Country and by Product Field (*cont.*)

Part B: Seven Industrial Product Fields in the Seven Nations, 1987

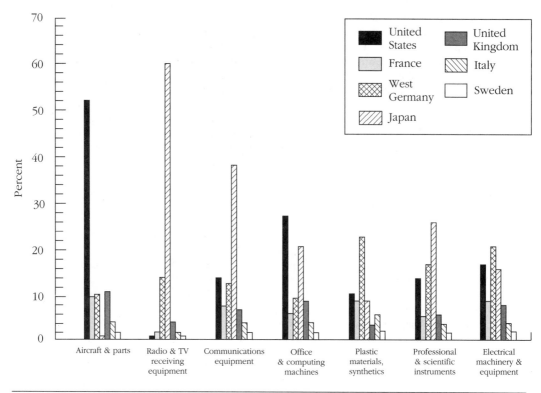

Source: *International Science and Technology Data Update,* Report #91-309 (Washington, D.C.: National Science Foundation, 1991), pp. 124, 126.

that were in the $2- to $5-billion range turned out to be optimistic by a factor of ten, but may yet be realized in the mid-1990s.[32]

Technology, Marketing, and Business Strategy

The road to success in technology-based industries and to penetration of markets is full of potholes and dangerous curves. Navigating the road is made easier by learning from the past and by observing some road signs, especially as they relate to the marketing mix. The first rule is to perceive the idea as a complete product or system, not as a device or as an assembly of technical specifications. Distinguish

BUSINESS MARKETING IN PRACTICE ▰▰▰▰▰▰

Quality in High Tech: Philosophy and Practice

Bertram Laboratories of Somerville, New Jersey, is a small manufacturer of gallium arsenide wafers, which are the building blocks in auto-electronics. The company recently increased its market share, growing in excess of the industry average. While its primary customers are in the USA, it already exports a third of its production to Europe and Asia. This success did not come easily.

Dr. Les Polgar is Vice President of Marketing and Quality Control. "I am the only person I know of (in the industry) who has this dual responsibility, which prevents marketing from promising what it cannot deliver. I too was once a user and found that while crystal quality of the wafers was generally ok, the wafer finishing was not. So that needed to be changed."

"The first thing on my agenda in Spring 1988 was to assess and then improve all quality aspects of our products. The existing site lacked the requisite cleanroom so we built a new one and we moved there in early 1990. Soon after that quality improved dramatically. One of the first things I did as Vice President-Quality Control was to halt production! I think it was one of the most important things I ever did. People say it was ludicrous—how can you be proud of shutting down your own production? I knew the pain customers endure and

loss of credibility that Bertram Labs would suffer if it did not set such things straight. Quality became a key issue."

"We also restructured the operations. We tried to do too much in the past with limited resources. Now we are more focused in terms of both products and markets. We try to do a few things exceptionally well, then slowly build up control and expertise. This gives a solid foundation. When we send out so-called qualification wafers, we pick them almost at random from a lot. Others tend to send out their best. Another dimension of quality is standards and standardization. Again, we resist the temptation to fill or meet all requests. The concept of 'superclean' can be quantified in terms of the number of particles on the surface measured by a standard test."

"Our finished product tells only part of the story. You see the tip of the iceberg, but underneath that there is 90 percent which is all process know-how and applications."

Source: Roy Szweda, "Quality: Philosophy and Practice: Leslie Polgar of Bertram Laboratories in Conversation," *III–Vs Review,* 4,5 October, 1991, 40–42. Used with permission of Elsevier Advanced Technology, Oxford, UK, publisher of *III-Vs Review.*

always between specialties and commodities. Seek to assemble support from others, especially in establishing standards. In promotion, emphasize direct sales, support, and documentation. If you dare, you can charge what the market will bear; it is a good idea to price on value and to allow ample margins for distributor partners. Listen to the marketplace, especially the lead users; keep an eye on competitors; combine sophistication with common sense. Question any forecast that predicts a higher than 20 percent annual growth rate for ten years ahead.[33]

The integration of technology strategy with overall business planning is probably the cornerstone for gaining a sustainable competitive advantage and for achieving financial and other forms of success. This is not easy, but can be done.

The key is to match corporate resources with external requirements. The next step is to integrate innovation with production and marketing. The third link is to demonstrate competence in all fields to the marketplace. Early on, Celanese showed the way in tires when its polyester cord proved superior to Du Pont's nylon. More recently, Michelin did a good job with its radial tires, beating Goodyear's bias-ply tires. Another example comes from Nordson, a maker of advanced spray-painting equipment. This firm sticks with its core competence and follows a lily pond strategy of moving from one lily pad to an adjacent one, where its technological knowledge is still valid and has market applications.[34]

Matching technology and corporate strategy can be done along four lines: first to market, second to market, late to market, and a specialist or niche focus, as seen in Exhibit 8–16. Each alternative has definite implications for the different functional areas, as shown in the diagram. The four strategies also mean different constraints on the organization and different timing on market entry. A company must decide which path to follow, based on its resources and skills.

The first-to-market strategy is appropriate for a leading firm that is willing to make a heavy commitment to R&D spending and thereby hope to beat the competition. Examples are Hewlett-Packard in scientific instruments, Intel in electronic components, and 3M in advanced materials. The second-to-market strategy requires quick imitation of the pioneer's efforts and agility in both production and marketing. Some of the companies that followed IBM's lead in computer mainframes belong to this category, and one can cite similar occurrences in office equipment and telecommunication fields. Late-to-market strategy is not an innovating, but a cost-minimizing route. The company cited as an example is Tandy/Radio Shack in small computers and peripheral equipment. The specialist or niche focus is for firms that wish to serve small pockets of demand with special applications of basic technology. Silicon Valley Specialists did just that, with its high-performance integrated circuits. Silicon Graphics, another firm, also uses a niche strategy. It combines advanced computer hardware and software to create spectacular presentation graphics as well as special effects for films, such as those seen in *Terminator 2.*

THE ROLE OF TECHNOLOGY IN SELECTED MARKETS

Technology plays a role in both old-line and high-tech industries, in some cases rejuvenating the traditional industries, in others providing the impetus for early growth. Innovators, imitators, users, and others are intimately involved in all cases, and cross-fertilization occurs to the benefit of many. The key to profits is often a combination of inventive genius, patient innovation, and marketing muscle. Creativity in science and technology must be coupled with quality and efficiency of production and with the ability to commercialize and to bring new ideas, products, and processes to the marketplace. As noted, however, there are alternatives to being first out and first to the market.

EXHIBIT 8–16   Corporate Strategy and Technology Strategy

Typical Functional Requirements of Alternative Technological Strategies

Alternative	R&D	Manufacturing	Marketing	Finance	Organization	Timing
First to market	Requires state of the art R&D	Emphasis on pilot and medium-scale manufacturing	Emphasis on stimulating primary demand	Requires access to risk capital	Emphasis on flexibility over efficiency; encourage risk taking	Early entry inaugurates the product life cycle
Second to market	Requires flexible, responsive, and advanced R&D capability	Requires agility in setting up manufacturing medium scale	Must differentiate the product; stimulate secondary demand	Requires rapid commitment of medium to large quantities of capital	Combine elements of flexibility and efficiency	Entry early in growth stage
Late to market or cost minimization	Requires skill in process development and cost-effective product	Requires efficiency and automation for large-scale production	Must minimize selling and distribution costs	Requires access to capital in large amounts	Emphasis on efficiency and hierarchical control; procedures rigidly enforced	Entry during late growth or early maturity
Market segmentation	Requires ability in applications, custom engineering, and advanced product design	Requires flexibility on short to medium runs	Must identify and reach favorable segments	Requires access to capital in medium to large amounts	Flexibility and control required in serving different customers' requirements	Entry during growth stage

Source: From "Corporate Strategy and Technology Policy," by M. A. Maidque and P. Patel in *Readings in the Management of Innovation 2/e* by Michael L. Tushman and William L. Moore. Copyright © 1988. Reprinted by permission of Harper Business, a division of HarperCollins Publishers, Inc.

Computer Hardware and Computer Services

Those who envisioned the computer include such great pioneers as Charles Babbage, Alan Turing, Howard Aitken, John Atanasoff, Cliff Berry, and John von Neumann. But the modern era of computing is traced to the first large-scale digital machine, built by Eckert and Mauchly at the midpoint of the twentieth century. When the successor to Eniac, the Univac I, was delivered to the U.S. Bureau of the Census, even visionary thinkers did not foresee any proliferation. Reportedly,

BUSINESS MARKETING IN PRACTICE ■■■■■■■

State of the "Wired" Office, 1992: Outlook by Field

Multimedia. Opinions vary on the market growth of multimedia, a technology that combines text, graphics, animation, audio, and video on personal computers. But even conservative observers predict dramatic growth of hardware and software during the current decade, with the market in 1992 estimated in excess of $1 billion. Two factors aiding acceptance are greater cooperation and alliances among vendors and broader acceptance of international standards compressing and manipulating full motion video on the desktop.

Parallel Processing. Massively parallel processing computers will tackle a task with hundreds and even thousands of microprocessors. Potential buyers are recognizing that the task is not as daunting as they once believed. Much effort will go into developing software tools for debugging. Thinking Machines and Intel have sold machines to American Express and Prudential Securities for data processing.

Object Orientation. Object-oriented programming systems, which allow programmers to assemble applications in modular fashion, will find greater appreciation. Object orientation promises to simplify systems development and maintenance, because codes can be reused for a variety of applications. This technology allows businesses to adapt more quickly to critical changes.

CD-ROM. Riding the coattails of multimedia, optical discs will get a boost. Some analysts say the CD-ROM or compact disc/read-only memory will double its base in 1992 and approach critical mass in commercial acceptance. The number of CD-ROM titles will go from about 6,000 in 1991 to about 11,000 in 1992. Two alternate formats will be introduced by Philips and Commodore.

Graphical User Interface. Smoothing the human to computer interface will be voice recognition, speech synthesis, and pen-based computing. But it will be several years before applications using these interfaces are commonplace. In the interim, Windows by Microsoft will enjoy strong growth. Apple Macintosh interface will remain steady. IBM is pinning its hope on its long-delayed Presentation Manager.

Artificial Intelligence. This field will continue to join the mainstream as companies struggle for competitive advantage in a service-oriented field. Dynamic changes are expected in expert or knowledge-based systems, in neural networking, and in fuzzy logic. Custom applications will be introduced.

Source: M. Alexander and M. Siggins, "The State of the Office, 1992," *Computerworld,* special 1992 forecast issue, 25 (January 1992), p. 47. Copyright 1992 by CW Publishing Inc., Framingham, MA 01701. Reprinted from *Computerworld.*

Thomas Watson of IBM thought that a single computer would suffice for all the major scientific calculations and perceived no commercial possibilities. What brought the full flowering of the computer hardware industry was a whole series of inventions and innovations that reinforced each other. These landmarks include the transistor, integrated circuits, programming languages, timesharing, and networking capabilities. Then came further miniaturization and the appearance of mini-, micro-, personal, laptop and notebook computers. In this parade, the key was coupling increasing sophistication with declining costs; this, in turn, paved the way to broader applications and to acceptance of the computing machines by an ever-widening circle of customers.[35]

In the 1990s, computer services have become as big a market as computer hardware, in the form of software, integrated systems, data processing, and consultancies. The software packages became user friendly, and other services also made it easier to acquire, learn about, and use the machines in different settings. Applications now include agriculture and mining, where computers are used to calculate harvest yields and to find rich veins, respectively. The manufacturing sector would shut down without computers as they provide process control, regulate climate, and monitor fuel flow. In the service sector, computer hardware and services are used for many tasks, such as payroll processing, market research, and financial control. One of the most interesting and profitable applications is in airline reservation systems. American Airlines reportedly made more money from selling computer space on its Sabre reservation system to other airlines than from selling seats to passengers. United Airlines is trying the same with its Apollo reservation system. Each major U.S. airline reportedly makes over 10,000 changes per day in its ticket pricing to yield the highest daily revenues. This is just one of many instances in which advanced technology is coupled with aggressive marketing methods for a payoff.

Steelmaking: Old and New Ways

The great names of U.S. steelmaking are still struggling. U.S. Steel became USX, an energy company, by buying Marathon Oil; Bethlehem Steel and Inland Steel are laying off thousands; and others have merged or gone out of business. At the same time, small steel mills, such as Nucor, Florida Steel, Geneva Steel, and others are flourishing. Some are minimills utilizing scrap; others make small batches of special steel for selected market segments. All of these plants use a few major and many incremental innovations, ranging from improvements in casting to more sophisticated instrumentation. Others, such as Ryerson Steel, focus on service by saying, "We shall not only cut and shape the steel, we will even coat it and paint it for you."[36]

The major technologies having an impact on this industry include direct reduction of iron ore, continuing evolution of the electric furnace, and the possibility of plasma arc steelmaking. The goals in using these technologies is to accomplish one or more of the following objectives: more speedy, continuous production; cost reduction, including more automation; quality improvements; and reduced emission of pollutants. The steelmakers are also aware of competing materials and are committed to meeting that challenge by better service offerings, quick delivery, and aggressive pricing. They are determined not to be left behind, as were the large mills when they ignored innovations, such as the basic oxygen furnace, coming from abroad. One lesson learned: invest in innovation, then produce and market effectively.

Supertrains: Is There a Future?

Trains have been around since the nineteenth century, and today they still cater to passengers and freight traffic on all continents. Admittedly, the quality of the passenger service is higher in those nations where population density is higher. One reason for this is the subsidies given to the railroads. The Japanese Shinkansen, or bullet train, running between Tokyo and Osaka, and the French TGV line between Paris and Lyons could not have made it without state assistance. Both lines move twice as fast as the average U.S. or Canadian train. But subsidies may be phased out, and so railroads everywhere are trying to innovate and market their offerings to both passengers and freight shippers. In the United States, Amtrak now needs less support and has upgraded its tracks and stations as well as the level of speed and comfort offered in its coaches.

One of the promising new technologies in the field is maglev, short for magnetic levitation. The train levitates or floats just above the rails. The concept was first developed in the United States in 1960, but it was abandoned, only to be picked up by the Germans and Japanese, who developed two distinct forms of it. By the 1980s, maglev trains made some experimental runs, and the trains may make their appearance in Europe, Japan, and North America in the 1990s. The technology remains experimental, but interest has risen as airports and aircraft become more and more congested and as the hub and spoke system of flying in the United States is fraught with delays. The main obstacle to maglev trains, known as ground-based jetliners, remains the high cost of investment needed for both real estate right-of-ways and the rolling stock equipment.[37]

Other technological changes in this field include advanced electric locomotives, tilting cars to negotiate unbanked curves, fixed formation or unit trains, and high-speed trackbeds. Each of these represents a market opportunity for makers of rolling stock, rails, and instruments. However, supporters of passenger and freight movement on rails must convince the private or public sector to provide financing. Those who oppose aid to rail have failed to explain why past and current subsidies to the interstate system of highways and hence to trucks and passenger cars have merit.

Biotechnology: An Old/New Field

Biotechnology used to be more an art than a science, but it is mostly science based. Bacteria are still employed in the fermentation of food and beverages, as they have been for centuries. But gene splicing and other new life forms are having a major impact in both agriculture and food processing. Enthusiasm also ran high in the 1970s for utilizing biotechnology in drug making and in medical healing. However, potential problems arose in adapting recombinant DNA for large-scale production. This illustrates well the point that scaling up is as significant as learning and assimilating new knowledge. In short, what works in the laboratory may not work in the factory, at least not as easily or cost effectively.

In the 1980s, the focus in biotechnology shifted back to agriculture and food processing as commercial payoffs in the two areas seemed more attainable. In the 1990s, however, health care and pollution control loom as potentially rewarding applications. Artificial antibodies are used as tools for diagnosis and as purifying agents. New vaccines and genetically engineered hormones are appearing. Bacteria now can consume vast quantities of sludge or waste, thereby purifying water and wastewater. Genetic manipulation of crops and genetic engineering for making industrial chemicals are two promising possibilities. The promise of expanding markets and the rising demand for environmentally harmless goods are providing the stimulus in this field to venture capitalists and entrepreneurs. A measure of how "hot" this field has become is the number of new start-up firms. The absorption of some of these firms by larger companies indicates a drive toward growth and consolidation, but the shakeout phase is not in full swing.[38]

Medical Imaging: Equipment and Process

After the discovery of x-rays a century ago, progress was slow in exploring alternative means of viewing what is inside the human body. But in the past two decades, one can claim a technological explosion in the field of medical imaging. Such activity was spurred by many factors, including the desire to minimize intrusion or impact on patients. Funds devoted to health care and prestige/income considerations on the part of doctors and hospitals also played a major role. If the employer, government, or insurance firm is willing to pay, why not do another scan? This is a major ethical question, and we may yet see a backlash in the 1990s.

Improved image resolutions come from various techniques, such as axial tomography, nuclear magnetic resonance, and ultrasound. It is instructive to note that wording can make a difference in the diffusion of a product or process. The makers of nuclear magnetic resonance equipment found that the use of the word *nuclear* did not please many people, including doctors and patients, so they renamed it magnetic resonance imaging (MRI). The result was faster growth for this category. The total medical imaging market is estimated to be in the billions now. Several equipment makers are also aggressively marketing related software and services to users. This happens to such an extent that health care institutions now object to being locked in to a given software or service package or to tie-ins between equipment and follow-up offerings.

The marketing of medical imaging equipment and processes provides a good example of market segmentation by technical features. Hospitals and clinics in developing nations comprise the major market for conventional equipment, such as traditional x-ray and CT scanners. The health care facilities in the industrialized economies tend to purchase the latest equipment. In a similar fashion, small and rural clinics opt for the simpler, older units, whereas the large city hospitals specify the more sophisticated equipment. Aggressive marketing has reached the point where technical sales representatives accompany doctors and technicians into the operating room. The key negative factor on further growth is the increasing reluctance of employers, employees, or governments to absorb spiraling health care expenditures.[39]

SUMMARY

The translation of scientific knowledge into economic prosperity is the key factor in explaining the prosperity of industrialized Western nations. In this context, technology is seen as the intermediary force between science and the marketplace. Technological change turns out to be an extremely complex, ongoing process in which inventors, innovators, imitators, and users play major roles. Interaction and feedback are central to technological progress. Whereas science is universal, technology is local and specific; indeed, it should be appropriate to local needs and institutions. There are some hopeful signs that technology is now being used more for civilian purposes, including pollution control, than for development of weapons and products that are harmful to the environment. We should admit that technology can be abused and misused; value judgments have to be made at all times by all participants.

The relationship between technological change and industrial markets is meaningful and working in both (or many) directions. It is not just a one-way flow from inventors and innovators to marketers. Instead, imitators, competitors, and users make significant improvements themselves and provide needed feedback. Different nations have certain social and economic goals that are then reflected in both government and private sector funding patterns for research and development. The various measures of R&D are worth studying, as they provide insights on the rate and direction of innovative activities. The diffusion of new technology follows an S-shape curve, but before all potential users adopt the new process or product, another generation may come to the forefront. Rapid changes are especially prevalent in high-tech industries, where hype and hope govern decisions. Technological forecasting is still an inexact pursuit, but it is carried out as an aid to better business and market planning.

In the global economy, ample evidence exists that both competition and cooperation occur in the various fields of technology. It is not easy to transfer technology from one nation or group to another, but it is increasingly attempted and success stories can be cited. A culture of innovation, flexibility, and widespread education/training are key to successful transplants. Technology can also be used to gain entry into foreign markets via exporting, licensing, joint ventures, contractual arrangements, or direct investment. Both in transferring technology and in using it as a tool for market entry, special attention should be paid to the needs and customs of the developing nations and to local institutions. In the areas of chemistry and electronics it is easier to transmit the latest advancements, but large-scale engineering and manufacturing operations are not easily transferred.

Even in areas that can be called old line or traditional, such as steelmaking or rail transport, major technological progress, as well as many minor but significant improvements, is possible. Such "hot fields" as biotechnology, electronics, resource conversion, and advanced manufacturing and transportation are continuing to attract funding and entrepreneurs.

Key Terms and Concepts

commercialization
innovation
invention
research and development (R&D)
appropriate technology
lead users
diffusion

substitution
technological forecasting
technology transfer
high technology
research intensive
artificial intelligence

Discussion Questions

1. Exhibits 8–1 and 8–2 illustrate the difference between the classic and the modern view of invention-innovation and beyond. Investigate one specific industry and/or product line and show how the feedback mechanism shown in Exhibit 8–2 is improving old products and creating new ones.

2. The text and Exhibits 8–9, 8–10, and 8–11 offer information on how long it takes to diffuse new ideas, concepts, and methods and show certain time lags. Do you think there is any speedup now in the diffusion process— that is, any shrinking in the time lag? (Hint: you can find relevant items in articles published in *Research Policy* and *Technological Forecasting and Social Change* especially. Also check *Research Technology Management, Journal of Product Innovation Management, Technology Review,* and *High Technology Business.*)

3. The chapter refers to the role of technology in both highly industrialized and developing nations. Do you think that countries in Asia,

Africa, and Latin America should specialize in certain areas of technology and use such specialization to capture domestic and foreign markets? Explain.

4. We know that Japan, through its government, industries, companies, and associations, is highly skilled and also well versed in protecting its home markets while capturing foreign markets. Now take a look at how European, Canadian, and U.S. firms are trying to penetrate the telecommunication and construction markets in Japan. Focus on recent bids on major projects. (Hint: Austin Company of Cleveland is now a partner in an alliance to build new airports in Japan.)

5. Evidence cited in the text shows that R&D spending has a major impact on the sales of companies in many industries, but the influence is more complex and not as clear regarding profits. How do you explain this situation? Why can't R&D have a direct, positive, significant impact on the bottom line?

6. If some industries spend little on R&D, what are the sources on which they rely for inno-

vation? Attempt to trace the origins of technological change in fields in which small sums are spent on R&D. Discuss whether mature industries would benefit by spending more on R&D. (Hint: Look at the R&D scoreboard issue of *Business Week*, published every other year, or similar issues of other journals and trace a given industry plus leading firms over several years.)

7. If cooperation and alliances pay off, as in the case of R&D consortia and other arrangements (see text of Chapters 7 and 8), then why should companies maintain their own R&D laboratories? Discuss the pros and cons of joining a consortium and the topic of sharing technical information with other firms in the preproduction stage.

8. The quarterly statistical publication *Predicasts* collects all published forecasts on industries and product lines in the United States. (Note: Its global counterpart, *Worldcasts*, is much harder to find in college or public libraries.) Pick a specific industry or family of products, where 0.0 is shown in the base year—those are new products. Now look at the short- and long-range forecast years and check if the predictions came true or by how much they were off the mark. (Hint: If you go over a few years of issues, you will find the base year, the forecast, and the actual numbers.)

9. Is it true that technological improvements first occur and get implemented in the defense sector in the United States, especially in aerospace and electronics? What about the promised spinoffs by NASA, the space agency, and the Defense Department? Have they materialized?

10. Several exhibits in the chapter illustrate S-shaped diffusion curves. Can you plot technological changes of various kinds not shown here where this applies? Does the S-shape form apply to computers?

11. One of the key features of the high-tech marketplace is the existence of hype and hope. Hype is overblown promises; hope is desire that they will come true. Find selected articles in various journals (see question 2 for a list) and see if the hype and hope came true in some cases.

12. Rejuvenating old industries is no small task. The chapter gives attention to a major, old-line industry, steelmaking. Find another mature industry and see what technological changes occurred recently and whether they have led to a resurgence of sales by participating firms.

13. When should a firm choose patenting and when should it go another route, such as trade secrets, copyright, iron-clad agreements, etc.? What about licensing? When should a company consider that an attractive proposition?

14. Several companies are taking technology to the market and selling it outright in the form of ideas, licenses, etc. General Electric is known for doing this; it develops more new concepts than it can bring to market. Should large and small firms stay with their core technologies and not be concerned with developing too many ideas they cannot utilize in-house?

Endnotes and References

1. The "rich tapestry of technological change" is documented in many books, but the most thorough treatment is D. Sahal, *Patterns of Technological Innovation* (Reading, Mass.: Addison-Wesley, 1981). On "appropriate technology," see the pioneering volume, E. F. Schumacher, *Small Is Beautiful* (London: Blond & Briggs, 1973), as well as M. J. Betz and P. J.

McGowan, eds., *Appropriate Technology: Choice and Development* (Durham, N.C.: Duke University Press, 1984).

2. See the sources cited in Exhibits 8–1, 8–2, and earlier contributions such as E. Morison, *Men, Machines, and Modern Times* (Cambridge, Mass.: MIT Press, 1966); D. G. Marquis, "The Anatomy of Successful Innovations," *Innovation* 1 (November 1969): 35–48; and R. R. Nelson, ed., *The Rate and Direction of Inventive Activity* (Princeton, N.J.: Princeton University Press, 1964). For more recent contributions, see K. Gronhaug and G. Kaufmann, eds., *Innovation: A Cross-Disciplinary Perspective* (New York: Oxford University Press, 1990); and J. Cantwell, *Technological Innovations and Multinational Companies* (London: Basil Blackwell, 1989).

3. See Sahal, *Patterns of Technological Innovation,* and issues of trade journals in any given field for documentation on how innovations evolve and what role feedback plays. Titles of journals range from *Automation News* to *Robotics World,* from *Chemical Processing* to *Instruments & Control Systems,* and from *Metal Architechture* to *Welding Journal.* Industry associations and technical institutes also publish newsletters and bulletins that underscore the diversity of sources and the idea of circularity. See also, A. Namatame, "Dynamic Comparison of R & D Innovation Process Structures," *International Journal of Technology Management* 4 (1989): 305–315.

4. E. von Hippel, *The Sources of Innovation* (New York: Oxford University Press. 1988), and his earlier articles, "Users as Innovators," *Technology Review* 81 (January 1978): 31–39, and "Successful Products from Customers' Ideas," *Journal of Marketing* 42 (January 1978): 39–49. Hippel's findings are confirmed by recent studies conducted by staff members of the Institute for the Study of Business Markets at Pennsylvania State University, 1987–1992. On the role of individuals versus groups, see R. M. Knight, "Technological Innovation in Canada: A Comparison of Independent Entrepreneurs and Corporate

Innovators," *International Journal of Technology Management* 4 (1989): 273–281.

5. See the various issues of journals which focus on innovation of both products and processes: *Research and Development; Research & Technology Management; Research Policy; Technovation; Technology Review; Technological Forecasting and Social Change; Science; Scientific American;* etc. See also such books as B. H. Amstead et al., *Manufacturing Processes,* 8th ed. (New York: Wiley, 1987); J. B. Clark, *Basic Process Industries* (London: Gower, 1984); and J. E. Edosomwan, *Integrating Innovation and Technology Management* (New York: Wiley, 1989).

6. D. C. Mowery and N. Rosenberg, *Technology and the Pursuit of Economic Growth* (London: Cambridge University Press, 1989); P. Stoneman, *The Economic Analysis of Technological Policy* (London: Oxford University Press, 1987); N. Rosenberg and L. E. Birdzell, Jr., "Science, Technology, and the Western Miracle," *Scientific American* 263 (November 1990): 42–54; a longer version of this was later published as a book, with the same title.

7. See "Innovation: The Machinery of Growth, *The Economist,* January 11, 1992, pp. 17–19. Several paragraphs in the chapter rely on this excellent article.

8. This point is made in the article cited in endnote 7; in *World Development Report* (New York: Oxford University Press for the World Bank), published annually; and in many publications of the United Nations, the Organization for Economic Cooperation and Development (OECD), the World Bank, etc.

9. Statistics on R&D come from two key volumes: *Science and Engineering Indicators, 1989* (Washington, D.C.: National Science Foundation, 1989) and *International Science and Technology Data Update,* Report #91-309 (Washington, D.C.: National Science Foundation, 1991).

10. The role of technology in automotive and other transportation fields can be noted by observing how much electronics invaded the

engines and other parts of cars, trucks, ships, and planes. Chrysler just built a $1 billion technology center. General Motors acquired Electronic Data Systems and Hughes for their technology. Airbus planes now fly by wire, meaning computers.

11. Conversation with Dr. L. G. Polgar, Vice President, Marketing & Quality Control, Bertram Laboratories, Somerville, N.J., January 1992.

12. Based on the NSF sources cited in endnote 9 and data from OECD. In spite of this, a statistic often quoted is that the United States has ten times more lawyers per capita than Japan, whereas Japan has ten times more engineers per capita than the United States. These ratios may seem exaggerated and might change over time, but the implications are clear. For more details, see *National Interests in an Age of Global Technology* (Washington, D.C.: National Academy Press, 1991).

13. D. Pelz and F. Andrews, *Scientists in Organizations,* 2nd ed. (New York: Wiley, 1976).

14. Many volumes are available on this topic—for example, F. Betz, *Managing Technology* (Englewood Cliffs, N.J.: Prentice-Hall, 1987); L. W. Steele, *Managing Technology* (New York: McGraw-Hill, 1989); B. C. Twiss, *Managing Technical Innovation* (London: Longman, 1980). For a good collection of articles, see M. E. Tushman and W. L. Moore, eds., *Readings in the Management of Innovation,* 2nd ed. (Cambridge, Mass.: Ballinger, 1988).

15. The classics in this field are J. Schmookler, *Invention and Economic Growth* (Cambridge, Mass.: Harvard University Press, 1966); J. Jewkes et al., *The Sources of Invention* (London: Macmillan, 1958); and E. Mansfield, *The Economics of Technical Change* (New York: Norton, 1968). For more commentary on patents and patenting, see K. Pavitt, "Patent Statistics as Indicators of Innovative Activities," *Scientometrics* 7 (1985): 77–99; D. Schiffel and C. Kitti, "Rates of Invention: International Patent Comparisons," *Research Policy* (1978): 324–340; W. D. Reekie, "Patent Data as a Guide to Industrial Activity," *Research Policy* (1973): 246–264.

16. Sahal, *Patterns of Technological Change,* plus various issues of *Research Policy, Technological Forecasting and Social Change, Technology Review,* etc.

17. Key sources on this topic are R. D. Buzzell and B. T. Gale, *The PIMS Principles* (New York: Free Press, 1987) and the following articles: G. K. Morbey, "R&D Expenditures and Profit Growth," *Research & Technology Management* (May–June 1989): 76–85; and G. K. Morbey, "R&D and Its Relationship to Company Performance," *Journal of Product Innovation Management* 5 (1988): 191–200.

18. The classic on diffusion is E. M. Rogers, *The Diffusion of Innovations,* 3rd ed. (New York: Free Press, 1982). Some earlier works include M. Radnor, *The Diffusion of Innovations* (Washington, D.C.: National Science Foundation, 1978); and L. Nabseth and G. F. Ray, eds., *The Diffusion of New Industrial Products* (Cambridge: Cambridge University Press, 1974). Ray recently published many articles on the topic; see Exhibit 8–9 for one listing. For a marketing viewpoint, see H. Gatignon and T. Robertson, "Technology Diffusion: An Empirical Test of Competitive Effects," *Journal of Marketing* 53 (January 1989): 35–49.

19. "Innovation: The Machinery of Growth," *The Economist,* January 11, 1992, 17–19, cites evidence from the works of two U.S. economists, Kenneth Arrow and Edwin Mansfield. See also D. J. Teece, "Capturing Value from Technological Innovation," *Interfaces* (May–June 1988): 46–61.

20. "Innovation: The Machinery of Growth." See also E. B. Roberts, "Managing Invention and Innovation," *Research & Technology Management* (January–February 1988): 11–29; "Innovation in America," special issue of *Business Week,* July 1989; R. L. Kuhn, *Commercializing Defense-Related Technology* (New York: Praeger, 1982); C. L. Freeman and L. Soete, eds., *New Issues in the Economics of Technological Change* (New York: Cambridge University Press, 1990).

21. S. P. Schnaars, *Megamistakes: Forecasting and the Myth of Rapid Technological Change* (New York: Free Press, 1989).

22. On both the successes and failures as well as the methods of technological forecasting, see J. Marino, *Technological Forecasting for Decision Making,* 2nd ed. (New York: North Holland, 1983); M. J. Cetron, *Technological Forecasting: A Practical Approach* (London: Gordon & Breach, 1962); and J. R. Bright, *Practical Technological Forecasting* (Austin, Tex.: The Management Center, 1978). For a recent overview, see R. U. Ayres, "The Future of Technological Forecasting," *Technological Forecasting and Social Change* (July 1989): 319–326. This journal is obviously a key publication to consult on the topic.

23. Schnaars, *Megamistakes,* pp. 161–169; H. E. Klein and R. E. Linneman, "The Use of Scenarios in Corporate Planning: Eight Case Histories," *Long Range Planning* 14 (October 1981): 69–77; B. Rosen et al., "A Comparison of Approaches for Setting Standards for Technological Products," *Journal of Product Innovation Management* 5 (1988).

24. *Business Week* publishes annually an "R&D Scoreboard" issue showing R&D spending in both absolute and relative terms by industry sectors and for several hundred individual companies. Other journals also carry statistics on R&D. Several trade publications focus on new product and process announcements; some cut across industries—for example, *New Equipment News.* Both *Research & Development* and *Fortune* carry articles on "new products of the year."

25. Personal communication, based on lists compiled by S. A. Wolpert of Predicasts, Inc. in 1982, and W. M. Weiss of The Freedonia Group in 1992, both of Cleveland, Ohio.

26. See such volumes as M. E. Porter, *The Competitive Advantage of Nations* (New York: Free Press, 1990); *Technology and Global Industry* (Washington, D.C.: National Academy Press, 1987); various OECD Country Surveys; and A. C. Gross, "Competition in Global Environment Markets," *European Journal of Marketing* (Spring 1986): 22–34.

27. NASA occasionally publishes reports on the spin-offs from the space program, but the extent of such transfers may be exaggerated. For an outside assessment, see Schnaars, *Megamistakes,* p. 137; and J. G. Welles, "Contributions to Technology and Their Transfer: The NASA Experience," in H. F. Davidson et al., eds., *Technology Transfer* (Leinden, Neth.: Nordhoof, 1974).

28. R. K. Dixon, "Plant Biotechnology Networking in Developing Countries," in D. J. Webber, ed., *Biotechnology* (Westport, Conn.: Greenwood Press, 1990), pp. 87ff. See also next reference entries.

29. On technology transfer in general, see F. J. Contractor, *Licensing in International Strategy* (Westport, Conn.: Greenwood Press, 1985); E. Mansfield, et al., *Technology Transfer, Productivity, and Economic Policy* (New York: Norton, 1983); R. D. Robinson, *The International Transfer of Technology* (New York: Harper Business, 1988); A. C. Samli, ed., *Technology Transfer* (Westport, Conn.: Greenwood Press, 1985); and *North/South Technology Transfer* (Paris: OECD, 1981). See also D. Ford and C. Ryan, "Taking Technology to the Market," *Harvard Business Review* 59 (March–April 1981): 117–126; K. Young and C. Steigerwald, "Is Foreign Investment Transferring U.S. Technology Abroad?" *Business Economics* (October 1990): 28–30; and Gross, "Competition in Global Environmental Markets," on technology transfer in pollution control.

30. M. Horwich, ed., *Technology and the Modern Corporation* (New York: Pergamon Press, 1986); R. Brenner, *Rivalry in Business and Science Among Nations* (Cambridge: Cambridge University Press, 1987); A. J. Morrison, *Strategies in Global Industries* (New York: Quorum, 1990).

31. W. L. Shanklin and J. E. Ryans, Jr., *Essentials of Marketing High Technology* (Lexington, Mass.: Lexington Books, 1986) is the key primer in this field, postulating "megatenets" for high-tech operations. See also R. T. Moriarty and T. J. Kosnik, "High-Technology Marketing," *Sloan Management Review* (Sum-

mer 1989): 7–17; H. Bahrans and S. Evans, "Strategy Making in High-Tech Firms," *California Management Review* (Winter 1989): 107–128; and C. Beard, "High-Tech Launch Strategies in the U.K.," *Industrial Marketing Management* (May 1989): 125–138.

32. Documented in L. Teschler, A. C. Gross, and R. Hisrich, "Taking the Long View in New Product Introduction: The Case of Expert Systems," *ESOMAR Proceedings, 1990* (Amsterdam: ESOMAR, 1990): pp. 245–256. See also W. Davidow, *Marketing High Technology* (New York: Free Press, 1986) and recent issues of such journals as *AI Magazine, Expert System Newsletter,* etc.

33. Davidow, *Marketing High Technology*; Gross, "Competition in Global Environmental Markets"; Schnaars, *Megamistakes*; Teschler et al., "Taking the Long View in New Product Introduction"; and many recent volumes on business forecasting. See also various issues of the *Journal of Business Forecasting*.

34. Based on two lectures by W. Madar, chief executive officer, Nordson Corporation, Cleveland, Ohio, 1990 and 1991.

35. This section, like others that follow, is based on a combination of sources; the first item listed is the key source; the others are updates or elaborations. A. C. Gross, "The Information Vending Machine," *Business Horizons* (January–February 1988): 24–33; D. E. Raphael, "The Information Industry: A New Portrait," *Business Economics* 24 (July 1989): 28–33; J. W. Verity, "Rethinking the Computer," *Business Week,* November 26, 1990, pp. 42–54; personal communication with members of Harvard University, Center for Information Policy, 1988, and with W. Warner, Vice President, Information Technology Association of America, 1992.

36. W. T. Hogan, *Minimills and Integrated Mills* (Lexington, Mass.: Lexington Books, 1987);

M. Hersch, *Minimills: Steelmaking in the USA* (Cleveland: Predicasts, 1984); R. Hudson and R. Sadler, *The International Steel Industry* (London: Routledge, 1989). See also G. J. McManus, "Growth Still Sparks the Minimills," *Iron Age* (April 1990): 14–16, and P. D. Southwick, "Steel: A High-Tech Material and Industry," *Journal of Metals* (March 1987): 27.

37. R. G. Rhodes and B. E. Mulhall, *Magnetic Levitation for Rail Transport* (London: Oxford University Press, 1981), and *Magnetic Levitation for Advanced Transit Systems* (New York: Society of Automotive Engineers, 1989). See also D. Moynihan, "How to Lose: The Story of Maglev," *Scientific American* 261 (November 1989): 130; "Levitating Trains Return to America," *The Economist,* October 13, 1990, pp. 91–92; and articles in engineering journals.

38. W. E. Martineau, *Biotechnology Markets and Companies* (Cleveland: Predicasts, 1982); and W. Weizer, *Biotechnology Applications* (Cleveland: Predicasts, 1984); BCC Staff, *Needs of the Biotechnology Industry* (Stamford, Conn.: BCC, 1989); M. Knott, "The Biotechnology Race," *Process Engineering* (July 1990): 33–35; A. Gibbons, "Biotechnology Takes Root in the Third World," *Science,* May 25, 1990, pp. 962–963; and articles in many other science journals.

39. E. Hester, *Medical Imaging Market* (Cleveland: Predicasts, 1983), updated by other multiclient studies by The Freedonia Group, Frost & Sullivan, Leading Edge, et al. See also K. Fitzgerald, "Technology in Medicine," *IEEE Spectrum* (December 1989): 24–29; R. Dowell, "Electronics in Medical Imaging," *Electronics World & Wireless World* 96 (May 1990): 440–444; and other medical, business, and electronics journals.

9

PRODUCT DECISIONS AND STRATEGIES

CHAPTER OUTLINE

- To understand the necessity of developing new products despite the risks involved
- To understand the new product development process
- To learn the use of industrial design in product development
- To recognize the importance of niche marketing
- To identify international considerations in product development

The essence of good marketing is to be aware of the customer's needs. This is most apparent when dealing with the product-service mix. To the customer, the product is not an end in itself. Rather, it is a means to an end. The manufacturing firm does not buy nuts and bolts; it buys means of fastening or joining parts together. Thus the marketer of nuts and bolts must view these products as a means of satisfying the customer's need to fasten pieces. That need might just as easily and economically be fulfilled by welding or adhesives.

The business product must be viewed as a need satisfier. The **product-service mix** is a combination of the physical product, its functional features and specifications, plus an array of other want-fulfilling aspects. These include the brand name, trademark, design, packaging, instructions, installation, availability of replacement parts, repair and maintenance, warranties, and so on. More formally, the **product** may be defined as the array of utilities or benefits anticipated by the business buyer. The business buyer doesn't purchase an electric drill, but rather is buying holes of certain sizes and tolerances.[1] Viewed from the customer's perspective, the business marketer's product-service mix assumes many dimensions that, although not immediate to the function of the product, may be crucial to its ability to generate and sustain sales.

For example, a German firm introduced a new line of industrial lathes and succeeded in capturing a significant share of the market formerly held by a leading British firm. Both companies' lathes were functionally the same. The difference rested in the customers' perceptions. The German product was cleaner looking and generally more attractive in its design. What is more, it begged to be kept clean and new looking. Business buyers recognized this advantage over the austere British lathe, not only in the aesthetics of the German design, but also in its ability to induce machinists to develop better all-around housekeeping habits in the plant.

BUSINESS PRODUCTS CLASSIFICATION

Although there are many ways to classify business products, one useful method is to view them in terms of the selling company's product line approach. **Catalog items** are the company's own design and most often are manufactured in batches, maintained in inventory, and conform to specifications that the company publishes in its catalog. Thus they can be purchased "off the shelf." Some companies design product components in compatible and substitutable modules so that an individual customer's requirement can be met by assembling the appropriate modules. This is typical of companies that supply electrical control panels in which the customer's choice of instrumentation (say meters and switching devices) can be quite different.

Custom-made items include systems, complete products, and components. **Systems** are such items as a power-generating station or an office building, designed precisely to the customer's specifications or blueprints. Often such systems are constructed from a set of modular component products, where the buyer's performance standards are met by a unique assortment of off-the-shelf items that are assembled together. Such would be the case in the provision of warehouse racks or in the development of a computer system for inventory control.

An example of a **complete product** would be a multispindle boring machine for shaping truck or automobile engine blocks. It would be purchased by a single automobile manufacturer, meet that buyer's exact requirements, and would be of no use to any other firm. A **component** might be the metal casing on a gas or electric meter that has been cast and machined to the meter manufacturer's design.

Although all manufacturers of business and industrial products must provide associated services, such as spare parts maintenance, technical advice, delivery, and so on, some business-to-business suppliers offer only **services**. Examples include management consultants, architects, accountants, testing laboratories, software designers and advertising agencies. Services will be explored in depth in Chapter 10.

The Product Life Cycle

For about half a century, vacuum tubes were the basic unit in electronic equipment. But a new technology, the transistor, revolutionized the industry. The electronic vacuum tube had moved through the stages of a relatively long life cycle and died. Whether their life is longer, as in the case of standard fasteners and vacuum tubes, or very short, as in the case of a particular microchip model, all products move through a life cycle that can be illustrated by charting their sales volume over time from their first market launch to withdrawal from the market (see Exhibit 9–1).

The **product life cycle (PLC)** concept can be applied to technologies[2] or product categories, as in the vacuum tube instance; to product classes, such as regular versus radial automobile tires; to individual product items; and to brands. Obviously, the life cycle of a brand will fluctuate more widely and will be shorter in duration than that of a product category. A brand may be more readily outflanked by a competitor's product, whereas it may require a new technology to make a product category obsolete (for example, the 80386 computer chip has rendered the 286 chip obsolete).

EXHIBIT 9–1   The Product Life Cycle

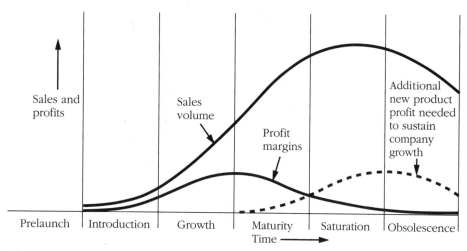

The product life cycle: note how sales and profits change over time.

Prelaunch.   Prior to product launch, the firm has made significant investment in research and development (R&D), pilot plant or prototype development, tooling, and so forth. These investments must be recaptured as the product begins to move through its life cycle. The prelaunch stage is not usually shown in the PLC diagram.

Introduction.   Typically the product is an unsought good when it is first launched. Potential customers are unaware of its existence or merits. The cost of marketing the new product is very high because of the heavy promotion required to inform the market and establish product awareness. It may be necessary to stimulate primary demand by seeking out applications and uses for the new product. Sales rise slowly, and production levels are low. Typically this means production costs are high and will be exacerbated by the need to eliminate "bugs" discovered during operation in the field and the need to do fine tuning. Profit margins are likely to be low at this stage. Innovators and early adopters are the main buyers. (The stages in the diffusion of an innovation are innovators, early adopters, early majority, late majority, and laggards.)

Growth.   The influence of early adopters begins to make an impact on the early majority, and both sales and profit margins begin to rise rapidly. Competitors begin to enter the market at a rapid rate, with an assortment of brands. This places downward pressure on price, which in turn may help to expand the market more rapidly.

Maturity.   While sales are still growing, their rate of growth is declining. Profit margins begin to fall because of the competitive pressures on price and the expansion of product designs. At this stage it becomes very important to provide good repair service and replacement part availability. Competitive pressures force inefficient suppliers out of the market, while firms that are farther down their experience curves are able to consolidate their positions. (With each doubling of production, the manufacturer's greater experience leads to greater efficiency and lower costs.)

Saturation.   Sales level off and become dependent on the state of the economy. In this stage, the number of firms remaining in the market is small. They concentrate their efforts on value analysis improvements and cost reduction techniques to improve their profitability. By this stage it is important to have other new products ready to launch if the firm wishes to sustain its growth.

Obsolescence.   Unit sales decline, never to regain their former levels. Obsolescence results from two main factors: a new and better product may be introduced to the market, or the needs, habits, or values of the customers may shift. The typewriter is becoming obsolete because the word processor is a substitute for the typewriter. Businesses increasingly prefer to use personal computer–based word processors and printers.

The Product Life Cycle as a Planning Tool

Marketers who graph their market and financial data against product life cycles have found the concept useful in formulating marketing strategies. This approach has been used at Westinghouse. The broad strategic guidelines circulated in the company appear in Exhibit 9–2.

PRODUCT OBJECTIVES AND POLICIES

In an industrial organization, the decision to manufacture one type of product rather than another, to offer one service or a range of services, to have a broad offering of products or just a few, to seek to be the leader in product technologies or to offer standard equipment at lower prices stems from organizational objectives. In Japan, Sord Computer was founded with the corporate objectives of offering the highest technology available and the greatest degree of user friendliness. Such corporate objectives establish the overall boundaries within which **product objectives** can be formulated. Product objectives set the long-run goals of the company for its product-service mix. Ideally, product objectives should be achievable, measurable, and consistent with strategic corporate goals and the marketing strategy. Thus, a product objective of Sord Computer is to seek out the newest and best technologies to incorporate into Sord products, no matter where in the world the innovation has originated. No "not invented here" syndrome at Sord![3] Another Sord product objective is to devote a great deal of time and attention to creation of software that will run on Sord equipment. From such objectives, product policies are developed.

Product policies give quick answers to recurring questions. For example, confronted by the question of whether to continue production of an existing computer line, given the availability of a faster microchip, Sord would opt for modification or redesign to incorporate the new device, as a matter of policy. Similarly Sord's policy toward revising and simplifying software would encourage more frequent modifications than its competitors, if the result were to make the programs easier to understand and use. Among the product objectives and policies to be established are decisions of how many product lines the firm should market (width) and how many items (depth) there should be in any product line.

Product Line Width

In western Canada there is a company that manufactures stone pickers. This piece of machinery removes large stones from fields so that a farmer's plows, diskers, seed drills, and cultivators will not be damaged when working the field. The company has no other product!

Contrast this to the approach of U.S. farm equipment manufacturers J I Case and John Deere. These companies have a broad range of products, including tractors, cultivators, combines, hay balers, rakes, wagons, and manure spreaders. The stone picker manufacturer is a single-product-line company. The other two are full-line agricultural equipment manufacturers. Both types are successful. They have chosen to offer wide or narrow lines on the basis of organizational objectives and capabilities and market expectations.

Product Line Depth

As a company grows, it finds that its expertise in a particular type of product can be exploited with little risk by expanding on the number of variations of that product. It is also usually able to broaden its customer base by offering more models or sizes of the basic product. Thus a wheel tractor manufacturer, although having a narrow product line—tractors—may have tremendous depth: offering equipment from the smallest low-horsepower garden tractor up to a gigantic machine used in western grain ranches to pull gangs of plows. IBM, well known for mainframe computers, added depth to its product line by introducing personal computers in the early 1980s.

EXHIBIT 9–2   Dynamic Competitive Strategy and the Product Life Cycle

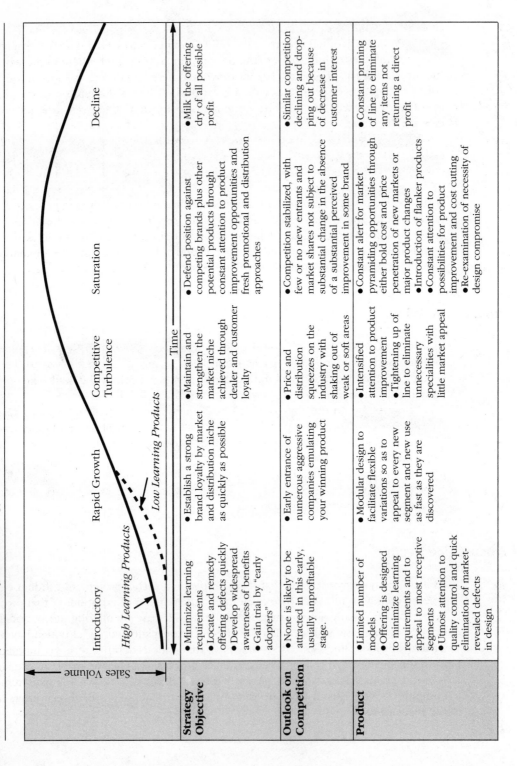

	Introductory	Rapid Growth	Competitive Turbulence	Saturation	Decline
Strategy Objective	● Minimize learning requirements ● Locate and remedy offering defects quickly ● Develop widespread awareness of benefits ● Gain trial by "early adopters"	● Establish a strong brand loyalty by market and distribution niche as quickly as possible	● Maintain and strengthen the market niche achieved through dealer and customer loyalty	● Defend position against competing brands plus other potential products through constant attention to product improvement opportunities and fresh promotional and distribution approaches	● Milk the offering dry of all possible profit
Outlook on Competition	● None is likely to be attracted in this early, usually unprofitable stage.	● Early entrance of numerous aggressive companies emulating your winning product	● Price and distribution squeezes on the industry with shaking out of weak or soft areas	● Competition stabilized, with few or no new entrants and market shares not subject to substantial change in the absence of a substantial perceived improvement in some brand	● Similar competition declining and dropping out because of decrease in customer interest
Product	● Limited number of models ● Offering is designed to minimize learning requirements and to appeal to most receptive segments ● Utmost attention to quality control and quick elimination of market-revealed defects in design	● Modular design to facilitate flexible variations so as to appeal to every new segment and new use as fast as they are discovered	● Intensified attention to product improvement ● Tightening up of line to eliminate unnecessary specialities with little market appeal	● Constant alert for market pyramiding opportunities through either bold cost and price penetration of new markets or major product changes ● Introduction of flanker products ● Constant attention to possibilities for product improvement and cost cutting ● Re-examination of necessity of design compromise	● Constant pruning of line to eliminate any items not returning a direct profit

High Learning Products

Low Learning Products

Sales Volume →

Time →

Category				
Pricing Objective	• To impose a minimum of "value perception" learning on the most receptive segments • High trade discounts and sampling advisable	• A price line for every taste from low-end to premium models • Customary trade discounts • Aggressive promotional pricing with prices cut as fast as costs decline due to accumulated production experience • Intensification of sampling	• Increased attention to "market broadening" and "promotional" pricing opportunities	• Defensive pricing to preserve product category franchise • Search for incremental pricing opportunities, including private label contracts to boost volume and gain an experience advantage	• Maintenance of profit level pricing with complete disregard of any effect on market share
Promotional Guidelines Communications Objectives	• Create widespread awareness and understanding of offering's benefits • Gain trial by "early adopters"	• Create and strengthen brand preference among trade and final users • Stimulate trial by all potential customers	• Maintain customer loyalty and strengthen dealer ties	• Maintain customer and trade loyalty, with strong emphasis on dealers and distributors • Promotion of greater use and frequency of use	• Phase out: keeping promotion just enough to maintain profitable distribution
Most Valuable Media Mix	In order of value: • Publicity • Personal "sales"	• Personal sales • Sales promotions including sampling • Publicity	• Dealer promotions • Personal "selling" to dealers • Sales promotions • Publicity	• Dealer-oriented promotions	• Cut down all media to the bone; use no sales promotions of any kind
Distribution Policy	• Exclusive or selective with distributor margins high enough to justify heavy promotional spending by them	• Intensive and extensive with dealer margins just high enough to keep them interested. Close attention to rapid resupply of distributor stocks and heavy inventories at all levels	• Intensive and extensive with a strong emphasis on keeping dealers well-supplied, but with a minimum inventory cost to them	• Intensive and extensive with strong emphasis on keeping dealer well-supplied at a minimum inventory cost to dealer	• Phase out outlets as they become marginal
Intelligence Focus	• To identify actual developing uses and to uncover any product weaknesses	• Detailed attention to a) brand position b) gaps in model and market coverage c) opportunities for market segmentation	• Close attention to product improvement needs, to market-broadening chances, and to possible fresh promotional themes	• Intensified attention to possible product improvements • Sharp alert for potential new inter-product competition and to signs of beginning product decline	• Information helping to identify the point at which the product should be phased out

Source: Westinghouse Form 20-2082 (9/79). This chart was originally conceived by Chester R. Wasson of St. Xavier College, Chicago. Reprinted by permission of Westinghouse Electric Corporation.

BUSINESS MARKETING IN PRACTICE ▇▇▇▇▇▇

A New Standard in Speed of Travel

Marketers who wish to sell ketchup to U.S. government and institutional markets will have to adjust their product consistency.

Washington has decreed that the best grade of ketchup—the type to be served in U.S. armed forces, schools, and jails—must flow at a rate of three to seven centimeters in thirty seconds. Previously, the limit was six to eight centimeters per thirty seconds.

When selling to such a large segment of the market as the federal government, marketers of ketchup can generate substantial sales volume by increasing product depth (in this case by adding a more viscous ketchup).

Source: (Toronto) *Globe and Mail,* April 3, 1991, p. A16.

Risk in Product Line Management

Expanding product line width or depth can be risky business. In manufacturing, a firm faces greater risk as the type of production requirements becomes less familiar. This is especially true in widening the product line. A company with resources in electrical-mechanical devices, such as switchgear (electrical controls and switches), faces quite different and unfamiliar manufacturing problems if it broadens its line to include electronic devices, such as microprocessor-controlled switches. The risk inherent in moving toward greater divergence in manufacturing is illustrated in Exhibit 9–3.

On the marketing side, similar risks are encountered as the traditional product line is extended (see the horizontal axis of Exhibit 9–3). Marketing risks result from lack of understanding of the needs of a new market segment, unfamiliarity with channel requirements, an untrained sales organization, and different methods of promotion. For example, Ampex, the firm that set the standard in magnetic recording equipment for broadcast studio use, ran into trouble when it added a line of tape recorders for the consumer market. The marketing functions of consumer research, advertising and sales promotion to the consumer market, and interacting with a country-wide network of retailers were too divergent from those on which Ampex had built its reputation in the broadcast industry.

Deepening a product line too far can involve similar risks because the needs, buying behavior, media use, and product use of the various subsegments of the market can vary substantially. For example, the buying needs of a thousand-acre rancher when it comes to buying a wheel tractor are quite different from the needs of the grounds superintendent of a golf course. In developing and managing product lines, the business marketer must assess the various strategic risks that may be associated with the product diversification and weigh them against its potential benefits.

EXHIBIT 9–3   Strategic Risk

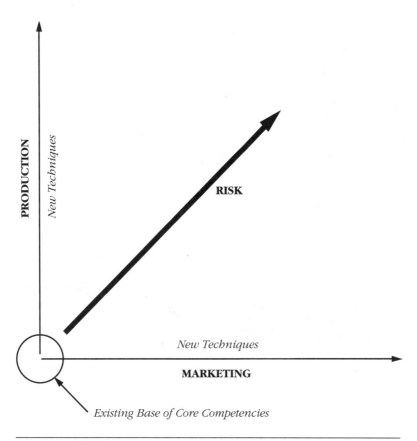

Source: Frank T. Troha.

DEVELOPING NEW PRODUCTS

The development of new products is a high-risk process. It is also a necessary process, and one that can bring significant rewards to a company. Without risk, firms in a competitive system produce no profits. **New product development** is risky because high capital investment typically is necessary to create and launch a new product, and the failure rate is high. Roughly one-half of the capital investment in new product development is expended on new products that are never launched or fail.

A study of fifty-one companies in several industries found that of every fifty-eight ideas or concepts of new products these companies generated, twelve made it past the preliminary screening test, seven showed sufficient profit potential, three were capable of further development, two passed the requirements of test marketing, and only one actually was launched.[4] A more recent replication of this study showed improvement. Seven new ideas yielded one successful new product launch.[5]

In the chemical industry the decay rate of new product concepts is even steeper. A study of twenty chemical firms by the Commercial Chemical Development Association found that to obtain one new product, an average of

- 540 possibilities in the idea stage were considered at the research level
- 448 were eliminated during screening conferences
- 92 were selected for preliminary laboratory investigation
- 8 were sufficiently promising to warrant further development
- 7 were dropped as unsalable or unprofitable before or during the prototype stage
- 1 survived and was placed in regular production.[6]

Even after a new product is placed in regular production, the risks of market failure are high. Failure can be defined in a number of ways. A commonly accepted approach is to define failure in terms of a product that does not meet the goals (sales volume, profit level, customer satisfaction, or market penetration) that management set prior to its market launch. Several studies in the past twenty years indicate that product success rates run about 65 percent successful in consumer goods and 75 percent in business goods.[7]

Management Attitudes Toward Risk

Despite the risks entailed in new product development, management seems to be relatively satisfied with current levels of success (see Exhibit 9–4). Indeed, they are quite pragmatic. They know that the odds are against them and that they will face disappointments, but they are willing to accept the risk.

As one executive of a large Japanese industrial manufacturing organization confided to a coauthor of this text: "Look at the batting averages of the most successful baseball players. If I can have a new product success rate of the same magnitude, I am happy."

The Necessity of New Products

With the high cost of examining and culling new product concepts, the substantial failure rate, lengthy development periods, and frequently slow payback of investment, why do business marketers bother to engage in new product development? They do so because it is essential to growth.

EXHIBIT 9–4 Management's Evaluations of Product Innovation Success Rates

Management Feeling Regarding Rate of Success	All Companies	Business Markets	Consumer Markets
Highly acceptable	37%	33%	44%
Disappointing, but still acceptable	52	57	44
Unacceptable	11	10	12

Source: David S. Hopkins, *New Product Winners and Losers* (New York: The Conference Board, Report No. 773, 1980), p. 7. Reprinted by permission.

No company can continue in a business very long with the same line of products. Business customers' requirements change over time as their own markets change. New technology forces industries to adopt innovations. For example, integrated circuits and microprocessors have revolutionized many industries quite beyond the electronics industry alone. The same is bound to happen in the new fine ceramics field and in optical fibers. Marketers recognize that a major implication of technological change is its impact on the product life cycle. High-tech products and processes typically have shorter PLCs. New markets evolve (such as biotechnology), and old ones die (such as vacuum tubes and mechanical cash registers).

BUSINESS MARKETING IN PRACTICE

Continuous Product Innovation

During the past ten years, Don Sheardown of Ontario Bus Industries (OBI) has transformed a $3 million bus repair company into North America's third-largest bus manufacturer, with sales of $124 million and manufacturing facilities in Mississauga, Ontario, and Utica, New York.

OBI's key to success has been its product innovation program. "Pretty well all our revenue comes from new products," states Sheardown. From the time Sheardown bought Ontario-based OBI in 1980, the company has developed imaginative new transit vehicles. Proven new products include the elongated Orion-Ikarus bus, which bends in the middle, and the Orion II, a small low-slung wheelchair transit vehicle for handicapped passengers. Upcoming products include natural-gas-powered buses and observation vehicles built for tour operators.

Product innovation has been vital to OBI's survival and growth in an increasingly competitive market. European competitors such as Volvo and Saab-Skania attempted to enter the North American bus market, found the competition too tough, and withdrew. As competition intensified, it was product innovation that kept OBI's assembly lines rolling. Says Sheardown, "If we had not been committed to developing new products and investing in research and development, this company probably would not be here today."

Source: Ian McGugan, "Innovation: By Choice Not Chance," *Small Business,* 9 (April 1990), pp. 20–27, and researchers Marlene DiGiuseppe, Tarek Dimachkie, Reena Lal, and Karen Vinter.

Loctite pushes a new product—an example of informative advertising for a new product.

Courtesy of Loctite Corporation.

Furthermore, as technological improvements are developed, business marketers who do not incorporate these improvements in their own products and processes find that their competitors, who have, are eroding their markets.

Thus it is not surprising that various studies have found that as much as 36 percent of companies' current sales and 32 percent of corporate profits come from new products introduced within the previous five years.[8]

THE NEW PRODUCT DEVELOPMENT ORGANIZATION

High capital investment, long development times, and high risk make it necessary for management to enter the new product development process with great care and detailed planning.[9] The starting point of the process is to structure the organization appropriately. Several approaches may be used for managing new products.

New Product Committees

Larger firms typically have a **new product committee** composed of top management from various departments, including R&D, production, marketing, engineering, and finance. Whether standing or ad hoc, these committees are responsible for screening new product ideas in the light of market opportunities and corporate objectives and resources. They approve new product plans and pass them on to a new product department. Members of new product committees come together on a regular basis, say once a month, to meet and make decisions, then return to their functional departments.

New Product Departments

The establishment of a **new product department** in a company gives formal recognition to the importance of new products to the organization. The department assumes responsibility for all aspects of the new product development process. It generates new product concepts, screens them, conducts business analyses, oversees engineering development and market testing, and brings the product to full commercial launch. After the launch, responsibility for the product is handed off to an ongoing operational division of the organization.

Product or Brand Managers

The **product** or **brand manager** assumes total responsibility for the continuing success or failure of a product or line of products once it or they have been launched. In firms without a new product department, the product manager also may be responsible for new product development.

Product managers establish the marketing strategy for their products, work with an advertising agency on promotional programs, set prices, supervise distribution, and usually work closely with the sales manager to ensure that the products under their managerial attention are receiving the amount and type of sales effort desired.

Venture Teams

Large organizations often find that bureaucratic rigidities can hinder the creation and development of new product concepts. New products can threaten old established relationships and methods in an organization.[10] The status quo is safer, and people who "rock the boat" are resisted. To insulate innovators from these restrictions, large organizations that wish to encourage innovation have put new product development into the hands of **venture teams**. In this organizational strategy, a group of specialists from different areas of the company are brought together and charged with the responsibility of generating new product concepts and concentrating on their development to the point where they are profitable in the market. At this stage, the new product may be transferred to the traditional marketing department. Alternatively, the new product may form the basis for a new corporate division (such as GE's Calma interactive graphics division, or Eli Lilly's Elanco division for veterinary pharmaceuticals) or even a newly created company.

The venture team differs from the new product committee in that it is an ongoing unit that may continue its operations for several years rather than disbanding after every meeting. Its organization is loose, and its activity is conducted separately from the traditional structure of the organization. Some venture teams are set up in "skunk works"—that is, in facilities that are geographically separated from the main line organization.[11] This gives them greater flexibility to operate along nontraditional lines and working hours and caters to the creativity and innovativeness of team members. Although reporting directly to top management, the venture team has an independent budget and complete freedom to conduct its operations as it best sees fit. The venture team is the *intrapreneurial* answer to the lack of entrepreneurship in bureaucratically rigid organizations.

THE NEW PRODUCT DEVELOPMENT PROCESS

The **new product development process** involves management of risk, idea generation, screening ideas, analysis of the commercial potential of the new product, testing prototypes, finalizing the product, test marketing it, then entering a full-scale market launch.

Managing New Product Development Risk

With the organization structured for new product development, management is ready to guide product concepts through to market launch, or abort the project if prospects begin to look less favorable. Five rules for managing the risk in new product development are proposed:[12]

1. Decrease investments as uncertainty increases. The greater the uncertainty, the less management should invest in the new product. That is, in the initial

stages of product development, when uncertainty is highest, the amounts at stake should be kept low.

2. Increase investments as uncertainty decreases. The stakes should not be allowed to increase unless uncertainties decrease.

3. Incrementalize the decision process. The new product "big decision" should be broken down into a series of small decisions.

4. Buy research information to reduce uncertainty. Each step in the series of small decisions should provide a point at which management can buy a glimpse of the potential outcome of the project.

5. Provide for "bail-out" points. Periodic "go/no go" evaluations throughout the new product development process offer the opportunity to kill the project before good money follows bad.

These rules make sense for large, sophisticated corporations. But for new or small entrepreneurs, lack of resources, "blind" faith in their new product and its market acceptance, and an urgency to get it to market often preclude a careful and measured risk evaluation. A quick and economical framework to help new entrepreneurs evaluate their risk in new product development has been suggested (see Exhibit 9–5). By evaluating the marketing factors in the center column, one can determine whether the new product exhibits a greater tendency toward the right column of effects (with which a small entrepreneur can cope) or toward the left column (which is better handled by a large corporation).

Idea Generation

A product idea is the starting point of the product development process (see Exhibit 9–6). The more ideas a company can generate, the better its chances. This is a case of more being better!

Idea generation must be managed. The first step is to increase the flow of ideas to the firm and keep them coming. Thus an individual should be appointed as "idea person" to assume responsibility for keeping the flow high and to act as a focal point, well known to everyone in the organization, to whom ideas may be directed.

Research by one of this text's authors among a number of companies suggested that the following sources of product concepts are most widely used in the Canadian chemical industry.[13] With the exception of the first source (because Canada has a large number of foreign-owned companies), these sources could be applied to other industries and to most companies in the United States.

- Importing concepts from a foreign parent company
- Close contact with and assessment of customer needs
- Association with government laboratories
- Association with university laboratories
- Efforts to utilize wastes and residues

EXHIBIT 9–5   A New Business Product Development Risk Evaluation Framework for New Entrepreneurs

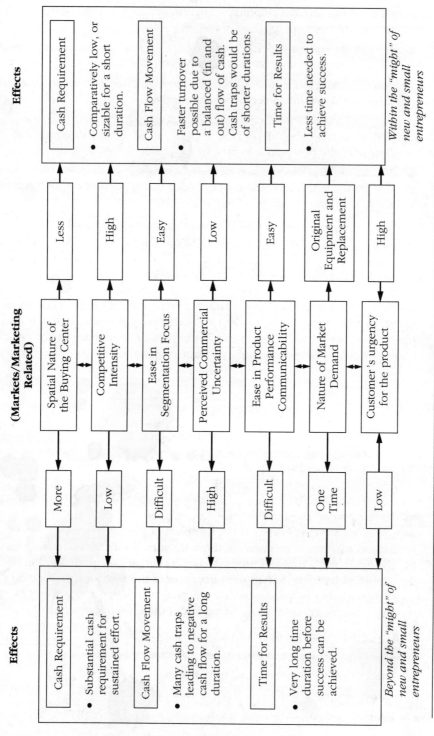

Effects

Effects

| Effects | (Markets/Marketing Related) | | Effects |

Cash Requirement
- Comparatively low, or sizable for a short duration.

Cash Flow Movement
- Faster turnover possible due to a balanced (in and out) flow of cash. Cash traps would be of shorter durations.

Time for Results
- Less time needed to achieve success.

Within the "might" of new and small entrepreneurs

Less — Spatial Nature of the Buying Center — More

High — Competitive Intensity — Low

Easy — Ease in Segmentation Focus — Difficult

Low — Perceived Commercial Uncertainty — High

Easy — Ease in Product Performance Communicability — Difficult

Original Equipment and Replacement — Nature of Market Demand — One Time

High — Customer's urgency for the product — Low

Cash Requirement
- Substantial cash requirement for sustained effort.

Cash Flow Movement
- Many cash traps leading to negative cash flow for a long duration.

Time for Results
- Very long time duration before success can be achieved.

Beyond the "might" of new and small entrepreneurs

Source: Reprinted by permission of the publisher from "Lessons from New Product Failures: Five Case Studies," by Sharad Sarin and Gour Kapur, *Industrial Marketing Management*, vol. 19, no. 4, November 1989, p. 311. Copyright 1989 by Elsevier Science Publishing Co., Inc.

EXHIBIT 9–6   The Sequential Product Development Process

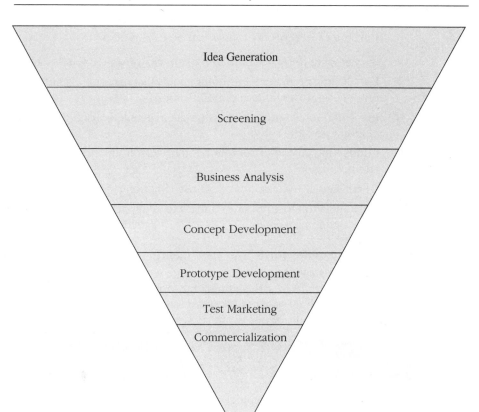

- Spinoffs, by-products, and sister products of product research
- Extension of existing products
- Seeking alternatives to high-cost imported materials
- Exploring possible areas of future innovation that might threaten existing markets

In general, there are two major sources of new product ideas: demand pull, and technology push—or, as the Japanese describe them, needs and seeds.

Needs. Customer needs and wants are the source of new product ideas that offer the greatest promise of success. If customers do not recognize utility in the business marketer's offering, it will not succeed. This source is underutilized, on average representing only 15 percent of new product ideas.[14] However, in the semiconductor, electronic subassembly, process equipment, and scientific instruments industries, most innovations are actually first developed by the customer.[15]

Customer's new product ideas can be exploited by:[16]

- Encouraging the sales force to pass on customer complaints and suggestions.

- Establishing permanent customer panels that meet on a regular basis to discuss product improvements and modifications.

- Involving "focus" groups of customers in problem-oriented discussions to help pinpoint possible solutions.

- Conducting customer surveys by mail, telephone, or visits to customer operations.

- Observing customers in product-use situations in their own workplace.

- Installing a toll-free hot line so that customers can call in with complaints and suggested improvements.

Seeds.   Customers usually can state their needs quite clearly in relation to the problems and weaknesses they experience with existing products. However, they have great difficulty in articulating what *might* be possible, because they are unaware of the technological possibilities and the potential applications of new scientific breakthroughs. Seeds are the new product ideas generated by technological research. About a third of new product ideas come from scientific and technical sources. Typically these sources are the R&D function and the engineering departments within the company. External sources include patents, patent and license brokers, private inventors, and university researchers. Emerson Electric kept a group of professors in engineering schools on retainer. Periodic meetings were held with this "braintrust" to ensure that Emerson people remained up to date with developments in the area.[17] Similarly, Technitron offers a grant to university researchers for commercially promising instruments.[18]

Other Sources.   Competitors' products often stimulate business marketers to come up with better innovations. Thus many companies routinely conduct competitive product analyses in which they purchase their competitors' products; evaluate their strengths, flaws, and novel features; and improve on them. Visiting competitors' booths at trade shows and carefully scrutinizing trade journals also lead to new ideas, particularly those suggested by foreign companies' products that haven't entered the domestic market and are not likely to do so for some time.

Suppliers also attempt to win customers by offering them new techniques and problem solutions. A supplier of cabs and cab components designed a state-of-the-art truck cab, far in advance of anything that the original equipment manufacturers (Ford, Mack, Kennilworth, or Navistar) had, in the hope that part or all of the cab would be adopted and built into one of the major manufacturer's own products.[19]

Employee new product suggestion schemes, offering monetary rewards to any company employee whose idea is accepted, are another good source of new prod-

EXHIBIT 9–7   Employee Suggestions

	Received per Employee	*Adopted*
General Motors	0.84	23%
Toyota	17.90	90%

Source: Reprinted from Charles J. McMillan, *The Japanese Industrial System*, 1984, p. 167, with kind permission of Walter de Gruyter, Berlin, New York.

uct and process ideas. This source has been tuned to a fine pitch by the Japanese, as Exhibit 9–7 comparing employee suggestions in GM and Toyota indicates.

Screening New Product Ideas

Screening is usually a two-step process consisting of a rough-cut stage and a fine-cut stage.

Rough Cut.   The first stage of screening a new product idea consists of a rough evaluation of the idea's fit with corporate image, current markets and distribution systems, company technical and production capabilities, present resources and markets, marketing skills, desired maximum or minimum sales volumes in units and dollars, and rough estimates of profit potential. During such a rough-cut screening, a small electronics company selling to the broadcast industry chose to eliminate a new home security alarm idea because it could not be sold through the company's existing nationwide distributor network.

Exhibit 9–8 shows the marketing criteria in a simple new product evaluation scheme used by a large steel mill. Notice the boundaries executives have set for the number of customers they consider optimal. Whereas one usually thinks that it is better to have a great many customers, steel mills prefer to sell in large quantities to fewer customers. Adding plus and minus points provides an overall score for the product. When several new products are evaluated in this manner, they can be ranked according to their total scores. Other criteria in this evaluation that are not shown in the exhibit include financial, R&D, production and engineering, and cyclical and seasonal demand aspects.

Fine Cut.   The short list of new product ideas that emerges from the rough cut is then subjected to a more finely tuned evaluation. At this stage each product is ranked according to its relative attractiveness on such dimensions as its product advantages, the potential of its market, its fit with the firm, and its future directions. Exhibit 9–9 is an instrument that has been used to assess managers' evaluations of the advantages of new products. Each product is given a score from 1 to 10 on each of seven criteria. These scores are weighted by the degree of confidence

EXHIBIT 9–8   New Product Profile Chart

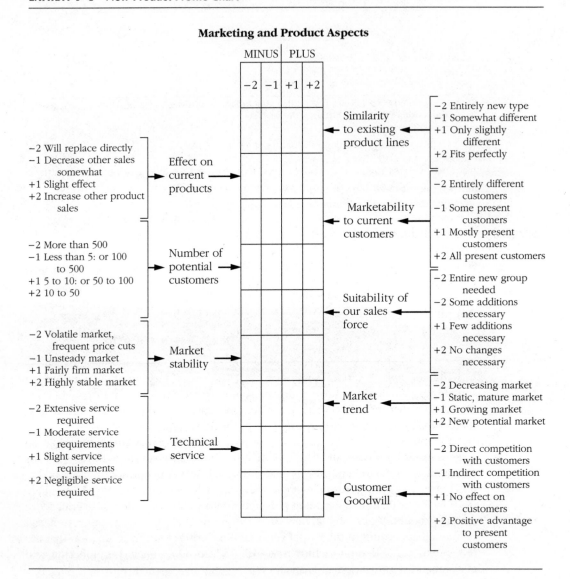

EXHIBIT 9–9   Fine-Cut Evaluation of Product Attractiveness

	Strongly Disagree	Strongly Agree	Confidence (0 to 10)
1. Compared to competing products, our product will offer a number of unique features or attributes to the customer.	0 1 2 3 4 5 6 7 8 9 10		_____
2. Our product will be superior to competing products in terms of meeting customers' needs.	0 1 2 3 4 5 6 7 8 9 10		_____
3. Our product will permit the customer to reduce costs when compared to what the customer is using now.	0 1 2 3 4 5 6 7 8 9 10		_____
4. Our product will permit the customer to do a job (or do something) that currently cannot be done with what is now available.	0 1 2 3 4 5 6 7 8 9 10		_____
5. Our product will be of higher quality—tighter specifications or stronger or will last longer or be more reliable, etc.—than competing products.	0 1 2 3 4 5 6 7 8 9 10		_____
6. Our product will be priced considerably higher than competing products. (10 = much higher; 0 = much lower).	0 1 2 3 4 5 6 7 8 9 10		_____
7. We will be the first into the market with this type of product.	0 1 2 3 4 5 6 7 8 9 10		_____

executives have in their ratings. When the seven weighted scores are added, the product with the highest summary score is considered most attractive. Management preferences and available finances for new product development will determine how many of the top-scoring products proceed to the business analysis stage.

Business Analysis

The number of new product ideas remaining is now small enough to be subjected to a more careful numerical analysis. The market size, growth rate, and sales potential for each product can be estimated using secondary sources. Estimates can be made of research costs, capital investment required, promotional support necessary, effects on cash flow and inventories, profit potential, payback periods, break-even requirements, and return on investment. It should be noted that at any given time, a firm will have a number of new product ideas in different stages of the ongoing process of development. Exhibit 9–10, the research project proposal, is a corporate example of one of the inputs to this process.

EXHIBIT 9–10   Sample Research Project Proposal

Project Proposal   Page 1

Division: _____   Date _____

Recommended by: _____   Project No. _____

Project Name: _____

_____

Objective: _____

_____

_____

_____

_____

Proposed Research Approach: _____

_____

_____

_____

_____

_____

_____

_____

_____

_____

_____

_____

_____

_____

_____

_____

_____

_____

_____

Estimated Return (excluding research costs)

_____

_____

_____

_____

EXHIBIT 9–10   Sample Research Project Proposal (*cont.*)

Page 2

Project Name: _____   Date _____

_____   Project No. _____

Project Participants: _____

A. *Person-Weeks Estimated to Complete Project:* Groups	*Estimated Person-Weeks*	*Estimated Cost*
_____	_____	$ _____
_____	_____	_____
_____	_____	_____
_____	_____	_____
_____	_____	_____
Total	_____	$ _____

B. *Capital and Expenses:*

Equipment _____   _____

_____   _____

Materials _____   _____

_____   _____

Others _____   _____

_____   _____

Total $ _____

Total Estimated Cost: • Staff and Expense (A and B Above) $ _____

• Less: Financial Support   _____

• Net Cost $ _____

Proposed Schedule: Start Date _____ Completion Date _____

Probability of Success: Excellent _____ Good _____ Fair _____ Poor _____

What Additional Development Work and Cost (Plant Equipment and Testing) Will Be Required Upon Completion of the Project Before It Can Be Applied?

_____

_____

_____

Project Approval   _____   _____

Division General Manager (or Delegate)   Research Director

_____   _____

Date   Date

Concept Development and Testing

The firm has now reduced the number of new product ideas to a manageable few. Management thoughts must be clarified about who the target market should be and how the new product will be positioned. (Recall our discussion of segmentation in Chapter 6.)

Research among potential customers will help pinpoint the needs of various segments with respect to the new product idea. These needs can be arrayed in perceptual maps of product spaces along relevant dimensions, where existing products and "ideal" products indicate unfulfilled needs. This information is used to find a possible position for the new product and to develop the product concept most likely to succeed.

A **product concept** is a description or representation of what the new product will be in its finished form. The product concept is rendered in drawings, models, or prototype form, along with a written description of its features, benefits, and probable price. The concept can be tested by further research with customers to gauge their preferences relative to competing products and the strength of their likelihood to purchase.

Prototype Development

If the concept evaluation is favorable, the product concept proceeds to engineering for its **prototype development** toward a final product. Concurrently, the marketing department begins work on packaging, promotional strategy, pricing strategy, and distribution strategy.

Trial or Test Marketing

In **test marketing**, a limited production run or prototype is sold in a small market area using the same marketing strategy that the firm anticipates using in a full-scale launch. If the test market is conducted in several circumscribed areas, variations of the marketing mix, such as different prices or promotion themes, may be used to test customer sensitivity or response to different approaches.

For many business products, the potential customer base is too small for test marketing. In such cases, one or a few customers may be selected for in-plant trials. Customer feedback may suggest product redesign, a change in price, or the use of direct mail rather than sales calls to identify the best prospects. The trial or test market is essential to determine the customer's evaluation of the product's value in use, whether the product performs as it should (there is a world of difference between performance tests in the company's own laboratories and performance under the customer's normal operating conditions), and the customer's perceptions (which may have little relationship to objective standards).

Commercialization

Assuming that the trial or test market is positive, product modifications and marketing strategy can be finalized, and the new product can be launched. This process is called **commercialization**. Smaller firms may wish to launch their new product in a sequential roll-out, say, starting in the Northeast and gradually expanding south and west. This approach conserves financial resources, gives the manufacturing plant time to work out unexpected bugs, and provides marketing with the flexibility to monitor and resolve problems as they arise with distributors, the field sales force, and customers.

For example, one manufacturer designed a small, slick, battery-powered vehicle intended to transport two or three passengers on plant tours, or for the use of foremen who were responsible for supervising physically large factory areas. Initial sales were excellent. But after a few months, sales fell off and many vehicles were returned to the manufacturer. The marketing department conducted field research into the problem. It was found that there were no service or comfort complaints and the vehicle was performing well. However, foremen complained that when they rode around the plant, the machinists would stop work and wolf-whistle or wave hankies. The problem was one of perception. The vehicle just didn't look masculine. Armed with this information, management went back to work and made the vehicle more rugged, angular, and masculine in appearance. The problem dissipated, and this firm now boasts a healthy sales volume and customer satisfaction.[20]

Most marketing publications present the new product development process as a sequential one, as shown in Exhibit 9–6.[21] Yet not all products go through every one of the stages. Some business products may be placed in full commercial launch without any test marketing being done. It is also important to note that the length of time spent in each stage may vary substantially from one business product to another, that some stages are likely to be concurrent, and that the sequence of stages might differ from one product to another. Exhibit 9–11 provides a more realistic representation of the process.

New Product Development and Marketing Strategy

Some researchers contend that traditional viewpoints of the product development process focus too much attention on generating a large pool of ideas from which a product may be developed and launched.[22] Other studies indicate that product failure is caused mainly by marketing inadequacies, and suggest that business marketing managers should concentrate their efforts on simultaneous and integrated development of both the product and the strategy processes. Thus the objective here is not to identify the "best" idea for further development, and then impose a marketing strategy just prior to the launch, but rather to eliminate ideas continuously as their marketing strategies become more developed.

EXHIBIT 9–11   The New Product Development Process

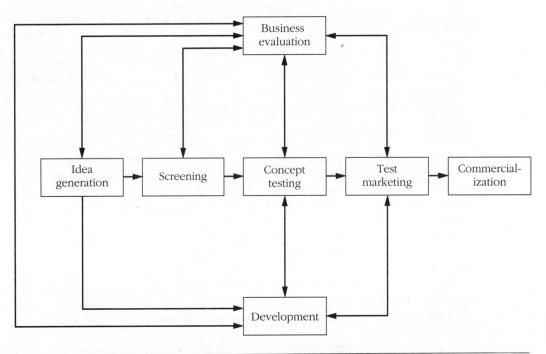

Source: MCB University Press Limited, Richard A. Moore, "Control of New Product Development in U.K. Companies," *European Journal of Marketing,* vol. 18, no. 6/7 (1984), p. 11. Reprinted with permission.

The **product development life cycle (PDLC)**, shown in Exhibit 9–12, shifts the emphasis throughout product development toward a greater attention to marketing strategy factors in determining a new product idea's worthiness for continued development. The industrial marketing manager begins the PDLC using very general marketing strategy dimensions to cull out unworthy new product ideas. Remaining new product ideas are subjected to more and more specific and better defined marketing strategy and tactical requirements and are further eliminated as they move through the PDLC. Because marketing strategies are developed and refined in parallel with new product development throughout the PDLC process, the inclusion of customer and competitor dimensions and their interactions with products (for example, positioning and product design) may lead to different products being launched than would be the case using the traditional product development process. The objective is to reduce the new business product failure rate, which has remained in the 20 to 35 percent range for more than a quarter of a century.

EXHIBIT 9–12   The Product Development Life Cycle

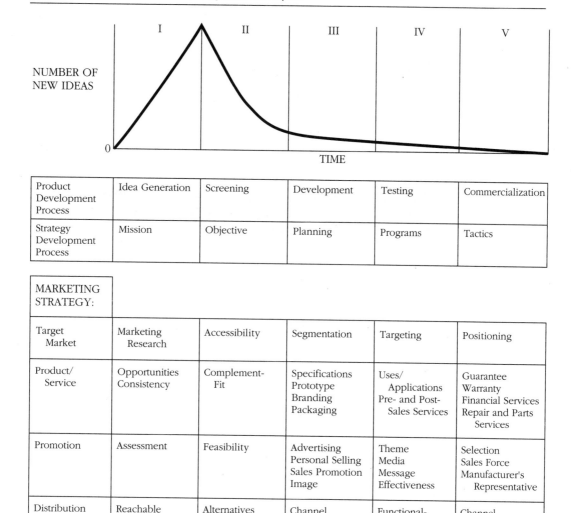

	I	II	III	IV	V
Product Development Process	Idea Generation	Screening	Development	Testing	Commercialization
Strategy Development Process	Mission	Objective	Planning	Programs	Tactics

MARKETING STRATEGY:					
Target Market	Marketing Research	Accessibility	Segmentation	Targeting	Positioning
Product/ Service	Opportunities Consistency	Complement-Fit	Specifications Prototype Branding Packaging	Uses/ Applications Pre- and Post-Sales Services	Guarantee Warranty Financial Services Repair and Parts Services
Promotion	Assessment	Feasibility	Advertising Personal Selling Sales Promotion Image	Theme Media Message Effectiveness	Selection Sales Force Manufacturer's Representative
Distribution	Reachable	Alternatives	Channel Availability Transportation	Functional-Separation Customer-Service Level Transportation-Modes	Channel Management Inventories Warehousing Transportation Rates Channel Selection
Price	Value	Consistency Pricing Policy	Cost/Revenue-Analysis Breakeven-Analysis	Profitability Target Return Pricing Terms	List Price Discounts Allowances Geographic

Source: Reprinted by permission of the publisher from "Simultaneous New Product Development: Reducing the New Product Failure Rate," by G. Dean Kortge and Patrick A. Okonkwo, *Industrial Marketing Management*, vol. 18, no. 4, November 1989, p. 303. Copyright 1989 by Elsevier Science Publishing Co., Inc.

DESIGNING NEW PRODUCTS

Design may be viewed as a decision-making process that coordinates resources into a planned, unified, and meaningful order to meet human needs. The design process not only transforms physical objects, but also human relationships to our many environments—physical, emotional, sociocultural, economic, and political.

The Europeans and the Japanese have long recognized the major competitive advantage created by good design of products. Unfortunately, most North American executives do not yet understand design as a critical business resource.[23]

As well as affecting the appearance of a product, design affects the ease with which a product is understood, used by the customer, and serviced and can be an important element in representing the identity of the company.

Industrial design is concerned with two important aspects of the product or service being created: function and aesthetics. *Function* refers to the efficient operation of that which has been designed—its ability to do the task well. *Aesthetics* refers to the morphological beauty of the design.

Some designs are good, others bad. One prerequisite for good design is functional efficiency. However, since people have to live with designs, the mere fact of efficient function is not sufficient for good design. The product or service must be aesthetically satisfying—pleasant and enjoyable to work and live with.

Although good product design requires functional efficiency and aesthetic appeal, it must also be remembered that the pursuit of these two basic aspects of design does involve consideration of a number of constraints. These would include, among others, the capabilities and resources of the firm, cost to the buyer, profitability, safety, and legal requirements.

Functional Design

Many North American firms have not achieved maximum productivity or efficiency in new product design and introduction. New products are entering the market with such rapidity that the business marketer has a prime advantage if offerings can be designed with a view to high productivity in manufacturing and consistent satisfaction of the customer. Furthermore, technological change and improvement are moving so quickly that for most products, the life cycle—the time when a company can recover its development costs and generate profits—is dramatically reduced. According to Robert Ferchat, president of Northern Telecom Canada Ltd., in the telecommunications industry, the life expectancy of a new system now is four years or less, compared with fifteen years a short time ago.[24] Manufacturing companies, therefore, need to adapt to life in the fast lane.

Technological expertise is no longer limited to a few nations or a few corporations; any successful product developed by one company quickly becomes a target for imitation and duplication by both domestic and foreign competitors. This surging, technologically adept competition reduces the time available to the in-

BUSINESS MARKETING IN PRACTICE

Product Development for World Markets

New product development for some product classes must be undertaken with global markets in mind. For example, General Electric is involved, among other activities, in the production and marketing of aircraft engines. This market involves huge risks in new product development. It requires tremendous up-front commitments to R&D, and substantial fixed investments in facilities, tooling and service. No single country's demand provides a large enough market to support a viable or profitable company. Therefore, it is necessary for General Electric to seek participation in global aircraft engine markets, and develop products accordingly.

Source: Robert Gillespie, "Canadian Competitiveness in a Global Environment," *Business Quarterly,* Winter 1990, p. 33.

novating company to generate the revenues for continued growth.[25] Ferchat states: "It means that new-product designs must be fully manufacturable from the word go. If a design is transferred to the plant floor, only to be sent back to the R&D team because it does not meet the capabilities of our plants in a cost-effective manner, then we have wasted valuable resources. . . . We have presented our competitors with a golden invitation to get the jump on us with their competitive products."[26]

A case in point is the South Korean Daewoo Corp. In 1984, the company was making plans to enter the personal computer business. By 1987 it was producing 15,000 units a month and exporting its product to North America. Starting from scratch, other firms might take twice as long just to build their markets in their home country.

It was not the speed with which Daewoo had advanced from the planning stage to full-scale production that is impressive; nor was it even the rapidity with which the company was able to capture a substantial share of export markets. The striking feature of the Daewoo assembly process was that it involved almost no testing or inspection until just before each personal computer was crated for shipment. At that stage, applications testing, with programs in English, was undertaken by workers on the line—mostly young high school graduates. The defect rate was close to zero without the overhead cost of multistage inspection and testing. In contrast, most North American high-technology manufacturers inspect and test their products at five or six different points of assembly, and each test involves expensive, highly skilled workers or costly technology.

The Daewoo example demonstrates that productivity starts with the design of a product. By ensuring that quality is built into the manufacturing process, a company can reduce its production costs and can provide the customer with a quality product at a highly competitive price. Well-designed products do what they are supposed to do, without reworking and without costly after-sales servicing in the field.

The successful company is one that can achieve maximum productivity, or efficiency, in the act of innovation, in new-product design, and in introduction to the market.

Industrial Design

Industrial designers are individuals qualified by training, technical knowledge, experience, and visual understanding to determine the materials, shape, color, surface finishes, and construction of products and systems that may be produced in quantity by industrial processes. Their responsibility is to help mold the product to suit all aspects of the human environment, from the product's conception and presentation on the market, through its convenience in use, through its ease of maintenance and storage, to its final disposal.

There is a difference between an engineer who creates a product to function properly and an industrial designer (probably also an engineer) who considers the aesthetic, ergonomic (how the machine is adapted to the limitations of the human body), and cultural impact of the product. In creating a control panel for an aircraft, for example, an industrial designer would use ergonomic principles to ensure that instruments can be identified easily, have the most visible types of readouts, generate the least strain on the pilot, and are placed on the panel in locations that identify naturally to the pilot and provide the least risk of error in use.

The Total Design Concept

Not all design involves products and services. One of the important ways in which the company achieves a competitive advantage is by designing a favorable corporate image—an impression of the company as a whole that reflects well upon its products and services. Dominion Foundries and Steel Limited attempts to instill confidence in the company behind the product through its slogan "Our Product Is Steel; Our Strength Is People." Ford uses the slogan "Quality Is Job #1." The overall design of such an image is called the **total design concept**. Essentially this concept is predicated on the philosophy that good design should permeate every single aspect of the company's operations.

The total design concept suggests that the corporate strategy should interpret and project the basic orientation and philosophy of the firm through the consistent and unified design of such facets of the company's operations as architecture of its plants, offices, warehouses, dealerships, franchised outlets, and retail stores—not only in building design, but also in interior design and exterior landscaping. The unity of the design theme should be evident in products, brand names and trademarks, corporate logos, graphics, signs, letterheads and communications, company publications, advertising, sales promotion materials, industrial and trade fair exhibits, community projects, and publicity. Company cars and trucks and even employees' uniforms should reinforce the design theme.

Toronto-based Frito-Lay Canada Ltd.'s 160 deliverymen were wearing brown polyester when the company commissioned designer Sally Fourmy & Associates Ltd. to design a new uniform. "They were dressed like truck drivers," said Ms. Fourmy, who also designed the new uniforms for the Toronto Blue Jays. Now they are dressed in collegiate-looking navy blazer, tailored gray slacks, a long-sleeved red wool sweater, a pale blue shirt, and a tie. They do drive trucks, but they also deal with customers—retailers and institutions. Frito-Lay recognized that they needed a more professional appearance, while still being able to bend, lift, and carry.[27]

It is obvious that the application of such a total design concept is tailored to generate the desired impact on a variety of the company's audiences, including employees, the local communities in which the company operates, unions, shareholders, various pressure groups, various levels of government, the general public, and of course, the company's customers and prospective customers.

PRODUCT DELETION

The area of product management to which the business marketer probably pays least attention is product deletion. Compared with the excitement of developing and launching new products, getting rid of outdated, ineffective, or obsolete products takes a back seat.[28]

The **product deletion process**, however, is just as important as the product innovation process, because candidates for deletion are obstacles to profitability. They consume too much valuable executive time, financial resources, and factory and warehouse space, and they generate hidden costs, all of which could be devoted to growth products and markets. For example, Sun Oil Company's Lubrication and Metalworking Materials Division spent four years redressing a product line imbalance. They cut metal-working oils from 1,150 grades to 92, lubes from 1,000 grades to 200, and greases from 225 grades to 29.[29] According to division manager William Naylor, "Most of those products were specific formulations for a single customer. The gradations were minute, but each required downtime in the refinery or mixing plant."

Typical warning signals of weak product performance include the following:

- Declining sales
- Declining prices
- Declining product profitability
- Increasingly effective alternatives or substitutes
- Devotion of excessive product management attention

Unfortunately, too many companies ignore these warnings. Products are maintained in the company's line because of concern that the customers who still buy them may be upset if they are no longer available, that their deletion may have a negative effect on sales of the firm's other products, or that the sales force or distributors will object to the loss of old familiar standbys. This suggests the need to establish a product deletion process that is just as comprehensive and thorough in examining candidates as the new product process is. In such a process, products should be evaluated against detailed criteria similar to those sampled in Exhibit 9–8.

Of course, there may be ways to revitalize a declining product: Production costs might be reduced through value analysis. Joint costs might be reallocated. The product might be repositioned or relaunched in a foreign market. The product might be made more profitable in its waning years by raising its price, by cutbacks in promotion expenses, or through more economical distribution, such as consolidating field inventories in a central warehouse. The drain on company resources might be reduced and customer demand still met by subcontracting production of the product to another manufacturer.

But when these alternatives hold little hope, the best approach is to program the product's elimination in such a way that the least disturbance is created for the company, its distributors, and customers and so that replacement and repair parts will still be available to customers. One technique for doing this is to authorize another (usually smaller) company, which can operate profitably serving the remaining core market, to take over the product. In a large-scale example of this type of deletion strategy, International Harvester sold off its entire agricultural business to J I Case so that under the name Navistar, International Harvester could focus its attention on the more profitable motor truck business.

DEVELOPING PRODUCTS FOR NICHE MARKETS

In a world beset with protectionism and threats of trade wars, it is easy to forget that powerful economic and technological forces are drawing the world together into a global market. To survive and prosper in the increasingly competitive global marketplace, many companies are learning to find and dominate "niche markets." For companies of all kinds and sizes, nichemanship is rapidly becoming the new business imperative.[30]

Simply defined, a **niche market** is a relatively small segment of a market that the major competitors or producers may overlook, ignore, or have difficulty serving. The niche may be a narrowly defined geographical area, it may relate to the unique needs of a small and specific group of customers, or it may be some narrow, highly specialized aspect of a very broad group of customers. In some cases, the niche market may actually be very large—particularly if the company operates globally.

The possibilities are virtually endless. So too are the opportunities, as effective niche strategies can be extremely profitable. Given the size and structure of our economy, nichemanship is likely to become increasingly important for business marketers. In any event, it is a phenomenon marketers can't afford to ignore.

By focusing on a niche market, companies develop an understanding of their customers' operations—and how those customers make money. This understanding in turn provides an edge when it comes to identifying opportunities for new products and marketing programs. Emphasis on niche marketing provides a very clear focus for the development of business strategies and action plans.

Nichemanship's Emergence

Earlier in this century, as businesses discovered assembly lines and economies of scale, successful marketing rested on products or services that met the needs of a broad base of consumers. These products were often mass produced, distributed widely, and advertised through mass media. The goal was products with broad appeal that could be priced attractively because of high volumes.

In its early years, the Ford Motor Company provided the classic example of this type of marketing strategy. From 1909 to 1926 Ford produced one major automobile, the Model T, and sold more than 15 million cars. Mass production brought the price down from over $3,000 to less than $900. But during this time, Ford offered the customer little choice—"Any color as long as it's black!"

Toward the end of this period, General Motors began to compete effectively with Ford by introducing new designs with superior performance. This strategy, called product differentiation, allowed GM to avoid direct competition with Ford and to command higher prices. But although GM's products were different, they too were aimed at the broadest possible customer base in several price ranges—and not really designed for a particular type of customer, aside from the obvious correlation with income brackets.

Market segmentation goes beyond product differentiation by identifying different customer groups and developing an understanding of their particular needs. One of the first examples of this was the image of the Buick as a "doctor's car."

A niche is simply one of the smaller segments in a market, such as the segment originally appealed to by the Honda Civic. The very small, economical car found a niche in a market made up of much larger vehicles. Successful nichemanship involves the ability to identify a segment with needs that closely match the capabilities of the company, and to design a marketing program that will reach the niche better than competitors can.

Determining Market Needs

In many business markets, there are important differences in the features that various market segments demand from suppliers of products and services. So manufacturers develop products that differ in quality, reliability, durability, and many other dimensions based on their perceptions of customer desires.

A truly creative business strategist can often identify new or previously unrecognized needs that will provide new ways of defining niches. Such a strategist was Jim Treybig. In the early 1970s, this marketing manager at Hewlett-Packard noticed that some of the computer customers he dealt with were very concerned about having a system that would continue to operate even if there was a failure somewhere in the computer. To a company such as American Airlines, which could lose more than $20,000 per minute if its reservation computer was down, high reliability was critically important. As Treybig thought about it, he realized that banks, hospitals, distribution companies, and even racetracks with computerized betting had an urgent need for such a high-reliability computer.

So in 1974, Treybig and three other Hewlett-Packard employees decided to form their own company to take advantage of the opportunity they had identified. They essentially linked two computer central processing units together. If one failed, the processing was automatically shifted to the other unit until the faulty one was fixed. Tandem Computers shipped its first computer in 1975, and by 1986 the company had a full line of "fault tolerant" computer systems and sales of about $800 million.

Targeting the Niche

Identifying a segment of customers with a distinct set of needs and then developing a product is not enough. Exploiting the niche market depends on targeting the customers accurately. Only then can marketing communication—whether personal selling, advertising, or publicity—reach them effectively. Company size, industry, and geographical location are key emporographic bases for targeting in the business sector.

Knowledge of the customers' business has earned Laidlaw Transportation a very strong position in a specialized market niche. The company is the largest operator of school buses and special education vehicles in North America, with more than 13,000 vehicles in service. While seemingly a mundane, mature business, it is consistently highly profitable for the company. By focusing on a niche like the education industry, Laidlaw has developed an excellent understanding of the needs of school boards and how decisions are made in these organizations. Thus Laidlaw is able to put together customized packages that meet the specific needs of a particular board.

As well as knowing the customer's industry, understanding the customer's approach to doing business provides an important means of targeting niche markets. In any one industry, different companies go about conducting their businesses in different ways. Some companies, for instance, want to contract out certain business functions, whereas others want to conduct almost all activities in-house.

In the late 1960s a Winnipeg accountant, Bill Loewen, found that many companies in many different industries would be delighted to have an outside company handling their complex payroll activities so that management could focus attention on what they considered to be the core functions of their businesses. In 1968, he founded Comcheq to provide a comprehensive range of payroll services to his clients. Initially small, this niche soon attracted some of the major Canadian banks and has become a major market in which Comcheq continues to retain a significant market share. By 1988 this market was considered so attractive that the Toronto-Dominion Bank acquired the Comtech Group International Ltd. payroll and accounting services division for $4 million, and Comtech changed the name of its other major division to Postech Corporation. The combined Comtech and Toronto-Dominion payroll operation processes more than 500,000 paychecks every payday throughout Canada.

Finding an Attractive Niche

Once a niche market has been identified and targeted successfully, its virtues are readily apparent. But since the market can be segmented into an almost unlimited number of niches, the real key is to find the most attractive opportunities. Some useful indicators of an attractive niche are the following:

- Customers in the niche should have distinctive needs. Otherwise, competitors serving similar segments may very well be able to serve the niche more economically.

- Customers in the niche should be easy to target. To target its efforts effectively, a company has to be able to locate the individuals or companies in the segment, to make its product available to them, and to communicate in terms that are meaningful to them.

- The niche should utilize the distinctive skills and resources of the company. The company must be able to do a better job of meeting the needs of the targeted niche than any of its potential competitors.

- The niche should be a protected one—there must be some barriers to stop competitors from easily entering and threatening the company in the niche. These barriers may be the result of specialized skills or products that are difficult to duplicate, low costs, or the close working relationship the company has been able to develop with its customers, making them unwilling to switch to another vendor.

- The niche should be large enough so that the company can make a reasonable profit by serving it—but not too large. A large and attractive niche invites competitors.

The Future for Niche Strategies

Several powerful trends suggest that nichemanship may be an increasingly important strategy for North American companies. Many business markets are breaking up into more segments, providing new opportunities for niche markets. The computer industry, dominated so long by IBM, is full of companies like Tandem, Cray, Compaq, and Digital Equipment—niche players that survive and prosper in competition with Big Blue. The following are some other data processing manufacturers and the niches they have exploited:[31]

Company	*Niche*
Burroughs	Hospitals
Control Data	Science and engineering
Honeywell	Process control
NCR	Retailing
Quantel	Professional football and basketball
Sperry	Government

Market fragmentation has been accelerated by the trends in many countries toward privatization of a variety of government services and the downsizing and restructuring of many corporations and their staffs. These trends are creating a host of new niche opportunities for firms to provide a range of products and services that are no longer available in-house.

Whereas one of the forces driving the fragmentation of many markets has been emerging customer needs, another driving force is the manufacturers themselves. Developments in production technology have made it far easier for manufacturers to cater to the needs of small markets with very small cost penalties. Flexible manufacturing systems (FMS) and computer integrated manufacturing (CIM) all mean that production volumes are less important than they once were in terms of cost. To state it another way, economies of scale can be achieved with smaller batches.

With production costs less of a constraint, the emphasis more than ever will be on smart marketing—staying close to the customer and providing the products, expertise, and service that the customer wants. With the inexorable trend toward the globalization of many markets, competing on a global scale will be not just desirable but inevitable for many business marketers.

DEVELOPING PRODUCTS FOR GLOBAL MARKETS

Business products lend themselves more readily to being marketed abroad because they frequently can be sold without any physical change. For example, the Timken Company manufactures roller and ball bearings in plants in Australia, Brazil, Canada, England, France, South Africa, and the United States and has a worldwide network of distributors. Timken assures customers that its components are uniform and interchangeable all over the world.[32] Most business-to-business marketers, however, must adapt their products to some extent if they wish to penetrate foreign markets.

Global Product Standardization

Product standardization permits a firm to market overseas at significant savings in costs, compared with adapting business products for different markets. Exporting a standardized product increases manufacturing volume, reduces unit production cost, and can enhance profits. Manufacturing a standardized product in several countries incurs no more R&D or design expense and can generate additional profits by offering more logistics alternatives.

Many business marketers attempt to extend their business products' life cycle when domestic sales have reached maturity by introducing them to new markets overseas without any change. Business products in the decline stage of their life cycle frequently can be rejuvenated by being sold in foreign markets that are at a lower level of economic development. For example, mainframe computers that have been superseded by a new generation in North America find ready markets in Pakistan and China. Similarly, good markets are found in Third World countries for used industrial equipment that is obsolete in economically advanced countries. An outdated alkaline manufacturing plant was dismantled in Canada and reassembled in India for $4 million—40 percent of the cost of a new plant.[33]

International Product Adaptation

The minimal degree of **product adaptation** for global markets may be simply changing the packaging and instructions to reflect the language of the foreign market. Dials and gauges may need to be converted to metric readouts. Ergonomic characteristics of the users may require modifications in positions of machine controls.

Telcom Research, a Canadian manufacturer of electronic time code equipment for use in videotape editing, ran into problems in attempting to market its products to television broadcasting stations in Germany. When the German company Siemens first entered the television field, its equipment was designed close to operating tolerances and ran hot. Thus instrumentation panels in control rooms were vertically oriented to allow heat dissipation by air convection. In North America, on the other hand, control equipment had greater tolerance, ran cooler, and therefore units were traditionally installed horizontally in control panel racks. Telcom Research equipment, although technically excellent, was not configured vertically, was enclosed in a metal box, and would have required physical redesign to penetrate the German market successfully.

North America is a market in which preventive maintenance and following operating instructions are common practices. In many other countries, however, such practices are not culturally ingrained. Thus equipment driven beyond its working limits fails prematurely. To succeed in such markets, equipment may need reengineering to withstand greater abuse than would normally be encountered domestically.

Business products typically require some adaptation because of the lack of universal standards. Some countries use the British units of measurement, whereas

BUSINESS MARKETING IN PRACTICE ▰▰▰▰▰▰▰▰▰

Caterpillar Develops Products for Global Markets

As a manufacturer of off-highway commercial and construction equipment, Caterpillar has recognized the need to be totally adaptable to different markets around the world. Both its people and its products are globally interchangeable. People can be transferred among plants, subsidiaries, and countries, and products and their components are completely interchangeable (a vital aspect for both international contractors and the armed forces).

Interchangeability of products and their components is a major criterion for Caterpillar's operations outside the United States. The company designs the basic product in the United States and adapts it to local conditions for complete functional, dimensional, and endurance interchangeability. This allows Caterpillar to begin production of a tractor in the United States, make its pistons in Japan, its crankshaft in France, and the final drive in Australia. This allows the international contractor and the military the advantage of purchasing parts, components, and, indeed, the entire product from several sources, and for different currencies.

Source: Robert Eucley, "Caterpillar's Ordeal: Competition in Capital Goods." Reprinted from *Business Horizons,* March/April 1989, p. 80. Copyright © 1989 by the Foundation for the School of Business at Indiana University. Used with permission.

others are metric. Power supplies operate at different voltages and frequencies and electrical currents, and hydraulic and pneumatic connectors abound in mind-boggling multiplicity. Electrical transformer leads in German components must, by law, be fixed to terminal strips, whereas in North America leads may be directly soldered to other components.

In adapting business products for export, 140 manufacturers reported the following product characteristics as usually important (in decreasing order):[34]

1. Function and attributes

2. Maintenance, after-sale service

3. Durability, quality, storage characteristics

4. Method of operation, power source, skill to operate

5. Ease of installation

6. Size of product

7. Method of shipment

8. Style

9. Color

Local factors rated by the same manufacturers as important in affecting the need to adapt business products for foreign markets were (in decreasing order):[35]

1. Customer expectations and preferences

2. Competitive offerings by local competitors

3. Competitive offerings by other exporters

4. Government regulations (for example, safety standards)

5. Stage of country's economic development

6. Economic status of potential users

7. Nontariff barriers

8. Culture (tastes, values, habits)

9. Climate and geography

One useful tool in evaluating what possible types of product adaptation may be required when marketing in different countries is a simple grid approach. Exhibit 9–13 shows a grid used by a marketer of business vehicles. In this approach, clusters of markets with similar critical adaptation factors (such as noise abatement requirements) can be identified.

Business marketers frequently debate the issue of whether to design business products to meet domestic requirements, capture the home market, and then

EXHIBIT 9–13   Product Adaptation Evaluation Grid for Business Vehicles

Items Subject to Regulation or Special Requirements	*Country A*	*Country B*	*Country C*	*Recommendation Regarding Impact or Importance*
Speed limits				
Dimensional requirements				
Front and rear overhang				
Turning circle				
Weight				
Steering				
Underride protection				
Tires				
Brakes				
Fuel tanks				
Wheel chalks				
Exhaust				
Noise				
Engine performance and transmission				
Miscellaneous				
Access to cab				
Visibility				
Controls				
Lighting and signaling				
Other				

Source: V. M. Yorio, *Adapting Products for Export* (New York: The Conference Board, Inc., 1983), p. 28. Reprinted by permission.

perhaps export at some time in the future; or to design, develop, and target their products for foreign markets from the start.

In a study of 203 new industrial products, products that had been designed and developed for worldwide applications and uses (beyond those found in the developer's own country) were called "international." Products that were created strictly for their home market were labeled "domestic."[36] As might be expected, the new product development process differed substantially between the "international" and "domestic" focused products. Critical activities in the innovation process (market research, product testing with customers, trial selling or test marketing, and launch efforts) shifted abroad and had a significantly higher international component for the "international" than for the "domestic" products. The success rate of "international" product designs aimed at global markets was 85 percent, compared with a 43 percent success rate for "domestic" designs aimed at the domestic market (see Exhibit 9–14). On all performance measures, the business products designed to meet foreign requirements and targeted at export markets were top performers by a substantial margin (see Exhibit 9–15). They also did better at home. In contrast, those products designed for the domestic market performed poorly. They had higher failure rates, lower profitability, smaller market shares, and slower sales growth.[37]

LINKING NEW PRODUCT STRATEGY TO RESULTS

A study of 122 business marketing firms encompassing the electrical and electronics, heavy equipment, chemicals, materials, and components industries identified five product innovation strategy scenarios in which the types of markets, products, and technologies chosen by the firms and the way in which they oriented and managed their new product programs generated a pronounced impact on corporate success and profitability.[38]

In the *balanced-focus strategy* (used by 15.6 percent of the firms), new products were aimed at high-growth, high-potential markets, against weak competition. They had a strong differential advantage, unique features, and commanded a premium price. Using state-of-the-art technologies and an R&D orientation, these firms nevertheless developed products that closely fitted existing company product lines and end uses. A strong marketing orientation guided the company's research and new product development programs. This strategy yielded the best performance: highest new product contribution to sales, highest new product success rates, and greater profits.

In the *low-budget, conservative strategy* (used by 23.8 percent of the firms), although spending little on R&D and generating imitative products with little differential advantage, the companies excelled in maintaining the highest technological and production synergy. Furthermore, their focused efforts were aimed at target markets that fitted well with the company's existing marketing resources: distribution channels, sales force, advertising, and marketing research skills. Their

EXHIBIT 9–14   Impact of Market/Product Orientation on New Product Success

Product Type

		International Design	Domestic Design
Target Market	Domestic	International product aimed at domestic market Success rate: 61.5% (23.7% of cases)	Domestic product aimed at domestic market Success rate: 43.1% (31.1% of cases)
	Nearest Neighbor	International product aimed at nearest neighbor market Success rate: 78.1% (18.3% of cases)	Domestic product aimed at nearest neighbor market Success rate: 45.5% (6.7% of cases)
	World	International product aimed at world market Success rate: 84.9%* (17.2% of cases)	Domestic product aimed at world market (3.0% of cases but too few to assess)

* Success rate differences statistically significant amongst market/product orientations at the 0.001 level, chi-square test.

Source: MCB University Press Limited. Elko J. Kleinschmidt and Robert G. Cooper, "The Performance Impact of an International Orientation on Product Innovation," *European Journal of Marketing,* Vol. 22, No. 10 (1988), p. 66.

EXHIBIT 9–15   Impact of Market/Product Orientation on Other Measures of New Product Performance

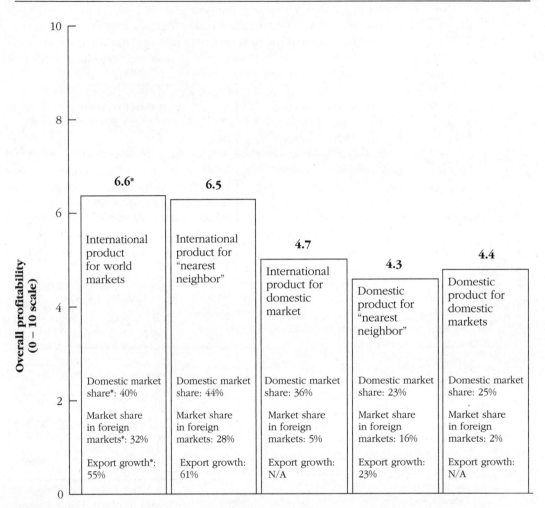

Note: The orientation "domestic product aimed at world markets" had too few cases for statistical analysis.

* means significant statistical differences on those measures (group means).

Source: Robert G. Cooper and Elko J. Kleinschmidt, *New Products: The Key Factors in Success,* Chicago: American Marketing Association, 1990. Reprinted with permission.

high new product success and low product failure rates resulted in an efficient, safe, and profitable, if low-luster performance.

In the *technologically driven strategy* (used by 26.2 percent of the firms), high technology, innovation, high risk, and technologically complex state-of-the-art sophistication characterized the new product programs. But the dominance of the technical product orientation and the lack of a marketing presence led to poor market need identification and targeting toward small, slow-growth, specialized low-potential markets with products lacking synergy with the firm's existing marketing resource base. Although new products during the past five years contributed a high percentage of corporate sales, these firms had the highest new product failure and kill rates and generated low profits.

A *technologically deficient strategy* was used by 15.6 percent of the firms studied. These, the smallest companies studied, produced low-technology, imitative, low-risk products relying on simple, mature technologies. New products didn't fit the production, R&D, and engineering technologies, skills, and resources of the firm. Market research, idea generation, and market need identification were passive. However, these companies aimed new products at existing customers, avoided new markets, and focused their program on products that were closely related to existing offerings. Their overall performance was poor.

A *high-budget, diverse strategy* was used by 18.9 percent of the firms studied. Although spending the most on R&D, these firms faced a technologically mature industry and did not produce innovative, technologically complex, or high-technology products. Their resources were dissipated by lack of focus, such as entering radically new markets, seeking new types of customers, requiring new advertising and promotion methods, and engaging new channels of distribution and sales forces (recall strategic risk, Exhibit 9–3). Although their target markets offered high growth potential, they were intensely price competitive, had a major dominant competitor, and consisted of potential customers who were satisfied with competitors' existing products. With no particular corporate strengths and weak marketing, these companies' diversity bred very poor results.

This research study clearly indicates that the type of new product development strategy selected by a firm will strongly influence the kind of performance outcome that can be expected. As mentioned earlier, too many firms enter markets without well-defined, consistent, and integrated strategies in place. Heavy investment in R&D alone won't do the job, any more than heavy investment in marketing without a unique customer benefit will. The most successful business new product strategy unites technological and marketing strengths in a synergistic, cohesive, and focused approach targeted toward the following:

- High-growth, high-potential, large markets
- Markets with weak competition
- Markets whose needs and requirements are familiar to the company
- Products that complement the firm's current product line
- Products with unique differential competitive advantage and superior quality
- Products with features and benefits that have strong customer impact

SUMMARY

Physical products are need satisfiers for customers. They may be catalog items (available off-the-shelf) or custom-made items. After prelaunch development, they move through the product life cycle stages of introduction, growth, maturity, saturation, and obsolescence. Attention to the position of the product in the PLC can aid strategic adjustment in the market.

Product objectives are derived from corporate objectives. They may be interpreted through policies which provide quick answers to recurring issues. Two important product objectives deal with the width and depth of a firm's product line.

Strategic risk is an important consideration in product line management. Despite the high risk involved in new product development, new products are necessary to remain competitive and to achieve long-run growth in profits. The rewards for successful new product development are significant. In terms of organizational structure, the new product development process may be orchestrated by a new product committee, a new product department, a product or brand manager, or a venture team. The new product development process encompasses idea generation, screening ideas, business analysis, concept development and testing, prototype and product development, trial or test marketing, and commercialization.

Industrial design, although not extensively used in North America, can help improve both manufacturing and marketing of new products. Industrial design encompasses both function and aesthetics, creating a product that works better, is easier and often cheaper to manufacture, is easier to use, and more pleasant to live with. A broader approach to industrial design, going beyond the design of the product itself, is the creation of a total design concept. Here, the corporate orientation and image is communicated through a comprehensive design theme that is incorporated in the company's architecture, landscaping, vehicles, employee uniforms, and all forms of its communication, as well as in its products and services. The use of a total design concept helps an organization achieve a differential competitive advantage.

When a product begins to enter the obsolescence stage of its PLC, executives may search for ways to rejuvenate it. If this cannot be done, then its elimination should be programmed. The product deletion process should be as thorough and as carefully planned as new product development.

Niche marketing involves selection of a small market segment where the marketer's resources and strengths can better match customers' requirements than can competitors'. Crucial to this approach is the precise targeting of customers who have unique wants. The niche should be large enough to generate reasonable profits, and the marketer should be capable of raising barriers to competitive entry.

Global standardization and international product adaptation are two approaches to product management in foreign countries. To sell business products in foreign markets some minor modification usually is necessary (conforming to foreign national standards, language). But a debate has long raged among marketers whether the best approach is to design for maximum product standardization across many countries (global standardization) or to customize (adapt) products to match the individual and specific needs of each country (international product adaptation). Research suggests that firms which start by designing and developing products for worldwide applications and uses, rather than designing them for the home market and then later adapting them to foreign market requirements, are more successful, both in their domestic market and abroad.

Among five possible product-market strategies undertaken by business marketers, the most successful involves selection of high-growth markets in which there is weak competition, the firm is familiar with customer requirements, and the new product complements the firm's product line and has unique advantages for the customer that competitors do not offer.

Key Terms and Concepts

product-service mix
product
catalog items
custom-made items
systems
complete product
component
services
product life cycle (PLC)
product objectives
product policies
new product development
new product committee
new product department

product (brand) manager
venture teams
new product development process
product concept
prototype development
test marketing
commercialization
product development life cycle (PDLC)
industrial design
total design concept
product deletion process
niche market
product standardization
product adaptation

Discussion Questions

1. Why is it important to screen new product concepts?

2. How can one use the product life cycle to formulate product strategy?

3. "Sell the Sizzle, Not the Steak." How would you interpret this expression in reference to business products? Give examples.

4. What are the causes of obsolescence of business products?

5. Test marketing is not widely used in business markets. Why? What alternative approaches can be implemented to evaluate new products?

6. What are the advantages and disadvantages of: (a) a narrow product line? (b) a wide product line?

7. Risk in product line management is an ever-present danger. Yet there are dangers in avoiding risk. Discuss.

8. Is niche marketing more or less appropriate in business markets as compared with consumer markets? Defend your position.

9. An industrial marketer with operations in Canada and the United States is considering developing a new line of products. What arguments favor targeting the North American

market? What arguments favor developing the products for global markets, even though the firm currently is not selling off-shore?

10. How would the new product profile chart in Exhibit 9–8 change if the company were manufacturing (a) ball bearings? (b) office furniture?

Endnotes and References

1. This was pointed out by Professor Theodore Levitt of Harvard University.

2. Barbara Krasnoff and Mel Mandell, "How High-Tech Products Can Achieve Profitable Longevity," *High Technology Business* (January 1989): 19.

3. The "not invented here" syndrome is common in North America. Firms tend to be uninterested in the inventions of others.

4. *Management of New Products* (Chicago: Booz Allen & Hamilton Inc., 1968), p. 11.

5. *New Product Management for the 1980s* (Chicago: Booz Allen & Hamilton, 1982).

6. Corley, H. M., ed., *Successful Commercial Chemical Development* (New York: Wiley & Sons, 1954).

7. *Management of New Products,* p. 11; R. G. Cooper, "Overall Corporate Strategies for New Product Programs," *Industrial Marketing Management* 14 (1985): 179–183; C. M. Crawford, "New Product Failure Rates—Facts and Fallacies," *Research Management* (September 1979): 9–13; C. M. Crawford, "New Product Failure Rates: A Reprise," *Innovation Management* (July–August 1987): 20–24.

8. D. S. Hopkins, *New Products: Winners and Losers,* Report No. 773 (New York: The Conference Board, 1980); R. G. Cooper, "The Performance Impact of Product Innovation Strategies," *European Journal of Marketing* 18 (1984): 1–54; *New Product Management for the 1980s.*

9. See, for example, David L. Kendall and Michael T. French, "Forecasting the Potential for New Industrial Products," *Industrial Marketing Management* 20 (1991): 177–183.

10. Don Frey, "Learning the Ropes: My Life as a Product Champion," *Harvard Business Review* (September–October 1991): 52.

11. T. J. Peters and R. H. Waterman, Jr., *In Search of Excellence* (New York: Harper & Row, 1982).

12. R. G. Cooper, *Winning at New Products* (Toronto: Holt, Rinehart, and Winston of Canada, Limited, 1986).

13. This research was done by Peter M. Banting, Ph.D., Professor of Marketing, McMaster University, Hamilton, Ontario, Canada.

14. B. V. Dean, *Evaluating, Selecting, and Controlling R&D Projects,* Research Study No. 89 (New York: American Management Association, 1968).

15. E. A. von Hippel, "Has Your Customer Already Developed Your Next Product?" *Sloan Management Review* (Winter 1987): 63–74.

16. Cooper, *Winning at New Products.*

17. Ibid.

18. Ibid., p. 74.

19. Ibid., p. 79.

20. This example was provided by the late Dr. W.J.E. Crissy, Professor of Marketing, Michigan State University.

21. See also, Robert G. Cooper and Elko J. Kleinschmidt, "New Product Processes at Leading Industrial Firms," *Industrial Marketing Management* 20 (1991): 137–147.

22. G. Dean Kortge and Patrick A. Okonkwo, "Simultaneous New Product Development: Reducing the New Product Failure Rate," *Industrial Marketing Management* 18 (November 1989): 301–306.

23. Peter Lawrence, "Products That Have Designs on Success," (Toronto) *Globe and Mail,* March 6, 1989, p. A7.

24. Ronald Anderson, "Focus on Quality Needed to Keep Up with Asians," (Toronto) *Globe and Mail,* May 14, 1987, p. 88.

25. "The Machinery of Growth," *The Economist,* January 11, 1992, p. 18.

26. Anderson, "Focus on Quality Needed to Keep Up with Asians," p. 88.

27. Barbara Aarsteinsen, "Uniforms Are Gaining Flair as Quality Image Pays Off," (Toronto) *Globe and Mail,* July 20, 1987, p. B6.

28. Douglas M. Lambert, *The Product Abandonment Decision* (Montvale, N.J.: National Association of Accountants, 1985), p. 131. See also George J. Avlonitis, "Project Dropstrat': Product Elimination and the Product Life Cycle Concept," *European Journal of Marketing* 24 (1990): 55–67.

29. "The Squeeze on Product Mix," *Business Week,* January 5, 1974, p. 54.

30. This entire section on developing products for niche markets was adapted from Federal Industries 1986 Annual Report, with permission. See also Robert E. Linneman and John L. Stanton, Jr., *Making Niche Marketing Work* (New York: McGraw-Hill, 1992).

31. Mack Hanan, *Re-Competitive Strategies* (New York: AMACOM, 1986), p. 49.

32. D. A. Ball and W. H. McCulloch, Jr., *International Business* (Plano, Tex.: Business Publications, Inc., 1982), p. 329.

33. "Used Factories Are Being Exported to Developing Countries," *The Wall Street Journal,* February 26, 1981, p. 1.

34. V. M. Yorio, *Adapting Products for Export* (New York: The Conference Board, Inc., 1983), p. 13.

35. Ibid., p. 7.

36. Elko J. Kleinschmidt and Robert G. Cooper, "The Performance Impact of an International Orientation on Product Innovation," *European Journal of Marketing* 22 (1988): 56–71.

37. Robert G. Cooper and Elko J. Kleinschmidt, *New Products: The Key Factors in Success* (Chicago: American Marketing Association, 1990).

38. R. G. Cooper, "Overall Corporate Strategies for New Product Programs," *Industrial Marketing Management* 14 (August 1985): 179–192.

10

BUSINESS SERVICES

OBJECTIVES

- To understand the nature of business services
- To recognize the need to segment business service markets
- To appreciate marketing differences between intangible services and tangible goods
- To learn the attributes of new service product development
- To recognize the importance of services in domestic and international markets

The *Service Industries Journal* defines *service* as any primary or complementary activity that does not directly produce a physical product—that is, the nongoods part of the transaction between buyer (customer) and seller (provider).[1]

Molly Maid is a consumer service that sends cleaning people to private homes. They bring their own vacuums, mops, dust cloths, and cleaning products. The same type of cleaning service (called janitorial work in business markets) is offered to business offices, hospitals, and schools by companies such as ServiceMaster. Both Molly Maid and ServiceMaster fall under the general classification of the "service industry." **Business services**, then, are part of the total service industry.

Primary business services are those that have a relatively small physical product component. Examples include machine rental and equipment leasing (both are forms of financial service); management consulting; office design; security surveillance; transportation; work performed by legal, accounting, and financial institutions; and so on. Even the local barber (a small business entrepreneur) may purchase scissors sharpening from a business service provider.

Complementary business services are those that complement or "accompany and enhance" the sale of a physical product. In this instance, the sale of the physical product is the principal focus of the business marketer. For example, the purchaser of a highly sophisticated system such as a mainframe computer installation may need training in how to use it. This training is a complementary service. Another example of complementary service is the provision of a technical specialist by the selling firm to help the customer determine engineering specifications for the product. The customer also would expect product installation, continuing adjustment and fine tuning, and maintenance. These services do not directly produce the product but complement it. In many industries, their provision by the business marketer in association with the sale of the product is necessary; otherwise, the customer would not buy the product.

How important is the service industry and, in particular, business services in the economy? Business services represent a high-growth market both at home and abroad. It is important to understand them because they require a different marketing perspective from physical goods.

GROWTH OF THE SERVICE SECTOR

Services are a rapidly growing sector of the world's developed market economies. Trade in services, which is currently valued at around $800 billion a year, has been growing by 12 percent a year.[2] The share of services in the gross domestic product (GDP) of developed countries grew from 55 percent in 1965 to 61 percent in 1985.[3] In the United States, service industries represented 69 percent of GDP in 1989,[4] constituted three-fourths of nonfarm jobs, and have generated more than 44 million new jobs since the 1960s.[5] Service providers in the United States generate more than half a trillion dollars of income every year, and over $100 billion of that comes from business services.[6] Between 1981 and 1989, service employment in the United Kingdom grew by 20 percent, whereas during the same period manufacturing employment decreased by 15 percent.[7] Similarly, in Canada, service employment between 1981 and 1989 increased 16 percent, whereas manufacturing employment decreased 6 percent. During the same period in the United States, service employment grew 21 percent, but manufacturing employment decreased 3 percent.

The following factors have stimulated such dramatic growth in services:[8]

1. Technological advances have created more complicated products that require more design, production, promotion, and maintenance services.

2. Management has hired outside specialist firms to provide "less critical" services that formerly were performed internally (such as janitorial and payroll processing services). Farming out such services has permitted executives to concentrate on their principal business. In addition, increased management sophistication and training have led to the desire to use techniques that may not provide sufficient work to justify full-time internal positions (marketing research and computer programming, for example).

3. Specialization by service providers has made some functions (like direct mail, marketing research, and executive recruitment) available at lower cost and better performance than can be provided by user firms themselves. This specialization is the result of service firms improving the equipment they use, achieving greater efficiency by becoming more capital intensive, adopting information technology, and consolidating into large, multiunit organizations.

4. Modern factories are becoming increasingly information- and service-intensive. This trend has reduced the proportion of wages paid for direct production work. For example, only 6 percent of labor costs go into direct production at Digital Equipment, and 10 percent at IBM.[9]

5. With increased size and efficiency, service providers have gone international. For example, the "Big Six" U.S. accounting firms have offices all over the world.[10] Major U.S. management consulting firms earn between 16 and 54 percent of their consulting revenues overseas.[11]

6. Deregulation has opened many service industries (airlines, banking, trucking) to more intense competition, generating greater innovation and expansion.

BUSINESS MARKETING IN PRACTICE ▪▪▪▪▪▪▪▪▪▪▪▪

The Swing Toward Services

Mention Westinghouse Canada, Inc., and an image arises of a dependent branch-plant manufacturer of turbines and motors. Wrong, says Edward Priestner, president and chief executive officer.

These days, Westinghouse Canada, based for eighty-five years in Hamilton, Ontario, garners the lion's share of its $800 million a year revenue not from manufacturing but from such services as selling and distributing electrical products, rewinding motors, managing industrial waste, and consulting on organizational development. The swing to service is a trend among most companies in the electrical and electronics industry, according to Priestner.

The service side of this manufacturing business tends to develop within the company's established areas of expertise. One of those is turbines and generators. "There are six hundred turbines with our name on them around the world. They need service, renewal, spare parts. We have to send people and keep jigs and dies on hand," says Priestner.

Another developing sphere for Westing-house is the handling and service of PCBs (polychlorinated biphenyls), a suspected carcinogen. Services in this area include maintenance of customer-owned apparatus that contains PCBs, decommissioning that apparatus and storing it safely on the owner's site (a developing business for the company), and transportation and destruction of the contaminated material. The last segment is growing slowly. "Nobody wants it in their area or on their streets." For the destruction of the PCBs, there are several effective technologies, both portable and stationary, and "we're in all of them," states Priestner.

Further down the road, he sees the company using its expertise and available technology to produce steam, destroy pathological waste from hospitals, and co-generate electricity and steam.

Source: Adapted from Patricia Lush, "Westing-house Shifting to Service," (Toronto) *The Globe and Mail,* Oct. 17, 1988, pp. B1, B3. Reprinted by courtesy of *The Globe and Mail.*

Recognizing these developments, a number of manufacturing companies are deliberately choosing to increase their involvement in the provision of services. Borg-Warner Corporation, which is one of the biggest suppliers of transmissions, clutches, carburetors, and other auto parts to the original equipment manufacturers (OEMs) of Detroit, as well as a manufacturer of heavy-duty plastics, chemicals, and industrial pumps, is one. The company has sought to reduce its dependence on the declining American manufacturing sector and is becoming a major participant in the services sector. In 1953, Borg-Warner began offering financing to its customers through its newly formed Borg-Warner Acceptance Corporation (BWAC). Soon, BWAC was providing credit service to other companies. Then Borg-Warner acquired Baker Industries, a New Jersey–based protective services firm that provides industrial plant security guard services and alarm systems and owns the Wells Fargo armored-car business. This move was followed by the acquisition of the Burns security-guard organization and the Pony Express courier service. Services now represent more than 50 percent of Borg-Warner's business.

In 1980, National Steel Corp. was the seventh-largest producer of steel in the United States. To avoid the intense competition from imports, the massive investment requirements, and the high labor costs of manufacturing, the company adopted a new name, National Intergroup, Inc., sold part of its steel business, and purchased a crude-oil shipping company and a pharmaceutical wholesaler. (It plans to sell the rest of its steel business.) After fifty years in the steel manufacturing business, National sees its future in the faster-growing service economy.

THE PRODUCT-SERVICE MIX

In economics, "pure competition" and "pure monopoly" are ideal concepts that are unlikely to exist in reality. Similarly, the concepts of "pure goods" and "pure services" cannot be found in the real world of business marketing.[12] Rather, most firms' offerings lie along a continuum that combines varying degrees of goods and services. In Exhibit 10–1, industrial wiping cloths are shown at the left, closest to the "pure good" end of the continuum. Wiping cloths are used to remove dirt and grease in manufacturing and machinery repair operations, inks from printing presses, and in janitorial cleaning situations. The wiping cloths are then disposed of. They are a very tangible, physical good. The "smallish" service component lies in the fact that they are delivered to business customers on a regular basis. In the case of uniform rentals, the service component of the transaction increases. Clean, pressed uniforms are delivered to the customer and exchanged for soiled uniforms. As we move toward the "pure service" end of the spectrum, the proportion of tangible, physical good in the total value purchased by the customer decreases, and the intangible element increases. For example, in consulting engineering, the physical component that the client receives may be a set of blueprints, representing the distillation of the engineers' problem identification, analysis, application knowledge, and experience. In personnel training, the trainee may not receive any tangible physical items. The training may be entirely through verbal communication and demonstration. For this reason, personnel training is shown at the extreme right as one of the business services that most closely approximates the "ideal" of a pure business service.

Virtually no tangible good is offered to business customers without some associated services. These services may not even be considered "services" by the vendor. Rather, they are perceived simply as part of the normal marketing activities of the firm. Examples include stocking adequate inventories, displaying the goods, or delivering them to the customer's location. Similarly, virtually no service is marketed without some physical good closely associated with the production or delivery of that service. Even a management consultant providing "ideas" gives the client a typed report in an attractive binder.

Because of this inevitable blending of intangible services and physical product components, marketers and academics often speak of the "product-service" mix rather than the product (in an offering where the good dominates) or the service

EXHIBIT 10–1   Goods/Services Continuum

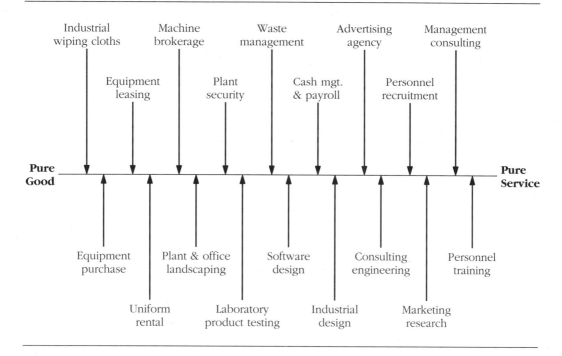

(where the good is peripheral to the offering). However, this is not the case in the business world. Even in predominantly service industries, such as insurance and banking, businesspeople refer to their services as "products." Thus, bankers refer to credit products (such as business loans) and cash management products (such as check reconciliation), whereas insurance marketers create new executive liability products. To avoid confusion, in this chapter the approach used in business will be adopted.

The term *service product* will be used to refer to the **core utility** (basic benefit) that customers purchase from a service provider. Typically, the offering of a service firm will include one or more service products, plus other minor goods and services associated with the production and distribution of the core service product(s).

CHARACTERISTICS OF SERVICES

What characteristics differentiate services from goods? The four traditional characteristics of services are intangibility, inseparability, heterogeneity, and perishability. In business marketing, two additional characteristics are added:

specialization and technology.[13] Together, these six characteristics can be represented by the acronym SHIPIT.

- S —specialization
- H—heterogeneity
- I —intangibility
- P—perishability
- I —inseparability
- T—technology

Specialization

Much more than in consumer marketing, the business marketing of services involves the provision of specialized, custom-designed bundles of services. Each distribution warehouse, office facility, or manufacturing plant is given a unique architectural design. The financial arrangements for each business are tailor-made to fit the particular cash-flow, credit, checking, and money-management needs of the individual business. The management consultant identifies the unique problems of the business client and recommends unique solutions.

Heterogeneity

Every time a business service is performed, the process and the customer experience will be different. Services that are provided by individuals (rather than machines) will vary, depending on which individual performs the service, and they will even vary with the same service provider from one job to the next. The service will also vary according to the degree to which customers or clients are involved in the production of the service. The degree to which the service organization designs the service delivery system to control variability will influence the heterogeneity (or quality) of the service experienced by the customer.

If customer uncertainty must be lessened, heterogeneity in services can be reduced by mechanizing, automating, standardizing, and rationalizing available options. However, heterogeneity may be desired by those customers who want customized service, rather than standard approaches that are less than optimal for their individual situation (say, in engineering design or in factory layout).[14]

Intangibility

The dominant characteristic of a service is its **intangibility**. It cannot be picked off a shelf, tasted, felt, or smelled. It is not a physical object. Rather, it is an activity performed by the supplier. An example is the provision of credit. Citibank may open a $500,000 line of credit to a business. The only tangible evidence of this is a contract signed by both parties. For the business marketer, the ephemeral nature of a service requires that ways be found to communicate that the service has been performed, that the service was provided at a particular level of quality, and that the service provides particular benefits to the customer. In other words, the marketer must give tangibility to the intangible. Tangible cues associated with the service help provide visibility. For example, a grounds maintenance firm might place a small sign on the plant or office lawn indicating that fertilizer has been applied. A sealed tag on a meter provides tangible evidence that the meter has been inspected. A date inscribed on a piece of electronic equipment indicates that repair has been done. In addition, brand-naming the service and building corporate imagery assist in communicating quality, as will be discussed later in this chapter.

Intangibility also means that the buyer cannot own a service. The payment is for use or rental. Among the benefits of nonownership are freedom from tying up capital, reduced labor, and reduction in management time.

Perishability

Unlike physical products that are manufactured and stored in inventory until a sale is made, services cannot be performed in advance and drawn later from inventory. Services are produced at the same time that they are used. Thus, if demand exceeds the capacity to provide a service (for example, accounting services at tax time), some clients will be unhappy. If demand falls short of the service firm's capacity, that amount of service and the revenue it might have generated are lost forever. Business marketers may build capacity to accommodate peak demands, but they then must seek other sources of business for off-peak periods. (Tax accountants often offset slack periods by engaging in management consulting.) It is no wonder, then, that the rule of thumb for breakeven on rooms in hotels is an occupancy rate of 60 percent. Another method of building business is to lower prices during slack periods (as is done with airline seat sales). This technique is difficult because of the interaction between price and perceived quality. The customer may think that the price cutter is cutting corners on quality of service.

Inseparability

Except where a service can be automated, as in electronic data transmission or automated teller machines (ATMs), a service usually cannot be separated from the personnel supplying the service. Services are produced and used (or consumed) simultaneously. Thus, the customer's perception of the service depends not only on the quality of the service product—that is, the actual service being performed—but also on the quality of the service delivery *experience*—that is, the manner in which the service is performed or delivered.[15] The service product must not only be provided in the *right place* and at the *right time,* but also in the *right way.*[16] The importance of this buyer/seller relationship cannot be overemphasized. In banking, to the business client, the account manager *is* the bank. The technical service representative repairing an office copier *is* Xerox. The van driver delivering parts *is* the parts organization.

Thus, in marketing services to business, the marketing mix (as represented by the four P's: product, price, promotion, place) requires that one more "P" be added: people.[17] Personnel policies need to recognize the importance of recruiting, training, and rewarding service delivery people to ensure that each point of contact with customers reinforces the service firm's objective of providing service quality. In other words, service firms should manage buyer/seller relationships rather than making transactions.

In addition, the service delivery person needs to be an effective salesperson: sometimes convincing a potential customer to buy the service, reassuring the customer during the performance of the service, seeking opportunities for more business, and ensuring that repeat business is retained after each performance of the service is concluded.

Technology

In the past, services have been viewed as a labor-intensive, low-technology industry, but times have changed. "The character and internationalization of many service industries have changed markedly in the postwar period, and any stereotype of services as low technology and domestic is long since obsolete."[18]

Two factors have changed the traditional view. As business markets involve more and more complex high-technology products, the services sector has had to keep pace in meeting customers' more sophisticated needs. Second, service providers are applying higher technology to their own operations. The *United States Banker* projects that by 1995 a third of all business transactions will occur via EDI (electronic data interchange).[19]

Computers and information technology have played a significant role in the service revolution—banks, insurance companies, and direct mail organizations are all industry examples of this. Using computerized legal databases, lawyers can now do more complete searches in hours than previously could be done in weeks. In addition, technology applied at the simultaneous production/consumption interface that characterizes services can be useful in two ways. It can reduce the heterogeneity of service (as in ATM application) while increasing delivery efficiency. It can also enhance the adaptation of the service to the individual customer's requirements (as in the use of diagnostic equipment).

SERVICE LIFE CYCLES

Just as physical products move through life cycles, so too do service products. There are some differences between the two, however.

Service Life Cycle versus Product Life Cycle

Because they usually involve only small capital expenditures and use existing delivery systems, service products generally are more quickly created than physical products and are easier for competitors to copy. Moreover, once it is in place, it is difficult to drop a service product. Customers and salespeople alike prefer the old familiar service product and resist its discontinuance. Corporate accounts often prefer to keep an existing service product because of the switching costs involved in the change to a newer service product. In the selling firm, management people may argue that "it doesn't cost anything to continue offering the existing service product."

Another justification of not dropping an old service product is that if it is retained, it will be available for potential future bundling with other services to match customers' wants better. For sophisticated services that are fully integrated into the firm's computer system, the high cost of cleaning out old programs can be a deterrent to dropping the service product. Furthermore, where it is important to maintain auditable files (as in insurance companies, banks, and stock brokerage firms), service product deletion may be next to impossible. Many management people don't want to spend a lot of time on the analysis and euthanasia of declining service products, and even more do not have a systematic service product deletion program. As a result, service products proliferate. Consequently, the **service life cycle (SLC)** has a shorter introduction period and a much longer decline stage than the physical product life cycles.

The Maintenance Service Life Cycle

A special case is the **maintenance service life cycle** covering the installed base of physical products that need repair and maintenance. This service life cycle is special because it depends on the volume of sales and durability of the physical products that it services, and it spans a different period than the product life cycle (PLC) of the physical product. The **installed base** represents the difference between (1) total shipments of new products (such as elevators, construction machinery, machine tools, industrial controls, trucks, and turbines) and (2) the reduction in products still in use (caused by their being scrapped, replaced by a substitute, upgraded, or cannibalized for spare parts). The installed base, then, generates a service cycle that may last ten times longer than the physical product life cycle (which is related to new product sales rather than useful product life).

The magnitude and importance of the maintenance service life cycle can be appreciated by the fact that repair services for electronic products alone are estimated to cost more than $60 billion annually, and they employ 400,000 people in the United States. In total, almost $200 billion (or about 6 percent of the GDP) is generated each year in maintenance service revenues.[20]

The maintenance service life cycle concept was created by George W. Potts, former director of strategic planning for the service division of Data General Corporation. It has four stages:

1. *Rapid growth:* from the first shipment of the new physical product to the peak of the product life cycle.

2. *Transition:* from the peak of the PLC to the peak of the service life cycle.

3. *Maturity:* from the peak of the SLC to the last shipment of new physical products.

4. *End of life:* from the last shipment of new physical products to the last unit of installed base.

Almost 70 percent of service revenues and 95 percent of service profits are generated in stages 3 and 4 (see Exhibit 10–2).

Rapid Growth.   During rapid growth, the organization focuses on the physical product's sales surge. Aggressively low service prices or long-term warranty serv-

EXHIBIT 10–2   The Maintenance Service Life Cycle

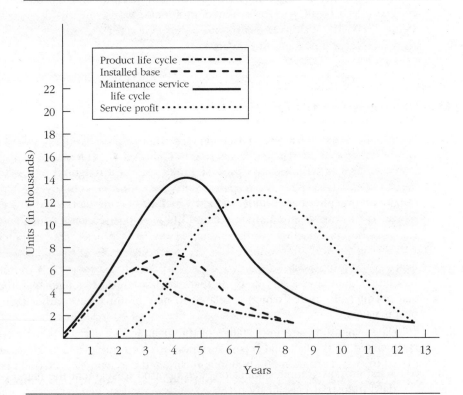

Source: Based on G. W. Potts, *Harvard Business Review* (September–October 1988): 33. Reprinted by permission.

ice enhance customers' cost-of-ownership comparisons between the firm's product and competitors' products. Rapid build-up of field inventories of spare parts and prompt repairs help build the company image. Laboratory-designed diagnostic procedures are improved using feedback from actual maintenance experience in the field. Heavy investment in training maintenance people and providing them with the highest-quality tools and product documentation generates satisfied maintenance customers, who subsequently spread the good news by word of mouth.

Transition. In the transition stage, maintenance service profits are modest but growing, while revenues from new product sales decline. Annual price increases for maintenance service are instituted early in the transition stage. In this stage, service resources and the acquisition of spare parts are carefully controlled to enhance service profits. Although training is more efficient now, the need for trained repair personnel continues to grow.

Maturity. In the maturity stage, all repair assets have been acquired. Revenues, cash flow, and profits are strong. This is the period of greatest service profitability. Programmed price increases continue. Premium service options may be introduced during this stage (service contracts, value-added options such as disaster recovery services offered by computer manufacturers) to defend against service competition that has been attracted to the market by high service prices. The firm begins to reduce its parts inventories.

End of Life. At the end-of-life stage, as much as 50 percent of the equipment that was shipped may still be in use. Service contract prices and service parts prices rise to keep pace with value offered to the customer and to preserve reasonable rates of return to the maintenance function. Inventories of spare and replacement parts are deliberately run down, and needed items are salvaged from scrapped equipment. At this stage substantial increases in maintenance service prices can be used to encourage customers to upgrade to the newer generation of product.

Examples of business products that have moved through all or most of the stages of the maintenance service life cycle include steam locomotives, mechanical calculators, vacuum tube radios, and early models of computers. Mechanical typewriters are now in the end-of-life stage of the maintenance service life cycle.

IDENTIFYING SERVICE SEGMENTS

In segmenting markets for services, marketers must address the same basic questions that are investigated for physical products:

- What common characteristics are present in important market segments?
- What emporographic dimensions can be used to segment the market—standard industrial classification (SIC), vertical market, geography, account volume, customer size?

- What expectations does each segment have?
- How well are these expectations being served? In what manner? By whom?
- How well can the firm satisfy these expectations?
- How much can demand be expected to fluctuate?
- What profit potential resides in exploiting each segment?
- What growth potential is possible/likely for each segment?
- How well does operating in any of these segments fit with the firm's service mission?

The goal of segmentation is to identify groups of customers with reasonably homogeneous needs and expectations that differ from the needs and expectations of other groups. From these groups, the service firm selects a target market, whose needs and expectations the service firm believes it can satisfy better than the competition.

Several differences can be found in segmenting business markets for services as opposed to physical products. Large firms tend to go after bigger core markets instead of identifying segments precisely and tailoring their marketing strategies to fit them. Large Canadian Schedule 1 banks (domestically owned) fit this pattern. In contrast, the best bet for smaller firms to survive is by seeking niches where they are protected against competition from larger firms with greater resources. Necessity causes the small firms to be better segmenters. Schedule 2 banks (foreign owned) in Canada exhibit this quality. They were not permitted to enter the Canadian market until recently. Their only method of competing against the Schedule 1 banks (which had thousands of well-established branches across the nation) was to find specialized niche markets that the domestic banks were not serving well. Thus, the Hong Kong Bank of Canada successfully captured the lion's share of business from immigrants from Hong Kong and from Canadian companies doing business with Hong Kong.

In service segmentation, the marketer must pay greater attention to customer *expectations,* whereas with physical products customer *needs* are the primary focus. In general, service segments tend to be narrower than those for physical products. Because customers' service expectations are highly personal, the more a service is standardized and routinized, the less likely are customers to feel that their expectations have been fulfilled.

A major difference between products and services stems from this personalized nature of services. Services tend to be **"high-touch" offerings**—that is, they provide the buyer with the warmth of human contact and with flexible adaptation to changing situations. (Bank tellers are an example.) If a marketer attempts to achieve productivity gains by substituting technology for labor, the result usually is a **"low-touch" offering**. (ATMs can't respond to the customer's questions or concerns.) Even though some customers may recognize the efficiency provided by "low-touch" approaches to service provision, others view them as cost-cutting and quality-reducing. Thus, another segmentation dimension is involved in service marketing that the business marketer cannot afford to ignore.

Even within a service segment, demand tends to be less homogeneous than it is for physical products. Service customers expect a unique experience. Service quality drops off sharply when demand goes beyond even such a small level as 75 percent of the capacity of the service firm.[21] When segmenting markets, the service marketer should take into account the tolerance customers will exhibit as segmentation progresses and the firm approaches its service-provision capacity.

Service segments should also be rated on their relative value to the firm. Since service markets tend to experience wide swings in demand, the most highly valued segments will require closer consideration during periods of peak demand, while service probably will have to be reduced for less-valued customers. Why bother marketing to less-valued customers at all? The answer lies in the perishability of services. During slack times, the less valuable customers provide an outlet for excess capacity. Thus, in segmenting service markets, it is important for companies to have the right mix of each type of customer grouping or to seek such groupings in subsegments.

Part of the segmenting process is the matching of a firm's competitive strengths with the segments exhibiting the greatest requirements for these attributes. Exhibit 10–3 shows the varying importance of bank service products to different industrial segments. This suggests that segmentation of banking services can be accomplished effectively along customer industry dimensions.

NEW SERVICE PRODUCT DEVELOPMENT

Service organizations require buildings, equipment, and legislated areas of operation. These are referred to as the **"hardware" component** of the service enterprise. In an existing service organization, new service products tend to have a major **"software" component**, in that they are generated by restructuring the conditions or definition of an existing service product. For example, when an airline introduces a new fare with more restrictions on time of departure and availability but at a lower price, that new service "software" is offered using the same "hardware" of existing aircraft, crew, booking facilities, and air routes. Hence, it is relatively easy to introduce new services, and they tend to proliferate, causing overload among service-providing employees and creating confusion for both staff and customers.[22]

This drawback suggests the importance of having clear objectives for new service product development and using a pretest market, or test-marketing a new service product prior to national launch. Few service firms use test marketing, however. Those that do any research on new service products do so in a limited way at one or two locations with minimal promotion. Their goal is to ensure that the new service product operates correctly rather than to determine or estimate customer response. Thus one objective in new service product development should be to conduct comprehensive marketing research prior to launch.

EXHIBIT 10–3   Banking Services Classified in Order of Importance Accorded by Industry Segments

	Agriculture Fishing	Mining	Construction	Manufacturing	Transport and Utilities	Wholesale	Retail	Financial, Insurance, Land	Services	Overall Service Rank	Total Respondents
Computerized payroll		6		2	5–6	6	5	1	2	4	66
Cash concentration		2		6	2	5	4	3	4	5	65
Lock box				7						15	7
Automatic funds transfer		3		3	3	2	1	4	1	1	122
On-line terminals (in office)			1							14	6
Check reconciliation		3–4		5					5	9	33
Preauthorized checks				6						10	27
Automated disbursements										12	12
Foreign exchange	1–2	4–5	3–4	1		1	7	5	3	2	82
Letters of credit	1–2	4–5	2	4	4	4	6	6		6	53
Cash-flow management					5–6					11	18
Investment services									6	8	30
General business information	3–4						3			7	38
Balance reporting		1	3–4	5	1	3	2	2		3	69
Cash management audit										17	5
Factoring A/R										13	9
Computer to computer link										18	2
Issuing checks										19	3
Merger and acquisition advice										16	5

1 = most important

Source: MCB University Press Limited. J. White, "Cash Management Services: Researching Segmentation Strategies," *International Journal of Bank Marketing,* Vol. 2, No. 2 (1984), p. 23.

Among the many new service product objectives are providing more service products for salespeople to sell to existing customers, having as wide a service product line as competitors, appealing to new segments of the market, and utilizing capacity during periods of slack demand. In one study, 34 percent of all new service product introductions had the objective of completing the service product line of the organization, 28 percent were copies of a competitor's existing service, and 28 percent were intended to support or enhance the firm's reputation.[23]

New service products, then, should be developed with clear objectives, test marketing, sales and profit goals, well-defined positioning, and periodic evaluation to determine their continued viability.[24] The service product evaluation process should identify candidates for deletion to prevent unnecessary proliferation of the service product line.

Positioning a Service

Just as products can be positioned uniquely in the customer's "mental map" of competing suppliers, so too can business services.[25] The position might be chosen to establish the firm as the best one among a number of competitors in the minds of agents who sell the service product. It might be chosen to appeal to the end buyer who wants lowest price, or to the customer who seeks highest quality and is willing to pay for it. The position may be to indicate that the service provider is a specialist in a particular narrow field of endeavor, such as aircraft engine repair. The firm may position itself as the quickest to respond to customers' requests, or as the only company offering worldwide availability. For example, an analysis of financial services offered by insurance companies to the professional market (composed of financial intermediaries, insurance brokers, and risk managers) in the United Kingdom and the United States, categorized these services into eight "positions," according to the intangibility, heterogeneity, and simultaneity characteristics of each service (see Exhibit 10–4). The study recommended six actions for financial service companies planning to implement a positioning strategy:

1. Deemphasize crowded positions. In financial services, one crowded position included eleven U.S. insurers, all claiming an "extra service to the intermediary" position.[26]

2. Support positions effectively. Claims should be substantiated with evidence. If claiming an "extra service" position, for example, show how this extra service is accomplished.

3. Occupy underexploited positions. The study found that in the United Kingdom no insurer was using the "technology" position.

4. Let artwork present the position. Although graphics in advertisements may be used as a "grabber" to attract attention, the attention should focus on a clearly presented position.

5. Consider branding. Brand names are not as widely used in service marketing

EXHIBIT 10–4   Positioning of Services

Service Characteristic	Positioning Strategy	Basis of Position
Intangibility	Offer a tangible representation	Organizational reputation and special capabilities: expertise position, reliability position, innovativeness position, performance position
	Offer an augmented service	Service product augmentation
		Provision of extra service (for example, more, better agents)
Heterogeneity	Offer superior selection, training, and monitoring of customer-contact personnel	"People" advantage, such as specialists
	Package the service	More attractive "bundle" of service products
	Industrialize the service-production process	Improved service product
Simultaneity	Use multisite locations	Improved accessibility for customer
	Customize the service	Extra attention to individual requirements
	Offer a complete range of service	Satisfaction of more customer needs (one-stop purchasing)

Source: Reprinted by permission of the publisher from "Positioning of Financial Services for Competitive Advantage," by Christopher J. Easingwood and Vijay Mahajan, *Journal of Product Innovation Management,* vol. 6, no. 3, 1989, p. 210. Copyright 1989 by Elsevier Science Publishing Co., Inc.

as in the marketing of goods, but an effective brand name can assist in consolidating a well-substantiated position. In the U.K. insurance industry, the firm GRE communicated exclusivity to its agents for a policy protecting a building and its contents that was aimed at the upper-end market by using the brand name "Select."

6. Look for mutually reinforcing main and support positions. Positions need not be unidimensional. For example, "expertise" and "customization" might provide mutually supporting positions, or a service product advantage may provide the direct reason to buy, whereas a company position provides more general support.

These ideas on positioning are not restricted to financial services but can be applied more generally to other services. In general, a successful service distinguishes a company from its competition.[27] Positioning is the technique that creates the distinction.

Branding Services

Service products are more difficult to brand than physical goods. For example, to what service product do you think "the Club," the brand name chosen by Air France, refers?[28] It probably doesn't mean much to you. Yet "Air France" does mean something. It conveys imagery and positioning of the airline relative to American Airlines, KLM, Singapore Airlines, and Quantas. The point is that the service organization typically assumes greater significance in the mind of the business customer than the individual service products it offers. That is, the firm's service products are usually perceived by customers as components of a single corporate brand. They can rarely stand alone under their own service product brand names. Thus, selecting a name for a service organization can be critical to a total marketing strategy because it is extremely costly and difficult to establish a brand name for the individual service products offered by the firm. In services, the company name *is* the brand name.

Four characteristics are associated with the strength of a service organization's brand name:[29]

- *Distinctiveness.* It immediately identifies the service supplier and distinguishes the firm from competitors.
- *Relevance.* It conveys the nature of the service or the service benefit.
- *Memorability.* It can be understood, used, and recalled easily.
- *Flexibility.* It not only encompasses the organization's current business but also is broad enough to apply to foreseeable expansions.

Visa is a good example of an effective brand name for a worldwide financial service because it communicates international access. Federal Express also provides a strong brand identity. "Express" suggests the speed of the service, as well as its nature. "Federal" implies a far-reaching enterprise and the possibility of governmental approval.

The service organization's brand name is reinforced by courteous employees, professional-looking uniforms, and consistent graphics on trucks, envelopes, and advertising. The comprehensive company colors and graphics are an important part of the branding program. However, no matter how good the corporate branding may be, the quality of the service determines the success of the image. If customers are not satisfied with the service, the corporate brand won't help.

Promotion of Services

Recall that promotion includes advertising, personal selling, sales promotion, and public relations and publicity. The final, crucial step is postservice follow-up.

Advertising.   Because services are intangible, they tend to be more difficult to advertise than goods. Thus, tangible cues that help the customer organization understand and evaluate the service are emphasized. These tangible cues are the things that the customer can see. The physical facilities of the service provider, the equipment used in providing the service, and the appearance of personnel are some examples.

Another technique is to make the service itself appear more tangible by personalizing it. This frequently is accomplished by featuring the service provider's employees in advertisements. For example, to promote their cash management products, Huntington Banks used the headline: "Because People Like Penny Bach Work for You . . . and the Huntington," then went on to profile Ms. Bach's experience, accomplishments, education, and personal interests. (She is Huntington's VP of cash management service products.)

A third approach is to focus on benefits. The Bank of Montreal, targeting small, independent businesspeople, advertises simplified, streamlined products, quick approval times, straightforward security arrangements, fixed monthly fees, clear, consistent pricing policies, and specialized account management teams.

One important advertising appeal is to cite the value added by the service, supported with factual evidence. For example, advertisements for the Ontario Co-op's Ration Right II Feed Balancing programs quoted survey evidence to show that dairy farmers who use this service get higher production: 478 kg. more milk per cow per year—over $200 more income per cow than those who don't use the service.

Another strategy is to build a favorable image for the service, and especially for the corporation behind the service. The Bank of Montreal reinforces its image by reminding business clients: "We created Canada's first currency. We set up her first foreign exchange operation. And we were first to implement 24-hour trading."

Service organization advertising is not only aimed at customers and potential customers. A significant benefit of the advertising is its role in influencing and motivating employees of the service organization.

Personal Selling.   The role of personal selling assumes greater importance when marketing services as opposed to products. Because of the intangibility of services, the salesperson (who is tangible) becomes part of the service—one of the visible cues with which the customer can identify. Furthermore, because of the need to identify unique customer requirements for many types of services, the salesperson frequently must have a high degree of technical expertise. Thus, for example, in a firm of consulting engineers, the only people who can sell the service are the engineers themselves, and usually they are the partners who own the firm. The same is true for accountants, management consultants, lawyers, and a range of other professional services. Indeed, the key to the marketing of professional services lies in the motivation of individual professionals.

When the services are performed by individuals (rather than machines), the quality of service provided is judged by the actions of the individual service provider as well as by the job that is performed. Thus, the service provider's interactions with the customer help to "sell" the customer. The delivery person for a

Photographs and testimonials from Pitt-Des Moines provide tangibility to Wausau's insurance services.

WHY A COMPANY KNOWN FOR ITS STEEL STRUCTURES CHOOSES WAUSAU FOR SUPPORT.

The St. Louis Gateway Arch. A 14,000,000 gallon water storage reservoir in California. Roosevelt Lake Bridge in Arizona. The storage vaults of Fort Knox — a few of the structures fabricated and erected by Pitt-Des Moines, Inc. What insurer has the service strength to support this company? Wausau Insurance. "We view our relationship with Wausau as a partnership, and we have a great

The service structure of Wausau is strong enough to support the needs of Pitt-Des Moines.

deal of respect for their professionalism and the high quality

For policyholders like Pitt-Des Moines, who need instant and detailed loss information, "Dial Wausau" provides direct access to PDM claims files in our computers.

of service they provide," says Richard Byers, PDM Vice President and Treasurer.

A good example of that service is "Dial Wausau," an on-line communications

link between Pitt-Des Moines and Wausau's claims department, providing immediate and detailed information on the activity of PDM claims. "Our company has realized substantial savings with Dial Wausau," concludes Mr. Byers. And that's how Pitt-Des Moines, a company known for steel structures, is made stronger with Wausau.

WAUSAU INSURANCE
A+ (Superior) A.M. Best Rating

Wausau Insurance Companies, 2000 Westwood Drive, Wausau, Wisconsin 54401 Telephone (715) 845-5211 A Member of the Nationwide® Group

Reprinted with permission from Wausau Insurance Companies.

courier service can reinforce or destroy the image of the service in the customer's eyes.

When the performance of the service involves interaction with and cooperation from the client (as it does in management consulting, architecture, contracting), the quality of the interaction may assume even greater importance than the actual performance of the task. This has led many firms in service industries to emphasize the importance of treating their interactions with customers as

BUSINESS MARKETING IN PRACTICE ■■■■■■■■

You Catch More Lawyers with Shrimp

The research insight was unambiguous: You catch more lawyers with shrimp than with peanuts. At least that's what a financial printer learned when it probed what customers really thought about its service. One lawyer said he switched from a competitor because the printer serves shrimp while customers wait to edit documents. His old printer only offered peanuts.

Though unexpected, that finding was hardly trivial to the printer. Successful business service marketers are learning that the customer's point of view—wholly rational or not—defines the quality of services they render. But many service providers, particularly professional service firms, still resist that market-oriented approach.

Source: Kate Bertrand, "In Service, Perception Counts," *Business Marketing* (April 1989), p. 44.

long-term relationships rather than as a series of transactions—in other words, more like a marriage than a date!

Training of personnel in the operations function (often called service delivery) is crucial to developing and maintaining such relationships. Marketing and operations are virtually inseparable in service industries. Brenda J. Weimer, North American customer service manager for the Plastics Division of Polysar Ltd. in Leominster, Massachusetts, points out that training service personnel how to interact with customers, even "how to shake hands, if necessary," is important if service representatives and others outside the sales function are to perform well on customer calls.[30]

Sales Promotion.   Sales promotion for services can be extremely helpful to the marketing strategy. Demonstrations and, where feasible, trials of the service help communicate the advantages of the intangible offering. John Henry & Associates, Inc., is a software developer located in Monett, Missouri, that specializes in the financial market. It designed a set of software programs that handles all the operations needed to run a small bank for use on Unisys mainframes. Unisys sells the software, and JHA provides sales promotion in the form of technical assistance and demonstrations.[31]

Giveaway promotional items, such as imprinted rulers, calculators, golf balls, pens, paperweights, Swiss army knives, and calendars, provide ready reminders in tangible form of the service organization's offering.

Public Relations and Publicity.   Public relations (PR) and publicity are widely used by business service organizations to create a favorable impression and to develop a receptive climate for salespeople. One financial institution, Canada Trust, has enhanced its public image through publicity generated by its "green account," whose earned interest is donated to worthy environmental causes. Forte Advanced Management Software of Carlsbad, California, a world market leader in integrated telecommunication management packages (in competition with AT&T, Switch-view, Northern Telecom, and MDR in the $180 million per year North American market), generates goodwill through sponsorship of user groups and educational seminars. Most business PR and publicity are developed through new product news releases to trade publications, through company researchers addressing technical meetings and publishing in technical journals, and by executives delivering speeches at high-level business and government meetings. Some business marketers obtain publicity through sponsoring sporting and cultural events, contributing funding for programs on national public radio and national public television, and releasing executives' time to organize charitable campaigns.

Postservice Follow-up.   Customer follow-up after a service has been performed is a crucial step in the promotion of services. "The big bucks aren't in making customers. They're in keeping customers. That's particularly true for business marketers, whose customers often have the potential to be life-time customers," says professor Michael LeBoeuf of the University of New Orleans.[32]

To keep customers, the service must be performed well. But more is needed. With little tangible evidence to go on, customers have to be *shown* that the job was done well. "Our customer service people are considered part of a proactive sales team," says Dow Chemical U.S.A.'s manager of customer service resources, Mitch Kern.[33]

IBM's Rochester, Minnesota, facility manufactures the AS/400 midrange computer. Three months after shipment, marketing representatives call AS/400 customers to determine their satisfaction. IBM's electronic customer support system offers remote testing and on-line hardware and software assistance. For stubborn problems, engineers are flown to customer operations to diagnose the situation first-hand. IBM estimates that a 1 percent improvement in AS/400 customer satisfaction worldwide generates more than $200 million in revenue over five years.[34]

Not only should service providers be trained to interact with customers but the service organization should also ensure that customers recognize and appreciate the fact that they have received good service. At Renex Corp., a Woodbridge, Virginia, computer interconnect company, technical service reps are treated like salespeople.[35] Customers evaluate their performance, and the service reps get substantial bonuses based on questionnaire feedback of customer satisfaction, including ratings of the rep's courtesy, responsiveness, and provision of clear instructions. One week after providing the service, the company does a telephone follow-up to make sure the customer's problem was satisfactorily resolved. Two days later it sends a thank-you card to the customer, restating the problem, when the customer requested the service, and the solution. This approach makes certain that customers remember Renex's good service, reminding them that the company solves service problems quickly and courteously.

Cross-Selling and Cross-Marketing

Finance, consulting, and accounting firms were among the first service providers to practice cross-selling. In **cross-selling**, the salesperson tries to maximize sales to a client who is purchasing one service product by selling other services.[36] Thus, a commercial banker who makes a loan to a business may then interest that client in a payroll management system or a corporate credit card.

Clearly, there are advantages to maximizing the returns from existing services—trading the customer up—before embarking on new service product development or seeking out entirely new customers. When accounting firms entered the management consulting business, the natural extension of cross-selling was cross-marketing accounting services to consulting clients, and consulting services to accounting clients. In **cross-marketing**, one strategic business unit (SBU) (or company) within a larger corporation markets the services of another SBU or sister company to its customers.

Today many corporations are tapping the advantages of cross-marketing the services of their different divisions. For example, PHH Corp. of Hunt Valley, Maryland, has eighteen operating units in three service groups: vehicle management, conducted by firms like Peterson Howell & Heather; relocation management, handled by firms like Home Equity (which looks after employee moves); and facilities management firms like Fantus.[37] When PHH acquired Avis Car Leasing, which rents vehicles for small corporate fleets, and Neville Lewis Associates Ltd., an interior design firm, it realized that its services were being sold piecemeal. Even though customers of one unit frequently required more than one of the services that PHH could offer, they weren't aware that PHH could provide those services through its other divisions.

In 1987, PHH created a corporate marketing department, united the various companies by prefixing their names with PHH (for example, PHH FleetAmerica, PHH Fantus, PHH Neville Lewis, etc.), brought eighty-five sales and marketing managers from all PHH divisions together for the first time (thereby initiating regular meetings), and rewarded salespeople for providing qualified leads for sibling PHH companies' services through a "Sharing Leads" program. This cross-marketing program brings in an additional $1 million in revenues to PHH each year.

Packaging Corporation of America, located in Evanston, Illinois, developed a cross-marketing strategy in 1988, building on strong ties with customers in five business groups (corrugated containers, paperboard, aluminum, plastic, and molded-fiber packaging). PCA bundled its packaging materials, services, and technical expertise to sell a full spectrum of packaging solutions to its twenty-five key customers. Until that time, even PCA's best customers usually didn't buy from more than one division. "A customer might be in the market for corrugated, folding carton, plastic and aluminum—all products we sell. But we'd only have one division in there," says George V. Bayly, marketing VP.[38] In the first six months, six national accounts started to buy from additional PCA divisions. PCA expects the cross-marketing program to generate an annual growth rate of at least 10 percent in national sales.

Pricing Services

Price can be an important indicator of service quality. When services are customized and their delivery involves a high degree of customer contact, each customer assigns a unique value to the service. Thus, one would expect business service providers to have wide latitude in both setting prices and varying them among market segments, and even among different customers. Those customers or groups of customers who value a service highly will be more willing to pay a higher price for it than others. Others may consider that the service provided is of a higher quality because it is priced higher than the competition.

Demand Management.   Price can be used to manage demand patterns. Since intangibles cannot be inventoried, and unutilized capacity means revenues are lost forever, a strategy of reducing price in slow demand periods and raising price in overcapacity periods may be used to stabilize demand. However, one must be careful not to allow lower prices to be interpreted as lower-quality service. The lower price should be explained to the buyer (as power utilities and telephone companies explain lower rates during off-peak demand hours).

Cost-based Pricing.   Research among seventy-one certified public accounting firms in Florida suggests that CPAs view their basic services as a commodity rather than a source of added value, unique to each customer.[39] Pricing practices of the CPA firms indicated that most firms (78.3 percent) charge a rate that is a multiple of the effective hourly rate paid to the staff member involved—a cost-based approach. Price changes are infrequent, mainly annual changes (80.3 percent).

For most services, however, marketers' cost measurements are a poor guide to pricing. In one study of service pricing, 61 percent of service firms couldn't measure the cost of introducing a new service because of difficulty both in allocating costs, since new services shared existing delivery systems, and in allowing for lost contribution resulting from cannibalization of existing services by the new service product.[40] That a wide range of pricing possibilities can be exploited by service marketers is demonstrated through the variation in delivery industry rates shown in Exhibit 10–5.

Value-based Pricing.   It is important to recognize that if an **augmented service**—that is, one that offers more than the minimum that the customer needs or has come to expect—is to command a premium price, it should be important to the client, different from that offered by competitors, believable, and recognizable upon delivery.[41] In a study of commercial delivery service between the United States and London, thirty-eight shippers ranked their preferences among DHL Worldwide, Federal Express, and Purolator Courier. Delivery time was discovered to be more important than either price or the delivery firm's reputation. Thus, the augmented service of overnight delivery, when compared to the expected two-day delivery service normally offered by competitors, could permit the only overnight

EXHIBIT 10–5   Delivery Industry Rates from Atlanta to San Francisco

Company Name	Deviation from Average Industry Price
UPS Next Day Air	− 51.07%
Pilot Airfreight System	− 37.05
CF Airfreight	− 5.20
Flying Tigers Air Cargo	− 4.40
Burlington Northern Airfreight	2.59
Federal Express	4.92
Airborne	11.92
Associated Air Freight	11.92
Purolator Courier	11.92
Emery Worldwide	11.92
DHL Worldwide Courier Express	14.25
Air Express International	28.24

Notes: 1. Cost is for a 10″ × 9″ × 12″ package weighing 10 pounds.
   2. Only firms specializing in business package delivery are included in this exhibit.

Source: Reprinted by permission of the publisher from "Pricing Augmented Commercial Service," by Roberto Friedmann and Warren A. French, *Journal of Product Innovation Management* (1987)38. Copyright 1987 by Elsevier Science Publishing Co., Inc.

delivery service provider, DHL, to charge a premium price 30 percent above its competitors' prices because of its greater value to the customer.[42]

Bundling Services.   As we mentioned earlier, most new services involve "software" changes as opposed to capital investment in "hardware." Since new investments in plant and equipment are not required, there are very low marginal costs in offering more service products to existing customers. When additional services are offered individually, they normally will be priced at a higher level than when they are "bundled," or packaged with other services. **Service bundling** can be used to obscure the proportion of the price contributed by any one service in the bundle. Thus, groups of service products may be bundled in different combinations to appeal differently to several segments within a particular market. Technimetrics, Inc., of New York bundles free consultations and other services with its financial databases, investor relations services, and microcomputer software, books, and research reports on trends in the investment community. Whereas competitors charge as little as $100 for undifferentiated databases, Technimetrics sells its bundled databases and customized services for premium prices of $2,000 to $5,000.[43]

Digital Equipment Corp. of Maynard, Massachusetts, is developing service bundles aimed at twenty-seven different markets to make it simpler for customers to use DEC service. Sun Microsystems, Inc., of Mountain View, California, introduced four separate service bundles, priced according to the level of service they included. The most elaborate provided customers with spare parts, on-site repair, software support, a designated account representative on service hot-line calls, and access to an on-line informational database.[44]

Support Services

Services provided by companies that manufacture goods are important in winning and keeping customers for the firm's physical products. Also, after-sales service can often yield higher profit margins than the original product sale. Many computer makers get as much as 25 percent of their total revenue from maintenance. Deere & Co., the Moline, Illinois, agricultural and construction equipment manufacturer, recognizes that farmers and contractors now purchase equipment based on calculations of overall possession costs (including purchasing cost, financing cost, fuel efficiency, cost of maintenance and repairs, cost of downtime, and resale value or disposal cost) rather than on initial purchase price. In addition, industrial contractors measure their profitability on an hourly basis and face nonperformance penalties when they miss deadlines.

In the agriculture sector, Deere is encouraging its dealers to open their own satellite sales and service centers to bring service closer to farmers. In both sectors "the key element is the availability of our parts and services to the customer," states Arden Esslinger, VP of the eastern U.S. region of Deere's Industrial Equipment Division.[45]

Third-Party Services.   An organization that services equipment that it does not manufacture is called a "third party." For some original equipment manufacturers, **third-party service** is a threat, stealing away lucrative service business that the OEM may wish to keep. Indeed, when IBM tried to lock users into IBM service and support of IBM networks by limiting outsiders' access to parts, training, and documentation, a consent decree was issued to permit third-party firms access to parts.[46] Strong third-party competition to the OEM's service operation arises during the maturity stage of the maintenance service life cycle and continues during the end-of-life stage.

For other equipment manufacturers, third-party service may be a blessing when the installed base of product is small but customers still require service. It is also important when the OEM is no longer manufacturing a product, or when the OEM has moved to a higher technology design and doesn't wish to be encumbered with servicing old apparatus.

Fourth-Party Services.   Both independent third-party service companies and OEMs often turn to smaller, specialized firms for **fourth-party service**. The smaller companies, called "fourth-party" maintenance firms, offer specialized care and extra services that generally are not available from third-party companies.

Caterpillar provides an example of the service component of a durable good.

Courtesy of Caterpillar Industrial Inc.

In the computer business, manufacturers and third-party service providers will do repairs at the customer's site, down to the "board level." If there is a problem with the circuit board, they remove it and may turn it over to a fourth-party firm. In Amery, Wisconsin, DMA, Inc., is one such fourth-party firm specializing in repairing circuit boards.[47] Another fourth-party firm is Dataserv, Inc., of Eden Prairie, Minnesota, whose third-party customers include TRW, Sorbus, Honeywell, and Control Data. Like most fourth-party firms, Dataserv buys, tests, and resells spare parts, and is less expensive and easier to deal with than the OEM. Dataserv has found a niche segment of the market and has successfully catered to it.

DIFFICULTIES IN MARKETING SERVICES

The characteristics of intangibility, inseparability, heterogeneity, and perishability not only describe services; they also encompass issues that can affect new service product development (see Exhibit 10–6). Some of these issues can create difficulties for their marketers. When asked by one researcher to evaluate various difficulties they had experienced, service marketers responded that their most serious problems had to do with the demand fluctuations experienced by services.[48] In periods of low demand, their perishability means they cannot be produced for

---

EXHIBIT 10–6   Issues Affecting New Service Product Development

---

Intangibility   —risk of conducting the development process too quickly
                  —risk of haphazard development process
                  —easy to copy competitor's product
                  —risk of new product proliferation
                  —risk of confusing customer with too many new service products
                  —risk of information overload with operations staff and customers
                  —difficulties in conducting R&D
                  —difficulties in conducting marketing research
                  —difficulties in conducting quantitative market research
                  —absence of a physical prototype to test-market
                  —slower market introductions
                  —effect of new service product on corporate image
                  —difficulties in measuring success
                  —difficulties in determining actual cost of new service product

Inseparability   —need for increased interorganizational involvement
                  —increased importance of delivery systems
                  —higher levels of customer input
                  —hard to allocate cost

Heterogeneity   —lack of standardized delivery system
                  —quality control becomes a success issue
                  —need to develop right level of standardization
                  —difficulties in concept testing
                  —need for more monitoring and control systems

Perishability   —difficulties in demand/supply management
                  —need for higher levels of integration among departments
                  —need to decide right mix between people and machines

---

Source: Scott Edgett, *New Product Development Practices in the Financial Services Industry: A Model of Successful Determinates for NPD,* University of Bradford, 1991, unpublished Ph.D. dissertation.

inventories, and their inseparability leads to underutilization of service providers. High demand strains human resources and reduces service quality.

Service marketing executives reported various methods of coping with demand fluctuation. In periods of high demand they were more likely to have their experienced personnel work overtime, to train existing employees in handling other tasks or functions, or even to hire extra part-time help.[49] The last thing they were willing to do was let work fall behind. During periods of low demand, they increased the number of their sales calls on customers, rescheduled employees, and used employees to perform nonvital tasks. The last thing they were willing to do was offer price reductions to stimulate demand. Recognition that marketing services involves solving difficulties that are different from marketing business products is important, and suggests that business service marketers should seek new and imaginative solutions to their problems.

EVALUATING CUSTOMER SERVICE

Measures of service performance differ between business marketers of goods and business marketers of services. Exhibit 10–7 indicates that service organizations focus more on customer complaints, the number of calls handled by each em-

EXHIBIT 10–7   Common Measures of Customer Service Performance

	Percentage of Business Firms Using Measure	
Service Activity	Manufacturers	Industrial Service
Number of customer complaints	41.6%	54.2%
Number of orders processed	62.0	47.2
Fill rate	32.9	43.1
Calls per employee	31.7	43.1
Time per call	23.1	41.7
Call waiting time	18.0	41.7
Time to answer calls	17.4	33.3
On-time delivery	42.8	26.4
Pricing/order entry accuracy	44.9	20.8
Back orders	41.6	18.1
Order cycle time	34.4	16.7
Number of inquiries	23.4	15.3
Stock outs	27.8	9.7

Source: Reprinted by permission of the publisher from "How a Customer Mission Statement Affects Company Performance," by Richard Germain and M. Bixby Cooper, *Industrial Marketing Management,* vol. 19, 1990, p. 52. Copyright 1990 by Elsevier Science Publishing Co., Inc.

BUSINESS MARKETING IN PRACTICE

"Bugs" Burger's Unconditional Service Guarantee

"Bugs" Burger Bug Killers (BBBK) is a Miami-based pest-extermination company owned by S.C. Johnson & Son.

Most of BBBK's competitors claim that they will reduce pests to "acceptable levels"; BBBK promises to eliminate them entirely. Its service guarantee to hotel and restaurant clients includes the following promises:

- You don't owe one penny until all pests on your premises have been eradicated.
- If you are ever dissatisfied with BBBK's service, you will receive a refund for up to twelve months of the company's services—plus fees for another exterminator of your choice for the next year.
- If a guest spots a pest on your premises, BBBK will pay for the guest's meal or room, send a letter of apology, and pay for a future meal or stay.
- If your facility is closed down due to the presence of roaches or rodents, BBBK will pay any fines, as well as all lost profits, plus $5,000.

In short, BBBK says, "If we don't satisfy you 100%, we don't take your money."

How successful is this guarantee? The company, which operates throughout the United States, charges up to ten times more than its competitors and yet has a disproportionately high market share in its operating areas. Its service quality is so outstanding that the company rarely needs to make good on its guarantee. (In 1986 it paid out only $120,000 on sales of $33 million—just enough to prove that its promises aren't empty ones.)

Source: Reprinted by permission of *Harvard Business Review.* An excerpt from "The Power of Unconditional Service Guarantees" by Christopher W. L. Hart, (July/August 1988). Copyright © 1988 by the President and Fellows of Harvard College; all rights reserved.

ployee, call waiting time, duration of the call, and time required to resolve a customer's request or problem and respond to it.

Such measures of service performance are of greatest use when they relate to the type of service performance desired by customers. Of course, care must be taken in assessing customer preferences to recognize that emphasis on various aspects of service varies from one market segment to the next.

In one general study, customers were asked to rate the importance of various service factors. The top five factors were reliability, responsiveness, assurance, empathy, and tangible aspects (for example, physical facilities, employees' appearance, etc.). Interestingly, when those firms scored their vendors on these factors, the items that were ranked as most important were the factors on which vendors scored the lowest. Meanwhile, the vendors received the highest scores on tangibles.[50] In other words, service vendors were not satisfying their customers' most important needs.[51]

The importance of service should never be underestimated. In the preceding study, 40 percent of respondents said they would change vendors because of poor service, whereas only 8.3 percent said they would switch because of price, and 8.3 percent said they would switch because of product quality.

INTERNATIONALIZATION OF SERVICES

At the beginning of this chapter we said that services represent a large and fast-growing segment of many nations' economies. From a global perspective, services are also having an increasingly strong effect on international business arrangements and trading patterns.

In 1991 the growth rate of global trade in services was 12 percent.[52] The share of a country's gross domestic product represented by services increases as the per capita wealth of the nation increases (see Exhibit 10–8). As a nation becomes more developed, growth in manufacturing and services is achieved at the expense of the primary sector (agriculture, fishing, mining and extractive industries), and services become an even more dominant sector. Service as a percentage of GDP ranges from 48 percent in developing countries to 69 percent in highly developed economies.[53]

World trade in services is highly concentrated. Three-quarters of world trade is conducted by twenty countries, with the top five world service traders (the United States, the United Kingdom, Germany, France, and Japan) accounting for more than 50 percent of global service exports and more than 40 percent of world service imports (see Exhibit 10–9).

The importance of trade in services to a country's balance of payments is illustrated by the trade figures for the United States (see Exhibit 10–10). As the goods balance of trade has declined since 1970, the services balance of trade has remained relatively strong and positive.

BUSINESS MARKETING IN PRACTICE

Commercial Real Estate Goes International

Today, more and more real estate firms are dealing with relocations to other countries. They may specialize in plant, office, and employee home relations. Since financial service companies have rapidly been moving abroad, advertisements should focus on major and medium-size accounting firms, investment banking houses, law firms, and advertising agencies.

In the marketing of international real estate service companies, two principal international real estate trade associations are active and highly involved: the International Real Estate Federation (FIABCI) of Paris and the Royal Institution of Chartered Surveyors of London.

Also participating in global real estate in a major way is the International Real Estate Institute, headquartered in Scottsdale, Arizona.

Other U.S.-based real estate trade associations that have attracted foreign real estate members are the International Council of Shopping Centers, Building Owners and Managers Association International, Urban Land Institute, and the International Association of Corporate Officers of Real Estate.

Source: Mary Alice Hines, "Marketing International Real Estate Services," *Commercial Investment Real Estate Journal* (Spring 1990), p. 41.

EXHIBIT 10–8   1988 Share of Services in GDP of Selected Countries

Country	Per Capita GDP as a Percent of U.S. GDP per Capita	Services as a Percent of 1988 GDP
Indonesia	3.5	40
Philippines	4.3	44
Turkey	7.5	46
Brazil	11.0	49
Italy	42.0	56
United Kingdom	56.0	56
France	63.0	59
Japan	70.0	57
Denmark	72.0	58
Canada	86.0	56
United States	100.0	65

Source: Adapted from Jacques Nusbaumer, *Services in the Global Market* (Boston: Kluwer Academic Publishers, 1987), and *World Development Report 1990,* The World Bank, pp. 182, 183.

EXHIBIT 10–9   Global Service Trade of the Heaviest Trading Nations

Country	Percentage Share of Total World Service Exports	Percentage Share of Total World Service Imports
United States	21.5	16.3
France	8.5	6.5
United Kingdom	7.3	5.1
Germany	7.1	6.9
Japan	6.4	6.6
Belgium-Luxembourg	4.7	3.8
Italy	4.0	3.2
Netherlands	3.6	3.1
Saudi Arabia	2.7	1.4
Switzerland	2.7	1.4
Spain	2.1	1.2
Canada	1.9	3.7

Source: K. Tucker and M. Sandberg, *International Trade in Services: The ASEAN Australian Experience* (London: Routledge Publishing, 1988), Table 2.4. Reprinted by permission.

EXHIBIT 10–10   U.S. Trade Balances (millions of dollars)

	1970	1974	1982	1984	1988	1989
Service exports	23,205	48,360	137,107	142,105	188,000	104,387
Service imports	20,186	33,708	103,897	123,944	183,000	90,946
Services balance	3,019	14,652	33,210	18,161	5,000	13,441
Merchandise balance	2,603	(5,505)	(36,389)	(108,281)	(127,000)	(122,840)
Net balance	5,622	9,147	(3,179)	(90,118)	(122,000)	(109,399)

Source: Adapted from "Services Trade Balances Continue Three-year Decline," *Business America* (July 8, 1985), p. 19; U.S. Department of Commerce, *Survey of Current Business* (March 1989 and Dec. 1991); and *International Financial Statistics Yearbook,* 1991.

The following factors have stimulated the internationalization of services:

1. As goods manufacturers go global, their service suppliers follow.

2. As goods manufacturers expand around the world, their global customers require information, product use, maintenance, and repair services.

3. As businesses, institutions, and other organizations around the world become more technically literate, there is greater opportunity for creating and delivering services globally.

4. Recent deregulation of tightly controlled industries in many countries has opened new markets to service providers (for example, Canadian banking, U.S. airlines and trucking).

5. The unification of the Federal Republic of Germany and the GDR and the independence movement in Eastern Europe have created new opportunities for service organizations.

6. The Canada–U.S. Free Trade Agreement, the European Community, and the various GATT (General Agreement on Tariffs and Trade Conference) Rounds to liberalize trade are reducing barriers that prevented free operation of foreign service providers in closed domestic markets.

7. Information technology and new telecommunication techniques are shrinking the globe through real-time data interchange. These developments are changing the way services are created and delivered and are changing the types of services that can be offered.

8. Many services are created and delivered through the purchase and use of goods (for example, programming services are stimulated by the purchase of computers).

9. A number of services are being embodied in goods, which makes it easier for the services to be traded (programs in diskettes are an example).

As service industries move into global markets, some countries have won competitive positions through their service industries. Exhibit 10–11 portrays patterns

EXHIBIT 10–11   Estimated Patterns of National Competitive Advantage in Selected International Business Service Industries

Service Industry	Denmark	Germany	Italy	Japan	Korea	Singapore	Sweden	Switzerland	U.K.	U.S.
Corporate training										xx
Hospital management										xx
Accounting/legal									x	xx
Advertising									xx	xx
Management consulting		x						x	x	xx
Construction			x		x			x	x	xx
Design service			xx							
Temporary help								x		xx
Industrial laundry & apparel supply	x								x	xx
Industrial cleaning (facilities/tools/equipment)							x			x
Equipment maintenance & repair							x			
Waste disposal & management										xx
Commercial banking				x				xx	x	xx
Money management		xx						xx	xx	xx
Reinsurance				x				x	xx	
Custom software/information/data									x	xx
Airport terminal service		x				x		x	x	
Shipping	x			x			x			
Port services		x				x				
Ship repair						x				
Logistics management								x		

Note: x = strong competitive advantage; xx = very strong competitive advantage

Source: Adapted with permission of The Free Press, a Division of Macmillan, Inc., from *The Competitive Advantage of Nations* by Michael E. Porter. Copyright © 1990 by Michael E. Porter.

of international leadership among selected nations in service industries that exhibit significant competition. For example, Italian design has become internationally renown. Switzerland has long been a global banker. And Singapore is well known for its ship repair services. U.S. firms have a very strong competitive advantage in management consulting. The percentage of revenues earned overseas by the ten largest U.S. management consulting firms exceeded $4.5 billion in 1987, providing around half the firm's revenues for McKinnsey, Coopers & Lybrand, and Price Waterhouse.[54]

Service firms that have appropriate competitive advantages increasingly are engaging in transnational trade. Internationalization of services may be accomplished by the following methods:

1. Exporting final services by selling them to independent buyers (e.g., Lloyds of London insures a U.S. ship).
2. Selling intermediate services to independent buyers (e.g., technology or management skills).
3. Foreign direct investment (FDI): a multinational enterprise (MNE) establishes a foreign subsidiary or affiliate, which provides services in that location and also may buy intermediate services from the parent firm.

The future for services, both domestically and internationally, is bright, given the magnitude and rapid growth rate of the service sector. Service marketing opportunities also are growing with the aid of new technologies. Less developed countries and medium developed countries, as they drive toward fuller development, will demand more services. In the future, business marketers will need to develop more fully their skills in providing the intangibles rather than, as in the past, focusing on physical products.

SUMMARY

In this chapter a business service is defined as the performance of an activity that does not directly produce a physical product. Typically, neither services nor products exist in isolation but rather are part of a product-service mix. Primary business services have a relatively small physical product component, whereas complementary business services accompany and enhance the sale of a physical product. Services have experienced dramatic growth worldwide in recent years, and many business marketers have changed their orientation from manufacturing physical products to provision of services.

Business services exhibit six characteristics: specialization, heterogeneity, intangibility, perishability, inseparability, and technology. Business services are different from consumer services because of their greater specialization and customization to meet customer requirements. Business services are heterogeneous because it is difficult to control the variability among service delivery personnel.

They are intangible and ephemeral, and cannot be owned. Their perishability makes demand management an important task, for they cannot be stockpiled. Perceptions of service quality are strongly dependent on the delivery experience, which is inseparable from the personnel who supply the service. Services have been transformed by technological developments, particularly the computer.

Service life cycles are similar to product life cycles discussed in Chapter 9, except that they usually have shorter introductory periods and longer decline stages. Of particular interest is the maintenance service life cycle. It is represented by four stages: rapid growth, transition, maturity, and end of life.

Of particular importance in segmentation is recognition that service market segments are less homogeneous. Hence the business marketer must pay attention to the service product's "high-touch" aspects and how they fit with customer expectations.

New service development usually centers on restructuring or modifying the "software" component of the firm's offering. Clear objectives, test-marketing, well-defined positioning, and branding are all important aspects of the new service development program.

In advertising services, the business marketer should use tangible cues, personalize the service, focus on the benefits the service provides, and reinforce the service image. In personal selling, it is important to recognize that the sales and service people are the tangible embodiment of the intangible service, and should be well trained. Sales promotion also involves providing tangible reminders of the service organization's offering. Public relations and publicity help to create a favorable impression of the business service firm and generate a receptive climate for the firm's salespeople. Post-service customer follow-up, extremely important because it provides more tangibility to the ephemeral, completes the promotion loop.

Width in the product-service mix permits cross-selling several services to the same client. When the service company has several divisions, or several affiliated companies, cross-selling can extend to cross-marketing. That is, one division (company) can cross-market a sister division's (or company's) offering.

Service product pricing involves several factors. Service product price may suggest a quality expectation to the customer. Price can be used to manage demand for the service. Service product cost measurements are difficult to make and are a poor guide to pricing. A far better guide is to price according to the value of the service in the customer's perceptions. Bundling of service products can obscure the individual prices of service elements in the bundle and offer the business service marketer greater pricing flexibility.

Goods-producing organizations usually have to provide support services to their customers. Such services offered by firms that are not OEMs are called third-party services. Fourth-party service firms do more specialized work for third-party firms and OEMs.

Marketing services involves more difficulties than marketing goods. The biggest difficulty is management of demand. Service quality is also difficult for management to measure and monitor, yet it is the principal cause of lost customers.

With a global service trade growth rate of 12 percent annually, with services representing an extremely large proportion of GDP in highly developed countries, and with services playing a more and more important part in developed countries' balance of trade, business service marketers possessing competitive advantages are in a good position to benefit by going international.

Key Terms and Concepts

business services
primary business services
complementary business services
core utility
intangibility
service life cycle (SLC)
maintenance service life cycle
installed base
"high-touch" offerings

"low-touch" offering
"hardware" component
"software" component
cross-selling
cross-marketing
augmented service
service bundling
third-party service
fourth-party service

Discussion Questions

1. Why are business services more difficult to market than business goods?

2. When an organization such as Westinghouse, Borg-Warner, or National Intergroup, Inc., decides to increase the proportion of its business that is generated by services, what changes would you anticipate in overall management philosophy and marketing management?

3. When would a marketer of business services choose to use high-technology equipment and a high degree of automation in the provision of the service?

4. Why might a business marketer choose to keep a service "high touch" rather than attempting to find ways to standardize and automate the service?

5. Why might business service marketers receive higher ratings from their customers on the tangibles associated with services offered (which customers consider to be less important) than on the intangibles (which customers consider more important)? Taking your suggested reasons, how could a service

marketer provide greater customer satisfaction?

6. A new company has recently been created to provide secure shredding of important and confidential business and legal documents and correspondence. As an adviser to the company, you have been asked to help identify an appropriate name for the service. What name do you recommend? Why?

7. As marketing manager for a nationwide system of highway tractor-trailer service centers, you recognize the importance of using advertising not only to win customers but also to motivate service center employees. Develop an advertisement for your service and indicate how it accomplishes both objectives.

8. You are the manager of a golf course that has a well-appointed, large clubhouse, an excellent chef, and several large rooms. How would you manage business demand for your facilities?

9. Jill Jenkins, chief librarian in a major city library system, has decided to erect a new

downtown library dedicated to business use. What should she do to ensure that the Downtown Business Library is successful?

10. Chuck Johnston has operated a successful advertising agency in Boston for ten years. He realizes that several of his clients are planning to set up operations in France so they can participate in European Community business. Once established there, they will need advertising agency services. Chuck believes that his company could offer his clients continuity of service and obtain additional work from them by establishing a branch agency in Paris. Suggest pros and cons regarding his plan to expand abroad.

Endnotes and References

1. David A. Collier, "The Customer Service and Quality Challenge," *The Service Industries Journal* 7 (January 1987): 79.

2. William Dullforce, "Services Pact May Be Seen as Milestone," (London) *Financial Times,* December 23, 1991.

3. John H. Dunning, "Multinational Enterprises and the Growth of Services: Some Conceptual and Theoretical Issues," *The Service Industries Journal* 9 (January 1989): 7.

4. *World Development Report, 1991,* The World Bank, pp. 208–209, 262–263.

5. James L. Heskett, "Lessons in the Service Sector," *Harvard Business Review* (March–April 1987): 118.

6. Roberto Friedmann and Warren A. French, "Pricing Augmented Commercial Services," *Journal of Product Innovation Management* 4 (1987): 33.

7. *Year Book of Labour Statistics, 1991* (Geneva: International Labour Office), pp. 396, 408, 447.

8. Although growth in services is undisputed, overinvestment in information technology and chronic inefficiency in U.S. service industries have prevented productivity improvement. See Stephen S. Roach, "Services Under Siege—The Restructuring Imperative," *Harvard Business Review* (September–October 1991): 82–91.

9. Leif Edvinsson, "New Business Focus," *The Service Industries Journal* 17 (April 1987): 197.

10. The eight largest U.S. accounting firms in 1989 were Arthur Andersen, Deloitte Haskins & Sells, Coopers & Lybrand, Touche Ross, Ernst & Whinney, Peat Marwick Main & Co., Price Waterhouse & Co., and Arthur Young & Co. They audited 90 percent of the corporations listed on the New York Stock Exchange. By 1991, after mergers and dissolutions, the top six U.S. accounting firms were Ernst & Young, KPMG Peat Marwick, Deloitte & Touche, Arthur Andersen, Coopers & Lybrand, and Price Waterhouse.

11. Kennedy & Kennedy, (Fitzwilliams, N.H.) *Consultant News* (June 1988): 2–3.

12. Dunning, "Multinational Enterprises and the Growth of Services," p. 5.

13. Ralph W. Jackson and Philip D. Cooper, "Unique Aspects of Marketing Industrial Services," *Industrial Marketing Management* 17 (1988): 116.

14. G. Lynn Shostack, "Service Positioning Through Structural Change," *Journal of Marketing* 51 (January 1987): 34–43.

15. Richard Germain and M. Bixby Cooper, "How a Customer Mission Statement Affects Company Performance," *Industrial Marketing Management* 19 (1990): 48.

16. Leonard L. Berry, "Services Marketing Is Different," *Business* (May–June 1980): 24–29.

17. Vaughn C. Judd, "Differentiate with the 5th P: People," *Industrial Marketing Management* 16 (1987): 241–247.

18. Michael E. Porter, *The Competitive Advan-*

tage of Nations (New York: The Free Press, 1990), p. 267.

19. Kate Bertrand, "High-Tech Product Sales Create Niche for Services," *Business Marketing* (February 1990): 25–26.

20. George W. Potts, "Exploit Your Product's Service Life Cycle," *Harvard Business Review* (September–October 1988): 32.

21. James L. Heskett, *Managing in the Service Economy* (Boston: Harvard Business School Press), p. 38.

22. Christopher J. Easingwood, "New Product Development for Service Companies," *Journal of Product Innovation Management* 3 (December 1986): 269.

23. Ibid., p. 273.

24. One study of 276 new service products, of which 150 were successes and 126 were failures, identified fourteen factors that are significant determinants of success. See Ulrike de Brentani, "Success Factors in Developing New Business Services," *European Journal of Marketing* 25 (1991): 33–59.

25. This section is adapted from Christopher J. Easingwood and Vijay Mahajan, "Positioning of Financial Services for Competitive Advantage," *Journal of Product Innovation Management* (September 1989): 207–219.

26. The firms were Aetna, CIGNA, Chubb, Fireman's Fund, General Accident, Hartford, Maryland Casualty, North America Reinsurance, Northbrook, Northland, and Utica.

27. William H. Davidow and Bro Uttal, "Service Companies: Focus or Falter," *Harvard Business Review* 89 (July–August 1989): 77–85.

28. "The Club" is the brand name Air France has given to its executive-class service.

29. Leonard L. Berry, Edwin E. Lefkowith, and Terry Clark, "In Services: What's in a Name?" *Harvard Business Review* (September–October 1980): 28–30.

30. Kate Bertrand, "Sales and Service: One Big Happy Family?" *Business Marketing* (December 1988): 38.

31. Kate Bertrand, "Harvesting the Best," *Business Marketing* (October 1988): 46.

32. Bertrand, "Sales and Service," p. 36.

33. Ibid., p. 38.

34. Frank Rose, "Now Quality Means Service Too," *Fortune,* April 22, 1991, pp. 102, 106.

35. Kate Bertrand, "Renex Recasts Its Service Image," *Business Marketing* (December 1988): 40.

36. The proliferation of personal computers in business offices, with their ability to store and retrieve documents, and the growth in electronic communication are threatening the business of the world's largest manufacturer of business forms, Moore Corp. However, by innovative cross-selling, the Chicago-based giant expects to take over many functions that its clients for business forms have been performing in-house, such as printing and database management. IBM and American Express are among business-forms customers that are expanding their purchases to buy Moore's long-term planning, electronic records management, mailing, and information management services. See Greg Boyd, "Managing Moore in a Paperless World," *Canadian Business* (September 1991): 60–63.

37. Tom Eisenhart, "PHH: Sharing Leads to Open Doors," *Business Marketing* (November 1988): 60–61.

38. Tom Eisenhart, "PCA: Packaging the Solution," *Business Marketing* (November 1988): 63–64.

39. Michael H. Morris and Donald A. Fuller, "Pricing an Industrial Service," *Industrial Marketing Management* 18 (1989): 139–146.

40. Christopher J. Easingwood, "New Product Development for Service Companies," p. 273.

41. Ibid., p. 36.

42. Roberto Friedmann and Warren A. French, "Pricing Augmented Commercial Services," *Journal of Product Innovation Management* 4 (1987): 41.

43. Kate Bertrand, "Technimetrics: Listening Be-

tween the Lines," *Business Marketing* (April 1988): 65.

44. Diane Lynn Kastiel, "Service and Support: High-Tech's New Battleground," *Business Marketing* (June 1987): 66.

45. Kate Bertrand, "Deere Reaches Out with Service Satellites," *Business Marketing* (December 1988): 41, 42.

46. Kastiel, "Service and Support," p. 62.

47. Diane Lynn Kastiel, "Where the Repair Experts Get Their Repairs," *Business Marketing* (June 1967): 64.

48. Valerie A. Zeithaml, A. Parasuraman, and Leonard L. Berry, "Problems and Strategies in Services Marketing," *Journal of Marketing* 49 (Spring 1985): 33–46.

49. Ibid.

50. "'Service' Means Serve-Us," *Business Marketing* (April 1990): 24, 25.

51. Similar results were obtained in a study of pump and valve manufacturers' perceptions of their metals suppliers' services. See Peter M. Banting, "Customer Service in Industrial Marketing: A Comparative Study," *European Journal of Marketing* 10 (Summer 1976): 136–145.

52. William Dullforce, "Services Pact May Be Seen as Milestone."

53. Dorothy I. Riddle, *Service Led Growth: The Role of the Service Sector in World Development* (New York: Praeger Publishers, 1986).

54. Kennedy & Kennedy, *Consultant News.*

11

BUSINESS PRICING

_____

- To appreciate the theoretical approaches to pricing provided by economics
- To understand the customer's perception of value
- To learn how to segment a market using pricing
- To become familiar with the pricing strategies used by business marketers
- To recognize the importance of price to the buyer
- To identify the different types of pricing
- To examine leasing in industrial pricing
- To become familiar with the process of competitive bidding
- To realize that a great deal of uncertainty surrounds pricing

The price of a product or service is crucially important to the seller. It determines whether a product will gain market acceptance, maintain its market position in the face of growing competition, and realize an optimum profit level. Yet marketing practitioners and scholars alike agree that pricing is one of the fuzziest and most difficult areas of decision making.

This state of affairs may be attributed to the elements involved in pricing that are unknown, beyond the firm's control, or simply clouded by much uncertainty. In establishing a price, one must estimate the costs involved. But to estimate the cost, the demand for the product must be known, which it rarely is. Beyond the firm's control are such economic conditions as wars, natural disasters, strikes, tax changes, and recessions or booms. But even more important to marketers is determining the value of the product or service to the customer, since prices should be market oriented. Yet even with extensive marketing research, until a product is launched acceptance is uncertain.

We begin this chapter with the theoretical foundations of price. We then present the "real world" considerations used to establish prices in business marketing.

MARKET CLASSIFICATION AND PRICING

From the perspective of management, one of the most important factors in pricing is the market in which the firm operates. The type of product and the number and size of competitors must be considered when setting prices. Pricing behavior that is rational and consistent with "scientific" principles in one type of market may be irrational and unscientific in another market. The appropriate starting point in pricing is to ascertain what type of market the business marketer is attempting to sell into.

Five theoretical forms of market structure are described here: (1) perfect competition, (2) monopolistic competition, (3) pure and differentiated oligopoly, (4) pure and differentiated oligopsony, and (5) monopoly. Although there are many differences among these five types of market structure, the major criteria used to distinguish them are the numbers of buyers and sellers, and the similarity of products sold by the sellers in the market. Exhibit 11–1 classifies each market structure form according to these two criteria.

In examining the implications for pricing, there are two ways in which these market structures may be ranked: in terms of degree of certainty and in terms of degree of control in setting prices of products. If the degree of certainty with which a firm can estimate the demand for its products is the criterion, perfect competitors and firms in monopoly markets can estimate their demand more precisely than firms in other markets. If, however, the market forms are ranked according to the degree of control that a firm has in setting the price of its product, firms in monopoly markets have the most control and perfect competitors the least.

In **perfect competition** no single firm has any control over price. This lack of control results from the large number of sellers, each producing exactly the same product. If a firm should raise its price above the prevailing market price, its product would be nonsalable. On the other hand, a perfectly competitive firm would not reduce its price below the prevailing market price because its offering is so small relative to the total supply that it can market its total output at the going market price. Commodities markets and widely held shares in the stock market are examples of perfect competition.

In a **monopoly market** there is only one seller. This firm has complete control of the market. It can formulate its pricing policy with little fear of losing sales to other firms, since there are none. Public utilities are an example of monopoly markets.

In the other three forms of market structure—monopolistic competition, oligopoly, and oligopsony—each industrial firm has some control over the price of its products and can alter its sales performance through nonprice competition such as advertising, sales promotion, product-service variation, channel of distribution changes, logistics strategies, and corporate imagery. However, a firm's freedom to change price is tempered by the possibility of competitive repercussions.

EXHIBIT 11–1   Market Structure

Market Configuration	Identical Product	Differentiated Product
Many buyers and sellers	Perfect competition	Monopolistic competition
Many buyers, few sellers	Pure oligopoly	Differentiated oligopoly
Few buyers, many sellers	Pure oligopsony	Differentiated oligopsony
Many buyers, one seller	Monopoly	

Monopolistic competitors have the greatest price-setting freedom. Since there are many firms in a monopolistic competitive industry, limited action taken by one firm is unlikely to make large inroads in the sales of any one rival. Hence, there is less fear of retaliation. Machine tool marketers are an example.

In an **oligopoly structure** there are only a few sellers. Thus, price changes initiated by one firm are likely to invite price retaliation. Marketers of cellular telephone service fit this category, as do petroleum refiners, and manufacturers of automobiles, steel, and tobacco. Unless it is an acknowledged price leader, an oligopolistic firm has limited pricing flexibility due to the uncertainty of competitive reaction.

Firms in **oligopsonistic industries** have pricing opportunities similar to those of monopolistic competitors. For example, a packaged food manufacturer selling to the central buying units of major corporate chain supermarkets is not very concerned about competitors' reactions to its pricing.

Economic theorists have devoted much time to explaining the behavior of firms in various market situations. If properly employed, this type of information can assist the seller in developing price policies and strategies that capitalize on market opportunities. For example, in a study of sixty-seven manufacturers of industrial goods that market only to industrial users, almost half (thirty-three) saw themselves as operating under perfect competition.[1]

The disproportionately high number of firms that perceive their markets as perfect competition is open to question for two reasons. First, few markets in

BUSINESS MARKETING IN PRACTICE

Oligopolist: McCain Foods Risks Price Retaliation

The U.S. French fry industry, already battered by a sluggish economy, appears headed for a price war.

The world's biggest producer of frozen fries, McCain Foods Ltd., of Florenceville, New Brunswick, Canada, cut its U.S. prices an average of 10 percent on curled, seasoned, and other specialty potato products that are increasingly popular at fast food restaurants. "We think we're the low-cost producer in this category," said Michael McCain, president and CEO of the McCain USA unit.

But the move risks retaliation by the Big Three of fries—the Lamb-Weston unit of Omaha-based ConAgra Inc., J.R. Simplot Co. of Boise, Idaho, and Milwaukee-based Universal Foods Corp.—which dominate the nearly $1-billion North American frozen-fry industry.

By slicing an average of 6 cents a pound off its specialty items, McCain hopes to grab a much larger share of the fast-growing U.S. market for fries coated with spices and other flavorings, where it now holds only about a 4 percent share. "The longer it takes competitors to respond, the more opportunity we'll have to capture share," stated Mr. McCain.

Typically, food service customers sign annual contracts for fries starting in August. The coated-fries business, which includes potato wedges and waffle-shaped and spiral-cut potatoes, represents about 12 percent of the U.S. French fry market.

Source: Reprinted by permission of the *Wall Street Journal,* © 1992 Dow Jones & Company, Inc. All Rights Reserved Worldwide.

today's economy are perfectly competitive. Second, fifty-four of the sixty-seven respondents identified themselves as leading producers of their products in the market. It therefore is likely that many of the thirty-three firms that saw themselves operating in a perfectly competitive market actually were participating in a monopolistically competitive market. Thus, these firms could enjoy far greater freedom in price setting than they believe possible.

PRICE-SETTING THEORY

Several methods of pricing are practiced by business marketers. Three pricing methods discussed here are (1) supply-demand pricing, (2) cost-plus or markup pricing, and (3) break-even pricing. Profit considerations are of paramount importance in all those methods. The methods differ in the emphasis placed on profit and in the importance of the role played by demand conditions. Since price setting in perfect competition requires no price decision by the individual firms (because buyers merely accept the market price), only the other market forms will be examined.

Supply-Demand Pricing

Supply-demand pricing places similar emphasis on both supply and demand factors. In this pricing method, it is assumed that firms are attempting to maximize profits. They accomplish this goal by determining a price where the extra revenue received from selling the last unit of product is equal to the cost of producing it (marginal revenue = marginal cost).

This demand-and-supply relationship implies that any increase in price would reduce both revenue and costs, but that the revenue loss would exceed the reduction in cost. Similarly, if price were reduced, both revenue and cost would increase but the increase in cost would exceed the gain in revenue (see Exhibit 11–2).

This method of pricing is an "ideal" that should be aimed for, but it is difficult to use in practice.[2] The cost of producing and selling additional units of a good or taking on a special job is difficult to ascertain. Even an approximation requires very detailed cost accounting, which is not usually found in small firms (for example, monopolistic competitors). A more important reason for the difficulty that firms have in implementing this method of pricing is due to the uncertainty surrounding the demand for the firm's product. It is difficult enough to forecast the demand for the product of an industry, especially in manufacturing. But forecasting is even more of a problem for a firm that must consider the influence of price on the actions of its rivals and other interested parties (including material suppliers, channel members, and the government), as well as the purchasing plans of its customers.

EXHIBIT 11–2   Supply-Demand Pricing

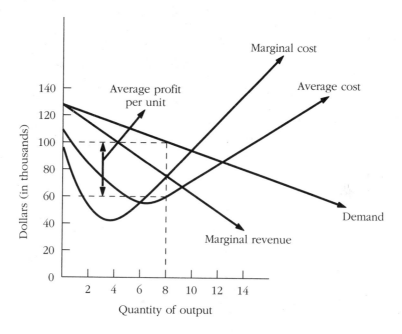

Best Quantity = 8
Best Price = $100

Demand illustrates the amount that can be sold at various prices.
Marginal revenue illustrates the additional revenue that can be obtained by reducing price in an amount necessary to sell each additional unit.
Marginal cost illustrates the cost of producing and selling each additional unit.
Average cost illustrates the per unit cost of producing and selling at various levels of output.

Thus, supply-demand pricing is best suited for a large firm that has the specialized staff necessary to estimate cost and demand relationships. However, it must be recognized that this approach offers little help in attaining long-run goals that are not consistent with short-term profit maximization, and implicitly assumes a homogeneous market with no segmentation strategies being pursued.

Cost-Plus Pricing

In **cost-plus pricing**, firms set prices on the basis of cost plus a "fair" profit percentage. Cost refers to average or per unit cost and may be based on actual, expected, or standard costs. The level of output (expected demand) used in computing cost is usually based on the quantity that is or could be sold at the current price. The profit markup is often set quite arbitrarily. Although many rationales are offered for its level, no one professes to want more than a "fair" profit.

The major objection to cost-plus pricing is that it is based primarily on supply conditions and pays little attention to the demand side of the market. This method of pricing does not attempt to measure the number of units that could be sold at different prices, precluding any possibility of increasing or reducing prices to increase profits. In addition, cost-plus pricing disregards the actions of competitors and places inordinate attention on a firm's historic costs.

The major advantage of this form of pricing is that it is simple. It appeals especially to firms that do very little market research. Many firms believe that cost-plus pricing is the safest method to follow, because attempts to estimate demand are frustrated by volatile buyers' preferences and unpredictable reactions by competitors. Indeed, according to one business pricing executive, "Most everyone uses cost-plus pricing."

Break-Even Pricing

Break-even analysis is often used to illustrate the relationship of costs and revenues to output, but it also can be used as a method of pricing. **Break-even pricing** is similar to cost-plus pricing in that it is primarily supply oriented; however, it does give some weight to demand conditions. Break-even pricing involves estimating a relationship between cost and output, and computing relationships between revenue and output at various prices. The points where the various revenues are equal to the cost are examined, and the firm selects the point that is determined to be the most readily attainable (see Exhibit 11–3).

Many of the criticisms that apply to cost-plus pricing apply to break-even pricing as well. For example, too much emphasis is placed on a firm's historic costs, and not enough importance is attached to forecasting demand. Many consider this pricing approach both crude and conservative.

Pricing Theory in Practice

In the study of manufacturers of industrial goods mentioned earlier, 55 percent of the firms used the cost-plus technique; supply-demand analysis was second in popularity, with 31 percent of firms using it; and 12 percent used break-even analysis. Use of supply-demand pricing increased with the size of the firm. This reflects the fact that large firms have cost accounting and marketing research departments that enable them to employ this more sophisticated and difficult method of pricing. Some firms use different methods of pricing for different products. The most important price-setting factors are production costs, competitors' prices, and marketing costs.

EXHIBIT 11–3   Break-Even Pricing

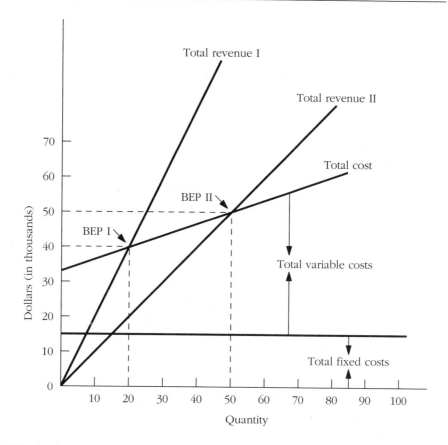

BEP = break-even point

Total cost illustrates the cost of producing at various levels of output.

Total revenue I illustrates the hypothetical revenue that would be obtained from selling various amounts at the higher price.

Total Revenue II illustrates the hypothetical revenue that would be obtained from selling various amounts at the lower price.

BEP I represents the break-even point at the higher price.   Output levels to the right of 20 units illustrate profits, and output levels to the left of 20 units illustrate losses.

BEP II represents the break-even point at the lower price.   Output levels to the right of 50 units illustrate profits, and output levels to the left of 50 units illustrate losses.

Although more than one-third of the companies saw themselves as price leaders (regardless of the pricing method they used), four out of every five firms in the study stated that competition has the final say. That is, after calculating what their price theoretically should be, they adjust their price to meet competitors' prices!

To the extent that this adjustment in price is downward, such behavior negates the value of identifying market structures and of conceptual pricing models. More importantly, it suggests lack of confidence in all of the other attributes of the marketing mix—unique technical product features, industrial design, quality of service, corporate image, and logistical advantages, for example—that the company has striven so intensely to achieve.

Nonetheless, comparing theory-based price with competitors' prices does recognize the dynamics of the market, which must be continuously monitored. And the use of this comparison recognizes that to be customer oriented, the business marketer must be aware that the buyer's perception of price within the context of the marketing mix may not be so readily appealed to by the mechanistic approaches suggested by economic theory.

Pricing Objectives

Because price is a visible aspect of the firm's operations, it should be consistent with the organization's overall goals.[3] A company like IBM, which has spent many years building a corporate image that communicates reliability and quality, will not spoil its reputation by competing on the basis of a low price. Thus, pricing objectives must be established by top management to ensure not only that the company's profitability is adequate, but also that pricing is complementary to the total strategy of the organization.

Among the many pricing objectives that a firm may adopt are pricing to

- achieve rapid cost recovery.
- support corporate imagery.
- achieve a target return on investment.
- maintain stability in industry prices and margins.
- maintain or improve market share (maximizing sales volumes or product adoption throughout the product life cycle).
- match, lead, or follow competitors.
- discourage entry of competitors.
- achieve or complement product differentiation.

Whatever long-range pricing objectives are established by top management, they set the framework within which more specific shorter-run pricing policies can be built.

BUYERS AND PRICE

In business markets, many products tend to be highly standardized, graded, and prespecified. Steel bars can be purchased from any basic steel mill, much like commodities, by a code number indicating carbon content. A one-quarter horsepower motor is designed by all suppliers to meet an agreed-upon industry specification. In such cases, price differentiation is difficult. Furthermore, for most industrial

Bell uses price to entice business subscribers for a customer call-in 800 number.

New 800 ENTRY

For only $25/month, keep in touch with customers, by letting them keep in touch with you.

Now any business can afford an 800 number. Bell's new 800 ENTRY. $25/month subscription fee.

Bell's new 800 ENTRY™ service can give you a big business presence at a fraction of the cost. For only a $25 a month subscription fee you

can have your very own 800 number. There is no minimum monthly usage charge, you pay only for the calls you receive.

This makes it easier for customers to call in orders, suggestions or complaints. And that means better customer service and increased sales.

800 ENTRY is one of a family

of toll-free services that make you more accessible to your customers. Find out more about Bell Canada's toll-free services. Call us.

1-800-565-5100
Long Distance Business Sense.

Bell
Answering your call™

Courtesy of Bell Canada.

purchases, the buyer is already familiar with some product whose price can be used as a reference in evaluating the price of a prospective vendor's product. It is against this "commodity" mentality that the business marketer must contend—using all available means to develop a differential competitive advantage. Only then can pricing be freed from the boundaries imposed by "reference" products.

Value to the Customer

The upper limit set on the supplier's price will be **value**, or **utility**, as perceived by the customer. Utility is the satisfaction obtained through use of a product or service. No wonder, then, that business marketers, after establishing their price on the basis of traditional economic approaches, almost invariably temper that price by a "look over their shoulder" at competitors' prices. Their customers have a fixed perceived value based on the "going market price."

It is not surprising to find little difference in competitive prices when products take on a commodity-like status. Thus, in most purchasing decisions in which the price spread is small, the final choice of vendor's product is generally based on attributes other than price. The typical attributes considered when choosing among suppliers are quality, service, and delivery, followed by price.[4] In evaluating vendors of five medium-cost (about $5) electrical components, fourteen industrial buyers primarily screened vendors on the basis of delivery and quality before requesting quotes.[5] In their final choice of supplier, these buyers first eliminated vendors on the basis of delivery dates and "significantly" higher prices. ("Significant" being in the range of only 5 to 7 percent above the lowest price.)

On the other hand, it is not sufficient for the supplier arbitrarily to build in additional quality in an attempt to hike the price of an industrial product, or even to compete at the same price as a competitor. A 5 percent higher efficiency in a 200 cfm (cubic foot per minute) compressor may not be valued at all by the customer, particularly if other components of the process cannot utilize the increased compressor efficiency. Even if, say, this greater efficiency led to a demonstrable saving in electrical power consumption, it may not be of significance to the customer. The values of the customer are unlikely to match those attributed to the purchaser by the industrial supplier.

Thus, in the traditional view, the upper limit to price is thought to be set by competition. To the extent that business products are viewed with a "commodity" mentality and compete among the same market segments, this will hold true. However, customers will pay more if they think they are getting better value.[6] For example, cable TV companies typically use splicing couplers to join home transmission wires. This eliminates expensive soldering. Installation costs one cent per coupler plus three cents for labor. One company dominated the individual coupler market until a competitor introduced a new line of couplers plus a special tool that could attach as many as sixteen at once. Although the multicoupler tool was expensive, the total installed cost of sixteen couplers was reduced by 28 percent.[7] Thus, the better value induced customers to pay more.

Comm/Scope is not afraid to say its Plenumax is more expensive than the competition.

Courtesy of Shepler/Coda Advertising Agency.

Similarly, the value of aluminum's light weight relative to strength, its ductility (plasticity), and its corrosion resistance make it a unique "skin" material in the production of aircraft. Even at much higher prices than those for which aluminum currently is sold, it would still be in great demand in the airframe market.[8]

In another example, very high-priced titanium pumps for extremely corrosive chemicals are greatly valued in processing plants where long production runs are planned and infrequent downtime for pump repair can be achieved. Whereas under similarly corrosive conditions, where there are frequent changes in the configuration of the manufacturing process, cheaper stainless steel pumps are within the value limit of the buyer, but titanium pumps exceed it.

In the highly competitive trade journal publishing business, rather than trying to deal with media buyers over rates, publishers remain competitive by "sweetening the deal" in the form of merchandising incentives, which provide added value to their advertisers. The incentives include paid focus group studies, direct mail, and editorial support.[9]

The business marketer is customer oriented when he or she can set a price at or below the customer's perceived value or raise the functional value of the offering to the customer beyond the barrier of a high price.

The Customer's View of Price

The business marketer's price is not synonymous with the buyer's cost. It is merely one aspect of cost. From the buyer's viewpoint, the cost of a purchase includes several factors, among them searching costs, transaction costs, start-up costs, postpurchase costs, and life-cycle costs.

Searching Costs.   **Searching costs** involve the expenses incurred in seeking out prospective suppliers. These include locating qualified suppliers, doing credit checks, visiting plants to inspect the supplier's facilities and capabilities, and analyzing the financial and management strength of the supplier. In the case of large purchases, the preparation of specifications, request for tenders, and analysis of bids are also costs. Often, these costs plus buyers' inertia preclude the consideration of potentially valuable new prospective products and suppliers.

Transaction Costs.   **Transaction costs** include the expense of negotiation, insurance, engineering and design, installation charges, and any initial technical training that may be required.

Start-up Costs.   **Start-up costs** may either be paid to a different supplier or be absorbed by the buyer, but are nevertheless expenses incurred by the purchase. The customer's facilities may have to be modified (as in the provision of air conditioning for a computer installation), additional space may be required, or additional power provided. Downtime may be lost during facility modification, product installation, run-in (initial operation) and debugging, or during training.

Postpurchase Costs.   **Postpurchase costs** include continued technical training, maintenance, and repair. It may be necessary to have back-up equipment or facilities. Incremental changes in taxes, interest on capital invested, and depreciation are likely. And operating expenses can change, encompassing such costs as labor, raw materials, inventory carrying costs, scrap rates, energy consumption, and space required by the new product's use. "We're really looking for lower 'total cost of ownership,'" states E. Michael Wood, supply manager, U.S.–area purchasing for Dow Chemical Co. of Midland, Michigan, "that incorporates a vendor's service, maintenance, and delivery."[10]

Life-Cycle Costs.   **Life-cycle costs** include the rate of utilization of the new product, decreasing productivity over time, the product's potential for technological obsolescence, and the expense of disposal. Technological obsolescence has become apparent in the case of computers, and disposal expenses related to chemical by-products of new processes and toxic or radioactive materials are of growing concern.

Large utilities are more likely to buy higher-priced electrical power distribution transformers that offer lower operating costs over their life cycle, whereas local municipalities, concerned with capital expenses and their political ramifications, frequently buy cheaper transformers with higher operating costs, incurring many times the total cost of the former during their life cycle. Such pricing segmentation opportunities abound.

More and more, the buyer's view of new acquisitions encompasses a panoply of factors beyond price, ranging from the total cost evaluation of alternative suppliers to the risk of a strike at the supplier's plant.[11] The customer-oriented business marketer recognizes that in the light of the buyer's extended view of costs, low price alone may not generate the anticipated sales volume. Indeed, a low price offering might be perceived as a high-cost noncontender because of its higher life-cycle costs. Thus, it is imperative to understand how the buyer perceives searching, transaction, start-up, postpurchase, and life-cycle costs relative to the supplier's price.

The strategic implications for industrial pricing based on customers' perceptions of the upper limit of value and the constraint of customer evaluation of costs of purchase are clear: it is important for the business marketer to research the market carefully and set prices within the context of a total marketing strategy.

PRICE SEGMENTATION

Different target markets can be identified based on customers' value expectations. Packaging equipment, for example, might allow a customer to expand into new fields, as in the case of aseptic packaging for milk and juices winning school and institutional restaurant and cafeteria business (due to their lack of refrigerated storage space), or it might extend the customer's market due to lower logistics costs (because refrigerated transport is not required).

Similarly, customers' different cost criteria may permit a seller to use **price segmentation**—that is, to segment markets and appeal to each segment with different prices. These prices correspond to the particular segment's view of price within the framework of its own particular costs.

There are four major ways to segment an industrial market:

1. *Intensity of product usage.* Life-cycle costs of a front-end loader to an eight-hour-a-day heavy user in a mining operation are more important than to a four-hour-a-day light user on a construction site.

2. *Geographical scope of usage.* Postpurchase costs of reliability and downtime are of less concern to a local contractor using earth-moving equipment than to a multinational company operating extensively in the Third World, where maintenance skills, repair service, and replacement parts are not available.

3. *Growth in the customer's business.* Fast-growing customers may be more receptive to cost-cutting new-generation computers, whereas slow-growing customers may be content with their current equipment.

4. *Nature of the application.* A manufacturer of off-highway vehicles, which have the disadvantages of high start-up and life-cycle costs, has a short-haul advantage in high-tonnage, slow-speed applications such as open-pit mining operations, compared to a competitor's vehicles that cost less to operate at cruising speeds under light or moderate loads.[12]

One of the easiest ways to segment a market using pricing is to require that buyers purchase a consumable good used in conjunction with a durable good.[13] IBM leased its early computing equipment with the requirement that they be used only with IBM cards. Rather than selling its equipment, Xerox leased its machines so that the company could require customers to use only the paper supplied by Xerox. Needless to say, the price of supplies in both cases carried a hefty margin. This approach permitted the companies to appeal to market segments that couldn't afford the initial high purchase cost of the durable equipment.

A similar technique is found in industrial strapping. The machine that tightens and locks the metal strapping around a crate is sold at something close to its incremental production cost. Of course, the strapping dimensions are unique to each manufacturer so that no other brand of metal strap can be used with the machine. The supplier's profit comes from the miles and miles of strap that are used in day-to-day operations!

PRICING STRATEGIES

Environmental factors, including the prevailing levels of technology in the industry, customer perceptions, intensity of competition, and barriers to competitive entry, as well as internal factors, such as efficiency of production and the need to recapture research expenditures expeditiously, affect pricing. Three pricing strategies—experience curve pricing; new product pricing, which includes price skimming and market penetration pricing; and product-line pricing—reflect the interplay of these various influences.

Experience Curve Pricing

It is well known that the direct labor hours required to perform a task decrease by a constant percentage as the number of times the task is performed doubles. This phenomenon, which applies across a wide range of industries, is called the *learning curve.* Purchasing agents have applied the concept in contract negotiations, both to encourage suppliers to increase their efficiency and to force them to reduce their prices. The Boston Consulting Group (BCG), working for the electronics and chemical industries, has shown that increases in productivity improvement as a result of learning are not limited to labor alone. Rather, they are quite general and can be found in most industrial activities, including administration, R&D, distribution, manufacturing, and marketing. BCG coined the term *experience curves* to describe this extended concept, showing that prices (in constant dollars) must be reduced as industry experience is accumulated in order to maintain competitive stability. A graphical representation of an experience curve appears in Exhibit 11–4. In **experience curve pricing**, the marketer bases pricing decisions on the product's current or anticipated position along the experience curve. If prices are not reduced in parallel with the inevitable cost reduction, instability develops until competition is attracted, thereby forcing a return to the experience curve. Thus, a high-price policy on the introduction of a new industrial product will have a limited lifetime until competition forces the firm to return to the industry experience curve price for its product. Alternatively, a low-price policy permits a firm to build volume sales, market share, and experience, thereby achieving lower costs than competitors. If all competitors are pricing their product at roughly the same level, then the firm with the most experience likely will achieve the largest market share and profits.

EXHIBIT 11–4   An Experience Curve That Is Plotted on a Linear Scale

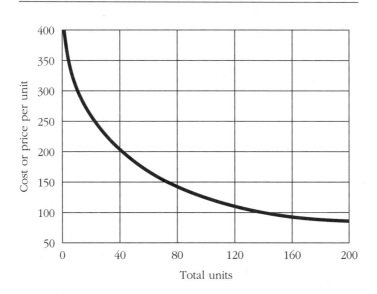

Here we see that as experience (represented by increased quantity of production) increases, costs are reduced.

Different products and different industries follow different experience curves. The experience curve for silicon transistors stabilized on a 77 percent slope. That is, with every doubling of cumulative production, their unit costs dropped by 23 percent. Integrated circuits have maintained a 73 percent slope. When plotted on a log-log scale the cost-volume, or price-volume, slopes produce a straight line (see Exhibit 11–5). The significance of this is that price or cost reductions are predictable.

The existence of the experience effect provides business marketers with an effective planning and pricing tool. Knowledge of a competitor's cumulative experience with a product can give the pricing executive an indication of the competitor's costs. The experience curve for a marketer's own industry can provide goals for cost reduction. Furthermore, comparison of competitors' prices with the price levels predicted by the industry experience curve can explain competitors' pricing behavior and help the business marketer to forecast future pricing actions and reactions.

It should be noted, however, that economies of scale and the experience curve may become less relevant to pricing strategies if manufacturing firms adopt

EXHIBIT 11–5   An Experience Curve That Is Plotted on a Log-Log Scale

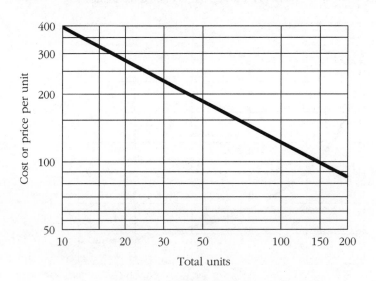

When the production quantities and their costs are plotted on a log-log scale, it can be seen that costs decrease in a constant ratio. This ratio is different for each product.   When this ratio has been identified it can be used to predict future values.

flexible manufacturing systems (FMS) that permit economical production of small lot sizes.

New Product Pricing

It is always difficult to price new products because of the uncertainty associated with their potential for success. Will customers really consider the new product of value? Will customers be willing to experience the disturbance to and possible interruption of their manufacturing operation in order to install a new piece of equipment? Will the prospect be willing to risk new equipment when things are going just fine with the old equipment?

These types of questions make **new product pricing** especially precarious. Thus, it is helpful to know that there are some conditions surrounding the adoption of new products that favor higher introductory prices, whereas other circumstances suggest choosing lower introductory prices. These circumstances or conditions are best illustrated by describing the extreme pricing strategies of price skimming (a very high introductory price) and market penetration (a very low introductory price).[14]

Price Skimming.   In **price skimming** the new product is priced close to the upper limit of value or utility as perceived by the industrial customer. To use such an approach, the following conditions should be present.

1. The buyer is an innovator or early adopter, a risk taker who welcomes new products. The buying company is probably known for its innovative stance.

2. The supplier has a patent or hard-to-copy innovation, such as software that is too difficult or time consuming to reverse-engineer, or a technique, such as the plate-glass manufacturing process, which, although technically easy to understand, requires operational know-how to be workable.

3. Variable costs are a high proportion of total costs. Thus, there are no economies of scale to be achieved. This condition exists in marketing of engineering services.

4. Barriers to competitive entry are high—whether they be financial, marketing, or other types.

5. The usage of the market is limited.

Because of a higher initial per unit profit potential, price skimming permits the business marketer to charge very high prices at the outset to recover heavy R&D and marketing investment costs quickly. But price skimming also acts as an invitation to competitors, so that eventually the marketer will have to reduce price to the experience curve norm. With careful monitoring of competitors' activities, this strategy can maximize profits over the product life cycle through price reductions that anticipate and may effectively prevent competitors' market entry.

Market Penetration.   In **market penetrating pricing**, the business marketer recognizes the following conditions.

1. With heavy fixed costs and low variable costs, the key to profitability is building sales volume and economies of scale quickly.

2. Many close substitutes are available; thus, a low price discourages competitive entry.

3. In this market, the customers are very conservative and traditional, and are unwilling to take risks.

4. The product is easy to copy and there are few barriers to entry by the company's competitors.

5. The market exhibits a high price elasticity of demand.

6. The size of the potential market justifies the risk of an extended period during which fixed costs must be recaptured.

A market penetration pricing strategy helps a company build a large share of the market quickly, with the resulting experience effect providing substantial cost advantages compared to competitors.

Product-Line Pricing

Most firms sell a range of products within each product line. These products are related to one another, marketed together, used together, and provide variations on the same general benefits required by the customer. Thus, **product line pricing** takes into account, on the demand side, the segments to which these products and services appeal and their impact on each other (complementarity and substitutability) and, on the cost side, their interactions with one another (joint costs, bundling possibilities, cannibalization).

The price of the entire line can support the image the company wishes to project. Westinghouse refused to put its corporate name on a fighting brand when its market for vacuum tubes was threatened by low-price Japanese imports. Alternatively, the low-end price in the product line might be used to attract marginal buyers and build total volume.

When a complementary relationship exists within the product line, the demand for one product may be enhanced by a lower price on another, as in the case of metal strapping mentioned earlier. The sale of medical testing equipment to hospital laboratories generates continuing business in the supplies used with it. And the sale of a crawler tractor generates a continuing demand for its fast-wearing metal treads as well as uniquely fitting accessories and repair parts. When pricing product lines, the business marketing manager must be aware that the sale of one item in the line may be influenced by, and may influence, the sale of other items in the line.

HOW IMPORTANT IS PRICE TO THE BUYER?

Despite many studies that rank price from first to sixth place in importance relative to other variables in the marketing mix,[15] a more realistic and practical viewpoint recognizes that the importance of price varies from situation to situation:

1. At certain times, price may be the single most important aspect of the marketing mix in winning an industrial sale.

2. At other times, price may weigh equally in importance with other variables in the business marketing mix.

3. At certain times, such as when a chemical processing operation will have to be shut down if the necessary raw material, product, or service is not received in time, price may be of little consequence.

Exhibit 11–6 lists the four most important factors in four different buying situations. Again, it is evident that the importance of price varies widely. Furthermore, when decision influencers from various departments of the organization (such as engineering, finance, or production) are involved, price will be viewed differently by each individual when evaluating a purchase.

EXHIBIT 11–6   Importance of Various Factors in Different Buying Situations

Buying Situation	*Four Most Important Factors*
A. Frequently ordered product; no significant problems in use	1. reliability of delivery 2. price 3. flexibility 4. reputation
B. Product training required	1. technical service 2. ease of use 3. training offered 4. reliability of delivery
C. Doubts about product performance in a particular application	1. reliability of delivery 2. flexibility 3. technical service 4. product reliability data
D. Difficulty in reaching agreement among all concerned	1. price 2. reputation 3. product reliability data 4. reliability of delivery

Source: Lehman, Donald R. and O'Shaughnessy, John, "Difference in Attribute Importance for Different Industrial Products," *Journal of Marketing,* Vol. 38 (April 1974), pp. 36–42. Reprinted with permission of the American Marketing Association.

Some general propositions will be helpful, then, in assessing the importance of price to the buyer in a given situation:[16]

Price tends to be more important when

1. the item is offered for the first time (new task);
2. the company needs to raise prices (thereby initiating a modified rebuy);
3. competitors reduce price (and try to win away the company's customers);
4. the buyer supplies a government agency that has a cost-of-purchase orientation;
5. decision influencers in the buying firm have difficulty in agreeing.

Price tends to be less important when

1. the item is bought on a regular basis (straight rebuy);
2. the seller has a high/unique reputation and the risk, cost, or difficulty created by product failure is high;
3. the cost of the item is insignificant relative to the buyer's budget;
4. the purchase represents an overhead or indirect cost to the buyer;
5. a governmental customer's budget has not yet been appropriated;
6. product training is required;
7. there is uncertainty about a product performing satisfactorily.

TYPES OF PRICES

There are many ways that prices can be stated. The following are some of the most common pricing approaches and the tactics associated with them.

List Prices

Typically in the business market, product catalogs contain no prices. This permits the production of large quantities of promotional materials—often expensive ones on high-quality stock with four-color reproduction—with no fear of wastage due to changes in prices. These catalogs are distributed to different classes of customer accounts and intermediaries. Price lists on single sheets can then be distributed to the various intermediaries or customers and can be revised from time to time, at little expense. For large companies handling many products and parts, the price list may be in the form of a book or a looseleaf binder with updates involving replacement of a few pages.

The prices in a price list are rarely those paid by customers. Rather, **list prices** form the starting point for calculation of a net price. Net price is a list price minus one or more discounts. Such discounts can be changed as frequently as required without the expense of printing a new set of list prices. The list prices can help a supplier camouflage price changes from competitors. List prices are also a useful guide to engineers and buyers who are estimating "ballpark" figures for proposals and in preparation of tenders.

Net Prices

The **net price** is, of course, the key price in the decision whether or not to buy. In arriving at the net price many types of discounts can be applied to the list price.

Trade Discounts.   **Trade discounts** are reductions from list price that are given to different groups of intermediaries or customers according to the range of functions they perform (stocking, advertising), the type of market to which they sell (OEM, retailers), and the volumes in which they purchase. A manufacturer of electrical lamps selling through three classes of domestic intermediaries, to overseas distributors, and directly to OEMs and government agencies might have the type of trade discount structure shown in Exhibit 11–7.

Trade discounts can be used as a competitive weapon. In most industries there is an accepted norm for the discounts offered to intermediaries. A business marketer selling through a distributor must recognize that competition includes not only similar products offered by other manufacturers but also quite dissimilar lines of items that are competing for the distributor's time and attention. Thus, the marketer may increase discounts to motivate the distributor to devote more effort on behalf of the manufacturer's product.

Cash Discounts.   **Cash discounts** offer the buyer an incentive to pay a slightly lower price within a short period of being invoiced. A typical payment term would

EXHIBIT 11–7   Typical Trade Discounts

Class of Customer	List Price Less a Discount of
Industrial distributor	15%
Manufacturer's agent	20
Wholesaler selling to retail accounts	10
Overseas distributors—hard currency markets	30
—others	25
OEM accounts	35
Government accounts	40

be 2/10 net 30, meaning that if the invoice is paid within ten days, an additional 2 percent can be deducted from the price. Beyond the ten days, the payment is the net price shown on the invoice. Usually a penalty of, say, 18 percent interest is charged on bills outstanding longer than 30 days. The cash discount encourages rapid payment and improves the seller's cash flow position. However, it becomes a problem when the customer is large and has a slow payment-authorization procedure. The customer may take the cash discount even though payment stretches significantly beyond the ten-day limit.

Cash discounts can be an important part of the marketer's pricing strategy. In the pharmaceutical industry, they are considered as important as stock replenishment frequency and even more important than lead time, consistency of lead time, and order placement policy.[17] Indeed, business marketers could segment their markets by offering an array of alternative cash discount terms so that the buyer could choose which one is best for the buying firm.[18] Such an innovative pricing approach might offer terms of, say, 2/10, 1.7/15, 1.3/20, 0.8/25, and net 30. Thus, a $1,000 purchase could be paid for with $980 at day 10, $983 at day 15, $987 at day 20, $992 at day 25, and $1,000 at day 30.

Quantity Discounts.   **Quantity discounts** encourage the customer to order in larger quantities. Volume price breaks are established, such as those in Exhibit 11–8.

The break points might represent savings the supplier can achieve in order processing, palletizing, or transportation. For example, a carload quantity is cheaper to ship than a less-than-carload (LCL) amount. A customer-oriented supplier might establish break points with such considerations in mind as the buyer's authorized dollar expenditure limits or annual usage rate.

Quantity discounts may be noncumulative or cumulative. **Noncumulative discounts** apply only to the quantity purchased on an invoice, on an order-by-order basis. **Cumulative discounts** take into account the volume (measured either in units or dollars) that has been purchased since the beginning of the current discount period. When the current order exceeds a break point, a larger discount is applied to the invoice.

The **rebate system** is similar to a cumulative quantity discount with the exception that no reduction is made on individually invoiced orders. Rather, a rebate

EXHIBIT 11–8   A Typical Quantity Discount Structure

Volume Purchased	Quantity Discount
Less than 100 units	0
101–300 units	2%
301–500 units	3.5%
501–1,000 units	4.5%
More than 1,000 units	5.25%

check is issued to the customer at the end of the rebate period, based on the total volume purchased during that period. In the rebate case, a procedure for updating the customer about the firm's current cumulative purchase status on a regular basis throughout the rebate period can provide an extra stimulus for additional sales.

Geographic Pricing

The geographical location at which a price is applied can be a competitive pricing technique. **Geographic pricing** means that the price may be quoted at the factory door, at the customer's receiving dock, or at some other location. The choice of which location to specify depends on the location of the competitors' plants, the bulk and density of the product, location of key customer accounts, industry norms, general competitive conditions, and the proportion of total price that transportation costs contribute.

FOB Factory.   FOB stands for "free on board." When goods are shipped **FOB factory**, the buyer pays the invoice price plus the cost of freight. This form of pricing is customer oriented in that the customer can choose which carrier will handle transportation of the goods. The choice may allow the purchaser to obtain a better freight cost than the supplier by consolidating shipments or by negotiating freight rates. The buyer may also choose among various transport modes to obtain the lowest freight charge (for example, rail may be cheaper than truck) or to obtain faster delivery (for example, courier or air freight). A logistically aware customer may make arrangements to utilize the buying firm's empty back-hauls.

FOB Destination.   The **FOB destination** pricing technique means that the supplier assumes the cost of freight (although this cost is built into the supplier's invoiced price). This frees the buyer from expediting arrangements, as the supplier handles all transportation arrangements.

Freight Equalization.   With **freight equalization**, the supplier assumes a portion of the cost of freight and charges only the remaining portion to the customer. The amount absorbed by the supplier depends on the distance between the seller's factory and the location at which freight is equalized. For example, because carbon electrodes used in electric melting of steel are made by only a few manufacturers and are extremely dense (therefore expensive to transport), manufacturers would not be able to compete beyond their local areas if they calculated delivered price based solely on transportation costs. Hence, they calculate delivered prices based on the transportation cost from the supplier's factory location nearest to the customer, whether it is their own or a competitor's.

CIF.   CIF stands for "customs, insurance, and freight" and is the most commonly used pricing format for international shipments. The **CIF price** includes FOB factory price plus all domestic inland charges and all ocean (or air) transportation and ancillary costs. The total of these costs is called the C&F (cost and freight) value. To the C&F value is added an all-risk insurance premium covering 110 percent of the C&F value, to arrive at the CIF price. This price is always quoted at the port of destination (for example, CIF Hamburg). Shipment from the dock or airport to the customer's plant is the buyer's responsibility.

LEASING IN INDUSTRIAL PRICING

Thus far, the pricing decision has centered on the sale of the product or service. It is important to recognize that a very powerful marketing alternative to outright sale exists—the lease. Roughly 27 percent[19] of all private-sector investment in equipment is financed through leasing in the United States, and about 10 percent in Europe and 5 percent in Japan.[20] Eighty percent of U.S. corporations[21] and 60 percent of U.K. companies[22] lease assets each year. Exhibit 11–9 shows that the trend toward leasing by business is growing. Worldwide, leases have increased in value more than sixfold since 1979.[23] Leasing has become a very important technique in marketing industrial equipment, ranging from batteries for forklift trucks to an entire $111 million aluminum reduction mill.[24]

A **lease** is a contract through which the owner of the equipment, in return for a periodic rental payment, allows the lessee to use the equipment. There are two types of leases. **Financial** (or full-payout) **leases** are intermediate to long-term, noncancelable contracts and are fully amortized during the term. The lessee pays operating expenses and assumes all liabilities for the equipment (production machinery). At the end of the term the lessee usually has the option to buy the equipment. **Operating leases** are short-term cancelable contracts that are not fully amortized. The lessor usually assumes expenses and liabilities of ownership, and a purchase option typically is not available to the lessee (trencher backhoe).

EXHIBIT 11–9   New Leasing Business Worldwide (billions of US$)

Region	1979	1980	1985	1990
North America	33.9	37.7	80.8	125.4
Europe	9.5	13.2	24.7	117.9
Asia	5.5	6.3	25.9	77.5
Australia/N.Z.	3.6	4.4	3.9	5.1
Africa	—	0.5	1.2	3.8
Latin America	—	1.5	1.6	1.9
Total:	53.0	63.6	138.1	331.7

Sources: T. M. Clark, Chief Executive, Mercantile Group Plc., Basingstoke, England; T. M. Clark, ed., *Leasing Finance*, 2nd ed. (London: Euromoney Books, 1991), p. 4; David J. Porter, "Leasing—Fighting for Funding in Recessionary Times," in *World Leasing Yearbook* (London: Euromoney Books, 1992), p. 2.

Economic benefits to the lessee include avoiding the cash purchase cost of the asset and concurrent financing arrangements, improved cash flows, more available working capital, protection from capital equipment obsolescence, and a better-looking balance sheet. Other advantages to the lessee include the ability to enjoy total deductibility of costs, no dilution of ownership or control, ability to finance small acquisitions, smaller after-tax cost compared to equity, investment tax credits for companies with low earnings or heavily sheltered earnings, and a greater tax shield than depreciation or interest.[25]

To facilitate customers' use of its products, an industrial manufacturer can act as lessor itself, forming a credit subsidiary to provide leasing (as has been done by J I Case and John Deere for farm equipment and Borg-Warner and Gould for pumps), negotiating the lease through a bank, or leasing products through a leasing company (such as U.S. Industrial Tools or General Finance Corporation).

Why should the business marketer become involved in the complicated process of leasing? There are several reasons. Leasing can expand the company's market to segments that otherwise might not be able to afford to buy the firm's products. A potential customer unable to invest $15,000 in a new forklift truck might be quite capable of affording to lease one at $300 a month. It also helps the marketer appeal to potential customers who have avoided outright purchase because of the risks associated with obsolescence or style change, incorrect selection of equipment, maintenance, and sporadic use.[26] The add-on of a service contract can keep the supplier in continuous contact with the customer, building preference toward the supplier's total product line and increasing the potential for future leases and purchases from the supplier.

In terms of pricing strategy, the business marketer can set the lease rate and the purchase price so that either alternative will generate the same return to his or her company. The marketer may use low lease rate pricing to encourage more customers to lease, thus binding lessees to the company's product line, generating closer contact between the sales force and the lessee, increasing sales of the company's other products, encouraging the lessee to trade up within the lessor's product line as the lessee's firm grows, and perhaps allowing the lessee to apply part of the lease payments toward purchase of newer or more expensive equipment. A method for segmenting markets through price breaks on leasing and payment schedules has been developed to help the lessor maximize profits.[27]

A danger in pursuing a leasing strategy is that business salespeople are usually specialists in the technical features rather than the financial aspects of their offerings. Thus, it might be more profitable for larger business marketers to create a financial specialist position in the sales organization.[28] Xerox Corporation, for example, has a consulting service representative (CSR), a marketing financial analyst who works with the customer's financial group in larger multiple-installation accounts to analyze the economic aspects of lease and rental options. Also at Xerox, a sold equipment representative (SER) aids customers who prefer purchase rather than leasing arrangements, providing assistance in analyzing the financial aspects of both installment purchase and outright purchase.

The pricing alternatives in outright sales of goods, installment payment for purchases, and leasing arrangements are extremely complex. Such strategies as those of Xerox recognize the quandary of the customer and creatively combine pricing with innovations in their total marketing strategy.

Pricing is no longer a technical problem that can be solved by applying a rule or even a complex mathematical procedure. It is a challenge to the creativity of the business marketer, who must use innovative approaches combined with insight into buyers' motivations.

COMPETITIVE BIDDING

A very large proportion of business transactions is brought about by the process of **competitive bidding**. This refers to situations where the buyer asks two or more competing suppliers to submit bid prices and associated data on a proposed purchase or contract. After evaluating the bids, the buyer decides which offer best meets the firm's needs and places the order. "Best" varies from buyer to buyer as each weighs offsetting advantages and disadvantages of prospective bidders' prices, delivery time promises, reputation for quality, past performance, and other factors. Competitive bidding is most frequently used when adequate specifications describing the item are available, competition is adequate (enough qualifying potential suppliers), the size of the proposed purchase is sufficient to create competitive interest, and sufficient time is available for carrying out competitive bidding procedures.[29]

The main reason for the buyer to use competitive bidding is to obtain the most reasonable prices. For example, when Robert McNamara was U.S. secretary of defense, he instituted competitive bidding to replace single sourcing, reducing ordinance purchase prices by roughly one-quarter. An example of the competitive bids quoted to McMaster University's Physical Education Department for the purchase of a whirlpool bath and valves (Exhibit 11–10) illustrates the typical range of prices.

Price reduction is not the only reason for seeking competitive bids, however. Other reasons include the following:

- Institutions spending public funds cannot be accused of collusion with suppliers to "rig" purchase price.

- The temptation for a supplier to illicitly influence the purchasing official is eliminated.

EXHIBIT 11–10   Competitive Bids for a Whirlpool Installation

Supplier:	A	B	C	D	E
Price:	$1,365	$1,200	$1,114	$952	$941

Source: Purchasing Department, McMaster University, Hamilton, Ontario.

- By cost minimization, the purchaser can increase the buying organization's profits.

- In a "straight rebuy" situation, competitive bids can be used as a check to ensure that the "in-supplier" is still charging a reasonable price.

- Price information can be obtained in the "new task" purchase situation, where there are no known norms for prices.

- The buyer can assess the range of prices in a market.

- The buyer can learn from whom and under what conditions lowest price is provided.

- The buyer can choose among various alternatives when design and manufacturing methods for complex equipment vary considerably.

- When the buyer doesn't want to repeat the entire purchasing process on each reorder of fabricated parts or materials but still wants some price leverage, competitive bidding can be used for, say, a year's requirements in a term contract purchase.

Since there are more reasons for conducting competitive bidding than price alone, the lowest price does not necessarily guarantee that a bidder will be awarded the contract. Indeed, it is a practice in some firms when evaluating the bid offers to eliminate the highest and the lowest bidder from consideration prior to beginning thorough bid evaluation. This eliminates bidders who (at the high end) may not really want the business anyway and who (at the low end) may have made an error in their submission.

There are three forms of competitive bidding procedures, ranging from the loosest or the least formal to the most formalized: informal bidding, open bidding, and closed bidding.

Informal Bidding

In **informal bidding**, the buyer may ask several salespeople to stop by the office. They are shown the requirements of the purchase, which they take away and use to estimate their price. If the job is simple enough, the buyer may describe its requirements to suppliers by telephone. The salespeople then telephone their price to the buyer and subsequently submit their quotation by mail. The buyer already may have awarded the job to one of them before the mail delivery of quotes arrives. This process is typical in printing of catalogs and other relatively uncomplicated purchases of no more than a few thousand dollars.

Open Bidding

In **open bidding**, a somewhat more formal process is followed. Specifications are drawn up, suppliers are contacted, and a final date for written tender submission is established. However, when an offer is received before the final date, the buyer is free to examine it, discuss it with the supplier, and even suggest changes and resubmission before the final due date. The danger in open bidding is that the contents of one supplier's proposal may be divulged to competing suppliers, as in: "If you can just shave another $350 off your quote, I'll be able to give you the job. Yes, that's how much Acme Fasteners' price was below yours." Or, "Gee Charlie, Apex Company came up with a great idea in their bid that cut the cost of this job by 10 percent. Here's what they did.... Can you match that?" Such disclosure of competitors' quotes is unethical and should be avoided.

Closed Bidding

In **closed bidding**, the supplier submits a written proposal in a sealed envelope by a specified deadline. Late submissions are not accepted. At a preset time and location all bids are opened and examined. Thus, there is no opportunity for their contents to be revealed to anyone before the bid-opening ceremony. Often this occasion is an open public meeting to which all bidders have been invited. Typically in this situation the supplier who wins the contract is the lowest "responsible bidder"—that is, the one whose bid meets all specifications.

Formal Bidding Procedures

Most private organizations and government agencies maintain a record of acceptable vendors, generally based on past dealings. They have been qualified on the basis of product quality, service and guarantee policies, prices, technical capability, overall reputation, and other criteria. It is most important for the potential supplier's organization to qualify for and get on the approved list if the marketer wishes to receive invitations to tender bids.

From this list, the buyer will select some or all of the vendors that match the firm's needs and send them a **request for quotation (RFQ)**, which is also called a **request for proposal (RFP)** or an **invitation to bid**. This form states all the requirements of the project, including specifications, quantity, weights, shipping specifications, terms and conditions of purchase, and date for formal opening of bids.

In proposals for building contracts and large projects, especially for governments, the bidder may be required to furnish a bid bond or certified check (say, 10 percent of the bid price) as a guarantee of good faith, and sometimes a labor and material performance bond (as much as 50 percent of the bid price), and insurance certificates. These protect the buyer from failure to complete the job and from lien claims against labor and materials. Since the bid is a legal offer, if accepted it becomes a legally binding contract.

Bidding Strategy

Competitive bidding is a costly process. It involves a great deal of marketing research to assess the customer's unwritten preferences and requirements (as well as those explicitly stated in the RFP). The potential for follow-on business must be assessed. Research is required to determine who the competitors on the bid are likely to be, including their performance on previous bids, their current plant utilization, and their expected bid price. Environmental appraisals are necessary to determine how current labor, economic, political, and financial conditions will influence the bid and the company's ability to fulfill its requirements throughout the duration of the contract. For these reasons, the development of a proposal resembles the process of preparing a carefully developed business plan.

Bidding Objectives

Objectives governing the development of bids should be established. Some of these will be derived from overall pricing objectives, whereas some will be specific to bidding. For example: Does the company wish to maintain its presence as a prospective supplier, even when the shop is working to capacity? If so, then it will be necessary to continue bidding on new jobs even though there is no intention to win the contracts. Thus, a high bid price would be indicated. Alternatively, to keep the shop fully utilized, it might be necessary to submit "low ball" prices on bids from time to time. Other objectives might include being uniformly competitive in all the company's markets, maintaining price stability, and using price to help maintain a particular corporate image. Part of the development of the proposal also will involve assessing the objectives of all competitors who are likely to bid.

Organizing for Bidding

The firm should be organized to bid effectively. The cost of preparing a bid is directly proportional to the job's total cost. Hence, a substantial budget should be allocated to support bid preparation. (In some cases, such as bidding on architectural design work, the customer will provide funds to cover proposal costs of a limited number of bidders.) Usually a **multiple buying influence (MBI)** is involved in developing the buyer's request for proposal. If the business marketer learns the "who's who" of the MBI early enough, valuable information can be provided to those people in the customer firm to help them design the specifications. It is common for an astute marketer to help the buyer write specifications that will qualify the marketer's own products and exclude those of competitors. At the same time, the marketer acquires greater insight into both the customer's "hard" (specified) and "soft" (or unstated) needs, and also builds some creeping commitment toward his or her firm in the process.

A significant organizational fault among contracting firms in civil engineering, building, and construction engineering is the employment of too few people as estimators.[30] The number of estimators can be as important to the bidding firm as the number of salespeople to a company selling goods at standard prices. In bidding, the higher the markup over costs, the greater the potential profit but the less the probability of success in winning the bid. To maintain shop volume, many companies choose to bid a low price at least occasionally. Thus, they may not maximize their profit. To optimize profits, it pays to increase the number of estimators and bid at a higher markup, as long as marginal estimating and sales costs of additional bids are more than offset. A study of six firms' actual and optimal numbers of estimators summarized in Exhibit 11–11 demonstrates this point. It can be seen that, grouped together, these six firms, by hiring a bit more than twice as many estimators, and incurring two and a third more estimating and selling costs, even with half the chance of winning bids at a higher markup, would earn an average of 58 percent more profit.

Last, an important organizational aspect is the assignment of people to follow up after the contract has been awarded to a competitor to find out why the job was lost. This provides valuable input about both the customer's priorities and the competitors' behavior, which can be used in preparation of future bidding proposals. IBM has formalized this process, holding monthly "joint loss reviews" (lost account discussions) with regional and branch personnel to analyze why business was lost and what corrective action can be taken.[31]

Bidding to Win Follow-on Contracts

Special pricing strategies may be implemented in situations where equipment contracts are large, component parts for the equipment are expected to be ordered

EXHIBIT 11–11   Analysis of Estimator Usage in Bidding

Total Number of Estimators		Total Volume of Bidding ($ million)	Average of 6 Mean Markups	Average of 6 Mean Success Probabilities	Total Estimating and Sales Costs ($ million)	Total Profits Expected After Estimated Sales Costs ($ million)
Actual	215	2,449	8.0	0.165	6.45	21.01
Optimal	434	5,322	12.7	0.085	15.10	33.20

Source: From "The Number of Estimators: A Critical Decision for Marketing Under Competitive Bidding," by Kenneth Simmonds and Stuart Slatter from *Journal of Marketing Research*, vol. 15 (May 1978). Reprinted by permission of the American Marketing Association.

for several years, some customization is required, and there is the chance of a follow-on contract. A **follow-on contract** is a repeat order from the customer. For example, if an injection molder wins the contract on the dies and the first run of a product, this firm has an excellent opportunity to obtain further runs, particularly if the molder retains possession of the dies.

The pricing strategy in such a situation might dictate sacrificing some profit with a low bid on the first contract in the expectation of winning follow-on business with a higher bid and a corresponding higher profitability in subsequent contracts. Determining the best combination of prices for the initial bid and the follow-on bid can be quite difficult.

Negotiation

After a competitive bidding process has resulted in a firm being awarded a contract, the buyer may decide to change the specifications or integrate some newly developed technology into the equipment. In other situations the job may be so complex, and have so many alternative solutions, that bidding is not feasible. Or it may take such a long time to complete that neither buyer nor seller can be sure of the amount or type of work involved.

In such an instance, price is arrived at through **negotiation**: the buyer and chosen supplier spend considerable time together working over the details of the job and eventually arrive at a mutually agreeable pricing arrangement. In one example of this, an African nation contracted a North American supplier to install a turnkey power distribution system in the country. Two years after work on the project had begun, negotiations were still under way!

In negotiation, any aspect of the marketing mix may be "up for grabs." Thus, the marketing manager must be thoroughly prepared and have not only technical information and costs but also negotiating skills, knowing when to concede an issue and when to draw the line.

PRICING UNCERTAINTY

At all times there is some degree of uncertainty in the determination of prices, especially the uncertainty of demand. However, this is a risk the entrepreneur accepts. A more troublesome risk is uncertainty about the availability of resources and their costs.

Until this point, our discussion of pricing has tacitly assumed that the labor, materials, and component supplies that are required to produce industrial goods and provide business services were available in adequate quantities and could be purchased at relatively stable prices. Thus, prices could be set and contracts could be bid for or negotiated with some confidence that the principal problems would center on customer and competitive reactions. Increasingly, however, this is not the case:

■ Westinghouse Large Power Transformer Division lost millions of dollars on an order that had been contracted two years earlier. At that time the fixed price contract had been estimated using an annual inflation factor of 6 percent for both materials and labor. By the time the transformer equipment was delivered, materials (which accounted for more than one-third of the quoted price) had skyrocketed by 435 percent.[32]

■ Electrical capacitor manufacturers flinched as the price of tantalum powder increased 300 percent in a twelve-month period.[33]

■ Manufacturers of high-tech electronic components have faced periodic production-stopping shortages of microprocessors.

All such instances affect costs, and thus the company's vulnerability in publishing firm prices and quoting on contracts. The following are some of the alternatives in dealing with these uncertainties:

■ Building and holding costly inventories of the items that might be affected.

■ Hedging, by buying futures on commodity exchanges.

■ Backward integration toward the source of supply (purchasing supplier firms).

■ Materials substitution. One manufacturer now uses tin alloy plating rather than gold plating for electrical terminals.[34]

■ Elimination of low margin products.

■ Investing in R&D. One manufacturer developed a new process to spot gold accurately on electrical contact points rather than spreading it.[35]

■ Unbundling of services. Manufacturers are increasingly charging for services separately rather than building them into product costs.

■ Writing fixed-price contracts valid for a limited time.

■ Delaying submission of quotations until the last minute.

■ Selling on a price-in-effect-at-time-of-shipment (PETS) basis. In a study of 153 purchasing agents, half of them stated that 80 percent or more of their vendors were selling on a PETS basis.[36]

■ Quoting on individual orders rather than publishing a price list.

■ Setting prices in anticipation of future costs.

■ Quoting current prices but including an escalator clause, which allows the buyer to compare base-prices among competitors. The escalator clause ties specific costs to a widely available published government or industry association index. If the index rises, then the prespecified portion of costs in the original price that was quoted is increased proportionately. (See the Business Marketing in practice box "Price Escalation—Coping with Cost Inflation.")

BUSINESS MARKETING IN PRACTICE ▰▰▰▰▰▰▰▰

Price Escalation—Coping with Cost Inflation

Because they are faced with lengthy bid and contract periods more often than their consumer goods counterparts, business marketers must be especially aware of the methods used to counter cost inflation. One method is to "firm" the bid price. That is, an allowance, or cushion, is built into the price to cover anticipated cost increases. Given the hazards of forecasting, this method can lead on the one hand to the marketer still having to absorb increased costs or on the other to the customer paying too much.

There is another method—one that is fairer to both marketer and customer. It boosts the marketer's price only after the marketer's costs are proved to have increased, and in proportion to the actual increase. That method is price escalation. In price escalation, the original contract price is increased in accordance with cost indexes published by objective third parties. Thus, the indexes are equally available to both marketer and customer and are influenced by neither.

Steam generators are a product class to which the method often is applied. The bid period for steam generators can exceed six months, and the ensuing contract period, two years. A major manufacturer of such equipment is Babcock & Wilcox, located in Cambridge, Ontario, Canada. Ian Anderson, Babcock's vice president, marketing and sales, describes the terms of a recent contract that provides for the base price of a large (600 megawatt) steam generator to be escalated as follows:

■   50 percent in accordance with a cost index for steel, the dominant material in steam generators. Although the steam generator is for a foreign customer, the index being used is published in Statistics Canada *Catalogue 62-011,* because the steel will be purchased in Canada.

■   40 percent in accordance with a labor cost index for the metal fabricating industry in the province of Ontario, where the shop work actually will be done (published in Statistics Canada *Catalogue 72-002*).

Anderson points out two practical considerations regarding price escalation. First is customer resistance. For policy or budgeting reasons, some customers want to know, *before* they award a contract, the exact number of dollars that they will have to pay. They will not only resist the marketer who proposes price escalation but also attempt to estimate the potential supplier's future price, using the marketer's own formula for the purpose. This estimated price is then used, in comparison with other suppliers' prices, to determine who gets the job. If the customer's inflation assumptions are higher than those of another supplier who did offer a firm price, the organization proposing escalation is put at a price disadvantage. As always, the marketer must know the customer! The second consideration is administration costs. The *administration* of a contract with complex escalation formulas is time consuming. As a result, both the marketer's and the customer's costs are increased.

Contributed by Terry Seawright, a business marketing lecturer and consultant in the Toronto, Canada, area.

■ Issuing new price lists or circulating surcharge notices as costs change.

■ Maintaining prices but reallocating scarce resources. Here, the volume of various products in the line will be adjusted to optimize total profits.

PRICING FOR EXPORT

Exportation of products offers new markets to previously domestically oriented firms. One advantage business marketers have over consumer marketers in exporting is that foreign customers' product evaluations are far more economically oriented and less subject to cultural peculiarities that may hinder market acceptance. A four-nation study by three coauthors of this text showed that the similarities in purchasing influences are quite strong.[37]

But the differences still exist! In pricing, however, they are not so serious. It is generally advisable to quote prices CIF the buyer's country in the foreign country's own currency, though this poses risks. Rolls Royce in the United Kingdom was stung to the extent of $66 million on jet engine export contracts that had been quoted in U.S. dollars. The pound sterling strengthened, and the dollar weakened in international currency markets.[38] The safest approach in selling export is to lock in the price quoted by short selling the foreign currency for the amount and date that the payment will be received.[39]

Unless export sales represent a large proportion of the firm's business, or the production facilities are strained, any revenue over the marginal costs of production and export will provide a contribution to overhead. Consequently, the business marketer has a wide range of flexibility in setting export prices.

SUMMARY

Knowledge of the forms of market structure—perfect competition, monopolistic competition, oligopoly, oligopsony, and monopoly—is helpful in understanding competitive pricing behavior. The traditional "economics" approaches of supply-demand pricing, cost-plus pricing, and break-even pricing provide further insight but have numerous limitations.

In practice, companies set pricing objectives that follow from and complement the total corporate strategy and objectives of the organization. Price objectives may seek to achieve other goals than simple profit maximization. From pricing objectives, shorter-run pricing policies are derived.

Despite a high degree of standardization in many business products, business marketers attempt to avoid commodity-like pricing by seeking nonprice differential advantages relative to their competitors. If successful, they are able to sell their offering at prices higher than their competitors'. The upper limit on price now becomes the customer's perception of value. Similarly, the marketer's costs become irrelevant to price determination (as long as they are recovered).

The customer's perception of value includes not only the price charged by the supplier, but also the buyer's searching costs, transaction costs, start-up costs, post-purchase costs, and life-cycle costs. Since perceptions of value can vary from one buyer to the next, it is possible to segment markets using different prices to appeal to different segments. Where purchase price and buyer's costs are important, four ways to segment business markets are according to intensity of product usage, geographical scope of usage, growth in customer's business, and nature of product or service application. Price segmentation can be used to improve profits significantly.

Three significant pricing strategies in business markets are (1) experience curve pricing, (2) price skimming and market penetration pricing for new products, and (3) product-line pricing. Experience curves are helpful in understanding competitors' pricing behavior, in setting cost-reduction goals and prices, and in forecasting future pricing actions.

Price skimming and market penetration are extreme high and low pricing strategies for new products. Conditions necessary for their implementation provide guidelines for setting new product or service prices. How much toward one or the other extreme the marketer should go can be determined through marketing research and by assessing how important price is to the customer.

When pricing product lines, the business marketer should be aware that the sale of one item in the line may influence and be influenced by the sale of other items in the line. Product-line pricing recognizes and takes into account the interactions of joint costs, bundling, cannibalization, and how product-line pricing affects segmentation.

The customers' perceptions are of greatest significance to the firm's ability to sell the product. The business marketer should recognize that the importance of price in the buyer's deliberations varies widely from situation to situation, and from one to the next member of the multiple buying influence (MBI).

Prices can be expressed as list price, net price, or a price that applies to a certain place of origin, geographic region, or destination.

An alternative to outright sale is leasing. This approach can expand the business marketer's sales into market segments where potential customers can't afford the high initial cost of outright purchase.

Another pricing approach is competitive bidding, where the buyer invites competing suppliers to submit prices on a specified contract. There are three types of competitive bids: informal bids, open bids, and closed bids. The latter two types follow formal routines. Competitive bidding can be costly to the marketer, who should have clear bidding objectives, taking into account what competitors' objectives may be. In addition to the need for well-researched customer and competitive intelligence, research tells us that most business organizations could improve their profitability by hiring more estimators and bidding on more jobs. Follow-up intelligence when contracts are lost will help improve the firm's bids on future quotations.

Often on a new competitive bid, where there is information that the customer will continue to place orders after the first contract expires, the business marketer will bid lower in the expectation that, as in-supplier, follow-on orders at higher prices will lead to desired overall profits. After the job has been awarded, negotiation between seller and buyer may be used to reestablish prices resulting from any changes in the terms of the competitively bid contract.

Uncertainty of demand in pricing can be aggravated in many circumstances by uncertainty in supply that can affect the business marketer's costs, sometimes with serious consequences when the firm has won a competitive bid or wishes to publish prices. A number of techniques can be used to reduce anticipated risks caused by uncertainty of supply.

One of the bigger risks facing business marketers who export is the high probability of changes in relative international currency exchange rates in the interval between the time the price is quoted and the goods are paid for.

Key Terms and Concepts

perfect competition
monopoly market
monopolistic competitors
oligopoly structure
oligopsonistic industries
supply-demand pricing
cost-plus pricing
break-even pricing
value (utility)
searching costs
transaction costs
start-up costs
postpurchase costs
life-cycle costs
price segmentation
experience curve pricing
new product pricing
price skimming
market penetration pricing
product-line pricing
list prices
net price
trade discounts

cash discounts
quantity discounts
noncumulative discounts
cumulative discounts
rebate system
geographic pricing
FOB factory
FOB destination
freight equalization
CIF price
lease
financial leases
operating leases
competitive bidding
informal bidding
open bidding
closed bidding
request for quotation (RFQ)
request for proposal (RFP)
invitation to bid
multiple buying influence (MBI)
follow-on contract
negotiation

Discussion Questions

1. What are the limitations of the theoretical approaches to pricing that are suggested by economists?

2. In what ways can the business marketer insulate the firm against downward pressure on price from buyers and competitors?

3. What objectives can be achieved by offering discounts to list prices?

4. Why is leasing a useful marketing tool?

5. What are the advantages and disadvantages of competitive bidding to the buyer? To the seller?

6. What factors make pricing for export markets different from pricing for domestic markets?

7. A number of pricing objectives are described in this chapter. Could these be classified under a limited number of headings, such as sales-related objectives, profit-related objectives, and competitive position objectives? What kind of structuring of pricing objectives do you think would be more useful?

Endnotes and References

1. Isaiah A. Litvak, James A. Johnson, and Peter M. Banting, "Industrial Pricing—Art or Science?" *The Business Quarterly* (Autumn 1967): 37.

2. Hugh M. Cannon and Fred W. Morgan, "A Strategic Pricing Framework," *The Journal of Business and Industrial Marketing* 6 (Summer/Fall 1991): 64.

3. Eunsang Yoon, "Pricing Imitative New Products," *Industrial Marketing Management* 20 (1991): 116–117.

4. Gerald Stiles, "An Information Process Model of Industrial Buyer Behavior," 1972, unpublished doctoral dissertation, University of Minnesota.

5. Lowell E. Crow, Richard W. Olshavsky, and John O. Summers, "Industrial Buyers' Choice Strategies: A Protocol Analysis," *Journal of Marketing Research* 17 (February 1980): 34–44.

6. Louis J. DeRose, "Meet Today's Buying Influences with Value Selling," *Industrial Marketing Management* 20 (1991): 87–91.

7. John L. Forbis and Nitin T. Mehta, "Value-Based Strategies for Industrial Products," *Business Horizons* (May–June 1981): 32–42.

8. Raymond Corey, *Industrial Marketing* (Englewood Cliffs, N.J.: Prentice-Hall, 1963), p. 217.

9. Alicia Lasek, "Restaurant Trade Magazines Serving Up Incentives," *Business Marketing* (February 1991): 18.

10. Tom Eisenhart, "Weighing More Than Just Price," *Business Marketing* (January 1991): 13.

11. These include penalties factored into price on the basis of past experience of delivery delays, expediting costs, subspecification reject rates, and the additional costs of training new suppliers, to name a few.

12. Forbis and Mehta, "Value-Based Strategies for Industrial Products," pp. 32–42.

13. Thomas Nagle, "Pricing as Creative Marketing," *Business Horizons* (July–August 1983): 16.

14. Joel Dean, "Pricing Policies for New Products," *Harvard Business Review* 54 (November–December 1976): 151.

15. J. Udell, "How Important Is Pricing in Competitive Strategy?" *Journal of Marketing* 28 (January 1964): 45–78; W. D. Perrault, Jr., and R. A. Russ, "Physical Distribution Service in Industrial Purchase Decisions," *Journal of Marketing* 40 (April 1976): 3–10; J. P. Guiltinan, "Risk-Aversive Pricing Policies: Problems and Alternatives," *Journal of Marketing* 40 (January 1976): 10–15; P. J. Kelly and J. W. Croaker, "The Importance of Price as a Choice Criterion for Industrial Purchasing Decisions," *Industrial Marketing Management* 5 (October 1976): 281–292; Peter M. Banting and Randolph E. Ross, "The Marketing Mix: A Canadian Perspective," *Journal of the Academy of Marketing Science* 1 (Spring 1973): 1–11; and R. A. Robichaux, "How Important Is Pricing in a Competitive Strategy?" in H. W. Nash and D. P. Robin (eds.), *Proceedings, Southern Marketing Association,* 1976, pp. 55–57.

16. Augmented and adapted from Michael V.

Laric, "Pricing Strategies in Industrial Markets," *European Journal of Marketing* 14 (1980): 314.

17. Michael Levy, "Diminishing Marginal Returns for Customer Service," *International Journal of Physical Distribution and Materials Management* 11 (1981): 14–24.

18. Michael Levy and Dwight Grant, "Financial Terms of Sale and Control of Marketing Channel Conflict," *Journal of Marketing Research* 17 (November 1980): 524–530.

19. M. Bruce McAdam, "Equipment Leasing: An Integral Part of Financial Services," *Business Economics* 23 (July 1988): 43–47.

20. "Japan's 1st Leasing Company Assesses Industry," *The Japan Times,* February 27, 1984, p. 5.

21. Ronald C. Lease, John J. McConnell, and James S. Schallheim, "Realized Returns and the Default and Prepayment Experience of Financial Leasing Contracts," *Financial Management* 19 (Summer 1990): 11–20.

22. Colin Drury and Steven Braund, "The Leasing Decision: A Comparison of Theory and Practice," *Accounting and Business Research* 20 (Summer 1990): 179–191.

23. The 1979 figures come from T. M. Clark in a presentation, "The World of Leasing," at the World Leasing Convention, Toronto, June 1987.

24. Peter Vanderwicken, "The Powerful Logic of the Leasing Boom," *Fortune* 88 (November 1973): 136.

25. Paul F. Anderson, "Industrial Equipment Leasing Offers Economic and Competitive Edge," *Marketing News,* April 4, 1980, p. 20.

26. L. Berry and K. Maricle, "Comsumption Without Ownership: Marketing Opportunity for Today and Tomorrow," *M.S.U. Business Topics* 21 (1973): 23–41.

27. Shmuel Oren, Stephen Smith, and Robert Wilson, "Pricing a Product Line," *Journal of Business* 57 (1984): S73–S99.

28. Paul F. Anderson and William Lazer, "Industrial Lease Marketing," *Journal of Marketing* 42 (January 1978): 71–79.

29. Lamar Lee, Jr., and Donald W. Dobler, *Purchasing and Materials Management* (New York: McGraw-Hill, 1971), p. 112.

30. Kenneth Simmonds and Stuart Slatter, "The Number of Estimators: A Critical Decision for Marketing Under Competitive Bidding," *Journal of Marketing Research* 15 (May 1978): 203–213.

31. Thomas J. Peters and Robert H. Waterman, Jr., *In Search of Excellence* (New York: Harper & Row, 1982), p. 162.

32. Bruce H. Allen, Ronald L. Tatham, and David R. Lambert, "Flexible Pricing Systems for High Inflationary Periods," *Industrial Marketing Management* 5 (1976): 243.

33. Barbara Bund Jackson, "Manage Risk in Industrial Pricing," *Harvard Business Review* (July–August 1980): 121–133.

34. Ibid.

35. Ibid.

36. Allen, Tatham, and Lambert, "Flexible Pricing Systems for High Inflationary Periods," p. 244.

37. Peter Banting, David Ford, Andrew Gross, and George Holmes, "Comparative Industrial Buying Patterns in High-Level Economies," *Demonstrating the Contribution of Research,* proceedings of the 36th ESOMAR Congress, 1983, pp. 121–141.

38. *Business Week,* October 19, 1979, p. 65.

39. Hedging is the act of protecting oneself against financial loss caused by future price fluctuations. Short selling involves selling something that you don't have but will acquire at the time you must provide its delivery. In this example of hedging, the U.K. firm would find a buyer who will pay an agreed-upon pound sterling value for the amount of U.S. dollars represented by the contract on the date that the U.K. firm receives payment in dollars. It is a short sale because the dollar sale is agreed to before the U.K. firm receives the dollars. No matter what happens to the exchange rate, the U.K. firm knows exactly how many pounds sterling the sale will yield.

12

DISTRIBUTION AND CHANNEL RELATIONS

- To explain the reasons for using intermediaries in the distribution channel
- To identify the various intermediaries that are used in business marketing
- To discuss typical practices and policies governing manufacturer–industrial distributor relations
- To explain why manufacturers' agents are used and discuss their advantages and disadvantages

Distribution is the term applied to the process of moving goods from producer to the ultimate customer. Distribution is usually thought of in terms of physical goods only. In marketing goods and services, however, much more than the simple movement of physical objects is necessary. Knowledge of who has the correct item, and credit, service, and technical information are a few of the ingredients that are also important. Thus, people and institutions are frequently involved in distribution without ever physically coming into contact with the product. Yet their contribution to distribution can be just as vital as the physical movement of the product.

THE DISTRIBUTION CHANNEL

A **channel of distribution** may be defined as a sequence of marketing institutions, including **intermediaries**, that facilitates transactions between producers and final users. The number of facilitating institutions can be very small when the producer sells directly to the user (no intermediaries), or quite large when several types of intermediaries perform successive operations in the product's distribution. The first scenario is called a **direct** (or **short**) **channel**; the second is an **indirect** (or **long**) **channel** (see Exhibit 12–1).

In the shortest direct channel, the manufacturer's employees deal face-to-face, or directly by mail or telephone, with the end users. Another fairly direct channel is created when the manufacturer operates sales branches and company-owned dealerships. In all these cases the manufacturer assumes total responsibility for all of the functions (maintaining inventory, delivering goods, providing information to customers, promotion, credit) necessary to satisfy customer needs. The manufacturer has greatest control over the quality of customer relationships, selling prices, service, and availability of product. But all this comes from a high investment in facilities, inventories, and personnel, which perhaps could be spent more profitably in the manufacturer's principal expertise: manufacturing.

Twenty years ago, Telcom Research, a small Ontario manufacturer of microprocessor-based digital electronic control equipment for the television broadcast-

EXHIBIT 12–1   Channel Length

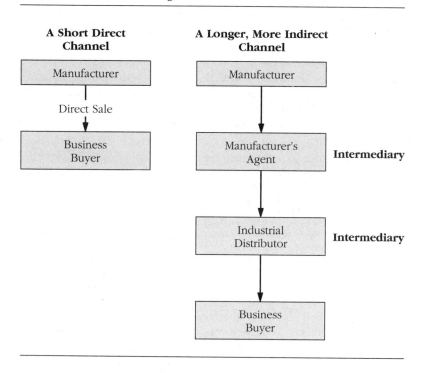

ing industry, had just begun production. After a few weeks of demonstrating his product, the owner-inventor realized that he needed a distribution channel for his product. He couldn't make enough sales calls himself, as well as keep his production shop going. He hired a salesperson, but after a year he found his sales costs were too high for the small number of orders being generated. After talking to a number of distributors, he realized that among their wide range of products, his equipment would be neglected. They had well-known, profitable products and would not be willing to push an unknown product with uncertain profit potential. Finally, he met a manufacturers' agent at the National Association of Broadcasters annual industry trade show. The agent had a limited number of broadcast-related products, was familiar with the technology, called on the appropriate mix of customers in California, and was willing to give the new line of control equipment aggressive promotion. The manufacturer started selling his product through this agent and was so pleased with the results that Telcom now markets its product through a nationwide network of twelve manufacturers' agents.

Like other business firms, Telcom Research found that there are many different methods of generating sales and delivering products and associated services to customers. The best alternative depends on a number of factors: the extent and frequency of customer contact desired, the availability of distribution channel members, their capacity to satisfy customer requirements, their willingness to devote time and attention to the product, and the costs of their services. Business firms selling to several market segments may need to employ separate channels for each industrial segment. For example, IBM uses direct distribution when marketing its products to large businesses. IBM can better satisfy large customers' requirements by discussing their needs face-to-face, then designing systems specifically to fulfill those individual requirements. In the large business market, IBM assumes all distribution functions itself, including making sales contact with potential customers, negotiating, carrying inventory, transferring title, communicating, and so forth. In marketing to small customers, however, IBM uses an indirect channel arrangement, shifting some of these functions to retail intermediaries called **value-added resellers (VARs)**. They modify equipment and install software for less sophisticated customers. Thousands of VARs who are spread across the continent and carry many computer-related product lines from a range of manufacturers can do a more effective and inexpensive job of contacting small customers than can Big Blue.

Although well-established and large companies may have used a particular business channel arrangement for many years, it is advisable to conduct a periodic channel audit and, if needed, restructure the channel. The **channel audit** is a comprehensive reappraisal of a company's approach to distribution. It identifies shifting customer emporographics and market behavior, reassesses costs of using different types of intermediaries, and evaluates changes in corporate distribution goals. It can suggest more effective avenues to the market. After such an audit, Ingersoll-Rand, which had traditionally sold pneumatic tools direct to industrial buyers, switched to using distributors who could provide faster service to a broader market.[1] Similarly, Aluminum Company of America (ALCOA), the largest aluminum manufacturer in the United States, diverted millions of dollars in annual small lot orders away from its own mills into the hands of a nationwide network of independent distributors some years ago. The result was better service to small lot customers and lower costs for ALCOA.

Until 1991, Apple Computers, Inc., sold its computers through 1,600 value-added resellers. To capture more small- to medium-sized business customers and department-level corporate buyers, as well as consumers, Apple changed its distribution approach to mass merchandising through authorized "superstores." Whereas VARs formerly handled all support services, Apple has assumed direct support for in-house programmers, MIS (management information systems) directors, and other sophisticated users, particularly in "mission-oriented applications" requiring seven-day, twenty-four-hour support. To complement the services and support provided by VARs, Apple has several telephone hotlines. A Software Development Answerline helps software developers creating applications for in-house corporate or institutional use. The Apple Technical Coordinator Answerline targets managers of "help desks" serving in-house populations of Mac users. And the A/UX Answerline supports users of Apple's A/UX operating systems software.[2]

Why Use Intermediaries?

Business marketers may choose to sell through intermediaries for a number of reasons, including the following.

Transaction Costs.   Every order incurs costs—contact costs, order-filling costs, expediting costs—and lots of paperwork. As in the case of ALCOA, when a company has a lot of small-value orders, these transaction costs can significantly reduce profits. By selling larger quantities to intermediaries, the manufacturer can reduce the proportion of transaction costs per sales dollar.

Inventory Costs.   When an intermediary carries inventory, the manufacturer can reduce its own levels of inventory. By reducing its inventory levels, the manufacturer reduces inventory carrying costs, which include storage costs, property taxes, insurance, cost of money invested in the inventory, and so on.

Limited Finances.   Even large corporations can have a difficult time raising enough money to operate a nationwide network of wholly owned local distribution outlets. Despite the high cost, some industries sell direct because customers demand personalized attention from the manufacturer, or their equipment is too sophisticated to risk less than optimal installation by intermediaries.

Narrow Product Line.   Few industrial manufacturers have a wide enough product line to generate a high ratio of sales to direct calls by their sales force. (This was the case for Telcom Research.) Excessive selling costs suggest turning the job over to intermediaries, whose broader range of products (because they handle distribution functions for a large number of manufacturers) generates higher returns per sales call.

Proximity.   Intermediaries offer much more immediate and local representation. Because they are closer to their customers, they are better able to ascertain their customers' needs and wants, assess their credit rating, and offer speedy delivery, service, and individual attention than an industrial manufacturer whose plant may be thousands of miles away.

Opportunity Costs.   Manufacturers often have begun operation on the basis of their technological and production expertise rather than on their marketing and distribution skills. Their return on manufacturing investment, then, tends to be much higher than on investment in distribution. Thus, it makes sense to let more efficient distribution specialists act as their intermediaries and then to invest more in the manufacturing side of the operation. Doing so reduces the manufacturers' **opportunity costs**—that is, the incremental gain foregone by not pursuing a higher-yielding alternative. A glance at Exhibit 12–2 suggests that in most industries there are key areas where the industrial firm should focus its attention. Forklift

EXHIBIT 12–2   Key Success Factors in Selected Industries

Industry	Factor
Forklift trucks	Product features
Semiconductors	Product quality
Aircraft	Product uniqueness
Bulk chemicals	Price levels
Cement	Physical distribution
Elevators	Customer service
Robotics	Manufacturing flexibility
Mining	Capital availability
Petroleum	Resource availability
Defense industries	Government relations

trucks, for example, are manufactured in various models, much like automobiles. Manufacturing design of product features is important, but distribution and sales can be handled by intermediaries, such as industrial equipment distributors. Cement distribution is characterized by large numbers of local mixers who deliver the product and pour it at the construction site. On the other hand, elevators are installed by the elevator manufacturer, whose reputation depends on continuous safe operation.

Types of Intermediaries

Each channel system is designed to provide certain specific functions or services. Channel length or complexity depends on the number of functions or services required and the manner in which they will be accomplished. Over the years, specialists have developed within channels when certain functions or services required greater attention than others.

To develop and use an efficient channel of distribution, one should be familiar with the various types of intermediaries available. The following sections describe the most common categories of intermediaries. The major functions performed by these various intermediaries are summarized in Exhibit 12–3.

Merchant Intermediaries.   Merchant intermediaries are wholesale industrial distributors who buy and own the goods they handle. The majority of these distributors provide the broadest range of services and are consequently called **full-service wholesalers**. They generally carry a broad line of staple, nonperishable items, accessories, and supplies and sell to retailers or industrial users. Their functions or services include stocking, delivery, credit, and promotion.

EXHIBIT 12–3   Functions Performed by Various Intermediaries

Intermediary Functions

X = Provides function
S = Sometimes provides function
T = Transfers title only

	Anticipates needs	Regroups goods	Carries stocks	Delivers goods	Grants credit to customer	Provides information and advice to customer	Provides buying function for customer	Owns and transfers title to goods	Provides selling function for manufacturer	Stores inventory for manufacturer	Reduces credit risk for manufacturer	Provides market information to manufacturer	Handles foreign transactions	Divides profit among customers	Does extensive promotion for customers	Provides display
Industrial Distributors																
General wholesale distributor	X	X	X	X	X	X	X	X	X	X	X	X				X
Import-export merchant	X	X	X	X	X	X	X	X	X	X	X	X	X			S
Voluntary group wholesaler	X	X	X	X	X	X	X	X	X	X	X	X		S	X	
Drop shipper or desk jobber					X	X	X	X	X		X	X				
Truck distributor	X	X	X	X	S	S	S	X	X	X	X	X	S			
Cash-and-carry wholesaler	X	X	X					X	X	X	X	X				X
Mail-order wholesaler	X	X	X		S	S	X	X	X	X	X	X				
Cooperative Marketing Associations; Other Dealers in Primary Products	X	X	S	X	X	X	X	S	X	S	X	X	S	X	X	X
Manufacturers' Sales Branches	X		S	X	X	X		T	X	S	X	X				X
Agents and Brokers																
Merchandise broker	S					X	X		X			X				
Manufacturers' agent	X	S	S	S		X	X		X	S		X	X			S
Import-export agent or broker						X	X		X			X				S
Auction business		X	S		S			X	T	X	X					X
Commission merchant		X	X	X	S	X	X	T	X			X				X
Selling agent						X	X	X		X		X	X			
Purchase agent or resident buyer	X					X	X									

Note: These functions are approximate, since individual intermediaries may perform more or less than indicated.

The **single-line wholesaler** restricts its offering to a certain type of product, such as industrial fasteners or chemicals, and provides more specialized service to industrial buyers.

The **specialty wholesaler** carries this concept even further and usually provides a great deal of technical information and selling functions along with the product. Distributors of industrial coating materials are an example.

Limited-function wholesalers do not provide as wide a range of services as the full-service wholesalers. This is because the customer does not require as extensive an array of functions or services and is unwilling to pay for unnecessary extras. The **cash-and-carry wholesaler**, for example, does not provide credit or delivery. Lumber distributors and food merchants are examples. The **drop shipper** (or **desk jobber**) does not physically stock products but orders goods to be shipped directly from manufacturer to user. A drop shipper, for example, might take orders for drywall board and have them shipped from the wallboard plant to the construction site of a large office tower. The **truck** (or **wagon**) **jobber** carries all its stock in a truck and provides quick, regular deliveries, usually of perishable goods, such as cutting tools.[3] The **mail order distributor** depends on a catalog to obtain sales. Distributors of test and measuring instruments usually fall into this category. **Cooperatives** split profits among their buying members. Agricultural supplies are sold by cooperatives. Farmers (business buyers) pay a membership fee to join. At the end of the year, this intermediary's profits are calculated, and each member receives a share of profit based upon his or her total dollar purchases during the year.

Agent Intermediaries.   In contrast to merchant intermediaries, **agent intermediaries** do not buy or own the goods they sell. Agent intermediaries also fall into several categories, characterized by the extent of their services. **Commission merchants** generally handle commodities and livestock, and are valuable to distant suppliers because of their wealth of local market information. **Manufacturers' agents** act as the sales force for several manufacturers who cannot afford their own sales forces. **Brokers** bring buyers and sellers together through their knowledge of market availability and requirements. Used machinery is often handled by industrial brokers. **Auction companies** provide display areas and facilitate negotiations among sellers and buyers.

CHANNEL STRATEGY IN PRACTICE

As channels of distribution develop and evolve, their structure becomes much more complex than the two channels shown in Exhibit 12–1. Different intermediaries join the channel, each performing different sets of functions for their customers. Also, one of the channel members assumes a leadership role to provide coordination and to fend off potential conflict in the channel. How consumer products, industrial products, and mixed products move through channels of distribu-

Profit potential of Lysol products is promoted to wholesale distributors and retailers.

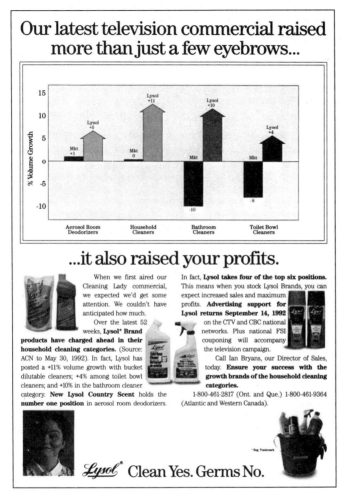

Courtesy of L&F Canada Inc.

tion is illustrated in the following industry examples. Multichannel marketing, channel leadership, and major business channels are also discussed.

Consumer Products in Business Marketing: Canned Foods

Business marketing know-how is applied to consumer products as they move through a channel of distribution up to the point at which they are purchased by a retailer, whose motive is to resell them at a profit. Canned foods, for example, are distributed through one of the most vast and efficient channel systems in to-day's market, providing high-quality goods at low prices. This is accomplished through high-volume sales at low markups.

The cannery operates for only a few weeks during the harvesting season. Since costs are critical, the canner attempts to gear production to orders received in advance from brokers, chains, and large wholesalers. The canner's large expenditures occur during the short packing season. Therefore, the canner wants to obtain revenue as quickly as possible. Since the canning firm cannot afford additional expenditures for a sales force, it relies on food brokers to sell its goods (see Exhibit 12–4).

The food broker represents several canned goods suppliers whose products become marketable at different times of the year. This intermediary obtains approximately a 2 percent commission from the canner for arranging sales to wholesalers and chains. The broker not only acts as a salesperson calling on wholesalers but also provides both canner and wholesaler with market and credit information, pioneers the introduction of new product lines, arranges shipments, and creates advertising and promotion deals.

Full-service wholesalers generally supply hospitals, schools, institutions, and hotels and restaurants, but their full range of functions (delivery, sales force, credit,

EXHIBIT 12–4   Distribution Channels for Canned Foods

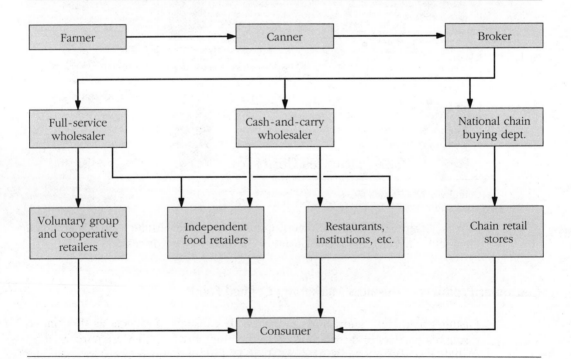

etc.) makes them costly. Retailers and restaurants that cannot buy in economical lot sizes, and small stores with low credit ratings, prefer to buy their canned goods from cash-and-carry wholesalers. This way the costs of credit, delivery, sales force, and other services are eliminated from the case price.

Voluntary group wholesalers organize a number of retailers to obtain the economies of quantity purchasing, cooperative advertising, uniform pricing, promotion, stock display, and routine ordering that are necessary to remain competitive with large chain operations. Such associations occur frequently in grocery, hardware, and drugstores. When the stores jointly own the wholesale warehouse, the arrangement is called a **retailer cooperative**.

The retail end of the channel includes grocery stores, delicatessens, department stores, and even drugstores. Chain stores handle the bulk of the business—more than a third—and supply their own large supermarkets. Their strength lies in their available finances.

An Industrial Product: Steel

Steel is used in one form or another in almost all industrial production. Steel is characterized by low price per pound (less than 10 cents on the average), high weight, and bulk. To attain economies of scale, steel is produced in large lots, and in most cases is formed on continuous rolling mills. Two-thirds of steel production is used by manufacturers to produce machinery, transportation, and construction equipment.

Because of steel's high transportation cost, difficulty of storage, and need to adapt to customers' specifications, four of every five tons of steel are shipped directly from the steel plant to the manufacturer. These large orders are solicited by the steel plant's own salespeople and assist the plant in planning long runs of specific grades and sizes of steel.

Smaller orders reach the steel plant through a different channel—the steel warehouse. Industrial steel warehouses (also called steel service centers) carry plates, bars, sheets, strips, and structural shapes, plus related items such as welding rods and grinding wheels. These warehouses group small orders and buy in larger lots from the steel plant. Their salespeople call on steel users and provide users with technical information. Steel service centers also semiprocess steel by performing cutting, bending, cleaning, heat treating, painting, and related operations. Their main service is fast delivery to the steel fabricators.

Oil field supply companies limit their steel stocks to casing, pipe, tubing, and steel wire rope for drilling firms. They also carry wide lines of other drilling equipment and supplies. Pipe jobbers buy in carload quantities, and they stock and sell plumbing and structural pipes. Pipe jobbers serve the plumbing and heating trades, mines and mills, and retail stores. Those supplying the plumbing and heating industry carry related lines such as fittings and fixtures, heating equipment, and tools. Mines and mills suppliers also handle boiler and machinery installations. Wholesale hardware jobbers sell wire fences, nails, galvanized sheets, and so on to

EXHIBIT 12–5   Distribution Channels for Steel

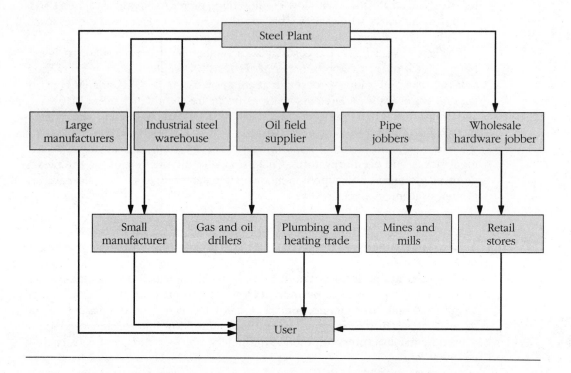

retail hardware stores and to merchants in farming communities. Exhibit 12–5 illustrates the main channels for steel.

A Mixed Product: Tires

Automotive tires represent what we might call a "mixed product"—that is, a product that is sold in both industrial and consumer markets. The automotive tire market is unusual in that wholesalers are rarely used. The market is too competitive, and wholesalers have not been considered capable of developing specialized tire dealers. The trend from a specialty to a convenience good in tires has fostered a proliferation of channels, shown in Exhibit 12–6.

Multichannel Marketing

These examples illustrate how different types of intermediaries arise to perform specialized functions. The use of two or more different channel structures by a manufacturer is not at all unusual and is called **multichannel marketing, dual distribution**, or **parallel channels**. A midwest manufacturer of auto parts, for

EXHIBIT 12–6   Distribution Channels for Automotive Tires

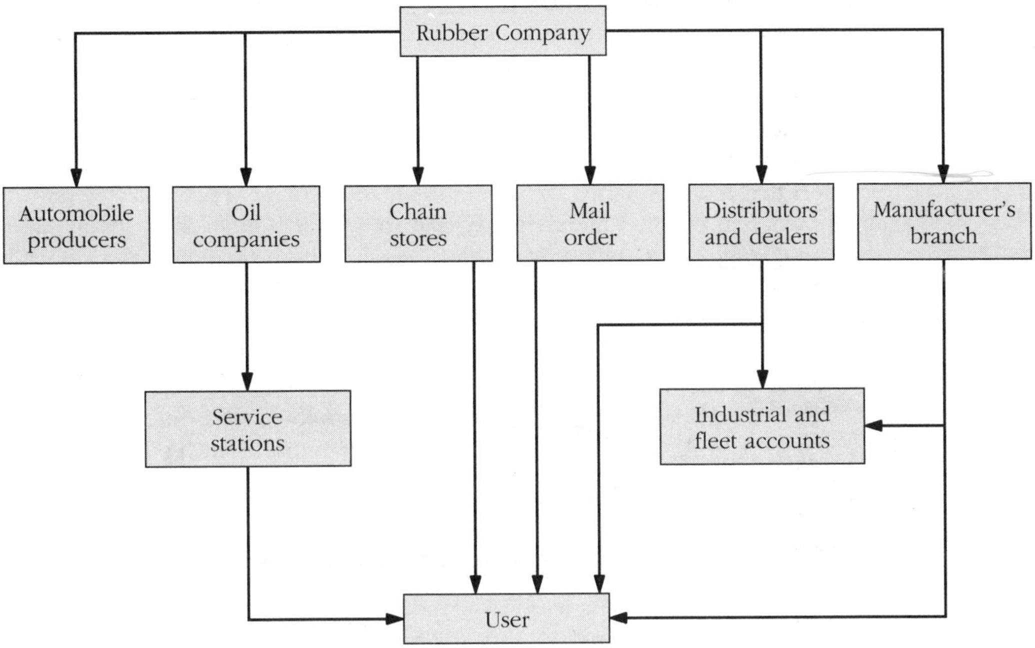

example, sells to the populous markets of the northeastern states through its own salespeople but to the sparse market in the western states through manufacturers' agents. A Canadian farm equipment manufacturer maintains company-owned stores in the concentrated farming areas of Ontario and Quebec but uses dealers elsewhere in the country.

Different channels are also used to sell to different classes of customers. One truck manufacturer sells to fleet accounts through its own branch offices, to smaller buyers through dealers, and to the federal government through a special Washington-based sales force. Refrigeration equipment is sold both directly to industrial buyers and through retail stores to consumers.

Selling through several stages of intermediaries is not unusual either. Usually the larger the number of customers making frequent small purchases, the more indirect (and longer) the channel becomes—large wholesalers selling to smaller ones, who in turn sell to still more specialized and localized jobbers.

Channel Leadership

The more indirect, longer, and more complex channel arrangements become, the greater the need for direction and coordination of channel activities. Each intermediary in the channel has its own goals and preferences for its stage of the operation. Unfortunately, these goals and preferences may be in opposition or at cross-purposes with one another, and can create **channel conflict**. The manufacturer would like its distributor to have ample stocks of the manufacturer's products on shelves. But the distributor doesn't want money tied up in any more than the minimal necessary inventory. Intermediaries complain continually that the manufacturer does not provide adequate advertising and product information; manufacturers protest that their jobbers don't use the material they provide. Manufacturers rarely feel that intermediaries are selling the manufacturer's products aggressively enough, whereas channel members say that they must spread their selling effort over a wide range of products to stay in business. Finally, manufacturers continually search for ways to obtain more market information. Channel members, on the other hand, fear that manufacturers will circumvent them and sell directly if they find out enough about the intermediary's customers.

These conflicts result in a power play for control over the channel system. As a result, the most powerful channel member ends up as the **channel leader**, director, or captain. As channel leader, a channel member is in a position to give directions to and make demands of other channel members (both forward or downstream toward the market *and* backward or upstream toward the supplier). The channel leader can dictate the amount of advertising, service quality, sales and promotion effort, and so forth, required from manufacturers, distributors, or retailers. The manufacturer of a national brand with a strong customer franchise can control the rest of the channel. Usually, the manufacturer is thought of as the channel leader; however, this need not always be the case. A strong merchant wholesale distributor may refuse to handle a manufacturer's product unless certain conditions are met. A manufacturer's agent with strong customer loyalty may dictate terms to the agency's suppliers (or principals). Power also can accrue to one party in the channel by default through indifference on the part of other channel members.

No matter how it develops, the emergence of a channel leader is necessary and of benefit to the distributive system. A distribution channel without guidance is directionless, with each member pursuing personal ends, frequently to the detriment of others. A channel leader can integrate the individual channel members into a coordinated unit, all performing together to pursue the same well-defined policies, and accomplish common objectives. This limits any short-term individual pursuits that could harm the channel system and assures a concerted effort toward overall continuing channel success.

The manufacturer can assume the role of channel leader if the firm develops a channel in which it is the strongest member or in which other members permit the manufacturer to direct policy. For example, a study of 324 distributors of office furniture and systems who could select their purchases from among 200 manufacturers found that distributors concentrated the bulk of their business with suppliers that they perceived to perform well and that allowed them adequate decision-making autonomy in their manner of doing business, while exerting reasonable control in other areas. Leading suppliers didn't offer the highest margins but did exhibit greater concern for giving the distributor long-term commitment, support, service, marketing help, and sales growth potential.[4] Often, however, the manufacturer is forced to relinquish control because another channel arrangement is more efficient, or the most desirable channel is not available. Many factors must be considered in developing a channel.

Major Business Channels

Although many different business channel structures may be employed, the most popular involves the manufacturer selling through an industrial distributor to the end user. In North America, almost three-quarters of all industrial products follow this route (see Exhibit 12–7). One-fifth of industrial unit sales are promoted

EXHIBIT 12–7   Percent of Unit Sales Handled by Intermediaries

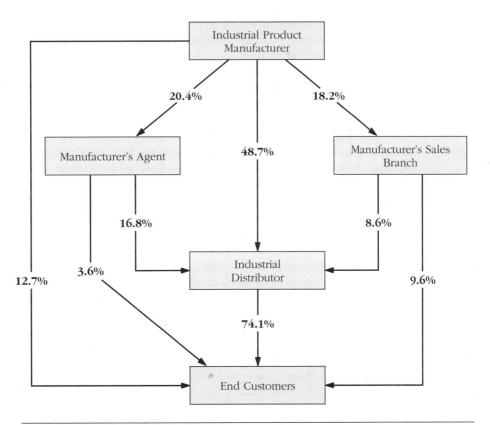

Source: Adapted from Robert W. Haas, *Industrial Marketing Management,* 4th ed. (Boston: PWS/KENT Publishing Company, 1989), 239.

through manufacturers' agents, slightly less through manufacturers' sales branches, and an eighth are sold directly from the manufacturers' head office or plant. Since industrial distributors and manufacturers' agents account for the majority of all business transactions, the remainder of this chapter will focus on them.

INDUSTRIAL DISTRIBUTORS

Handling almost three-quarters of all industrial products sold in the United States and selling $50 billion worth of goods, some twelve thousand industrial distributors are a potent force in marketing. Industrial distributors contact customers, provide delivery, may do some assembly or finishing of products, offer repair service, handle credit, and provide a wide product assortment to industrial buyers generally. Distributors take **title** (ownership) to the goods they sell. Hence they can set their own selling prices (and margins) for the goods, usually maintain adequate inventories, and even carry competing products. Distributors range from single-location owner-managed companies to multibranch corporations with more than a hundred locations across the nation. The typical outlet in a concentrated industrial market might serve an area as small as a twenty-five-mile-radius, whereas in sparsely industrialized or rural regions, the trading area could reach out as much as a hundred and fifty miles.

The average distributor sells around $2 million annually and maintains an inventory worth a half-million dollars. Average order size is between $100 and $200.

The distributor's outside salespeople act as "order getters," calling on customer accounts and prospecting for new customers, solving technical problems, and maintaining customer service. Although the distributor may be small in comparison with national marketers, the firm is likely to be a large, independently owned business in its own local community, providing a full range of service to its customers.

The distributor's inside salespeople, who have a high level of product expertise and stock availability knowledge, act as "order takers" by telephone. They also process orders, schedule deliveries, and answer customer queries. A growing percentage of women are now functioning as inside telephone and counter salespeople.

Products Carried

Distributors handle maintenance, repair, and operating supplies (MRO items) such as lubricants, paint, and machine parts to create immediate availability when required. They also stock original equipment supplies for OEMs, including such items as power transmission components, fasteners, and electronic memory chips, which become part of the manufacturer's finished product. Distributors also handle accessory equipment used in the operation of the customer's business, such as

EXHIBIT 12–8   Distributors Classified by Product Lines

- Mechanics' tools, power tools and accessories
- MRO items (lubricants, tapes, adhesives, welding equipment, paint, etc.)
- Pipe, tubing, valves, and fittings
- Cutting tools and abrasives
- Industrial rubber and plastic products
- Fasteners
- Fluid power (pneumatics and hydraulics)
- Power transmission equipment (belts, pulleys, gears, sprockets, couplings, clutches, drivers, brakes, etc.)
- Safety supplies
- Contractors' supplies (shovels, sledges, forks, hoes, jacks, ropes, chain, wire rope, etc.)
- Electric and electronic equipment
- Bearings
- Power equipment
- Ferrous and nonferrous metals

power tools and hoists, as well as machines such as lathes and presses that are used to machine metal and convert raw materials. Exhibit 12–8 lists some of the product lines carried by different distributors.

Broad Categories of Distributors

There are three broad categories of merchant distributors: general line, specialty, and combination house.

General Line Distributors.   General line distributors maintain inventories of a broad range of industrial items. To the trade, they are often referred to as "mill supply houses" and are known as the "supermarkets of industry" because of their extensive assortments. When customers have large annual requirements made up of small, frequent purchases, the general line distributors also establish specialist departments in some product lines. These specialist departments can provide customers with better service.

Specialists.   A limited-line distributor specializes in a narrow line of related products such as abrasives, cutting tools, or power transmission equipment. Surveys suggest that **specialty distributors** are growing in numbers relative to other distribution types.[5] The specialist offers customers a high degree of technical expertise, problem-solving capability, and application know-how. Some specialists perform special services such as assembly or submanufacturing to better serve customers and differentiate themselves from competitors. Steel service centers, for

BUSINESS MARKETING IN PRACTICE

An International Specialist Intermediary

The insides of a compact Eastman Kodak Co. printer are made in Japan, then shipped to Kodak in Rochester, N.Y., where they are paired with software. The interesting twist comes when a small, specialized intermediary, Brukar International Ltd. of Toronto, sells the printer back into Japan through its established distribution network.

"Kodak has bundles of money and a fabulous distribution system for film in Japan," says Carolyn Cross, Brukar's president. "But they can't sell a computer printer in the same store as film. We could do it more cost-effectively and faster. Kodak came to us because they knew we were good at what we do."

Source: Adapted from "Selling Computer Products to Japan," *The Financial Post,* Dec. 18, 1990, p. 18.

example, offer flattening, pickling (removing surface scale), cleaning, and cutting to length. A specialist distributor might receive rolled band saw stock from the manufacturer that is then cut, welded, and finished to the customer's requirements. Distributors that perform such special services must monitor their costs carefully to maintain their profitability.[6]

Combination House.   The **combination house** sells to other customers in addition to industrial manufacturers. It operates in both industrial and consumer markets. An electrical distributor may sell lighting fixtures to retailers and institutions in addition to the construction industry and manufacturers.

An Illustration of Manufacturer/Distributor Practices

Although it is not intended to be representative of practices in all industries, a description of the practices and policies of industrial manufacturers and their electrical and electronic distributors gives further insight into distributor operations.[7]

Criteria for Stocking.   Electronic distributors evaluate prospective principals (manufacturers whose products they consider adding to their line) on the basis of the following criteria:

- sales potential (based on established customer demand)
- reasonable margin (based on manufacturer's pricing structure)
- quality of product
- support services offered by the manufacturer
- reputation of the manufacturer (well known and well respected)
- product fit (product fits well with distributor's total line and strategy)

Use of Manufacturer's List Price.   Recall from Chapter 11 that list prices are used as a starting point from which various discounts are calculated to arrive at the price paid by the customer. Electrical and electronic product manufacturers typically revise their price lists once a year, although some revise theirs monthly. However, there is a wide range among distributors regarding whether they use list price to calculate the prices charged to their customers (see Exhibit 12–9). In selecting a distributor, manufacturers should ascertain what pricing approach the distributor will use.

Inventory Price Protection.   Eighty-four percent of electronics distributors say their current inventory generally is protected against decreases in price, and the manufacturer can be debited after product shipment. A claim can still be made by distributors who are not protected, if their volume is sufficient.

Quotes.   Electrical and electronic distributors contact their manufacturer for special **price quotations** if they encounter stiff competition (47 percent say), or if they are trying to close a large order deal (say 37 percent). The customer who wants a nonstandard product, needs an order in a hurry, or is particularly important to the distributor may ask for a special price quotation rather than using list prices.

Quotations are usually valid for thirty days. If the manufacturer fears that the quote may be used by the end-customer to win a price concession from a competitor, it might be valid for as little as one day. This prevents the customer from showing the quote to a competitor and using it as a bargaining point.

Distributor's Margins.   The difference between the cost of goods and their selling price is the **distributor's margin**. Margins in electronics cluster between 22 and 30 percent, with a range extending from 15 to 45 percent. One distributor, due to different competitive pressures, takes 22 percent in New York City, 24 percent in New Jersey, and 26 percent in Boston. Among the many reasons why dis-

EXHIBIT 12–9   List Price Usage in Electrical/Electronic Distribution

Situations Prompting Use of List Price	Percentage of Distributors
Usually use list price	21.1
Below certain $ or quantity order size	15.7
For small accounts	10.5
For new accounts	5.3
When competition absent	5.3
As a guideline only	10.5
Rarely or never use list price	31.6
	100.0

tributors might sacrifice their margins, the hope of landing a big order with a lower price is the most frequently mentioned (see Exhibit 12–10).

Promotion.   In most cases the electrical distributor pays at least part of the cost of promotion. Manufacturers take more responsibility for planning and designing product catalogs, product specification sheets, and trade journal advertisements than they do in paying for them. The degree of cooperative promotional effort between manufacturer and distributor is seen in Exhibit 12–11.

Sales Territory Allocation.   The territory in which a distributor represents a manufacturer can become an element of potential conflict if not clearly established at the beginning of the relationship. Twenty-two percent of electrical and electronic distributors report that they operate in clearly defined geographic territories. Some high-volume customers or customers with special technical service requirements in a distributor's territory may be designated as "house accounts" to be served directly by the manufacturer. Eleven percent of distributors indicate that manufacturers keep key accounts. Thirty-nine percent of distributors are free to sell to anyone. This could create problems if two distributors for the same manufacturer are competing with each other for the same customer's business.

Inventory Levels.   Seventy-one percent of electrical and electronics distributors maintain an inventory of all or most of the products they sell. The remaining 29

EXHIBIT 12–10   Margin-Cutting Practice in Electrical/Electronic Distribution

Circumstances for Sacrificing Margin	Percentage of Distributors
To obtain large-volume order	36.8
Competitive pressure on price	31.6
Large customer	21.0
New accounts	21.0
Slow-moving products/excess inventory	15.8
Delivery	10.5
To maintain strategic position	10.5
General market conditions	5.3
To meet quota	5.3
New product	5.3
New territory	5.3
Terms	5.3
Visibility	5.3
Credit	5.3
Warranty	5.3

EXHIBIT 12–11   Cooperative Promotion in Electrical/Electronic Distribution

Promotion Vehicle	Percentage of Firms Using	Planning & Design Responsibility (percent of firms)			Cost Responsibility (percent of firms)		
		Dist.	Mfr.	Both	Dist.	Mfr.	Both
Product catalog	90	47	35	18	35	18	47
Product spec sheets	95	22	67	11	22	44	33
Trade show exhibits	95	67	0	33	39	0	61
Trade journal advertisements	63	33	8	58	67	0	33
Incentive programs	90	65	6	29	53	46	41
Education seminars	95	39	11	50	39	11	50
Demonstration rooms	79	100	0	0	73	0	27

percent of distributors stock just those products that sell most quickly or that represent a substantial sales volume.

Suppliers usually want their distributors to carry at least minimum inventory levels. In electronics, the vast majority of the distributors studied (76 percent) dealt with manufacturers who set specific stock level requirements. These inventory levels are calculated on the basis of required inventory turns, sales forecasts, or percentage of sales. In most cases such designated products are popular items that sell quickly.

Manufacturers encourage their distributors to maintain inventory levels by requiring that the distributor place minimum order quantities or else pay freight charges. Some manufacturers conduct on-site inventory inspections and then offer suggestions regarding inventory levels. Once a distributor establishes a particular product line, the supplier might relax this inventory requirement. However, distributors sometimes feel that their manufacturers' suggested inventory levels are unrealistic and do not adopt them.

Frequency of Reordering Stock.   The frequency with which an electrical or electronic distributor reorders stock can vary from one product to another. For example, products such as programmable controllers might be ordered only when the one in stock is sold, whereas electrical supply items might be reordered daily. In general, a quarter of distributors order every week, a fifth once a month, and a third every three months.

Goods Damaged in Shipment.   Manufacturers' policies regarding goods damaged in transit to the distributor vary. In cases where the distributor is not permitted to return damaged items, the manufacturer of electrical and electronic products expects the distributor to make any necessary repairs. Eleven percent of distributors cannot return damaged goods. Seventy-eight percent return goods for full credit. The rest receive less than full credit when they return damaged goods.

Obsolete Inventory.   Two-fifths of electronic manufacturers allow return of unsold goods through a "stock rotation system" at year-end. These goods are traded for faster-selling items, but may be limited on the basis of a specified percentage of products ordered during the year or a specified proportion of the distributor's annual net sales. One-sixth do not permit unsold goods to be returned.

Incorrect Shipments.   Seventy-four percent of distributors report that incorrectly shipped items can be returned to the manufacturer for 100 percent credit and 21 percent report such goods can be returned but they receive less than 100 percent credit. Five percent said they cannot return incorrectly shipped items. Thus, a quarter of distributors are penalized for the manufacturer's error. This could be a cause of conflict between manufacturer and distributor.

Faulty Manufacturing.   For 83 percent of electrical and electronic distributors, faultily made goods could be returned to the manufacturer for full credit. The other 17 percent would receive less than full credit. In the latter case, the manufacturer encourages the distributor to do repair work on the spot, because the cost of returning the faulty item and shipping a good replacement far exceeds the cost of repair done by the distributor.

Incorrectly Ordered Items.   Incorrect ordering can be a simple error or, more likely, overoptimism on the distributor's part. The receptivity of manufacturers to returns is shown in Exhibit 12–12. Apparently manufacturers are more forgiving of distributors' ordering mistakes than their own shipping errors.

Feedback to Electrical and Electronic Manufacturers.   Most distributors submit monthly sales totals and inventory levels to their suppliers, except for very

**EXHIBIT 12–12   Incorrectly Ordered Goods Policies in Electrical/
Electronic Distribution**

Distributor's Redress for Incorrectly Ordered Items	*Percent of Distributors*
Goods returned for 100% credit	25
Goods returned for restocking fee up to 15% of product cost	12
Nonstandard products nonreturnable	44
Distributor cannot return goods	19
	100

slow-moving items that are reported annually. Distributors also submit information concerning their competitive weaknesses on an informal basis.

MANUFACTURERS' AGENTS

Second only to industrial distributors, manufacturers' agents handle almost 20 percent of all units sold in industrial markets. The manufacturers' agent is an independent business establishment that, on a continuous contractual basis in a limited or exclusive geographic territory, sells part of the output of two or more client manufacturers. The products handled are complementary or related to one another but are noncompeting. The agency does not take title (or ownership) to the goods in which it deals, has little control over prices, credit, or other terms of sale, and is paid on commission.

The main difference between a manufacturers' agent and a distributor lies in the "title." Because manufacturers' agents do not take title to the goods, they cannot set price and usually don't maintain inventories. The items they sell usually are shipped directly from the manufacturer's factory to the customer.

Manufacturers' agents are known by a variety of names, including manufacturers' representative, "rep," M/A, sales agent, and agent. Typically the "rep" has had many years of experience in a well-established company before becoming a manufacturers' agent. Indeed, the majority have been successful direct salespeople for large firms who escaped the bureaucracy of a corporate environment to go it alone. The majority of manufacturers' agents are one- to five-person operations covering a single metropolitan area, although some firms employ fifty or more salespeople and have sales territories spanning many states or even the entire nation. It is estimated that there are more than 30,000 manufacturers' agent organizations in North America, of whom about 10,000 belong to the Manufacturer's Agents National Association (MANA), which is headquartered in Laguna Hills, California.[8]

Trend Toward Manufacturers' Agents

Each year, for many years, the number of reps belonging to MANA has increased by about 10 to 15 percent.[9] This reflects the trend toward greater use of manufacturers' agents. There are several reasons for this trend, including manufacturers' rising selling costs, manufacturers' desire to sell into new industry segments and geographical territories, and rising travel costs for their direct sales force.

Sales Costs.   Industrial sales call costs have increased from $71.27 per call in 1975 to $259.00 per call in 1989.[10] This dramatic climb is not expected to slow.

Specialized Market Segments.   Industrial manufacturers are finding new sales opportunities in narrow market segments outside their traditional markets. For example, one hardware specialties manufacturer using a direct sales force to sell to distributors also sells to twenty-six specially defined markets (including marine equipment, rack jobbers, and OEMs) through manufacturers' agents.

Opening New Territories.   As industrial development expands into new geographical regions, industrial manufacturers have difficulty justifying the use of their direct sales force. Adolescent markets have insufficient sales potential to support direct selling. However, manufacturers' reps, who offer a much broader product assortment than any of their manufacturers can, provide industrial manufacturers a fixed cost of sales entry to such sparse markets.

Increasing Travel Costs.   When potential customers are widely separated or distant from the company's head office, the use of manufacturers' agents over direct selling has increased because of rapidly growing costs of travel.

Advantages Offered by Manufacturers' Agents

Manufacturers' agents as a distribution channel offer the manufacturer a number of potential advantages, particularly when compared with the manufacturing firm using its own direct sales force.

Predictable, Stable Sales Cost.   Manufacturers' agents are paid a straight commission on sales. Thus, the manufacturer knows exactly how much its sales expense will be. Commissions can range from 3 percent on very high-volume orders to 20 percent for products that require a lot of detailed attention, installation, and service, or that have an extended selling cycle. Rates are highest for products that take a lot of effort to sell or involve a lengthy specification and negotiation period to conclude the transaction. They tend to be lower for standardized products, and where the dollar sales volume is extremely high. Manufacturers' reps can be less expensive because they are paid only if they bring in orders. The manufacturer does not pay a regular salary plus benefits for orders that are not coming in, as would be the case with its own salespeople.

More Aggressive Representation.   Few corporate salespeople are paid on straight commission, but the manufacturers' agent is. This is a strong incentive for highly motivated, indeed maximum, effort.

Synergy in Complementary Lines.   Because a rep handles compatible products from several manufacturers, the sale of one product is likely to lead to the sale of others. Consider the example of a customer buying a signal lamp: the manufacturers' agent for the electrical instrument firm may also describe his or her related lines and often secures orders for sockets, panels, meters, or switches from the same customer during the same sales call.

BUSINESS MARKETING IN PRACTICE

GM Replaces Parts Catalog with Bull

Beginning in September 1993, workers at many GM dealerships will be finding the right parts for GM cars and trucks electronically—and faster and more accurately than in the past.

This development is the result of a decision by General Motors of Canada Ltd. to eliminate its paper parts catalog entirely, beginning with the 1994 model year.

Dealers will still be able to view the GM parts catalog on microfiche, but a more impressive, computer-based alternative is being offered by Bull HN Information Systems Ltd. With the new Bull Electronic Parts Catalog (EPC), the entire GM parts catalog for the past 10 years will be contained on just one compact disc—including parts numbers, explanatory text, charts, and diagrams.

Parts staff in GM dealerships will be able to access the Bull EPC disc catalog by means of a compact disc read-only memory player (CD-ROM) linked to a standard IBM-compatible 486 personal computer. Working much like an audio CD player, the computer-based CD-ROM player will use laser technology to quickly search for and display information stored on the EPC disc.

Certainly, one of the reasons Bull's new electronic parts catalog is easier to master than its predecessor is that it runs under the user-friendly Microsoft Windows graphical computing environment. The EPC system uses Intuitive Windows drop-down menus and on-screen prompts to quickly guide a clerk to the right component. And thanks to Windows' graphics capabilities, the system can display diagrams of most parts and magnify illustrations of smaller components by up to 200 percent.

An optional EPC feature uses an automobile's vehicle identification number to further narrow down the search for the right part. And whether or not the VIN is used, customer inquiries can be handled more quickly and efficiently with the EPC system than with GM's paper-based catalog.

In addition, Bull's new electronic catalog has been designed to link up with dealers' existing computer-based inventory control systems. As a result, it's possible to use the EPC system to compile a parts list for a customer and then switch to a connected inventory control system to see whether the parts are in stock.

The new EPC system is good for the environment, cutting back on the use of paper. It should also provide very tangible benefits for GM dealers—reducing training time for parts personnel and generating faster and more accurate responses to customers' inquiries.

Source: Murray Soupcoff, "Bull System Makes GM Parts Hunt Easier," (Toronto) *Globe and Mail,* September 2, 1992, p. B4. Reprinted by permission of the author.

Minimal Training.   The rep is an experienced professional salesperson, with an in-depth knowledge of a particular industry and territory. At most, the manufacturers' agent needs familiarization with a new principal's product line.

Instant Marketing.   The manufacturers' agent has an established market of regular customers with whom the firm has built rapport. For a manufacturer who is either introducing a new product (especially one that does not fit its traditional markets) or wishing to exploit sparse markets with mature products, the M/A is an "in-supplier" whose built-in customers offer immediate coverage in his or her territory.

Nurture for Small Customers.   Both manufacturers and distributors prefer to deal with larger-volume accounts. Thus, their smaller buyers often receive short shrift. Manufacturers' agents aggressively cultivate small accounts and develop new markets.

Reduced Sales Management.   Although reps are extremely beneficial for smaller companies, some quite large industrial manufacturers employ them. Manufacturers of commercial aircraft, for example, have used manufacturers' agents for years, as have Dow Chemical, W.R. Grace, McGraw-Edison, and Parker Hannifin. One reason is that the principal can be relieved of many sales management tasks. Using, say 22 reps across the country, which employ a total of 168 salespeople, a principal in effect deals with only 22 people without the hassle of establishing and operating 22 regional offices. Furthermore, the principal does not have to invest capital in 22 regional sales offices and have funds tied up until they become self-supporting.

Permanence of Representation.   All too frequently the young direct salesperson may cost the industrial manufacturer a couple of hundred thousand dollars to train, only to be lost to another firm just as he or she is about to become productive. On the other hand, the manufacturers' rep firm has its roots in its local territory, and its major asset is its customer base.

Disadvantages of Using Manufacturers' Agents

From the perspective of the business principal, the use of manufacturers' agents is not without some limitations, including the following:

Loss of Control.   As with direct salespeople who operate on a full commission basis, manufacturers' agents avoid any administrative or reporting functions that are not directly related to generating sales. There is no guarantee the agent will use the principal's promotional materials properly. The agent may exploit immediately profitable sales rather than maximizing long-run potential. The agent may devote more time to its other principals' products than the industrial manufacturer would wish. Solution: The principal should outline expectations clearly in its contract with the agent. Control needs are obviated if the manufacturer's products yield better than average profit potential.

Partial Attention.   Since the manufacturers' agent represents several manufacturers, it cannot give full attention to any one product line all the time. Indeed, the agent may devote more time to the other firms it represents than the industrial manufacturer would wish. This becomes particularly annoying when the manufacturer expects detailed call reports, extensive missionary selling, or extra pre- or postsale service. Solution: Such extra attention should be specified in the contract with the agent, specific fees for services should be negotiated, or higher commission rates should be established.[11]

Customer Patronage Preferences.   Some customers want to deal directly with the industrial manufacturer's own sales force; others have strong loyalty to a particular manufacturers' agent. Solution: Assess prospects' preferences before establishing a new representative.

Administrative Procedures.   Each rep has its own internal procedures. Thus, the proliferation of policies and procedures faced by a manufacturer may be equal to the number of reps the manufacturer deals with. Solution: Offer consulting assistance and be adaptable.

Government Contract.   Different government agencies have varying policies toward manufacturers' representatives. Solution: Investigate government agency policies and specify which government departments or agencies will be retained by the manufacturer as "house accounts." These house accounts should be clearly specified in the contract signed with the rep.

Circumventing the Agent.   The great fear of the manufacturers' agent is that the agency will build a substantial account from nothing only to have the manufacturer take it away from the rep and sell direct. This leads to secrecy by the rep about the agency's accounts. Alternatively, some industrial manufacturers who terminate a manufacturers' agent find that they also lose their customers because strong personal relationships keep customers loyal to their agent and their loyalty is transferred to the agent's new supplier. Solution: Maintenance of open communication between manufacturer and agent, together with clear conditions surrounding terminations, can reduce these potential conflicts.

SUMMARY

A channel of distribution is a sequence of institutions that facilitates transactions between producers and final users. Business marketers have a choice of selling directly to their customers or using intermediaries. Channel members may reduce total transaction costs, assume inventory responsibilities, reduce the manufacturer's financing requirements, provide more cost-effective market coverage, be better tuned in to local markets, and permit the manufacturer to invest in higher-return activities.

Channel length or complexity depends on the range of functions required and how they will be accomplished. Typically, the result is multichannel marketing. Direction and coordination of channels is assumed by a channel leader, whose activities may reduce potential conflict among channel members.

Industrial distributors are merchant intermediaries—that is, they take title (ownership) to the goods that they handle. Industrial distributors are a major force in business marketing. They include general line distributors, limited line (or specialty) distributors, and combination houses.

Another significant business marketing intermediary is the manufacturers' agent. Manufacturers' agents represent a growing trend in business marketing. Like other agent intermediaries, manufacturers' agents do not take title to the goods they sell. They offer manufacturers a number of advantages, including a known cost of sales, and quick entré to markets. Nevertheless, they entail disadvantages for principals, such as loss of control over their activities and little feedback of information about their markets.

Intermediaries, whether they are agents or merchants, have a special role to play in the distribution of business goods and services. They are the institutions and the people in the institutions between the manufacturer and the end user which form the critical behavioral side of distribution.

Key Terms and Concepts

distribution
channel of distribution
intermediaries
direct (short) channel
indirect (long) channel
value-added resellers (VARs)
channel audit
opportunity costs
merchant intermediaries
full-service wholesalers
single-line wholesaler
specialty wholesaler
limited-function wholesalers
cash-and-carry wholesaler
drop shipper (desk jobber)
truck (wagon) jobber
mail order distributor
cooperatives

agent intermediaries
commission merchants
manufacturers' agents
brokers
auction companies
retailer cooperative
multichannel marketing
dual distribution
parallel channels
channel conflict
channel leader
title
general line distributors
specialty distributors
combination house
price quotations
distributor's margin

Discussion Questions

1. What factors would lead a manufacturer to choose an industrial distributor rather than another type of intermediary?

2. What factors would lead a manufacturer to choose a manufacturers' agent rather than another type of intermediary?

3. Under what circumstances would a manufacturer choose to sell directly to end users rather than using intermediaries?

4. What sorts of policies might a manufacturer adopt to reduce the potential of channel conflict with manufacturers' agents in the firm's distribution channel?

5. Industrial distribution channels tend to have fewer intermediaries between manufacturer and end user than do distribution channels for consumer goods. Why?

6. What would be the explanation for the wide range of commission rates paid to manufacturers' agents?

Endnotes and References

1. Ronald Michman, "Trends Affecting Industrial Distributors," *Industrial Marketing Management* 9 (July 1990): 213–216.

2. Kate Bertrand, "Apple Bites Back," *Business Marketing* (August 1991): 12, 14, 16.

3. Cutting tools, such as drills, are considered perishable because they have a short useful life and are discarded when dull. They are also called consumables, for the same reason.

4. Roger J. Calantone and Jule B. Gassenheimer, "Overcoming Basic Problems Between Manufacturers and Distributors," *Industrial Marketing Management* 20 (1991): 215–221.

5. Michman, "Trends Affecting Industrial Distributors," pp. 213–216.

6. Tom Stundza, "Metal Service Centers Sing Bottom Line Blues," *Purchasing*, May 21, 1987, pp. 43–49.

7. This section is condensed from an unpublished research study conducted by Mc-Master University (Hamilton, Ontario) researchers Janice Long, Bruce Shaw, Bob Sommerville, and Adrian Zenwirt among nineteen members of the National Electronic Distributor's Association.

8. "MANA—A History That Continues to Write Itself," Manufacturers' Agents National Association (August 1990).

9. Ibid.

10. Cahners Advertising Research Report No. 542.1G (April 1991), based on a random mail survey of 4,000 business respondents.

11. Knowing what motivates a rep and developing a motivational plan can build a "special" relationship that encourages reps to "go the extra mile." See Edwin E. Bobrow, "Reps and Recognition: Understanding What Motivates," *Sales & Marketing Management* (September 1991): 82–86.

13

LOGISTICS MANAGEMENT

- To recognize the ways that logistics decisions affect a firm's competitive marketing advantage

- To understand the impact of logistics decisions on customer service

- To appreciate the impact of logistics decisions on the customer and the firm's operating efficiency

- To become aware of the interrelationships between changes in one aspect of distribution and all other aspects

- To understand how product and package design can affect logistics costs

A large sign at Navistar's parts distribution center proclaims:

THE RIGHT PRODUCT

AT THE RIGHT PLACE

AND THE RIGHT TIME

This statement encapsulates the job of the distribution system. Channel management assumes that the appropriate intermediaries have been established and motivated to interact with customers, but the channel cannot function without the efficient physical movement of the goods. This is accomplished through the logistics system.

LOGISTICS DEFINED

The industrial manufacturer's **logistics system** encompasses the total flow of materials, from the acquisition of raw materials and purchased component parts through to the delivery of a finished product to business customers. Logistics involves two major areas of the firm's operations: materials management and physical distribution management.

Logistics managers perform a wide variety of functions, all in an effort to ensure that the right product arrives at the right place at a time suitable to the customer's requirement. These functions, which will be discussed in detail in this chapter, include determining the appropriate location of facilities, forecasting and order management, transportation management, inventory management, warehousing, materials handling, and packaging.

Materials Management

For the industrial manufacturer, **materials management** entails the orchestration of purchasing, transportation, and receipt of raw materials, components, subassemblies, and supplies (see Exhibit 13–1). This activity might also be described as providing manufacturing supply service. The inbound material goes into stock and subsequently undergoes further finishing, processing, or assembly, all the while moving in and out of work-in-process stocking points—whether in bins, vessels, or tote boxes, or on skids. Throughout this acquisition and manufacturing process the term *materials management* applies to the logistical decision processes involved.

The various activities involved in obtaining products and materials from outside suppliers include requirements planning and scheduling, identifying sources of supply, requesting quotations, and placing orders. Logistics considerations may make it more cost effective for the buyer to transport the supplies rather than permitting the supplier to deliver. Orders are received, inspected, and stored. The materials management function may even include hedging and speculation on re-

EXHIBIT 13–1   The Logistics System

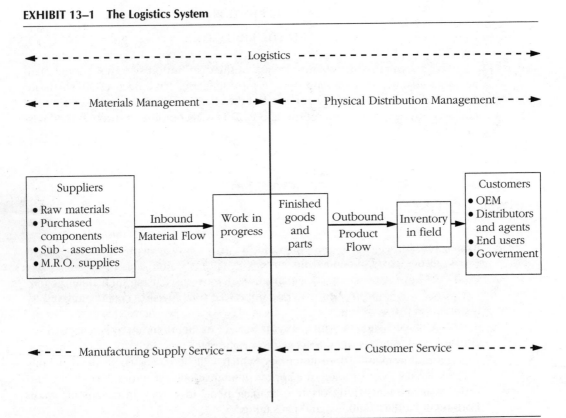

Source: Adapted from an unpublished diagram by Bernard J. Lalonde, Ph.D., The Ohio State University.

quired inventories.[1] Within the plant, materials management involves scheduling to meet manufacturing requirements and managing work-in-process storage and materials handling up to the point that the product is fully manufactured.

Physical Distribution Management

Once the finished product has been completed, logistical activities are termed **physical distribution (PD)** management. PD involves management of the finished goods inventories, both within and outside the plant, and everything else to do with the outbound flow of product to its final destination (see Exhibit 13–1). This activity results in the provision of customer service. Physical distribution also involves receiving and processing customers' orders, releasing goods from inventory, and handling and transporting the finished product within the firm's channels of distribution. PD requires coordination with marketing to ensure that customer service levels are appropriate, returned goods are properly processed, service parts are available, and promotional campaigns have total logistical support. To establish a customer service objective and manage logistics to achieve that goal involves financial commitment by management.

THE TOTAL COST APPROACH TO LOGISTICS MANAGEMENT

What costs are involved in the logistics operation of a firm? Typically they include the costs of performing a range of logistics activities, including the costs of planning and managing the logistics system; transportation of supplies to the plant and finished product throughout the distribution system; receiving, inspecting, and putting supplies in storage; maintaining inventories; processing customer orders; packaging; maintaining warehouses; and providing customer service (see Exhibit 13–3).

It is difficult to see these functions as being directly responsible for generating sales but easy to see that they are necessary to support sales and costly to perform. Hence, many management people evaluate their logistics systems according to the total logistics costs expended for any given sales revenue. This is known as the **total cost approach** to logistics management. Obviously, using such an approach, a manager would attempt to maintain or reduce total logistics costs compared to historical performance in the firm, compared to average performance in the industry, or in comparison with a similar firm in the same industry. For such comparisons the total logistics costs usually are expressed as a percentage of sales.

Logistics expenditures in the United States have been estimated to be as high as $650 billion per year and in 1990 accounted for 11 percent of total U.S. gross national product.[2] For individual firms, total logistics costs range from as little as 10 percent to more than 50 percent of gross sales. For example, electrical hardware and pharmaceuticals manufacturers' distribution costs are about 15 percent of sales, plumbing and heating product manufacturers's costs are 20 percent, petroleum products manufacturers run about 30 percent, and copper refiners' costs are 55 percent. A number of factors influence this proportion. Copper is heavy and low in value. Consequently, copper distribution costs are a high percentage of selling prices. The opposite is true of pharmaceuticals. Light in weight but high in value, their distribution costs are lower as a percentage of sales. The geographic scope of the firm's operation can also affect logistics costs, since transportation and branch warehousing costs mount the farther away customers are located.

As an item of cost, logistics often represents the highest single operating expenditure for the industrial manufacturer. Thus, it deserves careful managerial attention, not only to prevent unnecessary or excessive expenditure, but also in recognition of the fact that any saving in the logistics area adds directly to bottom-line profits for the firm. The impact of the profit leverage afforded by logistical cost reduction can be seen by equating such savings to the amount of effort in increased sales that would be required to generate the same profit (see Exhibit 13–2).

Management recognition of the profit-impact importance of logistics and exploration of methods of logistics improvement have been facilitated by high-powered computers that have made feasible some of the difficult analyses required to improve logistics activities. The overall objective of logistics management is to perform the functions assigned to logistics in the most cost-effective way.

Interrelationships of Logistics Functions

The various functions performed in a logistics system tend to be interdependent and interrelated. It is unlikely that a change in one element will not affect others and, therefore, the costs of the total system. These interrelationships are visually portrayed in Exhibit 13–3, which represent logistics activities as meshed gears. For

EXHIBIT 13–2 Profit Impact of Logistical Cost Reduction

If net profit on the sales dollar is 2.0 percent, then . . .

a saving of	*is equivalent to a sales increase of*
$ 0.02	$ 1.00
2.00	100.00
200.00	10,000.00
2,000.00	100,000.00
20,000.00	1,000,000.00

Source: MCB University Press Limited. Bernard J. Lalonde, John R. Grabner, and James F. Robeson, "Integrated Distribution Systems: A Management Perspective," *International Journal of Physical Distribution Management* (Oct. 1970), p. 46. Reprinted by permission.

EXHIBIT 13–3   Activity "Cogs" in a Distribution System

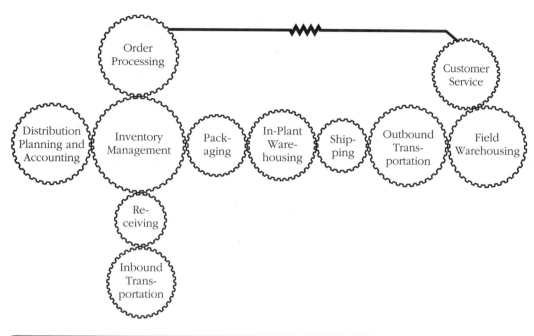

Source: From "Physical Distribution: Key to Improved Volume and Profits," by Wendell M. Stewart from *Journal of Marketing* (1965) 66. Reprinted by permission of American Marketing Association.

example, the marketing manager may decide to change the dimensions of the display carton containing industrial fasteners. The executive's reasoning might run like this: "If the container is displayed on the distributor's shelves, a thinner box presenting a larger surface at the shelf face will have more visual impact, and thus attract more sales." This change affects the corrugated shipping carton shape, which in turn affects how many cartons (fewer) can be loaded on a pallet. This may mean that space on loaded trucks is less fully utilized, and pallets cannot be stacked as high in field warehouses. Meanwhile, people supervising inventory records and accounting data can be confused because shipping cartons contain a different number of units, and the order-processing department may arbitrarily increase or decrease customers' order quantities to make them conform to the full unit size of the new cartons.

In a large corporation, where these functions are found in individual departments, the method of evaluating managerial performance typically exacerbates the problems of interdependency. The shipping department may accumulate shipments to take advantage of full truckload (TL) rates, which are cheaper than less-than-truckload (LTL) rates. Meanwhile, the customers are likely to complain about slow delivery.

Suboptimization

Suboptimization is the term applied to a situation in which one department's objective or function is optimized without considering the effect of the action on other departments or functions. For example, trying to minimize inventory costs by running inventory down to excessively low levels can result in stockouts, lost sales, time-consuming backorders, use of expensive premium transportation to fill orders, development of a bad reputation, and even lost customers. In this example, by trying to achieve optimal (lowest-cost) inventory levels, other areas of the distribution system are hurt.

This indicates how detrimental it can be to the firm if one area or activity pursues individual objectives without considering repercussions elsewhere in the system. In such situations, where a logistics activity in isolation is evaluated on its ability to fulfill management objectives, suboptimization results. The goal of logistics, then, is to manage the system to provide designated levels of manufacturing supply service and customer service at **least total cost**.

Cost Tradeoffs

Sometimes it takes an emergency to prompt distribution managers to consider alternative logistics methods and their cost impact on the total system. Xerox had always shipped toners, parts, and supplies for its copying machines by rail from Chicago to a California warehouse. When the warehouse suffered a fire, emergency shipments were air-freighted to customers. Later, when Xerox executives analyzed their costs, they recognized that the more expensive air transport could save the company millions of dollars without diminishing customer service because it was more than offset by the expense of operating local warehouses. They closed thirty-three warehouses as a result.

A **cost tradeoff** occurs when a change in the distribution system causes some costs to increase and other costs to decrease. In the Xerox example, transport plus warehouse costs using rail freight were traded off against transport plus warehouse costs using air freight. Evaluated solely in terms of transportation cost, air was prohibitively expensive, compared to rail. But faster air transport obviated the need for warehouses, reducing total costs. Evaluation of cost tradeoffs helps to identify the least cost method of operation among alternatives that provide a given level of performance.

Similarly, a fire changed Pilkington Glass methods of packaging sheet glass. In St. Helen's, England, Pilkington operated a box plant next to its plate glass plant. Sheets of plate glass were carefully crated in wooden boxes for shipment. During World War II, a German incendiary raid on St. Helen's razed the box plant. In a desperate attempt to keep shipments moving, blocks of plate glass were strapped together and laid against an A-frame on a flat-bed truck. They not only survived the haul to London, but Pilkington Glass has since saved millions in packaging expenses by abandoning wooden crates.

Obviously, distribution managers shouldn't wait for disasters to point out new directions. They should from time to time consider innovative options and the tradeoffs that might be generated (that is, conduct a **logistics audit**). But even with respect to proposed minimal changes, the tradeoffs and total cost implications should be evaluated before such changes are implemented.

CUSTOMER SERVICE

In Exhibit 13–3, we saw that the various distribution activities were interdependent. If a change in any one activity affects all the others, where should the distribution manager begin an analysis of the logistics system? From a marketing perspective, the answer is easy. The distribution system wouldn't exist without a customer. Hence, one should start to build the system by establishing the level of customer service the firm wishes to offer, then adjusting the rest of the logistics elements to provide it.

Customer service refers to a group of utilities or benefits the customer expects from the supplier. In logistics, these usually include such aspects as *on-time* delivery of *complete orders* in *good* condition (the right product at the right place and the right time). The **level of customer service** is the "batting average" of the firm in providing service—that is, the percentage of occasions the customer service target is met. Similarly, in evaluating an existing system, the logistics audit should begin with reevaluation of customer service objectives. The desired level of customer service, then, becomes the objective that all logistics activities, as an integrated system, attempt to achieve. The level of customer service also acts as a quality control standard against which the performance of the distribution system may be evaluated.

Of course, customer service is not cheap. The more service provided, the more it costs the business marketer. However, the customer firm may be willing to pay for these services rather than incurring the costs of fewer services. For example, if the business marketer consistently provides on-time delivery, the customer can save money by reducing safety stock, can order in a routine fashion, doesn't face expensive order expediting, and avoids the risk of production shutdown. In essence, consistent, on-time delivery enhances the value of the supplier's product-service mix and permits a higher price to be charged.

Elements of Customer Service

Customer service means different things to each customer. Most industrial buyers identify the following order-status factors as being important when dealing with suppliers:

- *order cycle time:* the elapsed time between placing the order and receipt of delivery

- *order cycle consistency:* the extent to which order cycle time varies,
- *order accuracy:* the degree to which items shipped meet order specifications
- *order completeness:* the extent that items ordered are totally filled when the order is assembled for shipment
- *order condition:* damage level at the time of receipt

A comparative study of the service expectations of ninety-eight pump and valve manufacturers in the United Kingdom and in Canada toward their suppliers of steel castings and forgings indicates a wide diversity and uniqueness of factors that can be included under the customer service heading (see Exhibit 13–4). This study indicates that although the ability to meet a quoted delivery date ranks number one in both countries, there are substantial differences in the other service expectations of customers in the two countries. For example, Canadian customers, unlike their British counterparts, place a high importance on price discounts. On the other hand, U.K. buyers are much more concerned about replacement guarantees than are Canadian buyers. The conclusion we should draw is that each customer is unique and has its own service expectations and requirements. Although some service factors may be of common concern to an industry (providing a basis for segmentation), it is dangerous to assume that customer service expectations will be similar among foreign markets and cultures.

EXHIBIT 13–4   Service Factors Classified According to Their Importance to the Customer

Service Factor	Percentage of Times Ranked in Top Five	
	U.K. (percent)	Canada (percent)
Ability to meet quoted delivery date	100	89
Prompt and comprehensible quotation	44	58
Provision of technical advice for problem solving	60	55
Discount structure on list prices	0	48
Technical after-sales service	24	44
Representation by supplier	28	41
Ease of contact with person in authority	48	38
Replacement guarantee	52	38
Willingness to manufacture a wide range	48	33
Pattern (or die) design service	12	25
Extended credit facilities	12	21
Availability of testing facilities	52	21
Provision of machining facilities	4	8

Source: MCB University Press Limited. "Customer Service in Industrial Marketing: A Comparative Study," by Peter M. Banting from *European Journal of Marketing,* vol. 10, no. 3 (Summer 1976), p. 139. Reprinted with permission.

Establishing Customer Service Policies

Although it is impossible to generate a universally applicable list of customer service elements, some general statements may be made.

Patronage.   **Patronage** is the state of being a regular customer. Customer service is an important determinant of patronage. In a study of 400 industrial purchasing agents in Europe, customer service was ranked second in importance after product quality among a list of supplier attributes.[3] This response confirmed results of an earlier study of 216 North American members of the National Association of Purchasing Management.[4] Dramatic evidence of the perils of allowing customer service to slip is that a 5 percent reduction in customer service results in a sales decrease of 20 percent.[5]

Segmentation.   The relative importance of customer service elements varies among industries, market segments, and individual customers. The difference in rankings between Canadian metal buyers in the pump industry and their counterparts in the valve industry illustrates this point (see Exhibit 13–5). Although both rank delivery reliability tops, valve manufacturers are more concerned about technical advice, ease of contact, and replacement guarantees, whereas pump manufacturers are more interested in discounts and after-sales service. The astute business marketer recognizes that markets can be segmented on the basis of differences in customer service elements.

EXHIBIT 13–5   Service Factor Ranked Order Comparison—Pump and Valve Manufacturers

Pump Manufacturers	Rank	Valve Manufacturers
Delivery reliability	1	Delivery reliability
Prompt quotation	2	Technical advice
Discounts	3	Prompt quotation
After-sales service	4	Ease of contact
Technical advice	5	Replacement guarantee
Sales representation	6	Discounts
Wide range of manufacture	7	Sales representation
Ease of contact	8	Wide range of manufacture
Pattern design	9	After-sales service
Replacement guarantee	10	Pattern design
Credit	11	Credit
Test facilities	12	Test facilities
Machining facilities	13	Machining facilities

Source: MCB University Press Limited. "Customer Service in Industrial Marketing: A Comparative Study," by Peter M. Banting from *European Journal of Marketing,* vol. 10, no. 3 (Summer 1976), p. 143. Reprinted by permission.

Customer Perceptions.   Customer perceptions, not supplier preconceptions, form the basis for setting customer service policies. The industrial buyer forms many expectations on the basis of industry "norms" for various aspects of customer service—for example, a seventy-two-hour order cycle for delivery of specialty lubricating oils and greases might be considered reasonable, based on typical practice in the market. A supplier who gratuitously offers forty-eight-hour service in such a situation may be spending money needlessly on a higher level of delivery service than his customers require or desire.

Profit Impact.   Customer service levels should not be established without considering their impact on costs and revenues. Some years ago, distributors of steel tried to outdo their competitors by offering customers more and more services. When delivery service was very high, they began offering extra treatments to the metals they sold. When this aspect of service was high, they began doing minor fabrication for their customers. Then they realized they weren't making money. Their trade association, the Steel Service Center Institute, had to offer an education program focusing on the cost-of-service concept to make distributors aware of the deleterious effects of offering more services without first costing them out.

How much should a firm spend on customer service to gain extra sales? Exhibit 13–6 shows how much a typical firm can improve its share of market for each $100,000 spent. Indicated too is the point of diminishing returns, at which additional expenditures will exceed the value of increased sales. Although the graph suggests a break point of about 85 percent, a company can determine its own figure only by studying specific conditions in its field. The nature of the product, geographic circumstances, transport characteristics, and other factors all affect the optimum service point.

Competitive Advantage.   Customer service can be an effective differential competitive advantage.[6] Nobody knows this better than Boeing, an aircraft manufacturer that ranks customer service high in winning and maintaining accounts.

> Nearly every operator of Boeing aircraft has a story about the company's coming through in a pinch. When tiny Alaska Airlines needed landing gear that could put a jet down on a dirt strip, Boeing was there. When Air Canada had a problem with ice clogging in some air vents, Boeing flew its engineers to Vancouver, where they worked around the clock to solve the problem and minimize disruption of the airline's schedule. Boeing's attention to customer relations has paid off. In December 1978, Alitalia lost a DC9 airliner into the Mediterranean Sea and the Italian national carrier vitally needed a replacement aircraft. Umberto Nordio, Alitalia's president, telephoned T. A. Wilson, Boeing's chairman, with a special request: Could Alitalia quickly get delivery on a Boeing 727? At the time there was a two-and-a-half-year wait for such aircraft, but Boeing juggled its delivery schedule and Alitalia got the plane in a month. Mr. Nordio returned the favor six months later, when Alitalia cancelled plans to buy McDonnell Douglas DC10s and ordered nine 747 Jumbos (from Boeing), valued at about $575 million.[7]

EXHIBIT 13–6   How Much Should You Spend to Improve Customer Service?

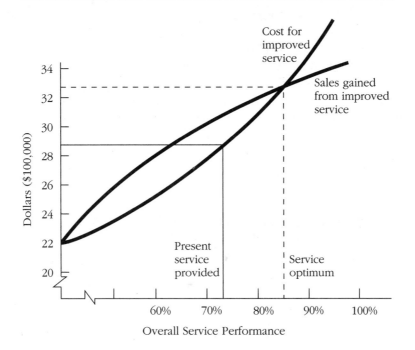

Cost Service Relations. How much should a firm spend on customer service to gain extra sales? Graph shows how much a typical firm can improve its share of market for each $100,000 spent. Indicated too is the point of diminishing returns, at which additional expenditures will exceed the value of increased sales. Although the graph suggests a breakpoint of about 85 percent, a company can determine its own figure only by studying specific conditions in its field. The nature of the product, geographic circumstances, transport characteristics, and other factors all affect optimum service point.

Source: Reprinted by permission from *Traffic Management Magazine,*
September 1982.

PLANT LOCATION

Location decisions can be very complex, and it is difficult to arrive at a standardized process of analysis. Manufacturing plant location decisions tend to center on finding the least cost of manufacturing supply service, production cost, and customer service.

Materials-Centered Locations

A plant location may be "pulled" toward sources of supply—a **materials-centered plant location**—for several reasons. The unique location of raw materials, such as in mining and extractive industries, limits choice. An industry may make a location decision based on the great weight loss in manufacturing or processing that leads to a reduction in total transportation costs. For example, sugar is only 18 percent of the sugar cane—the rest is fiber and water. Another factor is perishability of the material. The thirteen-month supply of tomato ketchup paste and other related products must be processed and packed during a short few weeks' harvest period.

Market-Centered Locations

Alternatively, a plant location will be "pulled" closer to the market under several circumstances. When the production of the finished product adds substantial weight, transportation costs may make some industries' products prohibitively expensive to ship to distant markets. Freight rates are substantially higher for the finished product than for the raw materials. Thus, **market-centered plant locations** can reduce overall freight costs. When the finished product is perishable, whether physically or technologically, it is better to locate closer to the market. Repair service facilities, for example, tend to be located close to the market they serve.

Terminus-Centered Locations

Historically, transportation facilities have had a strong impact on location. Sixty percent of Canada's steel output is manufactured in Hamilton, Ontario, because Hamilton's natural port facility provides the cheapest water transport of raw materials to the central Canadian market. Similarly, Pittsburgh and Youngstown are U.S. steel centers that are **terminus-centered plant locations**.

Other Factors

In some industries, transportation costs are relatively unimportant to plant location. For high-technology firms, "ambiance" (culture, climate, recreational activities, and schools) and "CEO attitudes" (grew up in a region) strongly influence location decisions.[8] Semiconductor industries are a case in point. The initial location of Fairchild Semiconductors and Texas Instruments was no doubt more a function of a pleasant climate than logistical costs. But the establishment of spinoff companies in "Silicon Valley" was due to external economies of critical industrial mass (that is, a concentration of suppliers and customers in the industry attracted other similar firms).

Production Costs

Factors that affect production costs can strongly influence the location decision. These include cost of land; taxes and subsidies; availability of stable, skilled labor; productivity levels and wage rates; labor laws; power and fuel availability and cost; and, most recently, insurance rates. Thus, availability of natural gas influences the location of glass factories, whereas aluminum smelters are located near hydroelectric sites.

Customer Service

The most recent example of the influence of customer service on manufacturing plant location is provided by the North American drive to imitate the Japanese just-in-time (JIT) system (discussed later in this chapter). Customers who have adopted this so-called "zero-inventory" approach require delivery of zero-defect supplies to feed their production lines directly, which can necessitate deliveries many times a day. Indeed, GM favors vendors that are close to its Flint, Michigan, "Buick City" plant.[9] And many of Delco Electronics' suppliers are moving their production plants closer to the Delco facility in Kokomo, Indiana.[10]

WAREHOUSE LOCATION

The number of warehouses in the logistics system is a function of the transportation cost savings from consolidating shipments and the level of customer service desired. Customer service usually can be improved by decentralizing supplier inventories to provide faster replenishment of customer inventories, thus permitting customers to reduce their inventories. However, this is done at the greater capital cost of physical warehouse facilities, the higher cost of increased safety stocks, the potential costs of more shorter-haul shipments, and even transshipments among warehouses. Thus, the business marketer must analyze the tradeoffs between achievement of least-cost warehouse configurations and maximum-service warehouse configurations.

Typically, an overnight run from warehouse to customer location would extend about 300 miles in radius. Thus, to serve the entire U.S. market would require about 40 warehouses.

Types of Warehouses

A firm with a large and stable-enough demand to fully utilize the facility will own a **private warehouse** to achieve low warehousing cost. This arrangement offers the ability to custom-design the work flow, equipment, and environment and provides the greatest direct control over operations. Private warehouses also often incorporate regional sales offices and service centers. A variation on the private warehouse is the construction of a dedicated customized facility that is *leased* to the firm. Leasing provides greater flexibility with no fixed investment.

A company wishing to have warehouse facilities in a market area with too small a demand to justify a private warehouse can rent space in a **public warehouse**. Such independent operations provide professional management of all the functions normally undertaken by private warehouses and offer the renter flexibility by charging according to the amount of work done and the amount of space required, typically on the basis of month-by-month commitments. This arrangement reduces the renter's capital investment and the risk of being locked in to an owned facility of fixed size or to materials-handling equipment that is subject to technological obsolescence. The use of public warehouse space is a particular advantage to a firm whose requirements may change due to seasonal demand or shifting markets, where promotional campaigns create unusual demands, and where alternative transportation opportunities may vary.

A **bonded warehouse** is a legally secure repository in which goods are temporarily stored for transshipment, for consolidation, or until taxes and duties are paid. It may be public or private. A **field warehouse** is a legally secure building or area within a building (whether a public or a private warehouse) where material is safeguarded by a bonded employee of a field-warehousing organization who issues receipts to the owner of the goods. The owner can then obtain loans based on the security of the field-warehoused goods (as represented by the receipts). Such goods are not released to the owner without authorization of the lending institution.

Warehouses can be production centered, market centered, or intermediately centered.

Production-Centered Warehouses

A **production-centered warehouse** is located at a manufacturing plant or close to several production facilities and primarily serves as a consolidation point to accumulate full trainload or truckload quantities for shipment at the lowest vehicle rate. These shipments may proceed directly to the customer plant or to other warehouses located in market centers.

Market-Centered Warehouses

The **market-centered warehouse** receives full vehicle-load shipments from the factory or production-centered warehouse and provides more certain on-time replenishment of customer inventories. It acts as a break bulk facility, receiving truck- or container-loads and reassembling shipments in smaller loads to provide the assortment that matches individual customer requirements—typically smaller quantities, in smaller delivery vehicles, for more frequent and timely short-haul deliveries to small distributors or manufacturing plants.

Intermediately Centered Warehouses

Intermediately centered warehouses may act as master distribution centers for regions of the country, utilizing lowest cost, full-vehicle-load in-bound transportation from factory locations across the nation and regrouping goods into appropriate assortments for shipment to local warehouses or directly to customers in the region.

Warehouses in Motion

Some companies recognize that in-transit inventory incurs costs and trade off some of the cost of a fixed site against utilizing a transit mode as a moving warehouse, even to the point of including limited processing on-the-move. One firm with continentwide markets loads train cars at the plant and adjusts their destinations as orders are received.

United Processors Company, which harvests watermelons and strawberries in the southwestern United States, experienced inventory buildups because supplies accumulated in advance of demand peaks in the East and Midwest. The company switched from truck transport to slower rail shipments, which meant that the produce could still be shipped at harvest time but not arrive until the market demand was strong. Thus, the railroad acts as a moving warehouse, reducing not only United Processors' warehousing costs but also its transportation costs.[11]

SALES FORECASTING

Forecasts of the anticipated sales of each product and in each market are critical to planning logistics. Typically, such forecasts are generated by the business marketing manager in large firms and then passed on to the logistics manager so that materials acquisition and PD plans can be coordinated with demand.

The goal of forecasting is to predict what products will be bought, when they will be needed, and where they will need to be delivered. **Product-market sales forecasts** typically deal with shorter time periods than strategic forecasts, generating predictions three months into the future to a year out. Such forecasts are continuously adjusted by what actually transpires in the markets as orders from agents, dealers, distributors, and customers are received and as customers inform the firm about changes in their own plans.

Product-market sales forecasts must take into account (1) cyclical components, including the impact of economic conditions as business activity heats up or cools down; (2) seasonal fluctuations, such as the increasing demand in winter for components used in the manufacture of air conditioners; and (3) trends, such as the steadily increasing demand in the late 1980s and early 1990s for microprocessors.

Of course, random components of demand, such as strikes, unusually severe winters, and catastrophes, cannot be forecast.

Time series forecasts, such as moving averages and exponential smoothing, are used when demand patterns historically have been relatively stable. In situations in which there appears to be a correlation between sales of a product and some other independent and leading factor, regression methods may be used for logistics forecasting. For example, replacement parts demand may be a function of the age of equipment in use.

ORDER MANAGEMENT

Logistics activities are initiated when an order is communicated to the business marketer. Orders may be placed by personal delivery, mail, teletype, personal telephone call, fax, or direct computer transmission (electronic data interchange, or EDI). A comparison of these methods illustrates the tradeoffs that exist among speed, cost, and accuracy. Generally, higher-speed transmission tends to be more costly, mechanical and electronic methods are usually more accurate than human methods, and accuracy varies inversely with the frequency of handling the information.

Efficient order management can provide more timely and accurate market intelligence in the form of sales reports. It can also improve cash-flow management, credit authorization, purchasing, production scheduling, and inventory control. Any higher costs associated with more efficient order management may be more than offset by the tradeoffs in other areas. For example, faster order cycles may reduce lead time sufficiently to justify less expensive transportation, while still delivering the goods within the customer's time constraints. In summary, efficient order management can reduce costs in the logistics system and may improve customer service.

TRANSPORTATION MANAGEMENT

At 40 percent of total PD costs, transportation of industrial products ranks as the most expensive functional activity in logistics (see Exhibit 13–7). The four transportation decision areas for both incoming and outgoing materials (in decreasing order of the dollar value riding on any one decision) are (1) FOB point, (2) mode of transport, (3) carrier approval, and (4) carrier selection. Exhibit 13–8 shows that higher levels of management are involved in the highest-dollar-value decisions—choice of the FOB point and selection of the mode of transportation, whereas lowest-dollar-value decisions (carrier approval and selection) are made predominantly by clerical and middle management.

EXHIBIT 13–7 Average Logistical Cost of Business Products, 1991

Function	Cost as Percent of Sales	Cost in $/CWT
Transportation	3.31	13.25
Warehousing	2.08	12.07
Inventory carrying at 18%	1.98	11.75
Customer service/order processing	0.63	4.75
Administration	0.38	2.78
Total distribution cost	8.18	43.32

Notes: CWT = hundredweight = 100 pounds. The columns do not add because the number of data entries for each statistic is different.

Source: Herbert W. Davis & Co. *Distribution Costs Database*. Reprinted with permission.

Modes of Transportation

The basic modes available for transportation are rail, highway, water, pipeline, and air. Choices among these modes involve tradeoffs in terms of cost, speed of movement, availability to serve desired locations, dependability to meet delivery schedules, capability to handle a shipment, and frequency of scheduled movement.

Rail. Railroads carry the greatest amount of freight (see Exhibit 13–9), typically because of the volumes of forest products, grain, chemicals, metals, and bulk

EXHIBIT 13–8 Management Levels Involved in Transportation Decisions

Decision Category	Management Level Category			
	Corporate Headquarters	Top Management	Middle Management	Clerical
Inbound				
FOB	2	7	3	1
Mode		6	6	1
Carrier approval		2	4	7
Carrier selection			3	10
Outbound				
FOB point	1	4	10	1
Mode		5	7	4
Carrier approval		1	4	11
Carrier selection			2	14

Source: Reprinted by permission of the publisher from "How to Determine the Composition and Influence of a Buying Center," by Melvin R. Mattson, *Industrial Marketing Management* (August 1988, vol. 17, no. 3), 213. Copyright 1988 by Elsevier Science Publishing Co., Inc.

EXHIBIT 13–9   U.S. Intercity Freight by Modes

	Percent of Ton-Miles	
Mode	1980	1990
Rail	37.5	37.4
Truck[a]	22.3	25.7
Oil Pipeline	23.6	20.4
Inland Water[b]	16.4	16.2
Air	0.2	0.4

[a]Truck traffic includes for-hire and private carriers, also mail and express.
[b]Water traffic includes both domestic and foreign traffic moving through U.S. rivers, canals, and the Great Lakes, but excludes domestic coastal and intercoastal movements.

Source: From *Transportation in America,* December 1991 Supplement, p. 10. ENO Foundation for Transportation. Used with permission.

materials that are handled over great distances. Rail shipments can accommodate a wide range of types and sizes of goods—dry, liquid, frozen, controlled atmosphere, and awkwardly shaped—in carload (CL) shipments of up to 30,000 pounds or in less than carload quantities (LCL). At an average rate of just a few cents per ton-mile, rail is an inexpensive transport mode. However, rail shipments have limited accessibility. Goods must be moved to and from railroad terminus points, unless shippers or receivers have spur lines into their plants or warehouses. Railroads primarily are used to transport low-value, high-density, large-volume shipments over long distances. As an indication of the large scale of a rail shipment, manufactured goods shipments by rail average 36 tons, whereas forestry, mining, and mining products average 62 tons per shipment.[12] Sensitive equipment may be damaged by the impact of rail cars being shunted in train assembly, so other modes are preferable for such shipments.

Highway.   The most popular mode of transportation is truck. Its importance in shipment of selected industrial products can be seen in the fact that more than 80 percent of the weight of all machinery, fabricated metal products, and rubber and plastic products shipped in the United States, and more than 90 percent of the total weight of leather and leather products, moves by truck.[13] Truck transport is the most available and accessible of the modes because motor vehicles are not restricted by terminal-to-terminal operation but can provide service from the shipper's loading point to the receiver's dock. Highway transport is used mostly for short hauls of high-value manufactured goods, because trucks have higher operating costs and less capacity than trains.

Pipelines.   Pipelines are limited to transporting gases, liquids, and slurries (suspensions of solid particles in a liquid), operate at a low speed (about 10 miles per

BUSINESS MARKETING IN PRACTICE ▮▮▮▮▮▮▮▮▮▮▮▮▮▮▮▮▮

Logistics Solutions Don't Always Work

The problem: Manufacturers typically buy grease in 400-pound drums, ten drums at a time. The drums require considerable physical handling, are nonreturnable, and create a disposal problem. On a production line, discarding partially empty drums at shift change rather than changing them during the shift wastes grease.

The solution: A grease supplier developed a logistically improved method for delivery, storage, and use of grease. The supplier purchased a tank trailer that would pump grease into the customer's plant, where it would be stored in 5,000-pound-capacity vessels and then piped to greasing stations on the production line.

The logistics savings: Bulk delivery was cheaper than drum delivery for the supplier. Customers could save 5 cents a pound in grease purchase costs, and eliminate wastage, drum handling, and disposal costs.

Market resistance: Customer adoption was so slow that three years after introduction, the specially designed bulk grease delivery truck still was underutilized.

The causes: The logistically better system failed due to poor sales training by the grease supplier. On the buying side, resistance to an unfamiliar idea by customers' engineering departments, misconceptions about the relatively small costs of adaptation to the new system, and fear of being tied to one supplier kept customers from switching over.

The moral: In evaluating a change to a logistics system, more than cost tradeoffs must be considered. The perceptions of people using the system are also important.

Source: Related to Peter Banting, Ph.D., Professor of Marketing, McMaster University, Hamilton, Ontario, by a corporate executive who requested anonymity.

---

hour), and have limited accessibility. Their third rank in ton-miles carried is mainly due to the huge volume of liquid petroleum products they carry.

Water.   The prime advantage of water transport is its capability to move very large shipments. Water offers lowest-cost transport, but at a slow speed and restricted access. Deep-water shipments are primarily intercontinental, whereas domestic shipments move along the coasts and through the Great Lakes, canals, and navigable rivers such as the Mississippi, Ohio, and Missouri rivers and the St. Lawrence Seaway. Water carriers primarily move low-value, high-density cargoes such as cement, chemicals, grain, mined items, and basic bulk commodities.

Air.   The least utilized and most costly (about 50 cents per ton-mile) freight mode is air shipment. The first large all-cargo air carrier was Flying Tiger. Other large airlines earn most of their revenue from passenger service. Air freight is confined to high-value items, emergency shipments, and perishable products (such as cut flowers). One advantage of air shipment is that pilots tend to land gently. This is a benefit to business marketers who ship computers, electronic equipment, and other sensitive devices that might be damaged by truck or rail shipment.

Trucking is a major mode of transportation.

Courtesy of St. Johnsbury Trucking Co. Inc.

Intermodal Transportation

When shipments are transferred among more than one mode, it may be possible to capitalize on the advantages of each mode. The most common intermodal shipment is placing a truck trailer on a railway flat car for a long haul, then hauling the trailer by truck from the train terminal for local delivery. Thus, door-to-door service is provided at a lower cost than by highway traffic alone. This is called trailer-on-flatcar (TOFC), or "piggyback." Other intermodal coordinated shipments are named "fishyback," for trailers loaded on ships or barges, "trainship," and "air-truck." Most intermodal shipments are carried in containers.

Containers are $8' \times 8' \times 20'$ or $8' \times 8' \times 40'$ standardized boxes into which palletized loads may be stacked, smaller items contained in corrugated boxes may be packed, and products that are awkward to handle may be blocked (braced by nailing blocks to the container floor). The standard sizes and fittings of containers make these unitized loads easier and cheaper to handle and move. Containers also protect contents from in-transit and handling damage, pilferage (they can be locked), and the elements, and can thus reduce the amount of protective packaging for the items being shipped. Some containers are insulated; they may be fitted with refrigeration units or heating units. They can easily be carried on appropriately adapted truck trailers, train flatcars, and ships. Loading and unloading the various modes is accomplished with appropriately fitted cranes and lift trucks. Containers are ideal for intermodal shipment but are more popular in international freight than domestic shipments.

In-Transit Processing

Transportation need not be simply movement of goods. Form value may also be created in-transit. For example, the cement truck mixes concrete on-the-move. Fish caught at sea are cleaned, filleted, and frozen on shipboard during the passage back to port. And tomatoes, picked green in Mexico, are sprayed with ethylene gas so that they ripen during their highway transport to the United States and Canada. These examples suggest that the high cost of transportation can be mitigated somewhat by creative analysis rather than viewing transportation as just an enhancer of time and place value.

The Small Shipment Problem

Small shipments generally are 1,000 pounds or less and are carried mainly by trucks. Small shipments are generated by low-density products (sometimes called "balloon" products), small orders from customers that are less-than-truckload (LTL) quantities, emergency orders, back orders, and service parts transport.

The magnitude of small shipments is illustrated by the volume of business handled by couriers. Federal Express, United Parcel Service (UPS), and several other companies specialize in small parcel delivery services across North America, offering door-to-door pickup and delivery in their own vehicles. Each day UPS moves 11.5 million envelopes and parcels weighing less than 32 kg (70 pounds) to, from, and within 190 countries around the world with a jet fleet of 162 aircraft. UPS carries twenty times the volume handled by the U.S. Postal Service.[14] The largest player among international courier services is DHL International Ltd. of Hong Kong, which controls 45 percent of the market outside of the United States.[15]

Small shipments represent a problem because they sustain the highest rates of loss and damage of any shipments; most of this damage occurs in handling rather than in transport. Thus, small shipments incur additional costs of reordering and higher insurance costs. A typical loss and damage sample is illustrated in Exhibit 13–10.

In addition to high loss and damage rates, small shipments cause a number of other problems for business marketers: order-processing costs are often higher than the value of the product, picking of small orders in the warehouse is as costly as retrieval of full pallet loads, and small shipments create congestion on the shipping dock, incur premium transport rates, and are usually unprofitable.

UPS expands its service in the small shipment market.

Our international passengers start clearing customs before our planes even land.

While we're flying your packages overseas, detailed shipment information is flying ahead on UPSnet, our global data network.

That gives UPS customs brokers in destination countries a sizable head start: from 2 to 36 hours. And that gives us extra time to sort out potential clearance problems before the packages even arrive.

As a result, UPS international shipments are well on their way while other delivery companies are still getting their paperwork in order.

What's more, this technology doesn't just make us faster and more reliable. It makes us more efficient. So we can deliver to over 180 countries and territories, usually for a lot less than other companies charge.

So next time you have an international shipment to send, just send it UPS.

After all, many companies can fly your packages overseas. It's what we're doing while they're flying that makes all the difference in the world.

We run the tightest ship in the shipping business.

Courtesy of United Parcel Service.

The business marketer can reduce this small shipment problem in a number of ways. At the risk of a tradeoff with the loss of some customers, minimum-order quantities might be raised. Volume discounts may be instituted, and customers may be encouraged to maintain safety stocks. Small orders can also be held up and pooled with other shipments, and back orders can be held for transport with the customer's regular shipment. Computer scheduling can help by balancing shipments and reducing back orders. Orders can be grouped, especially service parts orders, with regular product orders. Special packaging for small shipments, although more expensive, might be traded off against reduced loss and damage.

EXHIBIT 13–10   Small Shipment Loss and Damage

Mode Used	Percent of Shipments Experiencing Loss/Damage	Index of Relative Usage*
Truck	80.0	100
Parcel post	73.5	33
Rail	68.6	44
Express	66.7	13
Air	38.3	41
Other	87.5	5

*Index of Relative Usage: For every 100 small shipments transported by truck, 33 are transported by parcel post, and so on.

INVENTORY MANAGEMENT

Inventory costs are a constant concern of most business marketers for two reasons: they are the second largest cost in distribution, and they can add as much as 40 percent in extra costs per year to the value of goods being stored.[16]

One of the best-known studies of inventory carrying costs was conducted in 1955, and its conclusions are still valid (see Exhibit 13–11). Here the accumulated costs worked out to 25 percent of the value of the goods being stored. The largest component was obsolescence, followed by interest on money invested. It is easy to see that as the cost of capital varies, so too do inventory carrying costs. Conse-

EXHIBIT 13–11   Carrying Cost as a Percentage of Inventory Value

Carrying Cost Item	Percent of Inventory Value
Obsolescence	10.00
Interest	6.00
Depreciation	5.00
Handling costs	2.50
Transportation	0.50
Taxes	0.50
Storage facilities	0.25
Insurance	0.25
	25.00

Source: L. P. Alford and John Bangs, eds., *Production Handbook* (New York: Ronald, 1955), pp. 396–397.

quently, money borrowed at 12 percent (as opposed to 6 percent) would increase the carrying costs of inventory to 31 percent.

Given these high costs, wouldn't the business marketer wish to reduce inventories to as low a level as possible, thus freeing capital for investment elsewhere? The answer is both yes and no. On the materials management side, costly plant shutdowns may occur due to the unexpected shortage of a critical input. On the physical distribution side, an unavoidable stockout may result in a delayed sale and customer annoyance, loss of a sale, or even loss of the customer. Inventories, then, are necessary to cushion or absorb the effects of discontinuities among various elements of the logistical system. But there are a number of additional reasons for holding inventories (see Exhibit 13–12).

Types of Inventories

In any company, five types of inventory may be identified: cycle stock, in-transit stock, safety stock, speculative stock, and dead stock.

EXHIBIT 13–12   Twenty-two Reasons for Holding Inventory

- To provide customer service in the face of sales fluctuations and other problems
- To give customers assurance of availability
- To hedge against expected surges in sales because of promotions or price reductions
- To await shipment to fill a definite order
- To await shipment to fill an expected order
- To handle production variations
- To manufacture material in economic run sizes
- To allow for batch production
- To permit flexibility in plant scheduling
- To hold off increasing capacity
- To permit more flexible raw material scheduling
- To provide raw material storage
- To take advantage of favorable raw material price
- To take advantage of distribution costs or factors
- To hold material that is a by-product
- To store overruns or misruns
- To await disposition (as in the case of a canceled order)
- To keep storage equipment operational or from shutting down (as in the case of pipelines)
- To allow for errors in measuring and recording
- To protect against strikes and work stoppages
- To protect against hurricanes and other acts of nature
- To speculate against price and cost changes

Source: Reprinted by permission of *Harvard Business Review*. An exhibit from "Questions for Solving the Inventory Problem" by James I. Morgan, (July/August 1963). Copyright © 1963 by the President and Fellows of Harvard College; all rights reserved.

Cycle Stock.   Cycle stock is inventory required to meet basic demand under conditions of certainty. It is cycle stock for which economic order quantities (discussed in the next section) can be calculated.

In-Transit Stock.   In-transit stock refers to goods undergoing movement between fixed stocking points, such as warehouses. The concept of in-transit stock is important because funds can be tied up while goods are being transported. The cost tradeoffs may justify using a faster, though more expensive, mode of transport when, say, a transcontinental or international shipment is involved.

Safety Stock.   Safety stock is a buffer inventory held over and above cycle stock levels to cushion against unanticipated shortages of supply or uncertainties of demand. Safety stock levels are calculated on the basis of equating marginal savings of preventing stockouts to marginal carrying costs of additional inventory.

Speculative Stock.   Speculative stock is inventory in excess of normal requirements that is held in anticipation of price increases. The objective of holding speculative stock is to increase profitability on the basis of the change of value of the goods while they are being stored.

Dead Stock.   Dead stock is inventory for which no demand has been registered for a specified period of time. Typically, if warehouse space has alternative uses, dead stock should be scrapped.

Fixed Order Quantity

If the process of ordering were costless, the materials manager would maintain no inventory and place orders on a continuous basis to meet demand. Similarly, if inventory carrying costs were zero, the customer could hold huge inventories. But both inventory ordering and holding do have costs. The tradeoffs between inventory costs and ordering costs can be represented algebraically by the formula

$$EOQ = \sqrt{\frac{2RC}{I}}$$

where EOQ = the optimal order size in units (**economic order quantity**)

R = the annual requirement or sales volume in units

C = the fixed administrative cost of placing an order

I = the carrying costs of one unit of inventory

Thus, if a manufacturer of off-highway equipment requires 1,200 power transmissions per year (R) at a cost of $600 per unit, the cost of placing an order is $60

(C), and the average inventory carrying cost is 25 percent, the inputs to the *EOQ* equation would be:

$$R = 1,200 \text{ units/year}$$
$$C = \$60$$
$$I = \$600 \times 25\% = \$150$$

Thus,
$$EOQ = \sqrt{\frac{2 \times 1,200 \times 60}{\$150}}$$
$$= \sqrt{960}$$
$$= 30.9$$

Consequently, the economic order quantity (rounded) would be 31 units, and orders would be placed 39 times during the year, or roughly every 6½ working days (assuming 250 working days per year). Therefore, the EOQ is considered a **fixed order quantity**.

It is important to note that cycle stock EOQs will be affected by changes in requirements (or demand forecasts), by quantity discounts, and by other cost effects such as ordering several items jointly from the same supplier. Nevertheless, EOQ gives a reasonable estimate of order magnitude, even under varying conditions.

Fixed Order Intervals

An alternative to using the fixed order quantity approach (such as EOQ) is to order at a fixed interval, say every Tuesday, or maybe the fifteenth of each month. With this approach, order quantities are likely to vary with every order. A system of **fixed order intervals** permits better assignment of workloads and delivery schedules; however, it is more subject to stockouts. Therefore, this system requires close monitoring of minimum reorder quantities in case a stock low is reached before the scheduled reorder day. The alternative is to hold larger safety stocks. If the firm has a private truck fleet, fixed order intervals can permit purchases FOB origin for pickup by trucks that have made scheduled deliveries near the supplier, rather than having them deadhead home (return empty).

ABC Inventory Classification

A general rule of thumb known as the 80/20 rule states that 80 percent of sales volume is generated by 20 percent of the items in a company's product line. These percentages are not exact, of course, but they communicate that the relative importance of products in stock varies from item to item. In managing inventories there are always some fast-moving items, such as products in the growth stage of their life cycle, and some slow movers, such as accessories and products in the introduction, maturity, or decline stages. In **ABC inventory classification**, the general principle is to "go where your bread is buttered" by paying closer attention to those product line items that contribute most to sales or profit.

The ABC technique involves ranking all of the firm's items in decreasing levels of importance, then choosing arbitrary division points so that each product can be assigned into the A, B, or C group (see Exhibit 13–13). The greatest degree of managerial attention is devoted to managing A items, with less frequent review and analysis of the B group, and the least time spent on the C items. Since maintenance of high levels of customer service is very expensive, the ABC system may also be used to set customer service standards by product item. For example, the lowest stockout levels would be permitted for A items, moderate stockouts would be allowed for B items, and more frequent back orders the norm for C items.

EXHIBIT 13–13   ABC Inventory Classification

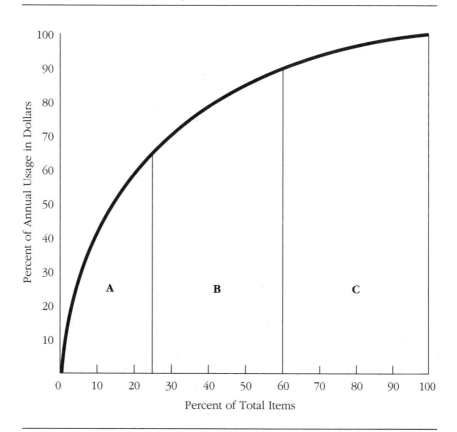

Clearly, judgment is important in managing an ABC inventory system. Some items, though low in sales volume or profitability, might be critical to maintaining customer relations (for example, an infrequently ordered bearing that, if unavailable, could shut down a customer's production). Such items should be classified A.

Inventory Reduction Through JIT

Since inventory carrying costs run between 25 and 30 percent of the value of the goods being stored, inventory reduction offers huge potential savings. In 1990, Asea-Brown-Boveri, Inc., one of the world's leaders in transformer production,[17] introduced **just-in-time (JIT) delivery** to its recently acquired transformer plant in Guelph, Ontario. A year later, in 1991, inventory had dropped 40 percent, stock turn had doubled, and the time needed to produce a transformer had shrunk 18 percent.[18] At General Motors' Windsor plant inventories turn once every 3.5 days, compared to twice a month before JIT was introduced. Each extra inventory turn produces $1 million in savings.[19]

Manufacturers are addressing this opportunity using three powerful techniques: (1) JIT delivery from their suppliers, which eliminates inventories by ensuring that materials arrive at the plant just before they are used; (2) computerized materials requirement planning (MRP) systems, which ensure that you don't order more than you need; and (3) electronic data interchange (EDI), the technology that allows intercompany communication between computers for instant order transfers and payments.

Inventory used to be considered a cushion against disaster. Now these techniques permit companies to view inventory of production inputs as a symptom of inefficiency that masks such underlying problems as variable input quality, lengthy production machine changeover time, inaccurate forecasting, poor scheduling, unreliable transportation, and inadequate information exchange with suppliers.

To obtain the supplier commitment necessary for JIT deliveries, the buyer must provide sufficient business to justify a supplier's extra attention. Thus, the supplier base shrinks and order size increases. For example, carriers used by GM's Windsor, Ontario, trim plant dropped to a reliable five from fifty.[20] The manufacturer has no inventory from which to substitute for faulty product inputs, misshipments, unavailability of parts, or damage. Thus, product input quality is higher, and back orders are reduced significantly. The supplier requires greater order lead times to meet JIT requirements. Thus, buyers' communication with suppliers improves after EDI is instituted; sales projections and information previously considered confidential are shared with the supplier. Working with the supplier, the manufacturer may make significant design changes as a result of JIT. Closer communication also leads to fewer sales calls from the supplier.[21]

Once a supplier adopts JIT, the firm is likely to encourage its second tier of suppliers to do the same. By 1995, 93 percent of the Canadian automobile parts suppliers will be using some type of JIT technique with *their* suppliers, four-fifths

Bar Code Is Taking Over

What if bar code had never been invented? How would our world be different today? Without grocery scanning, check-out lines would certainly be longer and food prices higher. Fewer product choices would be on the shelves, since store inventory could not be taken every day. Restocking from the distribution center to the local store would take an extra day or more without bar code carton labels and automatic laser scanning. Cars would cost more, too. Today's new Ford or Chevy has over twenty bar code labels on component parts, which are read by dozens of laser scanners from the time an engine block starts down the assembly line until your custom-made new Blazer is delivered to the dealer down the street.

Commercial use of bar code first began with grocery carton scanning for conveyorized order picking at a distribution center in early 1970. This application was followed within several months by the first of many automotive component tracking applications. Today, the bar code industry has grown to be a $5 billion international market for scanning and printing devices, label media, specialized software, and packaged application solutions. The bar code market is expanding at the rate of 25 percent per year, and over 90 percent of automatic data collection is now accomplished by bar code systems.

An acceleration in the spread of technology is sometimes provided unintentionally by government law or policy. This happened in the case of bar code. When the Environmental Protection Agency (EPA) began testing and certifying automobile engines to conform to the Clean Air Act, it was mandated under the act to impose a fine of $10,000 each time a car engine's serial number and component configuration were not recorded and made available for federal inspection. Not long after this bill was passed, an auto company was fined $90 million for failure to record 9,000 engine builds. This task is an easy one for bar code laser scanning, and it's called compo-

nent tracking, so all automotive manufacturers quickly installed bar code systems.

In the dozen years since this incident, auto makers have installed hundreds of additional component tracking systems, strictly for internal benefits. Today, bar code use begins when the auto manufacturer sends a purchase order to a supplier for components. The components are individually bar coded, and the shipment container is bar coded as well. These labeling procedures trigger the movement of the components from the manufacturer's receiving dock directly to the assembly line without intermediate parts storage. The reduction in inventory and its related carrying cost can generate savings of 10 percent or more of the manufacturing cost of complex products.

After automobiles are built, the need for detailed control procedures increases. Next, bar code ensures the matching of each auto with the proper transport carrier, and, if shipment damage occurs, bar code scanners record this information during delivery inspection. If product or warranty claims are made, or if a product recall is initiated, bar code is the tool that assembles all the claim records. Every new car built after 1990 has a bar code vehicle identification number (VIN) which can be scanned from outside the car with a handheld laser gun. This benefit permits law enforcement officials to establish a quick and error-proof record of the 21 alphanumeric characters that define a car, down to the serial number, country, assembly plant, and day that car was built. Many benefits throughout the product life cycle are possible through the use of a well-designed bar code data collection system.

Bar code is indeed taking over many important jobs in our society. When used intelligently, bar code can eliminate boring and error-prone activities and instead build a constructive bridge to efficient management.

Source: Adapted with permission from David J. Collins and Nancy N. Whipple, *Using Bar Code: Why It's Taking Over* (Duxbury, Mass.: Data Capture Institute, 1990), pp. 7–18.

will have computerized their materials flows, and virtually every supplier will be hooked into EDI.[22]

Although firms marketing under JIT agreements experience a reduction in competition, larger order sizes, higher prices, and greater profits,[23] perhaps their most significant gain is in the enduring strategic relationship that develops between the JIT supplier and the buyer. It creates an entry barrier to competitors. JIT requires relationship marketing and offers the marketer a monopoly position with the customer.

WAREHOUSE MANAGEMENT

Warehouses and distribution centers are buildings or dedicated areas within buildings where inventories may be safely stored to act as a buffer or cushion discrepancies of quantity or assortment among parts of the distribution system.

Warehouse Functions

A number of functions are performed within warehouses. After items are received from suppliers or from work stations in the plant, their quantities and quality are inspected. Then they are assigned appropriate stock identification codes, sorted, and put into storage. While being held in stock, their storage conditions are monitored. When needed, they are recalled from storage, assembled into desired assortments, and packaged. Inventory records are adjusted, and appropriate shipping and invoicing documentation is prepared. Sometimes light manufacturing and assembly are undertaken in the warehouse, as well as repair to items that have sustained minor damage.

Warehouse Design and Layout

Private warehouse construction and ownership is costly and limits the firm's flexibility to adapt to changes in the market. Yet where demand is large in volume and steady, the privately owned warehouse or distribution center can provide lower logistics costs than other alternatives (renting, leasing).

Space requirements are determined by forecasting demand and establishing economic order quantities, plus safety stock, and then converting these figures into cubic footage dimensions plus capacity for future growth. About one-third more space is required for nonstorage activities, including shipping, receiving and inspection, order picking and assembly, salvage and repacking, office space, employee cafeteria, shower, and restrooms and locker rooms.

In designing the warehouse, a number of tradeoffs must be considered. Rather than using fixed stocking points, higher space utilization can be achieved by assigning inventory to variable empty locations as space requirements (generated by changing market patterns, seasonal demand, sales campaigns) change, but this is at the expense of fast and accurate computer control and greater travel time. Highly mechanized warehouses offer speed and accuracy but have higher fixed investments, risk technological obsolescence of equipment, and are not adaptable to demand shifts, equipment breakdown, or power cuts when compared to labor intensive operations. High-rise buildings (one hundred feet or more in height) make better use of the cube than conventional twenty-five-foot-high buildings, cut aisle requirements, reduce land costs, and cut construction costs by as much as 80 percent, but at the cost of more expensive equipment and less flexibility. High-density storage (narrow and fewer aisles, greater rack height) utilizes cubic capacity at the cost of more expensive equipment and potential congestion. These are but a few of the tradeoffs. Indeed, each company faces unique tradeoffs that will affect logistical efficiency, flexibility, costs, and customer service performance. Some general principles of warehouse design and layout appear in Exhibit 13–14.

Materials Handling

The basic unit for movement of goods is the pallet—typically, a 40″ × 48″ hardwood platform containing slots into which forklift truck blades can be inserted for

EXHIBIT 13–14   General Principles of Warehouse Design and Layout

---

1. One-story warehouses usually are less expensive and more efficient than multistory facilities.
2. Straight-through materials flow is more efficient than when goods must backtrack.
3. Materials handling equipment, where appropriate, improves efficiency.
4. The ratio of aisle space to storage space should be minimized.
5. Whatever the height of the building, the cubic capacity should be fully utilized.
6. Order picking distances, handling, and movement should be minimized.
7. Faster-moving items should be stored close to receiving and dispatch docks, and slow movers farthest away.
8. Functionally related items that are usually ordered at the same time should be grouped together.
9. Physically similar items should be grouped together, for example, heavy items that require the same materials handling equipment, such as overhead cranes.
10. Fragile items should be grouped together.
11. Working stocks should be made more easily accessible by replenishing them from larger, more remotely located reserve stocks.
12. Special items should be separated for greater protection. For example, high-value items require security areas. Explosives, flammables, and toxic and radioactive items require safety equipment, such as shielding, better ventilation, and fire protection. Other items require environmental control over temperature, humidity, and lighting.
13. Stock should be rotated to avoid accumulations of older models, obsolescence, deterioration, or stale-dating.

---

lifting and transporting. On this pallet corrugated cartons or unpackaged items such as electric motors may be stacked to make a unit load. Other unit loads are created by strapping, shrink-wrapping, crating, use of slip sheets, wire cribs, tote boxes, and containers.

The most popular method of moving unit loads in a warehouse is by forklift truck. Many versions are available, including gas, electric, or hand powered, narrow aisle, high rise, and side loading. For high-volume movement, less flexible conveyors may be installed in the warehouse. Inclined low-friction gravity conveyors, rollers, and chutes, powered conveyors, drag lines, overhead tracks, cranes, and automatic guided vehicles are all part of the battery of materials handling devices that may be used.

PACKAGING OF GOODS

Packaging can be viewed from different perspectives. The business marketer usually is more concerned with the promotional value of packaging and whether the package meets the customer's requirements. But if a reasonable level of customer service is to be provided, the package should be viewed in the context of the entire logistical system, within both the marketer's own logistics network and the customer's. For example, will the package conform to the dealer's, distributor's, or OEM's logistical capabilities? Will customers be able to accept shipments and move them directly into their own warehouse or plant, or will shipments have to be unpacked and reassembled in a different format—put into tote boxes, repalletized, recoded, and so forth?

For purposes of this discussion we will examine some logistics aspects of one of the most widely used packaging devices—the corrugated carton. Typically, an industrial product, such as a small transformer, a gauge, or a quantity of fasteners, will be enclosed in a cardboard box. If the item is likely to be displayed on a dealer's or distributor's shelf, this container is printed in two or more colors for promotional effect. Then a quantity of these boxes is packed in a corrugated master carton or case. For storage or shipment, corrugated cartons are generally stacked on a pallet, four or more cartons high. Then pallet loads are stacked one on top of the other, several pallet loads high.

The first decision concerns the dimensions of the display box, for they will affect the design of the corrugated master carton. For example, one firm marketing powdered detergent in a $6^{5}/_{16}''\times 2^{1}/_{2}''\times 8^{7}/_{8}''$ display box was shipping 576 boxes per pallet when packed in corrugated cartons. This represented 70 percent pallet efficiency. In other words, 30 percent of the available space on the pallet was wasted, both in the warehouse and in the transport mode. The firm changed the display box size to $6^{1}/_{16}''\times 2^{1}/_{4}''\times 8^{5}/_{8}''$ and the new corrugated master cartons could fit 840 units on a pallet, achieving 92 percent pallet efficiency.[24]

Proper stacking of corrugated cartons is also important in the logistics system. Column stacking is best to utilize the maximum strength of the box. But if the cartons aren't perfectly aligned, the concentrated corrugated strength of the vertical flutes can no longer fully support the bulk of the load's weight. If three empty boxes are piled on top of each other only half an inch off perfect alignment, 29 percent of the carton strength is lost under compression. Since column stacking is subject to instability, stretch or shrink wrapping is a good way to maintain pallet loads in their unit load configuration throughout the entire distribution cycle.

Often corrugated cartons are stacked in an interlocking pattern in an attempt to improve stability of the load over column stacking. Stability may improve, but compression strength is reduced by 45 percent! If the pallet is stacked with corrugated cartons in such a way that the entire pallet surface is not covered (called underhang), the load can shift in transit. If one side of the pallet has cartons projecting beyond its lip (overhang) then cartons can be damaged and strength is lost. Going from a three-tier aligned stack without overhang to one with a single inch of overhang sacrifices 32 percent of stacking strength.

Another factor that reduces strength is humidity. As humidity rises, the carton absorbs moisture and load-carrying ability drops off dramatically. At 50 percent humidity, stacking strength is reduced to 80 percent of dry strength, whereas at 90 percent humidity, it is only 40 percent as strong. Fatigue also affects cartons. After thirty days under load, a corrugated carton retains only 60 percent of its original strength. The longer cartons are stacked, the more toppling becomes a concern. If humidity, fatigue, overhang, and misalignment coincide, the results can be disastrous. Exhibit 13–15 shows the combined effect of just two factors—temperature and humidity.

IMPROVING LOGISTICAL PERFORMANCE

Earlier in this chapter, the concept of logistics tradeoffs was discussed. The business marketer has a substantial role to play in optimizing logistics performance by

EXHIBIT 13–15   Effect of Temperature and Humidity on Compression Strength of Corrugated Cartons

Temperature		Percent Relative Humidity	Percent Difference in Compression Strength
°C	°F		
23.0	73	50	Base Level
27.0	81	30	+20
0.5	33	96	−73
27.0	81	90	−56

Source: MacMillan Bathurst, Toronto.

interacting with distribution channel intermediaries, customers, manufacturers, and other areas of the firm to facilitate tradeoffs that will bring cost and efficiency benefits to the firm.

Order Conditions

By smoothing order patterns and preventing congestion in the logistics system, customer service can be maintained at a high level more economically. Institution of minimum-order sizes helps to ensure that the costs of small orders are avoided. Using minimum reorder periods is another way of reducing small orders. When it is important to avoid technological or style obsolescence and perishability, maximum reorder quantities may be instituted. Similarly, delivery to individual customers on designated specific days can improve transportation efficiency by concentrating deliveries in geographic areas and leveling the delivery workload. Customer cooperation can be won to limit which products can be mixed in particular shipments and to agree on minimum lead times for ordering. Incentive price discounts can encourage customers to order in truckload (TL) and carload (CL) quantities. The business marketer may take the lead in helping small customers group their orders together so that shipments can be consolidated. Such approaches may be seen from the perspective of the business marketer's taking the initiative in *managing* customer orders rather than simply reacting to them.

Product Adjustments

The physical characteristics of an industrial marketer's products have considerable impact on the firm's logistics. For example, high-volume, low-weight products fully utilize the space parameters of the logistics system before the weight parameters are used up. This is especially true in transportation modes and in warehouses. An example would be bales of cotton loaded in a boxcar. Alternatively, low-volume, high-weight products use up the logistics system's weight parameters first, leaving excess volume available and unused. An example would be steel plate being carried on a flat-bed truck.

For lowest cost and highest efficiency, the business marketer's objective is to maximize utilization of both capacity parameters. Thus, an electrical equipment firm that ships motors (which fully utilize the weight parameter) could make use of the excess volume parameter by combining cartons of light bulbs in the shipment (but not on the bottom). Similarly, Steel Company of Canada combines shipments of barbed wire with chain-link fence—one is heavy and dense, the other light and bulky. Japanese suppliers ship auto engines and automobile seats on the same truck to their OEMs to achieve full cube-weight utilization. Such logistics thinking has led to the widespread change in packaging from glass to plastic containers to reduce weight. This is an example of **product adjustment**, where a change is made to the product to improve its logistical characteristics.

Many bulky products are shipped and stored in "knocked-down" condition—that is, disassembled—to make a compact package that is reassembled at the dealership or point of use. International Harvester (now J I Case) could mount only two fully assembled hay balers blocked on a rail flatcar for shipment to the West. Distribution logic suggested that by not completely assembling the machines, as many as six balers could be fitted on the same flatcar. However, the hay baler has a huge fly wheel that must be properly balanced on the finished machine; otherwise it would rip the baler apart. Since International Harvester dealerships could not afford to own expensive fly wheel balancing equipment for their individual small volume of hay baler sales, the finished machines had to be balanced at the factory prior to shipment. Investigation of the logistics savings led to the company completely building the machine, balancing the fly wheel, and then disassembling the machine for shipment and reassembly by the dealer. The extra labor was more than compensated by the tradeoff in lower shipping cost.

Product redesign for nesting or stacking is another product adjustment that can also achieve logistics economies. The Metal Cookware Manufacturer's Association surveyed 150 leading retailers and distributors, asking their reactions to pots and pans arriving from the factory with their handles unmounted. The switch would save freight, warehousing, and packaging costs, and could help cut cookware prices.[25]

When dense products are involved, excess metal may be trimmed and holes punched to eliminate unnecessary metal and reduce weight. One Japanese automobile manufacturer achieved economies by replacing the traditional solid crankshaft in its product with a hollow one. The redesigned "tubular" crankshaft not only brought logistics savings to the firm but also helped reduce the automobile's fuel consumption.

Another product adjustment technique is to concentrate products for storage and shipment. Rather than shipping bulky iron ore hundreds of miles from northern Quebec mines to southern Ontario, the Steel Company of Canada concentrates the ore into iron pellets at the mine site prior to shipment. Coca-Cola ships syrup concentrate to local bottlers around the world. The chemical industry would like to ship lubricants in concentrated form but is prevented by customers not having the appropriate equipment to heat and mix the product.

One company selling heavy polystyrene liquid switched to shipping pure polyester resin flakes by convincing customers that they could add their own (inexpensive) liquid styrene to make polystyrene. The supplier not only saved transportation costs but also was able to ship the flakes in inexpensive corrugated cartons rather than metal drums that cost $15 each.

Postponement of Commitment

The concept of **postponement of commitment** is especially useful in exploiting logistics tradeoffs. Here the decision to provide the product in finished form is delayed as much as possible, even to the very instant of purchase by the end user.

The result is reduced inventories, smaller safety stocks, fewer inventory control problems, reduced traffic, less capital equipment, and greater transportation savings. Some well-recognized examples illustrate the point. Sunoco is able to offer several varieties of gasoline by mixing an octane ingredient at the retail pump. This reduces the capital cost of several dedicated fuel tanks at each retail station and the logistics problems of inventory control over each variety. Similarly, paint retailers can hold smaller inventories of base paints, provide better product adaptation to customers' requirements, and offer better customer service when pigments are custom-mixed at the time of purchase. Manufacturing economies are achieved while still offering end customers variety of choice by shipping prefabricated building components. Similarly, building supply centers carry standard sizes of lumber that contractors then cut to the required specifications. In the computer industry, value-added resellers (VARs) assemble computer manufacturers' standardized components into specialized hardware for specific applications such as restaurant computer systems.

INTERNATIONAL LOGISTICS

International logistics offer the business marketer both opportunities and problems that are too expansive to cover in this book. Containerization is more extensively used in international shipment, with dedicated container ships providing frequent, fast, and regular transoceanic shipment and quick turnaround at ports. Free trade zones facilitate the transactions and physical flow of goods. Multinational firms such as Ford Motor Company can obtain materials and components anywhere in the globe, manufacture in some countries, warehouse in others, and sell in yet others.

Similarly, global competition is increasing. The decline in the U.S. dollar since the late 1980s attests to the Asian competition in domestic markets. Even close to home there has traditionally been competition in water carriage among the St. Lawrence Seaway, the Mississippi River, and West Coast ports for the North American grain export business.[26]

Two examples illustrate the special logistics considerations that affect international shipments. Canadian Canners (now DelMonte) made a shipment of canned goods to the West Indies. When the pallets were off-loaded from the cold ship's hold to the hot, humid dock, moisture condensed on the cans and all of the labels fell off. Unfortunately, the cost of identifying contents and relabeling the (now bright) cans was too high, and the shipment was scrapped. In the second example, alumina shipped from Jamaica is deliquescent—that is, it absorbs moisture from the air and eventually will dissolve and liquify.[27] This results in a weight gain by as much as one-third in transit. Consequently, alumina shipments must be planned so that cargo can be off-loaded at ports along the route of the ship's passage.

BUSINESS MARKETING IN PRACTICE ▮▮▮▮▮▮▮▮▮▮

Manufacturing Locations

Labor rates have a strong influence on the location of manufacturing facilities. National Semiconductor Corporation designs and fabricates computer chips in California's Silicon Valley. The chips are then transported to lower wage rate developing countries, such as Sri Lanka, Barbados, the Philippines, the Virgin Islands, and Panama, to be assembled and tested. Finally, the finished products are transported back to the United States and other countries for distribution to customers around the world.

Digital Equipment Corporation, the world's second-largest computer company behind IBM, has been able to save significant money by having components for its new line of personal computers made in Taiwan and assembled at several other facilities worldwide.

The U.S.–Canada Free Trade Agreement has encouraged a large number of Canadian firms to relocate their manufacturing facilities to the United States, where labor rates are lower. With the addition of Mexico in a North American Free Trade Agreement (NAFTA), there is little doubt that Canadian and U.S. companies will move some of their manufacturing plants to Mexico.

Sources: Roger Holmberg, "How High Technology Manufacturing Firm Manages International Distribution," *Annual Proceedings of the NCPDM* (1983), pp. 427–429; "Digital Unveiling a PC It Can Call Its Own," (Toronto) *Globe and Mail,* August 25, 1992, p. B3.

SUMMARY

The business logistics system involves the total flow of materials, from the acquisition of raw materials and purchased component parts (materials management) to the delivery of a finished product to business customers (physical distribution management). Among the various activities involved in logistics are facilities location, forecasting, order management, transportation management, inventory management, warehouse design, materials handling, and packaging. In logistical systems, suboptimization of any function to the detriment of the entire system is to be avoided. A minimum total cost approach, balancing the effects of many types of cost tradeoffs, is advised to achieve logistical efficiency for a specified level of customer service.

Customer service is the group of benefits the customer expects from the supplier, including on-time delivery of complete orders in good condition. The level of customer service is the quality standard set by the business marketer against which performance of customer service is evaluated.

An important determinant of logistical system costs is where warehouses and plants are located. Manufacturing operations may be materials centered, market centered, or terminus centered. Warehouses may be production centered, market centered, centered intermediately, or mobile.

Product-market sales forecasts are essential to planning and controlling the logistical system. Efficient order management can provide faster information flow and reduce costs throughout the logistics system.

The highest cost element in most logistical systems is transportation. The modes used include trains, trucks, pipelines, ships, and aircraft. Intermodal transport has been facilitated by the acceptance of standard containers. Occasionally the transport mode can accommodate in-transit processing. An expensive problem in business is caused by the need to make small shipments.

The second-highest cost in distribution is claimed by inventory. Inventories may be classified as cycle stock, in-transit stock, safety stock, speculative stock, and dead stock. Four approaches to managing inventories are use of economic order quantities, ordering at fixed intervals, setting different customer service standards in an ABC inventory classification, and use of just-in-time techniques. Inventories are maintained in warehouses. Many tradeoffs are made in the design and layout of warehouses, including the costs of mechanization versus the flexibility of the facility to adapt to changes in demand.

Packaging can enhance the promotional value of the business marketer's product while giving it protection. The logistical aspects of packaging, however, should be thoroughly considered to ensure that the goods can be moved and stored safely and efficiently.

Logistical performance can be improved if the business marketer actively manages customer orders rather than reacting to them. Similarly, greater efficiency may be obtained by combining shipments to take advantage of all the parameters of the transport mode or warehouse, and by product adjustments such as redesign or changes in the product's physical form. Postponement of commitment to the final form of the product is another technique for achieving greater logistical efficiency. The logistics alternatives available to a business marketer expand substantially when considering international markets. But so too do the potential problems that must be solved.

In this chapter we have shown that the business marketer who is familiar with the logistics implication of marketing decisions can use the logistics system to reduce costs, to operate more efficiently, to enhance customer service, and to achieve competitive advantages for the firm.[28]

Key Terms and Concepts

logistics system	level of customer service
materials management	patronage
physical distribution (PD)	materials-centered plant location
total cost approach	market-centered plant locations
suboptimization	terminus-centered plant locations
least total cost	private warehouse
cost tradeoff	public warehouse
logistics audit	bonded warehouse
customer service	field warehouse

production-centered warehouse
market-centered warehouse
intermediately centered warehouses
product-market sales forecasts
time series forecasts
cycle stock
in-transit stock
safety stock
speculative stock

dead stock
economic order quantity
fixed order quantity
fixed order intervals
ABC inventory classification
just-in-time (JIT) delivery
product adjustment
postponement of commitment

Discussion Questions

1. In what ways might a business marketer adjust the firm's products to achieve logistics efficiencies?

2. Given the interrelated nature of logistical activities, it is difficult to make a change in one facet—packaging, say—without creating negative results in other facets (warehousing, transportation, etc.). If you were analyzing possible changes in the distribution system (see Exhibit 13–3), which activity would you use as the starting point? Justify your response.

3. Automation of materials handling equipment in the warehouse can provide more efficient movement and storage of goods. What are the limitations of such automation?

4. Exhibit 13–2 lists twenty-two reasons for holding inventory. Yet the Japanese idea of just-in-time (JIT) reduces inventory to zero or very close to zero. Provide arguments for not holding inventory.

5. How can the logistics system create a differential competitive advantage for the business marketer?

6. When Alan Hall was appointed Canadian distribution manager for Pilkington Brothers, a British glass manufacturer, he visited the company's warehouses. There he found huge quantities of various sizes, colors, and thicknesses of plate glass in storage. Many of these were no longer part of regular production. When Hall asked warehouse foremen why these odd lots were being held in inventory, the typical response was: "You never know when a customer might call and want some of these." Hall returned to his office, examined the company's inventory records, and then ordered all of this glass to be broken up and disposed of. If you were in Hall's shoes, would you do the same? Why or why not?

7. United Parcel Service moves twenty times the volume of packages handled by the U.S. Postal Service. From a logistics perspective, what has given UPS such a great advantage over the Postal Service?

8. Does it ever make sense to give some customers poorer service than others deliberately? Explain why or why not.

9. What is suboptimization? Provide an example.

10. How would the promotional activities of the business marketer affect the logistics operations of the firm?

11. In what ways could the business marketer utilize the firm's logistics policies in its promotion?

12. Who in the firm should establish the organization's customer service objectives? Why?

13. Hilda Streng contends that transportation is the most important part of the logistics system. Do you agree or disagree? What are your reasons?

14. Which would you consider more useful from a marketing point of view: a fixed order interval system or a fixed order quantity system?

15. Would certain factors be more important

than others when locating a warehouse as opposed to locating a manufacturing plant? What would they be?

16. Discuss the difference between the promotional function of packaging and the protective function of packaging.

17. Cardboard cartons are used virtually everywhere. Why is it important to be aware of the impact of heat, temperature, and humidity on them? Is this purely a logistics problem, or is it also important to the business marketing manager?

Endnotes and References

1. *Hedging* is a means of protection against financial loss that involves a counterbalancing transaction. Thus, a logistics manager may buy or sell commodity futures as a protection against price fluctuations in commodities the firm will require at a future time. *Speculation* involves assuming a business risk in the hope of making a gain. For example, a logistics manager may purchase more inventory than is required for current production because the price (cost) of the goods is expected to rise.

2. John J. Coyle, Edward J. Bardy, and C. John Langley, Jr., *The Management of Business Logistics* (St. Paul, Minn.: West Publishing Company, 1992), p. 41.

3. Martin Christopher, David Walters, and Gordon Wills, *Effective Distribution Management* (West Yorkshire, England: MCB Publications, 1978), p. 27.

4. William D. Perrault, Jr., and Frederick A. Russ, "Physical Distribution Service in Industrial Purchase Decisions," *Journal of Marketing* 40 (April 1976): 5. See also Somerby Dowst, "CEO Report: Wanted: Suppliers Adept at Turning Corners," *Purchasing*, January 29, 1987, p. 73.

5. Bernard Lalonde and P. H. Zinzser, *Customer Service: Meaning and Measurement* (Chicago: National Council of Physical Distribution Management, 1976), p. 77.

6. Brian F. O'Neil and Jon L. Iveson, "An Operational Procedure for Prioritizing Customer Service Elements," *Journal of Business Logistics* 12 (1991): 157.

7. Thomas Peters and Robert Waterman, *In Search of Excellence* (New York: Harper & Row, 1982), p. 169.

8. Craig Galbraith and Alex F. DeNoble, "Location Decisions by High Technology Firms: A Comparison of Firm Size, Industry Type, and Institutional Form," *Entrepreneurship Theory and Practice* 13 (Winter 1988): 31–48.

9. Joan M. Feldman, "Transportation Changes—Just in Time," *Handling and Shipping Management* (September 1984): 47.

10. Robert Johnson, "An Idea from Japan May Offer Cities a Way of Recruiting Industry," *Wall Street Journal*, August 23, 1983, pp. 1, 29.

11. Ronald H. Ballou, *Basic Business Logistics* (Englewood Cliffs, N.J.: Prentice-Hall, 1987), p. 207.

12. Dudley F. Pegrum, *Transportation: Economics and Public Policy*, 3rd ed. (Homewood, Ill.: Irwin, 1973), p. 28.

13. U.S. Bureau of the Census.

14. "Package Limit Pondered," (Toronto) *Globe and Mail*, July 25, 1990, p. B18.

15. Andrew Allentuck, "Making a Mission Out of Parcels," (Toronto) *Globe and Mail*, July 9, 1991, pp. C1, C3.

16. Ronald H. Ballou, *Basic Business Logistics*, p. 242.

17. The others are Siemens of Germany and General Electric of the United States.

18. John Lorinc, "Inventory: Taking Stock," *Canadian Business* (April 1991): 49.

19. Ibid., p. 47.

20. Ibid.

21. Paul Dion, David Blenkhorn, and Peter Banting, "Buyer Experiences with JIT: Some New Roles for Buyers," *The Mid-Atlantic Journal of Business* 28 (June 1992):113–123.

22. John Lorinc, "Inventory: Taking Stock," p. 48.

23. Paul Dion, David Blenkhorn, and Peter Banting, "Buyer Experiences with JIT: Some New Roles for Buyers."

24. Bill Proctor, International Marketing Centre, MacMillan Bathurst, Inc., Toronto.

25. *Business Week,* September 7, 1974, p. 90.

26. Cecil Foster, "Outlook Improving for Seaway Shippers," (Toronto) *Globe and Mail,* August 23, 1988, p. B1.

27. Alumina is another name for aluminum oxide (Al_2O_3), which is used in the production of aluminum, abrasives, glass, and ceramics.

28. R. Graem Willersdorf, "Adding Value Through Logistics Management," *International Journal of Physical Distribution & Logistics Management* 21 (1991): 6.

14

BUSINESS MARKETING COMMUNICATION

OBJECTIVES

- To understand the key factors in effective business marketing communication, including the role of listening to customers
- To analyze the creative and administrative tasks involved in business advertising, including budget setting, message creation, ad agency selection, and media options
- To blend the various elements for an effective advertising campaign
- To describe the wide variety of sales promotion techniques, including catalogs, trade shows and fairs, and promotion to trade
- To identify the rationale for public relations, publicity, and sponsorship, and to show how each can contribute to a better corporate image and product positioning
- To demonstrate that both advertising and sales promotion play a major role in all aspects of preselling, especially in identifying potential sales leads through inquiries

Marketing is the most visible of all business functions. Accounting, finance, and labor relations are important, but it is marketing that creates contact with customers, both actual and potential. By linking the inside with the outside world, marketing becomes the linchpin for all organizational activities. Within the marketing domain, one activity is more visible and more vocal than others: communication, or promotion. Organizations have to talk to each other across space and time. They also must stand out in a crowded marketplace. Clients need to be informed about the product or service offered, its price, and its availability at different locations. The only way to do this is by speaking up and speaking out. Of course, good marketers must also be good listeners. Customer feedback is valuable and can act as a stimulus.

A strong argument can be made that in the highly developed countries—such as the United States, Japan, Canada, and the nations of Western Europe—there is too much information, there are too many options for communication, and the persuasive tone of messages is too heavy-handed. In such situations, creative communicators must find a way to be heard above the "noise" or the "clutter." This means recognizing that the task of communication is much more than just "getting the word out." The solution is likely to be a consistent, sophisticated campaign, using various advertising media, skillful personal selling, and appropriate publicity.

In contrast to the industrialized nations, there may be too few communication outlets and too many constraints on promotion in the developing nations in Latin America, Asia, and Africa. Airwaves for radio and television commercials, trade journals for print advertisements, and highways for the sales force may be few in number or even totally absent. In such cases, the task is to adjust to the circumstances in the short run and to build up the infrastructure for promotion in the long run. In fact, organizations can assist in building radio stations, starting trade journals, and sponsoring major events on a regular basis.

Under the impact of technology, marketing communication is reaching all parts of the world as individuals and organizations wish to keep in close touch with each other. In the 1990s, we see that data, voice, and pictures are being transmitted to and from the most remote corners of the globe. Members of the sales force and sample packages of the product can be sent quickly to any destination, be it San Francisco, Senegal, Seoul, or Stockholm. Although the major markets are still in the West and in the Northern Hemisphere, the fast-growing ones are in the East, the Far East, and the Southern Hemisphere. The messages and the media may differ, but business marketers should communicate with their target audiences in all promising locations.

THE COMMUNICATION PROCESS

Earlier in the text, especially in Chapters 3 and 4, we emphasized the idea that business marketing is a two-way street between buyer and seller and that, in a broader context, organizational marketing activities form an intricate web of relationships and transactions. At this point, we reconfirm this idea with the emphasis on two-way communication. Companies and institutions need to inform and persuade others, but they must also *listen*: listen for complaints, listen for suggestions, listen to requests for service support. Learning from clients is an excellent way of becoming a more skilled marketing communicator. It is crucial to hear both the substance and the tone of the feedback. By absorbing the content and style of what valued customers say, the marketer can prepare better messages and choose better media the next time.

The word *communication* means an electronic signal to a technician, a written memo to an office worker, and a visual aid to a teacher. Communication theory is taught in colleges of engineering and in schools of journalism. In marketing, **communication** implies beaming messages at clients. The goal is to move customers from being unaware to levels of awareness, interest, decision making, and the act of purchase. "New products must not only be created, they must be sold," and "Nothing happens until the sale is made" are old but valid slogans. However, marketing communication has evolved from being mere information or persuasion. It is seen today as a two-way bridge, as establishing trust, and as forging a social contract between the vendor and the user at individual, group, and organizational levels.[1]

Early models of communication defined the task as one of informing, persuading, and reminding. In a sequence reminiscent of electrical engineering, the source was asked to encode the message and send it through a channel to the recipient, who would decode it. Later on, using the tools of psychology, marketers spoke of audiences responding at cognitive, affective, or behavioral levels. By this, they meant that there would be a change in awareness, attitude, or action. Increasingly sophisticated models are being proposed, but the key components remain the same. Recently, feedback has been given more and more emphasis. Clearly, organizations must be attuned to what present clients and prospects are saying—or even implying.[2]

Factors in Effective Communication

The elements of good communication focus on certain key aspects: who, what, how, where, and to whom. The *who* refers to the source, usually the selling organization, which must know its own strengths and weaknesses as well as the opportunities and threats in the marketplace. *What* refers to the messages that are being sent, their content and style, in both electronic and print formats. *How* and *where* messages are to be transmitted refers to choosing among different mass media, personal sales calls, and sales promotion, or a combination of these. Finally, *to whom* is a call for defining the target audiences, including present and potential customers.

Consider the makers of computer hardware and peripheral equipment. In the 1960s and 1970s, large computers, known as mainframes, were specified by and acquired for centralized data processing or information centers. But in the 1980s and 1990s, thousands of microcomputers, terminals, and workstations have been requisitioned by and bought for all levels in an organization. Many such units are, of course, still connected to mainframes, but many others function in a stand-alone mode. In effect, information has been made available to many; power has been decentralized. So now makers of computers must speak to a larger and more diverse audience and must do so with new messages.

When a business marketer creates a message, many symbols, or codes, are used. For several years, IBM—the trustworthy, stolid "giant" of the computer field—used the clownish figure of Charlie Chaplin as "the little tramp" to signify that its personal computers were fun to use. Apple Computer continues to use its multicolor logo of a partially eaten apple as a visual reference. Its slogan for many years has been "The power to be your best." Apple also ran a famous "blockbuster" ad during the Superbowl 1984 football championship game introducing the audience to its line of Macintosh personal computers.[3] Microsoft, the leading software company, has a strong corporate signature, but its two slogans, "Making it all make sense" and "Making it easier" still need further penetration. Other high-tech firms use various symbols as well as comparative, down-to-earth cost and performance charts. There is a growing realization among business marketers that touting technical features is simply not enough anymore. Communication is a social process even from business to business; thus, emotional as well as rational appeals may be used. It is not unusual in the 1990s to see humor, fear, and friendly counseling as themes in advertisements.

The decision regarding how and where to transmit the message involves choosing among the available media. Traditionally, the two major categories were simply labeled personal and impersonal communication. The former refers to direct, face-to-face contact, involving members of the selling and buying teams as well as influential third parties such as opinion leaders. The latter refers to the use of mass media—that is, print and electronic advertising. A third category has emerged, with its own characteristics, but related to the two other groups. This is sales promotion, which encompasses publicity, public relations, trade shows, and sponsorship. The three major categories and their many subgroups are shown in Exhibit 14–1. Choosing among this wide array depends on the target audience, the cost of the media, and the characteristics of the product or service that is offered. We give examples and guidelines on how to make the selection in the following sections.

The Communication Mix

The most crucial requirement for an effective communication program is to blend the array of promotional options into a consistent campaign. The various tools must reinforce each other. In business marketing, the allocation of the promotion budget shows personal selling occupying the top rung, followed by sales promotion and advertising. Indeed, some claim that personal selling accounts for twice as much as the two other categories combined. When McGraw-Hill surveyed four hundred large companies in the 1980s, it found that marketing costs averaged about 9 percent of sales. About two-thirds of that, or 6 percent, could be attributed to personal selling, with the other third, or 3 percent, going to advertising and sales promotion.[4]

The McGraw-Hill report also revealed that large firms spend relatively less than small ones on advertising and sales promotion: 0.5 percent versus 4.4 percent of their sales. It seems that small companies must speak more loudly in order to be noticed. Print ads are dominant, followed by various sales promotion tools (see Exhibit 14–2). High-tech firms (electronics, aerospace, biotech) rely heavily on print ads, trade shows, and publicity. Old-line manufacturing establishments (chemicals, metals, transport equipment) spend heavily on direct mail and on brochures used by distributors. Such information enables managers in charge of communication to judge what the industry trends and averages are. What works well in one sector may not be appropriate in another. Of course, emulating one's rivals in a given field is not always the best solution; creativity often consists of being different from the pack and thereby standing out.[5]

Consider two small companies, a maker of industrial adhesives and a supplier of computer software. The product line of the former is considered old-line, whereas the latter is regarded as a provider of high-tech service. Yet both may stress the same theme in their mass communication—namely, "ease of application"—even though the theme has a different connotation for each company. The "ease-of-application" slogan must be mentioned in all journal advertisements and in news releases; it can also be used in radio commercials. (These two firms are not likely to advertise on television.) The slogan should be delivered by members

EXHIBIT 14–1   The Communication or Promotion Mix in Industrial Marketing: A Three-Way Classification Scheme

Traditional Advertising	*Sales Promotion and Publicity*	*Personal Selling*
Print Advertising	**Direct Mail**	One-on-one selling
		Group presentations
Magazines	Mailing pieces	Sales meetings
Journals	Mailed samples	Teleselling
Directories	Coupons, stamps	Bid hearings
Newspapers	Advertising specialties	Contract negotiations
	(novelties)	Missionary
Electronic (broadcasting) Advertising		Presentations
	Catalogs	
Radio		
Television	Buying guides	
Cable	Directories	
"Tie-lines"	Special listings	
	Brochures, flyers	
Outdoor Advertising		
	Exhibits	
Billboards		
Posters	Major fairs	
Display signs	Trade shows, expositions	
	Traveling shows, mobile vans	
Other	Specialty shows	
	Displays	
	Point of purchase	
	Handouts	
	Telemarketing	
	Publicity and PR	
	Sponsorship	
	Charity	
	Press releases	
	Annual reports	
	Seminars, speeches	
	Entertainment	
	Technical articles	

EXHIBIT 14–2   Allocation of Marketing Communications Budget of Large Business Advertisers by Specific Media

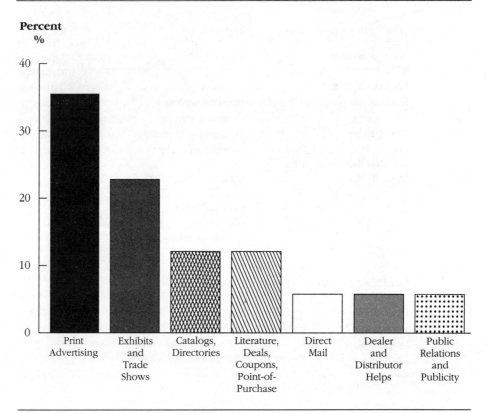

Source: *Survey of Industrial Marketing Costs*, Report 8015.7, a brochure from the Laboratory of Advertising Performance (New York: McGraw-Hill, 1985), p. 1. Reprinted by permission of McGraw-Hill, Inc.

of the sales force who call on clients at the factory or the office. It should also appear on the booth of each firm at the appropriate trade shows and on each company's packaging. The hallmark of superior communication is not just creativity but also consistency. Only then does the message get imprinted on the mind and acted upon by the client.

In contrast to small firms, large companies often gravitate to corporate image advertising and to the use of television. For example, Xerox spends about 90 percent of its corporate image budget on network television. However, its product line is also featured in print, with general consumer magazines and newspapers as outlets, not just trade journals and business weeklies. In a similar fashion, AT&T, the telecommunication giant, reaches its target audiences in diverse ways. These include network television ads, full-page ads in the *Wall Street Journal,* sponsorship of golf tournaments, and underwriting the "MacNeil-Lehrer Newshour" on public television. AT&T wages an intensive television ad campaign for subscribers against MCI and Sprint, emphasizing both corporate image and specific services.

Communication Strategy and Tactics

Both a grand plan and many small steps are needed to execute a successful communication program or even a single promotional campaign. The first step is **situation analysis**, or **environmental scanning**. This means looking at economic, political, and social trends and exploring their implications for promotion in general and for style of selling or advertising in particular. Global communication offers cultural challenges as well as new opportunities. In many Asian and Latin American countries, for example, it is considered rude to start with a sales pitch. In certain European nations, running comparative advertisements is frowned upon or even prohibited. Tradition may dictate using salespeople with technical degrees. Sweepstakes may not be allowed due to government regulation or industry association rules.

The next step calls for assessment of an organization's strengths and weaknesses. A large, profitable firm can afford to try diverse and expensive forms of promotion, as noted earlier. Such an organization can drive a bargain with ad agencies and with powerful media. It can also experiment with various incentives for its sales force and its clientele. A medium-sized firm offering complex equipment, such as automated assembly lines, should put personal selling at the forefront. A small sales team can be productive calling on large prospects; later, regional offices can serve a worldwide client base. Companies with mature product lines, such as electrical relays and switches, should use print ads, which serve as a reminder. When distributors are widely used, as in the case of parts and supplies, much of the promotional literature should be aimed at them in order to forge loyalty bonds and to present the picture of a partnership.

The next step in promotion, as in other facets of the marketing program, is the necessity to judge one's opportunities and threats in the marketplace. In communication, the battlefield is the mindset of customers, and the tools are ideas and concepts. Promises can be made, but they must be kept. Successful organizations can do this and remind the audience that indeed they have delivered the goods. Those who can back up their claims with ratings by independent sources have a convincing case. This is what one application software maker has done against its larger rivals: Borland showed how both *Info World* journal and J.D. Power, an independent rating agency, ranked its spreadsheet ahead of those by Lotus, Microsoft, and others.

Corporate goals, target audiences, and product characteristics deeply influence both the grand strategy and the many tactical steps of promotion. To illustrate, let us consider once again two key rival computer makers, IBM and Apple. Traditionally, IBM had sought to computerize the workplace in every sector of the economy using large mainframes. But now IBM sees itself as catering to many distinct segments, ranging from accountants to beauty salons, with a line-up of both large and small units. For example, in health care, IBM emphasizes the following goals and product/service benefits: (1) saving lives through increased accuracy, (2) increasing doctors' and nurses' productivity by calling up information quickly, and (3) saving money for hospitals and insurers by improved recordkeeping. Thus, its promotion is now multipronged, aimed at patients, the medical teams, health-care administrators, and financial consultants. Equipment and software are loaned out at no charge. Follow-up calls are made, and sophisticated ads appear in the right medical and trade journals.

Apple came to the computer industry much later and had a more modest initial goal: making its presence felt in the education sector. Its original line of Apple II computers proved very successful in many primary and secondary schools. Students, parents, and teachers were targeted in appropriate journals and via demonstrations. With its Macintosh computers, Apple invaded the college and university market by offering deep discounts to professors and students. Local journals served as inexpensive media to hammer home this point. More recently, Apple has chosen to compete with IBM and go after the industrial sector, especially certain white-collar offices. Personal selling to large firms and ads in major trade journals and business publications have accompanied this thrust. As the fields of computers, communication, and entertainment merge in the 1990s, Apple is getting ready and has forged an alliance with giant Sony. Its promotion campaign is likely to stress the theme of lifelong education, whether in school, college, home, or the workplace.

Communication Expenditures

How much effort and money should be allocated to the task of promotion and to the three major categories of advertising, personal selling, and sales promotion? How does the marketer choose among the different types of selling effort and among the various print and electronic media? There are several budget-setting procedures, and many firms use a combination of techniques. All major approaches rely on a mix of scientific method, experience, intuition, comparisons with similar organizations, and ease of implementation. Some of the detailed techniques for advertising are discussed later in this chapter.

Ideally, a marketing manager would like to see budgets established in line with the goals set for each promotional activity. Spending in each area would stop at the point at which the costs outweigh the benefits. The problem is that benefits are hard to quantify, and costs are not easily allocated. The ideal scenario is also colored by such practical considerations as what others are doing, what tradition dictates, what long-term contracts exist, and the size of the overall promotion budget. Although mathematical models have been developed for setting advertising and personal selling budgets (called ADVISOR and PAIRS, respectively), setting the communication budget as a whole remains a curious mix of art and science. Accumulation of experience, rules of thumb, and observation of rivals' action count for as much as strict rate of return or cost/benefit calculations.[6]

Evaluation of Communication

Let us assume that the grand strategy has been set: environmental scanning, corporate goal or mission statement, segmentation, target audience selection, product-market interface, and budget allocation have all taken place. Decisions must then be made on the media, the message, and the frequency of advertising. Choices have to be made between dispensing product information on the phone or providing it in person. Should technical advice include a sales pitch for supplementary services? Appearing at a large trade show must be weighed against exhibiting at several smaller ones, and comprehensive catalogs must be ranked against slim but more timely brochures. Such specific decisions must be made continuously; no grand plan can succeed without wise tactical steps. As the promotion unfolds, both in its overall design and in all the necessary day-to-day operations, an evaluation should take place on an ongoing basis. In other words, the short- and long-run goals and results of the communication process must be ascertained.

Several observers claim that the results of business promotion should be judged by increased sales. Scattered evidence exists that suggests major promotional campaigns do indeed have a major impact on sales. Aggressive personal selling or sophisticated counseling can result in measurable increases in shipments. More often, however, we have to be satisfied with measuring the impact of the communication on clients in terms of exposure, recall, or readership. In the case of sales promotion, we may have to be satisfied with counting inquiries. The long-range impact of communication, personal or mass, is especially difficult to judge.

Yet, whatever the yardstick, evaluation is necessary because it acts as a feedback mechanism to the organization and thereby affords an opportunity to modify policies and to change procedures. Looking at what went right and what went wrong serves as valuable input for the next time around. Furthermore, since promotional budgets are tight and since many choices are possible in terms of available media, accountability has become prevalent. Progressive firms learn from each promotional campaign and refine their strategies and tactics before undertaking new ones. For example, through trial and error, many high-tech firms found out that they must not only invent the future and bring forth new products; they must sell ideas, goods, and possible applications as well. Specifically, they have learned that their ads should not be filled with technical jargon but with lists of key benefits and offers of viable solutions to client problems.

BUSINESS ADVERTISING

There is fundamental agreement that advertising can inform, persuade, and remind members of an audience, be they readers, listeners, or viewers. In this context, the traditional role of **business advertising** is to make contact, to create awareness, to convince, and to maintain goodwill. A famous ad that McGraw-Hill has been running for decades on behalf of its trade journals closes with the punchline "Sales start before the salesman calls." But advertising does more than prepare the way for business marketers; it can replace personal selling, expand market share, and enhance profits.[7]

Does Advertising Really Work?

The key task of business advertising is to increase the overall productivity of the marketing program. Can it do this job? Four major studies have been undertaken on this topic in the United States, two in the 1970s and two in the 1980s. The first two surveys, by Morrill and by Manville, focused on the rationale of undertaking mass communication in the world of business organizations. The Morrill study encompassed 1,000 firms, 90 markets, and 26 major product categories. It concluded that when advertisements are run with sufficient frequency, there is almost always a payoff. Another key finding revealed that companies that advertised had 30 percent lower marketing costs than those that failed to do so. The Manville study of diverse industries and product lines demonstrated that the industrial sales force can reach only three or four out of every ten buying center members. Accordingly, advertising must fill the void.[8]

The two studies in the 1980s focused on the effectiveness of advertising. The first of these was sponsored by the Laboratory of Advertising Performance (LAP) of McGraw-Hill, a large publisher of trade journals. Although it may seem like a self-serving survey, the LAP findings are well regarded in the advertising community. The results of this survey showed that total marketing communication costs were a small portion of the total marketing program; as noted earlier, this figure came in at about 9 percent. Print advertising paid off handsomely, according to the LAP survey, with increases in awareness levels of 45 percent and 80 percent, respectively, for old and new firms. Stepped-up print advertising yielded significant increases in brand preferences and resulted in higher ratings for corporate images.[9]

The second major study in the 1980s was a two-year, $400,000 effort sponsored by the Advertising Research Foundation and the Association of Business Publishers (ARF/ABP) and forty-five individual organizations. It was probably the most thorough and ambitious project ever undertaken to measure the effectiveness of business and trade journal advertising in terms of sales. Yet it received a tepid reception at first, because some of its sponsors tried to claim too much, namely that "the more you advertise, the more you sell and the more you profit." A mere increase in ad spending is not the solution; indeed, a point of diminishing returns can be reached. What the ARF/ABP survey did show was that business and trade journal print ads produce more sales than would occur without advertising. In addition, the survey showed that increased frequency of ads, creative messages, strong commitment to the campaign, and support of dealers also have a definite beneficial influence on sales. In short, effectiveness is determined by a host of factors, not just increased spending.[10]

Segmenting and Targeting the Audience

Who is out there reading, hearing, and viewing the messages being beamed at them? These are important questions, but they still put the cart before the horse. The business marketer must first ask: To whom shall we send the message? Where is my target audience? Exposure is effective only when the message is delivered to a member of the target audience; otherwise, it is wasted. But how can one make the distinction? Existing levels of awareness, attitude, and buying action can delineate market segments and define target audiences. We can also get help by studying the profile of the audience subscribing to a journal or viewing a program; such data are collected by the media groups and market research organizations.

Recall that segmentation should take place at several levels, as shown in Chapter 6. At the macro and intermediate levels we are looking at industries, location, end-use patterns, buying situations, and benefits. These categories are illustrated for one family of machine tools in Exhibit 14–3. Note how the authors link the

EXHIBIT 14–3   Segmentation Basis and Implications for Advertising for Metal-Forming Machine Tools

Segmentation Basis	*Characteristics of the Selected Target Market*	*Implications for Advertising*
Primary benefit	Technical expertise	Primary message or theme of advertising should stress company reputation for expertise in solving manufacturing problems. Stress engineering capabilities and perhaps demonstration through case histories/examples.
Geographic concentration	Chicago, Cleveland, Detroit, Los Angeles, New York	Moderate advertising budget due to relatively small size of target market (plant size of 500+ and few number of companies in SICs 3711, 3713, and 3721).
Primary SICs	3711 (motor vehicles and passenger car bodies); 3713 (truck and bus bodies)	Combination of narrow target market, geographic concentration, and primary benefit sought suggests use of direct mail.
Secondary SIC	3721 (aircraft)	
Size of buyer	500+ employers	
Stage of buyer readiness	Immediate buy	Immediate buy stage calls for action-oriented copy (perhaps seek direct response through 800 number or return card).

Source: C. H. Patti & C. F. Frazer, *Advertising*. (Hinsdale, Il: Dryden Press, 1988), p. 205.

bases for segmentation with characteristics of the audience and the implications for advertising. In effect, segmentation assists the marketer in this situation not only with identification of various audiences, including those to be targeted, but also with choosing appropriate messages and the right media.

At the intermediate and micro levels of segmentation we focus on members of the buying center. A good example was the 1950–1970 study of engineers and scientists conducted by *Scientific American.* The survey showed that such professionals played a key role in the purchase of equipment for their laboratories. Armed with this evidence, the journal was able to attract advertisements from many instrument and other laboratory apparatus manufacturers.[11] Such analysis of buying center members can extend even to identifying their social styles and then tailoring the commercial messages accordingly (see Exhibit 14–4). Of course, the advertiser must identify the audience members before selecting the appropriate theme, message, and copy style. If the audience is diverse, different aspects can be emphasized to the different groups. For example, makers of process machinery— be it textile, food, or chemical—may stress low initial cost to purchasing agents, low operating cost to plant engineers and maintenance staff, and ease of use to those who operate the machines.[12]

EXHIBIT 14–4   Guide to Industrial Advertising Creativity According to Social Style

	The Driven	*The Expressive*	*The Amiable*	*The Analytical*
Approach should be	Straightforward, structured	Highly creative, imaginative	Strongly people-oriented	Detailed, orderly
Copy style should be	Concise, right to the point	Stimulating, rousing	Friendly, conversational	Precise
Emphasize product or service	Benefits directly affecting costs, production, etc., speediness of results	Innovations: exclusive or unusual features; sizzle, not the steak; status and recognition	Features minimizing chance and risk, features improving safety, features helping people	Features with details and data, process integrity
Impress them with	Short-term results, bottom-line expectations, control	Testimonials from recognized sources, short-term results	Buyer-seller "partnership," proof of claims, testimonials vendor service-oriented	Long- and short-term results (logic), proof of claims, testimonials, superiority of process
For action, offer them	Choices, options, custom design	Incentives, chance for personal recognition, speed of results	Guarantees, assurances, service support	Complete proposals, service, proof of salesperson's competence

Source: R. A. Kriegel, "Does Your Ad Talk the Way Your Prospect Thinks?" *Business Marketing* (July 1984), p. 94. Reprinted with permission of *Business Marketing.*

The Message: Content, Style, Outlet

Early texts on advertising gave a series of commandments on what makes for great copy, especially in print ads. The key points to remember were: (1) think of the reader and reward him or her with specific news, but avoid bragging; (2) tap your internal sources as well as your customers for ideas; (3) have a plan, have a headline that grabs the readers, and have a text that builds interest and inspires action;

Zippo advertises sales promotion devices.

Courtesy of Zippo Manufacturing Company.

and (4) make the illustration large and keep the layout simple. Recognizing the growth of electronic media, the general advice coming forth called for small, local firms to utilize radio and large, national firms to utilize television.[13]

In the 1980s, David Ogilvy, one of the giants of the advertising industry, issued his own set of commandments in regard to effective business advertising: (1) use testimonials from experts and reputable firms; (2) refer to demonstrations for effective comparisons; (3) proclaim your news, provide useful product information, and keep the layout simple; (4) promise a benefit in the headline, which has a readership five times that of the text; and (5) close the ad with a name, an address, a logo, and a coupon to achieve action.[14]

The most comprehensive advice for printed ads comes from an anonymous panel of judges called the Copy-Chasers. Every month, in the back pages of *Business Marketing,* this panel evaluates a series of ads taken from other trade journals or voluntarily submitted to them by advertisers and ad agencies. The panel is not reluctant to criticize poor ads, but it will shower praise on the ones it deems good. In either case, the explanation is highly detailed and accompanies a reproduction of the ad. The Copy-Chasers' criteria are listed in Exhibit 14–5. (Some of the ads reproduced in this book have been reviewed by this panel.)

What an ad conveys to an audience depends to a great extent on where it appears. So far we have focused on print ads that appear in newspapers and journals. In such cases, the reader has ample time to look over the ad, go back to it, or pass it along to other interested parties. In contrast, time is precious in electronic media, and there is no way to retrieve the message, so the point must be made quickly and precisely. Some firms do it well, some do it poorly, some do not do it at all. As a general rule, only large industrial firms opt for television. Let us consider some ads the three giant makers of commercial aircraft ran on television during the 1980s. The messages by Airbus, Boeing, and McDonnell Douglas were very similar; all showed an aircraft in flight and a voice talking about performance and safety. The audience sought after was not the public at large but rather airline executives, institutional investors, and frequent flyers. Not surprisingly, such an approach proved to be ineffective in terms of expenditures per prospect, so the aircraft firms switched to sending out videocassettes using a highly selective mailing list. On the other hand, TRW experienced a doubling in awareness level of its logo (from about 36 to 75 percent) as a result of a consistent campaign in the 1980s on network television. The slogan of this campaign was: "Tomorrow is taking shape at a company called TRW" (with the letters TRW expanding to the word *tomorrow*). The ads featured TRW as an integrated company, yet alluded to its strength in aerospace, automotive equipment, and information services. Large industrial firms that are diversified generally pursue such television ad campaigns, stressing both corporate and divisional strength.

Individual advertisements should convey a specific theme, whether they appear in print or in electronic media. At the same time, each ad and the sequence of ads should relate to the overall promotional goals of the organization. A recent research study showed, however, that industrial firms do a far better job of classifying their individual ads than they do on having them relate to the broad goals

EXHIBIT 14–5   Copy-Chasers' Criteria for Successful Industrial Print Ads

The Successful Ad...	Meaning...
1. Has a high degree of visual magnetism	It grabs the reader; has pertinent picture, arresting headline, etc.; a single component dominates.
2. Selects the right audience	Readers can readily identify the ad as a source of job information relating to their job interests. ("This is for me.")
3. Invites the reader into the scene	The illustration is tailored to the reader (design engineer—drawing; chemical engineer—flow charts; construction engineer—products at work, etc.).
4. Promises a reward	There is no bragging or boasting, generalizations, or clichés; the promise can be explicit or implicit, but it is, ideally, specific (for example, "Cut maintenance costs by 25%").
5. Backs up the promise	Hard evidence is shown that claim is valid: case histories, comparisons with competing goods, etc.
6. Presents the selling proposition in logical sequence	Components are arranged so that there is a flow from a clear entry point to the final closing; the layout is natural.
7. Talks "person to person"	The ad speaks to the reader as an individual, not as an organization; the terms are those of the reader, not the advertiser.
8. Is easy to read	The typography must be easy to read and pleasing to the eye (9 point or bigger, black on white, columns not too wide, etc.).
9. Emphasizes the service, not the source	The company name or logo should not be the biggest item; the reader must want to buy—or at least consider buying—before he or she is told where to buy.
10. Reflects the company's character	The ad conveys the company's "personality"; it portrays the firm as user- not maker-oriented, shows excitement, enthusiasm.

Source: "Copy-Chasers' Criteria," *Business Marketing* (January 1986), p. 104. Reprinted with permission of *Business Marketing*.

of the overall advertising effort. This survey analyzed a large number of award-winning ads and classified about 24 percent of them as trying to create awareness, 31 percent as attempting to arouse interest and desire, 28 percent as urging action or purchase, and only 17 percent as having no classifiable message. But when it came to matching these messages with broad corporate goals, only one-third of the ads could meet this criterion.[15]

Media: Print and Electronic

The traditional and favored medium of industrial advertisers is print. Using print rather than electronic media is in line with the characteristics of their target audiences. Technical staff, operating managers, purchasing agents, and top officers like to think things through and to compare competing claims. Within the category of **print media**, the choice usually falls on trade and industry publications. Publishing houses with a vested interest in such publications—for example, Cahners, Chilton, Edgell, McGraw-Hill, and Penton—extol the virtue of going down this road. They have done a convincing job of attracting industrial advertisers, as two-thirds of the advertising budget of large firms is allocated to such publications. McGraw-Hill at one time claimed that good print ads can outdraw editorial matter in trade journals. This publishing giant is also fond of pointing out that a print ad usually costs less than 50 cents per reader, as against $300 for a personal sales call, over $10 for a phone call, and $1 for a direct mail piece. Most important, the print ad paves the way for members of the sales force in both the short and long run.

Industry, trade, and technical journals run in the thousands. Titles range from *Aviation Week* to *Welding Journal*, from *Building Supply News* to *Pollution Engineering*, from *Automation News* to *Food Processing*. Specialized, narrow fields have two to three titles, whereas broader categories boast six to ten journals. It is traditional to categorize trade and industry journals into two groups. Those that are specific to a given industry, such as *Chemical Week*, are called **vertical publications**. Those that cover a functional area and hence cut across industry lines, such as *Purchasing World*, are called **horizontal publications**. Both types fulfill specific roles in terms of their readership; their editorials, articles, and advertisements fully reflect this situation.[16]

General consumer magazines and general business journals have grabbed some of the industrial advertising dollars of late. In the United States these include *Newsweek, Time, Business Week, Forbes, Fortune, INC.,* and others. In other nations they include the *Australian Financial Review, Canadian Business, Der Spiegel, The Economist, Paris Match,* and many more. Most of the ads in these journals by the auto, cigarette, liquor, and watch companies, along with airline, car rental, and credit card companies, are oriented toward households and individuals, including business travelers. However, some of the ads in these journals are also aimed at industrial users by the copier, computer, delivery, electronics, and insurance firms.

How effective are ads in the news and business weeklies that target business marketing organizations? Researchers have examined costs, exposure patterns, and other variables. The findings indicate that general consumer and business journals are useful when the message cuts across many industrial lines. These outlets are especially effective in carrying advertisements for information technology, office equipment, and business services. Recent ad campaigns by Hewlett-Packard, Epson, and CIGNA substantiate this point. Yet another possibility is the use of outdoor print media, such as billboards; they are popular for local services. Thus, some of the horizontal trade journals face rather strong competition for the ad dollars.

Just as general publications have captured some trade journal ads, so **electronic media** have invaded the traditional turf of both categories. Although a 30-second spot on radio or a 60-second ad on television seems to go by too quickly, each one can be effective for certain kinds of businesses. Radio is eminently suitable for local service organizations such as office cleaning, duplication, financial advice, and professional design. Business marketing executives are often on the

BUSINESS MARKETING IN PRACTICE ▬▬▬▬▬▬▬▬▬

A High-Tech Marketer Makes a Big Splash in Television Advertising

Sun Microsystems is a major producer of workstations, computers tied together in a network. Workstations are more powerful than personal computers but less complex than mainframes. The worldwide market for them is $7.3 billion—and growing fast.

Sun Microsystems spent $1.5 million in early 1991 on a one-day media blitz created by Anderson & Lembke, a division of Chiat/Day/Mojo, with the bulk of spending going for television. It used 30-second spots and was on for a total of 30 minutes during the day on the "Big Three" networks (NBC, ABC, CBS) and on cable channels. It also conducted a 3-month print campaign with an eight-page insert in the *Wall Street Journal.*

Some observers say a mass medium like television is a curious place for a company that this year will sell only about 200,000 computers at prices up to $500,000. "It seems an awfully expensive way to reach a limited audience," said Dan McCarthy, editor-in-chief of *Computer Publishing & Advertising Report.* However, Sun insists that the TV assault offered the most dramatic and cost-effective way to

launch a brand-building campaign. The blitz gave the "highest impact for the dollars available," said Mr. Brandt of Sun Microsystems. Sun expected the spot to reach 57 percent of U.S. households and 42 percent of its target customers, primarily senior-level corporate and computer department executives.

Sun has no plans to run the spot again in the United States but will consider using TV in future campaigns. The commercial will also run later in Germany, Japan, and the United Kingdom. Print ads will also appear in the United States and twenty-two other nations.

Why is Sun doing this? The company is competing against Hewlett-Packard and a coalition that includes Compaq and Microsoft to set a single standard for workstations. "They've got their products in place. What they've got to do is get their name out there. . . . They need to move fast," said Lisa Thorell, an analyst with Dataquest (a market research firm) and former Sun marketing executive.

Source: By permission from B. Johnson, "Sun Makes TV Splash," *Advertising Age,* April 15, 1991, p. 1.

---

road and listen to their car radios; after work, they may listen to sports or news shows. Television is the choice when the item is high-priced, widely used, or amenable to a visual presentation. Examples include computers, telecommunication, package delivery, and insurance. In addition, large manufacturers and service companies may sponsor sports events on network or cable television as well as cultural presentations on public television. Small firms are not as likely to have ads on nationwide television, but they may run spot ads on local stations.[17]

Statistics on advertising expenditures by industrial firms in various media are now widely available, so it is possible to make comparisons or to observe trends. Two key publications that carry the data are *Advertising Age* and *Business Publication Rate and Data.* The analysis of data from these volumes can reveal how different firms have distinct approaches to business advertising. For example, in recent years, Du Pont relied heavily on general magazines, whereas Union Carbide opted for spot television ads. For many years, Digital Equipment Company, or DEC, sponsored the "Nightly Business Report" on public television, but ran no ads on any commercial stations. Recently, DEC changed its mind, but several observers call the effort too little, too late. Recent upheavals at the firm appear to substantiate this point. Meanwhile, IBM continues to sponsor special shows on public television, and other computer firms contract for occasional spot ads on commercial or cable stations. Various service organizations routinely use distinct blends of print and electronic media. Such choices reflect differences in marketing goals, diverse target audiences, budget limits, and other variables.

Advertising Agencies

The **advertising agency** is perhaps best described by J. O'Toole, past head of the American Association of Advertising Agencies, as "one of those simple American inventions that, to the consternation of some and the benefit of many, has succeeded beyond the dreams of its originators and taken up residence everywhere in the free world."[18] Today we see much diversity in the field, which the pioneers did not anticipate. There is a trend toward mergers among large firms, but there is still much opportunity for small and medium-sized agencies. Some clients feel quite uncomfortable when agencies that represent competing products decide to merge; this is viewed as a conflict of interest. So one of the accounts is then withdrawn, and another agency, often a smaller one, will benefit. As a general rule, there is an affinity in size between advertiser and ad agency; giant manufacturing or service firms feel comfortable with large ad agencies, small companies with small agencies. Specialized boutiques or small shops emerge, established by creative executives who were squeezed out in a merger or who felt stifled in large agencies.

Advertising agencies perform many valuable functions: creating the actual ad, buying space or time in the media, conducting research, and managing the account in all its details. One of their chief contributions is bringing a different, creative perspective to the table. Agencies differ in style from workmanlike ("ads that sell, not just win awards") to those that stress the personal touch ("talk to a person, not a committee") or their far reach ("with offices around the world"). Because of the recent downturn in ad spending, agencies compete heavily to keep old or to gain new accounts. Advertisers are advised to shop around carefully, not just for the best price, but to understand the agency's approach and its past history of successes and failures. Asking for a full-scale sample presentation is now popular.

Among the largest agencies in the world are Leo Burnett, BBDO, DDB Needham, Grey, Lintas, and Young & Rubicam of the United States, WPP and Saatchi & Saatchi of the United Kingdom, and Dentsu of Japan. Large agencies involved heavily in business advertising in the United States include Bozell & Jacobs, Campbell, McCann-Erickson, and Ogilvy & Mather. Although mergers continue, especially among large agencies, small firms endure and creative shops are still being formed. Many medium-sized agencies specialize in handling business advertising, especially in the industrial heartlands of the United States (Midwest), Canada (Ontario), and Europe (the Ruhr and Rhine valleys, etc.). It is certainly evident that creative ads are being developed well beyond Madison Avenue in New York City.

The client-agency relationship is a complex one. Some relationships show longevity; others last for only a few years. Clients like to see continuity on the agency side; mergers or a revolving door for account managers can be unsettling. Agencies that fail to grow with the client's product line often lose the account. In addition, advertisers often take out their frustration over stable or declining sales by firing their ad agencies. A divorce between advertiser and agency can also occur over an honest disagreement about product positioning or message content. Choosing an agency carefully, establishing working rapport at all levels, and having periodic performance reviews should forge a mutually beneficial relationship that can endure for several years. But given a saturated marketplace and intense competition for accounts, switching agencies will not be unusual.[19]

Hewlett-Packard, a well-known maker of instruments, calculators, minicomputers, and workstations for engineers and scientists, sees its ad agency as an outside employee and conducts an annual evaluation. The items on HP's evaluation form are listed in Exhibit 14–6. Each item is ranked from exceptional to unac-

EXHIBIT 14–6   How Hewlett-Packard Rates Advertising Agencies

1. Client Contact

Frequency
Levels
Planning

2. Service

Availability
Urgency
Quality
Cost controls
Accounting and billing procedures
Efficiency

3. Creative

Client knowledge (marketing, technical, policies)
How creative (conforming to above points)

4. Creative Quality

Art
Copy
Enthusiasm

5. Media

Client knowledge (markets, audience)
Service
Media knowledge

6. Research

Interest
Cooperation
Capability

7. Personnel

Quantitative (number on job)
Qualitative

Ranking: Each item on the evaluation form is ranked from "exceptional" to "unacceptable," and each entry includes additional space for comments. Annual evaluation becomes the basis for continuing or terminating the relationship with the agency. The agency is given a chance for rebuttal.

Source: "How Hewlett-Packard Rates Agencies," *Business Marketing* (September 1985), p. 60. Reprinted with permission of *Business Marketing*.

ceptable, with space for comments. The agency is kept informed and is given a chance for rebuttal, both in a meeting and in writing. Out of such give and take, better campaigns are created for HP's family of products. An example of creativity is HP's logo of a colorful butterfly for its computer line. This is a whimsical, attention-getting design in sharp contrast to competitive ads that often feature dull computer screens or keyboards.

Expenditures: Absolute and Relative

What percentage of sales is spent on advertising in a given industry? How much will it cost to run an ad on the back cover of a national trade journal? What is the cost of a television commercial on the 6 P.M. local news? These and similar questions need to be answered before placing an ad and especially before mounting a long-run campaign. First, the general spending patterns of one's own business sector need to be taken into account. It may be smart to spend less or more than the industry average, but that average should be considered as a benchmark. Statistics on many industrial categories have been collected, and a sample is displayed in Exhibit 14–7. Expenditures by firms in different media are also available and can serve as rough guides.

EXHIBIT 14–7   Relative Advertising Expenditures, Selected U.S. Industries, 1991

Four-Digit SIC Code	Industry Sector	Ad Dollars as Percent of Sales	Ad Dollars as Percent of Margin	Annual Growth Rate (percent)
4513	Air courier services	1.2	9.9	11.7
3720	Aircraft and parts	0.6	3.1	2.8
7370	Computer programming, data processing	0.2	0.6	10.3
2750	Commercial printing	2.7	10.4	11.0
3530	Construction, mining, material-handling equipment	4.4	12.9	7.4
3510	Engines and turbines	1.3	6.6	(13.2)
2520	Office furniture	1.0	2.7	3.3
4813	Phone communications	2.3	4.9	3.1
2821	Plastics, resins, elastomers	0.7	2.4	(2.3)
4400	Water transportation	7.2	18.1	4.4

Note: Ad dollars as percent of sales = ad expenditures/net sales.
Ad dollars as percent of margin = ad expenditures/(net sales − cost of goods sold).
Annual growth rate = percent increase in ad dollars over previous year.

Source: Schonfeld & Associates, Lincolnshire, IL, quoted in *Business Marketing* (November 1991), pp. 113–114. That article lists about 180 categories.

There are several major publications on media circulation and on expenditures by such bodies as the Association of Business Publishers, the Business Advertising Research Council, and the Television Bureau of Advertising. The journal *Advertising Age* and its electronic sister, *Ad Age Yearbook,* carry useful data on the spending patterns of large firms. One of the most authoritative tools is the *SRDS* volumes published by Standard Rate and Data Service (SRDS). Detailed data are available on circulation, coverage, ad rates, editorial policy, and preparation requirements. These statistics assist companies and agencies in preparing the advertisement. The data are now available for both print and electronic media for both North America and Europe. A careful study of SRDS pays dividends by revealing not just financial figures but audience profiles too.

Consider a maker of process machinery whose target market consists of chemical manufacturers. The specific audience consists of plant engineers and supervisors, foremen and maintenance staff in large and medium-sized chemical firms. To reach them via print media, the marketing manager of the machinery maker looks at the circulation, cost data, and reading audience profile of the leading chemical industry journals. There are many choices, but to keep the illustration simple, assume that the two key contenders are *Chemical Week* (*CW*), published by McGraw-Hill, and *Chemical & Engineering News* (*CEN*), published by the American Chemical Society. A shortened version of the profiles of the two journals is shown in Exhibit 14–8.

Now comes the difficult part. The cost of a single ad on the back cover is $9,900 for *CW* versus $10,840 for *CEN,* and a full-page ad on the inside is $6,795 for *CW* and $8,100 for *CEN.* There are discounts for multiple insertions, on a sliding scale, with lower costs for more frequent appearances. But a more rational decision is to compare the **cost per thousand** subscribers. On this basis, the figures for the two back covers are $210 for *CW* and $83 for *CEN;* the choice seems clear: *CEN.* But other considerations enter. The manager may note that *CW* seems more oriented toward factory personnel, whereas *CEN* has almost 34,000 professors as subscribers. So the choice may yet be *CW* in spite of its higher per thousand cost. This is just a simplified version of what goes into the decision of placing ads in competing journals.

Now let us turn to electronic media with a specific example. Consider the situation facing an office supply company located in northeast Ohio, whose offerings cut across industry lines. The analyst for this organization thinks that the television audience of the local 6 P.M. news would be an appropriate target market for its 30-second commercials. All three network affiliates offer such local newscasts in Cleveland. There are definite differences, however, in terms of audience size, the actual dollar cost, and hence the cost per thousand viewers, as seen in Exhibit 14–9. Although Channel 8 looks like the best buy on the basis of the lowest cost per thousand, the analyst should do some additional work. It will be useful to find out what a series of commercials would cost over a year. Just as important, the analyst should try to get a detailed audience profile on each station. This may show the kind of people (by occupation, etc.) who watch each newscast. With this

EXHIBIT 14–8   Comparison of Two Leading U.S. Chemical Industry Trade Journals from the Viewpoint of Advertisers

Item	*Chemical Week (CW)*	*Chemical & Engineering News (CEN)*
Publisher location	McGraw-Hill Publishing Company, New York	American Chemical Society, Washington, D.C.
Editorial profile	*CW* reports and interprets the news for business and technical management of the chemical process industries.	*CEN* provides coverage of technical and business developments throughout the chemical process industries.
Representatives/ branch offices	1 in U.S. (used to be 6) 1 in W. Europe (used to be 4) 1 in Japan	6 across U.S. (used to be 9) 2 in W. Europe 1 in Japan
Commission and cash discounts	15% to agencies "on space, color, bleed and position"	15% of gross billing to recognized ad agencies "on space, color, bleed"
Frequency of publication	Weekly	Weekly

Advertising rates (as of 1/1/91)	Black & white
	  1 page/1 time: $6,795
	  1 page/18 time: $5,930
	  ½ page/1 time: $4,225
	  ½ page/18 time: $3,330
	Color (2 & 4 avail.)
	  4 color/page: $9,850
	Cover: $9,900
	Inserts (4 pages): $16,500
		Black & white
		  1 page/1 time: $8,100
		  1 page/26 time: $6,580
		  ½ page/1 time: $5,220
		  ½ page/26 time: $4,255
		Color (2 & 4 avail.)
		  4 color/page: $3,430
		Cover: $10,840
		Inserts (4 ×): 4 × $6,105

Circulation	Total: 46,741
	  paid 35,537
	  nonpaid 11,204
		Total:
		  paid 129,746
		  assoc. 108,333
		  status (ACS member)

Business analysis of circulation (partial)	Officers, executives and managers: 14,990 Works managers, supervisors, foremen: 5,683 Engineers, directors of development, chief chemists: 2,344	Officers, executives and managers: 10,171 Works managers, supervisors, foremen: 7,683 Engineers, directors of engineering: 7,366 Professors: 33,786

Source: Information taken from the March 24, 1991 edition of *Business Publication Rate & Data*, published by Standard Rate and Data Service.

EXHIBIT 14–9   Comparison of Three Midwest Television Stations from the Viewpoint of an Advertiser, 1987 and 1991

Television Station (Cleveland, Ohio)		Cost of a 30-Second Commercial during 6 p.m. Newscast (single insert; discount for multiples)	Audience Size (18 years old & over, to nearest thousand)	Cost/1,000
Channel/Call Letters	Network Affiliation			
Ch.3: WKYC	NBC	1987: $ 775	1987: 140,000	1987: $5.54
		1991: $ 600	1991: 128,000	1991: $4.68
Ch. 5: WEWS	ABC	1987: $2,000	1987: 341,000	1987: $5.87
		1991: $1,400	1991: 250,000	1991: $5.60
Ch. 8: WJW	CBS	1987: $1,200	1987: 270,000	1987: $4.44
		1991: $1,300	1991: 324,000	1991: $4.01

Source: Primary research conducted with sales and/or market research department of each station in 1987 and 1991 by one of the authors. Figures may differ from those shown by Arbitron, a television audience audit agency.

information, the company can make a far more intelligent decision regarding both a single commercial and a long-run campaign on the airwaves. If members of the buying center are not watching these newscasts, then the company should not advertise.[20]

Budget Setting: Theory and Practice

Several budget-setting methods exist, but each one represents a compromise between promotional goals on the one hand and available resources on the other. Methods that seem ideal in theory require either heroic assumptions or a costly collection of data. Furthermore, the empirical data in this field get dated quickly as changes occur in the economy or the specific industry. Competitors make new moves and can easily disrupt an ad campaign. It is also not unusual to find that desirable space or time have been taken: "Sorry, the back cover of our journal is sold through next year." Yet it is possible to arrive at workable solutions, often through a blend of methods and by noting guidelines developed over the years.[21]

Two simple budget strategies are the all-you-can-afford and the market-share approach. The former says: spend all you can without imperiling your financial base. Although this seems to be a safe method, it shows no relationship to the task that needs to be accomplished. Furthermore, it is not at all clear what is meant by the phrase, "all you can afford." The second approach says that spending should be in line with market share. But this requires knowing such data for each product in various industrial sectors. This thinking also implies that ad spending will maintain market share, which is simply not true, due to other determinants. There is an assumption that the present situation is a guide for the future, which again, is unlikely to be true.

Two other methods that seem desirable are the equi-marginal technique and the return-on investment approach. The former calls for spending up to the point where expenditures stop contributing to profits (where costs start to outweigh benefits). This is by no means easy to do and requires both unrealistic assumptions and extensive data collection. The latter approach does recognize the long-run benefits of advertising, but expected dollar returns cannot be easily estimated. Still, these two approaches impose important perspectives—namely, the idea of diminishing returns on the one hand and promotion spending as an investment on the other. Both approaches also alert us to the fact that as the product enters its mature phase, more advertising dollars may be needed to make a splash than in earlier stages.

In practice, three methods are widely used for several reasons: they make common sense, they are goal or competition-oriented, and they are relatively easy to apply. The first of these, the **objective-and-task approach**, looks at the ad budget from the perspective of what needs to be accomplished from the ad campaign and the placement of each single ad. The difficulty arises in agreeing on what the goal should be (such as awareness level versus possible impact on sales) and in determining the effort needed to get there (dollars and months needed). However, trial and error coupled with sophisticated models can do the job. Apple Computer used this technique successfully in its early days to track the impact of its ads aimed at schools.[22]

The second technique is the **competitive parity approach**. Here an organization takes a look at what other companies of the same size in the same industry are spending. Such figures can be obtained from the *SRDS* volumes, *Advertising Age,* or the research departments of large ad agencies and trade associations. (For given industrial groups, relative average spending patterns can be seen in Exhibit 14–7.) A troublesome aspect of this method is the assumption that other firms are in the same or highly similar situation and have identical goals or that the industry average is a good guide. These features may be unrealistic. However, there is merit in having roughly the same amount or percentage of ammunition as others of similar size as the battle unfolds for market share and recognition.

The third technique is the **percentage-of-sales** or **percentage-of-margin approach**. This is a variation of the previous technique and it is illustrated in Exhibit 14–7 for a sample of specific industrial categories. This technique is easy to administer and, like the previous one, has a fiscally conservative bent. But this approach treats advertising as a function of sales, whereas mass communication should be the factor influencing sales. In truth, either chain of causation seems simplistic. Still, the technique has commonsense appeal and can serve as a starting point in a stable environment.

A survey of the budget-setting practices of large advertisers revealed that the objective-and-task approach has been the most popular. About 65 percent of the firms surveyed used it. However, later researchers found that many firms made the claim just because it was expected of them. Other popular approaches were the percentage-of-sales method, quantitative techniques (not specified further), and the competitive parity approach with 53, 51, and 24 percent, respectively. That the percentages add up to well over 100 percent implies companies use several techniques.[23]

As in other fields, quantitative methods are being used increasingly to "drive" advertising budgets. One of the well-known models for budget determination is ADVISOR, which includes over forty variables.[24] Some of the key variables are product life cycle, purchase frequency, quality/uniqueness, market share, sales concentration, and customer growth. The analysis in this model focuses on three key ratios: marketing budget to total sales (M/S), advertising spending to marketing budget (A/M), and advertising spending to sales (A/S). The two professors who pioneered this ad budget model discovered that these ratios averaged about 7, 10, and 0.7 percent, respectively, across a number of industries. Although ADVISOR is a useful technique and an impressive model, the findings apply mostly to large organizations.

Advertising Effectiveness

There is no single measure of advertising effectiveness. Indeed, there is disagreement over what should be measured, when, and with what tools. As in budget setting, quantitative models do exist, but it is not possible to define accurately the impact of marketing communication in general or of advertising in particular. We can, however, conduct tests and attempt to gauge the impact of advertising in various ways. Pretests involve judging a print, radio, or television ad prior to its implementation, using a jury of experts or a sample of potential customers. The emphasis is often on judging the clarity of a simple message. Posttests involve aided or unaided recall and recognition measures. Here changes in awareness and attitude can be detected. One form of posttest is to review ads that have appeared in print. This is what the anonymous panel of Copy-Chasers does each month in *Business Marketing*, using the ten criteria listed in Exhibit 14–5.

An even more complex task than the pretest and posttest measures is trying to judge the direct impact of advertising on sales volume. This usually involves controlled experiments, which are costly; hence, only large firms attempt it. One example is the case of a chemical product, where Du Pont looked at sales increases between two control states and other states in the United States. Regression analysis is often used in such cases, with sales as the independent variable and past and current advertising expenditures as the explanatory variables. However, correlation still does not prove causation.[25]

Although it is difficult enough to measure the effectiveness of mass communication on product lines, assessing the impact of corporate image advertising is even more difficult. However, some results are emerging even in this area. According to a pioneer study in the 1970s, conducted by *Time* magazine, companies with corporate ad campaigns consistently received higher marks from executives than those that did not undertake such activity. Such "lift factor" differences ranged from 5 to 35 percent on a variety of measures, such as "leader in its field" and "responsive to clients." TRW, the large, diversified firm active in both the defense and civilian sectors, conducted an effective corporate image campaign in the 1980s. It claims that its identity rating rose from 34 percent in the early 1970s to about 80 percent by the end of the 1980s. Whether a better corporate image translates to higher sales or profits is another matter. In the recessionary early 1990s, firms are cutting back on ad spending, especially for corporate image.[26]

Creative Considerations

Would the promotion staff of a business organization and its advertising agency prefer to win prestigious awards for a single commercial, to be remembered for a series of memorable ads, or to be touted as having contributed to increased sales? The answer, of course, is all three! Creative advertising can and does work at many levels, from a catchy headline to the design of the overall copy, from the placement of the ad in a certain medium to the crafting of a yearlong campaign. Although creativity has been called the soul of advertising, it is difficult to define what constitutes a creative ad or a blockbuster message.

Some of the great names in advertising have attempted to define the elements of a creative ad. Thus, George Lois said he would like to see "purity of design." Back in the 1960s, David Ogilvy said he was opposed to "too clever" concepts for business communication, but since then he has mellowed. Still, he advocates precise steps and calls ads creative when they differentiate a product sharply from others and when they generate solid inquiries. Owens-Corning ran a well-regarded campaign for its insulation material. The company turned a commodity into a specialty by making its insulation pink and obtaining rights to a cartoon character, the Pink Panther, for its long-running series of television advertisements.[27]

The Campaign: Putting It All Together

In sports there is a difference between being player of the week and being the most valuable player over a season. The truly great players, of course, perform well year after year. The same holds true for business advertising. A superbly crafted **advertising campaign** with a central theme is superior to one clever ad. It is also bound to have a cumulative impact on the audience. Successful campaigns are long-range advertising efforts encompassing the various facets cited so far. They are carried out not only by large firms and their advertising agencies but also by smaller firms and their agencies. The following two stories focus on a medium-sized ad agency, Liggett-Stashower of Cleveland, and its work on behalf of two distinct organizations, Picker International and Ridge Tool. In both cases, the agency set the tone for the overall promotion and then adjusted the campaign as conditions changed.[28]

Picker International is a maker of complex medical imaging equipment; it competes against larger players like General Electric and Philips. Its target audience consists of radiologists in hospitals, a highly educated group. In the late 1970s, the company's ads emphasized high quality and performance. Then, as cost containment hit the health care field in the 1980s, the text and the tone of the ads shifted to productivity and money-saving aspects. The first print ad that cited specific prices resulted in major orders from those who had originally thought they could not afford a Picker scanner. The campaigns of the 1970s and 1980s also emphasized that the equipment aided in eliminating unnecessary surgery for patients, another key issue in the health care field. The key slogan remained "The diagnostic difference." This slogan conveyed the idea of benefits to the medical staff.

Ridge Tool, a subsidiary of Emerson Electric, is a maker of high-quality pipe tools targeted at plumbers. The tools are considered state-of-the-art and have an excellent reputation among users. Ridge Tool is the overwhelming favorite with plumbers and holds an enviable market share. However, the company wanted to expand its line of plumbing tools to others without alienating its traditional audience. So advertising campaigns had to be aimed at the oil, marine, and other industrial markets. Ridge Tool was also interested in reaching the maintenance staff of hotels, schools, and hospitals. In each case, separate campaigns were drafted by Liggett-Stashower to cater to the "drain maintenance requirements" of the specific end users. Distinct target markets received distinct appeals for the same product line. Follow-up studies indicated that this technique was useful; the audiences were "captured." This is the hallmark of a well-crafted campaign.

SALES PROMOTION

Between mass communication and personal selling lies the vast domain of **sales promotion**. This is a truly diverse field that includes direct mail, catalogs, trade shows and fairs, telemarketing, dealer aids, sweepstakes, and publicity of all kinds. Each of these categories contains some aspect of advertising and some aspect of personal selling. Although the variety is bewildering at first glance, each component has a specific role to play, and each one is action-oriented. Sales promotion is not as intimate as personal selling, but it is more direct than traditional advertising. At its best, sales promotion grabs the client with specific appeals.

When an organization sends out coupons in a direct-mail campaign, offers buying allowances, holds contests, or exhibits at a trade show, its objective is to generate action in the short run. It is asking for inquiries, sales leads, contacts, or just favorable comments—the sooner the better. It is true that some items, such as catalogs, have a long life, but frequently dispatched discount price sheets make them actionable and up-to-date. This illustrates another point—namely, that most sales promotional tools go beyond communication. Thus, contests combine product and promotion, cash rebates focus on pricing and promotion, and free samples or service demonstrations combine all three, making them especially effective.

Sales promotion is considered an integral part of the business marketing communication story, and many of its techniques have been around a long time. The great industrial trade fairs of Europe have attracted buyers for hundreds of years. Manufacturers and service organizations have used catalogs, brochures, and display kits for decades. The more flamboyant devices, such as sweepstakes, coupon redemption, and package deals are just making their appearance now.[29] These programs are aimed at various groups and individuals in the buying centers of large and small organizations.

Direct Mail

Use of **direct mail** in business marketing has certain key features: a small universe, a relatively high but affordable cost structure, and a focus on generating inquiries rather than sales. Prospects may number a few hundred or a few thousand, but they are all promising ones with nearly identical characteristics. This makes it easier to approach them with a uniform voice. Due to the higher cost of mailing lists and the difficulty in reaching those on the lists, it is common for business direct mail to cost about $1 per prospect, compared with 25 cents per prospect in consumer markets. Because the size of the typical industrial purchase is large, however, the relatively high cost of direct mail can be justified. The goal of the program is to yield inquiries or leads, not necessarily actual sales in the short run. The key idea is for recipients of mail to express interest and ask for more information, thereby forging the start of a good relationship.[30]

The growth of direct mail can be attributed in part to the much higher cost of industrial sales calls. This figure, as noted earlier, is about $300 per call in the United States, possibly more in other nations. This is no small sum when a large sales force is involved. Even phone calls cost over $16 in direct and indirect charges. True, the mailing pieces may not get to the right recipients every time, but when they do, they pave the way for the sales force. Mailings can be sent to many people at a given location, reaching all influential parties. Specially designed mailing lists from independent vendors are widely available, but they should be used in conjunction with inside lists of prospects.

Direct marketing agencies provide guidelines for achieving high response rates and avoiding mistakes in mail campaigns. These include using the proper letter format, providing coupons, not worrying about duplicate mailings, and including prepaid return envelopes. How to segment direct response markets, merge and purge lists electronically, and other useful information can be found in such journals as *Direct Marketing, Business Marketing, Marketing & Media Decisions, Sales & Marketing Management,* and others. The field has become so popular that there is concern, much the same as in advertising, with visibility. Distinguishing oneself is not easy. Thus, colorful envelopes, bold messages, unusual inserts, and incentives are becoming more frequent.[31]

BUSINESS MARKETING IN PRACTICE

Micromarketing Comes of Age—Targeting Key Customers by Using Receipts

Micromarketing is nothing more than using mail-order lists, census information, and historical buying patterns to help create the perfect prospect list. Once you have the list, you tailor your sales pitch accordingly.

Joan Silver runs Reeves A/V Systems, a $5-million-plus New York City company that sells and services a full line of industrial audiovisual equipment. About four times a year she does a mailing to 3,000 customers and potential customers. "Since direct mail is the only advertising we do, other than appearing in the *Yellow Pages,* I'd love to mail more frequently . . . but it is expensive." But Silver had a new $16,000 Sony video projection system in stock that she wanted the world to know about. How could she spread the word efficiently?

Silver did not have the money to set up a costly program. Instead, she sat down to analyze her receipts, meaning her invoices and purchase orders. She learned that while large firms (*Fortune* 500 companies) were significant buyers, they accounted for only 58 per-

cent of revenues. The rest came in from smaller companies. She also found that some large accounts became victims of mergers and cutbacks. Further analysis revealed that ad agencies and insurance firms were buying equipment for internal training and custom editing in-house.

Knowing all this gave Silver the clue to make a sales pitch to ad agencies and insurance firms who had not bought such equipment. "Since your competitors are bringing their production work inside, shouldn't you be thinking about it, too? We can custom design a system for you." Next she started classifying the products customers were and were not buying from her. "Some knew us for our equipment; some knew us for our service." She tailored letters to each group, underscoring Reeves's capabilities.

Source: P. Brown, "Paper Trail," *INC.,* Aug. 1990, pp. 113–114.

Telemarketing

Just as direct mail is not to be confused with mail-order selling, so direct marketing by telephone or computer—telemarketing—should not be confused with either direct selling or with market research using the same instruments. **Telemarketing** refers to an electronic link for voice or data with actual or potential clients. The purpose is not to sell them something now but to establish or to strengthen the relationship. The electronic link also can be used to solicit and to receive orders, but that is called *teleselling.* In telemarketing, the key consideration is to pass on new information, to generate inquiries, and to cultivate contacts. Of course, in the end, the two activities of telemarketing and selling do and should merge. At this stage, however, the central thrust is to forge loyalty bonds.

Telemarketing is a way of considering prospects and their needs. The creative marketer alerts its clientele to changes in products and prices; it can also offer service to customers both before and after the sale. For example, NCR uses telemarketing to introduce new products to top decision makers. Dow Corning uses telemarketing to identify small accounts that have large potential in the long run. Other large firms use telemarketing to alert clients to new service features, and still others offer maintenance contracts for products already sold.

According to practitioners, good telemarketing programs have the following features: specific cost and performance objectives, comparison of results against standards, structured format, and close supervision.[32] One popular feature in North America, which is now spreading across the globe, is the use of 800 numbers, which permit free long-distance calls to those calling to ask for assistance. Callers can also receive product, pricing, and dealer information. For the vendor, the 800 number is a chance to spot problems quickly and thus prevent dissatisfaction with service. Various studies indicate that requests for more assistance lead to increased sales of old products and yield ideas for new ones. Telemarketers should not just wait for incoming calls, however. Increasingly popular is **database marketing**, the development of prospects through list segmentation. Again, the central idea is to forge strong loyalty bonds for mutual benefit.

The revolution in telemarketing goes beyond telephone links. It involves computers and the linking of terminals or stations in a network. A simple yet powerful technique is **electronic data interchange (EDI)**, a technology that electronically links vendors and customers via dedicated tie-lines. The network can also link various branch offices and dealer locations. An example is shown in Exhibit 14–10. Such connections can handle inquiries, orders, complaints, price changes, and inventory adjustments. Other examples of two-way or multiple dialogue include aerospace companies searching for parts, food processors getting data on available fruits and vegetables, and furniture makers linking up with timber firms. Beside EDI, other forms of electronic ties include facsimile machines and electronic mail. Both fax and e-mail, which can put a distant message on a desktop for instant or subsequent retrieval, are growing in popularity.

Computerization of telecommunication means that all facets of the marketing program can be blended. Consider an industrial buyer trying to decide which abrasive to use in a specific grinding application. The sales rep can enter the request into an expert system routine on a laptop computer, which offers several alternatives in terms of operating and maintenance costs. The customer can then make a decision on the spot. The data can also be fed to a regional office, which can send out further information, even without a request. Meanwhile, headquarters can do demand planning, knowing which offerings are hot and which are not. The same logic applies to selecting health care programs for employees or for choosing among diverse office designs and decor.

Catalogs and Directories

Product catalogs, and **service directories** are silent partners to the sales force; they are both buying guides for the user. Placed on the right desk and updated from time to time, they serve both vendor and customer well. Catalogs are useful

EXHIBIT 14–10   Innovative Telemarketing in Action: Tie-lines with Clients (Use of Dedicated Computer Lines)

PRICE CHECK

This function lets you see the price you will be charged for any particular item. Simply enter the manufacturer and our part description or your part description. The system will display the manufacturer with our part description, your part description, your price for that item, and the unit of measure.

```
PRICE CHECK        DATE 10/10/93
                   TIME 08:00:00

MANUFACTURER _____ AND/OR
PART DESCRIPTION _____

        AND/OR

YOUR PART _____

    AND HIT RETURN




    F1      F2         END
```

```
PRICE CHECK        DATE 10/10/93
                   TIME 08:00:00

MANUFACTURER    _____
B1 PART DESC    _____
YOUR PART DESC  _____
YOUR PRICE      ____ __ UM __

   NEXT MANUFACTURER AND/OR
        B1 PART DESC_____

        AND/OR

YOUR PART DESC _____



    F1      F2         END
```

BACKORDER REVIEW

This function will enable you to review any backorders you may have on file with your servicing branch. This file may be reviewed in three ways: Key nothing on the first screen, and the system will begin the display with your first item on file. Key the manufacturer and the Bearings, Inc., Dixie Bearings, Inc., or Bruening Bearings, Inc. part description, and the system will display the entire file beginning with the item requested. Enter only a manufacturer, and the system will display all of your backorders for that particular manufacturer.

```
BACKORDER      DATE 10/10/93
REVIEW         TIME 08:00:00

MANUFACTURER _____ AND/OR
PART DESCRIPTION _____

        AND/OR

YOUR PART _____

    AND HIT RETURN




    F1      F2         END
```

```
BACKORDER      DATE 10/10/93
REVIEW         TIME 08:00:00

QUANTITY       _____
MANUFACTURER   _____
PART DESC      _____
OUR PO#        _____
B/O DATE       MM/DD/YY
REQ'D DATE     MM/DD/YY
YOUR PO#       _____

QUANTITY       _____
MANUFACTURER   _____
PART DESC      _____
OUR PO#        _____
B/O DATE       MM/DD/YY
REQ'D DATE     MM/DD/YY
YOUR PO#       _____

    F1      F2         END
```

Note: Other uses involve: (1) Memo to branch office; (2) Inventory review; (3) Addition to pricing contract; (4) Stock check; (5) Order entry; and (6) Product review

Source: "Omnex C, A Complete Customer Service System"; brochure issued by Bearings, Inc. of Cleveland, Ohio, 1986.

for comparing technical specifications that describe physical characteristics and performance levels. They provide prices, warranty descriptions, and delivery terms. Inserts can be mailed out announcing new products and seasonal discounts. Catalogs can also serve as user manuals; some are translated for foreign buyers. They are liked by manufacturers who offer much variety, such as makers of plumbing supplies, electronic components, office goods, and aircraft parts.

Catalogs and directories are not cheap; they cost between $25 and $90 each. Thus, the marketer has to be careful in placing them. Key prospects are often identified before printing takes place. Direct mail, insert cards, and members of the sales force are used to find potential users. To save money, only part of the volume is given out if the client shows no interest in the remainder of the offerings. Splitting catalogs works well where geographic segmentation occurs. For example, the thick *Official Airline Guide* is now available on a city-by-city basis at a low unit price. A firm headquartered in Atlanta and doing business frequently in Boston and Chicago needs to obtain only three booklets.

Directories can take many different shapes and forms. The metropolitan *Business Yellow Pages* provides listings by type of business and allows advertising; it is immensely popular among local small and medium-sized firms. The multivolume *Thomas Register/Thomcat* series is another example of business listings plus advertisements, including catalog pages, on a nationwide basis. According to the publishers of these two sets of volumes, buyers use them regularly to find new suppliers and to ascertain product availability and specifications. Some of the volumes are now becoming available in an electronic format. This means that one can think of combining certain features of catalogs and directories with aspects of telemarketing.

Catalogs and directories are frequently backed up by brochures or flyers. This supplementary literature is updated material, designed to bring the latest information on technical parameters or performance standards. However, brochures are often prepared in a hurry, so they tend to be more colorful than informative. The real problem with brochures and flyers is that too many of them reach the users. It is better to send them less frequently and to make them more meaningful. Several companies now send information via first-class mail. Promotional mail is sent third class, but it often includes a gimmick, a souvenir, or a small gift to catch attention.

Trade Shows and Fairs

Trade shows are vertical affairs that focus on one major industry, including the product and service providers, suppliers, dealers, and customers. If the industry is large, the show will include only certain subsectors. Conversely, if the industry is small, the show will include exhibits from related fields. The shows are usually sponsored by a trade, industry, or professional association, but each corporate exhibitor pays for its own display area or booth. The Instrument Society of America, for example, is the key force behind a trade show that features controls, meters, and other instruments by Foxboro, Johnson Controls, and hundreds of others. The Water & Wastewater Equipment Manufacturers Association (WWEMA) recruits makers of filtration, separation, and other treatment devices. If, by chance, not enough firms sign up, WWEMA may join forces with associations representing solid waste control or air pollution control firms.

There are now 750 major trade shows in Canada, over 9,000 in the United States (double the number ten years ago), and about 10,000 in Europe in any given year. Whenever a trade show grows too big, there is a tendency to have spinoffs, such as regional or local shows, yet the big one usually carries on. This allows for more choice of location, size of booth, and so on. Among the largest trade shows is the Paris Air Show, which features small planes, large civilian aircraft, military fighter planes, and aerospace components.

Aggressive selling is frowned upon at trade shows. Most firms prefer to do networking and soft-selling. They also observe the latest offerings of competitors, pick up useful gossip, and generate leads or contacts. Trade shows rank just behind advertising and tips from field representatives in yielding inquiries, and they rank just behind peer recommendations and personal selling in influencing the purchase decision. By not participating, an exhibitor must always wonder about missed opportunities.[33]

Fairs are horizontal affairs, usually covering several distinct industries. When a wide range of industries and products are displayed, we speak of **expos**, or major **expositions**. Selling does take place at fairs and expos, with orders solicited for high-priced items, including floor models. Fairs are an old tradition in Europe, but they have taken root now on all continents. In Europe, it is still customary to have a major industrial goods show in the autumn and a major consumer goods show in the spring. These are held in large cities that are crossroads between East and West, such as Budapest. The largest expo is in Hanover, Germany. It attracts over 6,000 exhibitors and 1.5 million visitors from over fifty countries. Materials, machinery, and components from old-line and high-tech industries are shown during eight days in April in two dozen large halls covering 5 million square feet.

Permanent exhibits, or marts, are also gaining popularity, although these demand an ongoing commitment from those who take space there. Such exhibits can encompass a wide variety of goods, though it is preferable that the building have a special mission. Booths are often spread over several floors with the displays clustered along aisles. Potential customers and distributors are invited to view new displays at any time or to make appointments with exhibitors. The famous Merchandise Mart in Chicago has acres of household furniture but also displays some office furniture and all-purpose sofas, tables, and chairs. Infomart in Dallas is a modernistic building showing off the latest in computer and communication equipment. Permanent halls for displaying health care apparatus have been proposed for Florida and Ohio, but they have been put on hold due to lack of commitment and financing.

Over the past twenty years, research has identified the rationale for attending trade shows. Generating sales leads is ranked as the top reason for participation. The companies exhibiting want the show to bring in genuine prospects, not sight-

World's largest industrial machinery trade fair invites large and small companies for exhibiting, meeting potential buyers, and looking over the competition. Attendance is a must.

ONCE A YEAR HANNOVER SERVES AS THE WORLD'S INDUSTRIAL MARKETPLACE

Make 1992 your year to visit the **HANNOVER FAIR.** This epic event is the world's most comprehensive exhibition of industrial equipment, components and systems. **April 1–8, 1992** It will draw 6,000 exhibiting companies and 480,000 attendees from 100 countries. Thousands of professionals travel from the U.S. each year to examine the world's newest industrial technologies...the latest innovations that can make your company more efficient and competitive. Whether you are buying or selling, observing or negotiating, the HANNOVER FAIR is the place to do it in 1992. Examine the state of the art, the state of the market, the state of the competition, and the state of the New Europe. In one place. At one time. April 1–8, 1992. Hannover, Germany.

HANNOVER MESSE '92

RESEARCH AND TECHNOLOGY · ELECTRICAL ENGINEERING AND ELECTRONICS · ENERGY AND THE ENVIRONMENT · PLANT ENGINEERING AND INDUSTRIAL MATERIALS · ASSEMBLY, HANDLING, INDUSTRIAL ROBOTS · SURFACE TREATMENT · TOOLS AND FACTORY EQUIPMENT · SUBCONTRACTING · PARTNER COUNTRY FRANCE

For further information:
Hannover Fairs USA, 103 Carnegie Center, Princeton, NJ 08540 Tel: (609) 987-1202, Fax: (609) 987-0092

DEUTSCHE MESSE AG, HANNOVER/GERMANY

FOR INFORMATION, CIRCLE NO. 56

Courtesy of Hannover Fairs USA.

seers. Other reasons to attend trade shows and fairs include introducing new products, surveying competitors, establishing technical contacts, and gaining corporate visibility. Statistics from associations and journals, such as the Trade Show Bureau and *Tradeshow Week,* indicate that there is no slackening of interest. The one exception is the slight decline in attendance at the largest trade shows; possibly, some have become too costly to attend and too cumbersome to visit all the exhibit booths.[34]

To find just the right trade show or fair/expo, an organization should study past records and projected figures on attendance, list of exhibitors, and physical layout. After the decision is made to participate, the characteristics of the exhibit become important. These include height of structure, seating, lighting, banners, multimedia presentations, product displays, brochures, refreshments, and give-aways. The cost can range from $90 to $180 per square foot, with total spending divided evenly into four parts: construction, space rental, services, and miscellaneous. Working with consultants or design firms is highly recommended, as they can assist in all phases, from initial sketch to final dismantling.

In evaluating trade shows, analysts suggest setting objectives in terms of target audience, messages to be conveyed, and geographical exposure. A glass bowl is a simple device to collect business cards, thereby tracking walk-in traffic and building a sizable list of potential buyers. Holding a daily raffle among the contributors encourages the depositing of business cards. Budgeting should take into account past experience and anticipated costs per square foot and per number of likely sales leads. Trade show surveys can yield insights on attendance, traffic density, buying plans, and recall of memorable exhibits. A cross-section of survey results is shown in Exhibit 14–11. It is possible to judge success on a number of criteria and to compare the results with those of previous years. Of course, the firm exhibiting should define its goals ahead of time and then judge accomplishments against its established standards.[35]

Promotion to the Trade

Although **promotion to the trade**—that is, promotion aimed at various interme-diaries—seems like a mundane task, it is absolutely necessary. Whether an organization works with distributors and dealers or with agents and brokers, it should view them as valued partners. Steel producers rely on steel service centers. Timken, the bearing maker, is friendly with Bearings, a distributor. Loctite is in touch with hundreds of outlets displaying its adhesives. Truck components make sure their parts are in stock at Truckstops of America. Software developers often cultivate both computer superstores and office equipment dealers. Large exhibit facilities and convention centers work closely with trade associations, travel agents, and individual exhibitors. A financial service firm builds strong relation-ships with banks, insurers, and financial planners. In short, building a network or alliance with others in distribution channels who influence your success is a must.

Trade promotion aimed at one's partners can take any of the forms cited so far, from direct mail to telemarketing, from sharing catalogs to cooperating on ex-hibit booths. Popular steps include running ads in journals read by distributors. Another friendly gesture is for the producer or provider of service to share the cost of advertising in a cooperative fashion, on a 50-50 basis. Dealer displays, sales kits, point-of-purchase displays, and specialty promotional items (pens, caps, rulers with logos) are welcomed by distributors. General Electric and Philips now pro-vide their own display racks to dealers handling their lines of industrial lightbulbs. Training and maintenance courses are also useful tools to build the relationship.

EXHIBIT 14–11   Selected Major U.S. Trade Shows Ranked by Various Indicators, 1989

Show with Highest...	Trade Show Name (abbrev. form)	Industry	Location	Registered Attendance[5]	Percent of '89 Audience
Net buying influences[1]	PGA Merch. Show	Golfing equipment	Orlando	8,435	98.0
	DesCon-A/E/C Sys.	Design, construction	Anaheim	21,058	96.0
	Natl. Assoc. of Brdc.	Broadcasting	Las Vegas	32,500	95.0
	Fed Micro	Government data processing	Washington, D.C.	21,752	95.0
	Pittsburgh Conf.	Instruments	Atlanta	12,081	94.0
Total buying plans[2]	PGA Merch. Show	Golfing equipment	Orlando	8,435	91.0
	Natl. Assoc. Brdc.	Broadcasting	Las Vegas	32,500	82.0
	COMDEX/Fall	Computers, personal	Las Vegas	na	82.0
	PC Expo	Computers	New York	na	82.0
	Fed Micro	Government data processing	Washington, D.C.	21,752	79.0
Audience interest factor[3]	Assoc. Oper. Rm. Nur.	Nursing/health	Anaheim	8,733	77.0
	Design Automation	Design equipment	Las Vegas	4,677	73.0
	IEEE/PES	Electrical enginering	New Orleans	5,186	64.0
	PC Expo	Personal computers	New York	na	64.0
	Info. Mgmt. Expo	Information management	New York	na	59.0
Traffic density[4]	DesCon-A/E/C Sys.	Design, construction	Anaheim	21,058	5.9
	TEXPO	Voice communication	San Francisco	6,881	5.7
	Uniforum	UNIX computer	San Francisco	18,316	5.3
	Assoc. Info. & Image	Information management	San Francisco	14,614	5.2
	TCA Annual Conf.	Telecommunications	San Diego	9,610	5.2

Notes: [1]Net buying influence: percentage of show audience who have final say, specify, or recommend for purchase one or more of the products exhibited.
[2]Total buying plans: percentage of exhibit visitors who said they were planning to buy the company's products as a result of what they saw at the show.
[3]Audience interest factor: percentage of audience at the show who visit at least two of ten exhibits from a selected group of exhibiting companies.
[4]Traffic density: average number of visitors who could theoretically occupy every 100 square feet of exhibit space during the time the trade show is open.
[5]Attendance figures represent number of registrants; this is not the same as the attendance reported by show management

Source: S. K. Swanby et al., "Trade Shows Poised for 1990s Growth," *Business Marketing* (May 1990), pp. 46–52. See also K. Swanby et al., "1989's Most Memorable Exhibits," *Business Marketing* (September 1990): 62–66, for a rating of top exhibits based on percent recall. For large shows, these companies ranked highest: Sony, Kohler, AT&T, General Electric, and IBM. For smaller shows: Pacific Bell, Apple Computer, Schlumberger, and AT&T.

BUSINESS MARKETING IN PRACTICE ▮▮▮▮▮▮▮▮▮▮▮▮▮▮▮▮▮

Breaking Down Stereotypes—How Three Young Women Handle Many Phases of an Equipment Business

A lot of male chauvinists ask Bob Kress of Cleveland why he brought his three young girls into the family business. He says he was not trying to make a statement. "My daughters take a back seat to no one. They're good at what they do." And what they do is help their father run Piping Equipment, Inc., an industrial supply house specializing in valves, pressure and temperature control devices, and actuators. The company provides parts for manufacturers, hospitals, and shopping malls, as well as for sewer and electric utility agencies.

Therese Kress handles outside sales, Holly Kress inside sales, and Kristine Kress Spelling accounting and finance. All three are under thirty years of age, but they already have a lot of experience. They go out and analyze problems at customer locations. They know their own warehouse, and they are learning every day on the job.

But the Kress daughters, while learning much from their father, also taught him a thing or two. They encouraged him to begin a direct-mail advertising program that includes a gift each month for customers or potential clients. One of their monthly fliers said: "The stage is set. The curtain is rising on another great year." It was accompanied by a bag of microwavable popcorn. Other innovative small gifts are sent out, not just ballpoint pens and calendars.

The monthly mailings are not just gimmicks. "They give out neat product information to us in the mail once a month," says Dave Houser, purchasing agent for Hyde Products, a manufacturer of units used in metal cutting. "They're also very service-oriented."

Source: Dana Canedy, "Daughters Handle Piping Business," (Cleveland) *The Plain Dealer,* May 3, 1991, pp. 1-E–2-E.

Although only 5 percent of the total industrial sales promotion budget is aimed toward dealers, the Specialty Advertising Association claims that "aid to the trade" almost always pays off and results in more inquiries.[36]

Other Sales Promotion Tools

Many other imaginative sales promotion techniques can be used by business marketers, whether old-line or high-tech, product or service oriented. Consider the situation in water treatment chemicals. The two leading firms in the United States, Betz Laboratories and Nalco Chemical, both publish handbooks. A giant French firm in the field, Degremont, also developed a massive volume, practically an encyclopedia of water and wastewater treatment. Experts in the company write these books, at times assisted by outsiders. Although there are subtle references to the company and its product line in each book, the emphasis is on giving practical, objective advice to plant engineers, technicians, and chemists involved in operations. Going a step further, Nalco Chemical developed a training videotape

This Microlog ad shows how one business successfully used Microlog's products

How WRC-TV Keeps 16,607 Armchair Athletes From Going Scoreless.

When WRC-TV in Washington, D.C. found its sports hotline sidelined by a faulty phone system, the station added Microlog's VCS 3500 to its game plan.

Now, WRC is able to give up-to-the-minute information on everything from football to the French Open. The system even polls viewers to get their opinions on major events and issues.

Hotlines are just one way the VCS 3500 helps improve performance. Newspapers can use it to provide stock quotes, weather, sports scores, horoscopes and soap opera updates. Radio stations can promote contests and provide information on local entertainment, sports

and traffic. And all forms of media can attract new advertisers and generate revenue with special programs using 800 and 900 numbers.

Whether your medium is TV, radio, or print, Microlog helps you reach a larger audience, faster and more cost efficiently than ever before.

We'll prove it with a FREE ANALYSIS of your present phone system. And we'll send you a free brochure explaining how Microlog works for media. Just call Kathy Mitchell today. 1-800-562-2822 In MD (301) 428-5227.

MICROLOG
CORPORATION
THE VOICE OF EFFICIENCY

© Microlog Corporation.

featuring a well-known sports figure as narrator. In the 1990s, celebrities and testimonials will be used increasingly in business marketing.

Companies offering data processing, computer consultancy, and software have used both traditional promotional techniques and unusual ones. Among their innovative practices is the encouragement given to technical staff on their payroll to develop articles for publication in various journals. Reprints of the articles are then sent to clients to enhance corporate image and service offerings. In this field, too, videocassettes as training tools are becoming popular. Even more popular are the free training seminars now espoused by even the largest companies, such as Apple and IBM. Some entrepreneurs have converted trucks into luxury vans and use them as mobile displays, sending them into small cities to reach clients who feel neglected by the big firms.

PUBLIC RELATIONS, PUBLICITY, AND SPONSORSHIP

Although public relations and related activities can be considered part of sales promotion, we are treating these subjects separately here for three reasons. First, they are becoming more and more distinct activities, with their own techniques, associations, and journals. Many PR firms see themselves as quite different from advertising agencies. Publicity spokespersons prefer to distance themselves from sales promotion specialists. Second, publicity and sponsorship can be considered integral parts of a broader campaign in which an organization seeks to create and maintain its image among more diverse audiences than is the case for sales promotion. (We shall look at various stakeholders, also called publics, who have no direct link to the organization yet can influence its success.) Third, measures of effectiveness in this field differ from those used in advertising and sales promotion.

What Constitutes Good PR?

How do we want others to view us? As an innovative, risk-taking firm or as an old-line, rock-solid organization? When companies work out the answer to these and related questions, the findings then become a basis for a **public relations (PR) policy**. The way an organization is viewed is influenced by personal and impersonal factors. The former includes everyone from top officers to delivery truck drivers, from the sales force member to the telephone operator (who, by now, may have been replaced by an answering machine). Inanimate objects, ranging from the logo of the company to the freshness of paint on its trucks, from the architecture of the building to the decor on the inside walls, also make a statement. This is called **corporate image** in the United States and **house style** in the United Kingdom. The task of the PR specialist is to coordinate it all for a consistent message.[37]

Just about every year, a picture of a giant tire appears in the middle of the business pages of metropolitan newspapers (see Exhibit 14–12). The caption says: "World's largest tire—once again made by Goodyear Tire of Akron, Ohio." Such publicity is worth more to Goodyear than many pages of paid advertising. It is news, and it is so treated by the papers and by the public. Who placed the photo? A PR specialist who is skilled at gaining free space and time in print and electronic media. But there is much more to PR than that. Textbooks on the topic now run to 600 pages, and topics range from having an employee information program to advice on what to do in a crisis situation. The key is to formulate appropriate policies in dealing with different audiences and diverse media.

EXHIBIT 14–12   Good Publicity for Goodyear Tire & Rubber Company: World's Largest Tire, Featured in Many Newspapers

Source: Goodyear Tire & Rubber Company, Akron, Ohio, 1986–87.

Dealing with Stakeholders

When Boeing unveils its new jetliners, it invites the top executives of airlines who placed orders to come to Seattle and greets them with marching bands and a reception. Airbus Industrie of Toulouse, France, does the same for its blue chip accounts on the festive occasion of the Paris Air Show. In similar fashion, but with more security and less hoopla, the makers of military aircraft show off their latest output to government officials. This is equally true for General Dynamics in the

United States, Dassault in France, and British Aerospace in the United Kingdom. Makers of the Falcon and Gulfstream executive jets unroll the red carpet for presidents and chief pilots. There is no better publicity vis-à-vis these **stakeholders** than impressing them with the roll-out of new products or the dedication of a new facility.

Makers of business products and services, however, must deal with many other stakeholder groups besides current and potential clients. These include suppliers, employees, and shareholders; opinion or community leaders, politicians, and government officials; and, finally, the editors, reporters, and analysts from the media and other groups, such as the financial community. They too should be invited to special events as appropriate. Each group deserves special attention. For example, employees may get news announcements and shareholders receive quarterly reports at their homes. Suppliers must be notified about changes in bidding procedures. Community leaders are sent annual reports dealing with corporate social responsibility, with special reference to charitable donations of money and time.

Good PR specialists should be equally adept at handling large and small affairs. The former include corporate mergers, plant openings or closings, major product announcements, the mounting of a lobbying campaign aimed at legislators or regulators, and the handling of environmental accidents. Many large U.S., Japanese, and European firms now maintain an office in Washington, D.C., to keep tabs on federal rules and regulations and to influence forthcoming legislation. In case of environmental disasters, damage control is the key PR phrase. As a general rule, speaking openly is far better than stonewalling and PR specialists can advise the company how to admit its error, show what is being done to rectify it, and maintain credibility. Finally, the PR specialist can advise corporate officials about many small matters, including travel at home and abroad. Cultural sensitivity is a must in foreign settings so that mistakes are avoided in dressing, gift giving, and other respects.[38]

Corporate Sponsorship

It is difficult to state where sales promotion ends and public relations activity begins. As a result, the two activities may be combined in one division, or there may be a single director. The overlap between the two fields is well illustrated by the growth of **corporate sponsorship**. This endeavor, like large fairs or expos, got its start in Europe, where companies have sponsored sports clubs for many decades, as well as major cultural events. Now corporate sponsorship is in full bloom in North and South America, the Pacific Rim, and other regions.

Although food, liquor, tobacco, fashion, and travel organizations are in the forefront of sponsorship activities, business marketers are also underwriting the cost of major sports, cultural, and community events. This is especially true for large companies in the fields of telecommunication, electronics, finance, and health care. Geographic coverage may be local or national, in rare cases even international. Corporate goals in sponsoring range from creating awareness to media exposure, from positioning a product to creating sales. Sponsors of sporting events tend to favor those sports that their target audiences (buying center members)

BUSINESS MARKETING IN PRACTICE ▬▬▬▬▬▬

From the Winner's Circle to a Trade Show—Saga of a Sponsorship

Cummins Engine is a large midwestern firm that makes engines for large trucks and construction equipment. It markets directly to businesses, not to consumers. So why sponsor a race car?

The answer is that a unique opportunity arose when Roger Penske, owner of a race car entered in the 1987 Indianapolis 500, found out that one of the car's key drivers and one of its sponsors had to withdraw from the race. Penske asked Al Unser, Sr., to race the car, but he still needed a sponsor, so he called on Cummins Engine's president, James Henderson, to "step in." He did so—to the tune of a six-figure sum. Why did Henderson and Cummins do this?

Al Unser was racing with a Cummins product in his car: the turbocharger on the engine was made by Holset Engineering, a Cummins subsidiary. Since the racing turbo was pretty much the same as the turbo found on all Cummins engine trucks, Henderson perceived a golden opportunity.

As luck and skill would have it, Unser won the race. The Cummins name was splashed across television screens and front pages all over the world. Henderson was elated. "What this tells people is that our turbocharger was chosen by the number one race team." Cummins took out ads in *Fleet Owner, Construction Digest,* and other trade journals to make the point with key users. In addition to trade press ads, the company bought booth space at trade shows and brought in Al Unser to sign autographs. Unser also chatted with customers and potential clients.

Although Cummins sponsored Unser for the rest of the 1987 season and thinks the tie-in was terrific, it has not sponsored other cars since then. However, it has a large hospitality suite at the race track, it displays the equipment at trade shows, and it continues to advertise in the journals cited, as well as others, such as *Heavy Duty Trucking.* It also has an ongoing relation with Hertz-Penske Truck Leasing.

Source: R. Sullivan, "From the Winner's Circle to a Trade Show," *Business Marketing* (May 1991), p. 20. Reprinted with permission of *Business Marketing.*

like: golf, tennis, and running. Some high-tech firms, wishing to project a daring image, may sponsor hang-gliding or rock-climbing events. Old-line manufacturers, in contrast, stick to safer sports such as softball or bowling. Banks and health care insurers often sponsor a special concert, ballet, or opera.

The sponsors of sports, artistic, and other events look to a number of measures when undertaking support: cost per customer, number of participants, media exposure, and changes in awareness levels. Some sponsors of auto races count the minutes their logos are visible on the cars and drivers during the televised race. Although many measurements can be made, the results are difficult to assess. Does underwriting an event change the positioning of a product? Research in the field indicates that corporate sponsorship is seldom effective by itself. It works best when combined with continuous ad campaigns and with a strong personal selling effort. It also works best when it is done on a year-in, year-out basis.[39]

In our research of sponsored events, we found that awareness was greatest when the sponsor's name was incorporated in the name of the event. For example, recall figures for the Budweiser Grand Prix and the Revco Cleveland Marathon were in the 75 to 85 percent range. For a 10K foot race, the Nutcracker ballet, and a river festival sponsored by Blue Cross, National City Bank, and BP, the comparable figures came in at 25 to 45 percent. A summary of recent corporate sponsorships is given in Exhibit 14–13. It reveals types of events sponsored, target audiences aimed at, geographic coverage, and objectives for various industry or product categories. Evaluation procedures in this field are still in their infancy.

EXHIBIT 14–13   Survey of Recent Corporate Sponsorships in Selected U.S. Industries, 1989–1990

Industry Group	Specific Product/ Service	Number of Events Sponsored	Basis for Target Audience	Types of Events Sponsored	Geographic Coverage	Objectives
Fashion accessories	Sunglasses	8	Lifestyle, demographics	Sports Community Fine arts	Regional National	Media exposure Image/ communications
	Watches	10	Lifestyle, demographics	Sports Community	All	Media exposure Image/positioning/ awareness
Food	Fruit juices	10	Demo- graphics	Sports Fine arts Community	All	Image/positioning/ awareness Sales
	Snack foods	9	Not stated	Sports	Regional Local	Image/positioning/ awareness Sales
	Fast food	14	Demo- graphics	Sports Popular arts Fine arts	All	Image/positioning/ awareness Sales
	Agricultural products	8	Lifestyle, demographics	Sports Community	Local Regional	Image/positioning/ awareness Sales
Travel, tourism	Domestic airlines	11	Lifestyle, demographics	Sports Community Fine arts	All	Media exposure Image/positioning/ awareness
	Car rental agencies	9	Demo- graphics	Sports Community	Local Regional	Media exposure Image/positioning/ awareness
Insurance	Life, health insurance	8	Demo- graphics	Sports Community Fine arts	All	Media exposure Image/positioning/ awareness

Source: *Special Events Report*, 10 issues from Jan. 30, 1989, to Nov. 19, 1990. Published by International Events Group, Chicago. The data are for specific companies and the results were compiled by A. Gross, R. Javalgi, and M. Traylor.

One effective tactic is to combine sponsorship with other affairs before and after the event. General Electric and Ameritech/Ohio Bell did this when they sponsored the performances of the Cleveland Orchestra in Europe on two different occasions. Dignitaries were invited to lavish parties before and after the concerts. These companies do not expect immediate increases in sales or a vastly changed corporate image, but they laid the groundwork for both, at home and abroad. In the long run, they do check on whether orders and inquiries originated from those in attendance. But what about small industrial firms? They can emulate GE or Ohio Bell by sponsoring local events or sports teams on a steady basis, then having a season-ending outdoor picnic. Again, the key is segmentation, targeting, and then positioning one's offerings.

SUMMARY

The communication process in marketing is both simple and complex. It is simple because the job consists mostly of information and persuasion. More specifically, it means taking business audiences from the awareness to the preference stage, then convincing them to make a decision about a purchase. But this is also a complex task, partly because the clutter, or noise level, has risen sharply and partly because marketers have to learn to be excellent listeners, not just speakers. In short, we have come a long way from the days when an industrial firm could run the same advertisement in a trade journal month in and month out. Today, the opportunities are many, but so are the challenges to find the right blend and the right message.

Many outlets and techniques are involved in the mass communication scheme of the 1990s: a wide variety of print and electronic media, numerous ways of getting the message created, and diverse ways of establishing rapport via sales promotion. Several budget-setting techniques are available, and the same applies to measuring the effectiveness of the promotion effort. Hundreds of advertising and public relations agencies stand ready to assist. They come in all sizes and configurations, offering general and specialized services.

Despite all the assistance, the business marketer must still be the final judge of what makes for a forceful message, a creative agency, and an effective campaign. Does the message convey benefits and solutions, or does it talk only about technical details and vague corporate virtues? Does the trade journal have a low cost per thousand subscribers and does it reach out to the right target audience? In the case of sale promotion techniques, the costs and benefits of participating in a trade show must be weighed, as well as telemarketing, catalogs, and promotional aids given to dealers. In the realm of public relations, the marketer has many choices: hosting financial analysts, sponsoring a sport or cultural event, or assisting a charity.

Progressive business marketers are in touch with their audiences and have become good listeners as well as good speakers. They know their various stakeholders as well as their competitors. Most important, they have mastered the art and science of mounting effective advertising and other promotional campaigns.

As a general rule, the successful ones have achieved both balance and consistency. Their advertising, sales promotion, and public relations efforts reinforce one another. The very best ones not only receive awards for their specific ads or campaigns but also can demonstrate the links between promotion and strategic corporate goals such as growth in sales, profits, market share, and image.

Key Terms and Concepts

communication
situational analysis
  (environmental scanning)
business advertising
print media
vertical publications
horizontal publications
electronic media
advertising agency
cost per thousand
objective-and-task approach
competitive parity approach
percentage-of-sales (percentage-of-margin)
  approach
advertising campaign
sales promotion

direct mail
telemarketing
database marketing
electronic data interchange (EDI)
product catalogs
service directories
trade shows
fairs
expos (expositions)
promotion to the trade
public relations (PR) policy
corporate image
house style
stakeholders
corporate sponsorship

Discussion Questions

1. The chapter suggests that business marketers should adopt some of the techniques used by consumer goods marketers: sweepstakes, coupons, two-for-one sales, tent sales, and the like. Discuss whether such adoption is suited for equipment, raw materials, supplies, components, accessories, or services.

2. Large firms often sponsor sports and cultural events as part of their public relations strategy. Should a small firm engage in sponsorship? If so, what kind and using what techniques?

3. Many large business marketers use print advertising. What about radio and television as the appropriate media for some business marketers? Which industries and which companies are likely to take to these electronic media?

4. The chapter cites evidence that industrial print advertising pays off rather handsomely in increased awareness levels. Do you think such mass communication also pays off in terms of changes in attitude levels? What about increased sales?

5. Corporate image campaigns and comparative ads are relatively new on the scene, but they are being used increasingly in the United States and elsewhere. What problems do you see with these two types of advertising? Why do you think there are objections to them in other nations?

6. Put yourself in the shoes of an ad agency executive who wishes to convince a business marketer that the firm should advertise in a business monthly journal that has only two-thirds the circulation of the top journal in the

field. What arguments can you cite in favor of your choice of the number two journal?

7. The Copy-Chasers of *Business Marketing* magazine are not afraid to criticize the short-comings of published ads. One of their heated debates concerned the use of young women in bikinis (or even less) to pose with forklift trucks and tools. Do you approve or disapprove of such advertising? Is it blatantly sexist? Why or why not?

8. Discuss the major advantages that direct marketing, trade shows; and catalogs have over traditional advertising. List them in order of importance. Now do the same for the disadvantages. Does sales promotion appear to be complementary or competitive to traditional print ads?

9. Exhibitions, trade shows, and fairs are now popular in the United States, but they have been popular in Europe for centuries. What explains their popularity on the European Continent? Do you think some trade shows in North America are getting too big and that the small exhibitors may be lost?

10. One of the cornerstones of marketing practice is that one should work *with* not *through* distributors. Should the manufacturer and distributor share the cost of an ad for a product? Should the maker of a product engage in advertising aimed at distributors?

11. Do you think that there are fundamental differences between high-tech and low-tech fields when it comes to advertising, sales promotion, and public relations? How can a low-tech marketer obtain a glamorous image?

12. Mobil, the giant oil marketer, has been in the forefront of advocacy advertising. It consistently runs one-quarter size "op-ed" pages in the *New York Times* and other journals. Its public relations chief, H. Schmertz, has written a book, *Good-Bye to the Low Profile*. Both the ads and the book seem combative, yet Mobil is highly respected. How do you judge such steps to influence opinion-makers?

Endnotes and References

1. See, for example, C. H. Patti and C. F. Frazer, *Advertising* (Hinsdale, Ill.: Dryden Press, 1988), and W. Wells et al., *Advertising* (Englewood Cliffs, N.J.: Prentice-Hall, 1989). There are also many criticisms of advertising; see, for example, M. Schudson, *Advertising: The Uneasy Persuasion* (New York: Basic Books, 1984). Promotion as a two-way bridge builder is discussed in B. B. Jackson, *Winning and Keeping Industrial Customers* (Lexington, Mass.: Lexington/Heath, 1985).

2. The levels of audience response are discussed in many marketing, psychology, and advertising journals and texts. See, for example, J. M. Bellizzi and J. Lehrer, "Developing Better Industrial Advertising," *Industrial Marketing Management* (February 1983): 9–23.

3. For the story of the blockbuster ad by Apple and related ads, see C. Dugas, "And Now the Super Bowl Lineup," *Business Week*, February 2, 1987, p. 35.

4. The advertising battle in various industries is documented in the pages of such journals as *Adweek, Advertising Age, Marketing and Media Decisions,* and *Sales & Marketing Management,* as well as industry and general business publications. A special issue, *Business to Business Media Buying & Planning* (Fall 1990) was issued by a joint venture of *Advertising Age* and *Business Marketing.*

5. The Laboratory for Advertising Performance (LAP), supported for many years by McGraw-Hill, issued several brief reports based on a sample of marketing managers in industrial companies drawn from the circulation list of *Business Marketing.* Unfortunately, LAP ceased operating at the end of the 1980s; see T. Eisenhart, "The Death of a Data Base," *Business Marketing* (May 1989): 38,39. The last of the key reports published include: #8015.5: "Major Industrial Companies Invest 8.9% of Sales in Marketing Costs"; #8015.6:

"Investments in Marketing Costs as a Percent of Sales Vary Across Industries"; #8015.7: "More than One-Third of the Marketing Communications Budget Is Spent on Print Advertising"; and #8015.8: "Marketing Communication Costs Average 1.73% of Sales Among Major Industrial Companies." Another comprehensive source is *Advertising Age Yearbook* (Chicago: Crain Communications, annually), published in hardbound format until 1984 and in on-line electronic format thereafter.

6. For pioneering articles on expenditures and budgeting, see G. L. Lilien, "Industrial Advertising Effects and Budgeting Personnel," *Journal of Marketing* 40 (January 1976): 20,21; G. L. Lilien and J. D. Little, "The ADVISOR Project: A Study of Industrial Marketing Budgets," *Sloan Management Review* (Spring 1976): 17–31. On the PAIRS project, see A. Parasuraman and R. L. Day, "A Management Oriented Model for Allocating Sales Efforts," *Journal of Marketing Research* 14 (February 1977): 22–33. For more recent contributions, see V. J. Blasko and C. H. Patti, "The Advertising Budgeting Practices of Industrial Marketers," *Journal of Marketing* 48 (Fall 1984): 104–110, and J. E. Lynch and G. J. Hooley, "Advertising Budgeting Practices of Industrial Advertisers," *Industrial Marketing Management* (February 1987): 63–70.

7. This famous ad features a scowling manager and the following text: "'I don't know who you are. I don't know your company. I don't know your company's product. I don't know what your company stands for. I don't know your company's customers. I don't know your company's record. I don't know your company's reputation. Now—what was it you wanted to sell me?' Moral: Sales start *before* your salesman calls—with business publication advertising."

8. J. E. Morrill, "Industrial Advertising Pays Off," *Harvard Business Review* (March–April 1970): 4–14, 159–169; and R. Manville, "Why Industrial Companies Must Advertise Their Products," *Industrial Marketing* (October 1978): 47ff.

9. For the list of the McGraw-Hill LAP studies, see endnote 5. Additional reports include #5255.1: "Brand Preference Decreases"; #5257.3: "Company Awareness Increases"; #5261: "Exclusive Ad Campaign"; #7020.7: "Advertising in Business Publications." On the ARF/ABP studies, see B. Donath, "ARF/ABP Study Confirms That Advertising Works," *Business Marketing* (November 1986): 74–90; and M. E. Ziegenhagen and F. F. O'Daly, "Where's the ARF/ABP Study Value and Real Value for Clients?" *Business Marketing* (April 1988): 88–93.

10. The ARF/ABP study is a landmark one, yet its findings remain controversial. For further discussion on what constitutes success, see the following items: the Yankelovich, Skelly, and White study for *Time* magazine (issued only internally in 1981); S. G. Cort, *Effective Business to Business Advertising Frequency* (New York: Advertising Research Foundation, 1983); P. Korgaonkar et al., "Successful Industrial Advertising Campaigns," *Industrial Marketing Management* (May 1986): 123–128. At the international level, see D. Dana-Haerl, "What's Different About Business to Business Advertising?" *International Journal of Advertising* (Spring 1986): 175–182; and D. M. Peebles and J. K. Ryans, *Management of International Advertising* (Boston: Allyn & Bacon, 1984).

11. The *Scientific American* study first appeared in 1950, but its latest version came out in 1970: *How Industry Buys* (New York: Scientific American, 1970). Its findings were confirmed later for the chemical and paper industries in R. Erickson and A. C. Gross, "Generalizing Industrial Buying: A Longitudinal Study," *Industrial Marketing Management* (July 1980): 253–266 (for the U.S.), and in P. Banting et al., "Generalizations from a Cross-National study of the Industrial Buying Process," *International Marketing Review* (Winter 1985): 64–74 (for other markets).

12. This point is also emphasized in Chapter 6. Although the underlying theme, product, and corporate image may remain the same or

similar, differing points will be stressed to different audiences. The Business Marketing in Practice box on page 205 describes how Marvin Windows catered to three audiences: remodelers, dealers, and architects. The message to the first group emphasized ease of installation and windows that fit existing spaces; to the second, the contribution to profits and low inventory holdings; to the third, the idea of functionality and decoration.

13. F. Messner, *Industrial Advertising* (New York: McGraw-Hill, 1963), and N. A. Hart, *Industrial Advertising and Publicity* (New York: Wiley & Sons, 1978), are the two pioneering books. For further specific details, see J. M. Bellizzi and R. E. Hite, "Improving Industrial Advertising Copy," *Industrial Marketing Management* (May 1986): 117–122; and L. C. Soley, "Copy Length and Industrial Advertising Readership," *Industrial Marketing Management* (August 1986): 245–252.

14. D. Ogilvy, *Ogilvy on Advertising* (New York: Random House, 1983), pp. 137–142. See also G. M. Zinkham, "Rating Industrial Advertisements," *Industrial Marketing Management* (February 1984): 43–48.

15. D. R. Glover et al., "How Advertising Strategies Are Set," *Industrial Marketing Management* 18 (March 1989): 19–26.

16. The most comprehensive list of trade, industry, and technical publications (of a vertical and horizontal nature) can be found in *Ulrich's International Periodicals Directory* (New York: R. R. Bowker, annually). To relate industrial categories and trade journals, see *Predicasts F & S Index: USA, Europe, and International*, where the first section is organized by SIC code. For an analysis of one facet, see L. E. Swayne and T. H. Stevenson, "Comparative Advertising in Horizontal Business Publications," *Industrial Marketing Management* (February 1987): 71–76.

17. AT&T, Federal Express, IBM, and many other large industrial firms have been heavy advertisers and/or sponsors of television shows on commercial and public networks as well as cable. For an analysis, see J. W. Kaumeyer, "When Should Business/Industrial Advertisers Use Broadcast TV?" *Business Marketing* (April 1985): 106–115. *Advertising Age* annually lists the media spending patterns of large companies.

18. J. O'Toole, *The Trouble with Advertising: A View from the Inside* (New York: Times Books, 1985). For details on the relationship between industrial advertisers and ad agencies, see two articles by D. L. Kastiel, "What Agencies Find Most Irksome," *Business Marketing* (September 1986): 58ff; and "Marketers Want Partnership with Agencies," *Business Marketing* (January 1987): 86ff.

19. M. G. Harvey and J. P. Rupert, Jr., "Selecting an Industrial Advertising Agency," *Industrial Marketing Management* (May 1988): 119–127; B. Donath, "Making the Right Agency Choice," *Business Marketing* (September 1986): 66–72; D. Kent, "When to Fire Your Agency and How to Avoid Needing To," *Business Marketing* (September 1985): 54–66. Both *Industrial Marketing Management* and *Business Marketing* have articles on this topic almost every year. For managerial aspects, see J. McNamara, *Advertising Agency Management* (Homewood, Ill.: Dow Jones Irwin, 1990). In recessionary times, a change of agency is more frequent: "More Advertisers Are Consolidating Their Accounts" and "Recession Blamed for Account Losses," (Cleveland) *The Plain Dealer,* July 9, 1991, p. 2-F (based on *New York Times* and Associated Press reports).

20. The data cited in the exhibit and text came directly from the three local television stations affiliated with the three major networks in Cleveland, Ohio. Arbitron and Nielsen can supply nationwide data in the U.S.

21. See endnote 6 for articles on this topic, as well as C. H. Patti and V. J. Blasko, "Budgeting Practices of Big Advertisers," *Journal of Advertising Research* (December 1981): 23–29; and S. W. Hartley and C. H. Patti, "Evaluating Business to Business Advertising: A Compari-

son of Objectives and Results," *Journal of Advertising Research* (April–May 1988): 21–28.

22. E. Largon and C. Dolan, "Apple Stages Elaborate Courtship of Press," *Wall Street Journal,* January 23, 1984, p. 21; and C. Dolan, "Apple Faces Selling New Computer," *Wall Street Journal,* May 3, 1984, p. 27. The large computer and related office equipment makers have been heavy advertisers in the *Wall Street Journal* year in and year out.

23. Hartley and Patti, "Evaluating Business to Business Advertising," admit that "advertising practitioners only partially adopted the conceptual standards of objective setting and evaluation set 25 years ago." In short, many companies still look at percentage of sales, competitive parity, and other shortcut techniques rather than to the objective-and-task method.

24. See endnote 6 for articles on this topic.

25. "Who Says Ad Impact Cannot Be Measured?" *Sales Management,* April 19, 1962, pp. 37–43, documents this pioneering, well-executed experiment by Du Pont. Other experiments have been carried out subsequent to this project and reported in such journals as *Business Marketing, Industrial Marketing Management, Journal of Business and Industrial Marketing, Journal of Advertising,* and *Journal of Advertising Research.*

26. See T. H. Garbett, *How to Build a Corporation's Identity and Project Its Image* (Lexington, Mass.: Lexington/Heath, 1988); M. F. Hartigan and P. Finch, "The New Emphasis on Strategy in Corporate Advertising," *Business Marketing* (February 1986): 42–49; S. Bullard, "TRW's Campaign Gets Cheers," *Crain's Cleveland Business,* October 21, 1985, pp. 116–123; P. Botwinick, "The Image of Corporate Image," *Public Relations Journal* (November 1984): 12–16; G. R. Dowling, "Managing Your Corporate Image," *Industrial Marketing Management* 15 (May 1986): 109–115; A. B. Fisher, "Spiffing Up Your Corporate Image," *Fortune,* July 21, 1986, pp. 68–76.

27. Owens-Corning was able to get exclusive use of the color pink for its fiberglass as part of its trademark. This innovative idea was then matched with the licensed use of the Pink Panther character. For other prize-winning ads, see "The Best Ads," *Adweek/Marketing Week* (special supplement to *Business Marketing*), May 22, 1989, pp. 43–44. See also F. C. Poppe, *The One Hundred Greatest Corporate and Industrial Ads* (New York: Van Nostrand Reinhold, 1983).

28. Personal communication with John Morton, senior vice president, Carr-Liggett (now Liggett-Stashower), a major industrial advertising agency in Cleveland, Ohio, January 1987. Subsequent conversation with the agency revealed that the Picker account has left.

29. J. Roberts, "It's Time for Industrial Marketers to Use Consumer-Type Promotions," *Marketing News,* October 28, 1983, p. 6. In recent years, more articles on this topic have appeared in the pages of this magazine, a publication of the American Marketing Association.

30. Figures are cited for the 1980s in W. Cohen, *Direct Response Marketing* (New York: Wiley & Sons, 1984), and F. F. Gosden, Jr., *Understanding Direct Marketing* (New York: Wiley & Sons, 1985). For more recent data and insights, see R. G. Ljungren, *Business to Business Direct Marketing: A Handbook* (New York: AMACOM, 1988), and M. Gross, *The Direct Marketer's Idea Book* (New York: AMACOM, 1989). For a linkage to strategy, see T. J. Sims and H. E. Brown, "Increasing the Role of Direct Marketing in Industrial Marketing Strategy," *Industrial Marketing Management* (November 1979): 294–301.

31. The judicious use of lists is a must; see M. Schwartz, "Database and Merge/Purge," *Direct Marketing* (July 1985): 56–59; B. J. Hansiota, "List Segmentation," *Business Marketing* (August 1986): 64–76; and R. G. Ljungren, *Business/Industrial Direct Marketing: Four Major Functions,* Release #1630.2 (New York: Direct Marketing Association, 1984). The Direct Marketing Association and Hoke Communication are two key groups promoting the use of direct mail. Like house-

holds, some industrial users are complaining about the volume of such mail.

32. R. L. Bencin, *Strategic Telemarketing* (Windsor, Conn.: Swansea Press, 1986); M. Roman, *Telemarketing Campaigns That Work* (New York: McGraw-Hill, 1983); and J. L. Pope, *Business to Business Telemarketing* (New York: AMACOM, 1983) are three useful books on the topic. For articles, see R. Voorhees and J. Coppett, "Telemarketing in Distribution Channels," *Industrial Marketing Management* (April 1983): 105–112; J. Coppett and R. Voorhees, "Telemarketing: Supplement to Field Sales," *Industrial Marketing Management* (August 1985): 212–215; J. Marshall and H. Vredenburg, "Successfully Using Telemarketing," *Industrial Marketing Management* (February 1988): 15–22; and E. Johnson and W. Meiners, "Telemarketing: Trends, Issues, and Opportunities," *Journal of Personal Selling and Sales Management* 7 (November 1987): 65–68. AT&T, MCI, and other companies in telecommunications have issued reports on the topic. As with direct mail, there are objections to the volume and the "tone" of telemarketing. Note the distinction made in the text between telemarketing and telesales (and, of course, marketing research via phone).

33. See T. Bonoma, "Get More Out of Your Trade Shows," *Harvard Business Review* (January–February 1983): 75–83, and the "Trade Show Trends" articles each May in *Business Marketing*. See also, "Fair Advantage," *Industry Week,* August 18, 1986, pp. 39–41; D. Phillip, "Hanover Fair," *High Technology* (March 1985): 57–66; L. R. Thomas, *European Trade Fairs* (Washington, D.C.: U.S. Government Printing Office, 1981); *Trade Shows: A Major Sales and Marketing Tool* (Monterey, Calif.: Business Research & Communications, 1988).

34. Compare P. Banting and D. Blenkhorn, "The Role of Industrial Trade Shows," *Industrial Marketing Management* (October 1974): 285–295; *Trade Show Bureau Research Report #19* (New Canaan, Conn.: Trade Show Bureau, 1983); and "Average Growth of Trade Shows," *Tradeshow Week,* November 10, 1986, pp. 1–19. Updates can be obtained by looking at the more recent publications of the Trade Show Bureau, recent issues of *Tradeshow Week,* and a series of papers on international trade fairs published by the Centre for International Business Studies, Dalhousie University, Halifax, N.S., Canada, in 1991–1992.

35. S. Cavanaugh, "Setting Objectives and Evaluating the Effectiveness of Trade Show Exhibits," *Journal of Marketing* 40 (October 1976): 100–103; R. Kerin and W. Cron, "Assessing Trade Show Function and Performance," *Journal of Marketing* 51 (July 1987): 87–94. For some practical guidelines, see R. Konikow, *How to Participate Profitably in Trade Shows* (Chicago: Dartnell, 1983).

36. Specialty advertising is discussed in R. W. Haas, *Industrial Marketing Management,* 4th ed. (Boston: PWS-Kent, 1989), pp. 353–354; R. G. Ebel, "Specialty Advertising," *Industrial Marketing* (February 1982): 80–81; P. Seelig, "Advertising Specialties," *Incentive Marketing* (May 1987): 104–108; C. Madden and M. Caballero, "Perceptions of the Specialty Advertising Industry," *Journal of Business & Industrial Marketing* 2 (Fall 1987): 42ff.

37. R. T. Reilly, *Public Relations in Action,* 2nd ed. (Englewood Cliffs, N.J.: Prentice-Hall, 1987).

38. See recent issues of *Business & Society Review, Public Relations Journal,* and the various newsletters of environmental groups, such as NRDC, Sierra Club, etc. For industrial firms, the handling of the PR aspects of major disasters is crucial (compare the explosion at the Union Carbide plant in Bhopal, India). See J. McNutt, Jr., and A. Gross, "An Integrated and Pragmatic Approach to Global Plant Safety Management," *Environmental Management* (May–June 1989): 339–346.

39. A. C. Gross, P. Shuman, and M. B. Traylor, "Corporate Sponsorship of Arts and Sports Events in North America," *Proceedings of the 40th Congress of ESOMAR, the European Society for Opinion and Market Research, Volume 1* (Amsterdam: ESOMAR, 1987), pp. 535–561, excerpted in *European Research* (November 1987): S9–S13. The long version carries insights on measuring the effectiveness of sponsorship, case studies, and references to the U.S., Canadian, and European literature. See also *Sponsorship: Its Role and Effects* (New York: International Advertising Association, 1988).

15

SALES FORCE MANAGEMENT

OBJECTIVES

- To appreciate the importance of planning for identifying potential sales and deploying the sales force

- To identify the most common techniques for organizing the sales force

- To learn about the issues related to sales force administration: recruitment and selection, training, supervision and motivation, and compensation

- To describe the control procedures that are necessary to monitor sales force performance

Effective management of the sales force requires planning, organizing, administering, and controlling. All four tasks must be carried out thoroughly because errors at any stage will affect the other stages and result in a sales force that, at best, cannot operate effectively and, at worst, may jeopardize the firm's marketing objectives.

Planning involves deciding how to define the firm's markets in terms of variables that the sales manager can later use to structure the sales force. Structuring, in turn, involves deciding how the sales representatives are to be assigned to the customers and products in such a way that they can do an effective job of servicing their accounts and developing new business.

In the organizing stage, the manager actually implements the decisions reached in the planning stage. The most common techniques for organizing the sales force are the customer-based, product-based, territory-based, national account–based, and inside/outside sales–based approaches.

Administering the sales force requires involvement in recruitment and selection, training objectives and techniques, supervision and motivation, and compensation systems. Recruitment and selection are concerned with hiring the right kind of sales representatives for the job. Managers must consider costs and revenues, competitive concerns, customer demands, and the personal characteristics of the potential employees. Training focuses on ensuring that sales representatives have the necessary skills and knowledge to perform their jobs effectively, and the objectives of supervision and motivation are to ensure that management provides the necessary guidance and support to aid salespeople in their jobs. Finally, administration of compensation systems involves knowing whether it is more advantageous to pay salespeople on the basis of straight salary, bonuses and commissions, or some combination of the two.

Controlling, the last task required in sales force management, is important because the sales manager needs to measure how well salespeople are fulfilling their objectives. If performance levels are found wanting, adjustments may have to be made in planning, organizing, or administering policies. This is why Exhibit 15–1 diagrams these four tasks as a feedback loop—each task affects the other.

**EXHIBIT 15–1   Sales Management
Functional Tasks: A Feedback Loop**

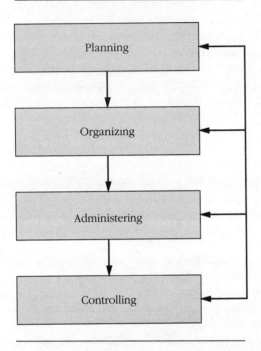

SALES FORCE PLANNING

Sales force planning involves a series of analytical procedures and decisions designed to achieve the most effective use of the firm's salespeople. It is important that sales force planning be conducted carefully at the outset because this will help to reduce management's need to subsequently "tinker" with the selling system.

Two key management tasks need to be conducted sequentially in the planning stage. First, the vendor's existing as well as potential sales must be identified and evaluated through analysis of its markets, or **planning and control units (PCUs)**. (A PCU can be defined on the basis of products, accounts, customer classifications, prospective customers, territories, sales regions, or any combination of such variables.) Second, deployment of the sales force must be determined by assessing the current needs and future sales potential of the customers of the firm. The deployment decision is basically concerned with determining how much sales effort should be devoted to customer accounts in the firm's various PCUs.

Planning and Control Units

Developing information on the planning and control units involves two steps. First, management has to decide on the appropriate basis for describing the units (for example, customers, products, territories). Second, the criteria by which the PCUs are to be evaluated have to be established.

In the first, or definition, step the selection of the appropriate components of the PCU depends on the judgment and experience of management and the senior sales staff. The PCU can vary among industries as well as among individual firms, and even within the different kinds of territories that comprise a given industry. In the industrial seals and packing industry, for example, vendors may define their PCUs according to industry type (paper mills versus chemical producers) and territory (east, central, west). Some furniture manufacturers, on the other hand, distinguish between PCUs based on the wholesale versus retail status of the distributors and whether they sell expensive furniture lines or cheaper furniture products. In the financial services industry, some banks have established retail and commercial account PCUs, while others have done just the opposite and merged these two previously separate groups into a single unit.

In the PCU evaluation step, management and senior sales representatives again rely on their collective wisdom to identify variables that have historically been good predictors of sales potential. These criteria are then used to evaluate how attractive a PCU is as a source of sales. Unfortunately, there are no universally applicable variables that describe all sales situations. However, brief descriptions of some of the more common variables used to evaluate the sales potential of territory-based PCUs follow.[1]

Economic and Environmental Variables.   Included in this category are variables that provide indications of the general health of markets that are relevant to the PCU. These highlight general trends that can affect the ability of accounts within a territory-based PCU to buy products. For example, aircraft manufacturers monitor general economic variables like consumer disposable income and airline bookings, because these variables have an impact on the ability of suppliers to sell passenger jets to the airlines.

Competitive Variables.   The number of direct and indirect competitors active in a sales territory, the number of competing brands, and the number of salespeople and support staff representing competitors in a territory are all variables that indicate the level of competition in a PCU. Vendors evaluate a PCU on the basis of these variables in order to gain insight into the amount of competitive pressure under which their sales force must function.

Customer-Related Variables.   The dollar and volume contribution of accounts, their growth rate potential, and the assortment of the vendor's products that they purchase are all examples of variables that will affect the manager's evaluation of a particular PCU's attractiveness.

Territory-Related Factors. The concentration of major and minor accounts in a territory, the geographical dispersion of the customers, and the sales potential associated with a particular area are some of the variables used to evaluate a territory-based PCU. These variables provide an indication of the sales force effort that will be required to generate sales and to service accounts in the area. Small accounts that are widely dispersed over a territory clearly decrease its attractiveness, due to the low volume of sales usually associated with small accounts and the large overhead and inefficiency associated with operating a sales force in a territory where accounts are widely scattered.

Company Variables. The vending company's marketing strategy and the tactics it employs in pursuit of those strategies are examples of variables used to evaluate the firm's ability to respond to market opportunities and threats in its sales territory. Vendors who employ well-developed strategies and tactics will also tend to carefully define the role of the sales force within their organization as well as the functions to be carried out by the individual sales representatives.

Sales Force Variables. Included in this category are variables that can be used to evaluate the characteristics of the vending firm's sales management and sales representatives as well as the sales force's organization and policies. Well-trained and motivated front-line sales managers and sales representatives, together with good sales force management practices and monitoring of performance, mean that the accounts in the territory will be properly developed and maintained. This contributes to the vendor's sales strength in the territory, making it more attractive to senior management.

Sales management must clearly define which variables are to be used to evaluate the PCU sales potentials. This avoids the problem of different people applying different criteria in evaluating accounts or even changing the criteria in the midst of carrying out their PCU evaluation task.

Just as a territory-based PCU can be evaluated by means of specific criteria, so can the individual customer accounts that comprise a PCU. Once the key evaluation criteria variables are determined, management and staff can then evaluate individual accounts on a five-point scale (see Exhibit 15–2). Since all of the factors that serve as evaluation variables may not be equally important, however, the sales management and sales staff must also weight each factor. These weights are distributed among the variables such that they total 100 points (see Exhibit 15–3). The weighting factors for each of the evaluation criteria are then multiplied by the rating scores on those criteria for each of the accounts. The result is a weighted rating score for each of the evaluative criteria for each account. These weighted rating scores are totaled for each account and divided by 100 to provide a sales effort allocation index. This index can serve as the basis for planning the deployment of the vendor's sales force.

EXHIBIT 15–2   Rating Scores of Accounts on Key Factors

Key Factors	Rating Scores (5 = excellent; 1 = poor)		
	Account 1	Account 2	Account 3
Competitive pressure	3	5	2
Account familiarity	2	1	5
Multiple buying influence	5	3	5
Purchase assortment	4	5	3
Account potential	5	2	1

Source: Reprinted by permission of the publisher from "An Approach for Allocating Sales Call Effort," by A. Parasuraman, *Industrial Marketing Management* 11 (1982), p. 77. Copyright 1982 by Elsevier Science Publishing Co., Inc.

Sales Force Deployment

The objective of **sales force deployment** is to determine the combination of sales force size, sales territory configuration, and selling effort allocation that yields the greatest productivity in the performance of the sales staff. The deployment structure is actually determined by making a series of sequential and interrelated decisions.[2]

Setting the Total Level of Selling Efforts.   This decision is addressed first because the fundamental problem confronting the sales manager is to determine the

EXHIBIT 15–3   Computation of Sales Effort Allocation Indices

Key Factors	Factor Importance Weight	Weighted Rating Scores*		
		Account 1	Account 2	Account 3
Competitive pressure	30	90	150	60
Account familiarity	10	20	10	50
Multiple buying influence	10	50	30	50
Purchase assortment	20	80	100	60
Account potential	30	150	60	30
Total	100	390	350	250
Sales effort allocation index		3.90	3.50	2.50

*Weighted rating score = rating score shown in Exhibit 15–2 X factor importance weight. For example, in Exhibit 15–2, account #1 received a 3 rating on the factor of competitive pressure. Multiplying the rating of 3 by the factor importance weight that the vendor ascribes to this factor in Exhibit 15–3 yields a weighted rating score of 90 (3 × 30).

total sales force size that will produce the desired level of total selling effort. In order to answer the question "How much selling effort is needed?" the manager must first complete the analysis of the firm's planning and control units. Once the manager understands the nature and magnitude of the account needs that must be serviced in all of the vendor's PCUs, the total size of the sales force can be determined.

Organizing the Selling Effort.   The specific deployment decisions here involve designing the sales districts or regions in which the sales force will operate and then designing the individual sales territories within the districts so that each sales representative will know the geographical area or areas for which he or she is responsible.

Allocating the Selling Effort.   A number of allocation decisions must be made in this stage. First, the manager must decide how much sales effort to allocate to each trading area. This will be determined by the size and needs of the existing accounts as well as the potential to increase sales in the area. The number of sales calls are next allocated to the individual accounts in the trading area because some customers require more sales force servicing than do others. Sales calls must also be allocated to prospects so that the customer base in the trading area can be expanded over time. Yet another allocation decision must be made concerning the amount of sales call time that is to be devoted to the various product lines within the vendor's total product mix. Finally, the manager must decide how much time the sales representatives should devote to each of their sales calls.

The last stage in the manager's sales force deployment task involves calculating how many sales calls are to be allocated to each account. This can be determined by the following process (see Exhibit 15–4).

1. The **sales effort allocation index** for each of the three accounts shown in the last line of Exhibit 15–3 is reproduced in Exhibit 15–4 under the column "Sales Effort Allocation Index." More realistically, however, suppose that we have a total of 100 accounts and that when the sales effort allocation indices for each of these accounts are added together we get a grand total of 415.5.

2. The sales effort allocation index for *each* account is, in turn, divided by the total allocation index points for *all* accounts (for example, 3.9 for account 1 ÷ 415.5 [total allocation index points] = 0.009). This number represents the fraction of the total sales effort that will be allocated to account 1.

3. Finally, assume for ease of calculation that 1,000 sales calls are to be allocated within the sales territory for the coming year.

4. If management can allocate 1,000 sales calls, then account 1 receives 0.009 × 1,000 (calls to be allocated) = 9 sales calls.

It must be kept in mind that market conditions change constantly and, as a result, deployment decisions must change with them. Thus, the sales manager must

EXHIBIT 15-4   Allocation of Sales Effort

Account Number	Sales Effort Allocation Index (weighted rating score ÷ total allocation index points)	Fraction of Sales Effort to Be Allocated[a] (sales effort × total allocated calls)	Number of Sales Calls to Be Allocated[b] (per account)
1	3.9	0.009	9
2	3.5	0.008	8
3	2.5	0.006	6
.	.	.	.
.	.	.	.
.	.	.	.
100			
Total	415.5	1.000	1,000

[a]The fraction was obtained by dividing each sales effort allocation index by the total of all the indices (415.5); each fraction was rounded off to three decimal places.
[b]Number of calls to be allocated was obtained by multiplying the fraction of sales effort to be allocated by the number of available sales calls (1,000).

Source: Reprinted by permission of the publisher from "An Approach for Allocating Sales Call Effort," by A. Parasuraman, *Industrial Marketing Management* 11 (1982), p. 78. Copyright © 1982 by Elsevier Science Publishing Co., Inc.

continually monitor her or his current sales force deployment and, if necessary, redeploy sales calls.

Sales Resource Opportunity Grid

Another method for arriving at a sales force deployment figure is the **sales resource opportunity grid**.[3] This technique assesses the total industry sales potential available from the account and the firm's ability to capture a share of the sales potential from that account. A high total industry sales potential coupled with a strong organizational sales position makes the customer a prime candidate for allocation of the company's sales resources. On the grid, the sales staff evaluates the attractiveness of the firm's accounts on a seven-point rating scale. The actual determinants are the size and sales growth of the account as well as the number of competing brands purchased by the customer. The firm's sales organization position is based on trade relations with the account, the number of the firm's products stocked by the account, and the type of shelf space given by the customer to the firm's products. The accounts are then classified according to their degree of attractiveness for purposes of sales force deployment. According to the grid analysis, there are four possible segments to which an account could be allocated based on its evaluated sales potential (see Exhibit 15-5).

EXHIBIT 15–5   Sales Resource Opportunity Grid

		Sales Organization Strength	
PCU Opportunity	**High**	*Opportunity Analysis:* PCU offers good opportunity since it has high potential and sales organization has strong position. *Sales Resource Assignment:* High level of sales resources to take advantage of opportunity.	*Opportunity Analysis:* PCU may offer good opportunity if sales organization can strengthen its position. *Sales Resource Assignment:* Either direct a high level of sales resources to improve position and take advantage of opportunity or shift resources to other PCUs.
	Low	*Opportunity Analysis:* PCU offers stable opportunity since sales organization has strong position. *Sales Resource Assignment:* Moderate level of sales resources to keep current position strength.	*Opportunity Analysis:* PCU offers little opportunity. *Sales Resource Assignment:* Minimal level of sales resource and selective elimination of resource coverage. Possible elimination of PCU.
		High Low	

Sales Organization Strength

Source: Reprinted by permission of the publisher from "Steps in Selling Effort Development," by Raymond LaForge and David W. Cravens, *Industrial Marketing Management* 11 (1982), p. 187. Copyright 1982 by Elsevier Science Publishing Co., Inc.

The grid is useful for examining a firm's current sales resource deployment patterns and for assisting in the determination of redeployment plans. This is accomplished by considering the number of accounts allocated to each of the appropriate priority segments. When the number of accounts assigned to the high-priority segment(s) exceeds the capacity of the sales calls, a redeployment decision is suggested. Similarly, if the number of sales calls devoted to a lower-priority segment is excessive, the grid analyst would suggest redirecting some of the sales effort to the more attractive segments.

The sales resource opportunity grid should be structured using a cost/benefit approach. The more segments that are identified for purposes of classifying accounts, the more accurate the deployment. If management decides to reduce the number of sales territories, smaller segments can be combined. It should also be noted, however, that the more segments that are produced for classification purposes, the greater the cost of the deployment analysis. Development of the sales resource opportunity grid, therefore, must be undertaken with a clear understanding of the costs associated with acquiring the benefits.

As sales organizations become larger and more complex, and as the need for greater sales force efficiency develops, especially as a result of increased global competition, the sophistication of PCU and deployment analysis will also increase. Most large corporations already employ sales force planning procedures and as computer software programs make the deployment task easier, even more companies will find it worthwhile to undertake sales force planning.

ORGANIZING THE SALES FORCE

The task of organizing the sales force to maximize efficiency and performance should be based on a combination of considerations. The firm's marketing objectives must be clearly addressed in organizational decisions regarding the sales staff. More importantly, however, the organizational structure is greatly influenced by the firm's customers as well as competitive (and other marketing) environmental factors. The choice of approach should reflect the manager's decision regarding the structure of the firm's PCUs.

A number of organizational approaches can be used. In addition, it is possible to combine the best aspects of the various approaches as long as care is taken to ensure that such hybrid organizational structures do not incorporate characteristics that contradict each other. Five of the most common approaches useful for organizing the sales force are discussed here.

Customer-Based Organization

The **customer-based approach** uses customer- or industry-based characteristics as the criteria for organizing the sales force. For example, some computer software developers have concentrated on servicing small accounting firms that specialize in providing tax preparation and electronic tax filing for clients. These characteristics include customer size, industry classification (manufacturing SIC code), or the orientation of the end markets served by the customer (that is, whether the firm's customer supplies other manufacturers, retailers, wholesalers, or final consumer users).

There are two major advantages to the customer-based organization. First, it allows the sales staff to specialize by customer classification. The sales staff consequently develops a specific expertise suited to the particular customer group(s) with whom it deals. Second, the sales representative is in a better position to establish a bond with the buyer and/or buying group because specific customers are assigned to specific salespeople. On the other hand, the customer-based approach to sales staff organization requires that a sufficient number of customers exist who can be grouped on the basis of their similarities. Otherwise, the number of purchasers may be too small to justify the approach.

Product-Based Organization

In the **product-based approach**, salespeople are assigned their responsibilities based on a specific product or product group. This approach is similar to the customer-based organization structure in that it fosters the development of specific areas of expertise. In this case, however, the sales representative's orientation is toward a specific product's characteristics, applications, and technical parameters as they relate to the customer's markets and processing requirements. Producers of aircraft wing assemblies, for example, have benefited from mini-computer manufacturers who specifically design their machines to interact with the robot technology used in the construction of wing struts. The salesperson's technical knowledge and skills thus become an important attribute in the total product package. Purchasing loyalty is fostered because the customer's buying group considers the salesperson's advisory capacity an important resource that can be accessed by using the vendor's product or product group. Depending on contractual agreements between the buyer and the vendor, the technical knowledge and skills of the salesperson can be marketed as a service distinct from the product. This allows the vendor to bill for sales staff expertise and therefore create a separate profit center that can be offered as a complementary service to the physical product.

The disadvantages of the product-based approach are primarily financial. Dissemination of specialized product-related knowledge to the sales staff can be expensive for the firm—both from the standpoint of absorbing actual educational costs as well as the costs incurred while employees are undergoing training instead of making sales calls. Also, depending on the range of different products purchased by the customer, the vendor may have to absorb the costs of multiple sales calls to one account. This is because the customer may purchase different, unrelated products from the vendor, and each product group may require a different sales representative. Thus, sales staff costs for a given territory may be increased because multiple "product specialists" cover the different product users in the area. This is clearly less efficient than using one representative to cover all of the customers in a geographical region.

Territory-Based Organization

In the **territory-based approach** to structuring the sales force, the representatives are traditionally given the responsibility for a defined geographical region. The employee is usually expected to maintain the vendor's competitive position with its current customers as well as to develop the region's sales potential through the cultivation of new customers. This structure is comparatively easy to administer since the designated rep and no one else is responsible for developing and maintaining the territory. Thus, the problems of different specialized representatives operating in the same area are avoided and the possibility of a given customer feeling overwhelmed by too many sales staff from the vendor's firm is reduced. Additionally, the possibility of one representative failing to develop an account because he or she felt it belonged to a different representative in the company is reduced. Territory assignments also tend to be comparatively less expensive with respect to travel time and costs. Since only one rep is active in the territory, the costs of multiple reps moving through the same geographical region are avoided. Finally, the interaction between the single territory representative and his or her customers contributes to a closer liaison with buyers than when different representatives call on the same accounts. A greater familiarity with the customer's needs and the idiosyncratic characteristics of the individual buyer can also establish a stronger buyer/seller bond and customer loyalty. Food products distributors such as Standard Brands and General Mills commonly use territory-based organizational structures because of the many retail food outlets they must service in each of the geographical areas.

The major problem with the territory-based structuring of sales staff is that the representative must to some degree become a jack of all trades. The salesperson must possess the requisite skills and knowledge to sell the firm's complete product mix effectively to the entire spectrum of the firm's customers. When the size of the company's product mix is limited and the customer base is small, the territory approach may be quite reasonable for organizational purposes. Care must be taken, however, as the product mix and customer base become larger. The manager must also be aware that territory-based systems can sometimes compromise the effectiveness of the salesperson in attracting new business as well as in introducing new product applications to current customers. This problem can occur because of inadequate technical knowledge of the firm's products: the broad-based product knowledge demands of territory selling can cause the rep to develop only a passing familiarity with some of the firm's product lines.

National Account–Based Organization

The rationale for the **national account–based approach** is compelling. National accounts usually constitute a large percentage of the sales demand for the vendor's products or have the potential to absorb large quantities of output. They are often characterized by large sales volume, sophisticated centralized buying center structures, multiple branch locations, and a position of competitive dominance in their particular trading environment. Thus, the customer is often one of the more important and larger competitors in a given industry or geographical trading region. Companies like Dow and Digital Equipment Corporation have used national account selling as a way to deal with some of their larger customers.

Structuring the sales force to deal with national accounts involves the creation of a marketing group whose objective is to tailor the vendor's selling function to suit the needs of the national account. This involves the establishment of a selling and sales support team that can interact with the customer's counterparts. The sales rep, for example, interacts directly with the buyer, whereas the vendor's engineers, marketing specialists, computer specialists, and key decision makers interact with their opposite number in the customer's organization. In order to maintain an organized and consistent interactive relationship with the customer, a national account manager is often appointed to fulfill a coordinating function. The rationale is that a much stronger bond can be created with the national account because the vendor's staff develops opportunities to interact with and influence those individuals in the customer's organization who are in a position to affect purchasing decisions.

The difference in structure between a customer- or product-based organization and a national account–based organization is shown in Exhibit 15–6. Organization by national account allows the vendor to communicate with and respond to the customer's needs on as many levels as possible. The goal is to ensure that, by meeting the customer's requirements, the vendor will be in a position to grow with the national account and thus not only increase sales but also establish multiple close relationships with the customer's organizational personnel, thereby building a more effective entry barrier for competitors. It is important, however, that managers carefully consider the risks of devoting much of their sales force effort (not to mention production) to one or a few large accounts. Loss of major customers who absorb much of the firm's resources and sales volume can be catastrophic if the company is not sufficiently diversified.

Inside/Outside Sales–Based Organization

Because of escalating sales call costs over recent years, some business marketing organizations have begun using an **inside/outside sales–based approach** through telemarketing. One of the major objectives of telemarketing is to reduce the firm's reliance on field, or outside, sales representatives. This allows outside sales personnel to concentrate on developing new accounts and visiting the firm's key customers. The inside sales staff then often takes over a range of the outside sales rep's duties. Soliciting repeat orders from current customers, checking on inventory problems, handling customer complaints, resolving shipping and delivery date issues, and maintaining contact with marginal customers are just a few of the activities that can be handled through telemarketing systems. Telemarketing differs from traditional inside sales structures in that telemarketers are more than order takers. Further, telemarketing systems often make use of computer programs that can carry out a range of interactive functions, such as automatically checking customers' inventory positions and even assisting inside sales staff in answering technical questions from customers and inquiries from prospective buyers. Georgia-Pacific, among other building materials suppliers, maintains telemarketing contact with its customers.

The costs of providing the necessary hardware and software support systems required to convert a traditional inside sales operation into a telemarketing system can be substantial. As a result, managers must be reasonably sure that the cost and efficiency advantages they can expect to acquire as a result of the conversion will pay off in the end.

EXHIBIT 15–6   A Customer-Based or Product-Based Organization and a National Account-Based Organization

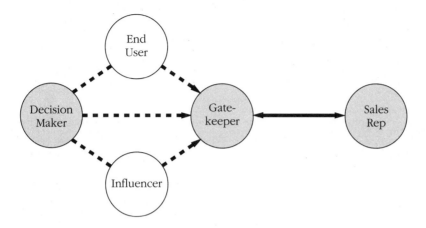

Part A. Typical relationship between seller and buyer when the selling organization is set up by geography or product. The interaction occurs primarily between the sales representative and the gatekeeper and does not occur with others in the organization who influence the gatekeeper.

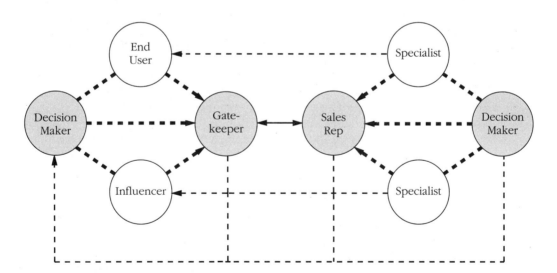

Part B. The interaction going on between seller and buyer in an organization set up with national account marketing. The team of salespeople focuses on the team of buyers and is able to reach the decision-making entity as well as the influencers.

Source: Reprinted by permission of the publisher from "Why Major Account Selling Works," by John Barrett, *Industrial Marketing Management* 15 (1986), p. 69. Copyright © 1986 by Elsevier Science Publishing Co., Inc.

SALES FORCE ADMINISTRATION

Administration of the sales force involves the management tasks of recruitment and selection, the establishment of training objectives and techniques, supervision and motivation, and the implementation of compensation systems.

Recruitment and Selection

Sales staff recruitment and selection are influenced by the current structure, resources, and objectives of the sales department and the firm, the requirements of the firm's customers, and the competitive environment (including the labor market) in which the firm operates.

Unfortunately, there are no convenient generalizations that the sales manager can rely on for guidance when deciding whether to hire experienced sales personnel or "green" recruits. This very basic first decision can, however, be partially resolved through consideration of cost/revenue considerations, competitive concerns, and customer demands.

Under cost/revenue considerations, it is generally accepted that experienced sales personnel can generate sales more quickly than inexperienced staff, albeit at a higher cost. Further, expenses related to intensive training programs can be minimized or avoided through hiring experienced sales representatives.

Competitive concerns are another issue. In industries such as raw materials processing or commodities markets, experienced sales personnel are routinely raided by competitors and even the firm's customers. The new employer thus gains access to his or her new sales representative's trading contacts. Less experienced staff are not subject to these same raiding pressures. Hence, the employer who uses fewer senior personnel may not have to increase compensation in order to retain staff.

Finally, depending on the specifics of the firms and industries involved, customer demands, or insistence on dealing with experienced sales staff, may force the employer to recruit at certain minimal skill and experience levels. Constraints of this sort tend to arise when the sophistication of product and/or processing technologies, such as chemical manufacturing or computer hardware and software applications, requires the use of experienced sales personnel.

Criteria for Selection.   Having made the decision to hire either an experienced or inexperienced sales representative, the manager must next address selection procedures. Selection criteria for different industries and companies may vary, but sales managers generally look for employee motivation, the ability to relate to people, appropriate skills and technical knowledge, information acquisition skills, the ability to "self-manage," the ability to negotiate, and the potential for adaptive selling strategies.

Evaluation of potential employees is far from an exact science. One interesting evaluation device is the self-monitoring scale—a psychological evaluation tool that can help determine whether a sales rep can adapt his or her selling behavior to changes in the sales situation. The questions in the self-monitoring scale are intended to determine whether the sales rep is motivated to practice adaptive selling, has the skills to use adaptive selling techniques, and shows a general tendency to practice adaptive selling.[4] Research underlying the self-monitoring scale suggests that representatives who are flexible enough to change their sales presentations as the selling situation requires tend to be more effective than their colleagues who do not possess these adaptive characteristics.

Ultimately, however, the sales manager must consider the nature of the particular selling job that the sales rep is being asked to carry out. Since good buyer/seller interactions often depend on the personalities of the customer and the vendor, the skills and characteristics of the potential sales rep should match as closely as possible the type of selling situation for which the job candidate is being considered.

Interviewing Techniques. Job interviews should attempt to determine the degree to which the candidate already possesses (or has the ability to efficiently acquire) the selection criteria established by management. Structured interviews ensure that the candidate (as well as the interviewer) methodically moves through a predetermined set of questions designed to aid in evaluating the candidate's strengths and weaknesses. In the structured interview approach, all of the job applicants are asked the same questions. This helps to foster a more consistent evaluative procedure, particularly if multiple interviewers are conducting the job search. The structured approach is also amenable to the type of questioning that relies on obtaining the applicant's response to work-related scenarios. In this case, the interviewer can prepare in advance questions that are designed to elicit the applicant's reaction to a hypothetical business marketing problem or opportunity.

Unstructured interviews, on the other hand, do not follow an imposed regimen. Rather than asking a set of predetermined questions, the interviewer encourages the applicant to talk freely. A skillful interviewer can learn a great deal about the applicant through this interviewing technique.

Whichever technique or combination of techniques is adopted, most firms also use a pattern of multiple interviews. This procedure ensures that the most promising applicants are interviewed by a number of people. The most common interview pattern usually begins with an initial screening of the candidates by the personnel department. Successful candidates are then interviewed by the appropriate department managers.

The advantages of the multiple interview procedure are that the applicant is evaluated by more than one screening agent in the firm, reducing the chance of bias, and is evaluated on a number of different attribute levels, including psychological characteristics, social interaction, and technical expertise concerning product knowledge.

Training Objectives and Techniques

The objective of most training programs is to acquaint the less-experienced or less-effective salesperson with the techniques and bases of information of the more successful, experienced sales personnel. Training should be undertaken as early as possible and as often as necessary. The costs of ineffective sales staff are not only the outlay of salaries but, more important, the potential problems in lost goodwill, direct financial damage to the firm through inexperienced negotiations with buyers, and other sales-related errors.

Companies often delegate the training task to members of the sales management team and/or senior and successful sales representatives in the organization. External training consultants are also used to provide a more generalized perspective in areas such as sales techniques and new operational systems, such as computerization of office procedures.

The training programs should focus on the particular selling environment. Within any given selling environment are three general classes of information with which the sales rep should be familiar: industry-related knowledge, company-related knowledge, and sales skills–related knowledge.

Industry-Related Knowledge.   Three areas of industry-related knowledge are critical for sales reps: knowledge of the customers, knowledge of the competitors, and knowledge of the markets. Sales staff training should impart two important areas of information about the firm's customers. First, the salesperson should be made aware of the characteristics that comprise the profile of the company's current major customers, including customer size, members of the buying center and other key people, customer purchases by product line as well as estimates of purchases from competitors, and the customer's derived demand profile—that is, information regarding the customer's dependence on *its* customers. Inexperienced sales personnel should also be taught how to organize and maintain their own customer profile system as an ongoing aid to effective selling. The advent of desktop and laptop computers has already made customer profile and other management information systems much more viable decision-making aids, since data can be kept up-to-date and much more accessible.

Sales personnel need to have as much detailed information as possible regarding current and potential competitors. The most important information concerns the advantages and disadvantages that characterize competitors' products relative to the firm's offerings. Comparisons should cover the firm's prices, products, distribution, and promotion versus that of the competitors. Further, trainers should take care to include direct and *indirect* substitutes as sources of competitive threat.

Finally, knowledge about industry trends is useful not only because it helps place the activities of individual customers in perspective but also because it helps the sales rep anticipate the future buying behavior of various market segments. Training should concentrate on trends of major market segments as well as changes in customer production techniques and uses of the vendor's products, changes in

Advances in selling include having the right technology to work with the sales force, and automating for higher productivity.

Courtesy of Brock Control Systems, Inc.

industry distribution systems, industry changes in technology, and management information systems.

Company-Related Knowledge.   Training should ensure employee familiarity with the company's marketing mix—its products, pricing, distribution, and promotion policies. This includes knowledge of the relevant complementary and substitute products that are also sold by the firm. Information of this type helps the salesperson grasp the importance of selling a product package as opposed to an individual product. Training should also familiarize the sales rep with different product attributes (including advantages and disadvantages), primary applications, alternative applications, role in the customer's manufacturing process or final product output, and the potential for product alteration to match customer needs.

Training in company pricing should include information on price lists, discount policies, credit terms, financing arrangements, and pricing policies for custom orders or other special requests that might be made by customers.

Training requirements related to distribution channels can be undertaken at two levels. First, sales staff should be made aware of the channel members the firm uses for distribution. Key issues of concern are the roles and procedures by which the channel members fulfill their obligations in the distribution network and the potential for channel conflict. Second, the salesperson should be familiar with the day-to-day operational logistics decisions, including rates charged by public car-

BUSINESS MARKETING IN PRACTICE

How Not to Rep

How important is the sales force to a vendor's organization? The regional general manager of a major bank related the following unfortunate but true story.

One of the bank's newer account managers recently called on the treasurer of a large U.S. corporation in an attempt to gain access to that firm's significant volume of financial business. The representative began the interview with a seemingly innocuous question. "So what can I do for you in the way of financial services products?" That question unleashed a vehement attack from the treasurer, who countered first with the question, "I don't know—what do *you* think you can do for me?" The sales call went downhill rapidly from that point as the treasurer explained that although the bank's financial products and prices were more than acceptable, it was clear the sales representatives didn't know anything about their potential customer's business or financial needs. As examples the treasurer noted that the bank had changed its account managers four times in the last twelve months and that he was sick and tired of teaching rookies about his business and industry. Further, the treasurer pointed out that he knew more about the bank's service

products than did the account managers who were trying to sell to him. Finally, he noted that the account managers predictably showed up during the last week of each month because they were simply meeting the bank's monthly quota for potential or new customer sales calls. The interview concluded with the treasurer's decidedly caustic remark, "It is clear you people don't care about us—why the hell should we care about you?"

The bank's regional general manager related the story as an example of how poor planning, organizing, administration, and control of the sales force can effectively negate the entire marketing function of even the largest organization. The bank's total marketing mix was in fact one of the better programs developed in the financial services industry. Unfortunately, the performance of its sales force made a mockery of the bank's commitment to serving its customers.

How can we avoid the kind of marketing disaster described here? An understanding of the principles that underlie sales force management is fundamental to achieving effective sales force representation.

riers, delivery lead times required, transportation routing, and the potential for stock damage associated with the use of various carriers.

Though the promotional programs of the firm are determined by management, trainers must still ensure that the sales staff is familiar with such programs when they affect customers. Examples usually include cooperative advertising programs offered by the manufacturer to customers and volume-related discount programs designed to coincide with the business marketer's other promotional efforts.

Effective training must also include those operational aspects of the company that affect the marketing function of the firm. Sales staff often require information about the firm's accounting procedures as well as production techniques and scheduling. The general rule for inclusion of such material in the sales staff training program is whether the particular operational aspect of the firm directly or indirectly affects the customer. If it does, chances are the customer will expect the salesperson to know the answer.

Sales-Related Knowledge.   Sales-related knowledge includes those selling skills and personality characteristics that help persuade buyers to buy. Of course, no single approach is effective in all buyer/seller interactions. At best, the manager can hope to develop a number of basic skills and personality attributes that the sales rep can then adapt as needed. Two of these skills are concerned with human relations and negotiating. Human relations skills have gained a great deal of attention from many sales organizations, especially over the last two decades. This is because of a general trend away from selling-oriented approaches in favor of customer-oriented approaches. The distinction between a **customer orientation** and a **selling orientation** is important because the former selling style is conducive to a longer-term close relationship between the buyer and the vendor.

The **Selling Orientation–Customer Orientation (SOCO) scale** attempts to identify selling styles and to assess whether or not a particular style is consistent with a collaborative relationship between the buyer and the seller.[5] The SOCO scale was developed and validated based on the responses of salespeople; a replication study using the same scale items was also conducted using the assessments of industrial products buyers.[6] The scale's statements were altered in the replication study to fit the industrial buyers' perspectives because they provide insight into those selling characteristics perceived to be customer oriented rather than selling oriented (see Exhibit 15–7). The statements specify the actions that might induce a buyer to perceive a sales rep's behavior in a favorable light (customer oriented) or as adversarial or manipulative (selling oriented). Management should consider using the items in the SOCO scale in their training programs.

The customer-orientation approach is similarly reflected in the need to develop sales representatives' negotiation skills. *Negotiation* is the process through which representatives of the buyer and seller develop the terms of exchange that will commit their organizations to a binding contract with each other. Current trends in sales training tend to stress collaborative rather than adversarial approaches to negotiating. The sales representative's role is to assist the buyer in resolving his or her company's purchasing problems in order to promote a collab-

EXHIBIT 15–7   SOCO Scale Statements

1. Salespeople give accurate representations of what their product will do for me.
2. Salespeople try to get me to discuss my product needs.
3. Salespeople apply selling pressure even though they know the product is not right for my company.
4. Salespeople imply that things are beyond their control when they really are not.
5. Salespeople try to influence me through information rather than by pressure.
6. Salespeople that call on me are customer-oriented.
7. Salespeople spend more time trying to persuade than they do trying to discover my product needs.
8. Salespeople try to help me achieve my purchasing objectives.
9. Salespeople answer my questions about their products as honestly as possible.
10. Salespeople agree with me only to please me.
11. Salespeople treat me as an opponent.
12. Salespeople try to figure out what my needs are.
13. Salespeople have my best interest as a customer in mind.
14. Salespeople take a problem-solving approach in selling to me.
15. Salespeople will go as far as to disagree with me in order to help me make a better purchase decision.
16. Salespeople recommend the product best suited to solve my problems.
17. Salespeople stretch the truth in their product representations.
18. Salespeople talk first and listen to my needs later.
19. Salespeople try to convince me to buy more than I need.
20. Salespeople paint rosy pictures of their products to make them sound as good as possible.
21. Salespeople try to provide for my organization's satisfaction.
22. Salespeople make recommendations based on what they think they can sell, not on the basis of my long-term satisfaction.
23. Salespeople try to find out which products would be most helpful to me as a customer.
24. Salespeople are always looking for ways to apply pressure to make me buy.

Source: From "Measuring Customer Orientation of Salespeople: A Replication with Industrial Buyers," by Ronald E. Michaels and Ralph L. Day from *Journal of Marketing Research* 22 (Nov. 1985), p. 445. Reprinted by permission of the American Marketing Association.

orative long-term interaction between the buyer and the seller rather than a one-shot deal in which the salesperson attempts to extract as much as possible from the buyer while conceding as little as possible in return. Using a **collaborative negotiating style** means that the sales rep now needs more training in the following areas:

■ Determining the customer's purchasing needs.

■ Developing information acquisition skills in order to learn more about the buyer's business.

- Designing strategies to maximize the long-term satisfaction of the buyer.

- Developing the technical and product knowledge skills needed to assist the customer in using the vendor's product(s).

- Developing new applications and markets involving those products.

Of course, not every buyer (or seller) is predisposed toward a collaborative approach. In such situations the sales representative who uses a collaborative approach may emerge from the negotiation with a less than satisfactory contract— the result of being victimized by a shrewd buyer devoted to an adversarial style of negotiation. Management must therefore stress the importance of being able to alter negotiation approaches as conditions dictate.

Supervision and Motivation

The role of management supervision in the structuring of a well-motivated sales force is best determined by considering the nature of the selling environment and the sales tasks the staff must carry out. No individual supervisory style is superior to any other with regard to establishing employee motivation. Consequently, the marketing manager's best strategy is to be aware of the range of supervisory strategies available and to incorporate the various techniques when and where situations dictate. The key to establishing a good supervisory relationship with the sales staff is flexibility combined with consistency.

For example, the general sales manager of an American/Japanese integrated forest products manufacturing company was responsible for supervising two types of lumber traders. Less aggressive and/or inexperienced junior traders sold the firm's output on a regional basis; senior traders were responsible for establishing international contracts with customers. Following the rejection of a series of "unified" supervisory approaches in which both groups of traders were treated identically, the manager ultimately had to develop two different approaches. Junior traders wanted and needed close supervision with clearly stated performance criteria and well-defined "selling procedures." This approach was the antithesis of the one that proved to be successful in motivating the senior traders. The senior traders produced best when allowed to operate almost as autonomous sales units within the division. Due to their experience, specialized expertise, and diverse international contacts, the senior traders responded best when assigned the responsibility for selling the output of "their own mill"—and then being left alone to develop their own procedures and selling strategies. The general manager somewhat ruefully discovered that, unlike junior traders, the more he left the senior traders alone, the more they produced.

Although no single supervisory style suits all situations, certain issues are common to all styles. For example, feedback from management is always important to the salesperson. **Outcome feedback** stresses the communication of performance-based information (for example, whether or not the salesperson has met some management objective such as sales or profit requirements). **Cognitive feedback** focuses on a discussion of the reasons *why* the management objective was (or was not) met.[7] The cognitive approach to feedback may be more useful than the outcome approach because the manager can focus on the specific job-related reasons that led to the salesperson's successful (or unsuccessful) performance. This information can then help the sales representative adjust specific aspects of his or her job performance or reinforce successful job-related behavior.

Turnover is one aspect of employee motivation with which most sales managers must deal. Turnover among sales representatives is partly a result of the large number of external contacts the salesperson is exposed to on a constant basis. Sales staff can be lured away by competitors, by other vendors who sell products that are complementary to the sales representatives' product line, and even by customers.

There exists a point at which turnover may become unacceptably high. Excessively high turnover rates signal motivational difficulties in the sales force. The problem may be caused by anything from inadequate remuneration to poor supervisory performance. It is important to appreciate that turnover costs do not just include losses associated with training; much greater penalties can arise. Sales staff who join competitors can often take with them key customer contacts as well as vital inside knowledge about their former employer's current products, new products, and marketing strategies. These factors can be very detrimental to the sales effectiveness of the organization.

Many firms, therefore, monitor their turnover rates closely and often conduct exit interviews in order to establish the reasons that motivate sales staff to leave. The objective of this approach is to gain an understanding of sales force discontent and to correct the causes.

Finally, **span of control** is based on the number of telephone and personal contacts between members of the sales staff and their supervisor, as well as the number and skill levels of the sales reps reporting to each supervisor. Large, young, inexperienced sales forces require that the supervisor maintain close contact by keeping the span of control small. It can later be increased as the experience and selling skills of the reps improve and they require less close supervision. The supervisor can then manage a larger number of sales reps without the risk that employee morale will suffer and lead to an increase in turnover.

Compensation Systems

Compensation systems for salespeople are generally based on straight salary, incentive systems (commissions and/or bonuses), or some combination of salary plus incentive. The compensation structure is determined after management has considered the nature of the selling task and the characteristics of the sales staff involved. Each type of remuneration has various advantages and disadvantages, and it is important to match the right remuneration system to the appropriate selling context.

Straight Salary.   Straight salary, in which the salesperson receives a set amount of income on a regular basis, has a number of advantages. First, it provides security for junior sales staff who are in the process of developing their selling skills and customer base. It also provides a financial operating base for sales staff assigned to the development of new customers and/or market segments, where there may be a long lead time between developmental efforts and sales revenues. Straight salary allows sales staff to provide many of the selling support activities that may be instrumental in retaining customer loyalty but that do not directly generate purchase orders. Finally, salary structures are easier to administer and plan than incentive systems.

On the negative side, straight salary structures do not provide a direct link between sales dollar (or profit) generation and a personal reward structure for the employee. Sales staff remuneration is not, therefore, directly linked to employee performance. The result may be that employees have little incentive to work harder at generating sales revenues.

Incentive Systems.   Unlike straight salary, an incentive system with commissions and bonuses does provide a direct link between reward and performance. Sales staff are motivated to work harder at generating sales and profits because of the direct impact on their commissions. Commission systems are generally valued by senior sales staff. This motivates the more experienced salespeople to realize their potential for higher incomes by generating sales. Commission systems are also relatively easy to administer.

Incentive systems do have some disadvantages. Employees may tend to concentrate on direct sales-generating behavior at the expense of longer-term support activities. Lag times between selling efforts and sales responses may leave salespeople with little income. Also, pure incentive systems may cause employees to become too aggressive and oriented to closure of the sale before the customer's buying process has been completed. This can cause customer irritation over what is perceived as a pushy sales staff. Commission systems may also cause friction among employees when a coordinated group selling approach is necessary. The problem develops in attempting to determine which employee actually deserves the commission. Finally, junior sales staff may suffer initially until they have developed a substantial customer base from which they can generate sales revenues.

Combination Systems.   A salary plus commission and/or bonus has the potential to provide the best characteristics of salary and incentive systems. Security aspects of a salary floor are provided (especially for junior staff), whereas incentives to generate maximum sales efforts are maintained by the commission structure. The salary component of the remuneration structure allows employees to fulfill the nondirect sales-oriented activities necessary to maintain good customer relations without suffering major financial penalties. The incentive component ensures that a reward system is in position to motivate employees to expand their sales base. The combination approach allows flexibility in tailoring the salary and incentive components to accommodate the firm's current sales environment as well as management plans to alter that environment.

Administration requirements, however, are more complex than those required for either a pure salary or pure incentive system. Too much emphasis on either the salary or the incentive component could skew employee behavior. The result could be a combination system that achieves very few of management's goals because the desired balance between employee behavior flowing from the salary component versus the incentive component has not been achieved.

SALES FORCE CONTROL

One of the major objectives of the sales force control system is to improve productivity. The sales force can be made more productive by improving the ability of the reps to increase sales while holding the costs associated with the generation of those sales constant, or by reducing the costs of producing sales without decreasing the generation of sales volume. In terms of practical application for management purposes, then, the control reports tend to concentrate on monitoring the direct generation of sales and gross profits and the costs incurred by the salesperson in the process of generating business. Two control reports that are useful in monitoring these factors are the sales representative's evaluation report and the sales call efficiency report.

Sales Representative's Evaluation Report

The objective of the **sales representative's evaluation report** is to monitor the performance of sales reps on the basis of their monthly averaged sales contribution and their monthly averaged gross profit (GP) contribution. The purpose of the report is to provide the marketing manager and the sale reps with a clearly defined set of criteria to aid in the assessment of the sales reps' performance. There are, however, some limitations.

The sales representative's evaluation report should be used when management has sufficient reason to believe that the specific sales territories or branch outlets in which its reps operate are roughly similar in terms of competitive forces and market opportunities. To the extent that this condition is not met, sales reps whose average monthly sales and gross profits are ranked against each other in the report may have vastly different sales opportunities and/or competitive constraints. A manager who does not specifically take into account such differences would not only be remiss in his or her ethical responsibility to the sales reps but also might misjudge the relative performance of individual representatives based on the report information.

The report should also be used when the manager needs a performance-based input measure that contributes *in part* to such decisions as the following:

- Compensation levels for salaried (or partly salaried) reps.

- Quota adjustments for sales reps.

- Identification of those sales reps in need of training to improve their sales skills.

- Identification of those reps who should be terminated due to substandard performance levels.

Report Structure and Calculation.   Exhibit 15–8 illustrates the sales representatives' evaluation report for the North American Division of International Pressure Packing, Inc. The information in the report is relatively easy to acquire since the yearly sales dollars value and number of units sold by each representative can be collected through the firm's invoicing system. The representative's unit sales are then multiplied by the gross profit associated with each of the products they sell to yield their gross profit contribution. The yearly sales and gross profit data are then divided by the number of months in the current year that were worked by the representative (column A) to yield the average sales per month (column E) and the average gross profit per month (column G).

The performance ranking of the representative relative to his or her colleagues is indicated in the sales rank column (column D), and the gross profit ranking appears in column F.

The gross profit to sales ratio (column H) is obtained by dividing the rep's monthly average generated gross profits (column G) by the corresponding monthly average sales (column E). The sales rep's gross profit to sales ranking is shown in column I.

Finally, any extra duties in addition to those of acting as a full-time sales rep are listed in column J. This addendum is necessary because some reps may fulfill other activities in the organization such as providing extra technical advice to their colleagues and/or customers. This, of course, would reduce the amount of time devoted to developing sales and/or gross profits for the firm.

Interpretation.   Depending on corporate orientation, the ranking of the sales reps (and hence the related rewards and/or sanctions) can be based on average monthly sales or average monthly gross profits. Alternatively, management might prefer to emphasize the gross profit to sales ratio in a "quasi-efficiency" index of the representatives' abilities to maximize their gross profit returns as a function of generated sales dollars (columns H and I). Because the sales force objectives can change from time to time, the manager may have to alter the evaluation basis from sales generation (to maximize the firm's market share) to GP growth (a cash flow orientation) or some combination of the two. Whichever evaluation technique is incorporated, it is important that all sales reps be aware of the basis for their assessment well in advance.

EXHIBIT 15–8   Sales Representative's Evaluation Report: Analysis of Sales Representatives Ranked According to Average Sales Dollars Per Month and Average Gross Profit Per Month as of December 31, 1991

Basis Month Avg. (A)	Name (B)	Location (C)	Sales Rank (D)	Average Sales Per Month (E)	GP Rank (F)	Average GP Per Month (G)	GP to Sales Ratio % (H) = (G)/(E)	GP/ Sales Rank (I)	Other Duties (J)
12	J. E.	Chicago	1	425,295	1	64,078	15.1	5	
12	H. W.	New York	2	367,470	3	54,338	14.8	6	
12	B. V.	Los Angeles	3	362,261	5	47,967	13.2	7	
12	R. P.	Boston	4	361,965	4	45,995	12.7	8	
12	R. R.	Dallas	5	361,852	6	36,915	10.2	11	
12	R. L.	Montreal	6	252,486	10	26,863	10.6	9	
11	H. V.	Denver	7	243,916	12	15,252	6.3	14	
12	B. L.	New Orleans	8	242,736	11	15,800	6.5	13	
12	G. W	Miami	9	237,322	7	36,817	15.5	4	
12	W. E.	Toronto	10	230,106	8	36,716	16.0	3	
12	K. M.	San Francisco	11	230,006	2	61,372	26.7	2	
12	G. N.	Columbus	12	218,316	13	12,442	5.7	15	
12	B. J.	Houston	13	216,712	14	11,887	5.5	17	
12	A. P.	Vancouver	14	215,041	16	11,702	5.4	18	
12	M. K.	Seattle	15	214,018	18	10,359	4.8	19	
12	M. M.	Detroit	16	212,566	20	9,616	4.5	20	
12	R. T.	Seattle	17	211,827	15	11,729	5.5	16	
12	D. H.	Buffalo	18	108,424	9	34,266	31.6	1	RSR
8	Y. M.	Toledo	19	104,871	17	10,861	10.4	10	
6	E. F.	Madison	20	104,140	19	9,773	9.4	12	RSR

RSR = resource sales representative, a technical specialist who acts as a resource person to other sales staff and customers in addition to maintaining some of his or her own sales accounts.

Subject to the constraint of comparability between sales territories and/or branches, the data from the report can be used to (1) question differing performance levels between sales representatives in similar selling situations, and (2) draw the manager's as well as the sales rep's attention to the importance of producing not only a significant sales dollar volume but also of generating the commensurate gross profits. The objectives are to improve the sales skills of the lower-ranked reps and to temper what seems in many instances a corporate obsession with market share per se rather than the development of a market share position capable of meeting profit requirements.

The sales representative's evaluation report is a control system that concentrates on the salesperson's ability to generate sales and/or gross profits as a measure of productivity. A second approach to monitoring sales force productivity focuses on efficiency through controlling the costs of generating sales.

Sales Call Efficiency Report

A basic report for monitoring expenses involves comparing sales representatives' costs per call. The calculations are straightforward in that basic data recording the number of calls per time period (usually one year) and the salesperson's cumulative field expenses for the same period are collected (see Exhibit 15–9).

The advantages of analyzing the sales force activity on a cost per call basis are that (1) sales representatives are encouraged to become more aware of the expenses they incur in the process of generating sales, and (2) management can more effectively compare the sales expenses for different sales reps, even when those expenses are also a function of the differing levels of sales call activity by each individual.

The major disadvantage is that the cost per call data can be misleading, especially when comparing sales reps across different sales territories. This is due to the differing sales expense structures as well as the differing concentration and sales volume potentials of accounts in different areas. Some reporting systems attempt to remove such disparities by entering adjustment factors that account for selling cost variations among different markets as well as differences in the concentration and nature of accounts in the various trading areas.

A good example of a reporting technique that attempts to incorporate the preceding factors is provided by the **sales call efficiency index (SCEI)**.[8] The index provides a way to assess the sales call costs of the firm's sales reps, even though they operate in different regions with differing sales opportunities and costs

EXHIBIT 15–9   A Comparison of Sales Representatives' Costs per Call

Salesperson (A)	Field Sales Expenses (B)	Number of Calls per Year (C)	Cost per Call (D) = (B)/(C)
Rep 1	$27,999.51	253	$110.67
Rep 2	$28,532.25	272	$104.90
.	.	.	.
.	.	.	.
.	.	.	.
Rep n	x	y	z

Source: Adapted from Richard Kern, "Survey of Selling Costs: Onward and Ever Upward," *Sales and Marketing Management* (Feb. 1986), p. 33.

of doing business. The SCEI formula shows the factors that are included in calculating sales call efficiency:

$$\frac{\text{total direct sales costs} \times \text{weighted per diem index}}{\text{calls per year} \times \text{territory concentration factor}} = \frac{\text{SCEI cost}}{\text{per call}}$$

where:

1. total direct sales costs = sales rep's base salary + bonus or commission + auto expense + travel + entertainment expenses + other expenses

2. weighted per diem index = selling costs (meals, lodging, auto rental) index in the rep's sales territory or city divided by the average for the United States (for example, if the selling cost index for Boston in 1991 was 134, dividing this into the American average [100] yields a weighted per diem selling cost index of 0.75).

3. calls per year = the sales rep's calls in one year in his or her territory.

4. territory concentration factor = average calls per day for the firm's total sales force divided by the average calls per day in the individual rep's territory (for example, if the firm's total sales force averaged 5 calls per day while the rep serving the Boston area averaged 7 calls, then the concentration factor is 5/7 = 0.71 for the Boston rep).

An example using hypothetical total direct sales costs and calls per year demonstrates how the preceding formula affects the comparison of two sales reps—one in Memphis and the other in Boston. Using the *unadjusted* calculation of costs per call in which the weighted per diem index and territory concentration factor are not considered:

	Total Direct Sales Costs	÷ Calls Per Year	= Unweighted Cost Per Call
Boston representative	$74,000	1,350	$54.81
Memphis representative	$59,200	850	$69.65

Using the SCEI formula, the adjusted cost per call for the Boston representative: $\dfrac{\$74,000 \times 0.75}{1,350 \times 0.71} = \underline{\$57.90}$

and for the Memphis representative: $\dfrac{\$59,200 \times 1.30}{850 \times 1.66} = \underline{\$54.54}$

Note: The weighted per diem index for Memphis = 1.30, and the territory concentration factor = 1.66.

Note how the spread between the unadjusted cost per call for the two sales reps is reduced once the territory concentration factor and the weighted per diem index are factored into the calculations.

Other evaluation systems attempt to control for various facets of the marketing environment. The benefit of such reports is often found in the greater degree of detailed information that can be used to assess the salesperson. No single sales force evaluation report can hope to control for the myriad intervention factors that could bias a comparison of the relative performances of the firm's sales representatives. Ultimately, the responsibility for ensuring that representatives are evaluated fairly lies with the sales manager.

SUMMARY

Planning, organizing, administering, and controlling comprise the fundamental tasks the sales manager must perform if the sales force is to function effectively. Good management requires that each of these tasks be carried out thoroughly. Additionally, the policies and objectives developed during each of these four tasks must be consistent with those developed in the other task stages. If this is not the case, conflicting objectives and tasks are likely to be introduced into management of the sales force. This chapter introduced three issues in sales force planning: defining and analyzing planning and control units, sales force deployment, and the sales resource opportunity grid.

Organizing the sales force logically relies on good initial planning so that sales representatives will be able to effectively service the planning and control units. Organizational structures include customer-based, product-based, territory-based, national account–based and inside/outside sales–based approaches. These bases for organizing can in fact be combined to make the configuration of the sales force more accurately fit the planning and control units it must serve. When combining these bases for organization, however, care must be taken to ensure that they do not conflict with each other.

Sales force administration includes recruitment and selection, training objectives and techniques, supervision and motivation, and compensation systems. The tasks associated with these issues constitute the day-to-day job of the sales manager. As with planning and organizing, care must be taken to ensure that the component tasks of administration are consistent with each other, as well as with the planning and organizing objectives. Salespeople must be recruited and trained, keeping in mind the type of accounts with which they will be expected to deal. Similarly, supervision and compensation must be structured so that they mesh with the kind of salespeople who have been selected and the tasks to which they have been assigned.

Finally, control procedures are necessary to monitor sales force performance and to signal the need for changes in the planning, organizing, and administering tasks of the sales manager. The sales representatives' evaluation report and the sales call efficiency index are examples of how a salesperson's performance can be monitored by the manager.

According to a popular axiom, "You get only one chance to make a favorable first impression." We might add one more thought: "The sales force is the vendor's last chance to make a favorable impression on the customer." This is because it is the sales representative who provides the final link between the buyer and the seller.

Key Terms and Concepts

sales force planning
planning and control units (PCUs)
sales force deployment
sales effort allocation index
sales resource opportunity grid
customer-based approach
product-based approach
territory-based approach
national account–based approach
inside/outside sales–based approach
customer orientation

selling orientation
selling orientation–customer orientation (SOCO) scale
collaborative negotiating style
outcome feedback
cognitive feedback
turnover
span of control
sales representative's evaluation report
sales call efficiency index (SCEI)

Discussion Questions

1. Name three of the six determinants of sales potential that are used in evaluating a planning and control unit. Why do you think a sales manager would be interested in these determinants?

2. What is deployment planning, and what problems is it designed to resolve?

3. Outline the objectives and two of the four hypothetical situations of the sales resource opportunity grid. If an established and competitively dominant firm enters a region of low business opportunities, what would you recommend?

4. What factors would you consider when deciding to use a product-based versus territory-based approach in organizing your sales force?

5. What are the benefits and disadvantages associated with an inside/outside sales organization?

6. What are the characteristics of a national account–based organization? Do you consider it to be the best type of organizational structure? Why or why not?

7. What is the difference between a selling orientation and a customer orientation? Is a customer orientation always superior to a selling orientation?

8. What sales situation would cause you to prefer a salary system over an incentive system as a means of remunerating your employees?

9. In the sales representative's evaluation report, why is it useful to calculate a gross profit to sales ratio?

Endnotes and References

1. Adrian B. Ryans and Charles B. Weinberg, "Territory Sales Response," *Journal of Marketing Research* 16 (November 1979): 453–465.

2. Raymond LaForge and David W. Cravens, "Steps in Selling Effort Deployment," *Industrial Marketing Management* 11 (1982): 183–194.

3. Ibid.

4. Barton Weitz, Harish Sujan, and Mita Sujan, "Knowledge Motivation and Adaptive Behavior: A Framework for Improving Selling Effectiveness," *Journal of Marketing* 50 (October 1986): 186.

5. Robert Saxe and Barton A. Weitz, "The SOCO Scale: A Measure of the Customer Orientation of Salespeople," *Journal of Marketing Research* 19 (August 1982): 343–351.

6. Ronald E. Michaels and Ralph L. Day, "Measuring Customer Orientation of Sales People: A Replication with Industrial Buyers," *Journal of Marketing Research* 22 (November 1985): 443–446.

7. Weitz, Sujan, and Sujan, "Knowledge Motivation and Adaptive Behavior," pp. 174–191.

8. Richard Kerr, "Survey of Selling Costs: Onward and Ever Upward," *Sales and Marketing Management* (February 1987): 10–33.

16

EVALUATION AND CONTROL

- To identify those characteristics of a marketing information system that help to make it a useful and efficient source of data for managers
- To determine the data input requirements and analytical techniques used to obtain the output needed for decision making
- To describe the range of information reports that can be expected from an adequate decision support system
- To discuss the uses of macro and micro reports
- To demonstrate the procedures used to analyze micro and macro report information and to pinpoint specific problems within the vendor's total marketing organization

Just as accountants need balance sheets and plant managers need production data to operate efficiently, marketing managers require information to anticipate and respond to market threats and opportunities. A decision support system effectively acts as the monitoring and signaling device that alerts management to the need for change in the marketing organization.

Who needs a marketing decision support system? The answer is virtually every business marketing organization that realizes the importance of constantly monitoring its products, customers, and sales operations in order to assess performance, detect change quickly, and pinpoint the cause of that change as soon as possible.

THE MARKETING DECISION SUPPORT SYSTEM

The objective of the **marketing decision support system** is to provide an integrated system of information acquisition and analysis based on the firm's own *internal* data sources.[1] This system is not intended to meet all of the firm's information needs. External environmental impacts, for example, require a totally different set of data and analysis and are outside the scope of internal monitoring or control systems. Constructing a broadly based internal decision support system is not easy. Hardware and software advances in information handling and processing, however, have greatly reduced the time and capital costs that plagued earlier efforts to develop large-scale systems.[2]

The marketing decision support system is designed to incorporate a number of characteristics that are helpful in monitoring and controlling business marketing functions. These are system integration, the ability to aggregate and disaggregate company data, and analytical efficiency.

System Integration

System integration means that all employees of the firm whose decisions can directly or indirectly influence the company's marketing operations should share their data, insights, and opinions with marketing management. Accounting, engineering, and production departments, for example, have all too often operated independently of the marketing department. Accounting data, however, directly affect customers through credit limits and billing procedures. Similarly, engineering directly affects product design, and production affects scheduling, which determines when products will be manufactured for sale. Closer coordination between marketing management and all of the other company departments on whom they depend means customers are better served.

A number of advantages can be derived from an integrated system. First, those employees who can affect (or be affected by) marketing decisions are made aware of the interdependence of all activities in an effective marketing operation. The objective here is to minimize the type of decision making in a vacuum that can happen in any organization. The brand manager has as much need for detailed data reflecting product item sales as the branch manager who actually sells to the customer because decisions by one manager affect results achieved by the other. An integrated system is most easily achieved when each of the decision participants has access to information regarding the performance of his or her function as it relates to the total marketing process. Second, benefits of teamwork in decision making are maximized when employees are given the necessary information to coordinate their actions on a continuous basis (rather than on a "one-shot" basis, as often occurs in new product launches, for example). Third, problem solving can be enhanced when different functional specialists are encouraged to offer their

BUSINESS MARKETING IN PRACTICE ▪▪▪▪▪▪▪▪▪▪▪▪▪▪▪▪

Problem Solving with Data Integration

The divisional manager of a major building materials supplier was under tremendous competitive price pressures in one of his distribution channels. Contractors were switching from cedar to cheaper species of wood used in the construction of housing. The situation was eased considerably when the brand manager, together with the mill's general manager, was able to increase the percentage of 8- and 16-foot 2 x 4 studs included in a standard rail car. Contractors heavily favor these lengths because North American houses are built with 8-foot ceilings. Using the preferred 8- and 16-foot lengths (cut in half) reduced the contractor's costs of wasted wood on the construction site. Modifying the product to better suit contractor needs helped to reduce the divisional manager's price disadvantage problem. The solution was actually suggested by the general manager based on production figures from his mill's operating database. Integrating production information with the divisional manager's data on contractor buying patterns provided the solution to the problem.

own unique perspectives and solutions. These solutions may not be readily apparent to others who have different backgrounds, as the story in the Business Marketing in Practice box on page 612 shows.

Aggregating and Disaggregating Data

The ability to **aggregate** (combine) or **disaggregate** (break down) **data** in the firm's decision support system determines the extent to which management can provide micro (detailed) as well as macro (broad-based) reports for purposes of analysis. A micro unit of analysis refers to the smallest denominational unit under consideration, such as a single customer branch or product item. A macro unit of analysis deals with larger groupings or aggregations of data that are used in reports for evaluating such things as entire customer segments, company divisions, or groups of products. Microsoft, which serves a large range of different customer segments with differing software needs, must monitor all of its diverse markets.

The capability to provide both macro and micro information is a desirable attribute of the decision support system because different problems may require the data to be reported in different ways. Sometimes data may need to be further broken down (disaggregated) to isolate and determine the source of a problem. Other times data must be combined (aggregated) to determine how widespread a problem is or whether it has spread to other areas of the marketing operation.

The major issue regarding the design of this capability in the decision system usually revolves around the costs versus the benefits of implementing a report structure that allows a full breakdown to the micro level of analysis, such as information at the individual customer or sales representative level. The major costs are in establishing the software support and, to a lesser extent, the appropriate computing capacity and on-line operation of the system.

Analytical Efficiency

Analytical efficiency is concerned with the ability of the decision support system to detect abnormally good or poor performance in the marketing organization as early as possible; to trace the nature of the problem to the smallest appropriate level with as little loss of time and effort as possible; and to collect information needed to determine the extent to which the problem has spread to other components of the distribution system. If, for example, a problem is detected within one channel group or class of products, management must quickly assess whether related channel members or products have also been affected, since rapid detection and reaction are often necessary for purposes of damage control.[3] Conversely, if the sales of a product or sales territory exceed all expectations, management will want to determine the cause in order to duplicate similar good performance in other products or territories.

Ultimately, the ability to locate and determine the extent of problems is crucial in convincing all managers to make use of any decision support technique. The system must yield the necessary information and produce it quickly with a minimum of effort or it won't be used.

The marketing decision support system can be applied to all sizes of organizations from small to large—wherever the potential for complex marketing structures arises. It is not uncommon, for example, to have networks that simultaneously use direct sales systems from the production facilities or head office, branch sales on a regional basis, and designated independent distributors acting on behalf of the firm (both domestically and internationally). Adding to the complexity is the often substantial mix of products and/or services that have come to characterize the sales offering of larger firms. Du Pont, for example, controls companies producing more than 1,700 products.

INPUT REQUIREMENTS AND OUTPUT REPORTS

The decision support system can best be described through consideration of the data input requirements that are required to feed the system and the output reports that are generated as a result.[4] A major rule of thumb to remember when designing the support system is that the more detailed the data that are entered into the system, the more detailed will be the output reports that can be subsequently analyzed by management.

Data Input Requirements

Due to the evolution of accounting practices, most customer invoices now include a significant amount of information that is highly valuable to marketers if they collect it in a meaningful and timely way. Standard data include the following:

- customer name, address, and location codes
- the vendor's branch and division identification (address and/or identification code)
- sales representative's identification (contract signature and/or identification code)
- date of transaction
- product description (name of item and/or product identification code)
- quantity purchased
- itemized as well as total value of goods sold to the customer
- discounts granted to the customer because of large volume purchases, prompt payment, or damaged stock claims

In addition to data from invoices, accounting and production systems often contain information such as customer identification codes based on SIC classifications or other internal company codes, customer credit limits, operational cost figures, and product performance data. Gross profits, product margins, cost of goods sold, inventory turnover and maintenance levels, and discounts by product item are common examples of operational cost and product performance monitoring data. Through combining invoice and internal company data a powerful array of marketing-monitoring reports can be produced.

By combining the invoice information with the firm's internal records, a sample of a customer input file can be developed (see Exhibit 16–1). Note that the customer input file contains both "current month" as well as "year-to-date" information. This is because it is useful to provide both current and historical records of the customer's purchases.

The selection of which customer input variables to maintain in the firm's records will, of course, vary according to corporate data needs. Most companies, however, include at least the product unit volumes and related sales and gross profit dollars associated with each customer's purchases. The information concerning the company's product performance with a given customer might also prove useful. The Business Marketing in Practice box below illustrates how valuable the accumulation of data can be.

By maintaining prior-year files, a company can make comparisons across time—both at the micro level (for changes in the purchasing profile of individual customers) and at the macro level, where the customer sales data are compiled into larger classifications to monitor changes in sales territory and product line sales.

BUSINESS MARKETING IN PRACTICE

Fighting Fraud with Data

A paper products supplier received a $2,500 claim from one of its East Coast customers. Rather than incur the extra cost of physically inspecting the damaged stock, the vendor often settled with some of its larger customers by simply granting a discount off the contract list price. One of the sales representatives, however, became suspicious when reviewing the total number of discounts granted to the client by other divisions of the seller's company.

A review of the customer's file indicated numerous claims made across all of the firm's divisions in the preceding eight-month period—but not more than two from any single division. A trace of the boxcar in question subsequently revealed that it was still 1,200 miles from the customer's plant at the time the client asked for the damaged stock discount. The customer was in fact going bankrupt and attempting to forestall the problem through fraud. Without the central customer file recording all discounts granted, it is unlikely that the sales reps' suspicions would have been aroused enough to trace the location of the shipment.

EXHIBIT 16–1 Customer Input File

Data Input Requirements for the Customer Profile

1. customer name, address & location codes
2. customer group classification code (3- or 4-digit SIC code)
3. branch and division identification code

4. sales representative identification
5. transaction date
6. customer credit limit

Year: 1992

Year: 1991   Year: 1990

Product Description		Product Item Unit Volumes		Sales Dollar Value		Product Performance Data			
						Gross Profit Dollar Value		Discounts Granted	
Product Identification Code	Product Description	Current Month	Year to Date	Current Month	Year to Date	Current Month	Year to Date	Current Month	Year to Date
01 02 • • • • • n	item description • • • • •	number of units	number of units	$ • • • • •	$ • • • • •	$ • • • • •	$ • • • • •	$ • • • • •	$ • • • • •
				$ Total Sales		$ Total Gross Profits	$	$ Total Discounts	$

Same Data

Format as for

Current Year: 1992

Source: Reprinted by permission of the publisher from "Developing and Using a Data Base Marketing System," by Lindsay Meredith, *Industrial Marketing Management*, Vol. 18, No. 3 (November 1989), p. 248. Copyright 1989 by Elseviere Science Publishing Co., Inc.

Exhibit 16–2 describes the data input levels that underlie the various macro and micro reports shown in Exhibit 16–3. The input data shown in Exhibit 16–2 are organized into eight different levels starting with the most detailed information on the individual product items sold to each customer in level 1. Moving upward through the levels, the data become more and more aggregated until total company sales and gross profits are summarized in level 8. The input information is arrayed in this way because it allows the manager to enter the structure at any level and either combine data to look at the "big picture" through macro reports or to look at more detailed information on individual products and customers through micro reports.

For demonstration purposes, Exhibit 16–2 shows the breakdown of the data levels for just one of the firm's divisions starting at level 7. Of course, all of the firm's other divisions would follow a similar pattern for disaggregating their data levels. The components of the product item performance analysis shown in level 1 are also intended for demonstration purposes. Depending on the organization, management may choose to collect other product performance information than that shown in level 1.[5]

Report System Output

For ease of reference the eight data input levels from Exhibit 16–2 are also reproduced in column A of Exhibit 16–3. The macro and micro reports that can be generated from the eight data input levels are shown in columns B and C of Exhibit 16–3.

Interpretation of the macro and micro reports is straightforward. If, for example, a manager wanted to compare the organization's various branches according to the different assortments of products they sold, then the micro report "Branch Sales and Gross Profit by Product Item" would be prepared. These data could then be used to examine which particular product items were most important to each branch in terms of sales and gross profits. If, on the other hand, management simply wanted to determine which branch was least important in contributing sales and gross profits to the company, then the macro report "Branch Sales and Gross Profit by Total Product Sales" would be useful. This information could then be used to help determine where the firm might cut back to help reduce overhead. Note that the reports allow for the inclusion of data related to gross profits in addition to sales information. This reflects a growing concern that perhaps more data related to profitability at all levels should be included in reporting systems.[6]

The content of each report is generally evident from its title. A number of the more detailed reports, however, may require further explanation. Consider, for example, the output reports that flow from the customer sales category shown as level 3 in column A. The micro report "Customer Sales and Gross Profit by Customer Group by Branch" shown in column C could be used if the manager wanted to determine how important some given customer is within the branch's customer

EXHIBIT 16–2   Data Input Levels

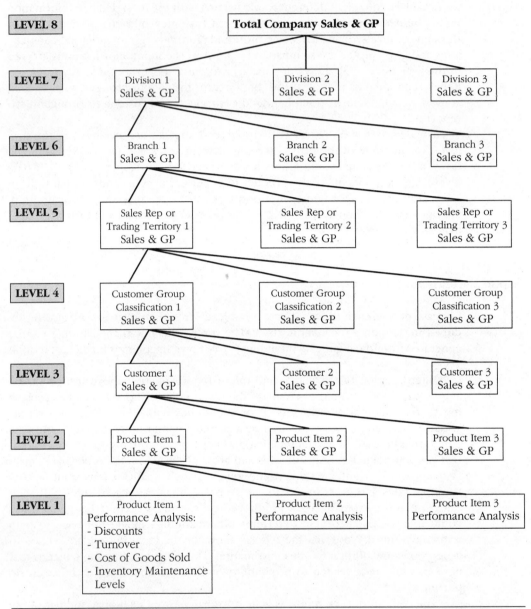

Note: GP = gross profit

Source: Reprinted by permission of the publisher from "Developing and Using a Data Base Marketing System," by Lindsay Meredith, *Industrial Marketing Management*, Vol. 18, No. 3 (November 1989), p. 250. Copyright 1989 by Elsevier Science Publishing Co., Inc.

EXHIBIT 16–3   Macro and Micro Report Generation

Data Input Levels (from Exhibit 16–2) (A)	Macro Reports (B)	Micro Reports (C)
8. *Total company sales*	Total firm sales & GP by division Total firm sales & GP by customer group Total firm sales & GP by product line Total firm sales & GP by division by customer group	
7. *Division sales*	Division sales & GP by total branch sales Division sales & GP by individual branch Division sales & GP by customer group Division sales & GP by product line	Division sales & GP by sales rep or territory
6. *Branch sales*	Branch sales & GP by customer group Branch sales & GP by total product sales	Branch sales & GP by sales rep or territory Branch sales & GP by customer Branch sales & GP by product item
5. *Sales rep or territory sales*	Sales rep or territory sales by customer group Sales rep or territory by total product sales	Sales rep or territory sales by customer Sales rep or territory sales by product item
4. *Customer group sales*	Customer group sales & GP by total product sales	Customer group sales & GP by product item
3. *Customer sales**		Customer sales & GP by customer group by branch Customer sales & GP by total product sales by branch Customer sales & GP by product item by branch
2. *Product item sales*		Product item sales & GP by customer group by division Product item sales & GP by customer group by branch

(*continues*)

EXHIBIT 16–3   Macro and Micro Report Generation (*cont.*)

Data Input Levels (from Exhibit 16–2) (A)	Macro Reports (B)	Micro Reports (C)
1. *Product performance analysis*		Product item performance by division
		Product item performance by branch
		Product item performance by customer by branch

*References to customer group sales and customer sales should be interpreted as sales made by the firm to these classifications.

Source: Reprinted by permission of the publisher from "Developing and Using a Data Base Marketing System," by Lindsay Meredith, *Industrial Marketing Management*, Vol. 18, No. 3 (November 1989), pp. 245–257. Copyright 1989 by Elsevier Science Publishing Co., Inc.

group classification based on that particular customer's proportional sales and gross profit contribution to the firm. Such information could be very useful in deciding the firm's negotiating stance toward the service demands of the customer. If the customer accounted for a very substantial sales and gross profit contribution to the branch compared to the other customers in that particular group, then the manager might be more inclined to provide a higher level of service than would be given other buyers who contributed very little in the way of sales and gross profits to the branch.

Similarly, the "Product Item Performance by Division" report would allow a product manager to review the performance of a given product item on a divisional basis to determine whether that item is meeting corporate expectations on any or all of the performance criteria suggested at the bottom of Exhibit 16–2.

REPORT APPLICATIONS

The application of macro and micro reports is determined by the marketer's analysis objectives. **Macro reports** are used to provide an overview of the firm's total marketing operation and to act as general monitoring devices that will alert management to changes occurring in the firm's environment. **Micro reports** are used to help managers narrow their analytical focus to specific areas of the marketing operation in order to identify causes of problems and to assist in the day-to-day functioning of the marketing organization.

Macro Report Applications

Macro reports are useful in four specific areas of analysis: general monitoring of the firm's marketing activities, identification of general trends affecting specific marketing functions, early warning of marketing threats and opportunities, and damage control assessment.

General Monitoring of Marketing Activities.   The objective of the macro reports in this capacity is to provide executives with an overview of the company's performance at a very broad level (for example, company and division total sales) as well as to offer summary information to branch and product managers concerning performance of their operating entities.[7]

Identification of General Trends.   Because of the manner in which output is displayed, the reports can offer insights into short-run sales and profit trends applicable to various levels of data consolidation. Although one must be wary of making decisions based on short-run data, such information can certainly provide cause for investigation of abnormally good or bad sales and profit trends.[8] The typical areas where short-run trends can offer insights are sales changes in geographic trading areas (division and branch), major product lines, and channel member group buying patterns. Lotus Development Corporation, because of its differing international markets, would be interested in general sales trends affecting its various divisions.

A three-year data history is usually sufficient to pick up short-run trends in these variables because it allows for changes to become fully developed.

Early Warning System.   Because the reports can be applied at any of the levels identified in Exhibit 16–3 and can provide output on current-month as well as year-to-date data, management can gather information on a timely basis. This aspect becomes important when a quick reaction is required to counteract market changes not favorable to the firm (for example, attempted market penetration by competitors). Similarly, when new marketing opportunities develop, management will want to detect them quickly and deploy resources to capitalize on their occurrence. The story in the Business Marketing in Practice box on page 622 illustrates how macro reports can serve as an early warning system.

Damage Control Assessment.   **Damage control** refers to the need for management to quickly determine the cause of a problem and how widespread it is so that immediate action can be taken to prevent the problem from getting any bigger. Damage control assessment helps the manager pinpoint the problem so that a solution can be developed to specifically target its cause. The example in the Business Marketing in Practice box on page 622 is also useful for demonstrating the damage control aspect of the report system. Because of the macro/micro feature in the reports, the firm was able to adopt either a wider or narrower focus as

BUSINESS MARKETING IN PRACTICE ■■■■■■■■■■■■■■■■

A Macro Report Pinpoints Sales Problem

A large U.S. multinational active in Canada noticed a decline in its central division current-month sales when in fact the commodity market in which it sold was known to be expanding rapidly. An investigation down to the branch and customer group levels discovered that a number of the retail customers in specific branch trading areas were being offered extremely favorable prices by another U.S. producer attempting to gain a foothold in the central division. Because the market threat was quickly pinpointed by geographic trading area and customer group, the multinational was able to respond immediately by instituting price cuts that countered the market-penetration strategy of the potential invader. The report system in this instance told management which customers and trading areas were most vulnerable to competitors, thus allowing the firm to undertake specific price cuts without generally depressing margins throughout its national distribution system.

conditions dictated in an attempt to determine how much of its distribution system had been affected. Once certain branches of the central division were found to be under heavy price competition, the firm checked the performance of neighboring branches to determine if the competitive pricing problem had spread to them, and it broke down branch sales by product item to determine if all or just some of the product mix was under competitive price threat. (It was determined that only three major product items out of a total mix of 169 product lines were suffering from the competitive price cuts.)

Micro Report Applications

Three analytical areas in which micro reports can be helpful are problem cause identification, micro market component evaluation, and on-line sales decisions.

Problem Cause Identification.   Although the macro reports are useful for indicating that a problem may exist, they may not offer sufficient insight into the *exact nature* of the problem. The micro levels of analysis, however, can provide the firm with a trail to follow that may lead to specific customers or product items that can then be investigated in depth. The objective here is to trace the problem to its source as quickly and with as little wasted resources as possible. The macro reports help to answer the question "Is there a problem and how widespread is it?" whereas the micro analysis addresses the question "How and why did the problem develop?"

Micro Market Component Evaluation.   Through the micro reports it is possible to evaluate the performance of individual customers, products, and sales representatives. This capacity of the report system is more appropriate for use by supervisory management responsible for day-to-day operations of the firm. Senior management, however, uses the micro reports when interdivisional comparisons at the micro levels are undertaken.

On-Line Sales Decisions.   One of the advantages associated with the decision support system is that sales representatives or branch management can access current and past sales records of individual customers. These data not only can help to reacquaint the vendor with the customers' current purchasing habits but also bring changes in those purchasing habits into sharper focus.[9] Honeywell's telemarketing organization would find customer-specific data quite useful for on-line sales decisions. (See the Business Marketing in Practice box below for an example of why micro reports can be helpful in on-line sales decisions.)

REPORT ANALYSIS PROCEDURES: A CASE STUDY

How can a manager detect a marketing problem using macro reports and then progressively narrow the scope of the search for the cause through micro reports? The following case study of a large pipe fittings manufacturer is based on the data given in Exhibit 16–4 and illustrates the procedures used to follow the "data trail" from a macro problem to its micro source. (The name of the company has been deleted, and the locations of branches and the data presented have been altered to preserve confidentiality.)

BUSINESS MARKETING IN PRACTICE ▮▮▮▮▮▮▮▮▮▮

Use of Micro Report Could Have Saved Company $47,000

The sales analyst of an integrated forest products producer became suspicious when reviewing the purchasing profile of one of the branch's largest customers. Historically, the industrial user bought only the vendor's premium quality products for remanufacture in his plants. The purchasing pattern changed dramatically, and the client suddenly began to concentrate on the vendor's poorest and cheapest grades of lumber. Branch and head office personnel ignored this change because sales volumes continued to remain large and current credit checks indicated no financial problems. The sales analyst's requests for further investigation were ignored. With virtually no warning the customer was placed in receivership by a competitor, and the vendor suffered a bad debt in excess of $47,000. The sales analyst's company now routinely reviews marked changes in customer purchasing behavior, having discovered that even relatively current credit checks can provide dated information.

EXHIBIT 16–4 Data for a Macro Report: Sales and Gross Profit by Division by Customer Group Year-to-Date, 12/31/91 to 12/31/92 ($000)

Eastern Division

Customer Group/SIC (A)	Sales 1992 (B)	1991 (C)	Percent 1992 (D)	1991 (E)	1990 (F)
1. 100–290 Retail	3,352.9	2,542.9	11.4	11.0	10.5
2. 300–390 Wholesale	6,982.6	5,964.2	23.8	25.8	26.8
3. 400–690 Industrial	19,059.0	14,610.0	64.8	63.2	62.7
4. Total All Groups	29,394.5	23,117.1	100.0	100.0	100.0

Central Division

Customer Group/SIC (A)	Sales 1992 (G)	1991 (H)	Percent 1992 (I)	1991 (J)	1990 (K)
1. 100–290 Retail	2,408.2	2,394.2	9.8	12.2	8.7
2. 300–390 Wholesale	6,854.3	5,338.0	27.9	27.2	31.6
3. 400–690 Industrial	15,306.4	11,892.7	62.3	60.6	59.7
4. Total All Groups	24,568.9	19,624.9	100.0	100.0	100.0

Western Division

Customer Group/SIC (A)	Sales 1992 (L)	1991 (M)	Percent 1992 (N)	1991 (O)	1990 (P)
1. 100–290 Retail	6,559.3	5,248.6	22.4	13.6	10.3
2. 300–390 Wholesale	9,721.8	9,609.6	33.2	24.9	20.5
3. 400–690 Industrial	13,001.4	23,734.6	44.4	61.5	69.2
4. Total All Groups	29,282.5	38,592.8	100.0	100.0	100.0

Total United States

Customer Group/SIC (A)	Sales 1992 (Q)	1991 (R)	Percent 1992 (S)	1991 (T)	1990 (U)
1. 100–290 Retail	12,320.4	10,185.7	14.8	12.5	11.5
2. 300–390 Wholesale	23,558.7	20,911.8	28.3	25.7	22.9
3. 400–690 Industrial	47,366.8	50,237.3	56.9	61.8	65.6
4. Total All Groups	83,245.9	81,334.8	100.0	100.0	100.0

Macro Report Interpretation

Exhibit 16–4 demonstrates the type of data that can be used for a macro report. For purposes of discussion, only the firm's year-to-date data for sales are shown. The complete report would also normally include "current-month-only" sales as well as all related gross profit information.

The customer groups are indicated in column A. The classification codes in this column are those developed by the company for its own internal purposes. These customer, or channel member groups, could also easily be categorized by SIC codes. This would allow the added advantage of collecting data on individual firms that could then be meshed with secondary industry-wide data produced by governments and industry associations.

To compile a macro report, a manager would begin with the firm's "Total United States" sales figures, then use the information in columns Q and R (the current and prior-year dollar sales) to gain perspective regarding the size of the contributions made by the various channel groups.

The data in columns S, T, and U are analogous to "market share" figures that represent the percentage of the company's total sales that move through a given customer group. Thus, the 1992 total company sales (column Q, row 4) are $83,245.9 million. The proportion of total sales volume that moves through the industrial channel members is in column Q, row 3 ($47,366.8 million). A ratio of the sales volume of the industrial customer group to that of the firm's total sales yields 56.9 percent (column S, row 3). This represents the percentage of total company sales in 1992 that are accounted for by members of the industrial channel. Column T, row 3, showing the 1991 percentage of company sales that moved through the industrial channel members, is determined in a similar fashion. The 1990 sales percentages (column U) are gathered from the prior-year report. The same analysis is applied to the firm's eastern, central, and western divisions in exactly the same fashion.

To interpret the data, the manager first scans the firm's total sales information. If no major sales changes are evident, the analysis is terminated. Note, however, that in this case study the industrial group of customers' sales has slipped from $50,237.3 million in 1991 (column R, row 3) to $47,366.8 million in 1992 (column Q, row 3). Further, the percentage of total sales generated by the industrial channel members indicates a declining (albeit *short*) trend—from 65.6 percent in 1990 to 61.8 percent in 1991, finally slipping to 56.9 percent in 1992 (row 3, columns U, T, and S, respectively).

In the case study, this information motivated further analysis. A brief review of the three divisions' industrial customer groups quickly isolated the problem in the western division. Although the percentage of sales accounted for by the industrial customer groups in the eastern and central regions continued to climb, that for the western division declined markedly.

The next step in the analysis automatically led to another macro report. This time "Total Product Sales by Branch by Customer Group" for each of the branches in the western division became the subject of interest. Although this report is not shown, management discovered to its dismay that serious decreases in sales revenues were evident in three of the six western division branches. The sales problems were again concentrated among the industrial customer group.

Once interpretation of the macro report determined where the problem was located and what general customer groups had been affected, micro report identification was needed to focus on what products and customers were causing the sales problem.

Micro Report Interpretation

Micro reports and analysis were used to pinpoint the origin of the sales problem in the case study. The three western division branches showing marked sales declines were San Francisco, Los Angeles, and San Diego. Since the macro report led the managers to suspect the industrial customers classification group, a micro report, "Branch Sales by Customer," was prepared on the individual customers in this group for each of the three branches.

The individual industrial customer total purchases from each of the three branches appeared to be normal until data on a number of chemical processing buyers were encountered. Only three or four of these customers dealt with each branch, but they accounted for a large total sales volume. Another micro report detailing the individual product item purchases by each of these customers revealed a marked decrease in their purchases of pipe seals and packing.

Once the individual customers and product items had been identified, further investigation quickly revealed that cheaper Japanese substitute seals and packing products were achieving substantial market penetration among the chemical processing customers. Management discovered that although the firm's customers continued to purchase (in order to qualify for the company's technical expertise), they were also buying heavily from the Japanese because of price advantages. Once the nature of the sales decline problem was understood, the firm moved to a system of surcharges for the technical expertise if the customer did not purchase a required minimum level of inventory from their branches.

A final micro and macro report analysis was conducted when the problem and its cause were discovered. All related products, customer groups, and branch territories were examined to determine if the new Japanese competitors had managed to make further inroads into the company's markets. Fortunately they had not, and the company's new policy of charging customers for its technical expertise when volume purchases were not forthcoming served as a very effective defense against further market penetration by the Japanese.

Exhibit 16–5 provides a flow diagram of the interpretative path from the macro through to the micro reports analysis used in our case illustration. Once the data collection hardware and software are in place it can be seen from the exhibit how quickly management can move through the analytical process and how easily data can be aggregated upward for a sales overview or disaggregated downward to focus on specific sources of problems.

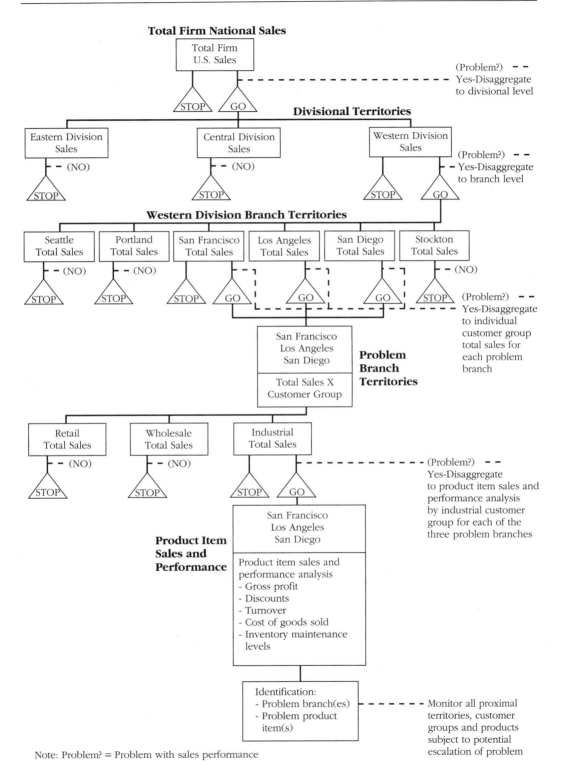

Note: Problem? = Problem with sales performance

SUMMARY

The marketing decision support system is designed to provide a broadly based internal source of information that can be used to address a majority of the marketing problems and opportunities that confront the business marketer. Although a full-range internal information system may require considerable work to establish, it has definite advantages over piecemeal reporting structures that can leave large information gaps in the firm's decision-making input requirements.

Decision support systems, however, must be designed with the user in mind. Data output must be made available to all employees whose decisions can affect the customer. This characteristic is the system integration requirement. The ability to aggregate data in order to examine the big picture and to disaggregate data so that problems can be traced to their source is the second characteristic of the decision support system. The third requirement of a good system is that it be efficient to use. Analytical efficiency is important because the system must be fast and easy to apply or employees simply won't use it.

Data input requirements and report output provide the structure of the decision support system. The data input must be arranged in levels, or tiers, beginning with the individual customer and product item purchases. These data can then be progressively compiled (aggregated) upward through the various data levels until total company sales for all products are reached. This procedure allows for the production of micro-level reports about individual customer product purchases and macro-level reports that describe customer groups, product groups, branches, and company division performances. The micro and macro reports have different applications in the organization. Although each of these reports provides different information to the manager, their real value is realized when they are used in conjunction with each other.

The use of decision support systems is expected to grow dramatically because of the increasing complexity of competing in global markets with larger product mixes and more diverse groups of customers.

Key Terms and Concepts

marketing decision support system
system integration
aggregate data
disaggregate data

analytical efficiency
macro reports
micro reports
damage control

Discussion Questions

1. What are the three characteristics of a marketing decision support system? Which of these do you consider the most important? Why?

2. How can accounting, engineering, and production decisions affect the marketing department of an organization? Give examples.

3. Which is more important, the ability to aggregate data or the ability to disaggregate data? Explain.

4. Why would a sales manager be interested in the macro reports "Sales Representative or Territory Sales by Customer Group" and "Sales Representative or Territory by Total Product Sales"?

5. How could a manager use the micro reports "Branch Sales and Gross Profits by Product Item" and "Customer Group Sales and Gross Profits by Product Item"?

6. Given all of the macro and micro reports in

Exhibit 16–3, which do you think would be most useful to a *small* business marketer? Justify your answer.

7. Assume the "early warning" characteristic in one of your macro reports indicated that a competitor was attempting to penetrate the market held by two of your fifty coast-to-coast branches. What steps would you take to isolate and identify the nature of the problem?

8. Why would a manager want to aggregate data upward from the individual customer or product item level?

Endnotes and References

1. Lindsay Meredith, "Developing and Using a Data Base Marketing System," *Industrial Marketing Management* 18 (November 1989): 245–257.

2. Linda M. Applegate, James I. Cash, Jr., and D. Quinn Mills, "Information Technology and Tomorrow's Manager," *Harvard Business Review* (November–December 1988): 132, describe the current and anticipated advances in computer data processing. These improvements in processing speed and data capacity will make large database analysis much easier in the near future.

3. Donald W. Jackson, Jr., Lonnie L. Ostrom, and Kenneth R. Evans, "Measures Used to Evaluate Industrial Marketing Activities," *Industrial Marketing Management* 11 (October 1982): 269–274.

4. See William G. Ouchi, "Theory Z" in A. Parasuraman, *Marketing Research* (Reading, Mass.: Addison-Wesley, 1986) for a somewhat different description of the input and output elements that comprise a marketing decision support system.

5. William H. Newman, James P. Logan, and W. Harvey Hegart, *Strategy* (Cincinnati, Ohio: South-Western Publishing, 1989), Chapter 23, suggest that the choice of variables that management decides to monitor should be influenced by considering those that are most likely to change and influence the firm's position in its industry standing.

6. Jackson, Ostrom, and Evans, "Measures Used to Evaluate Industrial Marketing Activities," pp. 269–274.

7. Philip Kotler, William T. Gregor, and William Rogers III, "SMR Class Reprint: The Marketing Audit Comes of Age," *Sloan Management Review* 20 (Winter 1989): 49–62, suggest that internal evaluation of the firm be conducted through marketing audits that review company marketing objectives, organization, and implementation. The marketing decision support system would clearly play a useful role in conducting such audits.

8. See Robert R. Reeder, Edward G. Brierty, and Betty H. Reeder, *Industrial Marketing*, 2nd ed. (Englewood Cliffs, N.J.: Prentice-Hall, 1991), p. 430, for a discussion of "management by exception." This technique relies on the practice of management by focusing only on information that suggests unusually good or bad performance.

9. Lindsay Meredith, "Developing and Using a Customer Profile Data Bank," *Industrial Marketing Management* 14 (November 1985): 255–268.

17

BUSINESS MARKETING STRATEGY, PLANNING, AND IMPLEMENTATION

- To understand the factors involved in designing a marketing strategy
- To learn the six general strategic orientations useful in developing a particular strategy for the firm
- To be able to describe the procedure by which a marketing strategy is developed and explain the problems associated with the various stages of the marketing plan construction
- To become familiar with strategy centers and contingency planning

The subtitle of this chapter could be "Managing the Proactive, Not the Reactive, Firm." The essence of a proactive marketing strategy lies in planning the future operations of the firm in an attempt to anticipate market developments and position the firm and its products so as to capitalize on the evolving marketing environment; hence, strategy, planning, and implementation are crucial steps. Reactive firms, in contrast, do not tend to exhibit forward planning and strategic positioning activities. Rather, they simply react to their current marketing environment as conditions require. The problem with such reactive management styles is that they inevitably lead to "crisis management" situations in which the organization becomes trapped in dealing with one marketing emergency after another. The first step in avoiding the problem of a reactive organization is to identify the factors that can affect the firm. These factors play an important role in correctly designing a strategy that will aid in creating proactive organizations.

FACTORS IN STRATEGY DESIGN

Marketing strategies can no longer be developed solely on management's "gut feeling" for the potential of the marketplace and on what the competitor down the street is doing. If this statement sounds like an exaggeration, think about the marketing myopia of America's big three car manufacturers as they fiercely competed with each other and left the market wide open for the Japanese and other small car producers.

How does a manager analyze the myriad factors that can have a dramatic impact on the firm and the market? Exhibit 17–1 provides a checklist of general factors that should be part of any marketing strategy. Some of these factors will be irrelevant in some marketing environments, but in others they may be crucial.

Macroenvironment of the Firm

The firm's **macroenvironment** is composed of sociocultural, economic, political-legal, and technological factors. Each can dramatically affect a business market.

EXHIBIT 17–1   Factors in Strategy Design

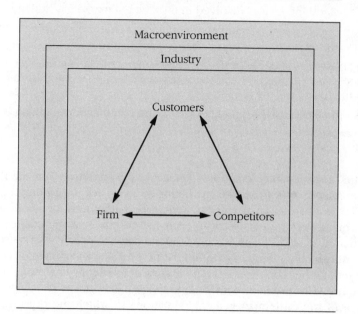

Sociocultural Factors.   Sociocultural variables include many of the factors that are typically analyzed in consumer marketing, such as consumer lifestyles, values, and attitudes. Shifts in sociocultural variables and in consumer tastes in general are of interest because the mechanism of derived demand can ultimately affect the demand for the business marketer's products and services.[1]

Economic Factors.   Commonly monitored economic factors include international exchange rates, domestic inflation rates, interest rates, and economic cycles. These factors can affect consumer demand as well as the business marketing organization's ability to compete both globally and domestically.

Political-Legal Factors.   Chief among the factors in this category are those related to changing international trade agreements and the development of trends that affect the business marketing competitive arena. Deregulation and government intervention through legislation regarding both consumer and environmental protection are expected to affect business marketing strategies throughout the coming decade.

Technological Factors.   Of all the environmental variables considered germane to strategy development, technology has perhaps attracted the most attention in recent years because it can cause profound market shifts at a very fast rate. The result is that some firms and industries quickly grow to international significance, whereas others disappear just as fast. RCA, once a vacuum tube manufacturer, was quickly displaced by Sony's transistor production at the beginning of the computer age.

Characteristics of the Industry

The next level of analysis concerns **industry attractiveness**. Both the good and the bad characteristics of an industry must be considered to realistically assess the firm's potential in a particular market. As with macroenvironmental factors there exists a broad range of variables useful to consider when evaluating an industry.

Market Size and Growth.   Size gives an idea of the total sales dollar value associated with a market, and growth gives an indication of industry sales potential in the future. Markets must be a minimum adequate size to generate a sufficient return on sales. They should also exhibit some potential to grow if the vendor is to increase sales without having to continuously fight competitors over market share.

Vulnerability/Defensibility.   Vulnerability and defensibility refer to an industry's insulation from or exposure to external threats. These threats could take the form of encroachments from indirect substitutes manufactured in other industries or from foreign competitors producing direct substitutes. Also worthy of consideration are the potentially negative effects caused by government regulation or changing consumer tastes.

Stability/Volatility.   Stability and volatility involve a dynamic assessment of the industry over time. The data of interest include industry-wide sales dollars, unit volume sales, profit-based measures (such as return on investment), and the entry and exit of competitors.[2] Analysis of these data can identify problems like cyclical patterns and seasonality in sales and profits. Stable industries are generally preferred by vendors because volatile fluctuations around the industry's medium- to long-term growth trend clearly indicate the need for increased emphasis on careful planning and the formulation of strategies.

Primacy/Dependency.   **Primacy** and **dependency** describe the balance of power between (1) the vendor industry and its customers and (2) the vendor's suppliers and the vendor industry. The term *primacy* implies a position of dominance for vendors in the bargaining relationship, whereas *dependency* means that members of the vendor industry are vulnerable to the demands of their customers and/or suppliers. When members of a highly concentrated industry (oligopoly) deal with firms in a very competitive industry, the primacy lies with the oligopolists because they have a much larger choice of firms with whom to bargain. Industries that produce output that is dependent on the sales of complementary products made by others may find that their demand is dependent on the decisions and successes of firms in other industries. For example, defense avionics producers are dependent on manufacturers of military aircraft.

Diversification Potential.   The **diversification potential** is the ease or difficulty with which firms can alter or add to their product line to penetrate other markets. The greater the diversification potential of an industry, the easier it is to reduce risk because the marketer is able to spread the organization's output over a number of different (and preferably independent) markets. If one of its markets should collapse, the firm may still be able to survive on the basis of its other ventures. Companies like Dow are well diversified in the chemicals industry.

Research and Development Requirements.   R&D requirements are increasing in importance as a prerequisite for survival in a significant number of industries. Technological innovation can offer tremendous marketing advantages but, at the same time, can create a high-risk environment. Specifically, sudden shifts in the direction of innovations can leave research-oriented firms with an unrecoverable investment in their R&D activities if they are unfortunate enough to pursue the wrong line of research. Consider the problems encountered by the producers of computer tapes and tape drives when the technology began shifting to disk drives for data storage and retrieval.

Customers and Competitors

The center of Exhibit 17–1 shows three participants, all of whose actions must be carefully considered in strategy formulation. The double arrows connecting these three players in the marketplace indicate not only that each of the participants can affect the others but also that each can in turn be affected by the others. The reason is that other organizations in the marketing environment can initiate strategic choices of their own as well as respond to the decisions implemented by the business marketer's firm. The implication for the marketer is that in assessing customers and competitors it is also important to evaluate the ability of these groups to respond to the vendor's actions.

Customers.   One useful way to evaluate customers is to define those buyer characteristics that are of value to the vending firm and then evaluate customers on those characteristics. Alternatively, customers can be grouped according to the firm's segmentation criteria, and the analysis can be conducted on a segment-by-segment basis. Because not all of a customer's (or segment's) attributes will be of equal importance, the marketing manager and sales manager should develop a weighted ranking scheme that assigns a numerical value to the purchaser's characteristics.

Exhibit 17–2 provides an example of a customer or segment evaluation system. Column A shows the weighted values that the vendor has assigned to each of the customer attributes. (The weighting system may change from time to time to reflect the vendor company's changing priorities and objectives.) Column B indi-

EXHIBIT 17–2 Customer Performance Evaluation

Customer Attributes	Attribute Importance Weighting Value (A)	Customer (or Segment) Performance Eval. Score (5 = excellent; 1 = poor) (B)	Weighted Score (C)	Maximum Attainable Score (D)	Percent of Achieved Maximum Performance (E)
Sales dollar volume	9	5	45	45	
Gross profits	4	2	8	20	
High margin purchases	3	1	3	15	
Cross-selling potential	7	4	28	35	
Low turnover purchases[a]	2	4	8	10	
Low service demands	2	3	6	10	
Low damaged stock claims	2	2	4	10	
Product modification ability[b]	5	5	25	25	
Technology strength	5	4	20	25	
Purchasing Profile			**147**	**195**	**75.4%**
Market share in trading area	9	4	36	45	
Market share growth	6	3	18	30	
Sales growth	5	2	10	25	
Diversification potential[c]	5	4	20	25	
Market Position			**84**	**125**	**67.2%**
Net worth	4	5	20	20	
Credit position	6	5	30	30	
Management ability	5	4	20	25	
Customer Stability			**70**	**75**	**93.3%**
Alternative supply sources	8	1	8	40	
High switching costs	5	1	5	25	
Cooperative advertising potential	2	2	4	10	
Customer loyalty	6	1	6	30	
Dependency/ Primacy Status			**23**	**105**	**21.9%**
Customer's Total Values	**100**		**324**	**500**	**64.8%**

[a]*Low turnover purchases* means the manager is interested in whether or not the customer purchases some of his/her company's slower-moving product lines.
[b]*Product modification ability* evaluates the customer's ability to further process or alter the vendor's products. These purchases are especially attractive to vendors whose production systems yield a range of different product qualities.
[c]*Diversification potential* assesses the customer's ability to develop by moving into new markets.

cates the actual ranking applied to each of a particular customer's attributes. These customer evaluation scores fall between 1 (poor performance on the attribute) and 5 (excellent performance). Multiplying the attribute weighting value (column A) by the customer's evaluation score (column B) produces the customer's weighted score on each particular attribute (column C). Column D shows the maximum attainable score the customer could receive on each weighted attribute. Finally, column E gives the customer's percentage achievement on the four major categories of evaluation chosen by the vendor. In this example, the customer attained 75.4 percent on the attributes comprising the purchasing profile, 67.2 percent on market position, 93.3 percent on stability, and 21.9 percent on dependency/primacy status. The total score of 64.8 percent represents the customer's overall evaluation.

The customer performance evaluation makes it easy for the vendor to spot potential problems. In this case the attributes that make up the dependency/primacy status variable scored very low (21.9 percent). The evaluation in this case is a warning to the manager that although he or she is dealing with a reasonably attractive customer (total score of 64.8 percent), either the buyer has little commitment to suppliers in general or the vendor has failed to establish a solid trading relationship.

Depending on the vendor company's sales base, the performance evaluation system may be too time-consuming for widespread application. In this case the evaluation can be conducted on a segment basis or applied only to major customers. The customer performance evaluation system is also value-judgment based. Its weaknesses lie in the potential for selecting irrelevant customer attributes, incorrectly assessing the importance of those attributes that are chosen, and failing to produce a realistic customer evaluation score on each attribute.

Competitors.   It is imperative for the firm to decide what kinds of customers and segments it wants, but it is equally important to determine whether the customers want the firm. Consequently, the analysis now must switch to the other side of the equation. Two key ingredients must go into deliberations regarding the strategy of attracting customers:

1. What vendor attributes do the customers think are important in making their decision to buy?
2. How does the vendor's product measure up against the offerings provided by competitors who also want to attract those customers?

These questions can be addressed by gathering information from customers and from carefully evaluating the competition. The answers to these questions will help the firm determine its comparative advantages and disadvantages relative to competitors. Customer interviews can determine the major attributes they use to evaluate suppliers, and customers as well as competitors can help establish the strengths and weaknesses of a firm and its products.

Exhibit 17–3 illustrates the evaluation technique by which the vendor's firm is compared to competitors and ranked by the attributes that customers consider to be important. The format and analysis are similar to that used in the customer performance evaluation except that the final two columns of Exhibit 17–2 have been eliminated.

Column A in Exhibit 17–3 shows the weighting values that customers place on their suppliers' attributes. Column B shows how they rank the vendor on each of the attributes. Columns C, E, and G provide the weighted scores achieved by the vendor's firm and those of two competitors.

The figures in these columns demonstrate the different marketing positions occupied by each of the three organizations. Note, for example, that competitor 1 appears to be using price competitiveness and delivery reliability, whereas the vendor's firm has adopted a wider marketing strategy based on product, delivery, and service quality, together with an emphasis on technological strength and the ability to produce custom specifications for purchasers. Exhibit 17–3 emphasizes the point that it is possible for the marketer to choose among a series of different strategies in order to position the firm in the marketplace.

The supplier performance evaluation can be used to reposition the vendor's firm to maximize those strengths the customer values and to minimize the firm's weaknesses as compared to its competitors. By understanding customers and competitors, the marketer can formulate the strategies necessary for survival.

The supplier performance evaluation can be misleading in two ways. First, the analyst must establish a wide definition of competitors. Setting too narrow a definition of who competes with the vendor's firm will cause potentially significant marketing threats to be ignored. The manufacturer of Next computers must not only consider the makers of other workstation systems when evaluating their competition, but also producers of powerful personal computers like IBM's. Second, the performance evaluation system provides a useful position summary of the firm and its competitors *at a point in time.* Only the naive manager would fail to continue monitoring competitors over time. When the vendor's firm undertakes changes in its marketing strategy, competitors will often respond with counter-strategies of their own. Thus, competitors' market positioning must be continually monitored because their marketing mix changes can adversely affect the vending firm's strategies.

STRATEGY SELECTION

The problem with strategy selection for the business marketer is that the choices of strategies and combinations of strategies for the firm are almost limitless. However, there are six major strategic orientations that all managers should be aware of: organization-based strategies, competitive-based strategies, environmental management strategies, contingency strategies, military-based strategies, and value-based strategies (see Exhibit 17–4).

EXHIBIT 17–3   Supplier Performance Evaluation

Supplier Attributes	Attribute Importance Weighting Value (total allocated points = 100) (A)	Supplier Performance					
		Vendor's Firm		Competitor 1		Competitor 2	
		Evaluation Score (5 = excellent; 1 = poor) (B)	Weighted Score (C) = (A)×(B)	Evaluation Score (5 = excellent; 1 = poor) (D)	Weighted Score (E) = (A)×(D)	Evaluation Score (5 = excellent; 1 = poor) (F)	Weighted Score (G) = (A)×(F)
Price competitive	6	1	6	5	30	1	6
Product quality	11	5	55	2	22	4	44
Product assortment	4	4	16	2	8	4	16
Service quality	7	5	35	3	21	5	35
Delivery reliability	8	5	40	4	32	5	40
Distribution coverage	3	3	9	3	9	1	3
Promotional expenditure level	5	3	15	1	5	5	25
Co-op advertising support	6	4	24	1	6	5	30
Marketing Mix Performance Variables			200		133		199

	Weight	Rating		Rating		Rating	
Market share	6	2	12	3	18	2	12
Market share growth	5	3	15	2	10	4	20
Financial strength	3	3	9	4	12	1	3
Technological strength	9	5	45	2	18	2	18
Customized production capability*	9	5	45	1	9	1	9
Relationship marketing orientation	12	3	36	1	12	5	60
Raw materials access	6	2	12	4	24	2	12
Supplier Profile			174		103		134
Supplier's Total Value	Σ100		374		236		333

Customized production capability refers to the supplier's ability to produce products that are specifically tailored to the customer's specifications.

EXHIBIT 17–4   Strategic Orientations

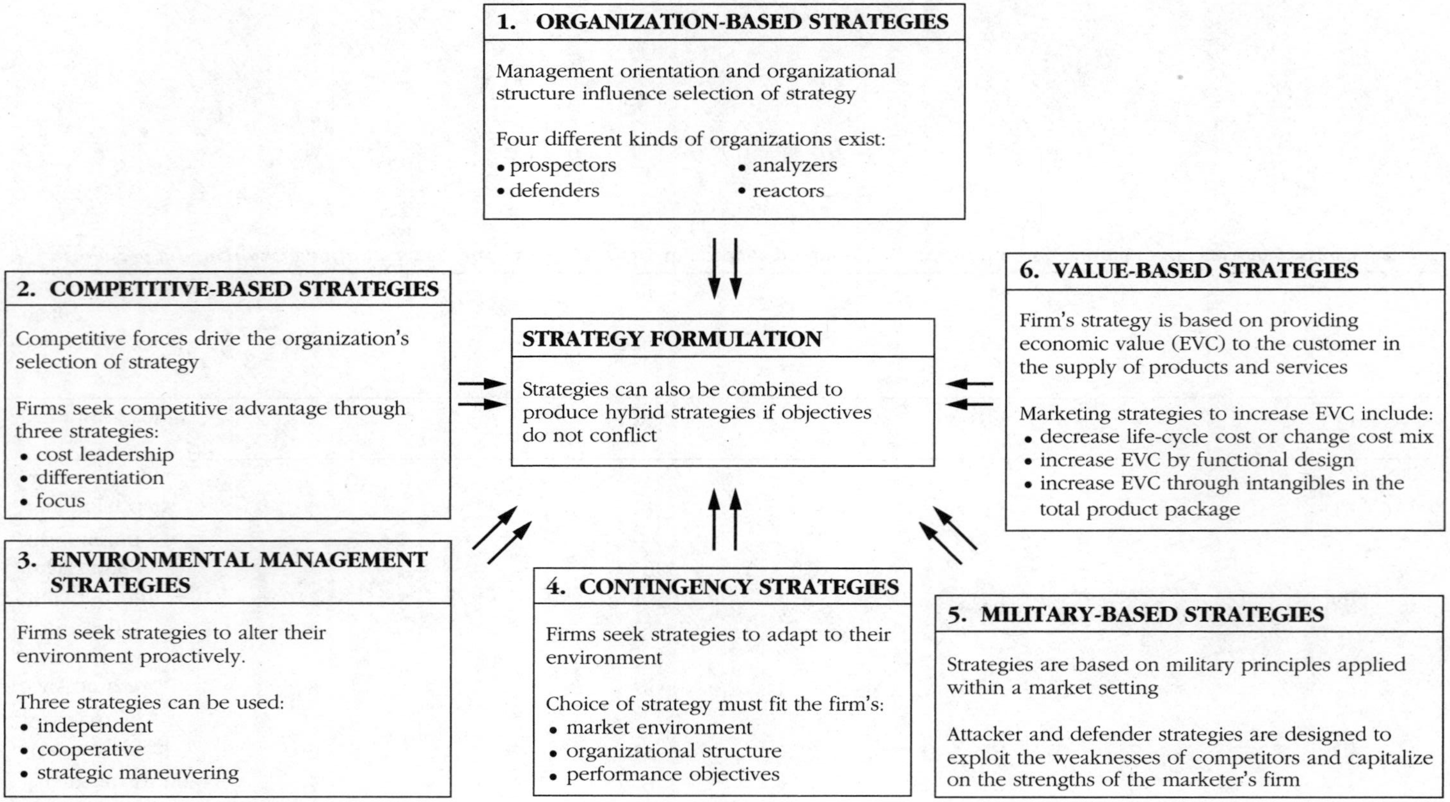

1.   ORGANIZATION-BASED STRATEGIES

Management orientation and organizational structure influence selection of strategy

Four different kinds of organizations exist:
- prospectors   • analyzers
- defenders   • reactors

2.   COMPETITIVE-BASED STRATEGIES

Competitive forces drive the organization's selection of strategy

Firms seek competitive advantage through three strategies:
- cost leadership
- differentiation
- focus

3.   ENVIRONMENTAL MANAGEMENT STRATEGIES

Firms seek strategies to alter their environment proactively.

Three strategies can be used:
- independent
- cooperative
- strategic maneuvering

STRATEGY FORMULATION

Strategies can also be combined to produce hybrid strategies if objectives do not conflict

4.   CONTINGENCY STRATEGIES

Firms seek strategies to adapt to their environment

Choice of strategy must fit the firm's:
- market environment
- organizational structure
- performance objectives

5.   MILITARY-BASED STRATEGIES

Strategies are based on military principles applied within a market setting

Attacker and defender strategies are designed to exploit the weaknesses of competitors and capitalize on the strengths of the marketer's firm

6.   VALUE-BASED STRATEGIES

Firm's strategy is based on providing economic value (EVC) to the customer in the supply of products and services

Marketing strategies to increase EVC include:
- decrease life-cycle cost or change cost mix
- increase EVC by functional design
- increase EVC through intangibles in the total product package

Organization-Based Strategies

The organization's structure, processes, and management predisposition help determine the firm's strategic intentions.[3] These factors combine to establish the business's propensity for adaptive behavior in the marketplace. Firms displaying an external, or market environment, orientation are probably more committed to product market change than their internally oriented counterparts. There are four kinds of organizations: prospectors, defenders, reactors, and analyzers.

Prospectors.   *Prospectors* have the most adaptive capability, and they devote resources to identifying new market opportunities. R&D expenditures and an emphasis on monitoring market change allow these organizations to adopt an aggressive product market position. Broadly defined markets and an innovative orientation are also components of the prospector attitudinal profile. Computer companies like Apple and Next fit this profile.

Defenders.   *Defenders* adopt a conservative strategic orientation with tightly defined market segments, minimal commitment to adaptive capabilities, and an emphasis on operational efficiency. Effective cost controls allow these organizations to compete on the basis of price. The desire for market stability and a limited resource commitment to innovation complete the defender profile. The American steel manufacturers during the 1970s fit this category.

Reactors.   *Reactors* are also low in adaptive capability, not so much because of overt strategic choice but because they lack the ability to monitor and evaluate market change. The source of this weakness is poor strategy formulation by management and an organizational culture oriented to the status quo. Southern U.S. coal mining firms fit this profile.

Analyzers.   *Analyzers* have a strategic orientation that encompasses aspects of both prospectors and defenders. Analyzers seek market niches that supply a stable source of demand and an opportunity to develop efficiencies, but they also monitor market activities in search of opportunities to develop new products. Defense industry firms like Lockheed are analyzers.

Competitive-Based Strategies

The drive for competitive advantage induces managers to search for strategies that will forestall such market threats as new entrants, substitute products, and aggressive direct competitors.[4] This leads to developing entry barriers, focusing on growth markets, and raising the buyer's switching costs, respectively. Three underlying strategies comprise the competitive-based approach:

1. *Cost leadership strategies* allow the organization a competitive advantage because operational efficiencies permit it to offer lower prices to its customers.

South Korean brake assembly manufacturers, for example, have taken market share away from some suppliers to the Japanese car industry through price competition.

2. *Differentiation strategies* refer to tactics of attracting customers through better product quality, superior design characteristics, and superior service.

3. *Focus (or niche) strategies* are used by the organization to attract a specifically defined segment. Companies using a focus strategy can also achieve their objectives by selectively applying cost leadership or differentiation techniques. Swedish suppliers of high-quality newsprint have taken market share away from Canadian firms in some markets of the British newspaper business using this strategy.

Environmental Management Strategies

Environmental management strategies are based on the idea that an organization should adopt a proactive approach in dealing with its environment.[5] The strategy is designed to *alter* the firm's environment so that it more closely fits the organization's structure and objectives. Three types of strategies can be used to change the firm's environment: independent strategies, cooperative strategies, and strategic maneuvering.

Independent Strategies.   Included here are a number of techniques. Competitive aggression is used in an attempt to drive competitors from the marketplace. Public relations and voluntary action are used to demonstrate good corporate citizenship and thereby diffuse criticism of the organization. Firms in the forest products industry, for example, widely advertise their reforestation and antipollution efforts. Weyerhaeuser has actively communicated its programs in responsible force management. Legal/political action is used to lobby government and, more recently, to file civil suits in an attempt to silence individuals who publicly criticize corporations. Vendors may also discourage undesirable types of customers (called **demarketing**)—for example, by refusing to grant credit.

Cooperative Strategies.   These strategies are designed to coopt (neutralize) the aggressive behavior of competitors or other participants in the marketing environment. Trade associations are sometimes used as a way to encourage friendly relationships between competitors and to lobby governments.

Strategic Maneuvering.   This strategy includes entering "environmentally friendly" markets and diversifying as a means of spreading risk. Tobacco manufacturers, for example, have expanded into real estate because of the controversy surrounding cigarette consumption.

Contingency Strategies

Contingency strategies are almost the opposite of environmental management strategies. Contingency theory stresses the importance of using strategies that help the organization *adapt* to its external environment as opposed to trying to *alter* the environment to fit the firm's needs.[6] Contingency strategy also suggests that management, in its strategy design, must seek *alignment* among four variables: organization type (prospector, defender, analyzer, or reactor); marketing tactics (market scanning, product development, pricing analysis, distribution intensity, advertising); the marketing environment (market volatility versus stability); and the organization's performance requirements (increased market share versus return on investment).

The key issue underlying a contingency-oriented approach is that the manager has to match the choice of strategy to the firm's marketing environment, organizational structure, and performance objectives or face the very real possibility that the strategy will never be effectively implemented. Consider, for example, what would happen if a reactor-oriented firm interested in short-term profits tried to compete in the very volatile and innovative market environment of computer chip manufacturing in California's Silicon Valley. Results would likely be disastrous because reactors are poor at anticipating and reacting to technological change. Further, highly innovative markets require long-term commitments to R&D, and this fact is not consistent with a short-term profit approach.

Military-Based Strategies

Military-based strategies help the manager allocate limited corporate resources in order to maximize their effectiveness.[7] Resource allocation is made within a competitive setting—either for purposes of launching an effective attack against competitors or to establish an effective defense against the attack of aggressive competitors.

Most attack strategies work on the principle of the aggressor concentrating resources on some aspect of the defender's market. The objective is to overwhelm the defender's resources and thereby acquire the defender's market. Flank attacks, for example, require that the aggressor develop specific strengths that can then be focused against the defender's weaknesses. Two effective flanking measures are *geographical attacks,* which concentrate on trading areas that are not effectively serviced by the defender, and *segmental flank attacks,* which are launched against market segments that the defender has failed to cover effectively. The European Airbus consortium, for example, concentrates on penetrating Boeing's medium-range, high-capacity aircraft market with its A310 model aircraft.

Guerrilla warfare uses a strategy whereby the attacker launches a series of small, diversified assaults on the defender's markets in an attempt to secure gains. The attacks are best launched against small, weakly defended markets that the defender may be less inclined to protect. The technique is often used by smaller firms against larger rivals with the key requirement that it costs the defender more to protect the market than to abdicate its control. Trust companies and insurance firms like Aetna have taken market share from some national and international banks by concentrating on commercial loans to a few very specialized industries that the large banks are not prepared to invest in servicing effectively.

Some defense strategies rely either on developing a broad range of resources with which to repel the attacker or on concentrating those resources in specific areas as a precaution against likely attack. Still other defensive strategies rely on counterattacking the aggressor or even the potential aggressor.

Mobile defense strategies, for example, rely on expanding the firm's marketing base and/or diversifying into new markets. The rationale is that the firm can develop a broader resource base that either will be used to help defend the product/market under attack or as a source for a counterattack against the aggressor. IBM now sells computer systems as opposed to its earlier concentration in mainframe computer manufacturing. This broader product and service base means that potential aggressors must now become experts not just in computer manufacturing but also in total system design and installation.

The *flank-position defense* is used when firms anticipate future challenges to their business or when they want to protect some vulnerable aspect of their market. This is a proactive defense strategy because preparations are laid prior to the onset of an aggressor's attack. The rationale is that attackers may be deterred from assaulting apparently defended markets, or, in the event that an attack is launched, the defender is "armed" and waiting. Now that the Canadian financial services market has recently been deregulated, for example, Canadian banks are preparing for attempts by life insurance companies to enter some of their markets.

Value-Based Strategies

Economic value to the customer (EVC) is the fundamental premise underlying value-based strategies.[8] EVC means that the marketer must first evaluate all of the customer's costs (purchase price, startup costs, and postpurchase costs) related to buying a product. Next, the selling price of the vendor's product is compared to that of a reference product offered by competitors. Finally, through comparison of the incremental value of both products, the marketer can establish a price that reflects the relative value of the product to the customer. The concept of incremental value means that the marketer is interested in the potential value of the product *to the customer,* as opposed to simply asking "How much did it cost us to make this product?"

The major strategy implications for pricing are, first, that the EVC may vary between customers and segments, and, second, that customers who associate a high relative incremental value with the marketer's product may in fact pay a higher price than that asked by competitors. How can the incremental value of a product be increased to its customers? There are three approaches.

1. *Decrease life-cycle costs or change the cost mix.* Some customer resistance to high initial purchase prices can be overcome by introducing product attributes that decrease the product's overall life-cycle costs. Others who want a low purchase price can be served by products that are cheaper but have higher long-term operating costs. Vendors can also design products to incorporate some of their customers' value-added component into the product purchase—that is, decrease the customer's labor or material costs through technology and automation.

2. *Increase incremental value through functional redesign.* This can be accomplished by designing changes to increase the customer's operating capacity, improving the customer's output quality, expanding the application flexibility of the vendor's product, and/or increasing the product's functions so it can be used in new situations.

3. *Increase incremental value through intangibles offered in the total product package.* Vendors can also differentiate and increase the EVC of their products by creating intangible attributes that customers value. Superior service, delivery schedules, technical advice, and financial assistance to aid customer purchases can be useful value-enhancing strategies.

Depending on the organization and its marketing environment, many aspects of the preceding strategies can be combined to produce **hybrid strategy designs**.[9] Management must take care, however, to ensure that the components of such hybrid strategies are internally consistent with each other; otherwise the marketing plan will be severely compromised.

THE MARKETING PLANNING PROCESS

Marketing plans provide the mechanism by which strategies are put into operation within the organization. As with many projects, it is often easier to conceptualize than to apply the concept successfully. The planning process plays an important role in marketing for this reason.

The **marketing planning process** can be divided into two stages. The first stage involves inputs to the marketing plan, and the second deals with actual development of the plan. Exhibit 17–5 shows how the input and plan development stages form a cohesive planning process.

Inputs to the Marketing Plan

The first stage of the planning process involves opportunity and threat analysis, the firm's market potential, marketing objectives, corporate and company constraints, and marketing strategies. These steps are shown as boxes 1 through 7 in Exhibit 17–5.

EXHIBIT 17–5   Business Marketing Planning Process

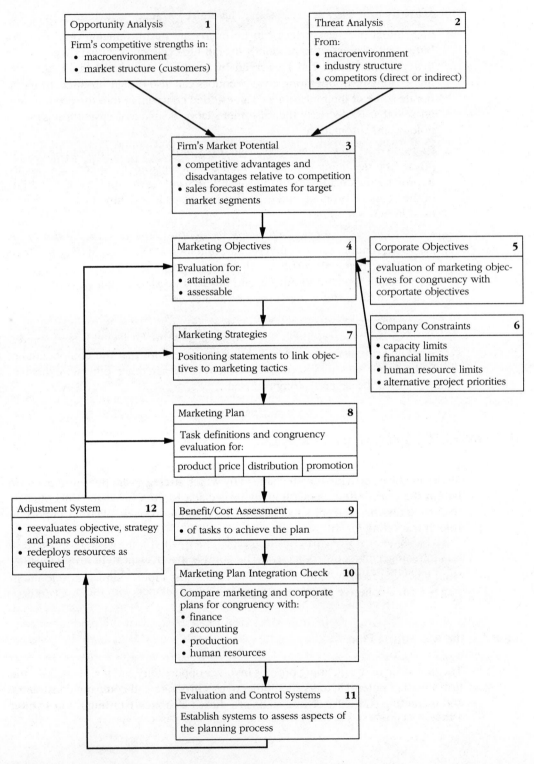

Opportunity and Threat Analysis.   The entire exercise of evaluating the macroenvironment, industry, customers, and competitors (Exhibit 17–1) is oriented toward providing the crucial information required to begin the planning process. Boxes 1 and 2 of Exhibit 17–5 are absolutely crucial to the planning process. An incomplete definition at this point will create errors that permeate the entire planning process. A complete description of the competition—especially the indirect competition—is especially important at this stage.

Firm's Market Potential.   The comparison of market opportunities and threats provides a key input to Box 3, where management seeks to identify its firm's advantages and disadvantages *relative to competitors.* Federal Express and UPS, for example, are well aware of each other's strengths and weaknesses. A common error at this point is to conclude that the firm is performing adequately, based solely on company personnel opinions. The problem is that customers may feel quite differently. A company that performs well but whose competitors perform *outstandingly* well may still be evaluated as mediocre by buyers. The second danger at this step is to overemphasize the firm's strengths and downplay its weaknesses, because the admission of inferior performance in many corporations carries with it the stigma of management inadequacy—and that can lead to disastrous consequences for the manager unfortunate enough to be identified as the weak link. Clearly, executive evaluation of strengths and weaknesses in the organization must be carried out in a nonthreatening manner if middle and lower management are to provide a balanced and realistic assessment of their operations. Marketing Objectives, Corporate Objectives, and Company Constraints. Boxes 4, 5, and 6 are dealt with collectively because marketing objectives cannot be developed in a vacuum. Marketers may develop objectives that, from their standpoint, are ideal. However, they may not be ideal from the corporate standpoint. In fact, corporate objectives may be severely compromised, as the story in the Business Marketing in Practice box on page 648 illustrates.

Note that Box 6 (Company Constraints) also includes the possibility of alternative project priorities. Related nonmarketing projects should also be considered because management must consider the entire range of alternative investments it can make to maximize profits. It is quite conceivable that alternatives such as modernizing production or restructuring company finances could offer a greater return than pursuing a marketing objective. The point is that management must consider *all* of its choices in setting marketing objectives.

The marketing objectives (Box 4) should be developed with the provisos that they be attainable and measurable. Attainable means that the firm is actually in a position to accomplish the objective. Measurable means that the objective is developed and stated in such a way that management can subsequently evaluate its actions in order to determine if the firm actually accomplished its goal.

Marketing Strategies.   The positioning statements that underlie the marketing strategy (Box 7) are important because they provide the link between the more widely stated marketing objectives and the specific tactics required to carry them

BUSINESS MARKETING IN PRACTICE

A Dream That Might Have Become a Nightmare

The executives of a U.S. multinational were approached by a paint manufacturer that wanted to deliver its product through the multinational's distribution system. It was a marketer's dream come true: the paint would be supplied on consignment (therefore, there would be no inventory carrying charges to the multinational). Further, this particular paint carried the highest markup and inventory turnover of any product on the market.

After careful consideration, the deal was rejected. What was wrong? Certainly not the marketing aspect of the offer. The product met the multinational's marketing objectives per-

fectly, and the product was virtually a foolproof moneymaker. The multinational's legal department, however, discovered some rather questionable behavior on behalf of the paint manufacturer's president with regard to stock manipulation.

Although the marketing objective of getting into the paint market was perfectly met by the offer, the corporate objectives of maintaining the multinational's substantial reputation and introducing a product into its mix that would not shortly be interrupted by legal proceedings and possible police action were considered to be more important—for obvious reasons.

out. Although marketing objectives are traditionally developed in the upper echelons of the organization, the specific tactics by which they are put into operation require the input of front-line managers. The positioning statements, then, specifically outline the strategies and tactics by which management intends to achieve its objectives. The executives of a medium-sized furniture wholesaler, for example, decided that they needed to decrease their reliance on the retail and interior design consultant segments of their market because of declining sales. They intended to accomplish this by setting an objective of attaining a 4 percent market share of the luxury furniture direct retail market in two of their five geographical trading areas (in other words, they proposed to enter the retail market themselves directly). Their positioning statement involved the tactics of penetrating the targeted markets by price discounting name brand high-line furniture products and communicating this information to upper-middle-class consumers.

A final check of the analysis and conclusions derived from the input steps should be conducted at this point in order to minimize the possibility that incorrect information will be transferred into the plan development stage.

Development of the Marketing Plan

The second and final stage of the planning process is actually developing the plan. The steps comprising development of the marketing plan are as shown in Boxes 8 through 12 in Exhibit 17–5. They include the marketing plan, benefit/cost assessment, marketing plan integration check, evaluation and control systems, and the adjustment system.

Marketing Plan.   The actual marketing plan (Box 8) is more specific than the objectives and strategies. Identification of the specific tasks required to pursue the strategies is very important at this stage because all members of the organization who will play a direct role in achieving the strategy need to outline exactly what functions they must fulfill. Further, when the specific tasks are identified, it then becomes possible to begin assessing the costs of the strategy.

Along with specific task definitions, management must cross-check for congruency all of the components that comprise the plan. Stated at the most basic level, the goals of the firm's prices, products, distribution, and promotion must not conflict with each other.

Bull emphasizes the benefits of good planning.

You've analyzed. You've agonized. You've listened to all the experts. And now that the future's here, where are

gets your current computers working together. We take what you have and make sure it works with what you need.

anyone could do it. But by solving tough problems for big companies and small companies and governments every-

IF EVERYONE WAS PLANNING FOR THE FUTURE, HOW DID THINGS GET SO MESSED UP?

you? Trying to cope with an unmanageable mishmash of computers. A system that has become more liability than asset. Are we overstating the problem? Not to the guy who's got to tell the boys upstairs exactly what went wrong and how much money he needs to fix it. But don't be rash. Before you do that, give us a call. We can develop a system that

Protecting your investment, eliminating waste, controlling costs. We don't have a crystal ball. But what we can promise you is an information system that builds in all the freedom and flexibility you need to be ready for the future. Whatever the future happens to be. Of course, we're not saying this is easy. If it were,

where, we've become one of the largest suppliers of information technology in the world. Call 1-800-233-BULL, ext. 2100. 1-800-268-4144 in Canada. After all, why have an information system that's confounded by the future. When you can just as easily have one that's completely at home there.

Worldwide Information Systems

Bull ♣

We solve the toughest problems in the world.

© 1991 Bull HN Information Systems Inc.

In the example of the furniture wholesaler described in the last section, one issue of concern in targeting the luxury furniture consumer was how upper-middle-income customers would respond to the idea of price discounting $10,000-$15,000 dining room suites by approximately 20 percent. Would they think the furniture was inferior because of the discount strategy? The distribution component also introduced congruency problems because name-brand luxury furniture manufacturers were likely to take a dim view of 20 percent retail discounts on their products. Further, the furniture wholesaler still supplied retailer and designer consultant accounts who would be directly affected by the wholesaler's discount strategy. Would these accounts drop the wholesaler as a supplier in retribution for this retail strategy?

The preceding example illustrates the detailed decision making that underlies a marketing plan. Each component has to be carefully defined and *all of the components must work together* if the plan is to succeed. Failure in just one of the marketing mix ingredients will very often result in a strategy that does not achieve the objective or—even worse—produces an outright marketing catastrophe. Thus, a major concern of the furniture wholesaler was what would happen if the firm failed to attract the luxury furniture consumer and simultaneously alienated its retail and designer accounts in the attempt to develop its own direct retail market. Fortunately for the marketing consultant in this case, the wholesaler was able to become a direct retailer and, because of other price discounting tactics employed, it also retained its retail and designer accounts.

Benefit/Cost Assessment.   As noted earlier, breaking down strategy and tactics into their underlying tasks allows management to assess the marketing costs required to attain the company's objectives. Assessment (Box 9) is needed so that (1) the costs of carrying out the strategy and plan can be compared to the value of their expected benefits, and (2) the cost/benefit ratios of various marketing strategies can be compared to each other. Using this portfolio approach, management can then select the strategy that appears to offer the largest expected benefits relative to its costs.

Marketing Plan Integration Check.   This step in the planning process (Box 10) provides a final check to ensure that the marketing plan can be successfully integrated with the planning systems used by other sectors of the corporation, such as finance and production. Just as there must be congruency between the marketing plan and overall corporate objectives, marketing strategies and plans must also mesh with those of all major departments within the corporation. Failure to establish congruency at the departmental level could result in either the marketing strategy being compromised or the plans of another department being compromised by the marketing group.

Evaluation and Control Systems and the Adjustment System.   These final stages in the planning process (Boxes 11 and 12) are designed to fulfill two functions. First, the evaluation and control system provides a way to measure the performance of the firm's plan. In the absence of a formal mechanism to assess whether the company is achieving its objectives, the chances of carrying out a successful strategy are greatly reduced. Second, the adjustment system is required to ensure that a structure exists for implementing changes to the strategy and plan if the evaluation system indicates substandard performance. The adjustment mechanism should, therefore, be capable of altering the company's strategies and plans if they are found to be inadequate. Additionally, however, adjustments may have to be made to the actual operating system through redeployment of the firm's resources. In this situation, the marketing plan may be considered sound, but resources may have to be redirected as changing market conditions dictate. In the fast-changing airline business, firms like American and United Airlines must be prepared to redeploy resources in response to competitive threats.

The planning process provides a formal structure by which management can implement strategies for change in an organized manner. Its value lies in helping the firm achieve a proactive and directed approach to developing the marketplace. In the absence of this process, the usual results are either a haphazard approach to planning or, worse, no planning at all.

STRATEGY IMPLEMENTATION

The most carefully developed marketing strategies and plans become a waste of time and energy if the organization is not strongly committed to careful implementation. The costs related to poor implementation of a marketing plan can easily extend beyond the damage associated with a strategy that fails to get off the ground. Poor implementation practices can compromise the firm's entire reputation, as the example in the Business Marketing in Practice box on page 652 shows.

Strategy Centers

A **strategy center** is a multifunctional management group established to oversee implementation of the firm's plans.[10] In this group are managers from marketing, sales, manufacturing, R&D, distribution, service, strategic business units affected by the plan, and corporate-level planners. The job of the strategy center team is to ensure that virtually every element in the corporate structure that is involved in the plan or will be affected by it has an opportunity to supply input during development of the marketing plan. The structure and membership of the strategy center depend on the complexity of the strategies under consideration.

There are at least three advantages to having a strategy center. First, all members of the organization are given an opportunity to bring their areas of expertise into the development of plans and strategies. This approach explicitly recognizes that many areas of the company outside of marketing can make a useful contribution to the development of sound marketing plans. Second, internal coordination of strategy implementation is improved because participation in development of the plan makes all of the parties aware of how interdependent they are. Finally,

BUSINESS MARKETING IN PRACTICE

Poor Implementation Practices Are Costly

A major battle between the head office marketing personnel and a senior field manager recently erupted during a private seminar for banking executives. The problem developed because head office marketing introduced a new financial service to target large corporate accounts. The product development process was very well executed and resulted in a new financial service that should have given the bank a substantial comparative advantage over its competitors. One difficulty, however, derailed the strategy. The senior field manager was on the verge of apoplexy because his commercial banking centers learned about the new product from their customers! The external implementation program carefully informed major corporate accounts of the new service.

The internal implementation program was a disaster because the bank failed to adequately inform its own account managers of the new product. What were the costs of this implementation fiasco? First, the new product failed to achieve the bank's strategic objective. Second, the credibility of the corporate account officers was badly damaged when customers had to inform them what products they were supposed to be selling. Third, the acrimony between the banking center field staff and head office marketing personnel reached an all-time high. Should this bank have done a better job of implementation? The corporate customers thought so, given that this particular financial institution typically controlled sales in excess of $400 million per year.

increased commitment by all members of the organization is obtained because their involvement in development of the plan produces a vested interest in making the plan a success.

Contingency Planning

Contingency planning is a technique of building alternative scenarios into the corporate plan so that if future market conditions differ from predictions, the plan can still be implemented. The approach works as follows.

The *most likely* scenario of future market conditions constitutes the core of the plan. Corporate plans and strategies are initially constructed on the basis of this scenario. Alternative scenarios, however, are spliced into the master plan at those points where management perceives the possible emergence of market conditions that may differ from those that they have predicted as most likely. These *less likely* alternative scenarios are characterized by having the distinct possibility of occurring. *Very unlikely* market occurrences do not enter into contingency planning, because the number of possible alternatives would be limitless. Alternative company strategies and plans are then developed and put in place to cover the eventualities of the less likely alternative scenarios. The result is a corporate plan that resembles a tree diagram containing a number of alternative strategies along with their own related plans for implementation. Should one of the alternative, less likely market scenarios emerge, management is in a position to react with its alternative strategy and a plan to handle that particular contingency.

Contingency planning is used so that even if the most likely scenario does not occur, management can continue operating under a set of plans and strategies that will offer guidance to the firm. This approach can be extremely useful in volatile and uncertain markets because it provides for flexibility in corporate objectives and, more importantly, helps to ensure that a strategy/planning mechanism exists to alter the marketing direction of the firm as conditions dictate.

SUMMARY

Designing a marketing strategy begins by first analyzing the macroenvironment and then progressively focusing on the firm's industry, customers, and competitors. These factors provide the inputs used to select the strategy best suited to the firm.

Strategy selection usually entails choosing one of the six most common strategic orientations: organization-based, competitive-based, environment management–based, contingency-based, military-based, and value-based approaches. Each firm must select the strategy best suited to its own situation, which could include hybrid strategies—that is, combinations of these six major approaches.

The marketing planning process is comprised of both the analysis of inputs to the marketing plan and the actual development of the marketing plan. It is through the planning process that a blueprint is created that will guide the firm in implementing its strategy.

Strategy implementation involves two concepts: strategy centers and contingency planning. These techniques increase the likelihood that a firm's strategy will be effectively implemented.

The major problem with strategies and plans reflects the same difficulty that pervades marketing in general: all of the strategy/planning components must function in harmony with each other in order to produce a successful outcome. In order to accomplish this, the single area that experience tells us is the most crucial is the correct identification of the factors that influence the strategy design. Doing this piece of analysis correctly and thoroughly makes the balance of the strategic planning process much easier and more reliable.

Key Terms and Concepts

macroenvironment	economic value to the customer (EVC)
industry attractiveness	hybrid strategy design
primacy and dependency	marketing planning process
diversification potential	strategy center
demarketing	contingency planning

Discussion Questions

1. How would your description of the silicon chip manufacturing industry differ from a profile for the flour manufacturing business? Use the industry profile variables discussed in this chapter.

2. How do sociocultural, political-legal, and technological determinants affect business marketers? Try to give examples of industries affected by each of these determinants.

3. All you have to do is beat your competition on price and you can corner the market. Agree? Disagree? Why?

4. Given the choice, which organization-based strategy would you prefer to adopt if you were in the pharmaceutical business: reactor, defender, analyzer, or prospector? Justify your choice.

5. Environmental strategies include the following options for the firm: competitive aggression, public relations, voluntary action, legal/political action, or demarketing. How could the business marketer operationalize each of these strategies?

6. How can you increase the economic value (EVC) of your product to the customer? When the EVC is not uniform across the firm's market segments, what are the implications for the business marketer?

7. How could departments outside of marketing help the sales manager serve customers better if they were included in a strategy center? Give three examples.

8. Devise a marketing plan for a product or service. Include two contingency plans to cover the possibility of alternative market scenarios.

Endnotes and References

1. Philip Kotler and Ronald E. Turner, *Marketing Management,* 6th ed. (Scarborough, Ontario: Prentice Hall Canada Inc., 1989).

2. A more detailed description of market volatility is provided in Daryl O. McKee, P. Rajan Varadarajan, and William M. Pride, "Strategic Adaptability and Firm Performance: A Market Contingent Perspective," *Journal of Marketing* 53 (July 1989): 21–35.

3. This section is based on material from Raymond E. Miles and Charles C. Snow, *Organizational Strategy, Structure and Process* (New York: McGraw-Hill Book Company, 1978).

4. This section is based on material from Michael E. Porter, *Competitive Strategy* (New York: The Free Press, 1980).

5. This section is based on material from Carl P. Zeithaml and Valerie A. Zeithaml, "Environment Management: Revising the Marketing Perspective," *Journal of Marketing* 48

(Spring 1984): 46–53. See also J. Pfeffer and G. Salancik, *The External Control of Organizations* (New York: Harper, 1978), for information on resource dependent strategies. Their strategic approach is basically environmental. Pfeffer and Salancik suggest, for example, that organizations can mitigate environmental constraints that limit management discretionary goals and objectives by avoiding highly competitive markets, using politically oriented strategies to soften the potential effect of government regulation, and striving for cooperative as opposed to antagonistic relationships with their competition.

6. McKee, Varadarajan, and Pride, "Strategic Adaptability and Firm Performance," pp. 21–35.

7. This section is based on material from Jack Trout and Al Reis, "Recycling Battles: Study the Classics to Avoid Checkmate in Business War," *Marketing Times* 25 (May–June 1978):

17–20. See also P. Kotler and R. Singh, "Marketing Warfare in the 1980s," *The Journal of Business Strategy* 1 (Winter 1981): 30–41.

8. This section is based on material from John L. Forbis and Nitin T. Mehta, "Value Based Strategies for Industrial Products," *Business Horizons* 24 (Summer 1981): 32–42.

9. Orville C. Walker, Jr., and Robert W. Ruekert, "Marketing's Role in the Implementation of Business Strategies: A Critical Review and Conceptual Framework," *Journal of Marketing* 51 (July 1987): 15–33.

10. Michael D. Hutt and Thomas W. Speh, "The Marketing Strategy Center: Diagnosing the Industrial Marketer's Interdisciplinary Role," *Journal of Marketing* 48 (Fall 1984): 53–61.

CASES IN
BUSINESS MARKETING

Case Planning Guide

Cases	1	2	3	4	5	6	7	8	9	10	11	12	13	14	15	16	17
1. Metropol Base-Fort Security Group	x																x
2. Morton International: From Salt to Airbags		x						x									
3. The Air Express Courier Industry		x							x								
4. Canadian Tillage and Harvesting Equipment Company Ltd. (A)					x												
5. Canadian Tillage and Harvesting Equipment Company Ltd. (B)			x		x												
6. Modern Purchasing (A)			x											x			
7. Modern Purchasing (B)			x	x	x												
8. Loctite: A Marriage of Technology and Marketing Skills				x		x											
9. Consolidated Glass International					x									x			
10. Falconbridge: The Corporate Image of a Mining Company					x									x			x
11. The Power Supplies Division						x											x
12. Honeywell: Builds on Synergy and Divsets a Division						x										x	x
13. Diebold: From Safes to ATMs to Software							x	x	x								
14. Avery Dennison: How to Do Marketing After a Big Merger							x	x	x								
15. Clifton Ceramics Ltd.							x										
16. Fiber Corp. Inc.									x								
17. Michigan Tanking										x			x				
18. Lee Steel Supply and Service										x	x						
19. General Controls and Electronics, Inc.											x						
20. Parker Instruments Ltd.												x			x		
21. Huntsman Chemical															x		x
22. Circuit Systems Group															x		x

Relevant Chapters

658

1. Metropol Base–Fort Security Group

Pat Haney, president of Metropol Base–Fort Security Group (Metropol), was sitting in his office contemplating the future direction of his company. Metropol, a leading Canadian security firm whose services included the provision of uniformed security guards, mobile security patrols, polygraph testing, insurance and criminal investigation, and a broad range of specialized services, faced a number of challenges that threatened its future profitability. "Increasing competition, especially from large multinationals such as Pinkertons, is further reducing already low industry margins," offered Haney. He was also concerned about Metropol's reliance on the commoditylike security guard business for 90 percent of its revenue. "We have to find some way to meaningfully differentiate our services from those of our competitors," Haney observed. "That is essential if we are to achieve the kind of growth we desire."

COMPANY BACKGROUND

Metropol was founded in 1952 by George Whitbread, a former RCMP (Royal Canadian Mounted Police) officer. In 1975, Whitbread sold the company to former Manitoba premier Duff Roblin. Haney came aboard in 1976 to run the Winnipeg operation, which was then 80 percent of Metropol's business. In the late 1970s and early 1980s, Metropol expanded into Saskatchewan and Alberta. In 1984, it took over the leading Alberta security firm, Base–Fort Security Group Inc. Haney believed this move offered economies of scale and helped to make Metropol a national company. Of Metropol's $30 million in 1985 revenues, 70 percent were in western Canada. Offices were maintained in all four western prov-inces as well as in the Northwest Territories, Quebec, and Newfoundland.

THE SECURITY INDUSTRY

Security products and services were purchased by individuals and businesses as a means of reducing the risk of loss or damage to their assets. The amount of security purchased depended on individuals' risk preferences, their perception of the degree of risk involved, and the value of the assets to be protected. Security therefore was very much an intangible product subject to individual evaluation.

The industry offered such services as unarmed, uniformed security guards, mobile patrols, investigations, consulting, and education, as well as hardware products such as alarms, fences, locks, safes, electronic surveillance devices (ESDs), and monitoring equipment. Most companies purchased a package combining various services and hardware systems. "It would not make much sense to have fifty television monitors and only one person watching them." Haney pointed out, "nor would it be wise to have fifty security guards roaming around a building that had no locks on the doors."

A number of factors contributed to the competitive nature of the security industry. All a firm needed to enter the business was to open an office. Start-up costs were minimal, and no accreditation was required by the company or its employees. Clients considered the cost of switching from one firm to another quite low, so the business often went to the lowest-cost provider. Most customers did not understand the difference in

This case was written by Stephen S. Tax under the supervision of Professor W. S. Good. Copyright © 1988 by the Case Development Program, Faculty of Management, University of Manitoba. Support for the development of the case was provided by the Canadian Studies Program, Secretary of State, Government of Canada.

services provided by the various competitors in the security business, which made differentiation very difficult. In studying the financial statements of the large multinational security firms, Haney found that most security companies earned pre-tax profit margins of about 4 percent on gross sales.

The 1985 security guard and private investigation markets in Canada were worth about $400 million retail. ESDs and other types of hardware added about another $400 million to this figure at retail prices.

Growth was expected to continue in the security field for a variety of reasons, including a general increase in the level of risk around the world, the rising cost of insurance, economic growth, technological innovation that created new security problems, and increasing sophistication among security system purchasers. The ESD and security guard segments were expected to outpace basic hardware sales growth (see Exhibit 1).

On the negative side was the industry's poor reputation regarding the quality and reliability of

EXHIBIT 1   Forecasted Market Growth for Security Guard and Private Investigation Services, Electronic Security Devices (ESDs), and Hardware Products in the United States, 1985–1995*

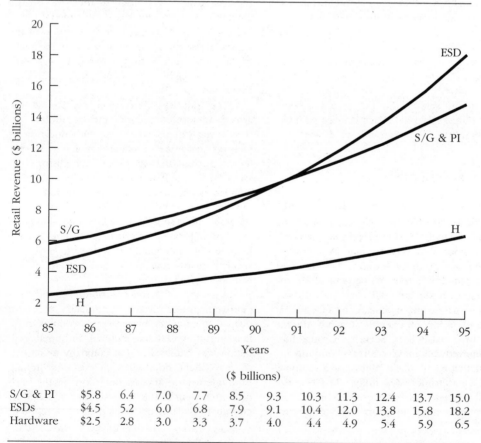

($ billions)

	85	86	87	88	89	90	91	92	93	94	95
S/G & PI	$5.8	6.4	7.0	7.7	8.5	9.3	10.3	11.3	12.4	13.7	15.0
ESDs	$4.5	5.2	6.0	6.8	7.9	9.1	10.4	12.0	13.8	15.8	18.2
Hardware	$2.5	2.8	3.0	3.3	3.7	4.0	4.4	4.9	5.4	5.9	6.5

*The Canadian growth rate for each type of service/product was expected to be similar to the U.S. pattern.

Source: Metropol Research.

its services. This perception threatened to limit growth and provide an opportunity for new competitors to enter the market.

COMPETITION

Metropol's competition came in both a direct and indirect form from a variety of competitors. "We compete with other firms that primarily offer security guard services as well as a number of companies that provide substitute products and services," observed Haney.

There were literally hundreds of security guard businesses in Canada, ranging from one or two ex–police officers operating out of a basement to large, multinational firms such as Pinkertons, Burns, and Wackenhut. Metropol was the third largest firm in the country, with a 7 percent market share (see Exhibit 2). It was the leading firm in western Canada, with a 25 percent share of that market.

Hardware products served as the foundation of a good security system. While items such as fencing, lighting, alarms, safes, and locks were to some extent complementary to the security guard business, they also competed with it: Firms could

substitute some proportion of either their security guard or hardware expenditures for the other.

Insurance had long been a favorite substitute for security and other loss prevention services. Business spent more on insurance than on all forms of security products combined. However, falling interest rates, a series of major disasters around the world, and a trend to more generous damage awards by the courts were making insurance a more expensive alternative. Faced with higher premiums, lower limits, and higher deductibles, businesses were likely to consider spending more on loss prevention products and services.

The various levels of government also provided some basic protection services to companies (fire, police, etc.). However, their services were geared more to personal than business protection. These government services tended to set the base level of risk in a community. Tight budgets were preventing these services from keeping pace with the growth in crime and the increase in the value of corporate assets. This provided the private security business with an opportunity to fill the void.

Businesses were spending almost as much for ESDs and related services as for security guard

EXHIBIT 2 Seven Largest Security Guard Companies Operating in Canada, Ranked by Market Share

Company Name	Canadian Revenue ($ millions)	Employees	Market Share
1 Pinkertons	$ 50	4,600	12.5%
2 Burns	30	4,500	7.5
3 Metropol Base–Fort	30	2,000	7.0
4 Wackenhut	12	2,000	3.0
5 Canadian Protection	12	1,700	3.0
6 Barnes	12	1,500	3.0
7 Phillips	10	1,200	2.5
Canadian total	$400	40,000*	100%

*In-house guards could raise this figure by as much as 100 percent. However, a better estimate would be 50 to 60 percent, as in-house accounts use more full-time staff. This means that there are more than 60,000 people working as guards or private investigators at any time. Further, with turnover at close to 100 percent annually, there are over 100,000 people working in this field over the course of a year.

Source: Metropol Research.

services. There were a number of different ESD products, ranging from small electronic gadgets to the very popular central station monitoring systems. ESDs were the fastest-growing segment of the security industry. The principal attribute of these products was that they provided accurate and reliable information to whoever was responsible for responding to a problem situation. Thus, to a large extent, these products were really productivity tools that enhanced the performance of security guards, the fire department, and/or the police force. They did tend to reduce the amount of security guard service needed. Some security-conscious firms with large-scale security needs hired their own internal (in-house) specialists. In most cases, they also hired guards from companies like Metropol to do the actual patroling.

The primary basis of competition in the security business was price. However, this was as much the fault of small, poorly managed firms and large multinationals trying to purchase market share as it was a fundamental characteristic of the industry. "I've seen companies bid under cost," observed Pat Haney, "and they did not necessarily know they were doing it. It is a very unprofessional business in that sense. If you offer superior service and give a customer what he wants, in most cases you don't have to offer the lowest price. Just recently the Air Canada Data Centre job went to the highest bidder. Lowering your price is very easy, but not the way to succeed in this business." However, since price was a key factor in getting jobs, cost control became crucial for making profits. Pretax margins of 4 to 8 percent quickly disappeared if unanticipated costs arose.

MARKET SEGMENTS

The market for security products and services could be segmented in a variety of ways, such as by type of service, type of business, geographic location, sensitivity to security needs, government versus private companies, and occasional versus continuous needs. Metropol segmented its customers and the rest of the market using a combination of the above bases, as outlined below and in Exhibit 3.

Large, Security-Conscious Organizations (Private and Public)

The common feature among these companies was their potential to incur heavy losses if security was breached. They typically had high-value assets, such as computers or other high-tech equipment, or valuable proprietary information, as in the case of research and development firms. These buyers were usually quite knowledgeable about security and rated quality over price. This group included firms in both local urban and remote, rural locations.

Organizations for Which Security Was a Low Priority

This group was dominated by local companies, commercial property management companies, and branches of firms that were headquartered elsewhere. They were less knowledgeable about security and tended to have limited security programs. They were price sensitive and principally utilized low-cost security guards.

Government Organizations

Government organizations (nonhospital) typically awarded contracts based on a tendered price for a predetermined period of time, usually one to two years. The price for these contracts was commonly in the vicinity of the minimum wage plus 5 percent.

Occasional Services

These included anything from sporting or entertainment events to social or emergency services. For example, they might include seasonal contracts, as with a CFL or NHL sports team, or one-time affairs. Wages paid to the security personnel were usually quite low, but profit margins to the firm were above average.

BUYER BEHAVIOR

The buyer of security services was commonly in the stronger position. This resulted from a multi-

EXHIBIT 3   Security Guard Service Market Segmentation by Gross Margin and Guard Wages

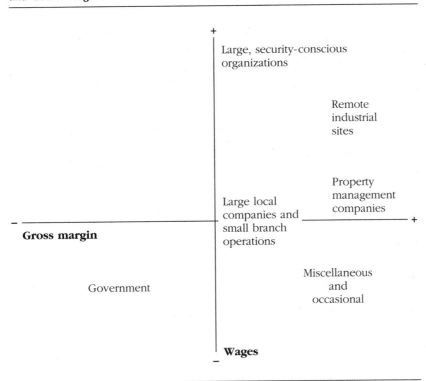

tude of firms offering what buyers perceived to be largely undifferentiated products and services and sellers trying to win business by providing the lowest price. Further, the cost of switching suppliers was low because of customers' perceived similarity of their services. It was also quite simple for firms to bring the security function in-house if they believed they could achieve substantial cost savings or other improvements in their security programs. In addition, some buyers tended to give security considerations a low priority in their budgeting.

Firms purchasing security products and services had three levels of decisions to make: (1) a general policy on the role and risk-cost framework that security would play in their firm, (2) a decision regarding the types of products and serv-

ices to be purchased, and (3) the selection of suppliers.

Each decision level involved new groups or individuals within the organization. Policy decisions were generally made at the senior executive level, while the product/service and supplier decisions tended to be made at the local level.

Most purchases were straight tender purchases based on a sealed bidding process. Firms for which security was a low priority and most government agencies tended to choose the lowest bidder. Companies that took a greater interest in the quality of their security programs considered attributes other than price when deciding on their security suppliers.

As part of a study on the security industry, Metropol surveyed buyers' ratings of the importance of several factors in choosing a security firm. It also had buyers rate Metropol's performance on those factors. Among the most significant decision-making criteria identified were consistency and reliability, availability of service representatives, and price. Metropol scored highest on the quality of its representatives and its customers' view of the firm's reputation (see Exhibits 4A and 4B).

METROPOL

Metropol organized its operations on a regional (provincial) basis. The Manitoba headquarters developed a centralized policy and operating guidelines procedure that was instituted in all offices. While sales representatives dealt with the day-to-day needs of customers, top management was involved in making sales presentations to large accounts.

Services

Despite Metropol's variety of services, supplying unarmed, uniformed security guards accounted for most of its revenue. Its sales revenue breakdown by service type was as follows:

Security guards	90%
Mobile security checks	8
Other (investigation, polygraph testing, retail services, consulting, and education)	2
	100%

Providing security guard services involved more than just sending guards to industrial or office sites. Metropol had to train, pay, uniform, and insure the guards. It also had to supervise and dispatch its people as well as provide reports to clients.

"We have attempted to provide greater value to our customers than our competitors have," stated Pat Haney. "For example, we have twenty-four-hour dispatch service, while all the other firms use an answering service. There is a $100,000 (annual) difference in cost, but we can respond much faster to any situation. Some customers will say they just consider price in their purchase decision but end up liking and buying the extra service."

EXHIBIT 4A   Customer Decision-Making Criteria—Survey Results

How important are the following attributes to you when making a decision on security services?

	Not Important			Very Important		Average
	1	*2*	*3*	*4*	*5*	*Score*
Consistency and reliability	—	—	—	3	14	4.824
Quality of service representatives	—	—	—	5	12	4.706
Price competitiveness	—	—	3	8	6	4.176
Company reputation	1	1	—	7	8	4.176
Emergency services	—	2	4	7	4	3.765
Full range of products and services	—	4	2	6	5	3.706
Consulting services	—	6	6	3	2	3.059
National coverage	4	4	6	2	—	2.375

Note: The survey was a convenience sample of Metropol customers.

Source: Metropol Research.

EXHIBIT 4B   Customer Decision-Making Criteria—Survey Results

How would you rate Metropol Security on the following attributes?

	Poor	Fair	Satisfactory	Good	Excellent	Average Score
	1	2	3	4	5	
Consistency and reliability	1	1	5	7	3	3.588
Quality of service representatives	—	2	—	11	4	4.000
Price competitiveness	—	1	4	10	2	3.765
Company reputation	—	—	2	10	5	4.176
Emergency services	1	1	6	7	3	3.556
Full range of products and services	1	2	7	6	1	3.235
Consulting services	—	4	5	5	2	2.944
National coverage	1	—	7	3	—	3.091

Note: The survey was a convenience sample of Metropol customers.

Source: Metropol Research.

Metropol also gave its guards special training on the procedures to follow in the event of such emergencies as bomb threats, hostage takings, and fire evacuations. Again, this was an attempt to differentiate its services from those of other security guard companies.

The mobile security business was contracted out to local firms. This market was not considered a growth area, and Metropol did not invest a great deal of resources in it.

Investigative and polygraph services were contracted out to a couple of ex-RCMP officers. Metropol had maintained these investigators on its staff at one time but found that demand for these services was not great enough to justify having the high-salaried people as full-time employees.

Education programs were another means Metropol used to create added value and increase switching costs for its customers. Haney explained, "We give seminars on such topics as 'The Protection of Proprietary Information' for our clients and even invite some companies we don't currently serve. We want our clients to realize that if they switch security firms they will be losing something of value."

Metropol did not sell hardware products such as fences, alarms, and locks. However, it could arrange the purchase of such equipment for its clients. It was presently considering working in conjunction with a systems engineer to enable the company to provide a total security package for its customers.

Costs

Metropol divided its costs into two groups: direct and administrative. A typical job had the following cost characteristics:

Direct costs	83–86%
Selling and administrative costs	8–9
Pretax profit margin	4–7

Given the above figures, cost control was a key success factor for Metropol and the security industry in general. Metropol's margins were, in fact, higher than the industry average of approximately 4 percent. "We use a job-costing process," volunteered Haney. "Every pay period (two weeks) we look at what we made on each job. We consider and analyze every expense item very closely to see if there was any deviation from what was budgeted."

Direct costs included wages, uniforms, bonding, transportation, and supervision. Metropol did a good job of keeping its costs as low or lower than its competitors, despite offering a higher level of service. Some of this was a result of economies of scale in purchasing such items as uniforms, achieved because of Metropol's comparatively large size. The company also did a superior job of collecting outstanding receivables within a two-week period.

Pricing

Prices were determined by identifying the direct costs associated with a job, allowing for a contribution to selling and administrative overhead and providing for a profit margin. Consideration was also given to any reason for pricing a bid either particularly high or low. "We once bid at very close to our direct cost for a job in a town where we had no competition to discourage other firms from entering that market," noted Haney. He also suggested that it was important to anticipate competitors' likely pricing strategy when bidding on a job as well as recognize that some projects had greater potential for cost overruns.

Promotion

Metropol individually identified the companies in each of its trading areas that were potential clients and concentrated its promotional efforts on that group. In Manitoba, this "club" amounted to about 500 firms.

Once these firms were identified, strategies were developed to either sell to those potential accounts that presently had no security service or become the logical alternative for those businesses using competitive services. "We want to put pressure on these incumbent firms to perform," explained Haney.

Metropol used, among other things, its educational seminars to stress to clients that it offered superior service. At times, firms using competing security companies were invited as a means of encouraging them to switch to Metropol.

Employees

Metropol employed almost 2,000 people, of whom 1,900 were security guards and 100 were selling, administrative, or management personnel.

Security guards came principally from three backgrounds: (1) young people (age 18 to 25) who could not find other work, (2) older people (50 to 65) looking for a second career, or (3) ex-military or police personnel who liked the quasi-military nature of the job.

Annual employee turnover in the security guard industry was very high, estimated to be in the vicinity of 100 percent. Metropol's turnover rate was in the same range. Reasons for the high level included a combination of low wages, generally boring work, and a lack of motivation or support from senior management.

"We have some employees who have been with the company for 15 years," Haney pointed out. "However, the wages we pay are based on our billing rate, which often allows for only minimum wages to be paid to our employees." Intense competition and clients who wanted to pay a bare minimum for security guard services forced companies to pay their guards the legal minimum wage. This caused high turnover rates, which evidently did not bother some clients. Other customers, concerned with employee turnover, specified a higher minimum wage rate, which the security company had to pay its guards. Haney liked this attitude because it allowed him to pay his people a higher wage and still be competitive.

Metropol's supervisors and customer service representatives (salespeople) did a good job servicing their accounts and handling any crises that arose. They helped maintain Metropol's reputation as a competent and reliable security company despite the generally poor reputation of the industry.

The Future

Pat Haney turned his attention to the future. He believed that the way business was conducted in the security guard industry would not significantly change in the near future. He did expect the business to become somewhat more professional, with guards trained in formal, standardized programs. The pressure on profit margins was expected to continue and perhaps even intensify as the larger, multinational firms fought for market share and smaller independents struggled for survival. Haney was thinking about how he could use

Metropol's present position and reputation in the security guard sector to expand into more profitable segments of the industry or improve the company's general standing within the guard sector. Some of the opportunities he was considering included

■ Geographic expansion
■ A focused strategy
■ Expanding the range of security products and services offered by the company
■ Diversification into service areas outside the security field
■ Serving the consumer home security market

Geographic Expansion. "To be a national company in Canada, you need a presence in southern Ontario," observed Haney. Even though many companies' security needs were handled at the local level, there was considerable potential for a national accounts program. To be involved in providing a national service, a company had to be active in the Toronto area, where most national companies' security decisions were made. In addition, the Ontario market offered substantial local business. Haney explained, "We handle Northern Telecom's security guard needs throughout western Canada, but not in Ontario. Northern Telecom has three times the business volume there that it does in all of the western provinces combined."

There were three ways Metropol could enter the Ontario market: by (1) purchasing a local security firm, (2) merging with another company, or (3) bidding on contracts in Ontario and opening up an office once a contract was obtained.

Haney believed that the merger method was the most appealing because it offered the potential for increased profits with virtually no additional cash investment. He had discussed the possibility with two firms that had head offices in Ontario and were also minor competitors in the Winnipeg, Edmonton, Calgary, and Vancouver markets. The western offices of the merged firm could be closed down and the business operated under the Metropol name. "The gross margin on their western contracts would go right to the bottom line," suggested Haney. "because all the current Metropol offices could meet their administrative needs and absorb any incremental expenses."

A restricting factor in this strategy was Metropol's limited product/service line. To provide a "complete" security package for any company on a national basis, it was necessary to offer the hardware and ESD packages in addition to the security guards.

A Focused Strategy. This alternative was really a continuation of Metropol's current strategy. Following this approach, Metropol's principal objective would be to become the fastest-growing security guard firm in western Canada, with the highest profit margin and return on equity, the lowest employee turnover, and the most satisfied customers in the business of providing contract, unarmed security personnel. This strategy required an increased emphasis on developing a formal marketing program and increasing the value added of Metropol's security guard and support services. Tighter control of costs and employee motivation would be critical success factors, as would be the need to carefully segment the market and identify the most profitable clients.

The strategy would be designed to match the distinct competencies and resources of Metropol with the needs of the marketplace. Pat Haney believed that while the strategy "sounded good," it would be very difficult to implement. "Even if you offer the highest-quality service, you might not get the job," he offered. "Too many contracts, particularly those involving the government sector and crown corporations, are based solely on price, and simply supplying a higher service level in the provision of security guards is not likely to change that."

Expansion of Security Products and Services. From the customer's point of view, there was an advantage to having one firm coordinate and provide the complete security coverage required by his or her business: The security system was more effective and efficient. If the customer had to contract with different firms for guards, fences, locks, lights, alarms, and ESDs, there was likely to be a lot of overlap and, in some cases, gaps in the overall system. Also, it was likely to be more expensive. Haney considered an investment in the production of hardware equipment much too costly given his firm's limited resources, but he was investigating the possibility of arranging a deal with a large, multinational distributor of security hardware and ESD products.

Haney explained, "We would like to have an exclusive relationship whereby they (large multinationals) would provide us, at wholesale, with all the hardware and ESD equipment we needed on a private-label basis (Metropol brand) and they would train our people. We could offer them our monitoring services and access to new markets." Metropol would package the system, which would include hardware, software, and people in whatever mix its clients needed. The products would be sold to the client or leased on a five-year arrangement.

The expanded product line strategy would deliver significant benefits to Metropol. Hardware and ESD equipment offered better margins than security guard services and, in some cases, were subject to becoming obsolete. This provided opportunities to sell upgraded systems. For example, television monitoring devices had already gone through several generations of change despite their relatively recent entry into the security product mix. Service contracts to maintain the equipment would provide another source of additional revenue. Finally, the need of these systems for close monitoring and servicing increased the dependence of the customer on Metropol. This higher dependence meant that switching costs for the customer were much higher than with security guard services. This would be especially true if the equipment were leased for a five-year period.

Diversification into Other Service Areas. This alternative would capitalize on Metropol's skills in hiring people for contract-type jobs and administering a payroll. Its current product line could be expanded to include one or all of the following additional services, which could be provided on a contractual basis: secretarial services, nursing care, janitorial services, or landscaping services. The commercial sector would continue to be its primary target market.

Several years ago, Metropol got into the commercial cleaning business, with poor results. "Businesses such as janitorial and landscaping services are beyond our particular expertise," revealed Haney. "However, we are looking at providing people and handling the payroll for temporary clerical or nursing services. In those cases, we would be taking our established skills to another market." Haney cited Drake International's experience as evidence that the strategy could work. That company went from providing temporary help to providing security guards.

The Consumer Market. Another alternative for Metropol would be to expand into the consumer market for security products and services. The major products of interest to residential customers were locks, supplementary lighting, fences, mobile home checks, house sitting, and alarm systems. This segment was growing more slowly than the business sector, but it still offered substantial opportunity.

Haney was currently exploring Metropol's opportunities as a franchisor of home alarm systems to the numerous small Canadian alarm system dealers. "We would become the Century 21 of the alarm business," Haney suggested.

The alarm business in Canada was made up of a large number of small, independent dealers and a few large multinationals. The "small guys" would buy their alarms from wholesalers in small lots, which precluded much discounting. They also had to contract out their alarm monitoring to their competition, the large multinationals, because they could not afford the central station monitoring equipment. In most cases, advertising and financing of installations for customers were too costly to be carried out on an extensive basis.

Haney thought a Metropol alarm franchise offered a number of important strategic advantages to independent alarm dealers: (1) By arranging with a large alarm manufacturer to produce a private-label Metropol brand alarm line, it could pass on volume discounts to its dealers; (2) franchises would have the Metropol name behind them; (3) co-op advertising would provide greater exposure; (4) an arrangement for consumer financing could be established; and (5) Metropol would set up a central monitoring system.

Consideration was also being given to making locksmiths subdealers of Metropol alarm systems. "Normally a customer must call a locksmith and an alarm specialist to secure his home," suggested Haney. "It would be more effective, especially from a selling perspective, if the locksmith could do both."

CONCLUSION

Pat Haney realized that the alternatives he was considering were not merely incremental changes in Metropol's strategy. In fact each option represented a distinct direction for the firm's future development. "We have to define our business mission more specifically," Haney thought. "Then we can choose and implement the strategy that best suits that mission."

QUESTIONS

1. What competitive advantages do market share leaders have in the security business?
2. What are the strategic strengths and weaknesses of Metropol?
3. Develop a generic corporate development model that a business might use in outlining its strategic alternatives.

2. Morton International: From Salt to Airbags

OVERVIEW AND OPERATING SEGMENTS

Morton International is a diversified company with three major operations that may be characterized as low-tech, medium-tech, and high-tech, respectively. These are (1) salt, (2) specialty chemicals, and (3) automotive inflatable restraint systems. The company was formed in 1989 as a result of the tax-free split-up of Morton Thiokol. The other component of the original business, aerospace propulsion systems, was retained and is now operated as Thiokol. Morton employs about 9,500 persons and has sales of about $1.7 billion annually. The salt segment accounts for about 28 percent of sales and 36 percent of operating profits; the corresponding figures are 62 and 58 percent for specialty chemicals and 10 and 6 percent for inflatable restraint systems.

The salt is marketed for human consumption under the Morton and Windsor labels (with the picture of a little girl holding an umbrella and the slogan "When it rains it pours"). The salt is also sold for animal consumption. In less refined form, it is marketed for highway and residential ice control, for municipal, industrial, and residential water conditioning, and for use in food and chemical processing. The specialty chemical segment line includes the following categories: adhesives and coatings for varied industrial uses, including metals, plastics, and packaging; electronic chemicals for semiconductors and circuits; various polymers; industrial heat stabilizers and biocides; reducing agents for bleaching paper; and metalorganic chemicals. The inflatable restraint units are essentially airbags for automobile drivers and front-seat passengers. These will be required on

This case is based on a longer report developed at The Freedonia Group, Cleveland, Ohio, in 1991; project director for that report was Ramune Kubiliunas. This version was developed by Andrew C. Gross of Cleveland State University, based in part on the TFG report and updated information.

EXHIBIT 1   Morton International—Results of Operations

	1988	1989	1990
Overall (million $)			
Net sales	$1,248.3	$1,406.6	$1,638.7
Pretax profit	179.3	151.2	214.5
Net income	112.6	97.1	134.8
Sales by Segments (million $)			
Specialty chemicals	874.1	935.4	1,021.5
Salt	356.9	420.9	454.2
Inflatable restraints	17.3	50.3	163.0
Profits by Segments (million $)			
Specialty chemicals	148.9	144.4	139.5
Salt	55.8	68.0	85.6
Inflatable restraints	− 1.7	− 5.0	15.3
Regional Breakdown Sales			
United States	874.1	968.6	1,140.8
Canada and Bahamas	116.5	156.5	179.9
Europe	235.0	260.9	296.9
Rest of the world	22.7	20.6	21.1

Source: R. Kubiliunas, *Morton International Corporate Intelligence, Report #C32* (Cleveland: The Freedonia Group, 1991), pp. 5–7. Based on Morton International reports.

all vehicles sold in the United States by 1994, and Morton is in a leadership position to fulfill this demand.

While Morton International derives about two-thirds of its sales from the United States, the company is now active in Canada and the Bahamas and shows increasing sales in Europe, though not in the rest of the world. The results of operations by segment and geographic area for the past three years are shown in Exhibit 1.

CORPORATE STRATEGY

For many years, Morton (and before that Morton Thiokol) pursued an aggressive and growth-oriented approach to business. The company's investments have enhanced its position in various markets; of its twelve major product categories, Morton claims to have market leadership in ten. Future growth is likely to come primarily from

current product lines, and selective acquisitions are another possibility. Morton plans to achieve a growth rate higher than those of the markets it serves with (1) new technology, (2) intensive technical support and nontechnical service, (3) strategic acquisitions, and (4) joint ventures.

To show its commitment to developing and commercializing new technical ideas, Morton devotes 6 percent of its sales to research and development. Key areas emphasized are adhesives, coatings, electronic materials, and inflatable restraint systems. Morton makes it a point to use economic downturns as periods for new product introductions. Industrial customers have more time and interest in evaluating new products in a recessionary economy. Morton believes that while its policy may be costly, it pays dividends when business picks up. The company also uses technology to achieve forward integration. For example, Morton has long been a producer of a family of compounds known as liquid polysulfide polymers. In the 1980s and early 1990s, it began to use these chemicals to make sealants for insulating glass and for aerospace applications.

A second area of emphasis in corporate strategy is technical support and other kinds of service. Morton is dedicated to providing such functions as a means of building loyalty bonds with customers (and, of course, thereby maintaining and possibly increasing market share). In the inflatable restraint system segment, Morton customizes its design for specific customers and for different models of cars. Morton is also able to provide just-in-time delivery. In the salt segment, Morton maintains market leadership via a widespread distribution network. By locating its facilities near transportation routes and key clients, it is able to deliver at low cost.

Morton plans to make strategic acquisitions that will enhance its existing product lines and geographic presence with complementary technology, manufacturing, or location. The idea is to make "nondilutive, enhancing" acquisitions. A recent example in this regard is the purchase of the coatings and adhesives business of Whitaker. This brought in a coil-coating process and customers, which proved to be complementary to Morton's existing offerings and clients. The purchase included two research laboratories and thirteen manufacturing plants and made Morton one of the largest and most diverse suppliers of high-performance coatings in the United States. In 1989–1990, Morton bought Dr Renger GmbH of Germany, which makes and markets industrial coatings for plastics and other materials, and the polyurethane operations of Sandoz-Quinn, also of Germany. Recently, Morton also swapped its copperplating and inking operations for the semiconductor resistance business of MacDermid, Inc.

A fourth element in the corporate strategy is participation in selected joint ventures. Morton formed a joint venture with Chemetall of Germany in 1990 to develop aircraft sealants for commercial and military markets. The new company, called Aerospace Polymer Systems, will operate facilities in both the United States and Europe. The other partnership is with the Bendix Division of Allied-Signal. This venture, called Morton Bendix, will supply passenger-side airbags for auto-

mobile manufacturers from a Tennessee facility. Morton is contributing the gas generant technical know-how, and Allied is contributing sensor technology.

INFLATABLE RESTRAINT SYSTEMS

The smallest but fastest-growing division of Morton is Inflatable Restraint Systems, or Automotive Safety Products. This segment designs, makes, and sells airbags to auto manufacturers. A driver airbag module is installed in the steering wheel and contains an inflator, bag, cover, and container. The front passenger-side airbag module has the same components, but it is installed in the glove compartment. In the event of a head-on collision, the bags inflate instantaneously and prevent injuries to front-seat occupants. Though currently about four times as costly as automatic lap/shoulder belts (about $400 versus $100), they are proving more effective and have been mandated for installation in U.S. cars by 1994.

During 1985–1989, Morton sold about 350,000 inflators to Mercedes-Benz, which pioneered their use and touted their effectiveness. The other major German, Japanese, and U.S. carmakers have since espoused the idea, albeit reluctantly at first. Currently Chrysler offers airbags as standard equipment in all its cars; Ford does so for 50 percent and General Motors for 20 percent of its cars. Manufacturers using Morton modules include Mercedes-Benz, Chrysler, Ford, GM, Toyota, Nissan, Mazda, Audi, and Saab. Morton has practically all of Chrysler's business; its market share among other European, Japanese, and U.S. carmakers ranges from 40 to 80 percent. Morton benefited from a recall in late 1990 by Ford, GM, Honda, and Mazda, which initiated such action on those of their cars containing airbags made by TRW. The TRW airbags leaked, exposing crash victims to sodium azide, a catalyst used to inflate the bags. Since TRW is Morton's prime competitor in the United States, Morton benefited from the recall of TRW airbags.

Although this segment contributed only about 10 percent of sales and 6 percent of operating profits for Morton in 1990, the rapid growth in demand and the company's dominant market share represent a major marketing opportunity in the coming years. Morton airbags installed so far (as well as current shipments) outnumber those of all competitors combined. The Freedonia Group estimates that the total value of U.S. auto airbags shipped should rise from $400 million in 1989 to $2.3 billion by 1994. Morton's dominance should continue as the company offers specific designs and performance standards for its customers. Because cars vary in size and shape, a computerized simulation program is required for the proper configuration in each make and model. Morton developed such a program and coupled this design/manufacturing capability with just-in-time delivery to each of its major customers.

The use of restraint systems illustrates a marketing situation where government, manufacturers, and users are coming into a general accord. First came conventional seat and shoulder belts, but manufacturers were reluctant to stress safety and many people did not belt themselves in. Then the states started mandating buckle-up laws. Next came automatic lap and shoulder harnesses, which moved into place when car doors closed, leaving no choice for drivers. Now the U.S. National Highway Traffic Safety Administration mandates that all new cars be equipped with front-seat restraint systems by 1994. It is likely that by the end of the 1990s such restraint units will also be standard equipment on all light vehicles, including trucks and vans. Automakers would like to see universal diffusion of airbags as quickly as possible. This would create a sustained demand and pressure on the manufacturing capability of airbag suppliers. Recalls may pose some setbacks, but the momentum is there and many observers expect that installations will be widespread and in line with new-car shipments.

The driver and front-seat passenger airbags offer good protection against injuries from head-on crashes. Some carmakers that shied away from safety ads in the past now show how airbags saved lives on television and in print. However, the current airbags are ineffective in side crashes and rear-end collisions. Protection of occupants in such cases is a challenge and represents an opportunity for car designers as well as airbag man-

ufacturers. The technical and economic aspects of such installations are formidable and remain to be worked out via design and testing.

THE AFTERMARKET FOR AIRBAGS

While it may seem desirable to install airbags on older cars, this is not likely to occur. Costs would be high, retroactive regulations are highly unpopular, and manufacturing capacities at Morton and TRW are already strained. (Currently Morton makes units at only two plants in Utah.) Even owners of older cars who desire airbag installations and are able to pay for them may not find suppliers and mechanics willing to undertake the tasks of making and installing such units. However, there is another aftermarket to consider: new cars that already experienced front-end crashes. The airbag can be used once; it cannot go back into its casing. Thus, a full module must be installed for the next round. This is undoubtedly a complex and expensive repair task (omitted, of course, if the car itself is not worth repairing).

Who will develop a relatively low-cost system for installing a new airbag? Where can such installations take place, and how quickly can they be done? Franchised new-car dealers, owners of used-car lots, service stations, and garage mechanics are pondering the answer to these and related questions. Morton and TRW may be reluctant to enter this field, because it is not their key market and because they are busy enough making airbags for new cars. Body shops may see a market opportunity, but mechanics will have to be trained to do the task.

QUESTIONS

1. Do you think it makes sense for one company to operate simultaneously in a low-tech field (salt), a medium-tech area (specialty chemicals), and a high-tech field (airbags complete with gas inflators, sensors, etc.)?

2. Should Morton take advantage of the recall problem of its key rival, TRW? Should it be

concerned with antitrust laws in attempting to gain market share?

3. Analyze and evaluate Morton's decision to become a supplier of airbags to Mercedes-Benz and then to a large number of other German, Japanese, and U.S. carmakers.

4. Suggest some creative and feasible ideas for making and marketing airbag modules for owners of cars equipped with airbags who have experienced one front-end collision. Who should undertake the installation of such systems?

3. The Air Express Courier Industry

OVERVIEW

This case focuses on domestic and international markets for air express courier services headquartered in the United States. The scope of the study is time-sensitive letters, documents, and packages under 100 pounds or about 45 kilograms, delivered in two days or less via an integrated air/ground network. Excluded are heavyweight cargo shipments regardless of mode of transport, ground-only courier services, and the activities of the U.S. Postal Service. The emphasis is on competition in the United States and the global marketplace, with further focus on marketing strategies and tactics.

Revenues for U.S.-based air express courier services were about $12 billion in 1990 and are expected to grow at slightly over 10 percent per year, reaching $21.5 billion by 1995. In terms of units, the total should rise from 665 million units shipped in 1990 to an estimated 1.2 billion units shipped in 1995. Therefore, the average revenue generated is about $18 per unit in both years. In the United States, as of 1992 the manufacturing sector accounts for about 55 percent of the value of shipments, service firms for about 25 percent, governments and nonprofit institutions for 10 percent, and consumer households for the remaining 10 percent.

THE IMPACT OF ENVIRONMENTAL FACTORS

The Macroeconomic Environment

The general level of business activity is a key determinant in the demand for air express courier services. When air express delivery came on the scene in the 1970s, the newness of the service, coupled with efficiency-enhancing benefits, attracted many customers and helped offset cyclical downturns. Now the service is almost universal, reliability is taken for granted, and technical innovations are fewer; in effect, the market has matured and competition has become very keen. Future demand for air express services will depend on general business conditions. The challenge of global competition, which is making U.S. companies more export driven, should have a positive impact on the couriers.

The industry study on which this case is based was written in late 1991 by Edward D. Hester at The Freedonia Group, Cleveland, Ohio. This case was developed by Andrew C. Gross of Cleveland State University in mid-1992.

Business Formations

The number of business establishments (companies, individual proprietorships, partnerships) in the United States rose from about 14 million in 1980 to 18 million by 1990. Some large firms have merged, others have restructured; on net balance, megasize firms now employ fewer people. Many displaced employees have become entrepreneurs, despite a recession, resulting in new-business formations. This has meant increased volume for the air express couriers, since even the smallest enterprises have occasional need for high-speed delivery to faraway places. The number of new U.S. business establishments should continue to rise, especially after mid-decade, reaching 20 million in 1995 and 24 million by 2000.

Technology

The birth of Federal Express in the 1970s heralded a major change in distribution techniques. This company, the pioneer in the field, introduced a hub and spoke system, with its hub in Memphis, Tennessee. A package shipped from San Francisco to Los Angeles on the West Coast of the United States still had to go through Memphis. At first glance, this seems absurd; on reflection, it was a creative idea that allowed a complete sorting process and subsequent night shipping. Federal Express also introduced the idea of convenient ground pickup and delivery using vans coordinated with its fleet of jet aircraft. This system allowed FedEx to make good on its advertising slogan: "When it absolutely, positively has to be there overnight." Today FedEx, UPS, DHL, and Airborne offer a wide variety of assured delivery in the United States and globally.

Another major technological breakthrough is tracking, which allows pinpointing of any letter or parcel through the entire shipping process. Effective tracking minimizes the likelihood that shipments will be lost, delayed, or damaged. Early on, tracking consisted of stickers with numbers; now all the major couriers offer state-of-the-art automatic identification technology using bar codes, laser scanning, and databases. Some of the more advanced tracking systems use satellite communications; this is expected to become more prevalent. Another increasingly popular feature is integration of the tracking function into larger computer networks that can handle documentation, accounting, invoicing, inventory, data interchange, and other functions.

Competitive Delivery Methods

Integrated air express couriers face extensive competition in the delivery of documents and small packages. Such competition comes from air cargo, airline, and air freight forwarding companies; private-sector motor and rail carriers; and the U.S. Postal Service, which has become more aggressive and now offers express mail at competitive prices, using various transport modes. But possibly the most threatening development is facsimile transmission, or fax. Facsimile machines connected to ordinary telephone lines can transfer a one-page document in seconds and longer ones in a few minutes.

When fax became prevalent in the United States at the end of the 1980s, observers predicted that air express delivery would become obsolete. Fax did cut down the volume of letters delivered, but the couriers' revenues remained robust. The fact that fax speeds up the flow of paperwork may even provide a boost to the air express business, since buyers expect quick dispatch of parts and other small packages. Still, on net balance, fax is a threat and air express companies are now moving into air freight delivery of heavier cargo.

Price Trends

After the oil crises of the 1970s, many observers thought it was only a matter of time until crude oil sold for $40 instead of $4 per barrel. But in the late 1980s and early 1990s, the price fluctuated in the $15-to-$25-per-barrel range and is not expected to go much higher, due in part to conservation measures and in part to availability of oil from diverse sources. Accordingly, the air express couriers may not face steep rises in jet fuel prices. However, in congested cities their fleets of vans are likely to encounter traffic jams and use more gasoline or diesel fuel. Furthermore, with many small and large businesses locating in suburbs, exurbs, and rural locations, delivery distances are likely to rise.

The increasingly global nature of document and small-package delivery necessitates the establishment of several hubs around the world and operating a fleet of aircraft capable of transocean hops. This means that firms must make heavy investment in such capital goods as aircraft, delivery vans or trucks, warehousing and sorting facilities, airport hangars, and maintenance bays. The infrastructure arrangements also call for dealing with customs officials, freight forwarders, airport officials, and regulatory authorities in many countries. Last but not least, to keep up with competitors and satisfy customers, significant sums will have to be spent on updating the automatic tracking systems. Some couriers, such as Emery Worldwide (a subsidiary of Consolidated Freightways), have already encountered these barriers. Even giant Federal Express has found the competition very keen in this regard in Western Europe and has pulled back, preferring alliances or partnerships to going it alone in unfamiliar markets.

THE PRODUCT/MARKET INTERFACE

Types of Goods Handled

Air express couriers deliver all sorts of letters, documents, and packages. From the simple format of a large envelope and a medium-size box, the package variations have evolved to all kinds of containers, from tubes to insulated boxes. These units are still classified by weight and, to a lesser extent, by size. Some companies are experimenting with packages above the old 100-pound limit. Pickup stations in large office buildings offer various envelopes that can be used by the sender and dropped off right there. The marketplace also demands time- and price-specific expediting. Accordingly, the couriers are experimenting with overnight, one-day, and two-day deliveries and various combinations of price points and discounts. In the early 1990s some companies, such as Airborne, moved toward economy, second-day

service; at the same time other firms, such as DHL, offered superpremium, one-day service.

Market Segments

The initial thrust for high-speed delivery of small packages came from the electronics firms and their customers. Chips and other electronic components are small in bulk and high in value; they are needed for quick installation if there is a demand for computers (whether original equipment or replacement). To be without computerization means a virtual shutdown for many businesses; to keep going, parts are of vital importance. Subsequent impetus for air express came from architects, builders, and contractors who wanted to bid on projects; these firms often work against deadlines or wish to make a bid at the last minute, so assured delivery on short notice is a must. Later on, a variety of component manufacturers, wholesalers, and retailers signed on to the idea that they could compete on the basis of time: Get there early and get there quickly, whether it is a solicitation or a fulfillment of an order. In some cases, shipping an item in an express mode became a matter of status; there are even stories of using a courier from one floor of an office building to another.

The International Marketplace

Air express expediting started in the United States, but this mode of delivery is now growing rapidly in other areas of the world. Europe and the Pacific Rim are expected to be the fastest-growing areas. However, the nations of Latin America and Eastern Europe have embarked on privatization and are welcoming investments from abroad. An example is Hungary, where the antiquated telephone system is being replaced in part by a cellular phone system with the aid of U.S. West. As a result, cellular phones and other communication equipment, parts, and components are in demand. Thus, air express couriers should find such countries ready for expanding their services, albeit slowly at first, because the payment mechanism and the convertibility of currency must also be in place.

COMPETITIVE STRATEGIES

The Struggle for Market Share

Following five years of extensive restructuring and consolidation, the air express courier industry is now dominated by a handful of players. Federal Express, the pioneer, is still the leading firm. It is followed by UPS, which has been the leader in ground delivery for a long time but aggressively expanded into air express. Next are DHL, Airborne Freight, a few smaller couriers, and passenger airlines for which this business is a sideline. (See Exhibit 1 for market share of U.S.-based couriers.) At the global level, DHL has the most extensive air and ground network. Another major global player is TNT, which started on a small scale in Australia but now operates worldwide, especially in the United States and Europe.

Because the United States is becoming a mature, saturated market, companies are looking at other countries and regions for expansion, as noted above. Specific steps taken include UPS's acquisition of a number of local courier operations in Europe (including Cuallado of Spain, Seabourne in England, and Prost in France) and Asia. Airborne Freight, emphasizing its low-cost business-to-business niche, opted for partnerships with local concerns. It has a dual agreement with Mitsui and Tonami Transportation for air express and freight delivery within Japan, but hopes to use the ventures as a launching pad for further penetration of the Far East. Federal Express chose to acquire several firms and to develop new air routes along with land-based delivery systems. Its purchase of Tiger International was made as much for foreign routes and landing rights as for delivery of heavier freight. Recently, however, FedEx pulled back from some of its less successful operations in Europe.

Using the Marketing Mix

All four components of the marketing mix come into play when intense competition prevails, as it does in this field. *Product/service* is in a state of constant improvement as the couriers strive for the best record in on-time delivery, package loss prevention, advanced tracking, and varied offerings in terms of package size and pickup and delivery times. For example, FedEx offers shipments up to 150 pounds and such ancillary services as COD (collect-on-delivery) to expedite payments to shippers. But proliferation of services adds to costs of operations and may confuse customers.

Pricing remains a competitive tool as the couriers continue to woo shippers, although the dynamics have changed from what was typical in the early days. In the current mood of cost containment, the couriers offer not just overnight but next-day, second-day, and other "time-deferred" delivery programs. Advanced technology is expensive at first, but once in place it offers economies of scale and the savings can be passed on to shippers. Companies that make frequent shipments of many packages are receiving volume discounts. Airborne and UPS are especially adept at targeting such users.

Place or *distribution* is used by the couriers as a means of gaining customers. Number of cities served in the United States and globally are selling points. Pickup points in cities also serve to attract clients. FedEx and UPS both play this game well, FedEx with its ever-present dispatch stations in office buildings and UPS by designating local businesses as package-posting points. (Of course, the U.S. Postal Service remains very visible with its branch stations and, as of late, special dispatch mailboxes.) Companies must think both globally and locally. In its bid for overseas expansion, FedEx increased its Far East capability by upgrading its San Francisco, Anchorage, and Tokyo hubs. UPS acquired small local couriers in Europe to enhance its ground delivery capability. Several companies are considering warehouse and inventory services.

Promotion takes the form of advertising, personal selling, and other sales promotion techniques such as sponsorships, sweepstakes, incentive programs, trade show appearances, and so forth. FedEx has captured television viewers with its imaginative early ads. UPS now stresses its far-flung network and its ability to deliver to remote locations. It emphasizes that what counts is door-to-door service and "total elapsed time" and cites its decades of experience in reliable ground delivery. Personal selling remains aggressive as the couriers attempt to woo purchasing agents

EXHIBIT 1   U.S.-Based Air Express Courier Services: Market Share by Company, 1990

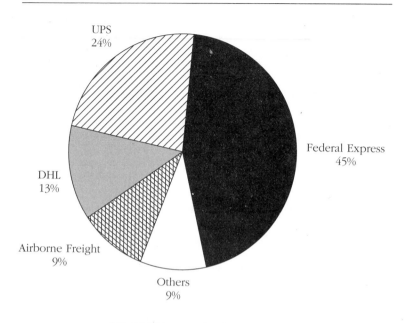

$11.9 billion total sales

Source: E.D. Hester, *Courier Services to 1995, Business Research Report #B277* (Cleveland: The Freedonia Group, 1991), p. 58.

and other influential people employed by major shippers.

EMERGING STRATEGIES

Although reaching maturity status in the United States, the air express courier industry is still in its growth stage elsewhere in the world. Accordingly, one key emerging strategy is *international diversification*. The leading U.S.-based couriers have invested in foreign expansion at a nearly frenzied pace. They wish to serve the international requirements of their U.S. clients as well as capture new ones abroad. To this date, the volume of business has not been sufficient to allow for full-cost recovery. As FedEx, UPS, and others found out, it is costly to establish foreign hubs, develop interregional and local delivery net-

works, and be in tune with different customs clearance and other legal procedures. The logistical aspects of international goods delivery are far more complicated than those in a single, large national entity such as the United States. But the major players have made commitments and have staying power; they now plan to step up their promotion activity to acquaint potential clients with the benefits of small-package air delivery.

A second strategy that is proving popular is *concentric diversification* into related areas. The quintessential example is the 1989 acquisition of Tiger International by Federal Express, which has allowed FedEx to offer air shipment from the smallest to the largest cargo, from overnight expediting to three-day-plus delivery. Another example, also in 1989, was the acquisition of Emery Air Freight by Consolidated Freightways, although the company was unable to compete successfully in small-parcel delivery and divestiture may be near. Australia-based TNT is another concentrically diversified air cargo carrier, with business units in general freight, air and ground express dispatch, logistics support, and contract distribution. Conglomerate diversification is not actively pursued by the air express courier companies.

Resource rationalization—meaning layoff of personnel, closing of facilities—has not been prevalent until now, as rapid growth had allowed vendors to expand. But the maturity of the U.S. market, overcapacity in certain international markets, and the general economic recession have forced couriers to consider this strategy. Federal Express is the most notable example. It has been encountering losses in Europe and sharply restructured its U.K. operations, including cutbacks in staff. Other firms are assessing their presence and plans for expansion in the United States and various foreign markets.

A final emerging strategy is *cooperation* in the form of *strategic alliances, partnerships, and joint ventures.* The fierce competitive environment excluded this mode until now, but the situation is bound to change with the maturity of the U.S. market and the cost of expanding in far-flung marketplaces outside North America. What is most likely is greater partnering activity between couriers on the one hand and other goods-moving companies such as passenger airlines, ground transport firms, air freight forwarders, and heavyweight-cargo carriers. The desire to expand market reach and to participate in a new but related business are the driving forces spurring such arrangements. A sample of various partnerships already undertaken is shown in Exhibit 2.

THE BOTTOM LINE

Regardless of the particular strategy pursued, surviving and growing as an integrated air express courier service requires access to substantial amounts of investment capital. Such funds can

EXHIBIT 2   U.S.-Based Air Express Courier Market: Selected Strategic Partnerships

Company	Type of Agreement	With Whom	Products Covered
AMR Corporation (American Airlines)	Code-sharing agreement	Cathay Pacific	Los Angeles/Hong Kong route
AMR Corporation (American Airlines)	Code-sharing agreement	MALÉV (Hungarian National Airline)	Zurich/Budapest route
Air Transportation Holding (Mountain Air Cargo & CSA Air)	Exclusive cargo service	Federal Express	Air delivery service under dry leases
Airborne Freight	Joint venture (Airborne Express Japan)	Mitsui & Company; Tonami Transportation	Express courier service
Airborne Freight	Operating agreement	British Rail (Red Star)	Line haul capabilities in the U.K.
Mail Boxes, Etc.	Air-shipping agreement	United Parcel Service Incorporated	
TNT Limited (Australia)	Joint venture	MALÉV (Hungarian National Airline)	
TNT Limited (Australia)	Joint operations	Aeroflot (former Soviet National Airline)	

Source: E.D. Hester, *Courier Services to 1995, Business Research Report #B277* (Cleveland: The Freedonia Group, 1991), p. 58.

EXHIBIT 3   Selected Air Express Courier, Air Freighters/Forwarders, and Passenger Airlines: Composite Financial Ratios

Item	Integrated Air Express Couriers[a]	Air Freighters/ Forwarders[b]	Passenger Airlines[c]
Net profit margin (%)	1.9	1.8	0.3
Return on equity (%)	8.3	11.3	1.9
Current ratio	1.1	1.1	0.7
Equity/assets (%)	32.2	31.4	26.2
Long-term debt/equity (%)	121.0	58.1	60.0
Capital spending/sales (%)	13.8	2.9	22.0
Price/earnings ratio	7.7	9.2	29.5
Sales per employee (000 $)	86.8	120.0	143.9

Note: Fiscal years vary.

[a]Integrated air express couriers sample consists of Airborne Freight, Federal Express, and TNT Limited.
[b]Air freighters/forwarders sample consists of Air Express International, Consolidated Freightways, and Pittston.
[c]Passenger airlines sample consists of AMR (American Airlines), Delta Air Lines, and UAL.

come from cash flow internally or from the outside in the form of borrowing funds or selling common shares. The leading couriers traditionally have had little trouble in the debt and equity markets, but capital availability may become a concern in the coming years. There is also pressure to consider diversification into related areas.

To gain insight on their financial situation, let us look at a composite set of financial ratios that show comparative data for the air express couriers, air freighters/forwarders, and passenger airlines. The ratios in Exhibit 3 are shown for illustrative purposes; their proper use requires recognizing their limitations, which include different methods of accounting for profits and the impact of multiple business units on consolidated results. In addition, extensive consolidation within the air transport sector in recent years reduced the pool of companies from which the samples can be drawn (this is especially true for the passenger airlines).

On the whole, however, the ratios illustrate clearly the difficulties that all firms related to the air transport sector have experienced as of late. Heavy capital spending, rapid expansion, a recession-induced decline in revenue growth, and debt payments have taken their toll on profit margins.

In short, profit margins are down and debt-to-equity ratios are up compared to other industries. Still, the air express couriers have done better than the airlines and are roughly even with the air freighters/forwarders. Their present weak financial position should improve by the mid-1990s, as couriers finish building their infrastructure and continue paying off their high levels of debt.

QUESTIONS

1. Select one of the key air express couriers—say, UPS—and develop a corporate profile of how it is competing in this fast-paced industry. Provide data on services offered, nations served, recent acquisitions, pricing policies, and other marketing activities.

2. Analyze the extent to which very small businesses—say, from zero to nine employees—tend to use the services offered by the air express couriers. Can such customers have any clout?

3. In a PBS file film entitled *Frederick Smith and Federal Express* (one film in the series, *Creativity,* by Bill Moyers), there is a comparison

of two series of advertisements used early on by FedEx. How do these two series differ? (If you cannot view the film, look at print ads. If you cannot get old ads, look at both recent TV and print ads.) Note: Why do you think Fred Smith got a C grade on his term paper at Yale in which he outlined the idea of Federal Express?

4. What would be a natural sponsorship for air express couriers? Do you recall a specific event or athlete sponsored?

4. Canadian Tillage and Harvesting Equipment Company Limited (A)

With sales of approximately 700 million dollars a year, Canadian Tillage and Harvesting Equipment Company (CTHE) is one of the foremost farm equipment manufacturers in Canada. The firm's home office is in Montreal, Quebec, with its manufacturing plant for harvesting equipment located in St. Jerome, Quebec; tillage equipment facilities in Oshawa, Ontario, and gasoline and diesel engine plant in St. Catharines, Ontario. The marketing, sales, and finance functions are centralized in the Montreal home office, and the products are distributed to exclusive dealers across Canada, either directly from the manufacturing plants or through transfer warehouses in Winnipeg and Halifax. In addition, a sales force working with the dealers operates from one district office in each province.

The district sales offices are responsible for maintaining emergency inventories of service parts; directing a small group of product specialists to train dealers in technical servicing of their products; checking dealers' orders and transferring them to the home office; following up on dealer invoices from the home office; extending credit to dealers' customers; conducting limited marketing research studies; and ordering and distributing dealer literature, catalogs, displays, service manuals, and other sales promotion materials. One important function of the district office is to organize for and participate in community fall fairs, plowing matches, and farm equipment shows. The district offices are also responsible for training the dealers in establishing sound accounting practices that conform to the company operating standards and provide data for sales analysis.

The district sales force is responsible for training and assisting dealers in effective selling techniques; educating dealers on product and service features; providing dealers with advertising materials from the home office; and assisting them in planning their promotional campaigns. Occasionally the district salesperson will travel from farm to farm with the dealer or the dealer's salesperson to handle difficult customer accounts, demonstrate new products and sales techniques, and gather firsthand information.

HOME-OFFICE SALES

Over the past seventy years, the dominant group within CTHE has been the sales department. At the turn of the century, one of the highest paid and most respected people in the organization was the "Blockman." In today's terminology, he would be classified as the "district sales manager." For the past six decades, the presidents of the company traditionally have followed the sales route, spending many years on the road working with dealers and their customers. Consequently, the overall tone of the organization is geared toward selling.

In 1992 Jack Weir, who had received a certificate in business from the extension department of McGill University, was promoted from eastern regional sales manager to the newly created position of dealer development manager. The major task facing Weir in his new position was to critically evaluate dealer territories, sales performance, contribution to the company image, promotional activities, service facilities, and inventory control procedures. Generally speaking, he was expected to completely revitalize and revamp the company's dealer network, which, while successful in meeting sales quotas, had been experiencing decreasing profit margins and generating a higher level of customer complaints than ever before in the company's history. One statement made by the president when assigning Weir his task was "I have a strong feeling that the trend to larger farms is shrinking the number of customers in our dealers' territories, and we must find a way to expand their territories and eliminate, perhaps, one-third of our present dealers."

MARKETING TO AGRIBUSINESS

Shortly after his promotion, the company sent Weir on a one-week continuing education seminar at Michigan State University to assist him in organizing and running his new department.

One of the keynote speakers at the seminar was Professor Everett M. Rogers, who discussed the "Adoption and Diffusion of New Farm Products." Professor Rogers stated that in the case of agriculture, diffusion is the process by which new farm practices or ideas are communicated from sources of origin, such as scientists and implement firms, to farmers. Adoption may be viewed as a mental process through which an individual passes from first hearing about a new idea to using the new practice on a full scale and incorporating it into his way of farming. Examples of new ideas studied are hybrid corn, wheat sprays, livestock feed additives, bulk milk tanks, pesticides, fertilizer, tillage practices, and new farm machinery.

EXHIBIT 1   Distribution of Farmers Among the Five Categories According to Time of Adoption

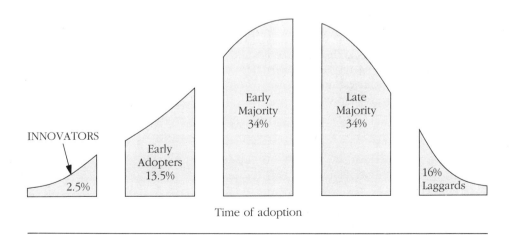

Time of adoption

EXHIBIT 2   Summary of Characteristics and Communications Behavior of Adopter Categories

| Characteristic or Behavior | Innovators | Early Adopters | Majority | | Laggards or Late Adopters |
			Early	Late	
Time of adoption	First 2.5% to adopt new ideas	Next 13.5% to adopt	Next 34% to adopt	Next 34% to adopt	Last 16% to adopt
Attitudes and values	Scientific and venturesome	Progressive	More conservative and traditional	Skeptical of new ideas	Agricultural magic and folk beliefs; fear of debt
Abilities	High level of education; ability to deal with abstractions	Above-average education	Slightly above-average education	Slightly below-average education	Low level of education; have difficulty dealing with abstractions and relationships
Group memberships	Leaders in countywide or statewide organizations; travel widely	Leaders in organizations within the community	Many informal contacts within the community	Little travel out of community; little activity in formal organizations	Few memberships in formal organizations other than church; semi-isolates
Social status	Highest social status, but their farming practices may not be accepted	High social status; looked to by neighbors as "good farmers"	About average social status	About average social status	Lowest social status
Farm businesses	Largest, most specialized, and most efficient	Large farms; slightly less specialized and efficient	Slightly larger-than-average-size farms	Slightly smaller-than-average-sized farms	Small farms; low incomes; seldom farm owners
Sources of information	Scientists; other innovators; research bulletins	Highest contact with local change agents; farm magazines; extension bulletins	Farm magazines; friends and neighbors	Friends and neighbors	Mainly friends and neighbors; radio farm shows

Some of the interesting observations articulated during this particular session were as follows:

■ Farmers who think they gain high status by planting straight rows are slow to accept contouring.

■ Innovators for one practice tend to be innovators for other practices.

■ Laggards and late majority farmers believe in "agricultural magic" such as planting crops or dehorning cattle by the signs of the moon.

■ Early adopters are willing to take risks and borrow money to realize profits through adopting high capital investment practices such as new farm machinery, sprinkler irrigation, or bulk milk tanks.

■ Older farmers tend to be conservative and laggards.

■ Early adopters and innovators are among the most highly educated farmers.

■ Innovators tend to have larger farms, higher gross farm incomes, greater farm efficiency, more specialization, and greater equity in their farms.

Exhibit 1 on page 681 shows the distribution of farmers according to time of adoption. Exhibit 2 (opposite) summarizes characteristics of the adopter categories. These exhibits appeared in the North Central Regional Extension Publication No. 13, entitled "Adopters of New Farm Ideas," which was distributed to the participants at the seminar.

REVIEWING THE SEMINAR

Upon his return to Montreal, Weir had to submit a report on the seminar to the president of CTHE.

In this report, Weir stated that there were certain limitations in the way CTHE's dealer organization was structured. Specifically, he stressed that the seminar made him realize that for years CTHE had been product oriented and, even further, sales oriented. The great majority of the company's efforts were spent "pushing" products at the dealers and relying on the dealers to "push" products at the farmers. In light of the new perspective he had acquired at the seminar, Weir suggested that perhaps the company's current difficulties were the result of too much emphasis on just selling and not enough emphasis on recognizing the characteristics of the company's ultimate customers— the farmers.

In his report, Weir strongly recommended that the company allot him a special marketing research budget to study the characteristics of the Canadian farm market. Until this time, the company simply had been analyzing sales and product performance.

QUESTIONS

1. Can the diffusion and adoption information Jack Weir was exposed to at the Michigan State seminar be applied with equal validity to Canada?

2. What questions should Weir attempt to answer through his marketing research?

3. Assuming that Weir is able to identify well-defined characteristics of his customers according to the adopter categories illustrated in the exhibits, how will this help him accomplish his dealer development program?

5. Canadian Tillage and Harvesting Equipment Company Limited (B)

THE CANADIAN FARM SCENE

Agriculture has been and continues to be a most important part of the Canadian economy. Agricultural production in 1991 involved $21.3 billion in cash receipts. The primary producer, the farmer, is becoming increasingly efficient, producing more food with less help. Current Canadian agricultural trends include a marked reduction in the number of farms and in the farm labor force, accompanied by increases in capital investment, specialization, mechanization, and output. From 1871 to 1971, the average size of Canadian farms increased from 98 to 463 acres. By 1991, the average farm size was 598 acres. These figures reflect the growth in farm size in the Prairie provinces. For example, in 1991 the average size of a farm in Manitoba was 743 acres, in Alberta 898 acres, and in Saskatchewan 1,091 acres, whereas the average farm size in Ontario was only 196 acres.

As farms increase in size through consolidation, incorporation of family farms, and specialization in crop and livestock production, a new breed of farmer is emerging—the agribusinessperson. This individual is a professional manager who is concerned with the same problems as the industrial manager, namely return on investment, inventory levels, purchasing policies, management of personnel, risk-taking priorities, selling and distribution strategies, and assessing market opportunities.

The dynamic changes taking place in agriculture strongly influence those who supply the farmer. The farm sector is rapidly becoming an extremely valuable market for both capital and consumer goods. The agricultural machinery and equipment manufacturer today caters to a multi-billion-dollar market ($2 billion in sales at wholesale to dealers in 1992). Dealers' customers are more sophisticated managers. More and more have college degrees and are supporting the scientific operation of the farm. Indeed, the old image of the "pungent barnyard operation" is rapidly being replaced by the sterile, hospital-like image of the modern farm.

These rapid changes in the Canadian farm market environment have been recognized by Canadian Tillage and Harvesting Equipment Company Limited. Jack Weir, dealer development manager for the $700 million sales farm equipment manufacturer, has engaged an outside marketing research house to determine the services farmers want from their dealers and how CTHE dealers perceive their customers' wants. In addition, Weir commissioned the same research house to profile his company's typical dealer.

THE RESEARCH FINDINGS

The marketing research firm surveyed the opinion of a representative sample of 300 farmers. The results of this survey indicated that the five most important services farmers expected from their dealers were as follows:

1. The dealer must have comprehensive facilities and well-qualified mechanics to adequately repair farm machinery.
2. The dealer should be not only capable but also willing to adjust machinery in the field

and to deliver emergency repair parts as quickly as possible, even after normal business hours.

3. The dealer should take the initiative in completely checking out equipment before the warranty has expired.

4. The dealer should provide information and advice, including training schools and "smokers," about product modifications, new equipment, and new operating techniques.

5. The dealer should be willing to offer price discounts for cash purchases.

A majority of the farmers also reported that they favored dealers who mailed unsolicited information about machinery and new developments on a regular basis, permitted them to try out new machinery on a trial basis before purchase, and occasionally offered special deals and discounts.

With regard to the dealers' attitude toward their customers' desires, the marketing research firm surveyed 133 CTHE dealers. The dealers ranked the following factors in terms of importance to their customers:

1. The dealer should provide effective service and repair facilities.

2. The dealer should maintain adequate supplies of parts.

3. The dealer should stand behind the products he sells.

4. The dealer should be known for honesty and integrity.

5. The dealer should be considered a friend.

6. The dealer should be an "independent" rather than a company-owned outlet.

7. The dealer should carry a full line of farm machinery and related equipment and supplies.

The majority of dealers surveyed believed that the farmer expected them to be technical consultants on the operation and repair of machinery and that the information and advertising literature supplied by CTHE was too general to satisfy their customers' needs for technical information.

The third study produced the following profile of the "typical" CTHE dealer: average age forty-seven, high school education, a business manager for fourteen years, situated in his current location for twelve years, and, in the majority of cases, sole proprietor of the dealership.

QUESTIONS

1. Critically evaluate the type of information Jack Weir commissioned and obtained from the marketing research house.

2. Compare farmers' expectations of the dealers with dealers' perception of the farmers' expectations. What does this suggest?

3. In light of the changing Canadian farming environment, do the research findings suggest how Jack Weir can design an effective long-run dealer development policy?

6. Modern Purchasing (A)

Business markets consist of people—people responsible for purchasing materials, services, and machinery at the right price for their operations. In the front line is the purchasing specialist who, in day-to-day buying, directly affects the economics of the firm in measurable dollars. In manufacturing, the bill for operating materials and supplies alone constitutes 55 percent of the end product value. A cost saving at the purchasing end, therefore, can exert great leverage on the profit and loss statement.

Markets are made up of buyers and sellers. Since buyers first have to be sold, it is good business to get to know them—who they are, what they do, and how to reach them. To get a better understanding of the people in purchasing, *Modern Purchasing,* a leading Maclean-Hunter trade publication, commissioned McDonald Research Limited to study the person responsible for purchasing in Canada's manufacturing industries. The research methods and procedures used were validated by the Canadian Advertising Research Foundation to ensure strict adherence to high standards of professional research. The results were expected to provide a reliable and revealing profile of the front-line people who are authorized by top management to purchase machinery, materials, and supplies for their firms.

The aim of *Modern Purchasing* in pioneering this major study was twofold: first, to maintain the editorial readership that can be obtained only through continuous research and understanding of the problems and needs of purchasing managers; second, to share this information with advertisers so that they can more effectively communicate with and sell to the people responsible for buying the right machinery, materials, and supplies for their plants.

OBJECTIVES OF THE STUDY

1. To define with reasonable precision the executive responsibilities of the "Management Core" for which *Modern Purchasing* is edited, as defined by *Modern Purchasing*: "The manager of the purchasing department or, if no formal purchasing department, the person in charge of purchasing"

2. To determine the degree and scope of purchasing authority engaged in by this management core

3. To determine the receipt and readership of *Modern Purchasing* among respondents

4. To gather information on actions taken as a result of readership

5. To gather information on subjects of interest that could form the basis of future *Modern Purchasing* articles

METHODOLOGY

The basic method was to conduct a face-to-face interview with each respondent after prearranging an appointment. Personal interviewing furnished the most practical approach in gathering readership information.

The Required Respondent

At each plant contacted, the interviewee was the person defined in objective 1. Interviews were not conducted among persons employed in plants where there were fewer than fifty employees. This eliminated very small operations, which do not come within the readership target of *Modern Purchasing.*

Sampling Method

The Standard Industrial Classification Code (Part I) of Statistics Canada (publication 6502-4; 11-3-64) lists all manufacturing industries (see subgroup codes 1011 to 3970). Statistics Canada was able to furnish its most recent list of all manufacturing plants within these industries. Subgroup codes 1011 to 3970 actually fall into 20 major manufacturing groups. The Statistics Canada computer printout furnished all listings of manufacturing firms within each group.

An equal probability random sampling method was used to select the sample, with the imposition of two restraints:

1. The sample was selected from within each of the twenty major groups in the same proportion as that group was represented in the sample universe.
2. Plants with fewer than fifty employees in all were omitted from the sample.

The imposition of the second restraint eliminated too many plants from the primary sample, and additional plants had to be chosen to obtain the desired sample size. Again, equal probability random sampling was employed in the same way. For practical purposes, one additional restraint was introduced for this and other studies of this series. If any plant appeared in the sample whose location was too remote for interviewing, that plant was eliminated. In the study, only two plants were considered inaccessible. Exhibit 1 lists the cities and towns across Canada where interviews were completed.

The sampling method involved the selection of a random number for the starting position and the selection of every *n*th plant for inclusion in the sample. With a target of 300 respondents, a total of 240 interviews were completed and considered usable.

Approach to the Respondent

Inasmuch as the required respondents were executives at the senior level, it was necessary to approach them in the most businesslike manner

EXHIBIT 1   Cities Where Interviewing Took Place

St. John's, Nfld.	Winnipeg, Man.
	St. Boniface, Man.
Halifax, N.S.	
	Regina, Sask.
Quebec, P.Q.	Saskatoon, Sask.
Three Rivers, P.Q.	
Charlesbourg, P.Q.	Calgary, Alta.
Ville d'Anjou, P.Q.	Edmonton, Alta.
Montreal, P.Q.	
Ottawa, Ont.	Vancouver, B.C.
Toronto, Ont.	Burnaby, B.C.
Kitchener, Ont.	New Westminster, B.C.
London, Ont.	Victoria, B.C.
Waterloo, Ont.	
Hamilton, Ont.	
Windsor, Ont.	

possible, to fit the interviews into their busy schedules at their convenience, and to conduct the interviews on a professional basis.

The following steps were taken to set up the interview:

1. The plant was contacted by telephone and asked (either switchboard operator or secretary) to furnish the name (with proper spelling), initials, and title used of "the manager of the purchasing department or, if no formal purchasing department, the person in charge of purchasing."
2. A letter from McDonald Research Limited was sent to the appropriate people advising them of the general nature of our inquiry and requesting their cooperation in setting up an appointment with a member of the field interviewing staff.
3. Approximately forty-eight hours after the letter was sent, the prospective respondent was called personally on the telephone by the interviewer who identified herself and requested an appointment for the interview.

If the respondent was unavailable, two return calls were made before dropping the candidate.

Interviewer Training

Because of the level of executive to be interviewed, it was essential that all field supervisors
be personally contacted before initiating the
study. Two senior project directors from Mc-
Donald Research Limited traveled east and west
in Canada, holding one-day seminars with groups
of field supervisors flown into central points (e.g.,
Calgary for all Saskatchewan, Alberta, and British
Columbia supervisors). The following topics were
on the agenda of each seminar:

1. A general explanation of the study
2. An explanation and discussion of the approach to be taken in obtaining the interview
3. An explanation and discussion of the makeup
   of the questionnaires and the method of conducting the interview.

Each field supervisor was also questioned individually to ensure that enough qualified personal interviewers were available for the study.

Pretesting the Questionnaire

When the final draft of the questionnaire (Exhibit
2) had been decided upon, a pretest among
twelve plants was conducted in the Toronto area
between May 31 and June 8. The results of the
pretest led to clarification of wording in the questionnaire. However, the basic concept and approach remained unchanged.

EXHIBIT 2   The Questionnaire

INTRODUCTION: Good morning, Mr. (or Ms.) _____ . We appreciate the opportunity to
talk to you. I'll try to use as little of your time as possible.

1. (a) First, would you please describe what areas and functions you are directly responsible for in
       your present position?
       (RECORD WORD FOR WORD) _____

   _____

   (b) For which of the following activities of companies like yours are you—(a) directly responsible
       for (b) share responsibility with others on or (c) have no involvement:

	Directly responsible	Share responsibility with others	No involvement
Traffic	☐ 11-1	☐ 12-1	☐ 13-1
Inventory control	☐ -2	☐ -2	☐ -2
Scrap disposal	☐ -3	☐ -3	☐ -3
Value analysis	☐ -4	☐ -4	☐ -4
Vendor rating	☐ -5	☐ -5	☐ -5
Make or buy	☐ -6	☐ -6	☐ -6

   (c) What other areas are you directly responsible for? _____

   _____ None ☐

   (d) In what other areas do you share responsibility? _____

   _____ None ☐

2. (a) What is the total number of employees in your purchasing department?

One	☐ 18-1	Four	☐ -4	Seven	☐ -7
Two	☐ -2	Five	☐ -5	Eight	☐ -8
Three	☐ -3	Six	☐ -6	Nine +	☐ -9

   (b) How many employees, if any, are there in other departments who report to you?

One	☐ 19-1	Four	☐ -4	Seven	☐ -7
Two	☐ -2	Five	☐ -5	Eight +	☐ -8
Three	☐ -3	Six	☐ -6	None	☐ -0

EXHIBIT 2   The Questionnaire (*cont.*)

3. (a) How many buyers at this location report to you?

One	☐ 20-1	Four	☐ -4	Seven	☐ -7
Two	☐ -2	Five	☐ -5	Eight+	☐ -8
Three	☐ -3	Six	☐ -6	None	☐ -0

   (b) How many buyers at other locations of your company report to you?

One	☐ 21-1	Four	☐ -4	Seven	☐ -7
Two	☐ -2	Five	☐ -5	Eight+	☐ -8
Three	☐ -3	Six	☐ -6	None	☐ -0

4. To whom do you report? _____

(JOB TITLE OR FUNCTION)

5. How long have you held your present responsibilities with this company?

Less than 1 yr.	☐ 23-1	5–6 yrs.	☐ -4	11–15 yrs.	☐ -7
1–2 yrs.	☐ -2	7–8 yrs.	☐ -5	16–20 yrs.	☐ -8
3–4 yrs.	☐ -3	9–10 yrs.	☐ -6	Over 20 yrs.	☐ -9

6. And how long have you been employed by this firm?

Less than 1 yr.	☐ 24-1	5–6 yrs.	☐ -4	11–15 yrs.	☐ -7
1–2 yrs.	☐ -2	7–8 yrs.	☐ -5	16–20 yrs.	☐ -8
3–4 yrs.	☐ -3	9–10 yrs.	☐ -6	Over 20 yrs.	☐ -9

7. Into which of the following age groups do you fall?

20–25 yrs.	☐ 25-1	46–50 yrs.	☐ -6
26–30 yrs.	☐ -2	51–55 yrs.	☐ -7
31–35 yrs.	☐ -3	56–60 yrs.	☐ -8
36–40 yrs.	☐ -4	61–65 yrs.	☐ -9
41–45 yrs.	☐ -5	Over 65 yrs.	☐ -0

(Hand Card No. 1 to Respondent)

8. Would you please read me the letter which represents the last stage of your formal education?

A—Public or grade school	☐ 26-1
B— Some high or technical school	☐ -2
C—Completed high or technical school	☐ -3
D—Post-secondary schooling (not university)	☐ -4
E— Some university	☐ -5
F— Completed university degree	☐ -6
G—Further study towards post-graduate degree	☐ -7
H—Post-graduate degree	☐ -8

9. (a) When salespeople call on your company, would their first contact normally be with another specific department or with the purchasing department?

   Other department ☐ 27-1   Purchasing department ☐ 27-2

If "Other Department":

   (b) Are these calls referred back to the purchasing department always, usually, sometimes, or never?

Always	☐ 28-1	Usually	☐ -3
Sometimes	☐ -2	Never	☐ -4

10. Mr. (or Ms.) _____, I am going to read you a list of items which may be used by your company. Would you please tell me first of all if your company uses the item. Also, here is a card (HAND RESPONDENT CARD NO. 2) which represents the degree you become involved in purchasing, once the need has been made known, and the type has been decided.

EXHIBIT 2   The Questionnaire (*cont.*)

Since there may be a difference in new orders versus repeat orders, we'll consider each separately. First of all, does your firm use _____ (NAME OF PRODUCT)?

List of Products:	Yes	No
Chemicals	☐ 29-1	☐ 31-1
Industrial lubricants	☐ -2	☐ -2
Electrical motors and/or controls	☐ -3	☐ -3
Fleet cars and/or trucks	☐ -4	☐ -4
Power transmission equipment (such as gears, V-belts, chains, etc.)	☐ -5	☐ -5
Maintenance equipment and supplies	☐ -6	☐ -6
Safety equipment and supplies	☐ -7	☐ -7
Materials (such as metals, plastics, glass, vulcanized fibers, rubber, etc.)	☐ 30-1	☐ 32-1
Materials handling equipment	☐ -2	☐ -2
Mechanical parts and assembly components (such as bearings, valves, pumps, fasteners, etc.)	☐ -3	☐ -3
Office equipment (such as furniture and business machines)	☐ -4	☐ -4
Office supplies (such as paper, forms, pens and pencils, etc.)	☐ -5	☐ -5
Packaging	☐ -6	☐ -6
Tools (hand and/or power)	☐ -7	☐ -7

Card No. 2

A—   The brand or manufacturer has usually been decided upon by the time I receive a requisition.

B—   I share in the decision on brand or manufacturer after consultation with others.

C—   I usually make the final decision on brand or manufacturer.

D—   I recommend brands or manufacturers.

E—   When brand or manufacturer is listed on requisition order, I usually provide alternates after investigation.

F—   When brand or manufacturer is specified, but not available, I have authority to select an alternate brand or manufacturer.

If "Yes": (Question 10)

Now consult the card and tell me which phrase describes your personal degree of involvement. Just call the letter opposite the phrase. Now which better describes your degree of involvement for new orders? For repeat orders? (REPEAT FOR EACH PRODUCT LISTED ABOVE)

		New Orders					Repeat Orders				
	A	B	C	D	E	F	A	B	C	D	E	F
	1	2	3	4	5	6	7	8	9	0	X	V
Chemicals 33												
Industrial lubricants 34												
Electrical motors and/or controls 35												
Fleet cars and/or trucks 36												
Power transmission equipment (such as gears, V-belts, chains, etc.) 37												
Maintenance equipment and supplies 38												

EXHIBIT 2   **The Questionnaire (*cont.*)**

		New Orders						Repeat Orders					
		A	B	C	D	E	F	A	B	C	D	E	F
		1	2	3	4	5	6	7	8	9	0	X	V
Safety equipment and supplies	39												
Materials (such as metals, plastics, glass, vulcanized fibers, rubber, etc.)	40												
Materials handling equipment	41												
Mechanical parts and assembly components (such as bearings, valves, pumps, fasteners, etc.)	42												
Office equipment (such as furniture and business machines)	43												
Office supplies (such as paper, forms, pens and pencils, etc.)	44												
Packaging	45												
Tools (hand and/or power)	46												
		1	2	3	4	5	6	7	8	9	0	X	V

11.   Within the past year or so, have you on your own initiative purchased or obtained any products or materials for trial and appraisal?

     YES   ☐   47-1   NO   ☐   -2

(Hand Respondent Card No. 3)

12.   Here is a ten-point scale. Would you please point to the figure on this scale which best describes your degree of involvement in the decisions to purchase capital equipment for your company. The higher the number, the greater your involvement; the lower the number, the less your involvement.

					48-					NO
FULL	9	8	7	6	5	4	3	2	1	0 INVOLVEMENT
INVOLVEMENT										AT ALL

13.   Here is a ten-point scale. Would you please point to the figure on this scale which best describes your degree of involvement in the decisions to lease capital equipment for your company. The higher the number, the greater your involvement; the lower the number, the less your involvement.

					49-					NO
FULL	9	8	7	6	5	4	3	2	1	0 INVOLVEMENT
INVOLVEMENT										AT ALL

Section II—Readership Patterns

14. (a) Do you ever receive any of the following publications?

         (CHECK (/) FOR EACH PUBLICATION RECEIVED)

         Canadian Purchasor ☐ 50-1   Modern Purchasing ☐ 50-2

EXHIBIT 2   The Questionnaire (*cont.*)

For Each Publication Received in Qu. 14(a), Ask:

(b) How many issues out of the last 12 would you say you have read?

Canadian Purchasor					Modern Purchasing				
One	☐ 51-1	Seven	☐ -7		One	☐ 52-1	Seven	☐ -7
Two	☐ -2	Eight	☐ -8		Two	☐ -2	Eight	☐ -8
Three	☐ -3	Nine	☐ -9		Three	☐ -3	Nine	☐ -9
Four	☐ -4	Ten	☐ -0		Four	☐ -4	Ten	☐ -0
Five	☐ -5	Eleven	☐ -X		Five	☐ -5	Eleven	☐ -X
Six	☐ -6	Twelve	☐ -V		Six	☐ -6	Twelve	☐ -V

Take Out Masked Issue

15. (a) I would like to leaf through this issue with you to find out what kinds of articles interest you most. Would you please point out any article or item that you have seen before?

	Seen article before -1	Glanced at -2	Read half -3	Read more than half -4	
Article #1					53
Article #2					54
Article #3					55
Article #4					56
Article #5					57
Article #6					58
Article #7					59
Article #8					60
Article #9					61
Article #10					62
Article #11					63

For Each Item Seen, Ask:

15. (b) Did you just glance at it, read about half or more than half of this article?
YES ☐ 64-1   NO ☐ 64-2

IF RESPONDENT RECEIVES MODERN PURCHASING, ASK:

16. (a) Is the copy of MODERN PURCHASING which you read also passed to other people in your company?
YES ☐   NO ☐

(b) IF "YES": What positions do they hold in your company? We do not want their names, just the position each holds.

_____

_____

_____

_____

_____

_____

_____

_____

_____

_____

Take Out _____ Issue of Modern Purchasing:

I would like to look at some specific articles and items with you, if I may.

Open at Article #1:

EXHIBIT 2   The Questionnaire (cont.)

For Each Article, Starting with Article 1, Ask:

19.   Do you remember looking at or reading any part of this article:

If "Yes":

Did you just glance at it, did you read part of it, or did you read it completely?

Record Below, and Continue Same Questioning for Each Article—Then Go to Qu. 20.

IF RESPONDENT SAYS HE OR SHE DOESN'T RECEIVE MODERN PURCHASING, OR DOESN'T KNOW, ASK:

17.   TAKE OUT _____ ISSUE OF MODERN PURCHASING:
I would like to leaf through some of the articles in this issue of MODERN PURCHASING to find out what articles interest you most. Would you please point out any marked article or item that looks interesting to you.

(Check Articles Mentioned)

Article #1 ☐ 65-1		Article #6 ☐ -6	
Article #2 ☐ -2		Article #7 ☐ -7	
Article #3 ☐ -3		Article #8 ☐ -8	
Article #4 ☐ -4		Article #9 ☐ -9	
Article #5 ☐ -5		Article #10 ☐ -0	

18.   As you know, articles and pictures in different magazines and different issues sometimes look alike. Now that you have been through the major parts of this issue, do you remember looking into this issue before or not?

YES ☐ 66-1 (go to Qu. 19)
NO ☐ 66-2 (go to Qu. 21)

For Each Article, Starting with Article 1, Ask:

19.   Do you remember looking at or reading any part of this article?

If "Yes":

Did you just glance at it, did you read part of it, or did you read it completely?

Record Below, and Continue Same Questioning for Each Article—Then Go to Qu. 21.

	Looked At or Read		If "Yes"		
	No	Yes	Glanced at	Read part	Read completely
Article #1	☐ 67-1	☐ -2	☐ -3	☐ -4	☐ -5
Article #2	☐ 68-1	☐ -2	☐ -3	☐ -4	☐ -5
Article #3	☐ 69-1	☐ -2	☐ -3	☐ -4	☐ -5
Article #4	☐ 70-1	☐ -2	☐ -3	☐ -4	☐ -5
Article #5	☐ 71-1	☐ -2	☐ -3	☐ -4	☐ -5
Article #6	☐ 72-1	☐ -2	☐ -3	☐ -4	☐ -5
Article #7	☐ 73-1	☐ -2	☐ -3	☐ -4	☐ -5
Article #8	☐ 74-1	☐ -2	☐ -3	☐ -4	☐ -5
Article #9	☐ 75-1	☐ -2	☐ -3	☐ -4	☐ -5
Article #10	☐ 76-1	☐ -2	☐ -3	☐ -4	☐ -5

To Be Asked of Readers of Modern Purchasing Only:
Hand Card No. 4 to Respondent

20.   Here is a list of the various things a reader might do as a result of reading a business publication. Which, if any, of these things have you done in the last twelve months as a result of reading something in the editorial or advertising pages of MODERN PURCHASING?

Requested prices or literature on products featured or advertised	☐ 77-1
Filed copies or articles for future reference	☐ -2
Marked articles or advertisements for special attention of others	☐ -3

EXHIBIT 2   The Questionnaire (*cont.*)

Otherwise investigated products featured or advertised	☐ -4
Made or recommended an actual purchase as a result of seeing a product featured in the editorial or advertising pages	☐ -5
Made changes in operation or methods as a result of information contained in the editorial or advertising pages	☐ -6
Used market reports as a guide to buying policy on various products	☐ -7
Investigated an advertiser as a possible source of supply	☐ -8

Can you think of any other action you have taken as a result of reading something in the editorial or advertising pages of MODERN PURCHASING?
(RECORD WORD FOR WORD) _____

_____

_____

Ask All Respondents:

21. (a) On which of the following subjects would you like to read more information?

Materials
management   ☐ 78-1

Value
analysis   ☐   -2

Data
processing   ☐   -3

  (b) On what other subjects connected with your job would you like further information?
(RECORD WORD FOR WORD) _____

22.   What are the major problems facing you in your job as a manager of purchasing?
(RECORD WORD FOR WORD) _____

23. (a) Are you a member of the Purchasing Management Association of Canada?
YES ☐ 79-1   NO ☐ 79-2

  (b) To what other associations, if any, connected with your work do you belong?

_____   _____

_____   _____

Hand Card No. 5 to Respondent

24.   Would you please mark the category into which your annual income from this company falls? Just indicate by the appropriate letter.

A—Under $30,000	☐ 80-1	D—$40,000–44,999	☐	-4
B—$30,000–34,999	☐ -2	E—$45,000–49,999	☐	-5
C—$35,000–39,999	☐ -3	F—$50,000 and over	☐	-6

Thanks Very Much for Your Cooperation

Conducting the Interview

The full-scale study was launched July 4, with interviewing to be completed by July 15. Specific article questions were based on the June issue of *Modern Purchasing.* Because of the summer holiday period, some of the executives were not available when initially contacted, and the inter-viewing period was extended by one working week. Completed interviews were returned to McDonald Research Limited by July 22.

Tabulation

Editing, coding, data entry, verification, computer tabulation, and report writing were done at

McDonald Research Limited under the supervision of a senior project director.

Translations

Interviewers in the province of Quebec and certain other areas of Canada where French-speaking populations exist (e.g., Ottawa-Hull, St. Boniface) were bilingual. Questionnaires were supplied to these interviewers in both English and French. In those instances when the respondent preferred, interviews were conducted in French.

A Toronto-based French translation firm retained by McDonald Research Limited translated questionnaires into French and rendered all verbatim and open-ended answers from the completed questionnaires back into English for inclusion in this report.

QUESTIONS

1. Evaluate the marketing research methodology employed.

2. What difficulties might be expected in the interviews?

3. Will the study, as described, achieve *Modern Purchasing*'s desired goals?

7. Modern Purchasing (B)

A Maclean-Hunter trade publication, *Modern Purchasing*, has conducted a study to obtain a precise profile of its market target readers—purchasing managers. This information is intended to help the magazine formulate editorial policy and also to provide its advertisers with useful guidelines to assist their promotional efforts.

Direct Responsibility	Percent*
Purchasing	75
Administration & management	24
Production management	15
Accounting & finance	12
Sales & sales management	10
(Many other activities were mentioned)	

*Adds to more than 100% due to multiple mentions.

THE FINDINGS HIGHLIGHTED

Profile of Purchasing Executives

Exclusive purchasing activity: 75 percent have purchasing as direct function

Seventy-five percent of the respondents were directly responsible for purchasing for their firm. Other direct functions of respondents included 24 percent administration and management, 15 percent production management, 12 percent accounting and finance, and so on.

Other Purchasing Duties

Direct or shared responsibility was reported by 87 percent of the respondents for company buying or brand selection decisions. Similar responsibilities were reported by 86 percent for inventory control; 76 percent for value analysis; 67 percent for vendor rating; 63 percent for traffic; and 55 percent for scrap disposal. Additional areas (other than purchasing) of direct responsibility were reported by 47 percent of the respondents.

Direct or Shared Responsibility	Percent*
Inventory control	86
Value analysis	76
Vendor rating	67
Traffic	63
Scrap disposal	55
Make-or-buy decisions	87

*Adds to more than 100% due to multiple mentions.

The majority report to top management

Seventy-nine percent of the respondents reported to one or more of the following: president, general manager, vice president, director or board of directors, owner, shareholders, and partners.

To Whom He Reports	Percent*
President	32
Vice president; owner; director	25
General manager	22
All other	29
No one	16

*Adds to more than 100% due to multiple mentions.

Professionalism of Purchasing
60 percent with firm more than 10 years

Sixty percent of the respondents had been with their present firm more than ten years, while 23 percent had been with their firm five to ten years. Actual time in their present job was as follows: 30 percent over ten years; 32 percent five to ten years; 38 percent four years or less.

Years of Service	With Firm (%)	In Job (%)
Over 20	33	12
16–20	12	6
11–15	15	12
5–10	23	32
3– 4	8	16
2 or less	9	22

Subordinate Buyers
55% have buyers reporting

Fifty-five percent of the purchasing managers had one or more buyers reporting to them at the plant where the interview was conducted, while 27 percent had buyers reporting to them from other locations of the company. Forty-seven percent of the purchasing departments had one or two employees, 29 percent from three to five, and 21 percent six or more.

Size of Purchasing Department	Percent
Over 6	21
3–5	29
1–2	47
No reply	3

Well-Educated Group

Sixty-one percent of the respondents had postsecondary school education, while 19 percent had graduated from university.

Education Attained	Percent
Postgraduate studies	6
University graduate	13
Postsecondary (incl. some univ.)	42
High or tech. school graduate	24
Other	15

A Well-Paid Occupation

The median annual income for respondents who replied lay in the range of $40,000 to $44,999. More than half (54 percent) reported receiving incomes of $40,000 or more annually from their companies, while 18 percent reported incomes of $50,000 or over.

Annual Income from Company	Percent
$50,000 and over	18
$45,000–$49,999	9
$40,000–$44,999	27
$30,000–$39,999	25
Under $30,000	21

Association Activities
57 percent are members of associations

Although 57 percent were members of various business trade associations, only 23 percent were members of the Purchasing Management Association of Canada. Forty-three percent did not belong to any association.

Purchasing Authority

Eight out of ten salespeople call on purchasing first
79 percent report salespeople contact purchasing first

Since the purchasing department's reason for being is to schedule and coordinate company buying of products and services in a central department, an important part of the purchasing manager's function is allocating time to suppliers and potential suppliers' salespeople. Seventy-nine percent of the respondents reported that these salespeople would normally contact the purchasing department first. In the instances where salespeople contact other departments initially, most (70 percent) are usually or always referred back to the purchasing department. This channeling of sales calls to purchasing ensures that the department fulfills its proper function of being the central company source of information on suppliers and potential suppliers of products.

Brand Decisions Among User Companies
73 percent new orders—76 percent repeat orders

Respondents' involvement in the vital area of brand or manufacturer selection was also checked after firm usage was established. Participation in brand selection averaged 73 percent on new orders, ranging from a low of 64 percent for mechanical parts and assembly components to a high of 79 percent for packaging materials. Repeat orders averaged 76 percent brand selection for the fourteen product categories respondents were questioned on.

73 percent appraise products

An important part of the purchasing manager's work is product appraisal. Seventy-three percent of the respondents said they had purchased or obtained products or materials on their own initiative in the past year for the purpose of trial and appraisal.

88 percent involved in capital equipment purchases

In the area of capital equipment purchases, respondents' involvement in decisions of this nature was checked against a 10-point scale. Seventy-four percent of the respondents indicated an involvement lying in the upper half of the scale, while 29 percent indicated full involvement. Only 12 percent reported no involvement. Sixty-six percent are involved in leasing capital equipment. (Of the 34 percent who stated they were not involved, it is not known if any or all respondent firms engage in leasing arrangements.)

READERSHIP

Seventy-eight percent of the respondents claimed to have received *Modern Purchasing*. Since the plants were selected for interviewing on an SIC basis (not from the magazine's own circulation list), the 78 percent receipt gives a true picture of total market penetration.

Receipt and Readership

Seventy-eight percent of the respondents received *Modern Purchasing*, and of these 72 percent had read one or more articles in the June survey issue.

72 percent read survey issue

Of the respondents who receive *Modern Purchasing*, 72 percent had read or looked at one or more articles in the June issue, three weeks after issue date. Sixty-eight percent claimed they read six or more issues out of twelve, while 47 percent read all issues.

66 percent pass *Modern Purchasing* to others

Two-thirds of the purchasing managers pass their copy to others. While assistant purchasing agents

Brand and Manufacturing Buying Decisions by "Purchasing" (Among User Firms)

	NEW ORDERS "Purchasing" Decides				REPEAT ORDERS "Purchasing" Decides			
	Purchasing Exclusively	Purchasing and Others	Total*	Others Usually	Purchasing Exclusively	Purchasing and Others	Total*	Others Usually
Chemicals	26%	47%	73%	27%	27%	47%	74%	26%
Industrial lubricants	22	44	66	34	26	43	69	31
Electric motors and/or controls	24	46	70	30	24	49	73	27
Fleet cars and/or trucks	30	41	71	29	28	45	73	27
Power transmission equipment (such as gears, V-belts, chains, etc.)	21	51	72	28	23	50	73	27
Maintenance equipment and supplies	27	45	72	28	28	47	75	25
Safety equipment and supplies	29	45	74	26	31	47	78	22
Materials (such as metals, plastics, glass, vulcanized fiber, rubber, etc.)	31	43	74	26	31	50	81	19
Materials handling equipment	26	51	77	23	28	54	82	18
Mechanical parts and assembly components (such as bearings, valves, pumps, fasteners, etc.)	21	43	64	36	24	46	70	30
Office equipment (such as furniture and business machines)	28	50	78	22	26	56	82	18
Office supplies (such as paper, forms, pens and pencils, etc.)	38	39	77	23	35	47	82	18
Packaging	37	42	79	21	34	47	81	19
Tools (hand and/or power)	27	45	72	28	26	49	75	25

*Average Purchasing Involvement New Orders 73%

*Average Purchasing Involvement Repeat Orders 76%

and other buyers were the most frequently mentioned secondary readers, the list of titles of pass-along readers indicates a wide and varied circulation on the pass-along list.

Readership Throughout Year of Those Who Receive *Modern Purchasing*	Percent
12 issues	47
6–11 issues	21
5 or less	19
Did not state	13

Action Taken as a Result of Reading *Modern Purchasing*

Receivers were asked about any action they took as a result of reading *Modern Purchasing* in the previous twelve months. Forty-nine percent had marked articles or advertisements for the special attention of others. Forty-three percent had requested prices or literature on products featured or advertised. Twenty-three percent had made or recommended an actual purchase as a result of reading an article or advertisement.

	Percent*
Marked articles or advertisements for special attention	49
Requested prices or literature on products featured or advertised	43
Filed copies or articles for future reference	43
Investigated an advertiser as a possible supply source	39
Otherwise investigated products featured or advertised	36
Made or recommended an actual purchase as a result of seeing a product featured in editorial or advertising	23
Made changes in operation or methods as a result of information in articles or ads	21
Used market reports as a guide to buying policy on various products	18
No action taken	19
Did not respond	7

*Adds to more than 100% due to multiple answers.

Respondents were handed a card with the following statements and asked to indicate their purchasing authority. The card contained the following statements:

A—The brand or manufacturer has usually been decided upon by the time I receive a requisition.

B—I share in the decision on brand or manufacturer after consultation with others.

C—I usually make the final decision on brand or manufacturer.

D—I recommend brands or manufacturers.

E—When brand or manufacturer is listed on requisition or order, I usually provide alternates after investigation.

F—When brand or manufacturer is specified but not available, I have authority to select an alternate brand or manufacturer.

For example the 26% for chemicals (see table on page 698) is based on those respondents who indicated, "I usually make the final decision on brand or manufacturer."

Capital Equipment		
Involvement in Decision	To Buy	To Lease
Full involvement	29%	26%
Substantial	45	28
Minor	14	12
No involvement	12	34
Salespeople First Contact		
Purchasing Department	79%	
Other Departments*	21%	

*70% of these are usually or always referred back to the Purchasing Department.

Trial and Appraisal of Products and Materials

Seventy-three percent of respondents have on their own initiative within the past year purchased or obtained products or materials for trial and appraisal.

EDITORIAL INTEREST

When asked about their job interests and major problems, respondents provided the editors of

Modern Purchasing with much interesting information that will prove useful in the preparation of future articles. Moreover, advertisers will be guided by these comments in determining copy approaches for purchasing executives and buyers. Subjects about which respondents would like to receive more information included:

- Control of production
- Purchasing and transportation for deliveries
- Inventory control systems
- Office methods
- Materials handling
- Packaging
- New products
- Plastics
- Costing, etc.

When asked what was the major problem facing the manager of purchasing, some of the responses included:

- Deliveries
- Transportation
- Training of people
- Selecting the right product
- Quality control
- Traffic and customs
- Scheduling
- Cutting down paperwork, etc.

QUESTIONS

1. How should *Modern Purchasing* use the findings in formulating its future editorial policy?
2. In what ways can the advertiser buying space in *Modern Purchasing* use this information to improve his or her marketing efforts?
3. What use can *Modern Purchasing* make of this information in attracting advertisers and advertising agency media people to use this trade journal in their advertising campaigns?

8. Loctite: A Marriage of Technology and Marketing Skills

TECHNOLOGY AND HISTORY

In 1953, Professor V. Krieble retired from the Department of Chemistry at Trinity College in Connecticut and began experimenting with various compounds. One of his patented inventions was an unusual anaerobic—a chemical that remains in a liquid state while exposed to air but turns into a tough, binding solid in the absence of air. This chemical, which he called "Loctite," would lock nuts and bolts against loosening from vibration. In the beginning, no one believed that a liquid could do the job that Loctite was claimed to do. But it did, and the result was phenomenal.

Today Loctite offers a series of "amazing chemicals" that keep metal assemblies together. These compounds can and do replace lockwashers, gaskets, tape, rivets, screws, and other mechanical fasteners. The adhesives and sealants the company offers rely on the fourth generation of

This case is based in part on a longer report developed in 1991 by Ramune Kubiliunas at The Freedonia Group, Cleveland, Ohio. It is also based on various Loctite publications, including annual reports, product brochures, catalogs, and journal articles. This version was developed by Andrew C. Gross of Cleveland State University in mid-1992.

anaerobics to provide very strong bonding. The compounds span a range of functions and perform well under adverse conditions in industrial, automotive, and consumer applications. Loctite's corporate strategy is research, diversification, and marketing "within its skills"; it is devoted to its family of specialty chemicals and will not enter into unrelated fields.

The company began test marketing its first products in the mid-1950s and was granted its first patent in 1959. Sales reached $1 million in 1961. In 1963, the company changed its name from American Sealants to Loctite. In the early 1970s, the company acquired Permatex, a famous name in automotive cements, and Woodhill Chemical, a marketer of household chemicals. Expansion continued based on internal growth, and the company has been highly successful in terms of sales, net income, and other indicators. Loctite joined the elite ranks of the Fortune 500 in 1990

(see Exhibit 1 for details). About 25 percent of Loctite is owned by Henkel (Germany).

CORPORATE STRATEGY AND TACTICS

Between 1985 and 1990, Loctite experienced excellent growth; sales grew at the rate of 17 percent per year and net income at 25 percent per year. The company is dedicated to maintaining this pace with a group of loyal employees around the globe. Indeed, Loctite benefited from being in foreign markets; today it derives 60 percent of its sales from outside the United States. Loctite expects its future growth to come from expansion beyond North America and Europe. It also plans to expand into electronics and medical markets, beyond its current emphasis on general industrial, automotive, and household applications. Loctite may make selected acquisitions in the future, but

EXHIBIT 1   Loctite Rankings in the *Fortune 500*

Fortune magazine ranks the largest 500 American industrial companies by sales volume for the prior year. *Fortune* also ranks the 500 companies by selected financial results and stock market performance. Shown below are the comparative rankings for Loctite Corporation among the Fortune 500 companies.

		Rank
Sales	$576.4 million	486
Profits	67.4	242
Assets	489.3 million	422
Stockholders' equity	320.2 million	317
Market value (3/8/91)	1,257.9 million	201
Profit as a percent of:		**Rank**
Sales	11.9%	32
Assets	13.8%	30
Stockholders' equity	21.1%	74
Earnings per share:		**Rank**
1990	$1.86	not calculated
% change from 1989	22.8%	not calculated
1980–1990 annual growth rate %	10.9%	101
Total return to investors		**Rank**
1990	30%	30
1980–1990 annual growth rate	17%	116

Source: *Fortune*, April 22, 1991, p. 305.

only if they fit in with its core businesses: adhesives and sealants. Its balance sheet now permits even a large acquisition. But the company will maintain its focus and diversify only within its skills.

Loctite is emphasizing new products, new applications, and market niches for existing products. It has doubled the rate of new-product introductions; in 1985 it derived 13 percent of sales from new products (those introduced in the past five years), and this figure rose to 25 percent by 1990. The company now sells more than 400 industrial and consumer adhesives, sealants, and related goods. There is some danger of product proliferation, but Loctite wants to maintain or even increase its research and development budget from the current 4 percent of sales. However, creation of new market niches is considered as important as creation of new products. A recent study indicated some 500 market niches for Loctite's products on a worldwide basis. The company often uses sophisticated psychographics to identify even small segments, which can then become target markets.

While Loctite "listens to the marketplace," it is also determined to be a leader in its field. Loctite developed liquid threadlockers, ultraviolet-cured adhesives, and "Super Glue" before there was any perceived need for these products. Then it went to work, aggressively promoting such compounds to industrial and household users through many distribution channels. Various incentive plans, volume discounts, and strong relationships with warehouse distributors, jobbers, and dealers characterize Loctite's operations. These strategies show the company's ability to combine new ideas, technical knowhow, and creative marketing.

BUSINESS GROUPS AND MARKET SEGMENTS

Loctite reaches its markets through three business or marketing groups: The North American Industrial Group, the U.S. Automotive and Consumer Group, and the International Group. The distribution of sales by the three groups is shown in

EXHIBIT 2   Loctite's Major Marketing Groups and User Markets

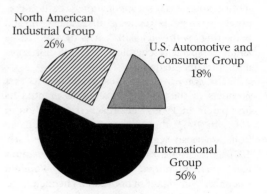

Part A. Loctite's Marketing Groups, 1990
(% of total)

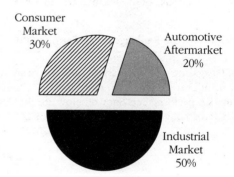

Part B. Loctite's Worldwide Markets, 1990
(% of total)

Exhibit 2, part A. All of the company's international operations (except activities in Canada, Mexico, and the Caribbean) are conducted by the International Group, which has shown the fastest rate of growth in recent years. Ken Butterworth, a chief executive, travels frequently around the globe and interacts with customers, employees, and suppliers.

Engineering or high-performance adhesives and sealants are the fastest-growing category of the adhesives and sealants industry in the United States. Loctite is well positioned in this category. Competitors in the United States are two specialty chemical firms, H. B. Fuller and Findley Adhesives, and a number of large, diversified firms, including Dow Chemical, Du Pont, General Electric, 3M, Monsanto, National Starch & Chemical, among others. For the latter group, adhesives and sealants are only a minor source of sales, which leaves the focused firms in a better position.

Loctite has three major user markets, as illustrated in Exhibit 2, part B: the industrial market, the consumer market, and the automotive aftermarket. The heart of the industrial market is the automotive manufacturing sector, which has reduced its purchases as of late. However, Loctite succeeded in reducing its dependence on the cyclical nature of the original automotive market from 15 percent in 1982 to 7 percent by 1990 in the United States and to 10 to 12 percent at the

EXHIBIT 3 A Typical Loctite Product/Application Matrix Available to Distributors

GASKET SEALANTS

Much as new engine designs require more advanced gasket makers, the underhood requirements of the 90's necessitate a superior sealant technology. Loctite offers a wide range of gasket sealants suitable for applications on both import and domestic vehicles of any model year or performance caliber.

	PART #							
PERMATEX® GASKET SEALANT GUIDE	**81997/ 81998**	**#1**	**#2**	**#3**	**#5**	**#9**	**#14**	**#97/98**
Import OE Endorsed	✔							
Non-Hardening Formula	✔		✔	✔		✔		✔
Hardening Formula		✔			✔		✔	
Thread Sealant	✔	✔	✔	✔		✔	✔	
For Gasket Positioning	✔					✔		✔
Gasket Sealant	✔	✔	✔	✔	✔	✔		
Temperature Range	600°F	400°F	400°F	400°F	350°F	400°F	300°F	450°F
Withstands High Pressures	✔	✔	✔	✔		✔	✔	✔
Sensor Safe	✔	✔	✔	✔	✔	✔	✔	✔

Source: *Loctite Auto + Consumer Group Product Catalog 1992* (Cleveland: Loctite Corporation) p. 4.

global level. The consumer market is doing well despite the recession in the United States, led by the single biggest product, "Super Glue," in all its various package formats. The automotive aftermarket is especially big in the United States, but Loctite hopes to expand its sales abroad.

MARKETING SEALANTS

As in adhesives, in the sealant market Loctite follows a policy of reaching both industrial users and households (the do-it-yourself market). In the industrial sector sealants are used mostly in construction, followed by other industrial segments and the automotive sector; percentage distribution in the United States is about 50, 25, and 25 percent, respectively. In construction, the sealants are used both in new buildings and for maintenance and repair of existing buildings of all kinds. In automotive manufacturing, the compounds are used in structural sealing applications. Silicones can replace gaskets, and synthetic rubber sealants are used to seal out moisture and dirt. About 20 pounds of sealants are used in the production of a medium-size car, a figure bound to rise as plastics substitute for metals. Other industrial applications include aircraft, rail, and marine equipment and other manufactured products, ranging from electronics to fluid power equipment (including professional maintenance and repair of such items).

While industrial users are the proving ground for high-performance sealants, these compounds are also used widely in the automotive aftermarket and by households. For such markets, Loctite packages its products in various kits for specialized applications. The merchandising of the product line, in all its variety, is aggressive, relying on quantity and special discounts plus offers of various incentive plans to a wide range of intermediaries: warehouse distributors, jobbers, and dealers. But Loctite could not achieve success by promotion alone. Accordingly, it extends technical assistance in the form of charts, tables, and other how-to advice. See Exhibit 3 for a typical matrix showing which sealant to use in which application.

Loctite seeks to motivate both its employees and its distributors. Company personnel are intimately involved in developing catalog items and in formulating promotional campaigns. There are seasonal variations in terms of what will be promoted and with what kind of theme, bonuses, and other forms of incentives offered to dealers. Recently the company featured T-shirts, jackets, videotapes, and other items as rewards. Loctite believes in marketing just the right product for the job, so it offers detailed assistance and advice to its managers, dealers, and ultimate users. The automotive aftermarket catalog now carries dozens of items in the sealant category alone, with specific applications pinpointed in great detail. As noted earlier, there is a possible danger of product proliferation, but Loctite knows both the garage mechanic and the do-it-yourselfer well.

QUESTIONS

1. How can a company survive by relying basically on a single technology, a single family of specialty chemicals, and a commitment to diversifying only within this core business?

2. Loctite is stressing growth in special niche markets and in moving aggressively in foreign marketplaces. What information do you think it is using to identify fast-growing markets?

3. Loctite has proven to be knowledgeable about its distributors and how to merchandise adhesives and sealants to them. Evaluate Loctite's merchandising program.

4. What would you include in internal memoranda to employees and in letters sent to outside distributors and dealers to keep them motivated? Would you use similar incentives and rewards?

9. Consolidated Glass International

INTRODUCTION

Consolidated Glass is one of the largest U.S. glass manufacturers. It is old, established, and viewed as a dignified, reliable corporation. It mostly supplies other industries with glass and associated products and makes few goods that are sold directly to consumers. It has a small subsidiary that manufactures tableware under the Consolidated brand name, but generally public awareness of the company and its products is not high. In industrial circles, however, the corporation is very well known.

In 1987, Consolidated decided to expand the sale of its products in the EC. It established an office in Brussels in 1988. Products that Consolidated sold successfully in the United States were selected to comprise the European product line. All of the goods were to be imported from the United States. A small team of technical representatives/salespeople was hired, and a sales program was begun to gain orders from industrial users.

By 1990, the Consolidated European operation had been less successful than Consolidated executives had hoped. Consolidated representatives were finding their task extremely difficult, were becoming somewhat discouraged, and were constantly being asked, "Who is Consolidated? What do they make?" It became apparent that Consolidated was little known in Europe, and this was hampering progress.

Rae, Johns, and Frey (RJF), a direct-mail agency, previously had engaged in tentative discussions with Consolidated executives, in both the United States and Europe, during a three-year period. RJF specializes in international direct-mail activities and has offices in New York, Toronto, London, and Amsterdam. In 1990, the agency was called in by Consolidated to advise on the use to which a direct-mail program might be put in Consolidated's situation.

DEFINING THE OBJECTIVES

Through discussions with Consolidated executives and technical representatives, RJF established that Consolidated had made no impact on the industries to which it was trying to sell in Europe. The representatives were trying to sell the products to buyers "cold." Consolidated had no "corporate image" in Europe, and there was no interest in its products.

RJF determined that Consolidated wished to become a major supplier of industrial glass products in seven of the European markets. The obvious first approach was to consider an advertising campaign.

This idea was rejected, because the product range was too narrow and specific, the target industries were known, and it would be expensive to reach the limited target audience since the campaign had to span seven markets in several countries. It was agreed that a direct-mail campaign would be mounted. The main objectives of the direct-mail campaign would be to

1. Establish a corporate image for Consolidated in the industries it wished to supply
2. Give Consolidated representatives/salespeople a prepared position and, if possible, obtain inquiries from prospective customers and invitations to call on them

A low-level media advertising campaign in trade journals also would be maintained as part of a long-term program to build up a presence. This

This case was prepared by Dr. David Corkindale, Cranfield School of Management, Cranfield, Bedfordshire, U.K. Copyright 1992 by Peter M. Banting, Ph.D., Professor of Marketing, McMaster University, Hamilton, Ontario, Canada.

was not closely coordinated with the envisioned direct-mail program. Consolidated stated it was interested in immediate recognition and sales response.

THE DIRECT-MAIL PROGRAM

RJF was given the responsibility of devising a program to achieve the agreed-upon objectives. From experience, it believed it was important to contact the most senior executives in companies, ideally managing directors (presidents) or manufacturing directors (vice presidents of manufacturing), since information about potential new suppliers travels down company hierarchies but rarely up. RJF also had found that the response to direct-mail-prompted inquiries was generally lower from purchasing managers than from more senior executives. In many cases, RJF asserted, purchasing managers wait to be told by others in the company to obtain information.

In consultation with Consolidated, it was agreed which countries and which industries were the prime targets for the campaign. RJF then set about establishing for each country the companies (by name) that fell within the industry classifications and the names and titles of senior executives in each company. This work was coordinated at RJF's Amsterdam office, where a record card index of details on many European companies is maintained. Information was abstracted from Consolidated's records and from specialist mailing lists and directory houses in each country concerned. A record card was established for each company to be contacted, listing key personnel and salient details on the company's products, outputs, and supply requirements.

A preselected target group of companies was drawn up based on the industrial segments that were assessed to be most worthwhile. RJF conducted interviews with Consolidated's executives to draw up the list. In all, a total of 8,036 key companies in 8 markets and 16 different industries was singled out for contact. Material in four different languages was needed. The program was launched in late 1990 and monitored over the succeeding year.

Details of the Plan and Material

Initially four mailings were sent out, a week apart, to several key executives in each of the companies selected. The letters included in the mailings were correctly titled and contained the same headline, but the text differed. Continuity was maintained in the sequence of letters and their content; they basically announced Consolidated's presence in Europe, the nature of the company, and its products. The main purpose of the letter was to invite the recipient to ask for further information via a reply coupon. The "further information" announced in the letter would be in the form of a Consolidated newsletter, which featured articles on the use of glass and new developments in the field.

Production of the Consolidated newsletter was coordinated by RJF, which advised on the layout and selected photographs from Consolidated's library. The newsletter was four pages long and contained short articles written by Consolidated Glass technical, development, and marketing executives. Each article had a reference code at the bottom, and the recipient was invited to send for further information on any topic of interest. A postage-paid card was enclosed with the newsletter. In both the newsletter and the subsequent material, recipients were invited to ask for specialist advice. The copy was intended to instill confidence in Consolidated's expertise.

Replies to the initial letters and the newsletter were sent by recipients in each country directly to a Consolidated Glass office in their own countries. RJF knew there was no international prepostage system and believed that if it had required all replies to be sent to Holland or Brussels and recipients to stamp their replies, this would have drastically reduced the response. Another advantage of having inquiries dealt with in the country of origin was that they would be processed quickly and with no language problems.

The Response

In the first year of the direct-mail program, a 21 percent response was obtained requesting copies of the newsletter. Analyses of the responses by

EXHIBIT 1 Response by Country

Country	Quantity Mailed	Quantity Response	% Response
United Kingdom	1,790	293	16.36
Germany	1,208	310	25.66
France	1,356	266	19.61
Switzerland—German	622	173	27.81
—French	465	81	17.42
Belgium—English	307	47	15.31
—French	410	93	22.68
Netherlands	706	101	14.30
Sweden	481	99	20.58
Italy	845	235	27.81
Various	116	48	41.38
Totals	8,306	1,746	21.02

EXHIBIT 2 Standard Industrial Classification (SIC) Code Explanation

SIC Code	Description
NO	No SIC Code
19	Ordnance and accessories
28	Chemicals and allied products
29	Petroleum refining and related industries
32	Stone, clay, glass, and concrete products
33	Primary metal industries
34	Fabricated metal products, except ordnance, machinery, and transportation equipment
35	Machinery, except electrical
36	Electrical machinery, equipment, and supplies
37	Transportation equipment
38	Professional, scientific, and controlling instruments; photographic and optical goods; watches and clocks
39	Miscellaneous manufacturing industries
73	Miscellaneous business services
82	Educational services
89	Miscellaneous services
91	Governmental

EXHIBIT 3 Response by SIC Code

SIC Code	Quantity Mailed	Responses	%
NO	435	52	11.95
19	13	6	46.15
28	110	29	26.36
29	3	1	33.33
32	152	94	61.84
33	45	8	17.78
34	394	46	11.67
35	822	160	19.46
36	3,072	632	20.57
37	1,405	243	17.29
38	1,454	331	22.76
39	53	8	15.09
73	61	27	44.26
82	22	8	36.36
89	28	22	78.57
91	121	31	25.61
Various	116	48	41.38
Totals	8,306	1,746	21.02

EXHIBIT 4 Analysis of Major SIC Code Response

Country	SIC	Mailed	Response	%
United Kingdom	32	33	27	81.81
	35	159	24	15.09
	36	496	103	20.76
	37	566	40	7.06
	38	242	71	29.33
	Rest	294	28	9.52
Germany	32	68	37	54.41
	35	107	32	29.90
	36	492	115	23.37
	37	153	19	12.41
	38	332	78	23.49
	Rest	56	29	51.78
France	32	21	17	80.95
	35	95	18	18.94
	36	565	85	15.04
	37	256	71	27.73
	38	193	44	22.79
	Rest	226	31	13.71
Switzerland—German/French	35	126	25	19.84
	36	327	94	28.74
	37	51	13	25.49
	38	386	72	18.65
	Rest	197	50	25.38
Belgium—English/French	35	114	16	14.03
	36	301	60	19.93
	37	108	27	25.00
	Rest	194	37	19.07
Netherlands	36	361	45	12.46
	37	54	8	14.81
	38	116	25	21.55
	Rest	175	23	13.14
Sweden	35	91	19	20.87
	36	212	37	17.45
	37	42	16	38.09
	38	74	16	21.62
	Rest	62	11	17.74
Italy	28	34	12	35.29
	35	79	23	29.11
	36	318	93	29.24
	37	175	49	28.00
	38	90	20	22.22
	Rest	149	38	25.50

EXHIBIT 5   Responses by Title of Respondent

Title	U.K	Ger.	Fr.	Swit.		Bel.		Neth.	Swed.	Italy	TOTAL
				Ger.	Fr.	Eng.	Fr.				
Directors	22.2%	30.3%	22.2%	26.6%	30.9%	10.6%	25.8%	26.7%	19.2%	24.2%	24.1%
Directors—Technical	2.0	4.8	10.5	6.9	14.8	8.5	17.2	2.0	8.1	13.6	9.4
Purchasing	8.2	11.6	13.5	19.6	11.1	21.3	20.4	15.8	12.1	14.5	13.2
R & D	12.0	14.8	12.8	8.7	12.3	8.5	9.7	3.0	6.1	6.4	10.1
Engineering	16.0	14.5	13.9	8.1	6.2	23.4	8.6	8.9	23.2	6.8	12.3
Technical	10.9	7.8	10.5	15.6	8.6	12.8	5.4	10.9	8.1	9.4	9.7
Unspecified	6.1	9.4	8.3	8.7	11.1	8.5	6.4	21.8	13.1	12.8	9.6
Various—Nontechnical	7.5	2.3	4.9	3.5	2.5	6.4	5.4	8.9	6.1	5.9	5.0
Various—Technical	5.1	4.5	3.4	2.3	2.5	—	1.1	2.0	4.0	6.4	3.8
Others	—	—	—	—	—	—	—	—	—	—	2.8
	100.0	100.0	100.0	100.0	100.0	100.0	100.0	100.0	100.0	100.0	100.0

country, SIC code within each country, and position of respondent within his or her company, together with SIC descriptors, appear in Exhibits 1 through 5.

On the reply cards contained in the initial letters and newsletter, respondents were asked to supply details of their positions, interests in Consolidated products, and the names and positions of others in their company who should receive details. In this way, Consolidated was able to build up its fields of contact and direct its representatives/salespeople to specific people within the target companies who had expressed interest in Consolidated products. All reply cards were sent to sales area managers by the Consolidated national office. Total response figures for each country were sent to RJF monthly so that the agency could monitor and coordinate developments.

FURTHER DEVELOPMENTS

Consolidated executives were very pleased with the first year's program. They believed that many useful contacts and orders had been gained through the program and that a firm base had been established to gain Consolidated the respect it was seeking. The newsletter idea was developed into a regularly produced publication, which was sent quarterly to all those originally requesting it. The whole program was repeated in the following year, when only those who had not responded at all during the first year were contacted, together with one additional industry category. Again RJF coordinated this program and analyzed responses.

QUESTIONS

1. Evaluate RJF's choice of respondents.
2. What conclusions may be drawn from the various response rates?
3. Evaluate the advantages and disadvantages of direct mail as a mass promotion medium.

10. Falconbridge: The Corporate Image of a Mining Company

OVERVIEW

Falconbridge Nickel Mines Limited is one of two major nickel mining companies headquartered in Sudbury, Ontario. The other company is International Nickel Company Limited (Inco). Falconbridge operates facilities in and outside Canada. It is engaged primarily in the mining and refining of nickel, but it is also involved in processing and marketing other metals and minerals. In the early 1980s, the company undertook a major restructuring and cost-cutting operation. In 1982–1983, an independent survey focusing on the corporate image of both Falconbridge and Inco was carried out by students at Laurentian University among local educators, politicians, the media, and the public at large. The results of the survey showed that both companies enjoyed relatively positive images with all four segments. This seemed surprising in light of the layoffs, operation cutbacks, strikes, and environmental damage that had occurred, but respondents recognized the ongoing contribution of these two large employers. Another survey, replicating the one of ten years ago, is being proposed now.

BACKGROUND

Falconbridge is an international resource enterprise engaged directly and through its subsidiaries and associated companies in the mining, processing, and marketing of metals and minerals. Its product family includes nickel, ferronickel, copper, cobalt, other base metals, certain precious metals, industrial minerals, and steel castings. Nickel is still the flagship product of the company; this metal is used as an alloy in coinage and in steelmaking, where it imparts higher strength to steel. The metal is used in other alloy applications, in electroplating, and as a catalyst. During the past thirty years, various metals have been found as substitutes for nickel. For this and other reasons, the company has faced cyclical downturns.

Falconbridge operations can be traced to the early part of the twentieth century, when a rich nickel lode was discovered in northern Ontario; mining and smelting operations followed in the greater Sudbury area. Falconbridge prospered, but demand for nickel dropped substantially after World War II and profits were depressed for several years. Demand rose once again in the 1950s; as a result, six new mines were brought into production and new processing facilities were built. Nickel sales increased sharply, but profits remained steady; however, dividends rose from $1.10 per share in 1959 to $3.50 by 1965. During the 1970s, increased competition came from mines and smelters in developing nations, which could produce nickel and other metals at lower prices. Falconbridge faced higher costs for labor, capital, and energy; nevertheless, it chose to invest in new facilities in Canada and the Caribbean. In the early 1980s, Falconbridge still faced increased operating costs, while prices for base metals fluctuated.

This case was written by Professor David Gillingham, currently Dean at Sup de Co (Groupe ESC Rennes), the Business School at Rennes, France. It is based on material developed in three student projects under his direction at Laurentian University in Sudbury, Ontario, Canada: Cameron et al., Doyle et al., and Chertow et al. This edited and revised version of the original case was developed by Professor Andrew Gross of Cleveland State University, Cleveland, Ohio.

OPERATIONS IN THE 1980s

In April 1982, William James was recruited as chief executive. His mandate called for making major changes and for running a "bare-bones operation." Features of this turnaround included elimination of fancy offices for top managers, cutting both staff at headquarters and operating personnel at the mines and refineries, selling off the corporate aircraft, and slashing both the research and development budget and the exploration budget by 50 and 75 percent, respectively. The results showed up in the bottom line. Although metal prices continued to fall in 1983, to about $2 per pound of nickel, the loss at Falconbridge was trimmed to $3.5 million.

THE COMPANY AND THE COMMUNITY

The cut in both operating and staff personnel was keenly felt in the company's headquarters town, Sudbury, and the surrounding area of northern Ontario. Despite the cuts in jobs, Falconbridge remained the region's second largest employer after Inco. Falconbridge also improved working conditions at its mining and smelter facilities, while advocating safety and espousing environmental concerns. Some of the steps taken during the late 1970s and early 1980s included emphasis on personnel safety equipment, provisions for filtered air in the smelting plants, and the reduction of sulphur dioxide emissions into the atmosphere. An energy conservation program and an industrial noise reduction project were also initiated. The company continued its charitable activities, including donation of equipment to hospitals. Falconbridge also provided funds and athletic equipment for local sports events.

CORPORATE IDENTITY AND CORPORATE IMAGE

The basic elements of corporate identity are the name and the logo of the company. The name and logo (also referred to as the *symbol* or *mark*) should appear on stationery, buildings, and vehicles and, of course, in advertising. Falconbridge uses its corporate symbol, the falcon, on all of its

printed material and in print media advertising. The symbol is readily recognizable, and its association with the company is obvious. It is readily recalled by the various stakeholders of the company. The corporate slogan, "Responsible developers of Canada's natural resources for over 50 years," was introduced in 1979 and is used in radio spots as well as in print. The logo and the slogan are used both within and outside the company.

Corporate image is a far broader concept than corporate identity. It is shaped over the years by both the company and many other "players." Such an image is formed from all the visual, verbal, and other components that a company generates. Also included are the items generated by others about the company, such as the media, commentators, and analysts. Put differently, corporate image embraces the product line, the behavior of the sales force, advertising and other forms of promotion, prices charged, and the views of the firm held by suppliers, customers, and the public.

Falconbridge conducts its promotional and public relations campaigns on many fronts. In addition to print and radio advertising, it uses public displays at shopping centers in Sudbury to influence local opinion. For example, it used various posters and photos to show how its plant noise abatement project was carried out. In the 1980s, Falconbridge also conducted tours of its operations for visitors during the summer months. These tours were advertised in newspapers and on posters located throughout the Sudbury area. The company sponsored a daily community service bulletin as well as a float for the annual Christmas parade.

METHODOLOGY OF THE 1982–1983 SURVEY

During 1982–1983 students in the Faculty of Business at Laurentian University conducted a survey focusing on the corporate images of Falconbridge and Inco. The results would allow the construction of two corporate profiles and then comparisons between them. The research objectives were to establish benchmarks for the corporate images of Falconbridge and Inco in the

EXHIBIT 1   Response Numbers by Sample Segments

Survey	General Public	Politicians	Media	Educators	Total
Falconbridge	69	42	10	83	204
Inco	118	12	12	23	165
Total	187	54	22	106	369

Note: The segment differences exist but are not statistically significant and must be interpreted with caution.

Sudbury area. The results would provide some guidance for the two firms in setting community relations objectives and allow measurement of progress toward those goals.

A questionnaire was constructed using multiple-choice and semantic differential scale questions to measure attitudinal and awareness factors. Attitudinal factors could aid in determining the image of the company held by various publics, and awareness factors could help in assessing what contributed to this image. Together the two sets would assist in formulating a communication strategy. The survey was administered using a mixture of mail and telephone interviews to four groups as shown in Exhibit 1. The overall response rate was about 26 percent.

The general public was surveyed using the phone directory, but educators, politicians, and the media were sampled on a convenience basis. The media sample was small, and caution was necessary for this segment. The results were likely to be representative for the other three segments. (Note: Since the two companies had few customers in the area, this public or stakeholder group was eliminated, and a study of employee attitudes was postponed to a later date.)

RESULTS OF THE 1982–1983 SURVEY

The results of the survey are summarized in Exhibits 2, 3, and 4. They show that both Falconbridge and Inco enjoyed relatively positive images with the four segments of Sudbury's population, with Inco slightly ahead of Falconbridge. Given the recent occurrence of layoffs and

EXHIBIT 2   Ratings of the Two Companies by Three Audiences

Politicians	Media	Educators
Rate F and I of equal importance to local economy	Rate F and I equal on safety aspects	Rate working conditions same at F and I
Rate union-management relations at F as better than at I	Rate union-management relations at F as better than at I	Rate F as more community minded than I
Rate F and I as being equally community minded	Rate F and I as being equally interesting	
Rate F as being a richer organization than I	Rate I as being richer than F	

Notes: 1. F = Falconbridge, I = Inco.
2. The segment differences exist but are not statistically significant and must be interpreted with caution.

EXHIBIT 3 Summary of Results for Multiple-Choice Questions, by Segment

Question

Multiple-choice question scale

Negative				Positive
1	2	3	4	5

In comparison to other mining companies how "safe":

Extremely un—	Less —	The Same	More —	Extremely —

How "concerned" about the environment:

Not —	Not very —	Somewhat —	—	Very —

How "important" to local economy:

Very un—	Un—	The Same	—	Very —

How community-minded:

Not —	Not very —	Somewhat —	—	Very —

How well do you think I/F treats its workers:

Very Poor	Poor	Average	Good	Excellent

What do you think of union-management relations:

Very bad	Bad	Average	Good	Excellent

Median Scores by Segment

Question	General Public		Politicians		Media		Educators	
	I	F	I	F	I	F	I	F
In comparison to other mining companies how "safe"	4	3	4	3	4	4	4	3
How "concerned" about the environment	3	3	4	4	3	3	3	3
How "important" to local economy	5	4	5	5	5	4	5	4
How community-minded	4	3	4	3	4	3	4	3
How well do you think I/F treats its workers	4	3	4	3	4	3	4	3
What do you think of union-management relations	3	3	3	4	2	4	3	3

Notes: 1. I = Inco, F = Falconbridge.
2. None of the differences in scores are statistically significant.

EXHIBIT 4 Summary of Results for Bipolar Scale Questions, by Segment

Scale	Median Scores by Segment								Scale
	General Public		Politicians		Media		Educators		
Zero (0) Score is:	I	F	I	F	I	F	I	F	Ten (10) Score is:
Poor working conditions	5	6	6	7	5	6	6	6	Good working conditions
Small	9*	6	10	7	9	7	9	7	Large
Not community-minded	7	6	8	8	8	5	6	7	Community-minded
Boring	6	5	7	5	4	4	5	3	Interesting
Poor organization	7	7	9	7	9	7	8	8	Rich organization

Notes: 1. I = Inco, F = Falconbridge.
2. *Significant difference between I and F responses.

facility closings, coupled with claims of environmental damage and labor disputes at the two large firms in the recent past, these results may seem surprising at first. The explanation may be that most respondents recognized the importance of the two large employers to the local economy in terms of good wages, benefits, and improved working conditions.

Regarding the two corporate profiles, Inco had a slightly more positive image. Inco was seen as being very important to the local economy, being community minded, giving good treatment to workers, offering slightly above-average working conditions, and being safer than other mining firms. Falconbridge was viewed as being important to the local economy, being somewhat community minded, providing average treatment for workers, offering above-average working conditions, and having the same safety record as other mining companies. The main differences in the samples of three groups (politicians, media, and educators) are summarized in Exhibit 2. Although Inco had a slightly more positive image than Falconbridge among the various segments and overall, the differences were not statistically significant. The top management of the two companies were pleased with the results of the independent survey and believed these findings would assist

them in formulating their public relations campaigns in the years to come.

QUESTIONS

1. Discuss and criticize the methodology used in the 1982–1983 survey conducted by the students at Laurentian University. Suggest ways of replicating or improving the survey.

2. In what ways can Falconbridge utilize the results in its proposed public relations work? Do you think the company is concerned that it finished slightly below Inco?

3. List a number of missions that corporate image advertising should accomplish. Suggest specific guidelines for a successful corporate image campaign. (Hint: Look at J. R. Gregory, *Marketing Corporate Image* [Lincolnwood, Ill.: NTC Business Books, 1991], pp. 197–200.)

4. If an environmental crisis such as a mining disaster should occur, what specific steps can a company like Falconbridge or Inco take? Do you think such damage control is effective? How would you arrive at fair compensation for the victims?

11. The Power Supplies Division

The Power Supplies (PS) Division of Hanson Enterprises, Inc. first applied its extensive knowledge of special-application space and military batteries to nongovernmental uses in the late 1960s. Until that time, the company had never attempted to market its pioneering battery products, mainly because the company's engineers had developed these products more as their own toys/inventions than as a business venture. However, even today, any visitor who enters PS's well-guarded plant in southern rural Indiana will be surprised to see that in the mid-1970s PS developed an electric golf cart with a range of more than 250 miles. About the same time, PS developed an electric car that achieved better than 140 miles per hour in an official time trial run in Utah, and in the late 1970s, a battery-powered racing boat. In the 1980s, the company developed compact batteries with the power to run medium-sized garden tractors, to start heavy construction equipment in cold weather to minus 40 degrees, and to provide emergency back-up power during electrical power outages for a wide range of potential uses.

COMPANY HISTORY

Hanson Enterprises, Inc. was established in the 1920s as a metal parts manufacturer in New Jersey. Despite some lean times and an ongoing battle with the national economic cycles, the company has grown and now has thirty operating divisions in a dozen states, Canada, England, Germany, Italy, and Egypt. Hanson Enterprises is engaged in the industrial manufacturing of thousands of different products in more than seventy plants and has a total corporate sales volume of about $950 million (1991). The company strategy is centered on divisional autonomy. The divisions operate fairly independently at relatively small plants, most of which are located in small to middle-size eastern and midwestern communities. Along with this philosophy of autonomous divisions, Hanson Enterprises stresses product quality and is known for its excellence in engineering and research.

HISTORY OF PS

The Power Supply Division was formed in 1952 as a government research facility for vacuum power tubes. In 1956, PS received a government contract to design and develop a battery to launch and guide a classified U.S. Army weapon. Over the next few years, PS won several military and space contracts. Since 1966, almost all of PS's sales have been related to military and space batteries and battery components. In 1990, the Power Supply Division was acquired by Hanson Enterprises. The division's prior parent had been forced into Chapter 11 bankruptcy in 1989 and chose to spin off PS as part of a retrenchment scheme. The old parent company was troubled by the division's strategic fit into the overall product/service theme and was happy to sell PS for cash. The new parent company changed the division's name from "Military Space" to "Power Supplies" (commonly called simply "PS" by its customers, competitors, and employees), hoping that the broader name would help propel the division out of its almost total reliance as a government job shop into commercial activities. Today, PS employs about 550 and is recognized around the world by the military and space battery industry

This case was prepared by Dr. Joseph W. Leonard, Assistant Professor, Department of Management at Miami University; and Dr. John Thanopoulos, Director of International Business and Professor of Marketing at the University of Akron. All names and places have been disguised.

as the leader in technical expertise and one of three co-leaders in dollar sales volume.

PS ACTIVITIES IN THE 1980s

In the late 1960s, PS spent significant amounts of capital to expand existing facilities, remodel old ones, and update its equipment. As a result, the division moved into late twentieth-century technology, and it started an era of overdependence on long-term loans. Capital expansion was necessary for PS if it was going to continue to compete successfully for military and space projects, but it was catastrophic for a series of PS's financial managers. Despite their competencies with internal processes, planning and control systems, and the like, these managers found themselves continually dogged by corporate management about the debt. As a result, there has been a considerable turnover of controllers.

The marketing area has also been plagued with management turnover; in fact, no contract manager lasted more than five years. The most outspoken, Bruce Jacobs, 1977–1982, with a Ph.D. in marketing, faced severe opposition for his Fun-Sun City electric car project. Although less flamboyant and less directed toward nongovernment jobs, the three contract managers who followed Jacobs also faced opposition and were all forced out.

THE ELECTRIC CAR PROJECT

In May 1980, a land-developing outfit in Arizona contacted PS to seek information and subsequently ordered 660 lithium battery systems at a price of $1,205.50 per unit, with delivery in early 1981. Fun-Sun City, Inc., the ordering firm, was in the land-developing business for retirement communities and recently had extended operations into the production of goods that potentially would be sold exclusively through their own captive markets. Fun-Sun City was operating five re-

tirement communities with a permanent population of 6,000+ residents and was producing an extensive line of products, ranging from T-shirts to paddle boats.

The latest product was to be an electric golf cart, oversized and with roadworthy specifications, planned to be marketed even outside the borders of the retirement community markets. The cart was designed to be used as a second family car, was fast (up to 30 miles per hour), and could travel 75 miles on one charge. The only reliable power unit that Fun-Sun City was able to find was the Li24N (lithium battery) system, patented and produced by PS exclusively.

Bruce Jacobs handled the sale with extreme care. He realized the potential of commercial sales* from the beginning, but he also realized that "rocking the boat is dangerous" in a conservative culture such as PS. "The life of a marketer in an engineering firm is pitiful," he said during the last days of January to Andy Parker, the division's controller, as well as Jacob's friend and ally. "First of all, you do not understand their [engineers'] language; then, they want to produce whatever toys fancy their minds; and finally, they want you to sell them. Now, I must say that they have ideas.... This Li24N, for example, was a very good one ... but it applies basically to military and space programs. It is much more than what they need in a golf cart."

"But this is what Fun-Sun City asked for, and they pay good money, too," interrupted Parker.

"Well, that's the point," continued Jacobs. "Golf carts do not need a space battery. They need a less demanding and a cheaper one. We must see the marketplace. The suppliers must see the real needs of the marketplace—if the buyers cannot see them. Otherwise, somebody from the competition will give Fun-Sun City a cheaper battery next year. Then, this nice door to commercial sales will close for us."

General Manager Joe Hinds walked in and heard the last part of the conversation. He did not say a word, but he deeply registered in his mind one further thought—to expand Jacobs' job de-

---

*PS considers all "nongovernment as end-user" sales to be commercial. Therefore, what PS considers as "commercial" many organizations would categorize as "industrial."

scription from contracts to a marketing direction. The general manager felt confident about his division. He had excellent engineers, high-level technology, good production facilities, competent product assurance and control workers, and an impressive backlog of military orders (April 1, 1981 backlog of $9.7 million, total 1980 sales of $18 million).

In spite of all the extensive orders and almost assured future business, however, the general manager also realized that profit margins were declining and that the only reason he could afford to make interest payments was that the previous controller had achieved all this modernization and capital expansion when interest rates were much lower than those of 1981. The competition was already bidding lower. What if this trend were to continue? New ways to benefit from the existing innovations and new markets had to be found. Old products had to be reexamined. Marginal use of resources had to be considered. The general manager knew that costs were increasing rapidly.

The whole PS division was truly thrilled with the new application of the Li24N. Further, one of the golf carts was given as a present to Jacobs (who, violating all existing unwritten practices, had accepted it and was using it for his transportation within the plant). When not being used, the cart was parked at the front entrance, and since it was "dressed up" with a blue jean outfit, it was carrying the name "NeDim" (new dimension versus "denim" for blue jeans). Jacobs had done an excellent job with the internal promotion of the new marketing dimensions (commercial products), and he had also instituted the "tiny" prize, which was 1 percent of the assured sales (over $5,000) arranged by any of the company's employees using existing batteries and new customers with commercial orientation.

However, in General Manager Joe Hinds' mind, there were some doubts about the whole approach of the "marketers." The "contracts" people were overperforming their roles. The atmosphere was like a continuous "fair" with flags, prizes, and gimmicks. Given the conservative climate at PS, the general manager faced a dilemma.

It was then that Hinds' secretary through the intercom announced that Jacobs was there to see him. Jacobs said, "Again violating the established guidelines, I assigned to Tony Tolbs the rather ambitious task of collecting potential leads for future commercial customers. Tony has worked on this project since November and has a thorough knowledge of most of our batteries with commercial application potential. I spent two days with him summarizing the information."

General Manager Hinds replied, "Bruce, I admire you. I like you. But you never follow my instructions. For your own sake, I expect that you better make sense. . . . Workers are trying to sell batteries. Your contracts people on the road wear funny T-shirts from Fun-Sun City, bought with our money. Good customers are complaining. I fear that some of your people do not give enough attention to our good old customers. For example, Jerry Day [Boeing Seattle, program manager on the Air Launched Cruise Missile] was upset last month when he and his crew were here and you were in Colorado trying to drum up some windmill battery possibility. I am discouraged, although I am persuaded that you are right."

TRANSITION PERIOD (1980s)

The next weeks were hectic for the contracts department. Jacobs and his staff were busy with contractual negotiations and meeting with regular customers on various problems such as schedule slippage and technical problems. As a result, Jacobs gradually slowed down his activities regarding commercial applications. PS did start limited production on two batteries for commercial applications. A few nickel cadmium batteries were produced and finally sold at a good profit for use in emergency lights. Some lithium batteries were produced on a speculative basis for fire alarm use; about half were sold, and the others were eventually scrapped out for parts. Jacobs was interested in a couple of other minor projects, but nothing materialized. Several months later, Bruce Jacobs resigned and went into college teaching. A month later, Jacob's ally Andy Parker resigned as controller and after two months was replaced by an outsider.

The remainder of the 1980s and early 1990s showed good sales (see Exhibit 1) and acceptable profits for PS. PS views the latest backlog figures

EXHIBIT 1   Sales Volume for Years Ending December 31 (in thousands of dollars)

Customer (end user)	1987	1988	1989	1990	1991	6/30 1992
U.S. Army	11,014	11,989	9,853	5,850	7,956	8,432
U.S. Navy	4,253	5,796	3,668	4,981	10,124	2,159
U.S. Air Force	7,524	11,489	13,896	8,420	7,121	2,966
Dept. of Energy	281	297	4,159	2,956	3,111	1,094
NASA	1,423	1,080	1,184	7,953	5,805	1,497
Foreign	6,839	7,945	6,120	9,842	7,160	7,856
Commercial	287	410	75	366	156	0
Unknown/Other	404	0	25	11	28	249
Total	32,025	39,006	38,980	40,379	41,461	24,254

as very good (see Exhibit 2). Corporate management was satisfied with the aggregate performance. With the exception of the controller and the contracts manager positions, there was little turnover among the managers of PS. A few commercial sales with end uses in marine searchlights, model airplanes, wheelchairs, photography equipment, and other applications came in the late 1980s (as noted in Exhibit 2). In spite of the unpredictability of foreign military sales and in-

creased domestic competition, sales flourished during the last half of the Reagan years. General Manager Hinds, however, was beginning to worry about foreign competition, the tightening of the space budget, and the continuing discussions about a tightening of military spending by the United States and its allies. Although the commercial satellite business for communications and television business was growing, PS's market share seemed to be sharply eroding. PS blamed the sat-

EXHIBIT 2   Current Backlog (in thousands of dollars), April 1

Customer (end user)	1987	1988	1989	1990	1991	1992
U.S. Army	5,325	4,796	4,122	6,740	3,262	6,497
U.S. Navy	546	799	844	836	396	6,644
U.S. Air Force	3,620	8,256	4,793	5,640	6,917	3,577
Dept. of Energy	0	290	3,350	1,746	2,985	38
NASA	5,890	5,982	4,686	5,019	4,717	7,958
Foreign	1,099	4,956	8,920	6,456	3,720	5,490
Commercial	0	410	54	306	167	55
Total	16,480	25,489	26,769	26,743	22,164	30,259

ellite battery business drop on changes toward less rigorous quality requirements and specifications and more emphasis on price and delivery terms. Although much of the satellite business is technically nongovernment, from PS's perspective these contracts are with the major aerospace firms so the administration, negotiation, and contractual process is about the same as with the standard government subcontracts.

The most recently departed contracts manager, George Marshall (1988–1990), experienced several minor run-ins with the general managers (both Hinds until his retirement and Jim Carr, the engineering manager who replaced Hinds as general manager) and all the assistant engineering managers. Many think that the 36-year-old Marshall lost his job because of what became known as the "samurai boondoggle." Marshall went to Japan in March 1990 to negotiate a contract to provide batteries for a golf tractor company. He allegedly spent most of his time viewing the cherry blossoms and, despite his international

business degree (actually he only had two international courses as a part of his general business major), returned three weeks later with nothing. For the record, Marshall actually left to go to work for his father-in-law's soft drink distributorship in another state.

THE REORGANIZATION OF 1990

The Power Supply Division was sold in mid-1990. Initially, very few changes occurred in the day-to-day or strategic direction for PS. The new parent seemed content and continued to monitor performance and use financial controls as the primary management control style.

It was reported that one stockholder of Hanson Enterprises expressed concern about the PS's batteries being used in both nuclear and nonnuclear bombs. A spokesperson for the corporation denied that the concern had ever been aired. Although there were a few protests against military

EXHIBIT 3   Organization Chart, August 1992

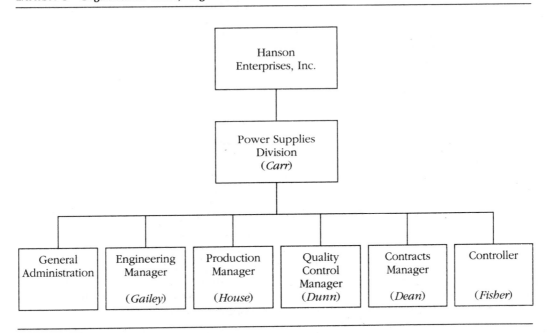

EXHIBIT 4   Executive Profiles, August 1992

Name	Title	Age	Years with PS	Education
Jim Carr	General Manager	62	27	B.S.M.E.
Herb Gailey	Engineering Manager	57	27	B.S. (Physics)
Bill Vernon	Assistant Engineering Manager	46	12	B.S.E.E.
John Ely	Assistant Engineering Manager	51	26	B.S.C.E.
George Sato	Assistant Engineering Manager	35	8	B.S.E.E.
Ralph Box	Assistant Engineering Manager	60	36	B.S. (Stat)
Chuck House	Production Manager	57	24	A.S. (Mech)
David Dunn	Quality Control Manager	45	16	B.S. (Math)
Leroy Dean	Contracts Manager	39	2	B.A. (Comm)
Ralph Arnold	Purchasing Manager	56	29	High School
Al Fisher	Controller	44	3	B.S.Ed., CPA
Sue Cook	Office Coordinator	61	40	A.S. (Acct)

production at the PS main plant during the Vietnam days, nothing has been reported in the past twenty years.

Hinds retired at age 65 just a month prior to the acquisition. He was replaced by Jim Carr, who had served as engineering manager for the past fifteen years (see Exhibits 3 and 4).

The work force breakdown for PS has remained about the same for the past 20 plus years. About one-third of the employees are white-collar (salaried), almost 80 percent having an engineering orientation. About 40 (7 percent) of the employees are administration, purchasing, accounting/controlling, personnel, and security. The remaining employees (about 325, all hourly paid) are production/assembly workers, maintenance workers, and first-line supervisors and technicians.

THE FUTURE

There appears to be increasing pressure from Hanson Enterprises for PS to improve its profitability. Subtle hints have recently surfaced in visits, communiques, and phone conversations. PS continues to receive inquiries for batteries for commercial applications, primarily related to energy conservation and clean air concerns. These interests include power supplies for lawnmowers, toys, robotics, forklifts (used in enclosed buildings), and both underwater and underground mining.

QUESTIONS

1. Does PS have the human resource base to successfully enter into commercial marketing? Why or why not?

2. Should PS forge ahead on all commercial fronts (i.e., enter into as many contracts as possible)? Or should PS zero in on a few potential commercial battery applications? How do product life cycle considerations affect the ultimate selection of battery products?

3. At what cost, in terms of overall human and financial commitment, can PS develop an effective commercial marketing organization?

4. Comment on Exhibits 1 and 2. Why do the numbers seem to vary so much?

12. Honeywell Builds on Synergy and Divests a Division

OVERVIEW

This is the story of how Honeywell returned to its roots, became a leaner company, used synergy for its marketing program, and spun off a profitable defense-oriented business unit. Like so many U.S. companies in the early 1990s, it tries to do more with less, including fewer employees and fewer divisions. It is likely to continue its aggressive restructuring and downsizing, its push into foreign markets, and its emphasis on renewed profitability.

Honeywell in one word means "control." Specifically, people in homes and offices associate the Honeywell name with the thermostat that you can set for a given temperature and then forget about it. But, of course, one can set a thermostat for different temperatures at different times of the day and thereby achieve more precise climate control. This was the core of the company, and climate control will still be the core in the years to come, though in far more sophisticated fashion. Honeywell tried to become a major player in the computer field in the 1970s and 1980s, but essentially has withdrawn from the field. In a similar fashion, it recently phased out its Defense and Marine Systems Business (DMSB) unit.

Honeywell will rely on three business segments in the 1990s, with each one generating roughly one-third of the total: home and building control; industrial automation and control; and space and aviation. Sales in the past three years were around $6.2 billion, with two-thirds originating from the United States. Return on equity was about 20 percent, and net income was running at about 5.5 percent of sales during the past two years. Corporate strategy emphasizes "unlocking shareholder value" and making divestitures rather than acquisitions. The marketing program, in the United States and abroad, stresses customer service and product quality. Honeywell always seeks to be on the "preferred list" of suppliers when it comes to control, automation, and avionics. During the past three years, the research and development budget was running at 4.4 to 4.9 percent of sales (see Exhibit 1).

LINES OF OPERATION: BUSINESS SEGMENTS

Home and Building Control represented about 36 percent of Honeywell's total sales in 1991. Products and services offered by this business segment provide climate control in single-family homes, apartments, office buildings, and other commercial structures. While most of the controls offered are for heating, cooling, and ventilating, others serve as fire and security alarms. Honeywell has derived steady income from this segment, but the market for such controls is mature; it is dependent for new business on new construction, which is volatile. Housing starts in the United States are not booming. With 20 percent office vacancy rates in many cities, construction of high-rises is in the doldrums. To enhance its position, Honeywell has embarked on the following marketing steps. First, it is pushing sales outside the United States, which now constitute half of the total. Second, it offers maintenance, training, and other

This case is based on a longer corporate intelligence report written by Edward D. Hester of The Freedonia Group, Cleveland, Ohio, in 1990; this version was updated and edited by Andrew C. Gross of Cleveland State University, Cleveland, Ohio, in 1992.

EXHIBIT 1   Selected Economic and Financial Indicators for Honeywell

Year	Sales (mil. $)	Net Income (mil. $)	Capital Spending (mil. $)	R&D Spending* (mil. $)	Return on Equity (%)	Return on Investment in Continuous Operations (%)
1991	6193	331	270	301	19.2	15.4
1990	6309	372	252	280	20.6	17.4
1989	6059	550	268	284	33.5	23.2

*In addition, Honeywell performed customer-funded research and development: $373 million in 1991, $418 million in 1990, $461 million in 1989.

Source: Honeywell annual reports, Standard & Poor's, Dun & Bradstreet, Moody, Value Line.

services. Third, the product line is being expanded and upgraded; examples include programmable controls and computer-based building management systems, with strong emphasis on energy savings.

Industrial Automation and Control supplies instruments, switches, sensors, monitors, and other types of control components to manufacturing industries (makers of appliances, autos, chemicals, food processing equipment, medical equipment, pulp and paper, textiles) and utilities (electricity, gas, water). This segment accounted for 26 percent of total sales in 1991. Half of the sales originated outside the United States, and Honeywell is aware that it must conform to emerging international standards. The key aspect of its corporate and marketing strategy is to upgrade the control system at existing locations and to install state-of-the-art equipment at new facilities. One of several new systems is "Batch Supervisor," which enables customers to alter process plant operations easily. Honeywell also sees major opportunities in solid-state sensors, including those that accurately recognize up to eight colors. Such advances require continued investments in research and development on the one hand and in various customer services on the other (e.g., educating and training users).

The Space and Aviation segment serves commercial, military, and space markets (aircraft manufacturers, defense contractors, defense ministries). This segment accounted for about 34 percent of total sales. About 40 percent of sales

are made outside the United States. Honeywell claims to be the leading avionics organization in the world. While in the past the defense portion generated profits, this segment has not been as profitable as others (see Exhibit 2 for details). Noting the end of the Cold War and resulting cutbacks in military spending, Honeywell is emphasizing the commercial side of the business. For example, it won the award to supply a digital avionics system to Cessna Aircraft for its Citation X, one of the most advanced business planes. Other projects range from navigation to communication systems. The marketing thrust in this sector involves soft-selling high-ticket items to several buying influencers, who range from chief executives to high-level defense officials, test and regular pilots, and regulatory agencies. Honeywell recognizes both the original-equipment market and the after-market. In the latter case, it was recently selected to insert state-of-the-art technology in aging aircraft, missiles, and ground vehicles for the U.S. air force. The modern plane is really more a bundle of advanced electronics than anything else, and Honeywell has profited from this trend.

KNOWLEDGE TRANSFER

Honeywell markets its climate controls to both home builders and owners of large buildings. The company sells automation and related controls to various industries. Finally, its avionics equipment

EXHIBIT 2   Major Business Segment or Divisional Data for Honeywell (in millions of dollars)

	1989	1990	1991
Sales by Line of Business			
Home and Building	2,077	2,197	2,249
Industrial	1,491	1,653	1,627
Space and Avionics	2,004	2,071	2,132
All Other	486	388	185
Operating Profits by Line of Business			
Home and Building	225	237	229
Industrial	137	220	224
Space and Avionics	111	200	226
All Other	21	19	(3)
Sales by Geographic Area			
United States	4,568	4,512	4,333
Europe	1,171	1,423	1,455
Other Areas	587	631	683
Duplications/Eliminations	(267)	(256)	(278)

Source: Honeywell annual reports, Standard & Poor's, Dun & Bradstreet, Moody, Value Line.

is used by both civilian and military aircraft. These dual or multiple applications represent technical and market opportunities for the company. Put differently, Honeywell is able to transfer knowledge *within* its key business segments from one application to another. For example, it is customary to install the most sophisticated equipment, including components and parts, in large commercial structures and in advanced military planes. Through feedback from users, the engineers and production people learn more about the functioning of such controls. They can then make improvements, including possible simplifications. Applications can be expanded to other markets, and the items can be produced at a lower cost. Both the users and Honeywell benefit.

In a similar fashion, knowledge can be transferred *among* business segments and *among* countries or regions. Honeywell, like other U.S. companies, has learned that research and development ideas can originate outside the main R&D laboratory. Indeed, innovative ideas often come from users in diverse locations. Honeywell is in-

stalling controls at a steel mill in India, a refinery in Korea, and a chemical plant in Taiwan. Sometimes regulations act as stimuli; for example, the drive toward uniformity in the European Community alerted Honeywell to design its "Batch Supervisor" automation system to conform to emerging international standards for batch operations design. Finally, Honeywell, like other firms, is now more willing to form strategic alliances with other companies. Such partnerships generally enhance learning. The company now has agreements with Bechtel (construction), DuPont (chemicals), Digital Equipment (computers), and several other firms. It has formed some joint ventures too, including one with an Italian company to supply the European space market.

DIVESTING DEFENSE-ORIENTED SEGMENTS

During the past four years, Honeywell embarked on a program of shedding many of its defense-oriented business operations. In late 1988, it sold a division that made electronic military simulation and training systems to Hughes Aircraft. In 1989, a division that produced infrared imaging products for military applications was sold to Loral. Other operations sold included signal processing and tactical defense communication equipment. Honeywell also sold some nondefense business operations and terminated or reduced its stake in certain joint operations, including those with Groupe Bull of France and Yamatake-Honeywell in Japan. In effect, Honeywell made an exit from the computer business.

The Defense and Marine Systems segment contributed about $1.4 billion to sales in the late 1980s, yet Honeywell announced plans to sell this division. Although profitable and well positioned in its key markets, this business segment—which involved ordnance, armaments, and marine-based weapons systems—did not fit in with Honeywell's concept of core businesses. The division was offered to several potential buyers, and it looked as though a sale would be consummated. After all, the division was making money and held a strong competitive position, with high market share. However, other defense contractors were reluctant to absorb the segment, since they were trying to reduce their exposure to the defense business. Accordingly, in 1990 Honeywell decided to spin off the segment to shareholders as a new company, naming it Alliant Techsystems.

The Defense and Marine Systems division manufactured armaments, munitions, and ordnance, as well as an array of marine and undersea electronic weapon systems. Contracts have been signed with the U.S. army, navy, and air force. There was hope that a buildup of conventional military forces in the United States and elsewhere (as opposed to nuclear, space, and missile forces) would aid this division. However, Honeywell came to the conclusion that the future looked uncertain for both offensive and defensive weapons. It may have also concluded that significant transfer of knowhow from this segment to its other divisions would not take place. Finally, while Honeywell enjoyed a good market share position, it simply found competition too keen. For example, other players in marine-related defense electron-

ics include E-Systems, Loral, Martin Marietta, Raytheon, Rockwell, Singer, and Westinghouse.

INTERNATIONAL ACTIVITIES

About 45 percent of the $6.3 billion sales in 1991 came from outside the United States. While close to three-fourths of foreign sales originated in Western Europe, the company maintains over thirty affiliate firms and works with over seventy distributors in ninety countries. Honeywell is eager to expand its activities in many regions, specifically Latin America, the Far East, and Eastern Europe. As developing economies move toward industrialization, Honeywell senses major opportunities for its line of automation and control equipment in both buildings and industries. While reducing its stake in the Yamatake-Honeywell joint venture, the company should find this operation a good way to penetrate the Pacific Rim. As noted earlier, it has already sold equipment in various nations of Southeast Asia. Honeywell also established joint ventures in the former Soviet Union and the former East Germany; these contracts should endure and allow the company to be a key player in revitalizing this region. Honeywell is an active participant in trade shows and fairs around the globe. Its Excel 500 climate control system for medium-size buildings won the "best technological product" award at a recent Paris trade fair.

QUESTIONS

1. Considering that Honeywell is still very active in the space and avionics markets, why did it decide to spin off its division that catered to the defense and marine markets?

2. The case points out that Honeywell benefits by working in related areas and transfers technical knowledge from one business segment to another. How can marketing knowhow be transferred in such instances between industrial and commercial markets? For example, is the marketing similar when selling controls to

manufacturing companies and when selling them to builders of new residential structures?

3. Based on your answer to question 2, discuss the similarities and differences when marketing the output of the avionics division to makers of military aircraft versus makers of civilian aircraft.

4. Do you think that Honeywell had an easy time maintaining its contract agreements when the former Soviet Union disbanded into the Commonwealth of Independent States and East Germany joined West Germany? Will its marketing strategy and tactics now change in Eastern Europe?

13. Diebold: From Safes to ATMs to Software

OVERVIEW

Diebold is a leading provider of automated teller machines (ATMs), also known as self-service transaction systems. In addition, Diebold makes and markets various customer transaction terminals (CTTs), a line of security equipment, and related software and services for these products. In 1991, sales were running at about $500 million and employment stood at about 3,900. Net income remained steady at about 7 to 8 percent of sales during the past six years; details on selected key financial indicators are given in Exhibit 1. Despite some difficulties, Diebold shows a strong balance sheet with little long-term debt. Unlike some other firms, Diebold has not burdened itself with unwise acquisitions. The company has strong positions in many of the markets in which it competes and should hold its own against giants like IBM, NCR, and Fujitsu. In fact, Diebold has forged a joint venture with IBM, called InterBold, to install advanced ATMs.

In the late 1980s and early 1990s, Diebold undertook a formal restructuring program in response to saturated markets and intense competitive pressures. The company has been able to reduce costs and to realign its operations. Measures included plant closings and consolidations, outsourcing, and investment in both computer-aided design and factory automation. A reorganization of the marketing effort included greater use of third-party, value-added resellers and manufacturers' representatives. This allowed a broadening of market coverage. Diebold also decided to cluster its retail-related businesses into a new unit, complete with its own product development efforts. The company rededicated itself to its core businesses, defined as ATMs, physical and electronic security, and systems and services for financial institutions. It is determined to serve them in a "user-friendly" fashion, e.g., providing networking capability for ATMs. Long-term plans call for cultivating high-margin activities and expanding in overseas markets, especially Europe and the Far East.

This case is based on a longer corporate intelligence report written by Edward D. Hester for The Freedonia Group, Cleveland, Ohio, in February, 1990; it was edited and updated by Andrew C. Gross of Cleveland State University, in June 1992. Used with permission of The Freedonia Group and Edward D. Hester.

EXHIBIT 1   Key Financial and Related Indicators for Diebold, Inc., 1980–1991

Year	Net Sales (mil. $)	Net Income (mil. $)	Capital Spending (mil. $)	R&D Spending (mil. $)	Capital Spending as % of Sales	R&D Spending as % of Sales
1980	346.9	21.2	3.7	5.6	1.1	1.6
1981	385.9	29.0	6.5	6.7	1.7	1.7
1982	427.6	41.5	10.7	8.8	2.5	2.0
1983	445.9	49.1	8.0	10.4	1.8	2.3
1984	474.3	56.9	10.8	13.4	2.3	2.8
1985	411.9	30.4	9.8	17.4	2.4	4.2
1986	417.4	34.9	14.9	14.4	3.6	3.4
1987	439.1	35.8	8.4	14.3	1.9	3.3
1988	450.6	35.8	8.2	14.2	1.8	3.1
1989	468.9	36.2	9.9	13.4	2.1	2.9
1990	476.1	27.1	22.2	20.3	4.7	4.3
1991	506.2	35.7	9.1	35.0	1.8	6.9

Source: Diebold annual reports.

THE PRODUCT-MARKET INTERFACE AND COMPETITION

Diebold was founded over a century ago, and its original product line consisted of bank safes, vaults, and chests. Such "bank fixed security equipment" still generates sales for the company, but given their maturity and the long replacement cycle, the demand for such goods is expected to decline even in real terms. However, building on its traditional expertise in bank security markets, Diebold established a strong position in electronic security, offering a full line of products ranging from access controls and local alarms to central station, multipoint security systems. To a greater extent than its other manufacturing businesses, electronic security holds good potential for large-scale penetration into nonfinancial markets.

Automated teller machines were Diebold's most visible product line in the 1980s and paved the way for the company's entry into related businesses. ATMs also assisted Diebold in penetrating foreign markets. In the United States, Diebold is the acknowledged market share leader in ATMs, with about 45 percent of the installed base. Die-

bold also claims to be the global leader in ATMs, with a 16 percent share. However, the U.S. market for ATMs is near saturation levels at banks and savings institutions. There is extensive price competition, and margins are being eroded. Diebold is responding to this situation on two fronts. First, it is moving aggressively to install ATMs in less traditional locations (supermarkets, workplaces, etc.). Second, it hopes to replace the first generation of ATMs at banks with newer machines.

At one time, non-ATM customer transaction terminals (CTTs) were touted as a major growth area for Diebold. CTTs are point-of-sale, electronic funds transfer, and automated fuel terminals. However, markets were slow to develop until now. Furthermore, Diebold faces intense competition in this field from NCR, IBM, Unisys, and others. Diebold's response has been to separate the retail-related activities from its other operations. In addition, Diebold hopes to show retailers that it has expertise to offer in automated self-serve technologies. This is in line with retailers' desire to lower their own operating costs.

Two key developments have been the joint venture with IBM and Diebold's move into software and services. In the joint venture, known as

InterBold, Diebold holds a majority stake. It shows the willingness of the two giants to forge a strategic alliance when doing so is to mutual advantage. In the move into software and services, Diebold is building on its strength in ATMs, CTTs, and electronic security systems to establish a growing business in applications software, systems development, and electronic equipment servicing. The service markets are natural complements to the hardware; furthermore, these fields show significant growth potential and tend to offer better profit margins. Yet Diebold has been able to offer competitive service contracts, in some cases with significant price cuts. Diebold succeeds by emphasizing two key aspects with which users are always concerned: networking capability and standardization. Other features include continuous availability (no downtime), reduced life cycle costs (low operating costs), and upgradability (newer equipment and services installed without a hitch).

RENEWAL IN CAPITAL SPENDING AND TECHNOLOGY

Diebold is moving from being a simple metal-bending manufacturer to an organization that emphasizes value-added engineering, factory automation, and a servicing orientation. Each step in the manufacturing operation is being evaluated; make-or-buy decisions are made constantly, and as a result outsourcing has increased. The company has also made some minority investments in smaller firms with which it does business, including Hidromex, a Mexican distributor of ATMs. In addition, it acquired certain assets from the EDS Division of General Motors, another provider of terminal equipment maintenance. But by and large, Diebold has chosen to expand internally and increase its capital as well as its R&D spending, as shown in Exhibit 1. Most important, Diebold is emphasizing automated or "focused" factories.

Diebold phased out most of the manufacturing activities at its century-old Canton, Ohio, plant and established more streamlined facilities in Newark, Ohio, and Lynchburg, Virginia. Diebold purchased computer-aided design equip-

ment and also invested in numerically controlled machine tools and robots. Another key step involves direct linkage between design and production as part of the move toward automated manufacturing. Automation extends to service activities. Diebold monitors customer equipment performance, tracks service calls, provides inventory control for parts, and expedites deliveries in a streamlined fashion.

As the overall product mix became more sophisticated and more technology intensive, Diebold steadily increased its research and development budget in both absolute and relative terms. As Exhibit 1 shows, R&D spending increased during the 1980s and currently is in the range of 3 to 4 percent of sales. Using Intel microprocessor chips, Diebold unveiled a series of advanced ATMs that reportedly provide a personal computer–compatible platform for the next generation of electronic banking transactions. Software packages are also developed for PC-based ATM network management. A new image-lift technology allows viewing the image of checks by depositors. Finally, a modern line of vaults and safes, as well as sophisticated alarm and monitoring systems, are now offered to financial institutions and other organizations.

In sum, Diebold is concerned with bringing technology to both its own process lines and its new product and service offerings. This is in contrast to some companies that automate their production lines but neglect the marketplace and other firms that spend little on rejuvenating their factories but still expect to produce high-tech goods. Diebold is concerned, of course, with its core customer base—mostly financial organizations—but it is looking for clients further afield. Last, but not least, the image technology example cited above shows that Diebold is correctly concerned not just with its own customers but with its customers' customers. This illustrates well the idea of relationship marketing.

SOFTWARE AND SERVICES

Diebold has learned a lesson from the computer industry, where certain large and small computers are on their way to commodity status. While neither ATMs nor electronic security systems have evolved to this point, there are similarities. Accordingly, Diebold is aggressively cultivating a software and service capability to support its core hardware business. The emphasis is on those goods that have a high performance-to-price ratio and on those services that enhance customer satisfaction. Even the most up-to-date equipment needs good servicing. In this way, Diebold can maintain strong loyalty ties with its varied clientele.

While Diebold does not break out its software- and service-related revenues separately, we estimate that these are now over $100 million, or more than 20 percent of total sales. The contribution to the bottom line is even more pronounced as the margin on ATMs and fixed security equipment have been eroding. The software and systems businesses in which Diebold competes comprise growth markets, with projected annual increases of between 15 and 20 percent per year through the mid-1990s.

Diebold provides both standard and application software and systems for ATMs, payment terminals, network transaction switching, and security monitoring. A typical package is PACE, designed to run on IBM and IBM-compatible personal computers. It performs both on-line and off-line operations, transaction processing, terminal control, and status processing functions. Put briefly, it helps banks and similar financial institutions to do their jobs more efficiently in terms of time and cost. A number of other packages facilitate network transactions. This is crucial because banks are linked in regional and national electronic fund transfer networks. It is now possible to link ATMs in local area networks (LANs). In Poland, Diebold has established what is believed to be the first ATM network in Eastern Europe.

On the service front, Diebold is providing postpurchase maintenance to clients and even to customers who bought competitive equipment from ADT and Mosler. Diebold claims to be servicing over 1 million pieces of equipment for over 13,000 customers in more than 50,000 locations. Service-related employment is now twice that for manufacturing for Diebold. Clients are served from 40 regional centers and 400 service locations. Services offered include equipment maintenance for ATMs, CTTs, and security equipment, including alarms of all kinds. Diebold is also offering security consulting, quality assurance, and disaster recovery. Based on a recent agreement with Tandem Computers, Diebold will provide service for workstations, terminals, and printers supplied by Tandem and other vendors. Diebold is also servicing the ATMs installed under its joint venture with IBM (InterBold).

INTERNATIONAL ACTIVITIES

Diebold, along with its U.S.-based competitors, is under increasing pressure to penetrate global markets to achieve above-average growth in revenues and net income. Diebold has responded to this challenge; its international revenues rose from 4 percent of sales in 1985 to over 10 percent by 1988. Further increases are expected in the 1990s, as Diebold expects to unfold a more aggressive service thrust. Until now, Diebold generated almost all of its overseas sales via export. It employed third-party distributors such as Philips. However, it is now moving toward local manufacturing or joint ventures. This, coupled with providing services, will necessitate a more local presence in various regions. Diebold recently purchased a 40 percent share in an ATM distributor in India. Other ventures include deals with companies in Eastern Europe, Latin America, and selected Far East countries.

While servicing the installed ATM and CTT base should generate maintenance contracts and subsequent revenues, Diebold thinks that significant growth potential exists abroad in electronic security markets. As companies become more concerned about safety and industrial espionage, counterintelligence measures must be taken. Diebold is ready to assist with alarms and other security equipment, as well as with security consultancy, monitoring, and maintenance.

QUESTIONS

1. Would Diebold have survived as a manufacturer and marketer of fixed security equip-

ment for banks, such as safes and vaults? What is wrong with the growth prospects in this field?

2. If Diebold made the right decision in moving toward ATMs and CTTs, why did it also move into security systems and services, including software, where there are many competitors and volatility is so great? Why not stay with dispensing terminals, specifically vending machines and the like?

3. Discuss the notion of networking and standardization, with special emphasis on why banks and other financial institutions demand these features from vendors of equipment and services.

4. How can Diebold penetrate international markets when it faced entrenched European and Asian competitors and got a relatively late start?

14. Avery Dennison: How to Do Marketing After a Big Merger

OVERVIEW

Avery Dennison was formed in October 1990 by the merger of Avery International and Dennison Manufacturing. The combined operation recorded sales of $2.55 billion in 1991. The new corporation is a leading manufacturer of pressure-sensitive materials, office products, and product identification items on a worldwide basis. Over 50 percent of Avery Dennison's sales are derived from areas where the company holds a number one or number two market share position, including heat transfer labels, office supply labels, diaper labels, three-ring binders, and retail apparel tags. The merger has made Avery Dennison the fourth largest office supplier in the world, behind 3M (Minnesota Mining & Manufacturing), Esselte of Sweden, and Acco World of American Brands. In other areas, competitors include Bemis, Scott Paper, Pitney Bowes, and Intermec.

While the merger has made Avery Dennison a powerful player in labeling products and other areas, the combined operation had to resolve a number of problems. Restructuring involved consolidation of certain product lines, divestiture of noncore businesses, reduction in employment, relocation of manufacturing activities, and integration of various operations. In the marketing area, decisions had to be made about all of the "4Ps" of marketing: product lines and services, promotion, pricing policies, and place or distribution strategies. Avery Dennison hoped to complete integration and consolidation by the end of 1992.

BEFORE AND AFTER THE MERGER

Prior to the merger, Avery International operated in two segments: Materials and Converting. The Materials Division featured a line of pressure-

This case study is based on a longer corporate intelligence report developed in 1991 at The Freedonia Group. Research analyst for the report was Trisha McKay; the project was directed by Ramune Kubiliunas. This edited and updated version was developed by Andrew C. Gross of Cleveland State University in 1991.

sensitive labels with the Fasson brand name. The Converting Division included office products and a subgroup, Soabar, which manufactured machines for imprinting, dispensing, and attaching preprinted tags, labels, and roll tickets. Before the merger, Dennison Manufacturing operated three lines of business: Stationery Products, Packaging, and Systems. Stationery Products was the largest segment; its output included various office products, such as binders and specialty highlighter pens. Packaging offered heat-transfer labels. The Systems Division operated in two markets: product identification (including printing equipment and accessories) and fastener equipment and supplies. This sector invested heavily in bar code imprinting capabilities for the retail market, including optical character recognition printers and readers.

At the time of the merger, Avery International accounted for 67 percent of total assets, 70 percent of sales, and 76 percent of net income and Dennison Manufacturing for the remaining 33, 30, and 24 percent, respectively. In fiscal 1989, Dennison's net earnings declined 22 percent over the previous year, though sales ran at a record level of $771 million. Increased development expenditures, product delays, poor management, and a slowdown in the global economy adversely affected corporate operations. However, Dennison had a number of promising products and technologies that blended well with the product lines and business strategies of Avery International.

The merger agreement, approved by the shareholders of both companies, was a tax-free exchange of stock and was accounted for as a "pooling of interests." An antitrust inquiry by the U.S. Department of Justice delayed the merger for about five months. Government approval was finally granted, but the delay caused confusion and concern and may have contributed to a deterioration of profits. The combined operations recorded sales of $2.6 billion in 1990, but net income was a meager $5.9 million—not even 0.25 percent of sales. The cost of restructuring and merger-related legal and banking expenses is put at $100 million. However, in 1991 the company began its realignment and consolidation. Since Avery was the dominant partner in the merger,

the restructuring applied Avery procedures and policies to the operations of Dennison, and this is reflected in marketing activities as well. The key to success will be the integration of complementary activities.

BUSINESS SEGMENTS AND OVERALL STRATEGY

The restructured Avery Dennison consists of three core business sectors: Pressure Sensitive Adhesives and Materials, Product Identification and Control Systems, and Office Products. These three divisions account for about 45, 25, and 30 percent of total sales, respectively. There may be shifting in these figures due to expansion or divestitures.

The Pressure Sensitive Adhesives and Materials segment benefited from the strong demand for such goods during the 1980s in both the United States and Europe. Offsetting the increase were lower sales of European specialty tapes at the start of the 1990s, due in part to the bankruptcies of three large specialty diaper tape customers in France. In addition, a slowdown in the automotive industries of both North America and Western Europe adversely affected this division. But in the current decade, a steady demand is expected from a wide variety of users in the auto, aerospace, appliance, consumer disposables, electronics, and health care sectors. Pressure-sensitive tapes, also known as unconverted or industrial roll tapes, are widely used by these industries for sealing, packaging, bundling, masking, decoration, and adhesive transfer. The tapes are classified by backing materials such as paper, cloth, plastic, and metal foil; Avery Dennison makes all of these as well as combination tapes.

In contrast, the Product Identification and Control Systems division manufactures and markets converted products. These include labels, tags, tickets, and automated labeling equipment. Avery Dennison is the market leader in heat transfer labels that are printed directly onto containers. The heat transfer process results in a natural or no-label look for plastic bottles, a feature valued by makers of shampoos such as Procter & Gamble. The division is also the market leader in the United States for apparel plastic fasteners and identification tags, which are widely used by retailers. Such tags and labels carry bar code identification. Bar code labels have penetrated many commercial and consumer markets because they help to control inventory, reduce labor costs, and identify products in a uniform way. Avery Dennison is able to provide complete bar code systems and services, including a printing press that can create virtually any image.

The Office Products division markets office supply labels, binders, notebook indexes, and similar stationery products; it also makes and sells highlighter pens. Office supply superstores are a major trend now, and purchasing in bulk allows these retailers to dictate terms to Avery Dennison and other suppliers. The marketing activities of this division are discussed at greater length in the next section.

Avery Dennison hopes to complete all restructuring activities caused by the merger in 1992. It is spinning off unprofitable product lines and integrating complementary operations. Noncore businesses divested in 1991 include a metallized paper unit and imaging systems, both from the Dennison side of the business. In contrast, there are significant opportunities for synergy in the combination of the two firms in several areas, including manufacturing, marketing, and logistics. Increased bargaining power vis-à-vis suppliers, economies of scale in the factories, opportunities in warehouse sharing, and sales force consolidations are emphasized in all of the divisions and corporate-wide. So-called "priority operating strategies" focus on increased market share and profitability, superior product quality, and enhanced customer service. Avery Dennison would like to achieve 25 percent of its sales from new products introduced in the past five years. Several independent analysts expect total sales to grow between 7 and 10 percent annually through the mid-1990s.

MARKETING ACTION IN THE OFFICE PRODUCTS DIVISION

This division was allocated about 40 percent of the restructuring costs upon the merger, which indicates that its various units, mostly those in

North America and Western Europe, required major changes as well as fine-tuning. Overlap and duplication occurred among the ten units. Decisions had to be made about which product lines and brand names to retain. In the United States, Dennison National, Dennison Monarch, and K&M are well-known brands for binders, notebooks, ledgers, business forms, and computer disks. Felt-tipped markers are sold under the Hi Liter and Click Hi Liter names. The Avery line is highly respected for its Label Pro color code, file folder, and correction tapes, Tabulabel for its data processing labels, and Aigner for its file guides. Avery Guidex and Avery Myers operate in the United Kingdom, while Dennison's Cheval-Ordex and Doret units enjoy strong market positions in France. These units produce office products (including desks, filing cabinets, and racks), stationery goods, and school-related products.

The Office Products division must make decisions about which brands to retain and which brands to phase out. The basic guideline was to retain the strongly established brands in each region or nation and possibly consolidate later on (other examples are Nissan phasing out the Datsun brand, BP eliminating the traditional Sohio name). Currently the focus of operations is on product quality, delivery, and responsiveness to market conditions. For example, the division expects to make forty-eight-hour deliveries to any major customer. A combined mass marketing organization has been formed to sell label, index, and binder product lines. The division is looking for strategic alliances. One example of such a partnership is the alliance with Hewlett Packard to market software, laser, and fax labels. This move is aimed at making the company a prime source to international customers.

A key challenge for Avery Dennison and its competitors is the rise of powerful vendors in the office market. Office supply superstores have been established regionally and nationwide in the United States by firms such as BizMart, Office Depot, Office Max, and Staples. They are also making their presence felt outside North America. Such superstores came on the scene in 1986 and since then have become powerful buyers of all kinds of office products, ranging from binders to writing instruments, from office equipment to software.

They are able to negotiate favorable terms with suppliers that allow them to keep prices down to the entrepreneurs, small companies, and households that flock to their stores. The shift to a white-collar society and the increased computerization of the office and the home account for the popularity of these superstores. They now reach only 20 to 25 percent of the potential market, with about 400 stores in operation; by the mid-1990s, these numbers could rise to 50 percent and 1,600 stores.

It will be interesting to see how negotiations evolve between powerful office product makers, such as Avery Dennison, and major office product distributors, such as the superstores. Currently the superstores are gaining market share as a channel of distribution at the expense of small stationery stores, direct sales, catalogs, and telemarketing sales. Professionals, small-business owners, and others enjoy wandering through the spacious aisles and selecting from among dozens of competing brands of stationery, binders, markers, software, and the like. Staples, Office Depot, and others will continue to exercise their clout in gaining lower prices from manufacturers. How can and how will Avery Dennison respond to this challenge? The answer lies in focused selling, im-proved merchandising, and reduced manufacturing costs. The company is also hoping to push certain key brands. The dangers include the fact that much of its product line is viewed by users as commodities rather than as specialty goods.

QUESTIONS

1. How do you assess the merger of Avery International and Dennison Manufacturing from a marketer's viewpoint? (Hint: Look at recent news items, not just company news releases, which tend to have a public relations cast.)

2. What would be the basis for your decision to retain certain brands and eliminate others in the merged operation? Would you undertake market research on this topic?

3. Discuss your promotion and pricing strategies aimed at the distributors of office products, specifically the office supply superstores.

4. Suggest specific, quantitative standards for Avery Dennison by which it can judge its performance for satisfying customers' demands and expectations.

15. Clifton Ceramics Ltd.

Alfred Deller, president of Clifton Ceramics Ltd. of Kingston, Ontario, was considering the purchase of a new technology from the Canada Centre for Mineral and Energy Technology (CANMET). The latter had developed a new process for making abrasion-resistant ceramic (ARC) tile from slag. It was February 3, 1985, and Deller was reviewing a background study prior to making a go/no-go decision on pursuing this technology.

SLAG AND ITS UTILIZATION

From the birth of the Iron Age, slag had been a waste product of iron-smelting operations. Blast furnaces often produced 500 kilograms of slag for each ton of pig iron. The interest of early iron-masters was restricted to the cheapest and quickest way of disposing it. This had led to huge slag hills, which blighted the landscape around great smelting works. The slag problem was immense. The annual production of blast furnace slag in the leading iron-producing countries of the world in 1981 is presented in Exhibit 1. Of course, since 1981, less slag has been produced because of the trend toward higher-grade iron ore and improved technology.

In Canada, slag had been primarily used in the construction of roads and as road bases and surfaces. Other uses for slag are presented in Exhibit 2. The primary treatment of slag was to crush it and use it as a building material.

SLAG CERAMICS: A DESCRIPTION

The simplest definition of a "slag ceramic" is a chemically modified blast furnace slag into which

crystallizing agents were added. The remelted product was cast in molds to give the required shape and then heat treated to produce controlled fine crystalline structures.

Among the desirable properties slag ceramics possessed were (1) excellent abrasion resistance, (2) scratch hardness of between 7 and 9 on the Mohs scale, (3) good resistance to weather and chemicals, and (4) a high crushing strength. On the negative side, slag ceramics appeared to be susceptible to thermal shock resulting from the freeze/thaw process.

HISTORY OF SLAG CERAMICS

Slag ceramics development work had been confined to the Soviet bloc nations, Great Britain, and, most recently, Canada, Exhibit 3. In Russia, the use of blast furnace and electrofurnace slag in the manufacture of ceramic tiles dated to the early 1960s. Originally developed to meet a government-inspired recycling plan, these "slag-sitall" tiles were found to have very desirable abrasion- and corrosion-resistant properties. Because the alumina that is used in traditional abrasion-resistant tiles was in short supply, the "slag-sitall" experiment was developed into a pilot plant operation.

The field of slag ceramics in the Soviet bloc nations had grown dramatically. The uses for these tiles in the Soviet economy included inside and outside facing of walls, industrial and home floor coverings, electrical insulators, sewer pipe, sanitaryware, and as abrasion- and corrosion-resistant protection for equipment in the mining and chemical industries, respectively.

Through the efforts of the British Iron and Steel Research Association (BISRA), the Russian technology spread to Britain and, in 1960, British scientists introduced "slagceram" and marketed it under the trade name Basramite. Available colors included black, gray, white, orange, brown, reddish-brown, and green. In industrial situations, it was used as a replacement for basalt in abrasive

environments. Specific applications included an abrasion-resistant chute lining for handling iron ore and coke, a tile floor in a busy office and office passage, an industrial floor exposed to heavy equipment, and a floor covering for use around a small furnace (at floor temperatures of 90°C). Other applications envisioned included stair treads, fence posts, lintels, tunnel lining, sea defenses (breakwaters), dams, nonskid road surfaces, paving flags, curbstones, guttering, and drain pipes. These applications were never tested.

Since this product was to be used extensively in the mining industry, the downturn in the economy in the late 1970s greatly affected mining and caused the project to be abandoned. For the British, the economics of the product were also a problem. The major cost was the energy required for the heat treatment of the tiles. Further, a plant needed to produce at least 300 tons of "slagceram" per day to break even, and it was believed that the demand for wear-resistant tiling would never reach that point.

SLAG CERAMICS IN CANADA

Though slag ceramics were introduced to the world in the 1960s, work in Canada began in 1980 when CANMET commissioned some research in the field. The production process for

EXHIBIT 1   World Slag Production, 1981

Country	Million Tons
U.S.S.R.	57.2
Japan	42.6
U.S.A	35.5
China	18.1
West Germany	17.0
France	9.2
Canada	5.2

EXHIBIT 2   Possible Uses of Slag

Road bases	Road surfacing
Railway track ballast	Concrete aggregate
Filter media	Slag wool for heat
Granulated slag in	insulation
cement manufacture	Slag ceramics

EXHIBIT 3   Comparison of Slag Ceramics

	Canada	U.K.	U.S.S.R.
Hardness (Mohs)	7.0–8.0	8.0–9.0	8.0–8.5
Coefficient of thermal expansion ($\times 10^{-6}$)	8.25	5.0	7.2
Abrasion resistance	Twice quartzite	Twice basalt	n/a
Modulus of rupture (lb./in.^{2}) (measure of strength)	8,000	20,000	20,000
Density (gm/cm^3)	n/a	3.00	2.71
Chemical stability in concentrated H_2SO_4	n/a	Lightening in color	99.70%
35% NaOH	n/a	Brown patches Surface lighter	83.64%

Note: n/a = not available.

slag ceramics included (1) ball milling of raw materials for two hours; (2) calcination of raw materials at 600°C for approximately eight hours; (3) melting at 1440°C and soaking for up to five hours; (4) nucleation at 720°C for ten hours; and (5) crystallizing at 900°C for three hours. Though the raw materials were cheap (72 percent slag, 22 percent sand, with the remainder being nucleating agents), this procedure required a large amount of heat. This would prove to be a key cost factor in commercializing the process.

By 1985, it was obvious that CANMET had more a product concept than an actual product. Two steps were necessary before commercialization would be feasible: (1) development of an improved slag ceramic with optimal composition, optimal heat application, and optimal properties and (2) development of a small pilot plant operation to expand and refine the laboratory process.

THE MARKET FOR SLAG CERAMICS

Given experience in other countries the possible uses for slag ceramic tile could be grouped into two categories: (1) abrasion-resistant ceramic (ARC) Tile and (2) industrial/home floor and wall tile.

Manufacturers of ARC Tiles

In 1985, no company in Canada manufactured ARC tiles. Thus, any company adapting this technology for use in Canada would have an abundant and cheap ($5 per ton) raw material supply and a monopoly in production. Annual Canadian sales of ARC tiles were approximately $4 million to $6 million. Demand was met by a series of wholesalers, the largest of which was Williams and Wilson Ltd. This firm filled approximately 60 percent of the Canadian demand, while a second wholesaler, Thermalloy Corporation, filled another 25 percent of demand. The remaining 15 percent was accommodated through contracting firms that provided a small amount of the tile as part of a larger job.

Most of the ARC tile used in Canada was imported from the United States, where annual sales averaged $50 million to $60 million. There were few manufacturers, and the top five accounted for 95 percent of sales. The largest producer was Coors Porcelain Company, located in Colorado. This firm produced about 40 percent of all ARC tiles in America. By production size, the other four companies were Champion Sparkplug (Michigan), Ferro Corporation (Ohio), Carborundum Company (Pennsylvania), and Diamonite (Ohio). There were also European companies that produced ARC tiles. The largest of these was Greenbank Terotech Ltd. of England.

The Abrasion-Resistant Materials Market.

In this market, there were many competing products. About 10 percent of the business did not go to tiles at all but to rubber and rubberized linings. The remaining business was divided among three types of ARC tiles: cast basalt, alumina oxide, and silicon carbide castings.

Cast basalt was made from volcanic rock. The rock was melted and cast into tiles. It was the cheapest type of tile and cost approximately one-third the cost of alumina tiles. The major drawback of cast basalt was the thickness of the tiles—1¼ inches. Though technology was improving and tiles ¾ inches thick could be produced, this thickness made them impractical for many applications. Cast basalt tiles accounted for little more than 25 percent of the abrasion-resistant materials market in Canada (though they were used extensively in the European market).

Alumina oxide tiles had a major share of the market, accounting for 50 percent of sales. These tiles were usually white or gray and came in a wide range of sizes and thicknesses. Exhibit 4 gives some of the tile costs. The only drawback to alumina tiles was their inability to be made in odd shapes or very small sizes.

When the latter situations arose, silicon carbide was often used. Though it cost more than alumina oxide, cost comparisons were difficult to make because silicon carbide was rarely cast into tiles but into small pipes and odd-shaped pieces. Most of the work was done to custommade specifications. As it was more expensive than alumina oxide tiles, it was never considered as a substitute but as a complementary material. Silicon carbide accounted for the remaining 15 percent of the abrasion-resistant materials market.

EXHIBIT 4 Costs of Various Sizes of Alumina Oxide Tiles

Size	Cost (Can$ F.O.B.)
6" × 4" × ¼"	1.56
6" × 2" × ¼"	1.62
6" × 4" × ½"	2.32
4" × 3" × ½"	1.56
6" × 4" × 1"	7.00
6" × 4" × 2"	13.00

Unlike rubber and rubberized linings, all ARC tiles suffered from an inability to withstand thermal shock. That is, in environments where there would be much heating and cooling, ARC tiles were susceptible to cracking and splintering.

Market Applications for ARC Tiles. The two largest users of ARC tiles were mines/smelters and power plants. In both cases, these materials were used as liners for chutes, hoppers, silos, bins, and raw material transport cars to protect metal surfaces from abrasion. In power plants, abrasion was from coal as opposed to iron ore. Power plants in Ontario, Quebec, Alberta, Saskatchewan, Nova Scotia, and New Brunswick used ARC tiles in their operations. The average contract size from these plants was $100,000 to $250,000 including installation costs.

Purchases made by mines/smelters were often in the "retrofit" area, and the number of these purchases was tied to the health of the industry. In the early 1980s, few companies were buying ARC tiles, but the economic condition of mines/smelters was expected to improve by 1990. Power plant purchases were unaffected by the economy and were part of a continuing effort to reduce costs and conserve resources. This part of the market could decrease in the future once all power plants had adopted ARC tiles for use in their systems, but this shrinkage was not likely to occur for two decades.

There were other, smaller users as well. Some of them had similar abrasion-resistant needs (i.e., grain-handling facilities and heavy traffic shop floors). Laboratories made use of the chem-ical-resistant properties of the material to produce a chemical- and spark-resistant floor. It was rumored that a major tile company was working with the Israeli military on a project using the impact resistance quality of ARC tiles as a nose-cone material in missiles. It was even suggested that ARC tiles could be used in bulletproof vests. Specially toughened alumina oxide tiles were used as armor cladding in helicopters, personnel carriers, and so on, and in flak jackets.

Industrial/Home Floor and Wall Tile

Slag ceramics possessed a distinct advantage in their abrasion and chemical resistance. If the material was to be used for industrial or home tiles, the need for chemical and abrasion resistance would greatly diminish. Thus, one of the competitive advantages of the tile would disappear.

The industrial/home tile market in Canada was divided into four types: (1) floor tile, (2) wall tile, (3) bathroom tile, and (4) mosaic ceramic tile. In 1984, 115 million square feet of industrial/home tile were sold in Canada. Dollar sales figures were unavailable. ARC material was most appropriate for use as floor tile or, synonymously, quarry tile. Both the Russians and the British reported using ARC material in this way.

Quarry tile was usually brown and unglazed in appearance. It had a strong crystalline structure and was very dense, making it ideal for use in high-traffic areas. In recent years, colored (green, blue, red, and white) and patterned quarry tile had entered the market through imports. Most commercial projects required the unglazed brown quarry tile only.

Quarry tile purchases were usually quite large. An average mall needed 100,000 square feet of quarry tile to cover its floor. Quarry tile was also very expensive. Because of this, firms were highly price sensitive. Alfred Deller believed that if this market was to be pursued, it was possible to reduce the abrasion and chemical resistance of ARC tiles to lower the price. A sample price chart for quarry tile is presented in Exhibit 5.

Manufacturers of Quarry Tile

In Canada, only one company produced quarry tile. Clifton Ceramics Ltd., located in Kingston,

EXHIBIT 5 Sample Prices for Quarry Tile

Size	Price ($)
2″ × 2″	3.20
4″ × 4″	3.20–3.55
4″ × 8″	3.30–3.63
8″ × 8″	3.60–3.90
4″ × 8″ Disc	3.45–4.10
8″ × 8″ Disc	3.75–4.12
Stair trim 8″	1.90

Note: All sizes quoted were ⅜″ thick.

Ontario, produced about 3 million square feet of quarry tile annually to help satisfy part of the annual Canadian demand of 11.5 million square feet. Its quarry tile was sold to commercial users for industrial floors, shopping centers, and lobby areas.

Clifton's major competition came from outside North America. Italy, West Germany, Spain, Brazil, Korea, Japan, and England all produced quarry tile and sold it in Canada. Korean quarry tile sized at 4″ × 8″ × ⅜″ sold for $2.65. The British version was approximately the same price as the Canadian tile, with an 8″ × 8″ × ⅜″ tile selling for $3.75. Foreign companies relied on cheaper prices to be competitive.

Noteworthy by its absence from the list was the United States. Though the United States produced quarry tile, it was not sold in the Canadian market because it was more expensive. Canadian distributors were unable to quote comparative prices. Higher labor costs, exchange rate fluctuations, and restrictive trade agreements were cited as problems affecting the pricing decision faced by U.S. manufacturers. U.S. firms offered a floor brick that competed with quarry tile as an alternative floor covering.

Clifton Ceramics believed it had two competitive advantages. For large orders that could not be filled from stock, quarry tile had to be shipped to Canada and could take from five to ten weeks to arrive. Clifton Ceramics maintained a three-week lead time for the production of any large order, making it fast and reliable. It also lobbied the federal and provincial governments to ask that any of their contracts for tile flooring request Canadian-made tile only. Since Clifton Ceramics was the sole manufacturer of quarry tile in Canada, tile for the job would have to be purchased from a distributor carrying its line.

CONCLUSION

Alfred Deller realized that the ARC tile–making process was incomplete and further development work would be needed. There were good reasons to develop the technology further: (1) A company producing ARC tile in Canada would be in a strong competitive position; (2) the inexpensive and abundant raw material could give a company a cost advantage in the market; (3) the social benefits of helping to clean up the environment could be an advantage for gaining government grants; and (4) tile manufactured by a Canadian company could have an advantage in getting contracts from government businesses (i.e., power plants).

There were also some disadvantages in carrying the work forward: (1) It might not be possible to develop an economical abrasion-resistant material from slag ceramics; (2) further development costs might exceed the company's budget; and (3) much of the groundwork development had been completed, but the risk inherent in the remaining research and development expenditures was probably high because setting up a pilot plant could be a considerably larger expense.

As he left the office that evening, Deller wasn't certain to which course of action he should commit the company.

QUESTIONS

1. Prepare a SWOT analysis (internal strengths and weaknesses, external opportunities and threats) for Clifton Ceramics Ltd. management.

2. Should the technology be developed further and marketed? Why or why not?

3. Should Clifton Ceramics pursue the ARC or quarry tile market? Why or why not?

16. Fibercorp Inc.

Fibercorp Inc., originally a manufacturer of synthetic fibers, located in Atlanta, Georgia, has grown into a diversified corporation. Company sales today are $554 million, and earnings are $48.7 million after taxes. The company's divisions include chemicals, paper, silicones, cellulose products, plastics, fiber materials, and consumer products.

Fibercorp's Central Research department conducts all basic research for the company, operates in liaison with the various divisions in developing specific products to the point of commercialization, and investigates any field problems that have been referred back to Central Research by division technical representatives.

Jim Dodge, newly appointed vice president of the Fiber Materials division, has had several exploratory meetings in recent weeks with Grant Holden, chief, Central Research. The broad objective of these meetings in Dodge's mind was to explore potential new product possibilities. Holden, however, suggested that Central Research had been so preoccupied with other projects that they had no new fibers to propose. He suggested that if Dodge were to identify a set of characteristics for a new material, the research group could establish that set as a project goal and develop the required new product within a reasonable period of time. However, if no specific project seeking specified fiber characteristics were established, the great volume of work currently facing Central Research would preclude any fiber research in the near future.

Dodge immediately called a meeting with his sales manager, Frank Pitts, and outlined the results of his interactions with Central Research. Fiber Materials division's sales were stagnant, Dodge pointed out. If the division was to show any medium-term improvement, a new product was needed—and fast! Pitts agreed and suggested that the upholstery market would be an ideal spot for a new fabric entry. This market had been growing steadily for several decades and was extremely receptive to new upholstery materials.

Jim Dodge was pleased with Pitts's suggestion, but when he pressed Pitts for details of the type of upholstery material Fibercorp should develop, he found that Pitts had no idea. "Then it will be your project to find out," said Dodge, "and report back to me in two weeks."

Pitts was worried. All his customers were mills that manufactured fabrics from Fibercorp fibers. Even as a consumer, he knew little about the requirements of upholstery buyers, for his wife had always made decisions about furniture purchases and reupholstery.

Nevertheless, he reasoned that if he could identify upholstery buyers' requirements and match them against the qualities of upholstery material currently on the market, he should be able to develop a set of characteristics for the ultimate in upholstery materials and, consequently, be able to specify the "ideal" set of characteristics for the new fiber Central Research would develop.

Pitts spent several days identifying the properties that different types of upholstery buyers expected of upholstery materials in general and the qualities of the various materials that were available on the market. He obtained this information by personally interviewing several furniture upholsterers. Information about one firm, Commercial Upholsterer, appears in Exhibit 1.

As a result of these interviews, Pitts was able to rate each of the properties expected by buyers on a five-point scale of importance and the qualities inherent in the materials on a five-point scale of excellence, as shown below:

The Rating System

Property Expected		Inherent Quality	
Extremely Important	4	Excellent	4
Very Important	3	Very Good	3
Fairly Important	2	Good	2
Slightly Important	1	Poor	1
Unimportant	0	Very Poor	0

Pitts figured that he could multiply the two figures together to obtain an overall score. Therefore, if the buyer considered a property such as water resistance to be extremely important (4), but the material—for example, corduroy—had a poor (1) inherent quality rating for water resistance, the overall score would be $4 \times 1 = 4$. If texture was rated very important (3) and the in-herent quality of the material—for example, bur-lap—was rated excellent (4), the overall score would be $3 \times 4 = 12$. The matrix developed by Pitts is shown in Exhibit 2.

Of course, Frank Pitts realized that different categories of clients exist among ultimate cus-tomers. Consumers have different requirements from those of contract customers. For example, uniqueness (having a different upholstery than the Joneses) would be more important to Mrs. Smith than it would be to the local school board. Among contract clients, the people who actually have to sit on upholstered furniture have different requirements from those of the people who make the decision about which material to buy. For ex-ample, cost of the material used would be impor-tant to the restaurateur but unimportant to the diner, whereas the diner would be more con-cerned about whether the material "breathed" than the restaurateur.

EXHIBIT 1 Commercial Upholsterer

Commercial Upholsterer is a medium-size firm engaged in repairing, refinishing, and reupholstering all types and styles of furniture. The repairing and refinishing side of the business accounts for about 25 percent of the company's sales volume. However, repairing and refinishing jobs generate a considerable volume of the company's more profitable upholstering business. In its advertising, the firm stresses the slogan "If your furniture isn't becoming to you, it should be coming to us."

Commercial Upholsterer has two classes of customers: contract and consumer. Contract accounts are all commercial or institutional organizations. Most are regular customers who are serviced once a year by Commercial Upholsterer, although about 20 percent of the contract business involves one-time "transient" orders. The major characteristic identifying contract accounts is the number of pieces of furniture that are reupholstered at a time. To qualify as a contract customer, the account must either represent a single upholstery order of ten items of furniture or enter into an annual service agreement. This agreement includes regular on-site inspection of all the client's furniture and repair, refinishing, and upholstering of those articles identified as needing such work by the Commercial Upholsterer inspector. Customers signing service agreements include offices, school, theaters, and larger restaurants. Their principal concern is durability.

In contrast, the consumer class of customer is mainly represented by home owners who want an individual piece, a suite of two chairs and a couch, or perhaps six dining room chairs reupholstered. In their case, style considerations in upholstery fabric are important. Although the individual order is for fewer units to be redone, consumer business commands a higher markup over cost and, consequently, is as important as contract business in generating income.

EXHIBIT 2   Currently Available Upholstery Materials

Properties	Importance Rating	Vinyl		Naugahyde		Smooth Leather		Suede		Corduroy		Crushed Velvet		Velour		Cut Velvet		Brocade		Cotton		Cotton Polyester		Nylon		Woven Viscose		Burlap		Rattan		Wool			
		Q	S	Q	S	Q	S	Q	S	Q	S	Q	S	Q	S	Q	S	Q	S	Q	S	Q	S	Q	S	Q	S	Q	S	Q	S	Q	S
a) Cleaning Ease—sponge																																	
—wash																																	
—dry clean																																	
b) Comfort—static charge																																	
—porosity																																	
—nonallergenic																																	
c) Resistance to—stains																																	
—mildew																																	
—shrinkage																																	
—snags																																	
—moths																																	
d) Durability—wear																																	
—seam integrity																																	
—cracks, splits																																	
e) Stability of—shape																																	
—color																																	
f) Appearance—texture																																	
—color range																																	
—luxuriousness																																	
—uniqueness																																	
—can accept patterns																																	
g) Coordinate Capability																																	
h) Initial Cost																																	
i) Maintenance Cost																																	
j) Ease of Installation																																	
k) Speed of Cleaning																																	
l) Profitability of Installation																																	
m) Profitability of Maintenance																																	
TOTAL SCORES																																	

Note: Q = inherent quality; S = importance.

Frank Pitts knew he would have to examine all of these influences to develop a complete picture. But he believed that at least the matrix he had developed would give him sufficient insights for the moment to guide his analysis of existing materials and to aid in identifying where new upholstery materials might be sought and what qualities they should have.

QUESTIONS

1. Critically evaluate the matrix approach to new-product development.

2. Outline an alternative technique by which Frank Pitts might identify new fiber product opportunities.

3. What is Frank Pitts's next step?

17. Michigan Tanking

On March 1, 1990, Brock Preston, branch manager for Michigan Tanking in Lansing, Michigan, was preparing the company's bid for a trucking contract. The bid, to deliver liquid fertilizer for Natural Fertilizers, also of Lansing, was due in two weeks, and Preston expected intense competition. Michigan Tanking won the last bid five years ago and had operated under that contract, in Lansing, to serve only Natural Fertilizers. Preston knew that if this bid was unsuccessful, the head office would close his branch.

COMPANY BACKGROUND

Michigan Tanking, a subsidiary of Hughes Trucking, was composed of a series of Michigan branches administered through a head office in Detroit. The branch office in Lansing consisted of eight truck drivers and the branch manager, who operated out of a rented office inside the Natural Fertilizers plant. The drivers were all members of the Teamsters Union, Local 141, and were paid on a combined basis of miles driven and time spent on delivery. Their average wage was approximately $13.29 per hour for a forty-four-hour regular workweek. The drivers were paid time-and-a-half for overtime (any hours worked over and above the forty-four-hour workweek). Benefits such as health insurance protection, a pension plan, unemployment insurance, vacation pay, and so forth were equal to 10 percent of regular wages and were paid over and above the weekly wages. No benefits were paid on overtime wages. The union agreement was coming up for renegotiation on January 1, 1991. Preston, who had an M.B.A. from Michigan State University, was paid a straight annual salary plus benefits and was not a member of the union.

The company transported liquid fertilizer in eight stainless steel tank trucks ranging in capacity from 3,200 to 5,800 gallons. The truck portion of each rig was leased from the Ryder Truck Company, while Michigan Tanking owned the tanker trailers. The lease for the trucks was scheduled to expire on the anniversary of the trucking contract with Natural Fertilizers (January 1, 1991).

Michigan Tanking's tankers delivered an average of eight to nine loads of liquid fertilizer a day, five days a week. Though many deliveries were local, drivers were expected to deliver loads of fertilizer throughout Michigan (including the Upper Peninsula) and to nearby states. As could be expected, spring was a peak season for deliveries, whereas the winter months experienced a decline in demand. During those months, drivers were allowed to take their holidays, and the tanker trailers were serviced.

The Lansing branch of the company existed solely to serve the delivery needs of Natural Fertilizers. Preston knew the company would not allow him to solicit outside contracts to increase revenue. Further, if Natural Fertilizers went out of business, or Michigan Tanking lost its delivery contract, the branch would have no other source of business and would be closed. Preston knew closure was possible; a Sarnia, Ontario, branch had been closed under similar circumstances a year ago.

COMPETITION

Michigan Tanking experienced competition from two other trucking companies: Ellsworth Transport of Mason, Michigan, and Billings Equipment Leasing of Okemos, Michigan. Both companies offered comparable service, but with lower per-mile rates than Michigan Tanking charged. One reason for the lower rate was the use of non-union labor by the two companies. Billings was the more aggressive company of the two. It had been formed little more than a year before and was operating with new equipment. Billings wanted the Natural Fertilizers trucking contract to give it more credibility. Management there could be expected to put in a low bid.

Natural Fertilizers also had the option to reject all submitted bids and purchase its own trucks for delivery. Tanker prices varied from $80,000 for the 3,200-gallon size to $120,000 for the 5,800-gallon size. The truck or cab portion could either be leased or purchased. Prices for transport trucks varied, depending on options, from $60,000 to $80,000. The company would also have to hire and train drivers and a dispatcher. Brock Preston estimated that it would take at least one year to make a new fleet of trucks run efficiently.

THE BIDDING PROCESS

Natural Fertilizers subcontracted delivery of its liquid fertilizer to trucking firms on a five-year basis. Over the period of the contract, the winner of the bidding process would be given first priority for all delivery assignments. If more fertilizer had

to be shipped than the trucking company could handle, Natural Fertilizers was free to hire extra trucks as needed to make those deliveries. This situation often arose in the spring and summer months, when drivers were working overtime to meet as many delivery schedules as possible. Yet they were still unable to meet them all.

While the sealed bids would be received on March 15, the actual contract would begin on January 1, 1991, and run for five years. In soliciting bids, Natural Fertilizers had made it clear to the three trucking firms that it wanted to lower its delivery costs from the $2.20 charge per mile that it currently paid. Each firm was attempting to come up with the lowest bid while maintaining adequate profit margins. Though timely delivery, friendly drivers, and good service were important, the winning bid would be the lowest rate charged, but only if that rate was acceptable to Natural Fertilizers.

THE PROBLEM

Michigan Tanking had been associated with Natural Fertilizers for twenty years, having won four consecutive contracts, but Preston knew that loyalty would be only a small factor in deciding the winning bid. Looking at a breakdown of the company's revenues and costs (Exhibit 1), he believed

---

EXHIBIT 1   Revenue and Cost Analysis for Michigan Tanking, Fiscal Year 1989

Revenues

Billings to Natural Fertilizers	$1,054,363

Costs

Truck drivers' wages & benefits	$357,042
Fuel	$117,111
Leasing costs	$142,612
Tanker maintenance	$102,754
Depreciation on tankers	$ 51,317
Administration and general overhead	$ 60,915
Total costs	$ 831,751
Gross profit from Lansing operations	$ 222,612

that the company's bid should be from 10 to 20 percent lower than the current rate to be competitive. The problem was further compounded by the uncertainty surrounding the bids of the other companies. His job depended on his coming up with a bid that attempted to maintain past margins and would win the five-year contract.

QUESTIONS

1. What bid should Brock Preston submit to win the Natural Fertilizers contract?
2. How can the parent company and the workers be persuaded to accept the bid?
3. What should be done if the bid is lost?

18. Lee Steel Supply and Service

Lee Steel Supply and Service (LSSS) is a medium-sized processor and distributor of rolled steel and aluminum products. The company was originally established as a dealer in scrap iron products in 1946. The initial facility in Buffalo, New York, has been expanded to include an 80,000-square-foot manufacturing plant, warehouse, and sales office. The total New York market is covered from this location. In 1957, a 30,000-square-foot warehouse and sales office was set up in Mississauga, Ontario, to service the nearby Canadian market. The company's present sales volume is $45 million, with 65 percent in New York and the remainder in Ontario.

THE PRODUCT MIX

The LSSS product line is classified into three basic categories:

1. Standard finished products: These include such items as cold-rolled slit coil, sheared-to-size blanks (which manufacturers employ directly in their production processes), and standard-size steel sheets.
2. Items preprocessed for inventory: Examples of products in this category are 28-gauge

$36'' \times 98''$ galvanized sheets and $60'' \times 120''$ 14-gauge hot-rolled sheet, as used in the manufacture of oil tanks.

3. Custom job processing orders: Recent custom orders have included 100,000 pounds of customer-supplied 43-inch, 22-gauge, cold-rolled coil to be slit into 8½-inch widths and 50,000 pounds of customer-supplied galvanized satin coat 32-inch, 24-gauge coil to be slit into 1½-inch widths. Although relatively insignificant in dollar volume, the custom operation accounts for almost 30 percent by weight of the metal processed by LSSS.

TECHNOLOGY AND PRODUCTION METHODS

The production process consists of three major operations: shearing, slitting, and cutting to length. Each of these job centers consists of a number of machines. This production flow presents scheduling difficulties because of the varied number of products and operations performed. Although machinery obsolescence is very low, monthly maintenance costs are high due to the need to keep equipment in working order.

Generally, there is a conscious attempt by LSSS management to purchase unusual, specialized equipment to produce specialized products. In this way, competition can be effectively eliminated for a number of products, which allows LSSS considerable flexibility in price setting.

CUSTOMER PROFILE

No major customers account for a large portion of volume. In fact, LSSS's largest customer represents only 4 percent of total dollar sales. Likewise, no single product contributes significantly to the firm's total revenue.

Most of LSSS's customers are located in the Buffalo and Toronto-Montreal area. Typically, product requirements for these two major markets differ considerably. Thus, separate sales strategies have been developed.

PRESENT INDUSTRY SITUATION

Early in 1991, Brian Matthews, general manager of LSSS, was somewhat pessimistic about future business prospects. The economy was almost one year into a recessionary period. Government action designed to tone down inflation had resulted in an unprecedented level of unemployment. As a result, 1990 dollar sales were down almost 8 percent below 1989, and 1991 expectations were poor.

At present, inventories and production are high throughout the industry, causing price deterioration in most product lines. Matthews believed that the possible Canadian steel strike, expected in mid-1991, would remedy this situation by increasing Canadian demand for LSSS's products. But if the strike failed to materialize, conditions could deteriorate, after the summer peak period, back to where they were at present.

GENERAL PRICING GUIDELINES

Essentially, LSSS uses a cost-plus basis in determining selling prices. A base processing cost is estab-

lished for each order, consisting of labor-machine costs (electricity, maintenance, and other variable costs). This figure is added to material and scrap freight costs and subtracted from the estimated selling price to set the gross margin for that particular order. The net margin is obtained by subtracting the fixed costs allocated to each order (plant overhead, marketing, paperwork, and administration).

To determine the cost of production for each order, the cost at each phase of production is calculated. Using a two-shift basis, the base processing costs of each machine are calculated per hour. These costs are revised monthly.

The various overhead costs are determined weekly and allocated to each order. To calculate these costs, the total plant production in hours is determined and each order receives a percentage of these costs in relation to its percentage of the total weekly production.

Price lists are accordingly established for the standard items produced. The production cost estimates are checked each month, but in each order-cost determination, changes are made only when long-term trends would justify them.

To facilitate this cost-plus basis of pricing, LSSS has a computerized recordkeeping system. Administration, sales, delivery, and other such costs are reported weekly. Each cost center within the plant reports its costs to the administrative department on a daily basis, and monthly production reports are subsequently prepared. The reports produced show breakdowns by customer, total order cost, total order price, and total gross margin.

The ultimate responsibility for pricing rests with Brian Matthews. Three people working in the administrative department report directly to him. In theory, the two people in administration at Mississauga report directly to him as well. In practice, these people nearly always act independently, since the Ontario market is distinct from that of New York.

ACTUAL PRICING

The pricing guidelines referred to above are often modified considerably in actual practice. The major factor affecting final price is the particular demand-supply situation existing at the time of sale.

Gross margins on orders to different customers vary widely—from 5 to 60 percent on standard items and up to 100 percent on custom orders. Generally, as the demand for a product rises, prices are increased for all except the best customers. Irregular or occasional customers are charged the highest price obtainable.

In general, the high-margin products are characterized by low turnover. They include small custom orders and sophisticated products that require specialized equipment. Low-margin products are high-turnover items and are produced in large quantities for two or three customers. Competitive pressure on these quantity products is the major factor for the lower margins. There is very little relationship, however, between gross margin and order regularity, customer size, and so forth.

Other criteria, although infrequently used, influence the pricing process. For example, prices may be lowered to obtain orders that will employ unused capacity, to fill delivery trucks, or to obtain very large orders.

The high dollar value of inventories, combined with handling costs, obsolescence, and spoilage (rust), results in extremely high inventory carry costs. As a result, "stress pricing," or selling at less than cost, will occasionally be undertaken to get rid of very-slow-moving items. Also, LSSS will sell a product as a "loss leader" to pick up sales of a higher-margin product.

Matthews frequently revises his price lists and sends them to all salespeople as a lower limit on which to base their quotations. One of the key factors by which he evaluates the performance of his salespeople is the price above this "lower limit" that the salespeople can obtain for their products.

SITUATION 1

LSSS has been requested by the New York State government to submit a quotation on work for a very large construction project. Although he is not certain of the exact figures, Brian Matthews thinks this could represent a sizable revenue, based on his present method of pricing. To his knowledge, four other firms have been asked to bid. Alternatively, Matthews knows that if the Canadian steel strike should materialize, LSSS will not have the capacity to handle both the contract and the expected heavy Canadian demand for his firm's products. In this situation, he would prefer to forgo the New York government contract, because the Canadian strike would generate large profits due to the short supply of metal. However, if LSSS does not win the contract and the Canadian strike does not occur, LSSS will most certainly operate only at a marginal profit level. Furthermore, if he wants to be certain of winning the contract, Matthews will have to submit a very low bid to the state, and this would result in quite low profits.

SITUATION 2

In an effort to expand market share significantly, Superior Steel, the major competitor of LSSS, has lowered the price of its rolled-steel products to a level below the cost price of similar products carried by LSSS. In pursuing this strategy, Superior Steel hopes to lower its fixed costs per order enough to permit it to undercut LSSS substantially in the long run.

SITUATION 3

Early in 1991, Brian Matthews was concerned about the discrepancy between LSSS's formal pricing policy and the company's actual pricing practices. He believed that the formal policy should be updated to conform more closely with current market conditions.

In May, Matthews hired a second-year M.B.A. student, Bill Witzel, to work on this problem as a summer project.

QUESTIONS

1. Evaluate the pros and cons of each alternative in Situation 1.

2. What pricing strategy should Brian Matthews employ in Situation 1?

3. Evaluate the alternatives available to LSSS in Situation 3 and design a suitable strategy in response to the Superior Steel move.

4. Provide a "business school" impression of LSSS's actual pricing practice in Situation 3 and suggest how the company can improve its pricing policy.

19. General Controls and Electronics, Inc.

THE ENVIRONMENT

General Controls and Electronics, Inc. (GCE), is a major manufacturer of substation control systems. Each system is designed specifically for one application, because many variations and options are available for use in a system. Thus, each installation requires considerable engineering design work before construction can begin.

Most orders are obtained through competitive bidding, with the lowest bidder receiving the order when all else is equal. GCE normally makes between 700 and 800 tender submissions during the year. District sales offices are instructed to respond to all public notices of invitation to tender and obtain the specifications for each. These bids have values from $10,000 to $1 million per unit. Some bids are submitted for several units in a particular job.

Because of the specialized nature of the equipment, the buyer must evaluate many factors, in addition to initial cost, to obtain the best value. Such factors as reliability, durability, ease of maintenance, efficiency, and adaptability must be considered in the decision. One factor is the ease with which the system can be expanded to handle larger units. Because some parts are central to the whole, costs can be reduced by the extent to which the unit can be expanded.

The special characteristics of the product require the industry to make large capital investments in heavy machinery. This leads to very high overhead. The unique features of each unit necessitate having the engineering department work out the final designs and interpret the specifications to make intelligent bids. Several persons are involved in the submission of bids and price setting because of the large number of bids that must be completely analyzed and processed during the year.

In the United States, there are three main competitors for GCE. These are Delta Electric Corporation, the largest U.S. supplier; Continental Controls, the smallest of the main competitors; and Old Dominion Systems, another relatively small firm. These four firms supply over 90 percent of the systems manufactured in the United States.

In the last five years, offshore competition in the industry has been increasing alarmingly. Today foreign firms are capturing more than 20 percent of the U.S. market, whereas as recently as a decade ago they received only 4 percent.

The market is composed of a large number of buyers. The product is sold to utilities through state and municipal governments, to private industry, and to contractors and commercial concerns; also, some equipment is available for special applications. Most of the orders are for one or two units. In the case of utilities, which customarily order at fairly regular intervals, most of the bids are submitted with little hope of substantial repeat business in the near future. In the past few years, market growth has been about 6 to 7 percent annually, although the rate is very cyclical. Currently, the company believes that business is starting an upswing.

Control systems represent a total U.S. market of some $1.4 billion, which is divided among the four major competitors roughly 40, 25, 15, and 10 percent for Delta, G.C.E., Old Dominion, and Continental Controls, respectively. These percentages apply to the 80 percent of the market left after foreign competition. As a result of the offshore competition and increases in productive capacity of the four U.S. competitors, the growth of capacity has exceeded the growth of the market, contributing to the generally low level of prices in the industry.

Marketing research conducted by the company consists mainly of interviews with principal customers' management conducted by GCE's pricing manager. During these annual talks, customers are asked to outline their projects for the coming year. In addition, general economic forecasts of the electrical industry are made available by the parent company. Each regional sales office of GCE also prepares a forecast of sales expected in its area. This information, plus the input from the various salespeople, is integrated into an estimate of the company's sales prospects for the coming year.

The most serious problem facing the company in recent years has been a deteriorating price level in the control systems market. Prices have fallen steadily over the past ten years, making it increasingly difficult for the company to operate profitably. Profit margins throughout the industry have been falling. Because of the high fixed costs and the general state of overcapacity, there has been a strong tendency to cut prices to keep shops full.

To make things worse, it is suspected that the offshore competition is "dumping" its product on the U.S. market (i.e., selling its product at a price that does not cover all its fixed costs in an attempt to minimize losses). Thus, a major concern of GCE pricing executives is to avoid upsetting the market in any way that might drive prices even lower. One objective, then, is to maintain price stability.

The company's formal pricing objective is to be uniformly competitive for all types of customers across the United States. The company submits bids on a considerable number of overseas orders, although with little success against the European manufacturers. In the last few years, GCE has received about 70 percent of its business from utilities, which comprise less than half of the total market. Some segments of the market are almost ignored by GCE, namely those requiring special applications or highly unusual design.

GCE has acquired a good name for its technical excellence and careful attention to meeting promised delivery dates. Especially well received is its line of Quickread components, a patented line of high-quality panel instruments.

All sales are handled by the field sales staff, except in very special cases. Salespeople are best able to serve the customer because of their close proximity to the market. They keep a careful watch for possible sales opportunities and tap the grapevine for any information that might prove valuable to the head office. In the case of tenders submitted to utilities and similar institutions, prices are normally made public. Everyone knows where the bids have been for each job. However, in the case of private industry, the buying decision is rarely made public. If GCE does not receive the order, it is often not possible to find out who did get the order, let alone the actual reasons why. So in the private industry sector, a company finds it much more difficult to know what the competition is doing. Occasionally information filters back through indirect sources, but its accuracy is often suspect, and indeed sometimes considered deliberately misleading. Although a report of all lost business is made by the sales representatives, they usually do not know why the order went to whomever it did. Nevertheless, they report what they do know and what they suspect.

THE RHODE ISLAND BID

On May 6, 1992, GCE received a set of specifications from the district sales office at Providence, Rhode Island. The specifications, prepared by the

Rhode Island and Providence Plantations Utilities Commission, were for five identical monitoring control panels to be installed singly in substations across the state. Because of the magnitude of the potential order (the Providence office estimate was approximately $1.3 million), the specifications were given to John Nicholson, P. Eng., senior bid analyst—major installations.

Nicholson was pleased to see a potential order of this size, for at a meeting with the department manager a week before he learned that the department was considerably below the forecasted shop "load" target set by senior management. At that meeting, he had been advised that the parent corporation was becoming increasingly concerned about profit expectations in the short term.

After an initial reading of the specifications, he recalled that the last contract with RIPPUC had been for nearly identical panels. A phone conversation with the Providence sales staff confirmed his idea that these panels would be installed in new substations as part of RIPPUC's network improvement program. This fact was important because it allowed greater flexibility in panel design. This would not be the case if the panels were to replace existing units.

Nicholson forwarded a copy of the specifications to the engineering department and requested that they "pull" the file on the last contract for comparison. In addition, he suggested the use of Paneline components for basic instrumentation.

GCE had two separate sets of panel instruments that it could use in its product. Quickread instruments were of the highest manufacturing quality and communicated precise information on electrical network performance. The Paneline instrument group was of somewhat lesser quality, but would feed back information reliably with slightly less accuracy. The principal advantage of Paneline instrumentation was lower cost, and Nicholson knew that RIPPUC historically had proven to be cost-conscious.

While the engineering department was preparing the quantitative data he required, Nicholson concentrated on the important qualitative information necessary for arriving at his ultimate bid price.

The actual performance of the U.S. economy was slightly below the forecast prepared by the president's Economic Council. Construction starts and the subsequent expansion of hydroelectric facilities to serve new developments were below expectations. Nicholson knew that it would be difficult to meet his "load" factor requirement (that figure having been derived from the economic forecast), and a major contract was a virtual necessity. Information from the district sales offices indicated that the situation existed throughout the industry. He expected that domestic competition would be composed of all U.S. competitors, namely Delta Electric, Continental Controls, and Old Dominion Systems. With a closing date of June 29, 1992, for the bid, he knew offshore competition was a possibility, provided they acted quickly.

Although shop loads for domestic firms were below normal at this point, a large number of bids currently were being evaluated by various utilities and industrial firms, and a number of these contracts were expected to be awarded while the RIPPUC bid was being prepared.

Examining the past performance of this customer, Nicholson noted the sales staff's view that RIPPUC engineers preferred GCE's control panels, largely as a result of the Quickread instrumentation. Two other factors also became apparent. RIPPUC showed a distinct preference for lowest tender if it expected future economic conditions would create a "tight money" market. Also, it seemed to favor bids that included components purchased from New England's growing electronics industry. Nicholson surmised his competition would have similar information and would include these considerations in its final price.

The specifications included a penalty clause, effective if the manufacturer awarded the contract had not delivered the control panels by the requested date. Penalty charges amounted to price reductions of 1.1 percent for the first ten days, 2.1 percent for the next ten days, and 4.4 percent for the following ten days, with contract cancellation at the option of the customer after thirty days. Although from a manufacturing standpoint it was unlikely that delivery would not be met, there were rumors that a railway strike would occur during the early months of the following year if the Brotherhood of Railway Engineers' union contract demands were not met. GCE's legal department advised Nicholson that any shipments embargoed during the strike and subject to penalty clauses would probably result in litigation between the company and the injuring party for compensatory damages—"a messy situation at best."

After consulting with appropriate line departments, Nicholson arrived at the following contract schedule:

Engineering/Drafting	4–6 weeks (8 max.)
Manufacturing	25 weeks
Testing	1 week
Shipping (normal conditions)	1 week
Plant Shutdown for Vacation	2 weeks
	33–35 weeks
RIPPUC Bid Approval	2 weeks
Total	**35–37 weeks**

Bid Closing Date—June 29, 1992
Delivery Date—March 31, 1993

Each firm within the industry published a price guide, revised periodically, that listed "book prices" for the various sizes of control panels and for components. The price guide allowed industrial firms and utilities to arrive at an approximate cost when determining control panel requirements. All firms engaged in bid submissions would attempt to add an appropriate margin to their product cost to arrive at a final bid price that was reasonably close to their published "book value."

During the past two years, offshore competition had upset the market by bidding considerably lower than "book price" figures, and GCE suspected this was a "dumping" practice. Nicholson knew the industry would shave its profit margin if offshore competition was expected on a bid. In this analysis, he had to determine not only the possibility of offshore competition in his own price determination but whether or not the domestic competition would price its bids in anticipation of offshore competition.

Continental Controls was known to occasionally submit an exceptionally low bid, by industry standards, if it badly needed work in its shops. Nicholson attributed its erratic performance to lack of bidding finesse, resulting from a less than complete understanding of environmental conditions. As a result, he believed he could not predict with any degree of accuracy the position it might take on this particular bid. In the past, Continental Controls had "robbed" him of contracts he thought were skillfully priced, by GCE standards.

He recalled hearing that Old Dominion Systems was expected to lose a major portion of its substantial export market in Canada as a result of an expansion in production capacity by Canadian manufacturers. This information came to him from a district salesman who had met a Quebec Hydro systems engineer at a recent convention in Montreal and had questioned him on the likelihood of future intercountry business. Prior to this time, Old Dominion Systems usually had been the highest bidder on domestic orders (when published figures were available). If Old Dominion did in fact expect a decline in export work, it had not yet established a pattern of highly competitive bidding in the U.S. market.

Nicholson did not expect that Delta Electric Corporation would be a serious bidder on this contract. Only yesterday it had received the largest of the bids currently under evaluation. That contract, coupled with a number of small industrial bids, probably would make it difficult for Delta to complete the RIPPUC panels by the delivery date. On past occasions, though, Delta, either by accident or design, had submitted a lower bid when its shops were very busy, and always managed to make the necessary delivery dates.

The threat of offshore competition on bid pricing was greatest when specifications were released for analysis far in advance of tender submission dates. Lengthy lead times allowed these firms sufficient time to receive, evaluate fully, and mail back their bids from considerable distances. Because the bids were to be submitted in a relatively short period of time in this situation,

Nicholson thought that only one firm, Europa Systemes, would be likely to submit a bid. While this firm was not considered the biggest "scavenger" in the offshore group, it occasionally would submit bids well below U.S. "book values."

The engineering department soon notified Nicholson that many of the design blueprints from the previous contract would be utilized with these specifications. They suggested the resulting time savings would allow them to work on exploratory designs. After a few weeks had passed, Nicholson was shown the final design to be recommended by the engineering department. The design had several advantages over the previous contract. It was lighter and would cost less to ship. The layout of the control system would allow easy interchangeability of component parts, and major servicing could be performed at the substation. Fifteen percent of the component parts could be purchased only from New England suppliers. Another 6 percent could be ordered from Rhode Island, but at greater cost.

The design had certain disadvantages. It was not possible to incorporate Paneline instrumentation into the control system, and the higher-cost Quickread controls would have to be used. Nicholson knew that the RIPPUC engineers would appreciate the design features. But he also knew that the bid must be approved by the commission members, a group of elected officials with no engineering background. He suggested that the engineering department prepare a design that was less efficient, but could use Paneline controls, as a possible alternative bid. Nicholson knew that regardless of the design chosen, he would have to include the extra engineering department expenses in his final price.

Finally, cost figures were derived for both the Quickread design and the Paneline design. These figures were $954,000, and $861,000, respectively. Neither figure included an overhead allocation of 11 percent required on every bid. In addition, the Paneline figure would increase by approximately $10,413 when the final shipping charge for that alternative was computed. This was the result of an error in determining shipping charges for the heavier Paneline control panels. Book prices for the Quickread panels and components totaled $1,285,232, and similar prices for the Paneline alternative were $1,186,241 in total. Nicholson checked the last contract awarded and found the acceptable price was 91 percent of book value. That panel had included Quickread instrumentation. Nicholson was now expected to cumulate his information into a final price for each of the two designs and present his rationale to the department manager and the general manager.

The greatest unknown was the anticipated performance of competition. If the other U.S. competitors expected offshore competition, they would tend to price lower than if they expected domestic competition alone. The general environmental conditions were not definitive, and judgment would be based on Nicholson's expertise. Necessity for shop load was a major factor, but the profit margin could not be ignored. Not only would short-run profits be affected; a low price could start a price competition of serious proportions on future bid submissions.

Nicholson was reasonably confident that the Quickread design was demonstrably superior to any potential competitive design. But he did not know to what degree this could be translated into higher price. While the Paneline design did not meet the specifications per se, it would do nearly the same job at a lower cost. Acceptance of this design would depend largely on the selling job put forth by the district salespeople.

Nicholson wanted the contract badly, but he did not want to leave any extra profit "lying on the table."

QUESTION

What price should GCE bid? Justify your answer.

20. Parker Instruments Ltd.

OVERVIEW

Parker Instruments Ltd. (PI) is a British firm that operates as a manufacturer and an importer/distributor. Its field is electronic instruments, and the imported products account for about 75 percent of sales. One of the companies Parker Instruments represents in the United Kingdom is Electro Industries (EI), a Canadian precision instrument firm. PI and EI have been working together for about ten years. The relationship between the two companies was good for a number of years. Then things started to go wrong, and this was accentuated by an accident that robbed EI of its top two executives. The time of the case is one year after the accident. George Parker feels strong ties to EI but is increasingly worried by the Canadian company's seeming indifference to its international operations in general and to the relationship with PI in particular.

George Parker locked the door of his car and walked across the parking lot toward the station entrance. Although it was a sunny spring morning and the daffodils and tulips provided welcome color after the grayness of winter, Parker hardly noticed. Within a few minutes the train from London would be arriving, and with it Bruce MacDonald, the export sales manager for Electro Industries—a Canadian firm that George's company represented in the United Kingdom. Parker would be spending the day with MacDonald, and he wondered what the outcome of their discussions would be.

PARKER INSTRUMENTS LTD.

George Parker was managing director of Parker Instruments Ltd., part of a small, family-owned U.K. group of companies. The company gained its first sales agency in 1923 (from a U.S. manufacturer), which made it one of the most well-established international trading firms in electronic instruments. PI sales were the equivalent of about $1 million, with 75 percent coming from imported distributed items and 25 percent from sales of its own manufactured items. The company had a total of fifteen employees.

PI was the U.K. distributor for fifteen manufacturers located in the United States, Canada, Switzerland, and Japan. Like many firms, it found the 80/20 rule held true; about 80 percent of the import sales of $750,000 were generated by 20 percent of the distributorships it held. With current sales of $165,000, the Electro Industries distributorship was an important one.

ELECTRO INDUSTRIES

Electro Industries was a younger and larger organization than its U.K. distributor. Located in southern Ontario, it was founded in the mid-1950s and had current sales of $2 million and a work force of ninety employees. EI had developed a strong reputation over the years for its high-precision instrumentation and testing equipment,

This case was prepared by Professor Philip Rosson of Dalhousie University, Halifax, Nova Scotia, Canada, as a basis for class discussion rather than to illustrate the effective or ineffective handling of an administrative situation. The names of the companies and persons have been changed, but in all other respects the case study is factual. Copyright © 1984 Philip Rosson.

and this led to considerable market expansion. The company had moved in a number of new product directions. The original products were very precise devices for use in standards laboratories. From this base it had more recently established a presence in the oceanographic and electric power fields.

As a result of this expansion, 80 percent of sales are now made outside Canada, split evenly between the United States and offshore markets. In the United States, the company had its own direct-sales organization, whereas indirect methods were used elsewhere. In the "best" fifteen offshore markets, EI had exclusive distributors; in thirty other markets, it relied on commission agents.

WORKING TOGETHER

EI and PI first made contact in New York City, and the two companies agreed to work together. George Parker was on a business trip in the United States when he received a cable from his brother saying that a representative of EI wanted to get in touch with him. Parker and his wife met the senior executive in their hotel room and, after initial introductions, settled down to exchange information. At some point, Parker, who had had a hectic day, fell asleep. He awoke to find that PI was now more or less EI's U.K. distributor, his wife having kept the discussion rolling while he slept.

The two firms soon began to prosper together. The distributorship gave PI a product line to complement those it already carried. Furthermore, the EI instruments were regarded as the "Cadillacs" of the industry. This ensured entry to the customer's premises and an interest in the rest of the PI product line. As far as EI was concerned, it could hardly have chosen a more suitable partner: PI's staff was technically competent, facilities existed for product servicing, and customer contacts were good. Moreover, as time passed, George Parker's long experience and international connections proved invaluable to EI. He was often asked for an opinion prior to some new move by the Canadian producer. Parker preferred to have a close working relationship with the firms he represented, so he was happy to provide

advice. In this way, PI did an effective job of representing EI in the United Kingdom and helped with market expansion elsewhere.

As might be expected, the senior executives of the companies got along well together. The president and vice president of marketing—EI's "international ambassadors"—and George Parker progressed from being business partners to becoming close personal friends. Then, after nine successful years, a tragedy occurred: the two EI executives were killed in an airplane crash on their way home from a sales trip.

The tragic accident created a management succession crisis within EI. During this period, international operations were left dangling while other priorities were attended to. Nobody was able to take charge of the exporting activities that had generated such good sales for the company. Although there was an export sales manager, Bruce MacDonald, he was a relative newcomer, having been in training at the time of the accident. He was also a middle-level executive, whereas his international predecessors were the company's most senior personnel.

From Parker's point of view, things were still not right a year later. The void in EI's international operations had not been properly filled. Bruce MacDonald had proved to be a competent manager, but he lacked support because a new vice president of marketing had yet to be appointed. A new president headed the company, but he was the previous vice president of engineering and preferred to deal with technical rather than business issues. So despite the fact that MacDonald had a lot of ideas about what should be done internationally (most of which were similar to George Parker's ideas), he lacked both the position and the support of a superior to bring about the necessary changes.

While the airplane accident precipitated the current problems in the two companies' relationship, Parker realized that things had been going sour for a couple of years. At the outset of the relationship, EI executives had welcomed the close association with PI. Over time, however, as the manufacturer grew in size and new personnel came along, it seemed to Parker that his input was increasingly resented. This was unfortunate, because Parker believed that EI could become a more sophisticated international competitor if it considered advice given by informed distributors. In the past, EI had been open to advice and had benefited considerably from it. Yet there were still areas where EI could effect improvements. For example, its product literature was of poor quality and was often inaccurate or outdated. Prices were also worrisome. EI seemed unable to hold its costs, and its competitors now offered better "value-for-money" alternatives. Other marketing practices needed attention also.

THE OCEANOGRAPHIC MARKET

One area where EI and PI were in disagreement was the move into the oceanographic field. George Parker was pleased to see EI moving into new fields, but wondered if EI truly appreciated how "new" the field was. In a way, he believed the company had been led by the technology into the new field rather than having considered the "fit" between its capabilities and success criteria for the new field. For example, the customer fit did not seem even close. The traditional buyers of EI products for use in standards laboratories were scientists, some of whom were employed by government, some by industry, and some by universities. By and large they were academic types, used to getting their equipment when the budget permitted. As a result, selling was "gentlemanly," and follow-up visits were required to maintain contacts. Patience was often required, since purchasing cycles could be relatively long. Service needs were not extensive, for the instruments were used very carefully.

In contrast, the oceanographic products were used in the very demanding sea environment. Service needs were acute, due not just to the harsh operating environment but also to the cost associated with having inoperable equipment. For example, ocean research costs were already high but became even higher if faults in shipboard equipment prevented taking sea measurements. In such a situation, the customer demanded service today or tomorrow, wherever the faulty equipment was located. The oceanographic customer was also a difficult type—still technically trained but concerned about getting the job

done as quickly as possible. Purchasing budgets were much less of a worry; if the equipment was good, reliable, and with proven back-up, chances were it could be sold. But selling required more of a push than the laboratory equipment.

When EI entered the oceanographic field, a separate distributor was appointed in the United Kingdom. However, the arrangement did not work out. EI then asked George Parker to carry the line, and with great reluctance he agreed. The lack of enthusiasm was due to Parker's perception that his company was not capable of functioning well in this new arena. Because PI was ill equipped to service the oceanographic customer, it was thought that there could even be repercussions in its more traditional field. Parker was unwilling to risk the company's established reputation in this way. However, while he preferred not to represent EI in the oceanographic field, he worried about a "one market, one distributor" mentality at EI.

THE CURRENT VISIT

George Parker had strong personal sentiments for EI as a company. In his opinion, however, some concrete action was required if the business relationship was to survive, let alone prosper.

Parker recognized the good sales of EI products, but also took note of shrinking profit margins over the last few years due to the increased costs PI faced with the EI product line. Since EI was slow to respond to service and other problems, PI had been putting things right and absorbing the associated costs more and more frequently. However, these costs could not be absorbed forever. Parker had been willing to help tide EI over the last difficult year, but expected a more positive response in the future.

George Parker hoped that Bruce MacDonald would bring good news from Canada. Ideally he hoped to drop the oceanographic line and rebuild the "bridges" that used to exist between his firm and the manufacturer. A return to the close and helpful relationship that once existed would be welcomed. However, he wondered if EI's management wanted to operate in a more formal and distant "buy-and-sell" manner. If this were the case,

George Parker would have to give more serious thought to the EI distributorship.

QUESTIONS

1. Discuss the role of overseas distributors and the value they contribute.

2. What benefits can be realized using overseas distributors compared to other methods?
3. What is meant by "commitment to international marketing"?
4. What is meant by "lip service to marketing"?
5. What should be done in the situation described in the case?

21. Huntsman Chemical

OVERVIEW

Huntsman Chemical is the largest privately held chemical company in the United States; in 1990 it had revenues of $1.6 billion. The company is 60 percent owned by the Huntsman family and 40 percent owned by Great Lakes Chemical, a publicly held Midwest manufacturer. Huntsman employs 1,600 persons who work in the southern, midwestern, and eastern states. Facilities outside the United States include plants in Canada, the United Kingdom, and, most recently, Russia.

Huntsman Chemical manufactures and markets various petrochemical products. It is a leading producer of polystyrene, styrene monomer, and polypropylene; other goods include specialty compounds and engineering plastics. All of these materials, in turn, are used to produce thousands of consumer items. The majority of the products are made in the company's wholly owned subsidiaries; others are made by affiliates and joint ventures. Huntsman also licenses its patented technology to other firms in several nations.

In the 1980s, the company's corporate strategy revolved around strategic acquisitions, joint ventures, vertical integration, and global expansion. In the 1990s, this strategy is expected to continue. The goal is to add about $750 million in sales, with an increase in employment of about 1,000 by the end of the decade.

OPERATIONS AND COMPETITION

Consolidated revenues for Huntsman Chemical rose from $1.2 billion in 1989 to $1.3 billion by 1990. Revenues came primarily from the sales of polystyrene, estimated at $500 million, and polypropylene, estimated at $140 million. Styrene monomer is used for the most part internally, but some excess production is sold off on the open market. Return on sales in recent years averaged around 3 to 5 percent. Exhibit 1 shows a breakdown of Huntsman's revenues exclusive of the captive styrene monomer consumption (estimated at about $400 million; hence the chart shows the breakdown for $900 million worth of revenues).

Huntsman Chemical is reportedly the fifth largest producer of styrene monomer in the

This case is based on a longer corporate intelligence report written by Teresa L. Hayes for The Freedonia Group, Cleveland, Ohio, in November 1991; edited by Andrew C. Gross of Cleveland State University, June 1992. Used with permission of The Freedonia Group and Teresa L. Hayes.

EXHIBIT 1   Percentage Distribution of Huntsman Chemical 1990 Revenues

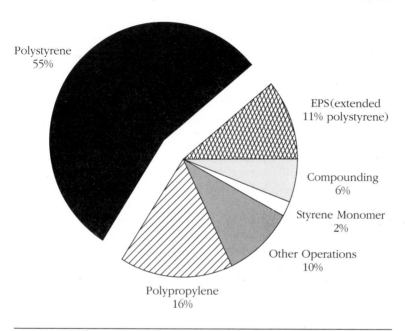

Polystyrene
55%

EPS(extended
11% polystyrene)

Compounding
6%

Styrene Monomer
2%

Other Operations
10%

Polypropylene
16%

Note: Distribution excludes captive styrene monomer use.

United States, with about 13 percent of industry capacity. Other leading producers are Cos-Mar, Arco Chemical, Dow Chemical, and Sterling Chemicals. While Hunstman is a leading producer of styrene, most of the output is used internally. Thus, the company is not a major player in the open or "merchant" market.

Huntsman is the second largest producer of polystyrene in North America, with 19 percent of total industry capacity. The leading producer is Dow Chemical, with 22 percent. Huntsman competes with large companies whose polystyrene operations constitute only a small part of their total business. Major competitors besides Dow and Huntsman are Novacor Chemical, Arco Chemical, Amoco, Chevron, Mobil, and Fina Oil. In the related field of expandable polystyrene, Huntsman accounts for 19 percent and Arco Chemical for 43 percent of industry capacity. Other producers are BASF and Scott Polymers.

In the field of polypropylene, Huntsman is among the ten leading producers in the United States and accounts for about 4 percent of industry capacity. Major producers of this material include Himont, Amoco, and Exxon Chemical; these three producers account for 50 percent of industry capacity. Demand in this field should rise at about 5 percent per year until 1995, compared to a projected annual increase of 3 percent for polystyrene and 2 percent for expandable polystyrene between 1990 and 1995.

CORPORATE STRATEGY

Huntsman Chemical followed an aggressive strategy for corporate growth in the 1980s, and this is expected to continue through the 1990s, although some of the growth may be generated more internally than in the previous decade. The corporate strategy involved acquisitions, joint ventures, vertical integration, and foreign expansion. Huntsman is not adverse to risk and seems to thrive in times of economic uncertainty, cashing in on the cautiousness and cost-cutting moves of other corporations. At the same time, Huntsman is careful not to add "fat" to its operations during boom times; thus, it is able to avoid massive layoffs in recessions. Such careful planning allows the company to be in an acquisition mode when other firms are selling off underperforming assets.

As a leading producer of polystyrene, Huntsman has accustomed itself to the cyclical nature of demand and has been able to adjust its supply to such cyclicality. During good times, the company concentrates on building cash reserves and on taking advantage of its capacity. It is also able to "fine-tune" its operations and get into an acquisition mode. As a privately held firm, the company pays lower executive salaries than the leading publicly held chemical manufacturers. It uses its funds to expand and upgrade facilities as supply-demand conditions warrant.

Acquisitions

Huntsman Chemical was formed in 1982 through the acquisition of business operations no longer thought profitable by other companies. The first step was the acquisition of the polystyrene business from Shell Chemical. Other operations were acquired from Hoechst Celanese, Russtek, and Potton. Exhibit 2 shows some of the strategic acquisitions in the 1980s and their results. This pattern may continue through the 1990s as Huntsman keeps looking for opportunities to purchase facilities at low cost that can fit into its current operations. The only danger is a very long recession, in which case the company could be loaded down with underperforming assets.

Joint Ventures

Huntsman also pursued selected joint ventures in both petrochemicals and thermoplastics with other leading firms, primarily General Electric. Huntsman's first venture with GE was for the production of polystyrene; other ventures involved engineering plastics and specialty compounds.

EXHIBIT 2   Strategic Acquisitions for Company Growth

Event	Result for the Company
Acquired Shell Chemicals' U.S. polystyrene business in 1983	Huntsman was founded and established itself as a polystyrene manufacturer
Acquired Shell Oil's U.K. polystyrene business in 1984	Established a European manufacturing presence and began global expansion
Acquired polystyrene, EPS, and styrene monomer operations of American Hoechst; acquired EPS operations of Russtek (U.S.) and Potton (Canada)	Became the largest North American producer of polystyrene and a leading producer of styrene monomer and EPS
Acquired the Shell Oil facility in New Jersey in 1987	Established the company as an important producer of polypropylene

The GE-Huntsman Corporation in plastics is a 50-50 venture producing specialized polystyrene and polyphenylene oxide. These materials offer good electrical and mechanical properties as well as dimensional stability over a wide range of temperatures. Such qualities make the materials useful for many applications: shower heads, sprinklers, switches, battery cases, electrical housings, printed circuits, instrument panels, wheel covers, body panels, appliance parts, and so forth.

Polycom-Huntsman is another 50-50 venture, in various custom plastics and a full line of color concentrates. The compounds made by this facility find applications in the manufacture of garbage bags, industrial film, detergent bottles, automotive and appliance parts, heater and air conditioner housings, and business machine parts. This joint venture, like those with General Electric, have allowed Huntsman to expand its product line offerings and to find new applications, while keeping development costs low.

A recent interesting joint venture is a partnership with AeroMar, a company formed by Aeroflot Soviet (now CIS or Russian) Airlines and Marriott Corporation. Huntsman-AeroMar began operations in July 1990 near Moscow Airport, making clear plastic tumblers used by the state airline. Some of the tumblers are sold for hard currency. The polystyrene plant is supplied with the basic materials from Huntsman's facility in England. Huntsman owns 51 percent of Huntsman-AeroMar, making it the first U.S. firm to own a majority interest in a Russian joint venture. A major expansion in capacity was announced in 1991, and the plant is said to be able to produce 50 million tumblers per year.

Vertical Integration

Huntsman has long-range plans for both backward and forward integration. The company moved "upstream"—that is, undertook backward integration—by purchasing the styrene monomer operations of Hoechst Celanese. This move provides a reliable "feedstock" for its polystyrene operations. Huntsman also plans to move "downstream"—forward—by moving into "high-end" engineering plastics and custom compounding. This strategy should complement its strong position in commodity-type products.

Foreign Expansion

Huntsman's activities outside the United States started in 1984 with the purchase of a Shell polystyrene facility in England; its latest foreign operation is the AeroMar joint venture noted earlier. Huntsman is actively pursuing joint ventures and licensing arrangements in such diverse locations as China, India, Singapore, and the Middle East. In 1991, the company licensed its polystyrene technology to Dongbu Chemical of South Korea.

ENVIRONMENTAL MATTERS

Huntsman is one of several companies that have banded together to promote plastics recycling.

Another goal of this consortium, known as the National Polystyrene Recycling Company, is to improve the image of polystyrene and other petrochemical compounds. The consortium, which includes Amoco, Chevron, Dow Chemical, Fina Oil, Huntsman, Mobil, and Nova of Canada, has set a goal of recycling 250 million pounds of "postconsumer polystyrene" annually by 1995. At least five recycling plants will be needed to accomplish this task. Jon Huntsman serves as the chairman of the executive committee of the Plastics Issues Group.

Showing its concern for environmental matters, Huntsman also eliminated about 60 million pounds of various materials from its waste streams; this saved the company $6 million in disposal fees and raw material costs. The company also has instituted recycling for solvents, cardboard containers, wooden pallets, scrap metal, and glass. At one location, the company reduced the amount sent to landfills by 80 percent in two years. Finally, Huntsman developed a garbage separator for trash from fast-food restaurants. The machine, which separates various types of trash with 97 percent accuracy, will be sold or licensed to a waste collection company.

QUESTIONS

1. Assess the corporate strategy of Huntsman Chemical, and contrast its preference for acquisitions, joint ventures, and licensing with possible internal growth.

2. How does Huntsman's concern for the environment make the company a better marketer? Why would it join competitors in the task of recycling and corporate image polishing?

3. What additional market opportunities for the clear plastic tumblers made in the plant near Moscow by Huntsman-AeroMar can you think of other than the current use by the state airline?

4. Develop a list of pros and cons for vertical integration by a petrochemical manufacturer, with special emphasis on marketing opportunities and threats.

22. Circuit Systems Group

Circuit Systems is a large U.S. electronics company. Through acquisition of Marshall Engineering and Spencerfield Electronics, both the size and scope of the company have significantly changed. The CS Group now consists of eight operating companies with current annual sales of 390 million, employing approximately 3,200 people, and with a total plant area in excess of 750,000 square feet. Of the eight companies, six are in the United States, one is in Canada, and one is in the United Kingdom. Sales are equally divided between consumer and industrial markets, with about 60 percent of the U.S. total being exported.

Products within the CS Group are technically oriented and range across a wide spectrum of the aviation and electronics industries. They break down into four basic categories: electronic systems, such as flight data recorders and crash position indicators; electromechanical assemblies for other electronics manufacturers; electronic components, such as circuit boards, radio frequency crystals, hermetic seals, and transformers; and industrial instrumentation, such as steel probes for basic oxygen furnaces and data loggers for aircraft.

In the four-year period from June 30, 1988, to June 30, 1992, prior to the acquisition of Marshall Engineering and Spencerfield Electronics, sales increased from about $5 million to $65 million and profits after taxes increased from $280,000 to $5 million. Research and development expenditures have always been significant in relation to revenue and in the 1992 fiscal year totaled $13 million, or 20 percent of sales.

Following is a description of the products and operations of the CS Group. The products and operations of the founding company are described first, followed by those of the seven subsidiary companies.

CIRCUIT SYSTEMS, INC.

Circuit Systems, Inc., is engaged in the design, development, and manufacture of aircraft location and recording systems, aircraft instruments, and some specialized electronic products.

Aircraft Location Systems

Upon release from the aircraft, the Crash Position Indicator (CPI) will descend slowly to the ground, whereupon it will signal the location of the downed aircraft. The CPI has so far produced the largest sales volume of any of CSI's products. It has been installed in a wide variety of aircraft of the U.S. Air Force Material Air Transport Command. While the CPI was initially fitted on aircraft that were already operational, it is now part of the standard specifications for U.S. air force transport aircraft and is installed as original equipment.

Aircraft Recorder Systems

CSI has developed four recorder systems: the accident data recorder system (ADR), the ADR contained in an airfoil (ADR/AC), a nonejectable accident data recorder system (ADR/NE), and a maintenance recorder system (MRS). The maintenance recorder system is specifically designed to determine the fatigue life of aircraft structures. It is limited to recording acceleration, air speed, altitude, calendar date, mission type, and aircraft weight. The recording tape can be played back on existing data processing equipment. The company received contracts from the Canadian armed forces for fifty systems to be installed in fighter aircraft and thirty-six systems to be included as original equipment in a new Lockheed long-range patrol aircraft.

Aircraft Instruments

In competition with leading U.S. and Canadian manufacturers, CSI has won design and production contracts from the armed forces for a number of aircraft instruments, including a new altimeter, which is currently in the final test stage.

Other Products

To reduce its reliance on the military market, CSI established a Special Products Department in 1990 to search for and develop products having primarily commercial and industrial uses. Close communications are maintained with various research agencies and government departments with a view toward finding such products. It is from these sources that CSI obtained licenses to further develop and manufacture an oxygen probe, a forestry survey radar altimeter, and an automatic fluoride analyzer. The oxygen probe has found acceptance among eight U.S. and Canadian steel producers.

SOLID STATE PRODUCTS

Solid State Products manufactures quartz crystals, quartz filters, and crystal ovens for radio communication equipment and for navigational equipment such as radar and sonar. Quartz crystals and crystal filters are used to stabilize frequencies and circuit elements in transmitting and receiving equipment, while crystal ovens maintain quartz crystals at fixed temperatures to permit more effective performance. These products are always made to customer specifications.

Solid State Products is a principal manufacturer of such components, and its sales to customers during the last ten years represented more than 35 percent of the North American market.

Approximately one-third of the company's production is exported, primarily to Western Europe.

Circuit Systems Limited

Circuit Systems Limited (CSL) carries on a manufacturing, repair, and overhaul operation for the products of CSI sold in Canada and also operates as a sales outlet in Canada. In September 1991, CSL began engineering research and development with respect to the application of electronics systems in the areas of medical electronics and pollution.

Aviation Electronics

Aviation Electronics manufactures components for the electronics industry. These components consist primarily of printed circuit boards and assemblies and also include terminal boards, nameplates, instrument panels, dials, and component boards made to customer specifications.

Grosvenor Industries Limited

Grosvenor Industries Limited is a United Kingdom company incorporated in 1973. All of its loan and share capital was acquired by CSI on June 7, 1990, for 5.5 million pounds sterling. Grosvenor produces flight data recorders, magnetic tape recorders, and industrial electronic products.

The Grosvenor flight data recorder, called the "aircraft data acquisition system" (ADAS), differs from those developed by CSI in that it is a wire recorder. It is capable of 200 hours of recording time and is protected by armor for crash survival. The ADAS is available in several versions suitable for different applications. The information recorded by the system when processed by the Grosvenor ground playback unit can be transcribed in chart form, on an electric typewriter, or on magnetic disks for processing by computer. Grosvenor entered the flight recorder market in 1987 when its ADAS was fitted to the British Airways fleet. Currently it is used by many other overseas airlines.

The magnetic tape recorders produced by Grosvenor are offered in a variety of models and are sold in commercial and military markets under the Grosvenor trademark. They are computer compatible, have a wide range of duration times, and accept either analog or digital signals. Grosvenor has produced tape recorders for more than fifteen years and has acquired a great deal of practical experience in a field that demands stringent electromechanical standards.

The industrial electronic products produced by Grosvenor include closed-circuit television systems, metering devices, and a highly sensitive temperature control unit. Grosvenor cooperated with Barclay's Bank Limited in the development of bank debit and credit card readers.

Interface Corporation

Interface Corporation, a New Jersey company, was incorporated in 1986. It is an independent manufacturer of glass-to-metal hermetic seals. These seals are sold to most U.S. manufacturers of sophisticated electronic communications, guidance and electronic control systems, and electronic components and modules. Because of its expertise in the techniques of heat treatment and glass manufacture, Interface is manufacturing the tip of the steel probe for CSI.

Marshall Engineering

Marshall Engineering was established in 1953 and incorporated in Pennsylvania in 1986. Prior to 1986, the firm primarily produced components for sound systems. Since then, Marshall has strengthened its engineering staff and improved and expanded its manufacturing facilities. These improvements have enabled Marshall to broaden its product lines to include a variety of electrical, mechanical, and other systems and components sold to a number of industrial and military customers.

The activity that currently accounts for the largest portion of Marshall's sales volume is the manufacture of mechanical assemblies for the U.S. armed forces. These assemblies are mechanical devices composed of sixty-five parts, most of which are produced in precision machine shops.

For many years Marshall has produced loudspeakers, tuners, amplifiers, and microphones for the home entertainment industry, as well as complete sound systems for industrial and commercial customers. Marshall has become an important U.S. supplier of components such as memory cores and drive units for high-speed printers used with computers. The company recently began assembling CD-ROM units and compact disk players produced for Marshall by suppliers in Taiwan and Korea. In 1990, Marshall acquired the assets of the transformer division of Oshowa Manufacturing. These transformers are being produced primarily for customers in the automotive industry.

Spencerfield Electronics

Spencerfield Electronics, a Utah company founded in 1983, is engaged, directly and through wholly owned subsidiaries, in the development and manufacture of electronic and mechanical components. Products include printed circuits for use in electronic, telephone, and computer equipment, a wide variety of instrument panels and precision dials for the automotive and aircraft industries, and flexible printed circuits for the automotive industry.

The Corporate Environment

Circuit Systems Group's strength lies in its product lines and worldwide sales potential. It has made a significant commitment to research and development. The major impact on the company in recent years has come from a conscious policy of acquiring sound companies in the electronics field.

Until now, each company in the group has maintained self-sufficient operations and a unique identity. The recent acquisition of Marshall Engineering and Spencerfield Electronics, however, has created some difficulties for the parent company. Corporate management is now considering a number of alternative ways to reorganize the Circuit Systems Group.

The corporate vice president in charge of manufacturing has submitted a proposal to rationalize the scattered and varied production operations as a way to increase production efficiency and minimize costs. He envisions all assembly operations being brought together under one department with centralized research and development, but retaining separate sales organizations so that the identities of the various companies remain intact in customers' eyes.

On the other hand, the senior marketing executive has responded that should any rationalization be implemented, its most beneficial effect would be having the sales personnel organized under a separate marketing company responsible for worldwide sales of all Circuit Systems Group products. But the controller has resisted this suggestion, because it would add yet another company to an already unwieldy group.

QUESTIONS

1. Discuss the various ways in which the company can be reorganized for greater marketing effectiveness (centralized versus decentralized; geographic, functional, product line, and industry grouping; etc.).

2. Describe the relationship between marketing control and financial accountability.

3. Given that the company is committed to a strategy of growth through acquisition, what impact will this have on its marketing efforts, and how would this affect the organization of the marketing function?

NAME AND COMPANY INDEX

SUBJECT INDEX